The Making of Japanese Manchuria,

1904–1932

Harvard East Asian Monographs, 196

The Making of
Japanese Manchuria, 1904–1932

Yoshihisa Tak Matsusaka

Published by the Harvard University Asia Center
and distributed by Harvard University Press
Cambridge (Massachusetts) and London, 2001

Printed in the United States of America

The Harvard University Asia Center publishes a monograph series and, in coordination with the Fairbank Center for East Asian Research, the Korea Institute, the Reischauer Institute of Japanese Studies, and other faculties and institutes, administers research projects designed to further scholarly understanding of China, Japan, Vietnam, Korea, and other Asian countries. The Center also sponsors projects addressing multidisciplinary and regional issues in Asia.

Library of Congress Cataloging-in-Publication Data

Matsusaka, Yoshihisa Tak.

The making of Japanese Manchuria, 1904–1932 / Yoshihisa Tak Matsusaka.

    p.   cm.

Includes bibliographical references and index.

ISBN: 978-0-674-01206-6

   1. Japan--Relations--China--Manchuria. 2. Manchuria (China)--Relations--Japan. 3. Manchuria (China)--History--20th century. 4. Imperialism--History--20th century. I. Title.

DS849.C6 M32 2001

951'.805--dc--21

                            00-049856

Index by the author

✇   Printed on acid-free paper

First paperback edition 2003

Last figure below indicates year of this printing

13 12 11 10

To Suzanne Lee

Acknowledgments

This book owes a great deal to my teachers and advisors in the United States and in Japan. I am indebted, in particular, to Albert Craig, my dissertation advisor, whose demands for intellectual rigor and conciseness of expression may not find adequate reflection in this study but nonetheless shaped my work ethic as an historian; to Andrew Gordon, whose counsel was instrumental in my decision to enter this profession; and to Steven Ericson, who introduced me to the historical study of railways. In addition, I must thank Harold Bolitho, who kindly agreed to read a long dissertation on a subject far from his own area of specialty. For invaluable training, along with timely and inspirational advice, I acknowledge Carter Eckert, Joshua Fogel, Cindy Hu, Mark Peattie, and Bob Wakabayashi. Among Japanese scholars, I am especially grateful to Kaneko Fumio, Hata Ikuhiko, Bannō Junji, Nishimura Shigeo, Kobayashi Hideo, and Kitaoka Shin'ichi. My colleagues at Wellesley College played an instrumental role in encouraging me to bring this work to timely completion. The opportunity to visit Northeast China in 1978 and travel by rail provided an important source of inspiration for this book. I express my appreciation to the Chinese People's Association for Friendship with Foreign Countries, the US-China Peoples Friendship Association, and, in particular, Richard Pendleton, for facilitating this trip.

Research for this study would not have been possible without the help of the staff of the Harvard-Yenching Library, the Japanese Section of the Library of Congress, the Japan Defense Research Institute Library, and the library of the Social Science Research Institute at the University of Tokyo. Professor Yamazaki Hiroaki served as my sponsor at the Social Science Research Institute, which provided invaluable support for many aspects of my work. Funding for various stages of research and writing was provided by a Foreign Language and Area Studies fellowship, a Fulbright-Hays Doctoral

Dissertation Research Abroad fellowship, the Mrs. Giles Whiting Foundation, the National Endowment for the Humanities, and Wellesley College. I am grateful to John Ziemer of the Harvard University Asia Center for his meticulous editorial work and to several anonymous readers for their valuable comments and suggestions.

Finally, I thank my wife, Suzanne Lee, and my son, Kenji, for putting up with my obsessive focus on this project for so many years, and my parents, whose stories of life in prewar Japan have given me glimpses into a world I cannot hope to see with my own eyes.

Y.T.M.

Contents

Appendixes

Reference Matter

Maps and Tables

Maps

Tables

Romanization and Railway Nomenclature

The majority of Chinese place-names in this book are rendered in the Wade-Giles system of romanization. Most others (for example, Peking, Nanking, Kirin) are written in traditionally established forms as they appeared in English-language treaty documents. The choice of this older system over the more commonly accepted *pinyin* is based on entirely practical considerations. Many of the place-names that figured prominently in the events examined in this study are no longer used. Such locations tend to be more recognizable to students of history who do not read Chinese if rendered in Wade-Giles rather than in *pinyin*. Others place-names were transliterated into older romanization systems based on local dialects (Mukden, Ssup'ingkai) and, in some cases, non-Chinese languages (Petune, Payintala). To rewrite them in *pinyin* based on *putonghua* (Mandarin) readings of the characters would, once again, detract from recognition. The quasi-colonial character of Manchuria during this era poses further difficulties. To render colonial place-names like Kwantung, invented and used largely by foreigners, into *pinyin* tends to naturalize them in a manner that would seem inappropriate. Such renderings as "Guandong Army" as opposed to "Kwantung Army" are somewhat jarring to the historian's eye, even though they are pronounced exactly alike. Dairen was a colonial city and written in this manner in all English-language documents produced by the Japanese.

It is common practice today, as it was in the early part of this century, to describe railways in China as well as Japan using one character drawn from each of the place-names of their termini. The Ssup'ingkai–T'aonan Railway, for example, would be commonly referred to as the Ssu–T'ao line. Such shorthand forms are not used in this book because they create more confusion than any benefits of brevity would justify. "Mantetsu," the Japanese character-acronym for the South Manchuria Railway, is avoided in favor of its official English initials, SMR. In all translations in the body of the text, "SMR" has been used as the equivalent of "Mantetsu."

Abbreviations

The following abbreviations are used in the text and notes (see the Works Cited, pp. 481–505, for complete bibliographic information):

CER	Chinese Eastern Railway
DK1	Bōeichō, Bōeikenshūsho, Senshishitsu, *Daihonei kaigunbu*, vol. 1
DR1	Bōeichō, Bōeikenshūsho, Senshishitsu, *Daihonei rikugunbu*, vol. 1
GSS	*Gendai shi shiryō*
MDN	Rikugunshō, *Mitsu dai nikki*
MGS	Rikugunshō, *Manshū gunsei shi*
Miyazaki 40, etc.	Sanbō honbu, Miyazaki shiryō, with item number
MSCS(A)	Kantō totokufu, Minseibu, *Manshū sangyō chōsa shiryō*, nōgyō
MSCS(C)	Kantō totokufu, Minseibu, *Manshū sangyō chōsa shiryō*, shōgyō
MSCS(M)	Kantō totokufu, Minseibu, *Manshū sangyō chōsa shiryō*, kōgyō
NGB	Gaimushō, *Nihon gaikō bunsho*
NGN	Gaimushō, *Nihon gaikō nenpyō narabini shuyō bunsho*
PMR	Peking–Mukden Railway
SMR	Minami Manshū tetsudō kabushikigaisha
SMR1	Minami Manshū tetsudō kabushikigaisha, *Minami Manshū tetsudō kabushikigaisha jūnen shi*

SMR2   Minami Manshū tetsudō kabushikigaisha, *Minami Manshū tetsudō kabushikigaisha dai niji jūnen shi*

SMR3   Minami Manshū tetsudō kabushikigaisha, *Minami Manshū tetsudō kabushikigaisha dai sanji jūnen shi*

TKN   Minami Manshū tetsudō kabushikigaisha, *Mantetsu tōkei nenpō*

TKS   Sanbō honbu, *Teikoku kokubō shigen*

YAI   Ōyama Azusa, *Yamagata Aritomo ikensho*

The Making of Japanese Manchuria,

1904–1932

Introduction

Japan's subjugation of Northeast China, a region known to foreigners as Manchuria, began in 1905 with the acquisition of a railway concession in the southern part of the territory, a prize of victory in the war against Russia. It culminated a quarter-century later in the creation of Manchoukuo, a vast realm the size of Alaska, severed from China and under complete Japanese control, that stretched from the Great Wall in the south to the Amur River in the north. The establishment of Japanese rule in Manchuria was, for the most part, an incremental process. Harnessing the possibilities inherent in the railway as an instrument of territorial control, the Japanese created corridors of imperial power running deep within the Manchurian heartland where they opened mines, built factories, and founded colonial settlements. Each addition to their growing portfolio of rights and concessions secured a new imperial bridgehead and created opportunities for colonization. In this manner, the Japanese gradually expanded their power and presence in the territory while steadily undermining Chinese sovereignty. During the 1920s, the process of encroachment entered a new phase with an attempt to create a Sino-Japanese condominium in Manchuria in partnership with the local warlord. The effort proved only partially successful, and in 1931, the Japanese army, growing increasingly impatient with what it considered half-way measures, finally resorted to armed aggression. The decisive importance of this military initiative to the consolidation of Japanese power in the territory is undeniable. In a larger historical context, however, the conquest of Northeast China must be understood as a protracted, decades-long endeavor in which the so-called Manchurian Incident of 1931 represents only a brief, climactic episode. The story of this remarkable imperialist venture, from its beginnings in the battlefields of the Russo-Japanese War to its denouement in the founding of the puppet state of Manchoukuo, is the subject of this book.

The quest for empire in East Asia forms one of the central threads in the history of modern Japan. A commitment to expansion emerged as an integral component of the young nation's adaptation to the predatory environment of the age of imperialism, a corollary of the same extraordinary process that transformed the country from a land of peasants and samurai overlords into a modern industrial society in the space of a single generation. As Japan matured and the pressures of Social Darwinian international competition receded, its imperialism developed an independent logic and momentum that ran counter to trends among the other Great Powers. Imperial aspirations clashed with the equally important foreign-policy goals of building friendly ties with China and maintaining harmony with the West, a dilemma that dominated the nation's diplomacy for much of the early twentieth century. The impact of expansionism on Japan's economic affairs was no less profound. The relative significance of economic motives for empire-building might be open to debate, but there is no question that Japan's vital trade and investment in East Asia, along with the outward migration of its people within the region, operated under a decidedly imperialist framework of special rights, gunboat diplomacy, and other "market constraints."[1] The issue of overseas expansion also formed one of the major fracture lines in domestic politics, a perennial point of contention within and among the multiple civil bureaucracies, the armed services, and the rival parties in parliament. It shaped Japanese thinking in broader ways as well. Before the 1930s, a popular culture of imperialism failed to take as deep a root in Japan as it did in Great Britain, as Mark Peattie has noted.[2] Nonetheless, for Japanese from all walks of life, empire provided a mirror in which they saw themselves and their place in the world—a head above their fellow Asians and equal to the mighty peoples of Europe and North America. Imperialism probably had its most profound influence on Japanese national development, however, in the arena of defense. Armed might, indispensable to acquiring and protecting an imperium abroad, led to the growth of a remarkably large military establishment for a country of Japan's limited means.

Manchuria represents one of several major expansionist thrusts that began in the late nineteenth century. Taiwan became Japan's first colony in 1895 and provided invaluable experience in the management of empire, a laboratory for colonial policy, and a training ground for a generation of imperial bureaucrats. Korea, over which Japan fought China in 1894–95 and Russia in 1904–5, lay at the heart of imperialist concerns until the conclusion of a protectorate treaty in 1905, which was followed by annexation five years later. Other undertakings included the colonization of Karafuto, as the Japanese called south Sakhalin, acquired in 1905, and the administration of the Caroline and Marshall islands, transferred from Germany to Japan in 1922 as a League of Nations Mandate. China emerged as a central focus of imperial attention early on. Competition with the other Great Powers for a share of the great wealth lying fallow in East Asia's largest and most populous country and for influence in shaping its future constituted, in the eyes of many Japanese leaders, a matter of national survival.[3]

Manchuria might be regarded as one facet of this activity in China before 1931. The nature of Japan's encroachments in the lands north of the Wall, however, diverged significantly from the general pattern of Japanese as well as Western imperialism in the south. During the late nineteenth and early twentieth centuries, China's relations with the outside world were governed by a multilateral system of treaties designed to maintain an equilibrium of foreign interests. This so-called Open Door system facilitated trade under Western rules while obstructing attempts at territorial aggrandizement. Such arrangements were satisfactory to those who sought to maximize commercial gains while minimizing long-term political and military commitments, an orientation characteristic of "informal imperialism."[4] As a signatory to these treaties, Japan officially denied any territorial ambitions in China, and in the lands south of the Wall, Japanese policies in regard to observing the rules of the Open Door were broadly similar, with the exception of a brief period during World War I, to those of the other Great Powers. In Manchuria, however, Japan attempted to circumvent these rules at every opportunity, with the goal of approximating, insofar as the international community would tolerate, conditions of direct territorial control. Unprepared to challenge the multilateral system overtly, the Japanese chose, in effect, to concede the question of Chinese sovereignty in Manchuria in the arena of high diplomacy while creating colonial realities on the ground.

A recognition of the distinction between Japanese policies north and south of the Wall is essential. Conflation of the two patterns of imperialism runs the risk of overstating the aggressiveness of Japanese activity in the south while understating its virulence in Manchuria. The difference is especially important in understanding the events of 1931. Many historians regard the Manchurian Incident as an event marking a sea change in Japan's China policies from a moderate commercial imperialism to an aggressive territorial expansionism. They have sought an explanation for this abrupt transformation in the extraordinary concatenation of three major crises at the turn of the decade: the triumph of revolutionary nationalism in China, the breakdown of international cooperation, and the onslaught of the world depression. A close look at the pattern of encroachment in Manchuria from 1905 on, however, suggests the possibility, if not the likelihood, of partition as an eventual outcome. The crises of the early 1930s provided an opportunity rather than any new need for seizing the territory. Indeed, given the colonial proclivities inherent in Japan's orientation toward Manchuria from the beginning, an attempt to illuminate the factors that restrained more aggressive action until 1931 presents as much of a challenge as an effort to identify those that caused it.

Insofar as Japan officially recognized Chinese sovereignty in the lands north of the Wall until the founding of Manchoukuo, the broad rubric of informal imperialism might be applied to its encroachments in the territory. Indeed, the legal framework of Japanese activity in Manchuria before 1931 relied on nominally economic rights legitimized by the multilateral treaty system. Japan was certainly not the only power to lay claim to railway and mining concessions in China. Narrower definitions of informal imperialism that take British practices as paradigmatic, however, would be misleading. Territory rather than trade lay at the heart of Japanese aspirations in Manchuria.

The uniquely creative manner in which the Japanese exploited purportedly legitimate economic rights in order to exert territorial control in Manchuria are well reflected in the operations of the extraordinary, semi-official corporation known as the South Manchuria Railway Company (SMR). This institution was established in 1906 by imperial ordinance for the ostensible purpose of managing the railway and colliery inherited from Russia. It was also charged with responsibility for administering a narrow strip of land along the right of way known as the Railway Zone. The SMR was formally chartered as a commercial organization, but for all intents and purposes, it functioned as an arm of the Japanese government in Manchuria. The principal mission of the company, although couched in formulations that emphasized the universally beneficial work of territorial development and Japan's desire to bring modern civilization to this supposedly benighted land, was nothing less than the colonization of Northeast China.

The SMR's promoters likened this institution to Britain's East India Company until it became clear that the comparison provided ready ammunition for international criticism; the parallel is useful in conceptualizing the purpose behind the SMR.[5] At the same time, the nature of its power differed from that of traditional colonial corporations. The East India Company served as a colonizing agency in South Asia through its direct control of land over which it exercised military and administrative authority as well as the rights of economic proprietorship. The SMR, in conjunction with the Japanese army, wielded comparable powers in the Railway Zone, but its total real estate holdings amounted to no more than 108 square miles. At the same time, its control over the railway network in the southern part of Manchuria endowed it with a power over territorial affairs that in time came to approach, at least in some respects, colonial rule. Military applications of railway technology allowed Japanese authorities to exercise a decisive hand in external defense as well as internal peacekeeping, and these circumstances, in effect, placed much of southern Manchuria under a state of virtual occupation. An effective monopoly over commercial transportation in the region enabled the SMR to direct the development of the territory's land and natural resources as well as patterns of migration and settlement. Exploiting the geography of Northeast Asia, the Japanese also used railway policies to enhance Manchuria's ties to colonial Korea while weakening connections to China south of the Wall. The railway had served as a vital nation-building tool in Europe and North America. In the hands of the Japanese in Manchuria, it became an instrument of imperialist reconstruction.

The colonization work of the SMR also entailed a wide range of activities beyond building and operating the territorial railway network. The company invested heavily throughout the modern sector of the regional economy, which it dominated from the outset. Its operations encompassed not only horse carting, warehousing, harbor works, maritime shipping, and international trade but also extensive mining and manufacturing. Particularly noteworthy was the SMR's diversification into heavy industries, which included ventures in iron and steel, chemicals, and machine building. Such initiatives were rare on the part of foreign investors in China, who generally emphasized light industry if they considered entering into manufacturing at all. The SMR's promotion of urban development within the Railway Zone also played an important part in the process of colonization. Company towns designed as models of imperialist modernity incorporated the latest techniques in city planning and functioned as centers of Japanese settlement and business activity. They also fulfilled a vital role in public relations by serving as showcases of the new technological civilization that the SMR claimed to be carving from Manchuria's wilderness.

The importance of Manchuria in the history of Japanese imperialism is widely acknowledged. The developments of the 1930s have been extensively studied in English-language scholarship. The Manchurian Incident is described in blow-by-blow detail by Takehiko Yoshiaki and Sadako Ogata. Mark Peattie's biography of Ishiwara Kanji offers insight into the motives of the principal architect of the military initiative and the founding father of Manchoukuo. The far-reaching impact of the seizure of the territory on Japan's foreign and defense policies and its contribution to setting the stage for all-out war against China in 1937 have been explored, among others, by James Crowley.[6] Studies of domestic developments in the 1930s link events in Manchuria to profound changes in society, politics, and economic affairs at home, including the rising influence of the army in all aspects of national life.[7] The construction of Manchoukuo, regarded by many as a social and economic experiment aimed at creating an imperialist utopia on the Manchurian prairie, has attracted special attention. Chalmers Johnson has popularized the notion that the lessons in heavy industrial planning learned by Japan's economic bureaucrats while serving in the territory during the 1930s found subsequent application at home. Louise Young's book not only delves into the political and economic construction of what she calls Japan's "brave new empire" but also examines the mobilization of the nation as a whole in support of this undertaking.[8]

In contrast to the 1930s, however, we know considerably less about developments in pre-conquest Manchuria. Diplomatic histories, in which the work of Akira Iriye figures prominently, have underscored the enormous weight exerted by Manchurian concerns in Japan's foreign policy from 1905 on. These studies also point to the near obsession on the part of Japanese policymakers with railways in the territory, an issue that was central to a long series of disputes embroiling Japan, China, Russia, Britain and the United States during the quarter-century before 1931.[9] Analyses of foreign investment further highlight the singular attention that the Japanese paid to this territory. Throughout the period between 1905 and 1931, well over half of the nation's capital commitments in China, Japan's largest field of overseas investment, were concentrated in the lands north of the Great Wall.[10] Beyond these broad contours, however, we know little about what the Japanese were doing in Manchuria and why they devoted such energy to this one region. Gavan McCormack's work on the warlord Chang Tso-lin is one of the few monographs exploring Japanese imperialism in the territory before 1931.[11] A number of writers have produced unpublished dissertations that examine aspects of the pre-conquest empire-building process, including Herbert Bix and Ken'ichirō Hirano.[12] These works begin to illuminate a fascinating area of inquiry, but they also raise a host of questions that indicate how much more remains to be done.

Japanese-language historiography, to be sure, offers far broader coverage and, for those who find it accessible, fills some of the empirical gaps in English-language studies. Not only does it provide a rich body of work on the Manchurian Incident and Manchoukuo, but it deals at length with developments before 1931.[13] Kitaoka Shin'ichi's seminal study of the army and continental expansion between 1906 and 1918, for example, presents a broad view of Japanese policy toward China, with an emphasis on Manchuria, and explores diplomacy, defense, and relevant problems in domestic politics in detail. He also takes a close look at railway development, trade, currency policy, and administrative practices in the territory.[14] Kaneko Fumio offers a comprehensive analysis of Japanese investment in Manchuria from the turn of the twentieth century to 1931 and examines the process of Japan's economic penetration of the region in depth.[15] A number of historians, including Kitaoka and Kaneko, have also explored the history of the SMR. The work of the Waseda University study group represents a pioneering effort in this field, and a recent collection of articles by Kobayashi Hideo and his colleagues have expanded on this scholarship.[16] Others have produced numerous articles on railway construction, immigration, industrialization, and Sino-Japanese collaboration. Of special significance are studies of military policy that link the sustained growth of the Imperial Japanese Army after 1905 to Japan's commitment in Manchuria.[17]

I seek to build on this base of knowledge by examining the interactions of defense, diplomacy, and economic policy in shaping the overall course of events and by offering a long view of developments between 1905 and 1932. Such an approach not only allows for an integrated analysis of imperialist behavior and how it changes over time but also opens the door to areas of inquiry largely beyond the scope of narrower treatments.[18] Taking advantage of this expanded investigative framework, I explore three overarching questions thematically throughout the book.

The first and most basic of these questions is why Japan pursued an expansionist course in Manchuria with such persistence during the quarter-century after 1905. An understanding of the impulses driving the quest for empire is fundamental to any study of imperialism, and most past inquiries have addressed this issue in one form or another. Answers that may seem adequate in accounting for any given initiative or phase of policy development, however, are far less satisfactory in explaining the larger pattern. Although strategic anxieties, for example, might well have pushed Japan into a policy of "forward defense" in Northeast China during the immediate aftermath of the Russo-Japanese War, the danger of a Russian "war of revenge" receded rather quickly, and the military value of maintaining the territory as a buffer zone diminished accordingly. Japan's initial commitment in Manchuria might also be explained in terms of the politics of imperialist rivalry in East Asia. Yet that rivalry began losing much of its steam in the years after 1905, and the declining need for Japan to match the moves of its fellow powers in the game of empire steadily reduced the significance of its claims in Northeast China as a geopolitical playing piece. A more enduring as well as cogent body of purposes might be found in the economic arena. However, the traditional imperialist quest for protected markets, cheap raw materials, and profitable investment opportunities likewise falls short in accounting for Japanese behavior. As a market for manufactured goods, China south of the Wall was far more important than the lands to the north throughout the period under consideration. Moreover, Manchuria provided few raw materials that were not freely available from other sources at lower cost and of a better quality. Opportunities for profitable business investment were even less relevant to Japanese concerns since ventures in the territory tended to offer substantially lower rates of return than enterprises at home.[19] The long-term value of Manchuria to Japan, whether assessed in strategic, geopolitical, or economic terms, was far from obvious, particularly when measured against the enormous costs entailed in an expansionist venture. What sustained this commitment over the course of 25 years is thus a problem that warrants careful examination.

The second question concerns matters of imperialist method. How the Japanese built a thriving, proto-colonial realm in Manchuria without the political and legal apparatus of formal rule is no less intriguing a problem than why. Their techniques in themselves were by no means original. The use of the railway as an instrument of empire, for example, had been well established by the late nineteenth century. In fact, the Japanese inherited not only the basic idea but also the physical apparatus they employed in Manchuria directly from the Russians. The successful use of this technique, however, cannot be taken for granted. The Japanese venture was singularly effective in exploiting the power of the railway for the purpose of territorial control and unsurpassed by any undertaking along broadly similar lines in the record of modern imperialism.[20] The combination of imagination, audacity, and technical skill embodied in the management of the SMR is noteworthy, particularly because the Japanese were not obvious candidates for such unusual achievements in this field. Railway construction was extremely costly and particularly difficult for a country with meager capital resources. Although railways offered the possibility of financial returns, their record of business performance in China was remarkably poor, a situation that led more than a few foreign investors to abandon their projects.[21] Lines managed for purposes other than profit, such as the SMR, were prone to large operating deficits. The Japanese overcame such problems early on and continued to pursue this strategy effectively in the face of increasingly inimical conditions. The decades after 1905 witnessed a marked rise in Chinese resistance to all imperialist encroachments. At the same time, the Great Powers became decreasingly tolerant of foreign behavior in China inconsistent with the principles of the Open Door. The fact that Japanese were able to navigate this treacherous environment and maintain an expansionist course in Manchuria without abandoning their nominal adherence to the multilateral system or precipitating a major armed confrontation with the Chinese before 1931 is quite remarkable.

The third question deals with the larger problem of continuity in the course of events spanning the Russo-Japanese War and the Manchurian Incident. Other than a common venue, how meaningful are the connections between the acquisition of a railway concession and the founding of a Manchurian state? At first glance, any direct link would seem rather implausible. These two developments represent qualitatively different types of imperialist encroachment and are, moreover, separated by two and a half decades of kaleidoscopic change in Japan and in its international environment. Whatever the original purposes in staking a claim in Manchuria in 1905, they are hardly likely to have retained their full relevance ten let alone twenty years later. The frequent changes of leadership characteristic of Japanese politics in the early twentieth century, as well as long-term shifts in the makeup and orientation of the governing elite, cast further doubt as to substantive continuities. Nonetheless, the existence of strong connective threads, if manifested only in the uninterrupted expansion of the SMR, are undeniable. An examination of the growth of Japanese power in Manchuria reveals a stepwise progression between 1905 and 1932 and points to an unmistakable evolutionary relationship between railway management and colonial rule. Manchoukuo's purportedly revolutionary program also has significant, preconquest roots in the heavy-industrialization program of the SMR. As Charles Maier notes, "in a time of upheaval, it is continuity and stability that need explanation."[22] This observation would certainly seem to apply to the history of Japanese Manchuria.

The question of continuity has broader ramifications for interpreting the record of Japanese imperialism. The expansionism of the Meiji era (1868–1912) has been well analyzed. The quest for empire during this period was an outgrowth of a predatory international environment and a corollary of the nation-building process of the late nineteenth and early twentieth centuries in which Japan self-consciously emulated Western models in both international and domestic affairs. The imperialism of the early part of the Shōwa era (1926–89) has likewise been described as a phenomenon of its time. This drive for conquest was shaped in part by the global depression and the concomitant rise of militarism in domestic politics. For these reasons, it is generally believed to have shared at least some features with contemporary Italian and German expansion.[23]

The empire-building process in Manchuria bridges these two distinct periods in imperial history. Along with the annexation of Korea in 1910, the founding of the SMR represents one of the last major initiatives of Meiji imperialism, whereas the Manchurian Incident of 1931 marks the opening act of Shōwa aggression. The larger part of Japan's undertaking in Northeast China, however, occurred during the Taishō era (1912–26). Indeed, granted the same chronological license often used in defining a "greater Taishō" era in domestic history that encompasses the first three decades of the twentieth century, we might describe the subjugation of Manchuria between 1905 and 1931 as the principal manifestation of a "Taishō imperialism." Characterizing Taishō imperialism in succinct terms comparable to those applied to its Meiji and Shōwa counterparts is difficult, and a simple extension of the boundaries of these two better-understood phases that absorbs the intervening period does not offer a meaningful solution. Few of the factors that explain Meiji expansion continued to exert influence much after 1905. Conditions that account for Shōwa imperialism had yet to emerge before the end of the 1920s. Although facile notions of the Taishō era as an interlude of liberalism have long been rejected by most scholars, these years nonetheless nurtured a greater faith in international cooperation, free trade, and the benefits of a domestic order based on market capitalism than seen during any other period in modern Japanese history before the end of World War II. Equally important, impulses toward aggressive empire-building, along with the power of the army and its allies in the bureaucracy, were never weaker than during this same period.[24] Taishō imperialism, then, does not readily lend itself to explanation as a product of its times. The material explored in this study will, I hope, shed light on this problem.

This book is the product of empirical research, whose findings I present in the form of a chronological account. At the same time, the telling of the story, along with its themes and emphases, reflects an underlying analytical framework that warrants a brief exposition here. In my efforts to explain the evolutionary dynamics shaping Japanese expansion in Manchuria, I have found particularly useful what might be described as an opportunistic and adaptive model of empire-building suggested in the work, among others, of David Landes and, more recently, Daniel Headrick.[25] According to this view, modern imperialism defies simple analysis as a "functionally rational" pattern of behavior in the sense of Karl Mannheim: a course of action determined by a predefined body of goals, logically geared toward achieving a desired outcome.[26] Instead, the expansionism on the part of the industrial states of the West that began in the 1880s must be understood as a response to opportunities in the environment, a speculative "scramble" to stake claims to whatever remaining tracts of territory, unsecured under Western international rules, that came within easy reach. Expansionist powers selected their targets, not by means of "rational shopping" in an imperial real estate market, but through a blind auction in which participants often bid for properties almost sight unseen.[27]

Given the nature of the process, imperialist statesmen seldom possessed clear plans for the territories they had seized. The formulation of imperial policy proceeded, in large part, through rationalization after the fact of acquisition, an approach that required policymakers to retrofit suitable goals and purposes to a line of action to which they had already committed themselves. Although taking into account the needs of the metropole and the constraints of the international environment, they adapted not only their

strategies, but also their aims and purposes to the conditions they encountered in their new holdings. Successful adaptation demanded considerable
creativity and an aggressive effort to explore the horizons of exploitable possibility offered by the land and peoples under their rule. The French concept
of *mise en valeur* aptly captures the underlying logic. The quest for worthy
uses of imperial assets, indeed, had taken on systematic form by the turn of
the century, represented in the practice of "scientific colonization" pioneered
by the Germans in Africa. This approach harnessed geology, botany, agron-
omy, and anthropology, along with the new field of tropical medicine, to the
task of managing an empire and discovering its optimum utilities.[28]

Adaptive rationalization in the formulation of imperial policy generated
two important corollary features of modern empire-building. First, it gave
rise to a diverse body of programmatic aims and strategies. Lacking specific,
predefined goals, policymakers readily entertained almost any proposal that
might put the territory to productive uses, so long as it remained within reasonable boundaries of cost, risk, and, within their cultural frame of reference,
ethics. Analogous to the diversification of product lines in large-scale enterprises, a multiplicity of programs ensured a more efficient exploitation of assets, as well as a broad base of constituency support. This encouraged a proliferation of goals.[29] Second, the process lent itself to a constant reinvention
of imperial policy over time. The self-consciously experimental orientation
of programmatic development, as suggested in the notion of "scientific"
colonization, accounts, in part, for this tendency. At a more basic level, it reflected the nature of adaptation as an open-ended process, one that would
continue as the framework of opportunity itself changed. The horizons of
possibility might expand or contract with shifts in the international climate,
developments in the metropole, or transformations in the periphery, some of
them the result of imperialist action. Technological innovations could lead
to new ways of exploiting territorial resources, just as the development of the
railway, telegraph, and shallow-draft steamer in the first half of the nineteenth century had created the basic framework of opportunity for the grand
expansionism of the second.[30] Over the long run, imperial policy might develop along lines entirely unforeseen and pursue goals bearing little resemblance to those embraced by an earlier generation of expansionists. This
propensity to reinvention endowed empire-building with an abiding relevance even as a changing world rendered many of its initial meanings and
purposes obsolete. Ironically, then, the very lack of a fixed and coherent

agenda for expansion from the outset might explain the enduring quality of many imperialist ventures.

The value of this model as an analytical framework in exploring the problems of motive, method, and continuity set forth in this study is two-fold. First, it directs the inquiry toward an examination of the opportunities facing the venture and how they affected the direction of development, not only during its startup phase, but throughout the duration of the undertaking. An understanding of imperialism as an art of the possible also recommends a careful evaluation of the causal relationship between ends and means. It is important to distinguish between a Manchuria policy formulated as a guide to action and one produced through the rationalization, after the fact, of behavior dictated by opportunity and circumstance. The model suggests that improvisation might have played a far greater role in shaping the venture than premeditated design. This framework of analysis, moreover, identifies targets of investigation that we might overlook otherwise. If the key to explaining the course of events lies in the nature of the opportunities the Japanese encountered in Manchuria, it is important to look beyond the conventional arenas of politics, economics, and national defense and consider as well the contribution of such factors as technology in shaping the horizons of possibility. The railway would seem particularly important as a technological source of opportunity, not only in the broad sense that Headrick describes but also in the more specific context of formulating a course of action in Manchuria. The versatility of the railway as an instrument of war, of economic development, and of territorial integration allowed for a wide range of imperial policy goals, from the modestly commercial to the more ambitiously colonial.

Second, this model describes a possible evolutionary logic underlying the course of events leading from the acquisition of a railway concession to the establishment of a Manchurian state. It accounts for a coherent pattern in the development of imperial power in the territory even in the absence of a grand design. Intended or not, the cumulative effects of activity steadily altered the horizons of possibility, and successive initiatives in the territory built on increasingly broad and elevated foundations. More important, this framework implies not only an evolution of power but also of motive and method. The process of adaptive reinvention offers an explanation for the persistence and continuity of Japanese activity in the territory despite conditions in the historical environment that might lead us to expect otherwise.

The venture retained its cogency over the course of a quarter-century because its aims and strategies changed with the times. The operation of such evolutionary dynamics requires the investigation to identify those specific adaptations responsible for sustaining the long-term relevance of the Manchurian endeavor.

An emphasis on opportunism, adaptation, and evolutionary change does not deny the contributions of imperialist volition. Even if opportunity and circumstance played a fundamental role in shaping the development of Japanese Manchuria, the course of action we observe was ultimately the result of choices made by groups in Japan with the power and the will to do so. An attempt to understand those decisions, how and by whom they were made, thus constitutes an important part of this study. The process involved a great many people, both inside and outside the councils of government, working in Tokyo as well as on the imperial frontier.[31] I focus on three institutional actors in this book: the Foreign Ministry, the Imperial Japanese Army, and the SMR. I have chosen these agencies because of their centrality to the empire-building process throughout the period under consideration and because they offer the most useful vantage points from which to recount the narrative as a whole.

The importance of the Foreign Ministry in shaping expansionist policy requires little elaboration, and given the existing body of work on diplomatic history, the institution itself warrants no special introduction.[32] Foreign Ministry sources have proved particularly valuable for this study, not only in illuminating the activities of diplomats themselves, but in providing a broader picture of developments on the ground as conveyed in the dispatches of Manchuria-based consuls. Although these sources are well known, they remain far from exhausted as far as the subject of Manchuria is concerned.

The army, likewise, is a familiar institution. Its development before 1931, however, has received surprisingly little focused study in English-language work.[33] We know of its role in foreign affairs primarily through the critical filter of diplomatic sources. In this study, I seek to explore army behavior more directly. A wealth of primary sources dealing with the military aspects of Manchuria policy exists. These include the Army Ministry's *Mitsu dai nikki* (Classified great daily log), a vast compendium of reports and proposals received by the ministry, as well as special compilations, such as the *Manshū gunsei shi* (History of the military administration of Manchuria), which deals with the army's occupation policies during the Russo-Japanese War and illuminates the foundations of the early postwar program in Manchuria. Major Koiso Kuniaki's seminal 1917 study on wartime autarky, a proposal that laid the basis for military-industrial policy in the territory from the 1920s through the early years of Manchoukuo, is another work of special importance. The operational planning records of the Army General Staff, which outline in detail strategies and tactics for prospective conflicts with Russia and China, have been particularly valuable. These documents provide foundations essential to an understanding of railway policy in Manchuria. Unlike Foreign Ministry sources, however, few scholars outside Japan have exploited this material to any significant extent in historical research on Manchuria. In introducing these documents, I hope to offer a fresh perspective on the problem of army imperialism.

The SMR was arguably the single most important agency in the frontline management of Manchuria before 1931, and as the least familiar of my three institutional actors to an English-language audience, it receives special attention.[34] I explore the nature of railway power and the company's colonizing mission in detail. I also examine the structure and strategy of the SMR as a business enterprise. Although the company was designed to serve as an instrument of national policy, it was simultaneously mandated to operate as a profit-making venture. The SMR's earnings, in fact, underwrote much of the cost of the expansionist undertaking as a whole. The logic of business management had significant consequences for the formulation and execution of imperial policy as well. It frequently constrained both the pace and the direction of the expansionist process, but at the same time, it also created unforeseen opportunities. Industrial diversification, for example, first emerged as an element of business strategy and was only subsequently rationalized by policymakers as a programmatic goal.

In order to support both its policy and its business functions, the SMR maintained a large research establishment that employed some of Japan's brightest economists, social scientists, agronomists, and engineers. Indeed, the company's researchers, particularly those working for the Chōsaka (Research section), might be described as Japanese Manchuria's brain trust. Voluminous publications and reports produced by the SMR's staff are some of the most important documentary source materials used for this book. They include not only studies of Manchuria's economic, social, and political conditions, but also policy analyses, often accompanied by recommendations for action. These documents offer information not available elsewhere, and they make it possible to flesh out our understanding of debates and decisions that appear only in telegraphic and often incomprehensible form in diplomatic and military records.[35]

The empire-building process, of course, involved a great many other players in addition to the diplomats, soldiers, and railway managers who figure most prominently in this narrative. In recent years, historians of Japanese imperialism have urged their colleagues to look beyond agents of the state and delve into the arena of imperialist civil society. They have also underscored the importance of exploring the cultural construction of empire in the realm of the popular imagination.[36] Louise Young's work on Manchoukuo demonstrates the significance of such approaches for the 1930s. Andrew Gordon's notion of "imperial democracy," born in the Hibiya Riots of 1905, points to possible directions for such a study of the pre-conquest period.[37] The need for work along these lines is unquestionable. Even within the domain of political history, there is much that remains unexplored. The question of parliament and empire, for example, warrants a far more lengthy treatment than offered in this book. So, too, does the institutional history of the SMR. The choice of actors and topics, however, is ultimately dictated by the nature of the questions posed by the inquiry rather than any absolute hierarchy of significance. My concern lies in problems of aim and strategy. I seek to illuminate the changing body of purposes and structures of power shaping the evolution of Japanese Manchuria, and my emphases follow from this focus.

I have framed this study within the context of Japanese history. At the same time, developments in Manchuria examined in this book unquestionably occupy a major place in the history of modern China. No comprehensive grasp of imperialism and its impact in this territory is possible without a detailed examination of events from a Chinese vantage point. Russian and Korean perspectives are important as well.[38] My primary goal, however, is to describe what the Japanese did and why they did it. Fortunately, the writing of history is a collective endeavor. In this spirit, I hope that this book will contribute a limited but significant piece to a broader understanding of Japan and its empire in East Asia.

ONE

War, Opportunity, and Empire, 1904–1905

By the turn of the twentieth century, the term "Manchuria" had become well established in the Western diplomatic lexicon as a description of the borderlands of the Ch'ing realm north of the Great Wall. The Yalu and T'umen rivers marked its boundaries with Korea in the southeast, and the Argun, Amur, and Ussuri rivers, its frontiers with the Russian empire. Narrowly applied, the term referred to the three administrative subdivisions of Heilungkiang, Kirin, and Shengking (later renamed Fengt'ien). Informal usage, however, often included the easternmost portions of Mongolia, which were closely linked by patterns of settlement, transportation, and commerce to Kirin and Shengking. In later years, these districts became part of Fengt'ien province and the special administrative region of Jehol, which also incorporated a portion of Chihli province (see Maps 1.1, 1.2). Broadly construed, Manchuria, or *Manmō* as the Japanese subsequently came to describe the territory, encompassed a vast expanse roughly a half-million square miles in size.[1] Encountering a rich but thinly populated land, foreign observers often drew comparisons to the Great Plains of North America. As in other border regions, the central government exerted less vigorous control in Manchuria than in the provinces of the Chinese heartland. Indeed, given its history as the ancestral home of the ruling dynasty, the authorities had deliberately limited the political and cultural integration of the territory with the realm south of the Wall. Owen Lattimore argues that they did so in order to keep their traditional domains fallow and to preserve the fading ethnic identity of the Manchu people.[2]

Manchuria offered a tempting target for Great Power encroachment in the age of empire; laying claim to spheres of influence in China or, where possible, carving off pieces of its periphery formed part of the "great game" in

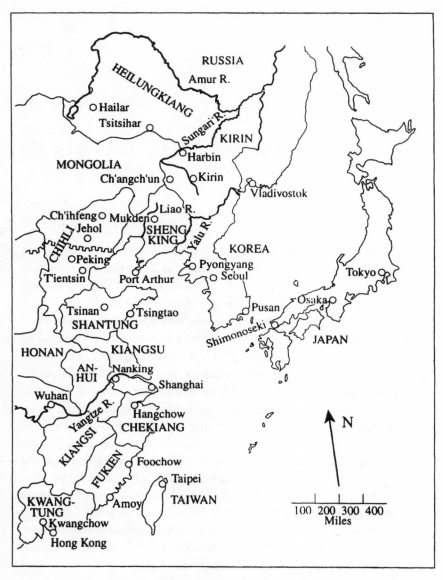

Map 1.1 East Asia in 1901 (based on Smith, *Century Atlas of the World*, map 107)

Map 1.2 Political boundaries in Manchuria and eastern Mongolia, 1901 and 1931. Political units as of 1931 are shown in italics (based on maps in Smith, *Century Atlas of the World*, map 107; Kaneko, *Kindai Nihon ni okeru tai-Manshū tōshi no kenkyū*, 18; Tōa keizai chōsakyoku, *Manchoukuo Year Book, 1934*).

East Asia. It is certainly understandable that the temptation might be particularly strong for Japan, which not only harbored expansionist aspirations but, as a result of the strategic geography of Northeast Asia, suffered deep anxieties about its security. From early in its modern history, the nation turned a vigilant eye toward Korea for the same reason. The fact that Manchuria might attract other powers magnified that concern and, if for no other reason, offered a powerful motive for pre-emptive efforts to secure control.

The existence of rational and cogent motives, however, is seldom sufficient to explain the actual course of imperialist action. In the final analysis, opportunity was often the paramount consideration. During the first decade of the twentieth century, Japan remained a country of very limited means, outclassed in both military and economic power by almost all of its prospective rivals in East Asia. Although the nation's governing elites had little difficulty discovering compelling reasons to seek control of neighboring territories, for the most part, they practiced empire-building as an art of the possible. Meiji leaders might seek imperialist solutions to the problems of defense, economic development, and geopolitical competition where circumstances permitted, but they were fully prepared to adopt non-imperialist solutions where necessary. The decisive importance of opportunity in the case of Japan's thrust into Manchuria is obscured by the ease with which the decision to secure a foothold could be rationalized after the fact as a natural, if not inevitable, course of action. An understanding of the nature of Japan's initial commitment in the territory, however, is essential not only to illuminating the origins of the venture, but also to explaining its subsequent development.

Meiji Imperialism: An Art of the Possible

The modern Japanese nation-state was itself a product of the age of empire, and its founding fathers were men of a decidedly imperialist persuasion. Japan's mid-nineteenth century encounter with the commercial expansionism of the West triggered a political upheaval that placed a group of young samurai reformers in power in 1868, who immediately embarked on an extraordinary program that would lay the foundations for the nation's rise as an East Asian power. Deeply impressed by their experience at the receiving end of gunboat diplomacy and the stinging humiliation of the unequal treaties imposed in the 1850s, Meiji reformers dedicated themselves to eradicating the weaknesses that had made their country vulnerable to foreign encroachment. They based their reconstruction program on contemporary Western models of power and prosperity, and as keen-eyed students, they could hardly overlook the apparent contributions of overseas empires to Western success.[3] Observations of the world around them offered clear evidence that "colonies," as William Langer put it, "were the sine qua non of national greatness."[4] It is hardly surprising then, that "enlightened" Japanese of the late nineteenth century came to internalize the values of imperialism and Social Darwinism along with those of industrial capitalism and constitutional government. The increasingly predatory environment in which the young Meiji state took form only confirmed the understanding that "eat or be eaten" formed the fundamental imperative governing even civilized international relations, and that expansion, in the long run, constituted a matter of national survival. In later years, other peoples in Africa and Asia would respond to foreign domination with a revolutionary anti-imperialism. Japan's overall response to the Western challenge distinguishes itself by its commitment to join rather than overthrow the very international system that had threatened its existence.[5]

However imperialist in outlook, the leaders of Meiji Japan were also realists cautious in their dealings with the outside world. With a profound respect for the power of the West and an acute awareness of Japan's relative weakness, they understood the great perils entailed in any premature adventures overseas. Empire might be vital to the nation's future, but competing with the likes of Britain, France, Germany, and Russia lay beyond Japan's capabilities for the time being. Itō Hirobumi (1849–1909) and Yamagata Aritomo (1838–1922), members of the original samurai oligarchy that had seized power in the Meiji Restoration and two of the most powerful figures in Japanese government until after the turn of the century, represented this circumspect orientation well. Itō, the more cautious of the two, constantly warned against imperial adventurism and repeatedly reined in the more aggressive impulses of some of his associates. In his view, it was far better for the Great Powers to regard Japan with benign indifference than with the dangerous respect afforded a serious rival. Yamagata might consider bolder action on occasion, but he, too, represented a voice of restraint, all the more important given his role as the nation's senior military leader. Although he was a soldier-statesmen engaged in all aspects of national policy, Yamagata dedicated himself first and foremost to the development of Japan's armed forces, never tiring of pointing out the myriad dangers confronting the nation in a hostile world. Yet the very conditions that necessitated a strong military also argued for great reserve in its use. Reckless action in an arena of rapacious imperialist rivalry could well prove fatal.[6]

The tension between well-developed expansionist impulses, on the one hand, and a strong propensity toward caution, on the other, produced a body of external policies that, at least through the 1890s, could fairly be described as "imperialist" in inclination. Yet placed in the larger context of contemporary events, Japanese actions in Asia represented little more than a pale shadow of Western behavior. In the 1870s, for example, Japan attempted to assert Great Power status with respect to China and to lay claim to the rights afforded signatories to the unequal treaties imposed on that country since the 1840s. Demanding the same privileges from China that the West had extracted from Japan was partly a matter of prestige, but it also had economic importance, since treaty powers enjoyed special commercial advantages. The Chinese, contemptuous of Japanese pretensions, understandably rebuffed such demands. Failure to win even China's respect represented a humiliating setback for aspiring imperialists, yet in a fashion characteristic of the Japanese of the Meiji era, they adapted to circumstances, devising alternative means to strengthen their economic position on the continent. Indeed, through a combination of active trade policies and the creative strategies of trading companies like Mitsui Bussan, Japan managed to do better than hold its own against Western commercial interests in China despite the lack of special treaty rights. Necessity forced Meiji leaders to invent effective, non-imperialist solutions to problems that stronger powers might have resolved with gunboats and bayonets. At the same time, granted a sufficiently attractive opportunity along with low costs and risks, even conservative leaders might act more aggressively. Japan's punitive expedition to Taiwan in 1874 and its emulation of Commodore Perry in the opening of Korea in 1876 offer examples of what Stewart Lone appropriately describes as the "sniping" imperialism of this era. These ventures seem to foreshadow the future directions of Japan's expansion, and in the case of Korea, strategic considerations played a part in drawing Japanese attention. At the same time, both Taiwan and Korea clearly constituted targets of opportunity. During the 1870s and 1880s, no other territories lay within the reach of Japan's very limited ability to project power abroad while remaining simultaneously outside the scope of Great Power interest. These initiatives, moreover, produced no lasting gains. Apart from settling the status of the Ryūkyū Islands, no fundamental adjustments in Sino-Japanese relations emerged as a result of the Taiwan Expedition. The Japanese continued to meddle in Korea for some time after 1876 in an attempt to "guide" the kingdom toward modernizing reforms modeled after their own. Yet when they encountered a vigorous challenge in the 1880s from a Ch'ing government determined to reassert its traditional claims of suzerainty in the territory, Japan backed down in order to avert a military confrontation. Before 1894, Japanese imperialism took form not so much as a program of bold thrusts but as a series of probing forays along lines of minimum resistance that withdrew quickly in the face of significant obstacles.[7]

National defense constituted the one area where a cautious Meiji leadership might undertake more forthright action and assume significant risks. In the early years, the concerns of Japanese strategic planners centered on repelling a direct invasion of the home islands. At the same time, military leaders understood that true security required the development of a capability to meet an enemy before its forces reached Japanese shores. A strategy of forward defense required the construction of a blue-water navy, a goal toward which Japan, with great sacrifice, had made considerable progress by the 1890s. At the same time, given the proximity of the Japanese islands to the Asian mainland and, in particular, to the Korean peninsula, an effective offshore defense entailed a continental dimension as well. In the words of a German military advisor, Korea constituted "a dagger pointed at the heart of Japan" and a mortal threat in the hands of a hostile power. Yamagata elaborated this concern into a strategic doctrine that defined an extended Japanese defense perimeter, or "line of interest," minimally encompassing Korea. The nation's security depended on excluding any potential adversary from a place within that perimeter, using diplomacy and, if need be, armed force. In Japanese thinking, Korea had left itself particularly vulnerable to encroachment, sufficiently weak to fall prey to Japanese gunboat diplomacy in 1876, and certainly easy pickings for any major power intent on seizure. Korea's ambiguous international status as a tributary state of China, making the kingdom neither a fully independent country nor an integral part of the Chinese empire, compounded the problem. Such ambiguity constituted an open invitation to encroachment, and Korea might well go the way of Vietnam, a tributary state that China had proved incapable of defending and had lost to the French in the war of 1883–85.[8]

Japan's defense policy demanded the exclusion of any potentially hostile power from the peninsula, but its greatest concern clearly lay with Russia. Russia presented a particular danger as a power with national territory in East Asia, sharing island borders with Japan to the north and a frontier with Korea near the mouth of the T'umen River. An ambitious scheme to build a Eurasian railway linking St. Petersburg with the Pacific coast, launched in the 1880s, increased Japanese anxieties. Soldiers and diplomats in the late nineteenth century regarded railways not only as economic instruments but as military facilities. The combination of steam locomotion and iron rails allowed for the high-speed deployment of large forces over long distances, a revolutionary development in land warfare perfected in a succession of mid-century conflicts. Strategic planners throughout the world had come to regard the establishment of a railhead in a territory as the equivalent of a military presence, the size of which could be readily measured by calculating the speed and carrying capacity of the line.[9] Before the inauguration of the Eurasian railway scheme, the vast distances separating the metropolitan centers of Europe from East Asia provided a source of some comfort to Japan's defense specialists. The "distance-shrinking effects" of a trans-Siberian line would enhance Russia's capabilities dramatically. Indeed, as if to play upon Japanese fears, rumors emerged that the builders of this railway sought an ice-free port in Korea as a possible alternative or supplement to a terminus at Vladivostok. Yamagata warned in 1888, "The day the trans-Siberian railway is completed will be the day crisis comes to Korea, and when crisis comes to Korea, all of the Orient will face upheaval."[10]

Although the pursuit of international prestige and economic opportunity no doubt contributed to Japanese meddling during the 1870s and 1880s, strategic interests dominated the growing preoccupation of Meiji leaders with Korea. Ironically, as anxieties about regional security escalated toward the end of the 1880s and the beginning of the 1890s, however, the Japanese retreated from their efforts to bring Korea under their sway in favor of non-imperialist solutions. In 1890, Yamagata called for the neutralization of the peninsula under international guarantees, envisioning a status for Korea comparable to that of Belgium or Switzerland. Insofar as this would exclude hostile powers from the area, neutralization constituted a diplomatic arrangement that would satisfy the demands of the "line of interest" doctrine. At the same time, it involved neither military intervention nor an assertion of Japanese imperialist prerogatives. On the contrary, neutralization would require Japan to renounce any particularistic claims.[11]

Unfortunately for all concerned, neither the Great Powers, the Chinese, nor the Koreans themselves found the notion of neutralization acceptable, setting the stage for the Sino-Japanese War of 1894–95.[12] Japan's principal aims in taking up arms lay in forcing China to relinquish its claims of suzerainty over Korea, clarifying the status of the kingdom as an independent state, and, not incidentally, clearing the field for Japanese influence. This action reflected the willingness of Meiji leaders to take significant risks in response to threats to the nation's security, as well as a rising level of confidence stemming from the development of Japan's armed forces. At the same time, to conclude that this war marked the beginning of a more aggressive Japanese expansion in Asia would overstate the case. Japan did, indeed, make significant gains, including a huge cash indemnity, Great Power status in its treaties with China, and, perhaps most important, its first colony—the island of Taiwan. During the war, Japanese policymakers had set their sights even higher, attempting to establish a form of protectorate over Korea, and demanding the cession of the Liaotung Peninsula from China, ostensibly for the purpose of further enhancing Korea's security.[13] At the same time, however, these aims and, in particular, the demand for Taiwan, which had no connection to either the causes or the subsequent conduct of the war, clearly represented opportunistic elaborations. Added to the agenda well after the initiation of hostilities, territorial demands reflected an inflated confidence fueled by a succession of relatively easy battlefield victories. Not surprisingly, such imperialist commitments proved quite tentative. Vigorous international opposition forced Japan to abandon the protectorate scheme in Korea and to honor its original promise to respect the kingdom as an independent state. The infamous Triple Intervention of Russia, France, and Germany in April 1895 compelled Japan to relinquish claims to Liaotung. Characteristically, Japanese imperialism had moved aggressively where it perceived opportunity, only to back off in the face of significant opposition. Wartime expansionism, in this sense, reflected the same pattern of probe and retreat exhibited earlier, albeit on a much larger scale than before. Meiji empire-building remained, even after the historic triumph over China, an art of the possible.[14]

Ironically, Japan received clear title to Taiwan, the most unequivocally opportunistic of its wartime claims, largely because no other power, China aside, had sufficient interest to object. The nation's first colonial acquisition thus represented a clear case of an expansionism moving along lines of minimum resistance. Indeed, given its provenance as a last-minute addition to the imperialist agenda, Japanese policymakers had no plans for the island and little knowledge of the territory they had annexed. As it turned out, Taiwan offered few short-term prospects for productive exploitation, and to aggravate matters, Japanese occupation forces confronted unexpectedly stiff resistance from the local Chinese population. Disappointment led some in Japan to contemplate selling the island to France. The government rejected the idea, and in time, Taiwan provided valuable lessons. When imperialists chose their targets on the basis of opportunity rather than rational need, the ability to make the best of whatever hand fortune dealt them, to effectively adapt policy aims to circumstance, constituted the key to success. Gotō Shinpei (1857–1929), one of the early civil administrators of the island colony, advocated precisely such an approach, chastising those inclined toward pessimism as shortsighted and fickle. Empire-building, a long-term proposition incompatible with a get-rich-quick mentality, demanded a commitment to development. Gotō introduced the European practice of "scientific colonization" to Taiwan, and through a program of economic research and planning, he managed to turn the situation around.[15]

That Japanese imperialism retained its opportunistic and circumspect qualities even after the war became clear in its response to the intensification of Great Power encroachment in China in the decade that followed, an era marked by the so-called scramble for concessions. Japan's victory over China provided the proximal trigger for this development, but the underlying trends had pointed in this direction for some time, reflecting the arrival in East Asia of a more aggressive form of Western imperialism that had overwhelmed Africa and Southeast Asia during the preceding decade. Foreign assaults on China's sovereignty, dating back to the Opium Wars (1840–42), certainly represented nothing new, but the unequal treaties imposed on that country during the middle of the nineteenth century had been formulated with the limited aim of integrating the Ch'ing realm into the Western system of trade and diplomacy and preserving an equilibrium among Great Power interests in the region. All participants in the treaty framework shared the common goal of opening Chinese markets as widely as possible as well as a stake in preventing any one of their number from acquiring special privileges, let alone closing off opportunity to its competitors by laying claim to pieces of Chinese territory. These arrangements ironically served to forestall China's dismemberment, despite its weakness in the face of overwhelming Western power. A preoccupation with commercial aggrandizement, moreover, militated against any action that might destabilize the Ch'ing government, which would most certainly prove bad for business, and imposed some measure of restraint on the behavior of the Great Powers. The postwar scramble represented a partial and, as it would turn out, temporary breakdown of this system. The new pattern of competition, which centered on the acquisition of railway rights, introduced an element of geographic particularism that fell well short of partition, yet lay the groundwork for such a possibility. In contrast to the general commercial privileges conferred equally upon all signatory powers under the multilateral treaty system and its "most-favored-nation" provisions, railway concessions, often combined with ancillary coal-mining rights and small leaseholds surrounding prospective harbor sites, constituted, by their nature, localized and exclusive claims. These qualities inevitably associated concession holders with particular regions in China. Railway agreements, moreover, even if not accompanied by full guarantees of a regional monopoly, at least contained provisions for restricted competition, making these associations all the more exclusive. In this way, the powers acquired what came to be known as "spheres of interest" in China, special rights in a geographic area usually described by the transportation watershed of concessionary railway lines and affirmed through reciprocal understandings among claimant governments.[16]

The nature of these spheres, the methods of exploitation applied, and the degree to which the foreign presence actually compromised Chinese sovereignty in the affected areas varied with the aims and orientation of the concessionary power. Some, like the French, who established themselves in south China, and the Germans, who staked out Shantung province, saw these arrangements primarily as a means of securing a competitive advantage over the British, who had come to dominate the China trade. The Russians, who moved into Manchuria, saw their sphere as a quasi-colonial realm that they might, in time, absorb into their Far Eastern territories through gradual colonization. The British, unhappy with the general trend but unable to stop it, lay claim to the Yangtze valley as a defensive reaction. Competing powers did not entirely set aside the existing agreements concerning open trade and the implicit commitment to uphold China's territorial integrity during this scramble. Joint action during the Boxer War of 1900, to which Japan contributed one of the largest military contingents, reaffirmed the value of multilateral cooperation. The United States objected strongly to the exclusiveness of the new arrangements, and in the Open Door Notes of 1899 and 1900, American diplomacy attempted to exert a restraining influence. Enthusiasm for concession hunting, moreover, would die down after 1905 as the powers began re-evaluating the costs and risks entailed in this practice. Nonetheless, during the decade straddling the turn of the century, the dismemberment of China appeared imminent to the more pessimistic among contemporary observers.[17]

Given its imperial aspirations and its economic interests in China, Japan had ample motivation to join this scramble. Komura Jūtarō (1855–1911), an ardent expansionist and foreign minister between 1901 and 1905, pressed for an active engagement, warning that if the Japanese failed to stake a claim of their own, they would find themselves excluded from future opportunity in China. He acknowledged that, at present, the demands of economic development at home would make any effort to invest in railways and mines abroad extremely difficult. The Great Powers, however, would not wait for Japan in carving up China and would leave nothing but scraps for a latecomer.[18] Others, particularly within the army, also called for a more vigorous expansionist policy.

Despite such pressures, a cautious senior leadership, chastened by the experience of the Triple Intervention, prevailed and opposed any line of action that might antagonize the Chinese further and attract unnecessary attention from the powers. They allowed some probing for concessions in Fukien, an advantageous target because of its proximity to Taiwan and its prospects for trade, and these efforts produced an understanding from China that it would not alienate the province to another power. However, having already given up so much to the Japanese during the recent war, the Chinese refused to concede any substantive rights that might have formed the basis for a sphere of interest. The army contemplated creating a pretext for military intervention to back Japan's demands for concessions, but Prime Minister Itō squelched the idea and forbade any further initiatives in Fukien.[19]

Although the scramble in China failed to elicit a Japanese imperialist offensive, it did provoke a strong, defensive response. Russia's acquisition of a sphere of interest in Manchuria presented cause for alarm, and the strategic situation unfolding in the north, indeed, contributed to a more cautious policy in the south. Concessions granted in 1896 and 1898, ostensibly in repayment for their role in the intervention against Japan, enabled the Russians to begin building a Manchurian railway network connected to the Trans-Siberian line. The Chinese Eastern Railway (CER), as they called their project, consisted, in part, of an east–west trunk line cutting across the northern part of the territory and providing a shortcut between the Lake Baikal region in Siberia and Vladivostok in Russia's Maritime Province. A

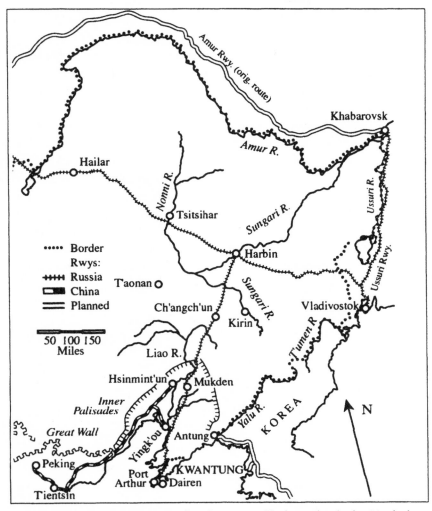

Map 1.3 Railways in Manchuria, 1903 (based on maps in Tōa keizai chōsakyoku, *Manchoukuo Year Book, 1934*; Smith, *Century Atlas of the World*, map 107)

north–south branch connected what would later become the junction city of Harbin and the seaports of Talien and Port Arthur (Lushun) in Liaotung. Ominously, the plans included another branch line extending to Korea's Yalu River border. Control of Manchuria would leave Russia well poised to wield the Korean dagger, a situation nearly as dangerous as an outright occupation of the peninsula (see Map 1.3). The Japanese clearly understood that, upon the completion of the Trans-Siberian and Manchurian railway network, the Russians could seize Korea at their leisure. The fact that St. Petersburg's representatives had acquired a leasehold on Liaotung in 1898, the very piece of real estate that they had forced Japan to retrocede three years earlier, compounded the threat. This development not only rubbed salt in the wounds of the Triple Intervention but granted Russia a secure base from which to launch an attack on Korea. Liaotung also offered an ice-free harbor at Port Arthur, well suited for a naval facility. Combined with a base to the north at Vladivostok, the tsar's Pacific Fleet would enjoy a commanding strategic position against the Japanese islands. Making matters even worse, the Russians began probing for additional naval facilities in southern Korea, along with railway concessions linking the northern part of the country with the Manchurian network. They also appeared to make headway, for a time, in expanding their influence in the Korean court. All in all, these developments represented nothing short of a Japanese strategic nightmare come to life.[20]

A War for the Open Door

The government in Tokyo adopted a number of measures to counter the growing Russian threat between 1896 and 1903. An unprecedented armament program, partly financed by the Chinese indemnity, was one major step. Naval construction plans sought at a minimum to balance the strength of the Russian fleet in the Pacific, and army targets called for a near doubling of standing force levels from seven to thirteen infantry divisions.[21] A second step took the form of a hardening of Japan's attitude toward Korea, following a brief hiatus in activity after the failed attempt at establishing a protectorate. This new approach entailed not only a resumption of pressure on the Korean government to align itself with Japan but also active efforts to acquire railway concessions and to establish a stronger economic presence. Such measures would counterbalance Russian encroachments and secure a firm defensive position on the peninsula in the event of war. Policy toward Korea during this period, particularly after 1901, signaled an important development in the history of Japanese expansion, marking the first time in which the nation's leaders came to regard an imperialist solution as a necessity rather than a discretionary line of action. Diplomats had considered reviving the idea of neutralizing Korea immediately after the collapse of Japan's wartime schemes, but once Russia entrenched itself in Manchuria, few saw it as a viable option. Indeed, a majority of Japanese leaders recognized that even with a stronger position in Korea, there would be no lasting security in the region unless they dealt with the problem of Manchuria. In this case, however, in sharp contrast to the imperialist solution envisioned for Korea, the Japanese pursued lines of negotiation that, in some form or another, entailed a renunciation of claims north of the Yalu River.[22]

Between 1898 and 1903, Tokyo explored two approaches to the Manchurian problem. One centered on the idea of a reciprocal recognition of spheres of interest along the same lines that the powers had worked out in China. Japan would acknowledge Russia's paramount position in Manchuria if Russia would, in turn, recognize Japanese claims in Korea. This scheme came to be known as "exchanging Manchuria for Korea."[23] The other entailed an attempt to loosen Russia's grip on Manchuria by enlisting the support of Britain and the United States, both of which found the practice of concession hunting problematic in general and Russian intentions in the north particularly troubling. Taking advantage of the American Open Door initiative, Japan hoped to forge an international coalition that would force Russia to moderate its activities. The underlying idea, taken to its logical conclusion, constituted an effort to neutralize the territory by encouraging broad multilateral engagement, thereby diluting Russia's exclusive position. Opening Manchuria, if successful, would certainly represent a positive development in itself, but even if the effort fell short, some Japanese leaders saw the possibility of using the leverage of a Great Power combination to persuade Russia to agree to the "exchange" scheme.[24]

Itō, who favored an exchange, and Yamagata, who leaned toward an Open Door strategy, pinned their hopes on a negotiated solution and continued to press both options despite indications that Russia was neither taking Japan seriously nor open to any meaningful compromise. Such intransigence fueled growing pessimism about the prospects of a peaceful settlement in some leadership circles. Skeptics noted that British and American interests in Manchuria remained largely commercial and that neither stood ready to undertake any serious risks in confronting Russia. The Open Door coalition thus lacked teeth, and the Russians appeared unlikely to respond with more than minor concessions in the area of trade. Britain, locked in rivalry with Russia elsewhere in the world, might consider taking a stronger stand, and the Anglo-Japanese Alliance, formed in 1902, appeared an encouraging step in this direction. The terms of the alliance, however, limited its deterrent value in any prospective Russo-Japanese confrontation, since it would become operative only if two or more powers attacked either signatory. Russia hardly required any military assistance in challenging Japan. Moreover, Britain had already compromised itself with respect to the particular problem at hand, having concluded a reciprocal agreement affirming Russian interests in Manchuria and British claims in the Yangtze valley. Foreign Minister Komura argued that, under these circumstances, no negotiations would result in substantive progress unless Japan made an open and unequivocal commitment to back its position with force. Komura and others also argued that the exchange idea, even if the Japanese could persuade the Russians to agree, would not offer a viable solution in the long run. Japan would never enjoy security in Korea so long as Russia remained entrenched in Manchuria. By the same token, since the dagger could point both ways, Russia could never relax its vigilance in Manchuria so long as Japan positioned itself in Korea. It would only be a matter of time, then, before Russia would seek to resolve the situation by taking possession of the peninsula. In the long run, war might prove unavoidable. Some in the armed forces, indeed, argued that Japan should strike first, before the Russians entrenched themselves too deeply and before they could take full advantage of a completed Eurasian and Manchurian railway system, scheduled to become operational between 1903 and 1904.[25]

The emergence of a group of responsible officials favoring military confrontation with Russia reflected mounting frustration with the standoff in Manchuria, as well as a growing generational divide within national leadership. Well aware of the need for an orderly succession, the samurai oligarchy that had ruled Japan since 1868 had groomed a number of promising men, roughly ten years younger, to take over when the founding fathers retired. Komura Jūtarō belonged to this successor generation. The inauguration of the cabinet of General Katsura Tarō (1847–1913) in 1901, the first organized without a member of the original oligarchy, marked the beginning of a formal transition. Despite their nominal retirement, however, Itō and Yamagata continued to maintain a tight rein on actual policymaking, much to the consternation of their protégés. A desire for greater independence and responsibility, however, provided only one source of tension. The younger men, of a rather different orientation and outlook, opposed the cautious policies of their seniors, particularly in matters of empire and national defense. The chronological gap between these leadership cohorts might seem relatively small, but given the scope and pace of change in the Meiji era, a single decade represented a major gulf in experience. The younger group had come of age in a Japan ascendant, trained in the ways of the West if not in Western institutions. For professional soldiers, diplomats, and statesmen possessed of the same skills and knowledge as their counterparts in Europe and North America, Western civilization held little of the mystique that had so impressed the older men born and raised in the late-medieval world of Tokugawa Japan. Although far from reckless or adventurist, men like Komura and Katsura tended to see the glass of Japanese power half full rather than half empty and believed that national progress demanded, in some instances, a willingness to take risks. The crisis with Russia represented one of those instances.[26]

A militant attitude toward the Manchurian problem ran particularly strong among the staff officers in the armed forces and the rising crop of young diplomatic specialists in the Foreign Ministry who organized themselves in 1902 into a loose, pro-war group known as the Kogetsukai.[27] The confidence of these men in facing the prospect of war against such a formidable adversary as Russia, which vastly outclassed Japan in material strength, rested on their professional and technical expertise and their faith in the modern science of politics and warfare. They acknowledged that fighting Russia entailed grave dangers but believed that with proper timing, diplomatic skill, and strategic brilliance victory lay well within reach. A war plan outlined at an army staff conference in June 1903 by Major General Iguchi Shōgo (1855–1925) reflected such thinking. Iguchi pointed out that in a conflict waged against Russia in Korea, Manchuria, and the waters of the northwestern Pacific, Japan enjoyed clear advantages in short lines of communication and the ability to concentrate its main forces at the battlefront quickly. If Japan struck first and neutralized the Russian fleet at Port Arthur and Vladivostok, the army could defeat the enemy's relatively small regional units in Manchuria and the Far East well before reinforcements could arrive from Europe by way of the still-incomplete Trans-Siberian Railway. Once Japan entrenched itself in Manchuria and seized control of the territorial rail network, the Russians would find themselves hard-pressed to launch an effective counterattack. Moreover, even if Japan lost the advantage of timing, Russia's dependence on the Eurasian rail link for supply would limit the size of the total force it could deploy in the East. The underdevelopment of Siberia, the Maritime Province, and Manchuria itself offered little opportunity for an enemy to exploit local resources. According to staff estimates, the Russians could sustain, at best, a quarter of a million troops in the region, a force that Japan, albeit by mobilizing its total armed strength, could more than match. The overall balance rested in the enemy's favor, and Japan could not hope to disable the military capabilities of its adversary permanently. In a regional conflict unfolding as anticipated, however, even limited Japanese success could force Russia to the bargaining table.[28]

Significantly, Iguchi did not envision Japan staking a claim to Manchuria in the anticipated peace settlement. On the contrary, he saw negotiations leading to the neutralization of the territory, including the internationalization of its railways and strict enforcement of the Open Door. Indeed, underscoring the fact that the lack of significant material stakes in Manchuria on the part of the international community constituted the primary reason why Japan found itself alone in its standoff against Russia, he argued that Japan should actively encourage Britain, the United States, and other Western powers to deepen their interests in the territory after the war. Neutralization represented a desirable settlement because even if Japan succeeded in dislodging the enemy and driving its forces across the Amur River, Russia would remain a formidable military power in East Asia, and it would be only a matter of time before it would seek to recover its losses in a "war of revenge." The postwar involvement of other powers in the region would discourage such an attempt, and should deterrence fail, a second war would pit Russia against a firmer and broader Open Door coalition. Even the more militant advocates of war, then, gave no serious thought to taking Manchuria at this time. Although decidedly pro-expansion, Komura concurred and did not look favorably upon an imperialist advance beyond the Yalu River. In fact, he saw these lands as too undeveloped and poor to offer significant economic value to Japan and believed it more productive to direct the nation's expansionist energies toward the richer areas in the south, namely, Fukien. Staking a claim in Manchuria, then, represented neither a strategically necessary line of action, so long as neutralization remained an option, nor an economically desirable one.[29]

At first, Itō, Yamagata, and their colleagues among the oligarchy met the arguments of the war party with skepticism. In their view, the notion of provoking hostilities with the likes of Russia simply defied common sense. They conceded the possibility of fighting a defensive war in Korea if need be and had supported a military buildup for this reason. Although the war party numbered several admirals among its ranks, the senior-most leadership of the navy evinced a particular reluctance to consider a conflict with Russia. Navy Minister Yamamoto Gonbei (1852–1933) argued in 1903 that Japan could survive without Korea, so long as it maintained the capability of protecting the home islands.[30]

Historians have pointed out that the Russians did not seek to provoke Japan. If so, it was certainly a measure of the failure of diplomacy on both sides and, in particular, of miscalculation in St. Petersburg that during the second half of 1903 even a cautious and reluctant senior leadership in Tokyo became persuaded that the war party might be right. In Japanese eyes, the Russians were inflexible. If anything, they had hardened their position in recent months, stepping up their encroachments in Korea. Iguchi and his colleagues argued that time stood on Russia's side and that a long delay would make the enemy's position all the stronger. Such arguments appeared compelling. By late 1903, Japan's armed forces made active preparations for military conflict, and with the prospects for a negotiated settlement receding, a first-strike strategy seemed to offer the only hope.[31] Well aware that they might be putting the nation's future at stake, Japan's leaders decided for war, and on February 8, 1904, the Imperial Navy launched a torpedo attack on Russian vessels at Port Arthur.

The war between Japan and Russia would last eighteen months, a bloody clash made all the more brutal by advances in military technology that foreshadowed the terrible loss of life in World War I. Given the long history of tensions in the region between the two countries, this confrontation was, perhaps, predictable, and in retrospect, Yamagata's warning of 1888 would seem prophetic. The belligerents fought over Manchuria and Korea. The opening of armed conflict probably sealed Korea's fate. However, Tokyo had slated Manchuria for neutralization in the event of a Japanese victory. Indeed, Japan's public pronouncements at the start of the war reiterated a commitment to the Open Door, and this stance encouraged the vital financial support of Britain and the United States.[32] Why the Japanese reversed themselves on Manchuria during the course of the war and decided to stake a claim to Russia's assets in the territory is the question to which we now turn.

Volte-Face

The line of thinking presented by Iguchi at the staff conference in 1903 formed the basis for Japan's military strategy. The navy's task was to destroy or paralyze Russian naval forces in the East as quickly as possible. For the first six months, the course of the conflict seemed to favor Japan even more than anticipated. Caught unprepared, the Russian Pacific Fleet suffered severe damage, and its surviving naval forces found themselves divided and bottled up in Port Arthur and Vladivostok. The land war also went surprisingly well during the spring and early summer of 1904 (see Map 1.4). The Japanese army occupied Korea at the outset of hostilities and, in May, defeated outnumbered Russian forces in the Battle of the Yalu River. Crossing into Manchuria, Japanese troops began moving toward the CER, building a temporary field railway behind them as they advanced. The army also landed forces virtually unopposed on the Liaotung Peninsula and the south Manchurian coast. In the battle of Telissu in June, the Japanese cut the lines of communication between Port Arthur and Russian forces in the interior of Manchuria. Japan had succeeded in mobilizing and deploying its forces quickly and had encountered only light Russian resistance. Early results exceeded expectations, and it seemed that the war might end sooner and with greater advantage to Japan than originally hoped. During the summer, the army began preparing for a decisive engagement at Liaoyang, a town on the CER some forty miles south of Mukden. Victory in this battle might well bring Russia to the bargaining table. Considering this possibility, Foreign Minister Komura drafted in July a proposal for terms that Japan would bring to peace negotiations with Russia.[33]

It is not entirely surprising that Komura, along with a growing number of army leaders, had undergone a change of heart during the early months of the war and become imbued with a new level of confidence fueled by success. He acknowledged this shift quite frankly in the preamble to his draft terms: "Before the war, we would have been satisfied with safeguarding Korea as our sphere of influence and affirming our existing rights in Manchuria.[34] Unfortunately, Russia would not accept these moderate demands, and this has led to the opening of hostilities. Under these circumstances, Japan's policy toward Manchuria and Korea cannot be expected to remain unchanged." The specific policy adjustment Komura had in mind entailed pressing for

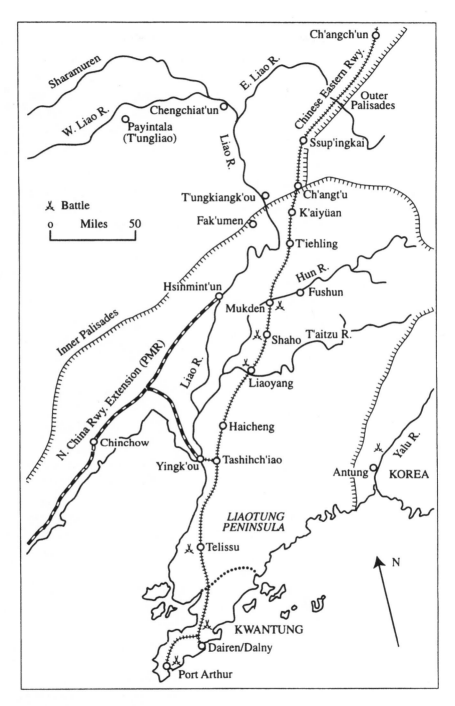

Map 1.4 Southern Manchuria during the Russo-Japanese War, 1904–5 (based on maps in SMRi; DRi, 103, iii)

the permanent transfer of all Russian concessions in the southern half of Manchuria to Japan: the branch of the CER running from Harbin to Port Arthur, the Kwantung Leased Territory, coal-mining rights at Fushun, along with all other ancillary properties and rights held by Russia. In making an argument for why Japan should present these demands, he stressed forthrightly the need for aggressive opportunism in advancing the nation's imperial interests.

In recent years, the Great Powers have been industriously expanding their claims in East Asia. Each seizes even the slightest of opportunities to acquire concessions for fear of being outdone by the other. For this reason, we, too, must avail ourselves of opportunity and develop our national strength by endeavoring, in this instance, to expand our claims in Manchuria, Korea, and the Maritime Territory.

The imminent partition of China made securing any and all concessions within Japanese reach essential:

If we carefully examine China's domestic and international situation, it is clear that in the long run, there is little hope for the country to maintain its independence and territorial integrity. Sooner or later, China will encounter its tragic destiny. We expect it will collapse and be carved up like a melon. Given that such an eventuality has an extremely important bearing on our interests and well-being, Japan must, at this time, prepare for the day when the partition of China becomes an active question. We must create the foundations in a timely manner in order that we may participate in this process from a position of strength.

Komura had raised these same concerns with great urgency at the turn of the century, only at the time Fukien rather than Manchuria had provided his target. The foreign minister's revised view may have reflected the philosophy of "bird in hand." Alternatively, a perspective of "sour grapes" may have informed his earlier negative appraisal of Manchuria. In either case, Komura's new course represented an unabashedly opportunistic volte-face.[35]

Given the past record of Japanese expansionism, this turn in policy was somewhat predictable, little different from the revision of aims during the early months of the Sino-Japanese War. As of the summer of 1904, Komura had come to believe that Japan had the ability to hold a piece of Manchuria on its own without the need to rely on neutralization to exclude the Russians. Territorial gains north of the Yalu River had not been a consideration in going to war. Once committed to this course of action, however, the marginal costs of pursuing aims that might otherwise never have warranted the

risks of armed confrontation became attractively low. Given such cost calculations, the flush of confidence emerging in the early months of the war
undoubtedly opened the eyes of many Japanese leaders to opportunities that
they had not seen before. An imperialist solution to the strategic problem
had become possible, and since, as the foreign minister pointed out, such a
solution allowed Japan to deal simultaneously with economic and with geopolitical concerns in China, it became highly desirable as well.

Komura's views enjoyed considerable sympathy in the cabinet during the
summer of 1904. Prime Minister Katsura offered a similar proposal for
peace terms, although he included a demand for a substantial indemnity
from Russia. Komura remained somewhat dubious about monetary compensation, an additional reason why he believed the transfer of concessions
important. Still, that responsible leaders even gave consideration to financial
reparations points to the marked rise in confidence at this juncture. What
Japan could ultimately demand at the conference table, of course, would depend on the actual military outcome. Accordingly, the cabinet appears to
have made no firm commitments. Nonetheless, establishing a Japanese
sphere in southern Manchuria had emerged as a working aim by the summer of 1904, and the cabinet authorized Komura to begin laying the diplomatic groundwork for the policy shift. The foreign minister anticipated
some difficulty with the United States, since President Theodore Roosevelt
(1858–1919) strongly supported neutralization and expected Japan to uphold
its initial commitments. Military administrators in the occupied areas of
Manchuria also began gearing their planning toward an activist postwar
policy in the territory, some even couching their expectations in terms close
to annexation.[36]

As it turned out, the optimism of July 1904 proved premature. The Japanese army, as anticipated, triumphed at Liaoyang in September, but serious
problems with logistics and supply, caused in part by the simultaneous initiation of the siege of Port Arthur, prevented it from exploiting its success
and forcing a deeper Russian retreat. The Russians, puzzled by this inactiv-
ity, counterattacked. The Japanese repelled the assault and began advancing
north along the CER, only to face the same problems encountered at Liaoyang in subsequent engagements. The Japanese army found itself bogged
down in what amounted to a two-front war. Delay represented a serious
problem, given a strategy that depended on speed and counted on delivering
a decisive blow against Russian forces in the East before reinforcements

could arrive in large numbers from Europe. The Baltic Fleet, which would not have entered consideration had Japan achieved a speedy victory, became a looming menace as it made its slow way toward East Asian waters. Emerging evidence that the Russians had managed to move more men into Manchuria and sustain much larger forces than expected provided additional cause for anxiety. After the army finally took Port Arthur in January 1905, it succeeded in advancing north more quickly, but in the Battle of Mukden in March, the Japanese confronted larger Russian forces in this single engagement than earlier estimates had predicted for total enemy capabilities in the East.[37]

The Japanese army scored yet another victory at Mukden, and the battle proved to be the last major engagement of the land war. Warships under the command of Admiral Tōgō Heihachirō (1837–1934) sank the Baltic Fleet in the Strait of Tsushima in May. The Russians had faced serious domestic trouble since the events of Bloody Sunday in January and sought to put an end to the conflict, indicating an interest in peace talks by the beginning of the summer. The situation turned once again in Japan's favor, and in an effort to strengthen the Japanese negotiating position, the army seized the island of Sakhalin in June. Peace talks commenced in August, mediated by the United States and held at Portsmouth, New Hampshire.[38]

The war ended in military success for Japan, but the difficulties encountered between the autumn of 1904 and the spring of 1905 had taken a severe toll on the confidence of national leadership. Senior officials, military and civilian alike, understood the marginal nature of Japan's victory. Had Russia retained the political will to continue the war, it possessed the material strength to do so. Japan, on the other hand, had come close to exhausting its resources. As a result, cabinet members and elder statesmen began having second thoughts about the wisdom of staking a claim in Manchuria. The idea remained on the table, and the proposals Komura outlined in July 1904 formed the basic terms Japan intended to bring to Portsmouth, but the underlying commitment to follow through had softened.[39] Meiji imperialism, after all, remained an art of the possible, and as of the summer of 1905, the possible seemed to have receded.

Yamagata's memorandum to Komura immediately prior to the veteran diplomat's departure for Portsmouth as Japan's ambassador plenipotentiary provides evidence of the flagging confidence with which the Japanese government entered negotiations. Yamagata assumed that Japan would proceed with plans to take over the Russian position in southern Manchuria, but his outlook on the postwar situation was markedly pessimistic, dominated by the anticipation of a war of revenge. "It would be appropriate to regard today's peace, in essence, as a long-term truce. Those who believe that a lasting peace has been established in the Orient are mistaken," he warned. Japan's prospects in a second war seemed poor. His assessment of Japan's military performance during the preceding eighteen months offered little to inspire confidence for the future.

That the timing of the war was propitious to us, that Russia was not adequately prepared for a conflict and suffered a surprise attack, are realities that we cannot deny. Yet as the war progressed, they expanded their transportation capacity with surprising speed and increased their troop strength, so that they were able to maintain at all times superiority over our own small numbers. For this reason, our endeavor to deploy both our active duty and reserve forces proved insufficient. We even had to create on short notice several new divisions and send them to the front. I do not believe that those not directly involved in these affairs can truly imagine the difficulties my colleagues and I faced.[40]

This assessment implicitly rebuked those military planners who had predicted that limited transportation facilities would keep Russian troop strength low and ensure Japan's regional numerical superiority. The basic strategy under which the army had fought this war, in other words, suffered from serious flaws.

Yamagata concluded that Japan needed to prepare for an inevitable second conflict. The nation could not count on the kind of optimistic assessments originally offered by the army staff. "We must accordingly expand our army and navy on a large scale and complete such preparations as will allow us to face the vengeance of our enemy, whenever it might come." The arms buildup Yamagata had in mind assumed breathtaking proportions. Although not specifying numbers in this document, he cited elsewhere a figure for the army of 25 standing divisions, double the number with which Japan had started the war. What Yamagata envisioned for fleet expansion is not clear, but the navy's own plans called for a core force of eight battleships and eight armored cruisers, each less than eight years old. This, too, represented a substantial increase from the force levels with which Japan had fought Russia. Such an armament program in a country staggering under a war debt of ¥1.5 billion, two-thirds of which was owed to foreign creditors, was a daunting proposition to say the least. It also became apparent, by the time negotiations began at Portsmouth, that Japan's chances of extracting an indemnity from Russia were negligible. Yamagata acknowledged that the costs of defense would pose a major challenge, but one from which the country could not afford to shrink.[41]

A position in Manchuria would, of course, serve to check Russia's "southern advance," and this would certainly contribute to Japan's security. The use of Manchuria as a forward base, however, would incur an additional set of costs. For one thing, the army would have to maintain a sizable permanent garrison in the territory. The development and exploitation of local resources might help defray some of these costs. At the same time, the railway, although representing a vital military asset, would prove to be a drain on finances. As a commercial undertaking, Yamagata regarded it as near hopeless.

The Russians originally built the Chinese Eastern Railway as a military line, and their experience clearly shows that revenues will hardly balance expenditures. Indeed, given the fact that we will acquire control of the line only south of Harbin and that freight north of Harbin will go directly to Vladivostok, our railway will not have access to the wealth of the interior. In addition, shipping on the Liao River is not something to be taken lightly. It has not lost its power as a fearsome competitor for our railway. For this reason, the line between Harbin and Port Arthur will serve us as a purely military facility used for the sole purpose of checking a southward advance by the Russians.[42]

As it turned out, Russian negotiators at Portsmouth refused to consider the cession of the entire southern branch, forcing Komura to accept a compromise in which Ch'angch'un became the northern terminus of the Japanese railway. The truncation of this line could only have deepened Yamagata's reservations.[43]

Nothing in Yamagata's memorandum suggests that he favored a reconsideration of plans to stake a claim in Manchuria. Yet it is clear that he thought the project would entail costs and risks that Japan would be hardpressed to sustain. Whatever Yamagata's personal convictions about Manchuria, it would certainly not come as a surprise if others, accepting his assessment, concluded that a forward policy in the territory might not be such a wise choice after all, and that the original goal of neutralization might offer the best course.

The Harriman Affair and the Manchurian Army

The so-called Harriman Affair offers evidence that senior leaders in Tokyo had begun thinking along such lines by the beginning of September, even as Komura exerted himself at Portsmouth to win Japanese demands. The American railway magnate Edward Henry Harriman (1848–1909) arrived in Japan on August 31, 1905. During the spring, Lloyd Griscom (1872–1959), the U.S. minister to Tokyo, had written to him suggesting the possibility of investment opportunities in Manchuria. Although not acting in an official capacity, Griscom's encouragement dovetailed with standing American commitments to the Open Door in Manchuria. The possibility that Japan's intention to keep Manchuria for itself might not be written in stone, despite Komura's tireless diplomacy, required no inside knowledge. Itō Hirobumi, one of the few leaders who openly dissented from the emerging consensus of the summer of 1904 and who continued to favor neutralization, had been pursuing his own informal diplomacy. In November 1904, in talks with a British official in Tokyo, he had cast doubts on Japan's interest in the territory. According to Claude MacDonald (1851–1915), British minister to Tokyo, Itō had expressed the view that Japan "neither wanted Manchuria, nor was she strong enough to maintain large garrisons indefinitely on the remote borders of that province." The British minister also reported that Itō had reiterated his view that the "administration of the railway by an international body was, in his opinion, the only method by which Manchuria could be securely preserved from subsequent Russian encroachment."[44] Griscom's perception of the possibilities and his advice to Harriman, in this context, had solid foundations.

Harriman had his own reasons for being interested in Manchuria. He had long nurtured the idea of building a global transportation network under his own control in which Manchurian railways, both Russian and prospective Japanese, would form a vital link. Harriman also had close ties with the banking house of Kuhn-Loeb through his efforts to reorganize the Union Pacific Railroad in 1898. Kuhn-Loeb, in turn, had played a major part in raising loans for the Japanese war effort. All of these factors conspired to bring the American businessman to Tokyo to discuss the possibilities of a joint Japanese-American venture to manage the railway under negotiation at Portsmouth.[45]

If the cabinet gave Yamagata's assessment any credence, it is not difficult to see the appeal of a joint venture with Harriman. It would allow for the revival of arrangements similar in effect to neutralization. A strong American presence in southern Manchuria would reduce the risk of war at least to some degree and force Russia to think twice before trampling American interests in a war of revenge. Moreover, American official opinion, while not opposed outright to Japanese intentions as conveyed by Komura, clearly viewed them with displeasure. This agreement would not only reduce the risk of war but also avoid friction with the United States, ensuring its continued support and friendship should the worst case materialize and Russia seek to recover its losses. Finally, cooperation would alleviate financial worries about managing the railway. Harriman would provide the larger part of the resources needed for reconstruction, since the proceeds of selling him a half-share of the railway would cover the funds Japan would have to put up, and he would supply the balance as part of his own share. Itō, not surprisingly, embraced this proposal. Inoue Kaoru (1835–1915), a member of the oligarchy known for both diplomatic caution and fiscal conservatism, reportedly told Griscom, "We would be very foolish to let such a great chance slip."[46]

Itō and Inoue worked to persuade the government to take advantage of this opportunity. Cabinet members proved sufficiently receptive to open serious negotiations. On October 12, Prime Minister Katsura and Harriman signed a "preliminary memorandum of understanding" for a joint venture. Under the proposed terms, a private syndicate, in which American and Japanese investors held equal shares, would take possession of the railway and ancillary concessions acquired by the Japanese government. Japan would retain the right to the military use of the railway in the event of an emergency, but otherwise the arrangement entailed a full partnership. The agreement did not involve the Kwantung Leased Territory, and this ensured that Japan would retain some measure of exclusive interest in the region, but the scheme, on the whole, represented a substantial retreat from visions of a Japanese sphere entertained in the summer of 1904.[47]

Had this deal come to fruition, the history of Japan, East Asia, and the United States in the twentieth century might have taken a substantially different course. The government abruptly suspended the preliminary agreement, however, only two weeks after its signing and formally renounced it in January 1906. Why the Japanese side abandoned the understanding has generated considerable speculation over the years, since documentary evidence is lacking. In 1930, Nagao Sakurō, a scholar exploring the history of colonial railways, offered one of the more interesting interpretations. Apparently perplexed by the notion that responsible officials would even consider a sale of the railway, he suggested that Komura and Katsura had conspired to dangle the possibility of a cooperative undertaking before the Americans, without ever intending to follow through, in order to soften their criticism of Japan's ambitions in Manchuria. The two had staged negotiations in October to allow Harriman and his backers "to partake of the aroma of the eel" while ultimately denying them the taste.[48] Reflecting the assumptions of his time, when the notion of Manchuria as a life-and-death issue for Japan had become firmly established, Nagao no doubt felt the need to find a consistent explanation.[49]

The available evidence, however, suggests another. The pessimistic assessment of the situation, on which the decision to work with Harriman rested, was substantially revised during the last months of 1905. By the beginning of the new year, Japanese leaders had recovered their confidence that the project was manageable. Komura, who opposed the Harriman deal in principle, appears to have orchestrated the abrupt suspension of the preliminary agreement by persuading the government to hold off any final decision on Manchuria until after the affirmation of the terms of the Treaty of Portsmouth through negotiations with the Chinese (Treaty of Peking). This step, no doubt, bought time for more careful and thorough deliberation. Forestalling a precipitous decision proved important because Itō and his colleagues had rushed the Harriman deal through the cabinet without leaving much opportunity for serious discussion and study. Komura had been detained in the United States by illness and had not participated in the initial deliberations. He had learned of the details of the agreement only after he arrived in Yokohama in October.[50] Apparently, the cabinet had also neglected to consult key army leaders, most notably members of the general staff still stationed in Manchuria with the expeditionary forces. Yamagata's negative views of the railway and economic prospects in Manchuria were based on a tour of the front in July 1905 and not on any systematic survey. This is not to suggest subterfuge on the part of Itō and his allies, but the decision clearly lacked the benefit of all the information available at the time, nor had it been reached after hearing the full spectrum of opinions. Broader discussion and deliberation in late 1905 revealed that expert opinion disagreed with the pessimistic assessments underlying the cabinet's receptiveness to Harriman. Two analyses were particularly important in promoting a more positive appraisal of both the military and the economic situation. One was a strategic study prepared by the staff of the expeditionary forces in Manchuria, known as the Manchurian Army, sometime between the end of September and the middle of November. The other was a report on an extensive economic survey of the territory under Japanese occupation, commissioned by the Manchurian Army but carried out by a civilian group headed by Ishizuka Eizō (1866–1942), an administrator "on loan" to the army from the colonial government of Taiwan.[51]

The Manchurian Army staff document, entitled "Key Considerations for the Postwar Management of Our Army," provided a detailed assessment of the Japanese military experience during the war and recommendations for defense policy in the future. It presented a far more optimistic view than Yamagata's in both of these areas and, in fact, obliquely criticized the elder soldier-statesman's opinions. The Japanese victory, in the view of the authors of this document, vindicated the bold strategy formulated in the summer of 1903. The fact that Japan had been able to force Russia to the conference table confirmed the proposition that "a small army can frustrate a much stronger enemy if it can continually maintain a superior force in the field of battle." The strategy admittedly required some major adjustments. Some of the problems Yamagata pointed out warranted serious concern. Yet the shortcomings resulted not from flaws inherent in the original war plan but from specific miscalculations and mistakes in execution, which lent themselves to ready correction.[52]

For example, Russian railway capacity had, as predicted, proved to be the limiting factor in the size and rate of enemy deployment. Japanese plans had dangerously underestimated the actual numbers, to be sure, but the problem had resulted primarily from poor intelligence and the lack of attention to quantitative analysis. "Whatever the means by which we derived our estimates of the transportation capacity of the Trans-Siberian Railway before the war, we now know they were ridiculous." Military analysts clearly needed to pay more attention to the "science of statistics." Strategists had also failed to foresee the ability of the Russians to adopt emergency measures that had allowed the enemy to double the normal capacity of a single-tracked line. Future plans would have to take such measures into account. None of these errors, however, changed the basic fact of the Russian army's absolute dependence on the railway.[53]

The Russians had also failed to concentrate their forces quickly, as anticipated in the original plan. Early Japanese successes owed much to this circumstance. The Japanese army, however, had failed to take advantage of this window of opportunity for three reasons. First, the siege of Port Arthur, which proved far more difficult and protracted an engagement than expected, had tied down a major part of the army's strength. Whereas strategists had planned for a northward-moving sequence of battles along the railway corridor, the conflict had devolved into a two-front war. Second, Japanese front-line units found themselves continually short of ammunition. Combat troops had expended munitions at an unprecedented rate, taxing the capacity of both stockpiles and production facilities. "Maintaining a superior force in the field of battle" required not just troops but actual firepower, and in this respect, the army had fallen short. Third, front-line units received inadequate replacements for their casualties despite the increasingly large numbers of fresh Japanese troops arriving in Manchuria. According to the staff analysts, this constituted the "greatest of our shortcomings in the recent war." The problem lay not in the total balance of numbers, as Yamagata seemed to suggest, but in the ability to place them where needed. This represented an organizational failing susceptible to correction.[54]

The Manchurian Army paper discussed other difficulties and miscalculations as well, including the ability of the Russians to draw more effectively upon local supplies than expected. Despite such problems, however, the Japanese had reason for confidence. The authors of this paper accordingly saw more modest needs for postwar defense than did Yamagata. True, the settlement at Portsmouth would not provide for a lasting peace, and a Russian war of revenge posed a serious danger. A second conflict, however, did not represent an immediate threat. Russia faced troubles at home and tensions in Europe. Its railway network in the East demanded considerable improvement, including the building of an alternative route from Siberia to the Maritime Province, given that the east-west trunk of the CER no longer provided a secure line of communication with Japan entrenched in southern Manchuria. It would take years before the Russians could even consider recovering their losses. In the meantime, Japan would have time to rebuild its strength.[55]

The Manchurian Army staff clearly saw some need for an arms buildup but criticized Yamagata's estimates as inflated. Adopting a perspective that would have warmed the hearts of fiscal conservatives in government, and most probably with that intent in mind, the authors of this paper called for budgetary "self-restraint" on the part of the armed forces. They emphasized the need "to guard against the temptation, in the afterglow of victory, to press for the rapid expansion of manpower and other military expenditures that would exceed the capabilities of our country and disregard the greater national interest." They warned that without a cautious approach to an expansion of military forces, "armaments meant to topple our enemies will, ironically, threaten our own downfall." Indeed, the postwar situation, in their view, demanded no further expansion of sea power. Admiral Tōgō's forces had effectively destroyed the enemy's navy, and many years would pass before the Russians could rebuild their forces to the point of posing a danger to Japan. Moreover, the renewal of the Anglo-Japanese Alliance in August 1905 as an offensive and defensive agreement would make the allies supreme in East Asian waters. These circumstances made a moratorium on naval spending possible. The army would require some expansion, but nothing on the order of a target of 25 standing divisions. According to the Manchurian Army staff, nineteen would suffice for the time being. Regularizing the four divisions created on an emergency basis during the war would add to the standing complement of thirteen. An adequate force level would require only two entirely new divisions. Moreover, unlike Yamagata, they believed a permanent garrison in Manchuria unnecessary. With Korea as a protectorate, troops stationed there could do double duty, provided good railway connections between Korea and Manchuria were established. A single military command covering both territories would prove more effective and efficient. A paring-down of the garrison in Taiwan, given the successful pacification of the island and the shelving of Fukien as an immediate target, would further lighten the burden.[56]

The control of railways and other facilities in southern Manchuria would also reduce both the costs and the risks of the postwar defense program. The building of new railway lines would strengthen Japanese operational capabilities, making it easier to threaten Harbin and much harder for the Russians to contest control. Under the ready pretext of ordinary commercial activity, the Japanese might also establish all manner of facilities designed for mobilization in wartime in order to support Japan's logistical efforts. The ability to draw heavily on local resources would enhance the advantage of short supply lines. The Manchurian Army staff also recommended postponing the permanent reconstruction of existing railway lines until Japan found itself in a better financial situation. The Russians had built the CER to their unique five-foot gauge, and in its efforts to make captured portions of the line operational during the war, the army had laid down temporary track of the narrow gauge (3'6") common in Japan. Japanese gauge would allow the immediate use of rolling stock brought in from the home islands. Plans formulated during the war in anticipation of a takeover had postulated the subsequent conversion of these lines to the English standard (4'8") used in China and Korea to facilitate the creation of an integrated continental network. This second conversion could wait.[57]

Overall, the authors of this paper argued that postwar defense, even assuming a Manchurian commitment, would entail substantially fewer costs than Yamagata suggested. Russia, moreover, did not pose a danger as acute as some believed. Presented by the army's strategic specialists, the argument carried weight, especially because the soldiers themselves called for restraint in military expenditures. That the army would actively work to deflate demands for additional divisions or to minimize its assessments of threats represented a rather unusual development, and it indicates an earnest effort to bolster flagging confidence, to allay financial anxieties, and to persuade Tokyo that an imperialist initiative in Manchuria lay well within the realm of military feasibility.

Strategic anxiety, however, was only one factor informing the government's pessimistic view. Yamagata had also presented a rather negative appraisal of economic prospects in Manchuria and had predicted that managing the territory, quite apart from military expenditures, would entail net costs. Here, the survey team led by Ishizuka offered reassurance, presenting arguments that the territory held far more economic promise than many believed.

Although staffed by civilians, the survey was sponsored by the army, and the initiative emerged as an outgrowth of the army's own economic research, conducted earlier as part of its wartime occupation and supply operations. By the summer of 1905, officers in charge of these operations began setting the stage for postwar policy.[58] Lieutenant Colonel Nishikawa Torajirō (1868–1944) of the Manchurian Army's supply and logistics staff, for example, ordered the quartermasters of the four subordinate army commands to undertake detailed studies of their areas of jurisdiction in July 1905. "In order to develop the wealth of Manchuria and establish the basis for reaping rewards after the war, we must first introduce Manchuria to the world at large," he explained. In his instructions, he called for the study of Manchurian society, history, land, politics, products, population, transportation, and culture.[59] Along the same lines, Iguchi Shōgo, in effect the army's quartermaster-general during the last stage of the war, submitted a memorandum in August to Manchurian Army commander Ōyama Iwao (1842–1916) proposing a systematic and comprehensive survey to prepare for the postwar management of the territory. Iguchi's note clearly reflects awareness of an uncertain commitment on the part of home authorities and the need to strengthen their resolve.

Regardless of what our government's policy may be regarding Manchuria after the settlement of peace terms, it is essential that we begin to lay the foundations for developing the wealth of Manchuria and securing new concessions. For this reason, I believe it is urgent that we begin investigating immediately the [potential] value of Manchuria. We should release these findings to the general public promptly in order to provide them with a reliable compass needle.

Iguchi underscored the importance of initiating such an effort prior to the troop withdrawals scheduled under the peace accords in order to allow for penetration of the more inaccessible and dangerous areas. He recommended the recruitment of civilian specialists, including experienced businessmen, to conduct the study. The army would provide escorts and translators.[60] Iguchi's proposal formed the basis for the organization of a large survey group in October, the majority of whose 75 members were drawn from the technical staff of the Ministry of Agriculture and Commerce. The appointment of Ishizuka to head the effort held considerable significance. He had come to Manchuria at the request of Kodama Gentarō, Manchurian Army chief of staff and simultaneously governor-general of Taiwan, in order to assist in the task of occupation administration. Along with his better-known colleague Gotō Shinpei, Ishizuka had formed part of the team of administrators responsible for turning around a rather unpromising situation in Taiwan by applying the methods of scientific colonization. A man of more appropriate background to conduct a study of the kind the army sought would have been difficult to find.[61]

Ishizuka and his group published the full results of the survey in eight volumes in August 1906, but well in advance of the final report, they issued a shorter, confidential compendium of their principal findings in December 1905. A favorable economic assessment of the railway formed the single most important conclusion of the preliminary report: "There are those who take a pessimistic view of the performance of the Chinese Eastern Railway, but the prospects for profitable development of the railway are ample." Yamagata had cited the Russian experience in his negative appraisal. The report pointed out, however, that the line had been open to regular traffic for only eight months before the war began, hardly enough time to draw definitive conclusions. Moreover, the authors noted that the Russians had given priority to shipping materials for the construction of the harbor at Talien and fortifications at Port Arthur. Railway authorities had accepted paying commercial traffic only intermittently, as military transportation priorities allowed. The past record thus offered a poor basis for appraisals of the line's potential. With the establishment of normal conditions, the survey group believed that the railway would generate more than enough business to cover the costs of operation. Interviews with local merchants and other potential customers pointed to great interest in the reopening of the line to civilian traffic. Large stocks of goods had piled up at station facilities. Merchants, who had relied on the Liao River in the past, indicated an eagerness to use rail service, since it offered greater reliability, safety, speed, and year-around access, a finding that challenged Yamagata's concern that river transportation would offer stiff competition to the railway. The two systems, in the view of survey members, would complement one another rather than compete. Goods like timber would probably continue to move by water, whereas most agricultural goods would be shipped by rail.[62]

Even as survey team members offered reassurances about the commercial viability of the railway, they carefully avoided portraying Manchuria as a land of milk and honey. If the Japanese were to reap the true benefits of a foothold in this territory, they would have to commit themselves to development and long-term investment. Moreover, they warned, immigrant farmers and small-scale merchants from the home islands would encounter difficulties in holding their own against local Chinese in the same fields of activity. They would have to find specialized areas of economic endeavor. The railway, however, could serve as a means of supporting Japanese business development, for example, by subsidizing freight charges. Raising sufficient investment capital in Japan might prove difficult at this stage, but tapping local sources presented some possibilities. The authors of the report favored the idea of a Japanese-controlled Manchurian bank and suggested that, given the lack of modern financial institutions in the territory and the urgent need, local Chinese depositors would be plentiful. They recommended a number of other measures as well. The feasibility of undertaking a venture in Manchuria without massive new investment on the part of the Japanese government, nonetheless, formed the principal thrust of even these cautionary remarks. As in the case of Taiwan, knowledgeable and creative management could place the new project on the road to self-sufficiency.[63]

The findings and projections of the survey group indicated quite clearly to policymakers in Tokyo that misinformation had led to pessimistic assessments. Although Manchuria did not promise great, short-term returns, neither would it become a financial liability for Japan. Ishizuka's team, made up of specialists, provided a credible, professional analysis pointing to the economic feasibility of securing a foothold in the territory. Combined with the Manchurian Army's strategic assessment, the experts in the field presented a much more optimistic picture of prospects in Manchuria.

No direct evidence links either the army position paper or the survey report to a reconsideration of the Harriman agreement. These analyses, however, deliberately sought to reassure anxious policymakers that the costs and risks entailed in a Manchurian venture ran significantly lower, and its benefits, much higher, than Yamagata and others had suggested. If, indeed, concerns about military and economic feasibility had led cabinet ministers to favor a deal with Harriman, then these reports constituted more than ample reason to change their minds. There is no doubt that the government took these findings seriously. By the beginning of 1906, official policy statements began incorporating proposals contained in both these documents. The Manchurian Army's paper provided some of the core elements of the Imperial Defense Plan promulgated in early 1907. Recommendations in the survey group's report may be regarded as the earliest known outlines of the program embodied in the South Manchuria Railway Company.

The Japanese government officially notified Harriman on January 16, 1906, of its rejection of the joint-management scheme. Precisely when the cabinet decided to drop the option entirely is difficult to say. Likely it came significantly after late October when Komura's insistence suspended the agreement, since that suspension rested primarily on diplomatic protocol rather than a more substantive policy decision. The cabinet had not taken the step of a preliminary agreement with Harriman lightly. The underlying reservations ran deep and could not have been addressed without considerable discussion and debate. Tokyo had erupted in riots protesting the inadequacy of Japanese gains in the Treaty of Portsmouth. The fact that responsible leaders were talking to an American businessman about selling a half-share in the railway at this time testifies to the seriousness of their concerns and their willingness to accept considerable domestic political costs.[64] The effort at persuasion evident in the Manchurian Army paper and the Ishizuka group's preliminary report also points to the substantial resistance and skepticism they sought to overcome. Not until the beginning of the new year was it possible to say with certainty that the government had resolved to pursue an activist course in Manchuria. Unmistakable evidence of that resolution emerged with the formation on January 1 of the Commission on the Management of Manchuria, a provisional interministerial agency headed by General Kodama Gentarō and charged to decide specifically what to do with the rights and facilities inherited from Russia.[65]

In the months that followed, the debate shifted from how, rather than whether, to manage Manchuria, and in the bustle of activity in 1906, little obvious trace remained of the hesitancy with which the government had approached the idea of a commitment in the fall of the previous year. Support for the Manchurian venture also soon spread to even those political and economic interest groups that were initially skeptical. An opportunistic, bandwagon effect seems to have been at work. They might have equivocated about the wisdom of going into the territory at first, but once the gates were opened, they had no intention of being left outside. Civilian bureaucrats, whatever their original convictions, all scrambled for a prominent place at the Manchurian table. Business leaders rushed to invest in Japan's new railway project and eagerly sought contracts to procure rails and locomotives.[66] In subsequent years, the notion that anything on the order of the Harriman agreement might have been considered became nearly unthinkable. Nagao's perplexity in 1930 is certainly understandable. Yet placed in the larger context of Meiji expansionism, vacillation over Manchuria and the uncertainty over the course the nation should take even after the historic triumph over Russia conforms to the established pattern of Japan's empire-building. The government ultimately based its decision to stake a claim in the territory on the calculus of a conservative imperialism, with its characteristic qualities of caution, tentativeness, and opportunism. The Manchurian Army and the Ishizuka group geared their arguments toward that calculus, and their efforts at persuasion were aimed not toward demonstrating the need or the desirability of an expansionist course of action but, rather, its feasibility. Insofar as Meiji imperialism constituted an art of the possible, feasibility formed the key consideration.

The Russo-Japanese War as a Turning Point

Although the logic of opportunity was decisive in Japan's acquisition of a foothold in Manchuria, there were indications in the immediate aftermath of the war that Japanese attitudes toward empire were changing. A number of historians have argued that the victory over Russia and the thrust into Manchuria signaled the beginning of a bold, confident, and self-directed expansionism that differed substantially from the cautious, tentative, and opportunistic initiatives of earlier years.[67] A rising confidence among Japanese leaders in the nation's power after 1905 is unquestionable. Although initial doubt about the substantiveness of the Japanese victory, as expressed by Yamagata, ran strong in official circles, the opposing view of the Manchurian Army increasingly came to inform subsequent assessments of the nation's military achievement. Self-assurance generated by such analyses differed qualitatively from the ephemeral confidence stemming from the victory over China a decade earlier. Russia, after all, ranked among the Great Powers. Changing perceptions of Japan by outsiders reinforced this sense of newfound strength. The Sino-Japanese War had not created as much international respect for Japan as hoped. The fact that Russia failed to take Japanese concerns about Manchuria and Korea seriously offered evidence of this. Following the war of 1904–5, few of the powers would repeat Russia's mistakes. Japan had won considerable admiration, some of it grudging, to be sure, and some of it mixed with anxieties about a new kind of "Yellow Peril" capable of wielding modern armies and battleships, fears the Russians had helped to encourage during the war.[68] The Japanese victory electrified the colonial world, and even many Chinese took heart at seeing a non-Western nation defeat a Western power. Japan had, in fact, altered the balance of power substantially in East Asia and had won a new freedom of action as a result. Of the two Western powers most interested in East Asia and capable of posing a serious challenge to Japanese aspirations, Japan had beaten one and formed a military alliance with the other.

Growing national self-confidence was also closely related to the changing of the guard in the top levels of military and bureaucratic leadership. The decision for war and the settlement in Manchuria were signal victories for the cohort of officials represented by Kodama Gentarō, Katsura Tarō, and Komura Jūtarō. They were even more important in elevating the standing of a yet younger group of military staff officers and Foreign Ministry officials who had formed the Kogetsukai. The political acumen and strategic brilliance demonstrated by Army Major Tanaka Giichi (1863–1929) and Navy Commander Akiyama Saneyuki (1868–1918) would win them key leadership posts in their respective services. The technical expertise of such junior men had been instrumental in enabling Kodama and Komura to overcome the caution of the elder statesmen. In this respect, the Russo-Japanese War marked the triumph of specialists and technocrats over the common sense of the oligarchs whose generalist, "jack of all trades" leadership had served the nation well in its early years. The elder statesmen had by no means faded from the scene and would exercise a powerful influence over national affairs for some time to come, but they no longer enjoyed the prestige and authority inherent in their status as founders of the Meiji state. Younger leaders ceased to behave as deferential protégés. Having demonstrated their competence and the soundness of their judgments, they were finally in a position to put their own ideas into action without the old former samurai peering over their shoulders.

Evidence of new attitudes toward imperialism might also be found in popular thinking as well. The war had a profound impact on Japanese from all walks of life. The human toll had been high, with the army alone suffering more than 60,000 dead and 130,000 wounded over the course of eighteen months, losses that made this conflict the most costly military undertaking in Japan's modern history until the outbreak of the China War in 1937.[69] The events of 1904–5 would form a dominant element in the historical memory of the decades to follow. The experience touched every adult citizen in Japan, combatant or not, and represented in many ways the equivalent of what World War I would mean to Europeans. The nation's resources, human and material, had approached a state of total mobilization toward the end of the conflict. All Japanese involved themselves in the effort, with villages proudly recording in commemorative books the numbers of boots, straw mats, and horses they had contributed. Even the Meiji empress rolled bandages. The "participatory dimension" of total war, as Arthur Marwick describes, gave rise to a new sense of citizenship.[70] Peter Duus suggests that "the Russo-Japanese War, at the deepest level, had made imperialists of all Japanese."[71] It is certainly true that as the most tangible outcome of the war, Japan's foothold in Manchuria came to be regarded as a monument to its sacrifices, the "crystallization" of the blood shed by Japanese soldiers. In time, many came to believe that the war had been fought for the primary purpose of securing that foothold. A Manchuria vested with such meaning, albeit after the fact, became a sanctified, politically untouchable issue. Moreover, the notion that Japan's position in this territory was the result of a frightful investment in blood and gold inevitably created expectations for proportionally high returns.

The strongest indication of a broader shift in Japanese thinking about empire, however, may be found in the army. In the view of the ascendant cohort in the officer corps, Japan had attained a level of national power concomitant with its aspirations and had closed the gap between will and way that had constrained expansion during the preceding decades. The quest for empire would no longer depend so heavily on the catch-as-catch-can of opportunity and circumstance but could be pursued based on more deliberate and farsighted designs. Such ideas were best represented by Tanaka Giichi who in 1906 outlined a grand program of continental expansion in which Manchuria was only the first step. Indeed, in the thinking of this ambitious young staff officer, the lands north of the Wall were essential to the empire's security, but the real prize in China lay in the rich lands to the south.[72] Not all were prepared to go as far as Tanaka. However, there is no doubt that the Russo-Japanese War marks the emergence in the army of a single-minded dedication to continental expansion that would form the core of its mission for decades to come.

How deep this change in attitudes ran within the Japanese polity as a whole, however, is open to question. Although dedicated imperialists figured prominently in the new generation of military and bureaucratic leaders, not all shared an aggressively expansionist outlook. Saionji Kinmochi (1849–1940), who alternated with Katsura Tarō as prime minister between 1906 and 1912, held many of the same positions as his mentor, Itō Hirobumi, on matters of empire. Admiral Yamamoto Gonbei, a member of the new cohort and the navy's most influential representative in political affairs, was, as we have seen, quite skeptical about continental imperialism. Moreover, although both of Japan's armed services had become increasingly self-assured in their capabilities in the aftermath of the war, they did not agree on the best ways to use the nation's military power. Tanaka and Akiyama became bitter adversaries in 1906 as their respective services locked horns over the question of continental versus maritime expansion.[73] Growing national confidence, moreover, led some leaders to question the need for further imperialist undertakings regardless of direction. Given newfound international respect, an invigorated alliance with Britain, and a secure base in Korea, Japan enjoyed, in their view, an unprecedentedly strong position in East Asia and no longer had any compelling strategic reasons for expansion.[74] As for popular attitudes, at least some of the pro-imperialist sentiment reflected in the Hibiya Riots was fueled by a postwar euphoria that proved to be transient.[75] Although there is no doubt that an imperial consciousness took deeper root in Japanese thinking than ever before as a result of the Russo-Japanese War, it is important to bear in mind that the war against China ten years earlier had also produced a surge of public enthusiasm for expansion.[76] Significantly, opposition politicians in the Diet, uncertain of the long-term directions of public opinion, declined to ride the wave of popular imperialist outrage expressed in the Hibiya Riots in a challenge to the government.[77]

The growth of parliamentary influence in national affairs is another development that served to brake aggressive tendencies of Japanese imperialism in the aftermath of the Russo-Japanese War. Since its founding in 1890, the lower house of the Imperial Diet had waged a protracted struggle to strengthen its influence over a government dominated by an aloof professional bureaucracy and cabinet ministers drawn from a small elite of founding oligarchs and their handpicked successors. Using their constitutional function of approving the national budget as leverage, parliamentary politicians had managed, over the years, to extract significant concessions over policy issues and political appointments. This process accelerated after 1906 as the power of the founding fathers declined. The new cohort of bureaucratic and military leaders remained no less committed to maintaining an elite government and limiting the role of the Diet than the original oligarchs. Men like Katsura and Saionji, however, could not assert the same kind of authority as their predecessors and had little choice but to compromise further. As bureaucratic governments came to recognize the impossibility of managing national affairs without the support of the majority party in the Diet, bargaining became almost routine, and Japan inched toward a form of parliamentary government. Under the de facto leadership of Hara Takashi (1856–1921), the Seiyūkai, which managed to sustain a stable majority after the Russo-Japanese War, proved most effective in playing this political game. By making itself indispensable to effective government, it won significant policy concessions and bureaucratic appointments for its members, along with a major voice in the formation of cabinets.[78]

Members of the Diet held a wide range of views on empire and national defense. The parties themselves, including the Seiyūkai, however, had no consistent platform on these issues, and their stands, more often than not, stemmed from considerations of tactical advantage rather than principle. At the same time, they demonstrated a general tendency toward moderation on matters of imperial expansion and armaments. The reason for this inclination had less to do with broad views of national policy than with their inherent fiscal conservatism as representatives of taxpaying citizens. For the most part, they limited their support for large-scale spending programs to domestic projects that would directly benefit their constituents. Whether or not they agreed with empire and armament in principle, such undertakings incurred enormous costs without offering the kind of tangible returns to local voters that, say, domestic railway projects did. Accordingly, they might endorse the idea of expansion in Manchuria, but they would not look favorably on any grand imperial schemes that would dramatically increase military and administrative expenditures.[79]

The trend toward a more aggressive expansionism evident in the army, then, was bridled by other domestic political forces. Although Japan's capabilities had increased, voices calling for restraint on a variety of grounds remained strong and limited the imperialists' freedom of action. In this respect, the broad dynamics of policy conflict did not undergo as radical a transformation after the war as might be expected. What did change was the intensity of the conflict. An emboldened army, less amenable to arguments for caution based on imperialist *realpolitik*, adopted a more intractable position in the post-1905 years. The decline of the oligarchs' influence, moreover, deprived the political process as a whole of a strong, authoritative center to which competing factions might defer. The emergence of empire as a destabilizing force in domestic politics must certainly be regarded as an important outcome of the Russo-Japanese War.

Incipient developments in the international arena also set obstacles in the way of an invigorated postwar expansionism. By 1906, events in Europe had already begun to exert a dampening effect on imperialism in East Asia. The Russo-Japanese War itself contributed to this trend by illuminating the danger of unrestrained competition for empire. In addition, the rise of militant Chinese resistance to foreign encroachment, inspired by Russia's defeat on the one hand and provoked by Japanese demands in Manchuria on the other, led a number of the Great Powers to begin reassessing the costs and benefits of concession hunting. The Americans and the British had expressed their unhappiness with the Japanese decision to renege on their commitments to the Open Door in Manchuria, a stance that hinted at a shifting attitude toward China. Insofar as the Social Darwinian dictum "eat or be eaten" had underpinned the logic of Meiji imperialism, diminishing Western appetites would begin to erode the cogency of this rationale for empire.[80] Although the army and others of like mind could no doubt find other compelling reasons for Japan to persist in an expansionist course, running against the tide of Western opinion entailed grave risks. Japan might be stronger and more confident than ever before but not sufficiently so as to defy the collective will of the Great Powers with impunity. The need for a circumspect approach to empire-building remained.

To be sure, the full implications of the changes in the international environment beginning to take shape were far from clear in 1906. Not even the more astute Japanese observers in the immediate aftermath of the Russo-Japanese War understood that the age of empire in East Asia was coming to a close. Moreover, in the heady, post-victory atmosphere of late 1905 and early 1906, when much of the nation was still gripped by imperialist fever, critics of expansion tended to keep their counsel. A direct challenge to a triumphant army, whose prestige was at an unprecedented high, would certainly not have been politically wise. Hindsight leads us to question the notion that the war resulted in a sea change in Japanese attitudes toward empire. Dedicated expansionists at the beginning of 1906, however, had every reason to anticipate an era in which Japanese dominion in East Asia would come within reach. General Kodama and his colleagues thus threw themselves into the task of mapping out a program for action in Manchuria with great optimism.

TWO

The Trojan Horse, 1905–1907

Dictated by the logic of opportunity, Japan's decision to stake a claim in Manchuria rested on a framework of possibilities rather than a body of clearly defined aims. At a broad level, the nation's leaders had little difficulty rationalizing the decision. Strategic geography, the "line of interest" doctrine, and the looming threat of a vengeful Russia provided strong grounds to justify the commitment. Moreover, aggressive concession hunting remained, at least in Japanese perceptions, the norm among the Great Powers active in China. Having failed to acquire a sphere of its own before 1905, Japan could only leap at the chance offered in Manchuria to even the score. For the more ambitious among Japanese imperialists, the thinly settled and undeveloped lands north of the Wall promised room for the nation's growth, and the fact that the territory was rather loosely controlled by the government in Peking made it vulnerable to encroachment in a manner not possible elsewhere in China.

Outlining a specific program that would yield tangible benefits worthy of the costs and risks involved, however, proved more challenging. Like other opportunistic imperialists, the Japanese had little choice but to adapt policy to circumstance. They could devise meaningful aims and strategies only after taking careful stock of the horizons of possibility defined by conditions in the territory, by the resources at their disposal, and by the political constraints limiting their freedom of action. The recommendations of the Manchurian Army and Ishizuka's survey group provided a solid point of departure, but much remained to be done in fleshing out a specific course of action. The most important question facing policymakers at the beginning of 1906 was how to make optimum use of the assets inherited from Russia. Early discussions produced no shortage of proposals, ranging from modest commercial schemes favored by moderates, such as Itō Hirobumi, to bold programs for colonization envisioned by Kodama Gentarō and his colleagues in the army. Although the Japanese were by no means bound to follow in the footsteps of their imperialist predecessors, Russia's original blueprints for the railway, designed with quasi-colonial aims in mind, weighed in favor of those calling for a more activist program.

In addition to the formulation of aims and strategies, two other tasks confronted policymakers in 1906 and 1907 that were in some respects more urgent. One was to create an administrative apparatus for managing Japan's Manchurian holdings and to clarify lines of bureaucratic jurisdiction. Whether Manchuria policy should fall under the primary authority of the army, the Foreign Ministry or some new colonial agency became a subject of heated debate, one outcome of which was the establishment of the institution that came to be known as the South Manchuria Railway Company (SMR). The other task was to revise the nation's defense policies to meet the needs of new commitments in both Korea and Manchuria. Substantial continental holdings made an adjustment in the balance between land and sea power unavoidable and inextricably tangled the question of Manchuria with rivalry between the army and the navy. The questions of administrative arrangements and revisions in defense policy proved to be highly contentious. The decline of the authority of the oligarchs had unleashed centrifugal tendencies within the Japanese polity and had fueled sectional conflict between compartmentalized agencies. These trends were reinforced by the technocratic orientation of the new cohort of leaders, which led them to define national interests in narrower terms than their generalist predecessors and to identify themselves closely with specific professional bureaucracies.

The Inheritance: Russian Designs

The early lessons of Taiwan underscored the importance of adaptability in policy. Circumstances encountered in the acquired territory would determine the particular path that empire-building efforts would follow. As in Taiwan, the social, economic, political, and natural environment of the vast lands north of the Great Wall would define the horizons of imperialist possibility. In the case of Manchuria, however, the Russian legacy represented an additional factor to consider, no less significant as a starting condition in shaping Japanese policy than the territory's other endowments. Indeed, the fundamental approach to developing programmatic aims and strategies in 1906 and the first few years to follow entailed nothing more or less than an inversion of the conventional logic of ends and means: an attempt to adapt Japanese purposes to the designs of their predecessors. Any understanding of policymaking in 1906 must thus begin with an examination of the original schemes underlying the Chinese Eastern Railway (CER).

The Russian venture in Manchuria represents an outstanding example of "railway imperialism." The application of railway technology in empire-building emerged as a permutation of its use as a tool of public policy in the metropolitan world, a function developed and perfected during the second half of the nineteenth century. The combination of steam locomotion and iron rails, introduced during the first half of the century, revolutionized transportation, offering service qualitatively faster, safer, more reliable, and cheaper by the unit than any other form of overland conveyance. Its ability to "shrink" distances unified and expanded markets, changed basic ways of doing business, transformed the nature of warfare, and began to alter the political and cultural geography of Europe and North America. Inspired by these effects, activist states quickly harnessed railways as instruments of policy in a variety of arenas, a step that contributed to the growing reach and power of the state itself in many instances.[1]

Among policy applications, military uses emerged early on; the first serious speculations about the value of railways in warfare date to the 1830s. In the German states, soldiers appear to have had a greater appreciation for the military potential of this technology than businessmen had for its economic uses. A series of wars in continental Europe and North America between 1859 and 1871 tested these ideas and produced a well-honed body of theory and practical experience in the uses of the railway as an instrument of war. The qualitative improvement in the speed of transportation across long distances led to new thinking about offensive and defensive strategies. Railways allowed for the long-range deployment of unprecedented numbers of soldiers in a very short time, making mobility and flexibility major considerations in military planning. Mobility, in turn, contributed to a new efficiency in the use of ground troops. A well-designed network could allow a relatively small force to defend or occupy vast territories, reducing the need for large, fixed garrisons. Strategic plans could count on rapidly concentrating troops precisely where needed, an advantage exploited in the Japanese military reforms of 1888, when the army shifted its structure from one based on regional garrisons to a more flexible divisional organization. Railways also broke new ground in military supply and logistics. Freed of the need to rely on local sources of provisions, troops could advance through barren lands and wage war in undeveloped territories. Old limits on the size of front-line engagements disappeared with the possibility of sustaining vast armies almost indefinitely through secure railways to the rear. As knowledge about the military applications of this technology became more systematized, it produced a body of unwritten conventions, assumptions, and understandings in international relations. Defense planners treated all railways, regardless of their nominal peacetime uses, as strategic installations representing a virtual military presence in the areas through which they ran. Data on speed and carrying capacity were used to calculate reliable estimates of how many troops an adversary might deploy in a particular region and how quickly they might do so. Such calculations played a major part in Japanese planning for the war against Russia.[2]

Railways, of course, served as vital economic policy tools as well. Even when run by private interests for purely business reasons, they produced sweeping economic changes in their service territories, intended or not. Because of their impact on entire communities, privately owned railways often faced strong pressures for public accountability and were regarded as economic agencies far too powerful to leave in the unrestrained hands of businessmen. In the United States, populist critics of private railway management often depicted companies in this field as territorial powers unto themselves, acting as states within states, and evoked feudal associations in the characterization of managers as "barons." Yet the same power that presented a danger if left in unregulated private hands also offered enormous potential to serve the public good. Railways, indeed, were one of the first objects of large-scale state intervention in otherwise market-oriented economies. They functioned not only as "engines of growth" but also as tools with which policymakers might direct the vectors of development with some precision. Through the administration of a regional transportation system, it became possible to exercise considerable managerial control over the economy of the service territory as a whole. Construction programs determined patterns of commercial integration, land and resource use, settlement, and urbanization. Freight rates could serve to fine-tune economic policy, much like tariffs and subsidies. Creative railway administration might even allow public authorities to redistribute the benefits of growth in the form of aid to distressed geographic areas and pork-barrel measures for select political constituencies.[3]

A corollary of the use of the railway as an economic policy tool, but as-suming a special significance in its own right, emerged in its function as an instrument of nation building. The new transportation technology inte-grated formerly fragmented regional and local economies into larger, more unified market areas. This development contributed significantly to the con-struction of nation-states in the nineteenth century. Some nationalists saw customs unions and connecting railway systems as preludes to political amalgamation. Improved transportation also facilitated the movement of people and ideas as well as goods, accelerating the integration and homog-enization of national culture in a manner broadly similar to that which Benedict Anderson postulates for the printed vernacular.[4] Railways enabled even illiterate people to "imagine" themselves as part of a larger national community, turning villages once worlds apart into virtual neighbors. They facilitated the sharing of ideas and values, the spread of fashions, and the de-velopment of uniform consumption patterns.[5] For Russia this technology played a vital role in binding together the vast continental expanse of its em-pire, a mission fulfilled by the Trans-Siberian line, one of the greatest proj-ects of the age. Railways could also nurture the distinct identities of neigh-boring countries. The Canadian Pacific Railway functioned as much to preserve Canada's nationhood with respect to its rich and powerful neighbor to the south as it did to integrate its own provinces.[6]

Given the far-reaching policy applications of the railway in defense, de-velopment, and national integration, it is not surprising that in an age of em-pire, efforts emerged early on to harness its potentialities as an instrument of imperialism. In formal possessions, railways served as arms of the colonial state, playing a vital role in pacification, defense, and the construction of new communities out of what often constituted no more than arbitrary polygons drawn on a map. These colonial functions were extensions of the same pur-poses at home, but in the marches of empire, they became all the more im-portant. Railways were the vanguard of the new "civilization" the imperialists sought to introduce. In many areas, the real influence of the colonial ruler exerted itself through the railway more than through any other single insti-tution, whether church, army, school, or business corporation. An impor-tant permutation of the imperial applications of this technology emerged in China and Korea as well as the Middle East, where expansionist powers sought to employ railways as instruments of empire-building outside the framework of formal rule.[7]

Any generalizations about the nature of foreign railway building in China and Korea warrant caution because of wide variations in purpose. Foreign entities undertook some of these projects primarily as investment opportunities, ventures driven, indeed, by the interests of the "coupon clipper." Some powers built lines to facilitate the expansion of their trade with China's interior; essentially this was an elaboration of the commercial imperialism dominant during the middle of the nineteenth century, modified by the particularist orientation that had come to inform the pursuit of trade by the late 1890s. The French scheme to open a "back door" from Indochina into the British-dominated trade of the Yangtze valley by establishing railway connections offers a good example. Britain, although one of the more active railway builders in China around the turn of the twentieth century, responded defensively for the most part, with the aim of protecting its commercial interests against plans such as those of the French. A few ventures, however, attempted to harness the potentialities of the railway as an instrument of territorial control in a broader fashion. Designed appropriately, a trunk line within a region staked out as a sphere of interest could turn that claim into more than a diplomatic fiction, establishing a significant measure of actual power on the ground. Creative administration offered a variety of opportunities to implement a protectionist commercial policy. It also provided the means to reconfigure historically evolved patterns of territorial integration, to strengthen distinct regional identities, and to establish new connections to the national, colonial, or leased territories of the controlling power. A railway sphere aggressively developed might thus serve as a halfway house to partition. Enhancing these possibilities, foreign railways in China also carried unmistakable military implications, whether intended or not, establishing an implicit armed presence, a latent state of occupation that a power might activate on demand.[8]

The Russian undertaking in Manchuria represents the most striking case of a "proto-colonial" railway imperialism. In scope, scale, and elegance of design, no foreign venture in China came close to the CER. Sergei Witte, the architect of both the CER and the Trans-Siberian, envisioned the Manchurian system, both literally and conceptually, as an extension of the Eurasian line, providing a shortcut between Chita and Vladivostok and offering the added benefit of connections to the ice-free ports of Port Arthur and Talien. It required no major conceptual leap to proceed from thinking about the CER as a branch of the Trans-Siberian to regarding Manchuria itself as a prospective addition to Siberia, a pocket of inconveniently non-Russian territory hampering communications in the Far East. Although some official circles in St. Petersburg regarded annexation as a possible remedy, Witte believed that his approach could reproduce effective control without the complications inevitably generated by formal demands for territorial cession, an idea often described as "conquest by railway."[9] According to Steven Marks, Witte saw the Trans-Siberian Railway as an instrument for colonizing Asian Russia, for bringing Russian civilization and power to a land that constituted a "wild East." In the case of the CER, a similar strategy of Russification could also apply to territory not formally Russian.[10]

Compared to other areas of China of interest to the Great Powers, Manchuria lent itself more readily to this kind of scheme because of its character as a frontier region, much like the American West in the second half of the nineteenth century. It encompassed an area roughly 400,000–500,000 square miles in size, depending on how imperial cartographers construed its western boundaries, and with only seven million inhabitants at the turn of the twentieth century, it remained thinly settled by Chinese standards. Commercial transportation in the area suffered from severe limitations. The two major navigable rivers, the Liao in the south and the Sungari in the north, remained frozen for much of the year and, even in the best of times, served only a portion of the territory (see Map 2.1). Primitive roads rendered travel difficult and became almost entirely unusable during the spring and autumn rains. Endemic banditry added serious hazards to any movement of people or goods. On the other hand, the land offered great potential for development. Fertile plains beckoned to farmers, and soy emerged as a major cash crop, particularly in the Liao valley, where the river made possible the shipment of crops to Yingk'ou, Manchuria's single commercial seaport before the coming of the Russians. Coal deposits existed in great abundance in various parts of the territory, particularly near Fushun. Such mineral wealth, however, remained commercially unexploitable without modern transportation facilities. All these factors tended to magnify the importance of railway power in this territory, essential for defense, law and order, and economic development.[11]

The relatively weak hold of China's central government over its northeastern border region also tended to enhance the opportunity for Russian encroachment. As the homeland of the ruling dynasty, Ch'ing authorities

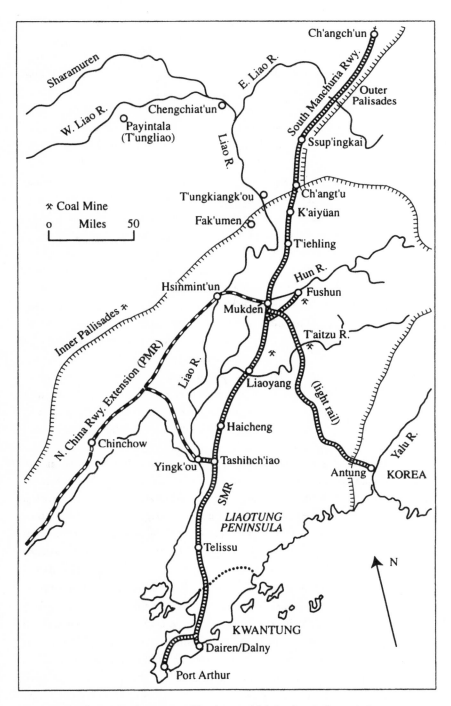

Map 2.1 Southern Manchuria, 1906. The Antung-Mukden line is shown in its permanent configuration as of 1909 plans. The route of the actual light rail and its connection to the SMR trunk was slightly different (based on a map in SMR1).

sought to preserve the territory as what Owen Lattimore describes as a "reservoir" of strength, keeping it distinct from China proper by placing restrictions on the immigration of ethnic Han Chinese to the region. A portion of the Liao valley within the so-called Inner Palisades was exempt from this restriction and formed, as a result, one of the older and more densely populated areas of settlement. Legal reforms gradually opened other areas to newcomers in the late nineteenth century, partly in an effort to raise revenue through land sales but also in response to the danger of foreign encroachment. The effects of a long history, however, could not be reversed quickly. Few major cities in Manchuria had existed for more than a century. Mukden, the original Manchu capital, represented the most important exception, and yet even this urban center dated back only to the seventeenth century. Han (ethnic Chinese) settlers founded Ch'angch'un, which eventually became the capital of Japanese Manchuria in the 1930s, as a permanent community in 1825. The institutions of government in the territory remained rudimentary. It was organized into three provinces with military governors, whose real political reach never penetrated far into the hinterlands. Endemic lawlessness reflected political underdevelopment, and most inhabitants had little choice but to rely on their own efforts to secure a modicum of order in the area surrounding their communities. For example, in the 1860s, local merchants, through their own fundraising efforts, erected a wall around Ch'angch'un to protect it from bandits.[12]

Manchuria, then, provided not only an environment in which the railway might play an extraordinarily important role but also one in which a foreign intruder armed with this technology confronted relatively weak competition from traditional native authority. To be sure, charges that a railway company was competing with the state for control of a territory were often nothing more than political hyperbole and in the United States, skeptics might well have dismissed the idea as a paranoid fantasy of turn-of-the-century populists. In Manchuria, however, the possibility held substance. Admittedly, the potentialities of railway power lent themselves to exaggeration even in this land. With the Japanese in mind, Owen Lattimore warned against "a tendency to assume that in Manchuria there is a clear field; that there is almost no necessity of making over an old civilization, with all its vested interests, social and economic, and that it is therefore an ideal territory for the introduction of 'modern civilization.'"[13] Still, if such a possibility existed anywhere in continental East Asia outside Russian national territory, it lay in Manchuria. From the beginning, Russia encountered in this region an opportunity far greater than that available to other powers harboring similar aspirations elsewhere in China. A number of geographic and strategic circumstances, as well as special provisions that the Russians managed to acquire for their project, magnified this advantage.

Russian interests, and in fact, the government itself, which worked through an entity known as the Russo-Chinese Bank, owned the CER outright. Direct ownership, which the Germans and French also enjoyed in their concessions in Shantung and Yunnan, respectively, contrasted with most other railway agreements, which entailed loans to the Chinese government as nominal owner and operator. In these "loan concessions," foreign entities commonly exercised managerial influence through the right, written into the loan contract, to appoint the chief engineer, traffic manager, and chief financial officer; they also held a mortgage on the railway's assets. Such terms endowed foreign interests with decisive authority over operation of the line, but the Russians enjoyed a more direct and uncompromised control over the CER. The one consolation offered the Chinese lay in the possibility of purchasing the system 36 years after its completion (1939).[14] The Russians also built the railway to their unique, five-foot gauge, which made the CER incompatible with the English standard, the norm in China and Korea. The special gauge, coupled with the fact that the network anchored itself in Russian national or colonial territory at all three of its termini—the border town of Manchouli in the west, Pogranichnaya in the east, and Port Arthur in the south—rendered the CER ideally suited to integrating the region with the Russian Far East. Provisions for a one-third discount on Chinese custom duties applied to goods crossing the Chinese-Russian border by railway enhanced this possibility. Only the British-financed North China Railway Extension, later renamed the Peking–Mukden Railway (PMR), linked the lands south of the Wall to those north. Ethnically and culturally, Manchuria might have close ties with Shantung and Chihli as a result of immigration, but from the perspective of transportation links, the territory enjoyed closer ties to Russia's Maritime Province and Trans-Baikalia. Russia, then, found itself in an excellent competitive position to shape the future of the territory[15] (see Map 2.2).

The strategic potential of the CER is so self-evident that it warrants little

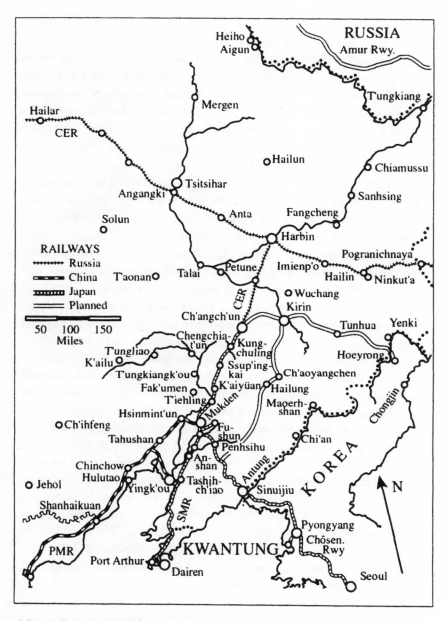

Map 2.2 Railways in Manchuria, 1906. Some planned routes are shown based on actual lines built subsequently (based on maps in Tōa keizai chōsakyoku, *Manchoukuo Year Book, 1934*; SMR, *Eigyō hōkokusho, 1923, 1928, 1930*; DR1, looseleaf).

comment. The railway virtually "hard-wired" the territory for occupation. Any moderation shown Japan in prewar negotiations may well have resulted from the fact that the system remained incomplete until 1903. The Russian military position in Manchuria, however, went beyond the virtual presence represented by the railway as a "dual-use" facility. The original treaty governing the CER granted Russia the right to station as many as fifteen railway guards for every mile of line. With a system running more than 1,500 miles, this provision sanctioned the deployment of a force the size of a Russian army corps deep within the Manchurian interior.[16]

The most unusual of Russia's special rights, however, rested in the Railway Zone, a narrow strip of land along either side of the track, enlarged around station areas. Although formally leased to the CER, the company exercised, for all intents and purposes, colonial control over these real estate holdings. The agreement gave the CER "the absolute and exclusive right of administration" in these lands, endowing the Russians with actual powers of territorial government, not only in the leasehold of Kwantung but well inside Manchuria proper. The total area of Russian colonial rule in Chinese lands north of the Great Wall remained relatively small, the Zone adding only a few hundred square miles to the 1,300 of the Leased Territory. In this case, however, size alone offers a poor measure of significance. Kwantung and the Zone represented some of the most valuable real estate in Manchuria, forming the axis of development and colonization. In the enlarged station areas, established, in some instances, alongside existing Chinese communities as in Ch'angch'un, the Russians had planned to build settlements complete with all modern amenities, including their own schools, hospitals, and public works. Although not completed before the war against Japan, the port city of Dalny in Kwantung, laid out on the radial grid favored by Russian designers, offered an early example of modern urban planning in East Asia. The Japanese would retain this basic plan when they renamed the city Dairen and completed its construction. The most striking effort in urban development, representing an attempt to build a new metropolis from near scratch, manifested itself in the junction city of Harbin, where the southern branch and the trans-Manchurian trunk of the CER met. In time, it would become a center of Russian power in the East.[17]

The Chinese Eastern Railway Company, which administered all Russian holdings in Manchuria with the exception of the Leased Territory, bears a family resemblance to the chartered colonial companies operating in contemporary Africa and Southeast Asia, which traced their institutional roots to Britain's venerable East India Company. The principal difference lay in the fact that most chartered colonial companies based their operations and their power on direct control of vast stretches of land. We might, indeed, conceive of such institutions as imperial real estate development corporations with their own police and administrative powers. Despite the CER's limited land rights, however, possession of the railway allowed it to exercise considerable indirect control over the territory within its transportation watershed. From a business perspective, railways and real estate management have long enjoyed an intimate relationship, with developers often switching their emphasis from one field of enterprise to the other as if they constituted interchangeable undertakings. This relationship provides a sense of the full extent of the CER's power. In its own way, it represented no less a force in Manchuria than the East India Company in South Asia.[18]

One final feature of the Russian railway venture warranting comment was its near-monopoly on railway transportation in the territory. In many respects, this arrangement formed the linchpin of the entire scheme. Railway power of the kind Russia hoped to exercise rested on the ability to hold the territory hostage to the exclusive services of its facilities, and the existence of any significant competitive alternatives to the CER would undermine that power. The Russian company had done nothing to "earn" this monopoly in the marketplace but had received it as a benefice written into the original agreement with China. The agreement stipulated that China would not build railways that had an impact on the interests of the CER, nor permit any other power to do so, without the express permission of the Russian authorities.[19]

All in all, the Russians had designed an apparatus in Manchuria capable of reproducing many of the functions of the colonial state by harnessing the power of a railway monopoly. The Chinese Eastern Railway Company constituted an agency competing, in effect, with Chinese authorities for control of the territory, not in the realm of high diplomacy, where Russia might concede the issue of Chinese sovereignty on paper, but on the ground. Defeat in 1905 thwarted the full implementation of Witte's grand designs, but in the portion of the system Russia retained after the war, Russification proceeded reasonably well until 1917. Harbin even today remains a Chinese city distinguished by onion-dome spires. As for the southern portion of the system, the Russians had, in effect, handed Japan a ready-to-start project in "conquest by railway."

Japanese Adaptations

Japanese accounts of the origins of the venture in Manchuria written before the end of World War II tend to obscure the Russian legacy, ascribing the basic design of program and strategy to the creative talents, farsightedness, and imperialist dedication of the nation's leaders. Such revisionism characterizes, in particular, the biographies of some of the men involved in planning in 1906, including those of Komura Jūtarō, Kodama Gentarō, and Gotō Shinpei, which depict their subjects as the primary architects of Japanese Manchuria. Accounts of Gotō's activities, for example, commonly attribute his inspiration for the SMR directly to the East India Company rather than the more immediate and obvious model of the CER.[20] Although there is little doubt as to the audacious imagination of Japan's imperialist statesmen, circumstances in 1906 demanded of them a creativity rather different from that demonstrated by Sergei Witte and his associates. The principal challenge facing Japanese policymakers lay in discovering the optimum applications for the turnkey project they had acquired. Japanese planners made some modifications in the inherited apparatus during the early years, to be sure, principally in the form of gauge changes, double-tracking, and connections with the Korean railway system. They also completed unfinished Russian projects, such as the construction of Dairen. But for the most part, they devised a program and strategy for Manchuria through adaptation and rationalization, by recasting Japanese policy in a mold created by the technology of Russian imperialism. Given the nature of this process, discussions in 1906, not surprisingly, generated a wide range of ideas.

The strategic elements of Manchuria policy emerged as the most clearly defined from the outset. The assumption of a probable second war against Russia lay at the center of the army's program. Reflecting the affirmative view of Japanese achievements during the recent conflict, military planners adopted a revised version of the strategy originally outlined in 1903, making adjustments for the shortcomings acknowledged by the Manchurian Army in its postwar assessment. Possession of what formerly constituted the southern branch of the CER would make an enormous difference in Japan's position, allowing the army to initiate a campaign against Russia from where the last war left off. Using the rapid-deployment and logistical-support capabilities of the railway, the army planned a quick strike against Harbin, where its forces would intercept the CER and dig in to prepare for a Russian counterattack. The importance of timing in this strategy dictated the reconstruction of the trunk line from Port Arthur to Ch'angch'un in order to accommodate high-speed trains and to enlarge its capacity. The army would deploy troops from Korea as well as Kwantung, and under certain circumstances, it would also consider making use of the PMR as a strategic line. Apparently for these reasons, military planners reconsidered their position of 1905 that a temporary narrow-gauge system would suffice and argued for the standard gauge, which not only offered higher capacity but compatibility with the Chinese and Korean systems.[21]

The establishment of Korean connections for the trunk line occupied a high priority in army plans. A temporary narrow-gauge railway from Antung to Mukden already existed and had been used as a military line during the war to support the advance of Japan's Yalu Army. Planners regarded a permanent replacement for this facility as indispensable, and negotiations with the Chinese in December 1905, culminating in the Treaty of Peking, incorporated this demand. The Antung–Mukden line enjoyed the same status as the Russian-built trunk, including provisions for a railway zone. A second proposal called for a connection between Ch'angch'un and the city of Kirin and, from there, to some point as yet unspecified on the T'umen River border (later designated as Hoeryong), where it would eventually connect to a port on Korea's northeastern coast. These lines would not only facilitate troop deployment from Korea to Manchuria, but, given Korea's status as a protectorate, established in 1905, also emulate the cross-border connections that the CER had enjoyed with Russian national territory. The Manchurian Army plan recommended one other route, on a more tentative basis, to run from some point on the Antung–Mukden railway to Kirin. Although such a parallel rail connection might compete for traffic with the Port Arthur–Ch'angch'un trunk, strategic logic argued that the more lines running north, the stronger Japan's offensive capability against the Russian position.[22]

Although railway development formed the most important element in the army's concept of using Manchuria as a forward base, the scheme went considerably further. A key element in the optimistic assessment of strategic prospects offered by the staff of the expeditionary army in late 1905 lay in Japan's ability to make use of a developed base in southern Manchuria in any future confrontation with Russia. Army planners thought in terms of creating a far-ranging complex of dual-use facilities that, like the railway, might operate as commercial ventures or public works under civilian management in peacetime but, once mobilized, function as military assets in the event of war. They considered the development of ancillary transportation particularly important and called for extensive Japanese involvement in shipping on the Liao River and in freight-hauling ventures using ox- and horse-drawn carts. Planners also favored the building of ordinary roads and bridges throughout the territory. In these efforts, army authorities sought to take advantage of temporary postwar occupation arrangements, which, under the Russo-Japanese accords for gradual troop withdrawal known as the Ssup'ingkai Protocol, would last until April 1907. They planned to levy taxes on local residents and initiate a series of infrastructural projects on their own. This scheme, not surprisingly, ran afoul of the Japanese Foreign Ministry, a dispute that we shall consider shortly.[23]

The army's idea of preparing southern Manchuria as a base for wartime mobilization also extended to sources of supply. For example, its program called for the development of modern meat-packing facilities, located in Kwantung and the Railway Zone, in order to alleviate problems with fresh meat supplies encountered during the recent conflict. Wartime experience in procuring military mounts and draft horses from local sources during the war inspired the idea of promoting horse breeding in the territory, an undertaking much more suitable for the broad expanses of Manchuria than land-poor Japan. One of the more curious ideas, not only entertained but set into motion under the occupation, involved a program of afforestation. Japanese authorities planned to create tree nurseries and begin restoring some of the woodland areas devastated during the war as well as those stripped as a result of overexploitation in the past. Occupation administrators had already established one nursery late in the war at Liaoyang. The army's concerns arose not only from the need to control erosion and protect water supplies but also from the desire to develop sources of fuel. During the harsh Manchurian winter, shortages of firewood in 1904 and 1905 had proved serious. Desperate Russians had seized Chinese boats on the Liao River and broken them up for fuel. Afforestation represented a rational and environmentally sound program, but it also suggests, even with the fastest growing of trees, the long time horizon of Japanese planning.[24]

One other military project of special note entailed a plan to build a network of local health centers and hospitals in Kwantung and the Railway Zone. The Russians' central medical facility in Dalny (Dairen) and satellite clinics in the larger station towns along the southern branch of the CER had inspired this idea. The Japanese army saw the possibility of using such facilities as modern military hospitals advantageously situated close to the prospective front lines in a future conflict. In order to ensure their development in peacetime to a scale that might be required in the event of war, the army proposed that these hospitals and clinics serve a large civilian clientele, both Chinese and Japanese, under normal circumstances. The promotion of civilian public health in the region, a desirable goal in itself, would also help Japan win international approval for its humanitarian effort and even cultivate goodwill among local Chinese.[25]

The general principle underlying the army's planning in the territory held that the value of southern Manchuria as a rear area during a military conflict increased in proportion to its development in peacetime. The basic idea stemmed from the well-established tradition of drawing upon local, frontline sources of supply, what Japanese army planners described as *genchi chōben*. The notion of systematically promoting economic development near prospective front lines in order to meet the demands of war, however, made the scheme in Manchuria rather unusual. In effect, it involved a unique synthesis of economic mobilization planning and field procurement, a plan to sow a neighbor's lands in order to ensure an abundant plunder should the need arise.[26]

The fact that these plans took advantage of "dual-use" undertakings such as railway construction, shipping ventures, agricultural development projects, and public health programs offered some special benefits worth noting. For one, they allowed the army to build and maintain military installations at little or no net cost to the defense budget. If these activities lacked commercial viability, their contribution to good public administration or humanitarian work provided ample justification. Moreover, although the commercial or public service functions of these ventures did little to camouflage their actual nature in the eyes of any informed observer, they did allow Japanese diplomats a plausible basis for denying any improper activity. Army Chief of Staff Kodama, in fact, described this scheme as one in which Japan would "secretly manage all manner of facilities under the public mask of railway management." Gotō Shinpei characterized Manchurian defense plans even more frankly: they were *bunsōteki bubi*, "military readiness in civilian dress." In this context, it would be fair to say that the army's plans amounted to a scheme to maintain a covert form of occupation. Railways provided the equivalent of a military presence. In addition, the Japanese would retain an entire complex of assets designed to support military operations, equivalent to what the occupation administration had created during the war. The army would honor the terms of the Ssup'ingkai Protocol and evacuate the territory completely by April 1907. At the same time, it would leave as a parting gift to the people of Manchuria a Trojan Horse.[27]

The quality of the Russian apparatus made possible Japanese defense plans calling for the maintenance of a covert or, perhaps more accurately, partially demobilized occupation of Manchuria. It also created an opportunity to carry out economic policies, better suited for formal colonial situations, that circumstances elsewhere in China would not have allowed. Although their plans were not nearly as developed as military proposals, policymakers and specialist advisors explored a number of important ideas along these lines. The Ishizuka survey group, for example, had recommended a developmental orientation toward extracting value from Manchuria, an effort that would bear fruit perhaps a generation down the road. Their analysis emphasized the high potential of the territory but cautioned that realizing economic gains would require long-term investment and the implementation of a far-reaching, activist economic policy. The leadership of the survey team by a colonial official from Taiwan, where the Japanese had pioneered precisely such an approach, bears reiteration. Economic policy in Taiwan, however, depended on unfettered Japanese political authority and the power of a strong and intrusive colonial government, advantages not available in Manchuria. The Russian apparatus, nonetheless, offered sufficient capabilities to compensate at least partially for this deficiency and to substitute for the economic policy functions of a colonial state.[28]

Ishizuka's group offered some preliminary ideas in this vein. The railway, of course, would provide the most important policy device, its economic power supplemented through the creation of special institutions, such as the Manchurian bank noted earlier, along with agricultural and commercial development agencies. The survey team also appears to have favored the idea of designating the civil administration of the Leased Territory to serve as the central economic planning organ for Japanese Manchuria. It is, perhaps, not entirely coincidental that, at the time of the survey, Ishizuka Eizō held the post of civil administrator in the occupation government and stood likely to fill the equivalent peacetime post in Kwantung, as he eventually did. This particular idea, however, did not get far since placing the Kwantung government in a position of substantial authority outside the Leased Territory proper would create serious diplomatic complications and lend Japanese policy too overtly colonial a coloring. A better solution, in the view of many, lay in turning over all economic policy functions to the railway agency itself, an approach that the Commission on the Management of Manchuria formally recommended in March 1906.[29]

Russian designs made it possible for Japanese policymakers to consider the pursuit of an essentially colonial approach to the extraction of economic value from Manchuria. Combined with the general conditions in the territory, they also opened the door to economic objectives that would have proven difficult to pursue elsewhere in China under more modestly constructed spheres of influence. The direct exploitation of land constituted one such goal. In the view of most contemporary Japanese, one of Manchuria's greatest resources was arable land. Many saw the acquisition of real estate abroad in order to make up for Japan's poor natural endowment as a particularly cogent reason for pursuing empire. The emerging land grab in Korea following the establishment of the protectorate in 1905 speaks to the enthusiasm for this prospect. Both the general public and official circles shared the perception that Manchuria, with its sparse population and broad prairies, offered even greater opportunities. "Manchuria is a big place," wrote novelist Natsume Sōseki (1867–1916) during a 1909 tour of the territory, invoking the image of "a thousand leagues of fertile plain" stretching before him. As a point of departure, following the Russian pattern, the Leased Territory and Railway Zone would provide a secure setting for large, permanent communities reproducing all the amenities of home, a favorable environment that might help overcome the general reluctance of Japanese to leave the comforts and familiarity of the motherland.[30]

Those with a better knowledge of actual conditions in the territory, for example, the authors of the 1905 survey, recognized the excessive optimism informing some of these perceptions of opportunities for immigration in Manchuria. Legal bars to foreign landownership in China, which might, of course, lend themselves to resolution through subsequent Sino-Japanese negotiations, presented one obstacle. The limited availability of arable but unworked tracts, despite appearances to the contrary, posed a yet greater problem, and even poor real estate commanded rather high prices. The vast, thinly settled prairies of Japanese visions actually lay in the Russian north. Moreover, even if Japanese won the right to homestead, competition with local farmers accustomed to lower standards of living and the harsh climate presented major challenges. Experts nonetheless regarded these problems as reason not so much to discourage the idea of settlement but to underscore the importance of a vigorous Japanese policy apparatus. Coherent Japanese power in the territory would render economic support to "pioneer" settlers, shield them from native authority, and protect their lives and property in a region where law and order left much to be desired.[31]

Policymakers engaged in thinking about economic prospects in Manchuria in 1906 did not limit themselves to long-term development and immigration. Those who viewed settlement and Taiwan-style economic programs with skepticism tended to emphasize more conventional commercial goals. Manchuria, of course, did not offer a particularly attractive market for Japanese exports, given its sparse population and relative poverty. Cotton cloth presented one significant exception. A relatively new export commodity in 1906, it found a pioneering customer base in the territory, benefiting from a government policy aimed at redeeming military scrip used to make local purchases during the war.[32] The strength of Japanese rights in the territory, however, compensated for weak commercial prospects by allowing for the application of what amounted to protectionist policies. Overall consumption of foreign goods in Manchuria might be low at present, but a strong policy could ensure Japanese dominance of the market, one that would undoubtedly grow even in the near term as a result of development associated with the railway. Komura Jūtarō had long emphasized the need for strong government support and protection of Japanese economic activity in China. "Japan is a country where private enterprise is still underdeveloped," he noted in 1901, arguing for an active policy in Fukien. "It will be many years before the private sector is up to the task." Japan's alignment with Britain and the United States during the interwar years, the "Open Door coalition," represented, as William Beasley suggests, a case of strange bedfellows. From the perspective of economic interests in China, Japan's orientation shared more with protectionist Russia than with its Anglo-American partners.[33] Three specific ideas about managed trade in Manchuria circulated at this time.

One scheme, abandoned quickly because of Great Power protests but nonetheless illustrative of intent, called for the use of the extended evacuation schedule allowed by the Ssup'ingkai Protocol to get a head start on commercial competition in the territory. The agreement had set the deadline for April 1907, and until that time, the Japanese army, at least in its own estimation, could maintain conditions approximating wartime occupation. These conditions, in turn, could serve as a pretext to exclude all commercial activity other than Japanese from the occupied areas. Although the army would subsequently bear the brunt of criticism for this scheme, the Finance Ministry appears to have worked closely with military authorities. Shortly after the battle of Mukden, the ministry issued a directive establishing a quasi-official body known as the "Manchurian Trade Cooperative." "Countering foreign competition and establishing Manchuria as an exclusive market for Japanese goods" formed the principal mission of this organization. A supplementary memorandum, in which the Finance Ministry requested the army's chief supply officer in occupied Yingk'ou to treat all incoming cargoes bearing the logo of the cooperative as "military goods," described one subterfuge for achieving this goal.[34]

Another idea envisioned the creation of a railway union with Korea, using the newly acquired protectorate as a secure "back door" into Manchurian commerce, much in the same way that the Russians planned to use their own territorial connections with Siberia and the Maritime Province, and the French, their railways from Indochina. In this context, the military lines connecting Korea, as proposed by the army, acquired a second important use. Commercial access to southern Manchuria would proceed principally through Japanese-controlled territory, and as a result, the overall direction of commercial development would likely orient itself toward Japan. Finance Minister Sakatani Yoshirō appeared particularly enthusiastic about the idea of a railway union. In a speech to the Diet in early 1906, he spoke of the potential benefits of such an arrangement as part of a larger postwar economic program for Japan.[35] Cross-border tariffs such as the Russians had obtained for the CER would further enhance the efficacy of railway connections, foreshadowing a full-blown customs union.

A third scheme, supplementing the plan for a railway union, entailed the establishment of the yen as a major, if not the dominant currency, in southern Manchuria. The redemption of military scrip, exchanged for silver yen certificates issued by the Yokohama Specie Bank, offered an immediate vehicle for this program. This policy had already helped promote the sale of Japanese cotton cloth. Concern that the lack of a unified currency in the territory made any commercial transactions difficult provided one justification for this plan. The coinage in use and its value varied from town to town. The larger aim, however, lay in strengthening Japanese economic dominance. Currency reform, combined with the plan for a railway and an incipient customs union, suggests that at least some Japanese policymakers seemed fully prepared to pursue the Russian idea of economic integration.[36]

A few of the more ambitious and visionary imperialists in leadership circles sought to push the process of integration beyond the economic level. The opportunities offered by the Russian inheritance encouraged them to think about Manchuria in terms approaching colonial possession. They believed that complete subjugation of the territory might lie well within the realm of possibility, given time, patience, and appropriate circumstances. In their view, the already strong version of an informal sphere they possessed provided the foundations for a further, incremental expansion of territorial control. In the years to come, they would demand additional railway rights, real estate, and mining concessions, build an ever-growing complex of economic and civic institutions, and, above all, settle large numbers of immigrants. Shortly before appointment to the governorship of the South Manchuria Railway Company in the summer of 1906, Gotō Shinpei articulated this idea, drawing upon developments in Korea as a model:

On the surface, our suzerain position in Korea today would appear to have been the product of victory in both war and diplomacy. In reality, however, this outcome was neither so sudden nor simply achieved. Our acquisition of suzerain status was based upon the past immigration of our people to Korea, giving us superior claim over other powers and creating a reality that could not be challenged with words or arguments. This experience should be applied toward the resolution of the Manchurian question.[37]

The questionable accuracy of Gotō's characterization of the process in Korea aside, these remarks nonetheless reveal much about his view of Manchuria. He envisioned Japan taking possession of the territory through the gradual creation of a new and indisputable reality on the ground, through a long-term process rather than a single event. That reality, once established, would render formal annexation a natural course of action.

Gotō's idea, to say the least, seems quite bold. It added yet another dimension to the concept of Japan's Trojan Horse in Manchuria. In later years Gotō would elaborate the notion of "military readiness in civilian dress" to give it a meaning close to Witte's idea of the "peaceful conquest of Manchuria." Many leaders with a more activist orientation toward empire-building took the scheme quite seriously, despite its audacity. As the prospective governor of the South Manchuria Railway Company, Gotō himself occupied a key position. Some writers credit him, as a trusted civilian aide and chief civil administrator of Taiwan, with exercising considerable influence over General Kodama, who in 1906 served concurrently as army chief of staff, governor-general of Taiwan, and head of the Commission on the Management of Manchuria. Kodama and other army leaders clearly favored this way of looking at Japan's future in the territory. Members of Ishizuka's survey group appear to have entertained similar ideas, referring, for example, to the promotion of settlement in the territory as a process of "transplanting Japanese power."[38]

Indeed, even those unwilling to go as far as Gotō and Kodama in looking toward annexation as an eventual goal nonetheless shared significant leanings in this direction. Policymakers advocating the long-term development of territorial resources, the permanent, large-scale settlement of Japanese immigrants, and the creation of a captive market in Manchuria might not have deliberately fashioned their schemes in order to produce an eventual, colonial outcome. Nevertheless, only the use of the extraordinary territorial power that the Russian apparatus had conferred on Japan rendered such goals attainable. Equally important, development, settlement, protection, and efforts at economic integration, even if pursued with limited aims in mind, objectively advanced the process that Gotō envisioned.[39] Progress in these areas, regardless of intention, would strengthen the Japanese presence in depth and breadth, quietly transforming the fundamental structure of territorial power.

The fact that responsible officials in 1906 thought in such terms stands in stark contrast to the attitudes among senior leaders who had advocated sharing the management of the railway with American interests in the autumn of 1905. A changing attitude toward empire precipitated by the war and the shifting balance of political power in government certainly may have contributed to the emergence of this bolder outlook. However, the adaptive process of policymaking, in which the capabilities of the instruments at hand, rather than autonomous choice, defined basic parameters in the formulation of Japanese goals, would seem to have played an even greater role. Boldness stemmed at least as much from the unusual quality of the opportunities confronted in Manchuria as from the intrinsic orientation of Japan's leaders. It is certainly difficult to say what the Japanese might have done if their inheritance from Russia had been more modest. There is no reason to believe that Japanese imperialists lacked the imagination and, given the emerging confidence of 1906, the audacity of their Russian counterparts. It is possible that, in time, they may well have arrived at similar designs on their own. Yet even given autonomous proclivities toward colonizing Manchuria, opportunity formed a major factor in encouraging the expression of these tendencies. In a sense, Japanese leaders in 1906 asked themselves not why they should follow in Russian footsteps but, rather, why not. This peculiar circumstance created serious difficulties for opponents of imperialist excess in the territory.

Opposition to colonization schemes at this time manifested itself in several quarters, including the navy, which we will consider as a special case. Among civilian leaders, Itō Hirobumi, predictably, emerged as the most outspoken critic of this trend. Itō held no cabinet post in 1906, and the power of the elder statesmen had, in general, declined, but he remained an influential figure in national affairs. Moreover, as Korea's first resident-general, a position he had assumed partly in an effort to restrain imperial policy on the peninsula, he had a particular basis for demanding a hearing of his views.[40] Itō feared that excesses in Manchuria would alienate Great Britain and the United States, generate hostility in China, and, relevant to his new bailiwick, cause complications in neighboring Korea. Japan had already received sharp warnings from British and American diplomats about maintaining freedom of commerce in the territory. Pointing to the army's obstruction of foreign business activity in occupied areas, its interference with Japanese diplomats and local Chinese officials, and its schemes for taxing local residents for infrastructural improvements, he prevailed upon Prime Minister Saionji Kinmochi to call an interministerial conference in May 1906 to discuss problems in Manchuria.[41]

At the beginning of the meeting, Itō read at length from a British protest to set the tone. He then proceeded to enumerate what he considered the army's transgressions. Chief of Staff Kodama, speaking for the army, justified some of the actions taken but did not appear inclined to put up an active resistance to Itō's demand that the army desist from activities injuring the interests of the powers or China's sovereign rights. It would seem that although army leaders might attempt to create advantageous faits accomplis during the window of opportunity offered by the Ssup'ingkai Protocol, they had not sufficiently invested themselves in such schemes to take on a major political fight with one of the nation's founders. Kodama's readiness to concede most of the specific issues that Itō raised seems to have frustrated the elder statesman. To judge from the transcript record, Itō had apparently intended to push the debate beyond these particular transgressions toward larger issues but failed to find a suitable opening. As if spoiling for a fight, he reiterated his concerns and criticisms even after army representatives agreed to put a stop to the objectionable activities cited, much to the consternation of the prime minister and other cabinet members present. "I would be prepared to agree with this [Itō's] overall argument in principle," noted Army Minister Terauchi Masatake (1852–1919), hoping to bring the discussion to a close. Itō replied, "To say that you have no differences in general is not good enough. I would like to see procedures and methods for implementation discussed." The senior statesman's frustration boiled over toward the end of the meeting, and he attempted to provoke a confrontation with Kodama. During the course of the conference, the chief of staff had used the expression, "managing Manchuria" (*Manshū keiei*) quite freely, and as the discussion wound down toward a close, he revealed what could be construed as the latent meaning behind the phrase by adding, inadvertently, a reference to Japan's "sovereign rights" (*shuken*) in the territory. Itō seized upon this slip of the tongue and eagerly took Kodama to task:

The way I see it, Chief of Staff Kodama and his colleagues are fundamentally mistaken about Japan's position in Manchuria. Japan's rights in the Manchurian region are those handed over by the Russians in the peace treaty. That is to say, this entails nothing more than the leased territory on the Liaotung peninsula and the railway. The term "managing Manchuria" became popular among our countrymen during the war. Today, officials and even businessmen speak readily of "managing Manchuria." But Manchuria is in no way part of Japan. It is no more and no less than one part of China's territory. We have no right to speak of exercising sovereignty (*shuken*) in a territory that doesn't belong to us. . . . The responsibility for administration in Manchuria belongs to none other than the Ch'ing government.

In order to forestall a confrontation, Prime Minister Saionji attempted to mollify Itō: "I don't believe that the term 'managing Manchuria' as used by Chief of Staff Kodama has such profound meanings. I used it myself in asking the chief of staff to undertake the responsibility of chairing the group on Manchurian affairs [the Commission on the Management of Manchuria]."[42]

Saionji certainly erred, or perhaps engaged in some disingenuousness, in reducing the difference between the two men to a matter of semantics. All things being equal, General Kodama would likely have preferred outright annexation of the territory. Given the same freedom of choice, Itō would have rather kept Japan out of Manchuria altogether. In a world of real political and diplomatic constraints, however, Kodama saw Japanese activity in Manchuria taking the form of railway imperialism. Likewise, Itō found himself unable to object openly to activity based on exercising legitimate rights inherited from Russia, a situation that likely accounted for his frustration at this conference. As he acknowledged at this meeting, "It is only natural that we should hold on to what Russia has handed over to us, and there should be no room for anyone to object."[43] Given the constraints on both parties, then, the gap over practical matters appeared substantially narrower than those over principle. Kodama called for maximizing the use of railway power. Itō sought to minimize it.

In this context, Saionji, whom some historians regard as a weak figure with a penchant to avoid confrontation at all costs, had good reason to seek to reconcile the two views.[44] Imperial activists like Kodama, Gotō, and Ishizuka approached Manchuria from a proprietary point of view and proposed policy goals that Itō and others favoring a more moderate course found disturbing. Yet in practice, particularly at this early stage, most of these ideas entailed nothing more than the exercise of former Russian rights, a framework Itō grudgingly accepted. Anything that went substantially beyond these boundaries, Kodama had been willing to concede. Indeed, setting aside rationales and looking only at the lines of action proposed, opponents found themselves hard-pressed to offer serious objections. Aggressive management of a railway enterprise to promote Japanese business interests and regional development in Manchuria, which would benefit local Chinese as well, hardly constituted activities that moderates could protest. No one could reasonably stand against planting trees, breeding horses, or setting up modern slaughterhouses and meat-packing enterprises. Nor did immigration as such to Manchuria offer grounds for objection, particularly in view of mounting hostility in the United States and other Western countries to the entry of Japanese immigrants in their own territories. In many respects, the audacity of Gotō's ideas rested in the purpose he ascribed to his proposed actions rather than in the actions themselves. In Saionji's view, the incipient confrontation at this meeting served no purpose. If General Kodama chose to describe operating a railway as "managing Manchuria," why should Itō object?

The possibility of casting even ideas like colonization in a benign light suggests that the subterfuge inherent in Kodama's notion of using the "mask" of railway management had internal as well as external applications. Itō's frustration and his reason for latching on to Kodama's slip about "sovereign rights" seem understandable in this context. Aware of Kodama's line of thinking, the elder statesman refused to accept at face value the general's agreeableness and his protestations of innocence. At a more basic level, however, the problem for Itō and the moderates lay in the fact that once they accepted the premise that Japan should retain and exercise its inherited rights, it became difficult to contain the corollary policies that the inheritance made possible. Had Kodama or Gotō sought to build from scratch instruments of railway imperialism comparable to what the Russians had handed over to Japan, the burden of demonstrating the need for such extraordinary measures would have fallen squarely on their shoulders. Under such circumstances, Itō's objections would no doubt have carried a great deal more weight. In the event, however, the moderates found themselves forced to demonstrate why Japan should not exercise the full capabilities of the tools it had acquired. George Lensen has described the transfer of the remaining trunk of the Chinese Eastern Railway in north Manchuria in the early 1920s to Bolshevik control as a "damned inheritance."[45] The phrase also aptly describes the dilemma facing Japanese policymakers of Itō's persuasion in 1906.

Bureaucratic Turf Wars and the Origins of the SMR

Policymakers and their advisors devoted considerable attention to the formulation of programmatic goals for Manchuria in 1906. The discussion generated a wide range of ideas, some modest, others quite ambitious. The diversity of proposals, indeed, formed another corollary of the adaptive nature of the policymaking process. In a sense, "What do we do with a railway in Manchuria?" formed the principal question confronting the nation's leaders in their efforts to clarify aims and purposes. The inherent versatility of railway technology, coupled with Manchuria's vast horizons of possibility, guaranteed multiple and divergent answers. Deliberations in 1906 failed to produce an overall consensus on this question. At the same time, however, the formulation of a set, programmatic agenda did not present itself as a pressing problem at this juncture. Action in Manchuria could proceed without agreement on goals. The lack of consensus or clarity as to overall purposes posed no obstacles to the operation of railways, mines, harbors, and the management of real estate concessions, at least on a provisional basis. Defining an agenda remained an issue of fundamental importance to the future of the venture, but in 1906 it did not constitute an immediately pressing task.

The problem of organizing the undertaking administratively, of demarcating lines of authority and jurisdiction, and of parceling out leadership prerogatives among contending groups in government, however, did not offer the same kind of leeway. The army's activity, which had precipitated the May conference, underscored the urgency of resolving these matters. The fact that occupation authorities had acted on their own and overstepped the boundaries of their authority, in fact, constituted the central issue for most of the high officials in attendance at the meeting, rather than broader questions of direction that Itō had hoped to raise. General Katsura pointed out at the meeting that the source of the problem lay in the lack of clear leadership.[46] All agreed on the need to establish unambiguous chains of command in Manchurian affairs as quickly as possible.

Part of the solution, worked out after considerable wrangling, called for the creation of three distinct sets of institutions as the front-line agencies for managing Japanese holdings in Manchuria. The most straightforward arrangement, involving little dispute since it followed diplomatic norms, entailed the establishment of a consular apparatus to manage the numerous treaty port concessions in the territory. The organization of a nominally commercial joint-stock corporation to manage the railway, the coal mines, and the Railway Zone, treated officially as a form of corporate real estate over which Japan exercised extraterritorial rights, represented a more complex solution but one also enjoying a broad consensus. The Commission on the Management of Manchuria had largely settled this issue in March, and an organizing committee formed by the government had produced articles of incorporation by June. Although commission chairman Kodama had preferred placing the railway under a special government bureau, he seems to have conceded the point without much protest, acknowledging privately the value of commercial camouflage in allaying the suspicions of the Great Powers. Majority stock ownership would ensure government control. Commercial organization would also offer added advantages in raising capital, not only in attracting share capital in Japan but also in borrowing funds abroad.[47]

The establishment of a Japanese military agency in Manchuria, which became linked to the question of the administration of the Leased Territory, proved far more controversial. The army insisted on stationing a division-strength garrison in Kwantung along with six guard battalions in the Railway Zone, which was permitted, in principle, under the Treaties of Portsmouth and Peking. Although military planners had eschewed the need for such a force in their arguments in 1905, they had since reconsidered. Such rethinking reflected the army's general tendency, evident in its demand for standard-gauge reconstruction of the railway, of backsliding on its fiscal conservatism and its moderate assessment of military needs of the previous year. To what degree this change of heart represented a serious reappraisal of Japan's strategic position in 1906 is difficult to say. The Russians appeared rather slow to evacuate their forces, and this presented cause for some anxiety. As it turned out, the delay resulted primarily from weather conditions and logistical problems in Manchuria as well as political difficulties at home. It is also not unreasonable to suspect that the army may have deliberately downplayed what it considered its actual requirements in 1905 in order to avoid frightening civilian leaders into the arms of Harriman.[48] With the commitment on solid ground by the beginning of 1906, the need for such self-restraint had substantially diminished. As we shall see, escalating rivalry with the navy may also have contributed significantly to this shift in attitude.

The establishment of a garrison in itself did not become a major issue of contention. The problem, rather, lay in the army's demand for the integration of the military command with the administration of the Leased Territory, creating a structure described as a *totokufu* (usually translated "government-general"). The governor of Kwantung would simultaneously serve as garrison commander. The army based its claim on the importance of the Leased Territory as a base area in a future war against Russia and the role envisioned for the government-general in mobilizing Japan's Manchurian assets in the event of a military emergency. The army bolstered its reasoned arguments, moreover, with a fait accompli. Taking advantage of the extended evacuation schedule, it had already established a working agency of the type it demanded, organized, in effect, as a partially demobilized version of the wartime occupation apparatus. Civilian leaders, particularly the professional diplomats, strongly objected to this scheme. Given the combined weight of the military argument and realities on the ground, however, they conceded the issue, with the proviso that a distinct, civil administrative apparatus be established under the government-general and that, apart from purely military affairs, the governor-general answer to civilian authority in Tokyo.[49]

The most difficult problem in devising an organizational structure for Japanese Manchuria, and in fact one not fully resolved at this time, lay in the area of broad policy oversight. Both the Foreign Ministry and the army made strong claims to jurisdiction. Diplomats argued that, regardless of some of the unusual features of Japanese holdings, Manchuria remained foreign territory and thus fell under their purview in peacetime. The soldiers disagreed. Although diplomats might do the talking in any formal representation of Japan's position to the outside world, the strategic importance of the territory and the continued military sensitivity of Japanese activity in Manchuria demanded overall army leadership. As a possible compromise, General Kodama had proposed, during the May conference, the establishment of a special agency for Manchurian affairs in Tokyo, operating outside existing ministerial chains of command. Itō, who favored the Foreign Ministry's claims, vigorously opposed the scheme, regarding Kodama's agency as akin to a "colonial ministry" and representing yet another attempt by the general and his colleagues to treat Manchuria as a Japanese possession.[50]

The government failed to work out a comprehensive settlement of the problem of policy oversight and coordination in 1906. By default, both the army and Foreign Ministry managed their respective front-line agencies more or less autonomously. Apart from some minor, cross-jurisdictional arrangements that, for example, placed professional diplomats responsible for external affairs within the Kwantung Government-General, the only source of overall direction came from the cabinet itself, which could do little more than provide very general guidance and exercise an occasional ad hoc intervention. One important exception to this arrangement, however, emerged in provisions for the supervision of the SMR. Given the importance of the railway to the venture as a whole, whatever agency in Tokyo acquired responsibility for directing company operations would dominate Manchuria policy. In this respect, the SMR lay at the heart of the dispute with regard to general leadership and oversight. Negotiations among all interested parties during the spring of 1906 produced a relatively simple, if inelegant, solution. All major agencies with jurisdiction over Manchurian affairs would enjoy a significant voice in supervising the company, but no single ministry would acquire paramount control.

Under these provisions, the cabinet exercised final authority over the company's operations. The prime minister appointed the top officers, titled the governor and the vice governor. The board of directors, though elected by shareholders, required cabinet confirmation. The articles of incorporation mandated a 50 percent share of all stock to the Japanese government, with an additional 1 percent reserved for the Imperial Household, guaranteeing the state a majority interest. The remaining 49 percent would be offered for public subscription. The company's top officers voted both the government and imperial shares. The army exercised authority over matters of direct military relevance, such as technical specifications for railway construction and rolling stock. The Kwantung governor-general would assume control over the company in the event of wartime mobilization. The Foreign Ministry supervised the company's external relations, including business negotiations with Chinese and foreign entities. The civil administrator assigned to the Kwantung Government-General provided proximal oversight with regard to internal business decisions and technical matters outside the army's concerns, but ultimate authority fell to the Communications Ministry. The Finance Ministry audited the company's books and supervised long-term capital expansion plans.[51]

Under these arrangements, the SMR would appear to have acquired the status of a cabinet agency. However, those who crafted this compromise had not intended to confer on this institution the autonomy, transcendent authority, and high prestige that would come to be associated with such status in later years. On the contrary, the contending ministries sought to maximize their own authority and had no intention of creating a center of autonomous power in Manchuria, particularly one in control of the all-important railway. They envisioned the company not as a policymaking organ but as the institutional custodian of Japan's principal assets in the territory. They expected managers to focus their attention on technical and business matters, as they would in an ordinary commercial venture. The appropriate authorities in the army, the Foreign Ministry, and the cabinet as a whole would retain control over issues of high policy.

Gotō Shinpei, recommended by Kodama shortly before the chief of staff's death in June 1906 for the post of the SMR's first governor, found this general perspective on the role of the institution unsatisfactory. He regarded divided supervision and the narrow scope of authority granted company officials as particularly problematic and made his own bid to define its place in the policymaking structure before agreeing to accept the appointment.[52] In many ways, Gotō filled the requirements of this post rather well. As one of Kodama's most trusted civilian aides, he appears to have been advising his patron on Manchuria policy issues since the autumn of 1905. Given his relationship with the army chief of staff and his appreciation of the military requirements for the management of Manchuria, he offered excellent qualifications from the army's point of view. From the Foreign Ministry's viewpoint, it certainly would have been worse to have a retired army officer as a candidate. Moreover, Gotō presented sound credentials as an effective administrator, and his experience in Taiwan had relevance for the task ahead in Manchuria. Having given a great deal of thought to problems of territorial policy, however, Gotō held well-developed views of his own regarding the proper role of the company that conflicted with those of the government. He envisioned the SMR as an entity comparable to the colonial corporations of Africa and Southeast Asia, an heir to the tradition of the East India Company, and he believed that it should have comparable prestige and authority. These institutions, he argued, functioned not as simple business enterprises but as agencies that "represented the state and accordingly exercised a measure of the sovereign power of the state." Their chief executives enjoyed the status not of business managers but of high-ranking policymaking officials, exercising final authority within the realm of company rule. He went so far as to suggest that "the South Manchuria Railway Company serves as a substitute for the government in the management of Manchuria."[53]

Gotō lobbied actively for his position, but ultimately without success. Nonetheless, he accepted the post and proved one of the more vigorous chief executives in the company's history. His vision of a powerful and autonomous SMR did eventually come to pass. Ironically, however, the source of the company's autonomy and power rested in those very aspects of the institutional arrangements he found most problematic. Divided jurisdiction and status as a cabinet agency provided the company with a measure of political neutrality and thus a tenuous institutional independence. Operating outside the direct chain of command of a powerful ministry gave the SMR a certain freedom of action it might not have enjoyed otherwise. The mundane business functions of the company played an even more important role in expanding its influence over policy. From the outset of the venture, all policymakers assumed that the railway would pay its own way and manage its own debts, a promise implicit in the 1905 survey report. Fiscally conservative members of the Diet, and in particular, the Kenseihontō, the main opposition party in the Twenty-Second Diet (December 28, 1905–March 28, 1906), had already raised objections to the high cost of railway building in Korea and had insisted on sound business management. They were clearly unprepared to subsidize Japanese railway operations in Manchuria. This assumption extended to all operations under the company's auspices. As Kaneko Fumio points out, the SMR's successful operation as a policy instrument rested on the premise of profitability.[54] Gotō, with his contempt for the businessman's role, had at first attempted to reject this premise, submitting to the cabinet at the beginning of his tenure a tentative ten-year budget that projected a deficit for the first few years. The Finance Ministry quickly disabused him of the notion that such a budget would pass muster.[55] In his quest for greater authority for the SMR, Gotō emphasized political status and an enlarged official mandate, and in this effort he appears to have been barking up the wrong tree and overlooked the power of the purse. Profitability as a basic precondition for the pursuit of policy would give company managers considerable leverage over the policy agenda itself. *Raison d'affaires*, rather than *raison d'état*, would form the basis for the SMR's influence in the councils of empire.

The emergence of a quasi-autonomous SMR, of course, only compounded the problem of fragmented jurisdiction and authority in Manchuria. The basic organizational solutions worked out in 1906 would endure well into the 1930s, but they satisfied no one entirely. Rather, they were accepted by all parties to the political bargaining that produced them as the least among possible evils. All agreed on the importance of unified leadership and policy coordination and regarded the lack of such unity as the bane of Japanese Manchuria. Yet all also seemed to agree that, as irrational as divided authority might be, the unification of policy under a rival agency represented an even less desirable outcome. Solomon's wisdom appears to have had little influence in the problems of Manchurian administration.

The Army, the Navy, and Manchuria

In the jurisdictional rivalries of 1906, soldiers and diplomats had little choice but to compromise. Nonetheless, the army had unmistakably emerged as the paramount player in Manchurian affairs. Indeed, whereas Komura had assumed the leading role in advocating the initial commitment during the war, the army's voice had dominated since the conclusion of the peace. Its strategic assessment of 1905 and sponsorship of the economic survey reflected a central position in decision making, further underscored by Kodama's chairing of the Commission on the Management of Manchuria and the appointment of Army Minister Terauchi Masatake to head the SMR's Organizing Committee in June 1906. Although a candidate acceptable to all parties, Gotō closely associated himself with his patron, General Kodama.

A number of reasons account for the army's extraordinary interest and activism in Manchurian affairs. Defense clearly played a central role in the undertaking as a whole, both as a policy aim and a precondition for all other endeavors in the territory. Moreover, the army, certainly no less than any other group in Japan at this time, embraced imperialism in its general outlook. Indeed, it would hardly come as a surprise to find that the men who had fought on the front lines harbored a strong, proprietary orientation toward a territory for which they had struggled meter by meter. Yet another consideration lies in the army's institutional stake in Manchuria. The decision to embark on this venture in 1905 constituted a commitment to build and maintain ground forces of unprecedented size. In Manchuria, the army had found a special calling, a mission that would demonstrate its value to the nation, justify its enormous demands on the country's limited resources, and guarantee its future in the Japanese political world.

In many ways, Japan's creation of a world-class army represents a somewhat peculiar development. As an island country whose first line of defense is the high seas, its economic well-being and security dependent on freedom of navigation, strategic logic would seem to dictate a primarily naval orientation. An ability to wage war on land, of course, would play a vital role in the event that the navy failed to halt an invasion before it reached Japanese shores and in the case of major internal disorder. The nation also needed the functional equivalent of marines to protect Japanese nationals and their property abroad, particularly in China. These considerations might well have led to the creation of ground forces of respectable size. Nonetheless, given the simple realities of strategic and economic geography, it would appear that Japan's future lay in the cultivation of sea power.[56]

Several factors contributed to deflecting Japan from this course. One lay in the early history of the modern nation-state. The army originated in the revolutionary force that overthrew the old regime in 1868, and it continued to serve as a vital prop of the fragile Meiji government in its early years.

These circumstances produced a tradition of army primacy that rational arguments alone could not easily overcome. The high cost of navy development in terms of hard currency expenditures for imported warships was another consideration. Navy expansion proceeded slowly, and Japan's security until the 1890s continued to depend on the army standing watch along its shores, a circumstance that further entrenched an army-first tradition. At the same time, the nation's military specialists understood that warships maintaining vigilance offshore would, in time, supersede the role of ground forces as the nation's first line of defense. All other things being equal, the rise of the Japanese navy implied the decline of the army.[57]

The emergence of security concerns on the continent rescued the army from this fate and accounted for its expansion well beyond a size that coastal defense or domestic peacekeeping might warrant. Yamagata's "line of interest" doctrine granted infantry divisions an offshore-defense role as important, in theory, as that assigned to cruisers and battleships. Indeed, given the assessment that the principal danger to Japan came from the continent by way of Korea, rather than a seaborne attack on the home islands proper, the army could make a case for a paramount place in defense policy. In 1882, it made its first steps toward expanding force size and revising its organization for the purpose of continental expeditions. Between 1886 and 1894, the express aim of developing a capability to fight China over Korea provided the impetus for major military reforms. These developments mark the beginning of the commitment to continental activism that would become characteristic of this service.[58]

The idea of a continental mission began to gel with the emergence of rivalry between the army and the navy during the interwar years. The Sino-Japanese War had proved that the navy was a respectable regional force and, for the first time, placed the nation's erstwhile second-string service in a position to challenge the primacy of its well-entrenched rival. By the turn of the twentieth century, the debate over precedence between the two services intensified. The navy argued that Britain, with the high seas forming its first line of defense, provided the best model for Japan. The key to the nation's security and its future success lay in sea power. The navy should, accordingly, receive priority in appropriations as well as a paramount place in strategic planning and leadership. Commander Satō Tetsutarō (1866–1942), a leading naval theorist influenced strongly by the work of Alfred Mahan and the author of one of the Imperial Japanese Navy's earlier expositions of strategic doctrine, propounded this perspective in 1902.[59] In an oblique challenge to the concept of a continental "line of interest," Satō pointed out that "in order to deploy our army abroad, we must first build a navy capable of securing the high seas." His superior, Navy Minister Yamamoto Gonbei, as we have noted, argued more forthrightly that Japan could forgo control of Korea from the vantage point of national security.[60]

Soldiers, not surprisingly, honed their own arguments for the primacy of their service. Going beyond the limited, defensive orientation of Yamagata's "line of interest," some officers began thinking about a more militant and positive continental expansionism in which the army would serve as an instrument of empire as well as national defense. This view ran strong among the emerging generation of professional officers, an example of which appears in the diary of then Captain Ugaki Kazunari (1868–1956), writing in 1903:

Newspapers as well as some military people have been debating the question of interservice precedence. The notion that because Japan is surrounded by seas in four directions, the navy constitutes the principal force is unworthy of consideration. This question must be settled by determining whether, in the future, we will seek the development and expansion of the Japanese nation on the high seas or on the continent. We must decide on the basis of where our interests are most likely to collide with those of another [power]. . . . If we are resolved that the Japanese nation will remain forever secluded on today's isolated islands, then we have no need for a vast army, making the navy the principal force. If, on the contrary, we wish to acquire a foothold on the continent, we must build, along with a navy needed to open the first barrier gates, an army that can rival those of the world's great powers. The army, in other words, would be principal, with the navy serving as an auxiliary force to support the army's operations.[61]

Although the rivalry between the two services escalated after 1895, other factors at work during the interwar period tended to mitigate tensions. Those members of the original Meiji oligarchy holding army or navy rank and directly engaged in military affairs retained a broader and more transcendent view of national defense than did their professional and, in many cases, more narrow-minded and doctrinaire juniors, and they played an important mediating role. Yamagata held the rank of marshal within the army and acted as its supreme leader, yet he generally favored a balanced development of the armed forces until later in his career. Saigō Tsugumichi (1843–1902), who held the equivalent rank in the navy, had started out as an army leader, occupying a position in the early years of the Meiji state corresponding to army minister. Such leadership restrained sectional tendencies to a significant extent. Perhaps an even more important mitigating circumstance, however, lay in the fact that during the interwar period, both services geared their defense preparations against the same prospective adversary, Russia. Each received extremely generous appropriations for this purpose, minimizing any reason to squabble over funds. Indeed, although doctrinal and sectional differences sharpened during the interwar period, the generational divide among military officers of both services, rather than the rift between army and navy, probably exerted a greater force in shaping military politics. In meetings of the war party held in 1902, men like Tanaka Giichi of the Army General Staff and Akiyama Saneyuki, his counterpart in the navy, who would become rivals in bitter doctrinal disputes of later years, sat together in the Kogetsu restaurant, comrades in arms.[62]

Victory in the Russo-Japanese War and developments in its immediate aftermath, however, aggravated tensions between army and navy. The changing of the guard and the associated rise of bureaucratic sectionalism contributed significantly. The common strategic mission shared by both services and the generous funding of the interwar era also came to an end. The authors of the Manchurian Army's 1905 paper warned:

Our army and navy each have their own postwar [arms expansion] plans. However, if each service concerns itself only with expanding its own realm, the development of our national economy will suffer. In the final analysis, armaments meant to topple our enemies will ironically threaten our own downfall. For this reason, the army and navy must engage in thorough discussions, taking into account our national objectives and the relative priority of the tasks facing us. Self-serving sectional (*gaden insuiteki*) behavior cannot be tolerated.[63]

Most important, however, Japan's commitments in Korea and Manchuria had introduced a fundamentally new factor in defense planning.

Permanent, continental commitments became pivotal issues in interservice relations because they unmistakably tipped the balance in favor of the army. Manchuria held special significance because Japanese claims in this territory made a land war against Russia the most likely conflict for which the nation had to prepare, and this strategic scenario gave the army primacy. Indeed, with the decision to establish a foothold in Manchuria, it would seem that Japan had embarked on the course that Ugaki had envisioned, and given the logic of the debate as framed in the interwar period, the commitment represented a triumph of the army over the navy. The army certainly lost no time in drawing such conclusions. With major acquisitions in Northeast Asia, Japan had become a continental power, and defense policy would need to reflect this reality. The authors of the Manchurian Army paper of late 1905 articulated the basic thrust of this argument. Starting from the premise of financial stringency, they stressed the possibility of defending the territory against Russia while holding down military expenditures to modest increases. Their call for a moratorium on naval spending, however, made it clear who would exercise self-restraint and who would enjoy the modest increases. The authors made no apologies: "There should be no dissension over the fact that priority in arms expansion must be placed on our ground forces." These remarks should put any appraisal of the army's fiscal conservatism and its calls to transcend narrow sectionalism in proper perspective.[64]

This line of argument, of course, did little to persuade the navy. Clearly, if Japan could get by without Korea, it could certainly manage without Manchuria and thus avoid any need for a major expansion of the army. The potential for a major political dispute appeared in the making, one that might well have seriously disrupted planning efforts for Manchuria in 1906. However, the navy found itself in a poor position to challenge the army's claims at this time, and its leaders seemed well aware of the fact. Although the army took maximum advantage of the opportunity to advance its institutional interests, Japan's commitment in Manchuria certainly did not constitute a Machiavellian scheme concocted for this purpose. The idea of securing a permanent foothold in the territory enjoyed broad national support. Like Itō Hirobumi, the navy had little choice but to reconcile itself to the unavoidable. Moreover, although the army's arguments about the strategic situation might appear self-serving, they did not lack merit. Russia retained a formidable capability to wage war on land, but Admiral Tōgō's fleet had destroyed its sea power at Tsushima. In 1906, Japan faced no foreseeable naval threat that a renewed alliance with Britain could not meet. Thus, when approached by the army for discussions about postwar defense plans in 1906, navy leaders were amenable to compromise.[65]

Negotiations during 1906 produced an interservice agreement promulgated in February 1907 as the Imperial Defense Plan. Although the army approached the bargaining from a position of strength, it had no desire for a confrontation or political deadlock, and rhetoric about the auxiliary role of sea power aside, it recognized the need for some degree of navy support for operations in Manchuria or Korea. Army leaders appeared unprepared to push institutional self-interest beyond certain limits. The agreement, accordingly, contained significant mutual concessions. Eschewing doctrinaire formulations about the primacy of one service over the other, it advanced the principle of parity between army and navy. It also called for the maximum independence of each service in operational planning, allaying any concern that the army thought of the navy as an escort force. The agreement endorsed in principle the navy's goal of building a core force of eight battleships and eight armored cruisers. In the same spirit, it revived and endorsed Yamagata's call for 25 infantry divisions. Achieving these force levels was contingent on the nation's financial condition, and both sides accepted fiscal restraint as unavoidable for the foreseeable future. The army's immediate target remained nineteen divisions. Compromises notwithstanding, however, the central thrust of the defense plan nevertheless reflected the army's dominant position and underscored the new strategic situation created by Japan's continental commitments. The preamble noted: "Having crossed the seas and established claims in Manchuria and Korea, we can no longer consider national defense to be a matter of planning military action within the realm of our island-nation. Unless we are prepared to take the offensive against our enemies overseas, our national security cannot be guaranteed."[66] The document set forth the premise that Russia posed the principal danger to Japan and the most likely scenario for conflict was a land war in Manchuria. Implicitly, these premises elevated the army to a position of first among equals. More important, as a political agreement, representing something on the order of a "treaty" between the two services, the Imperial Defense Plan gave formal sanction to the army's new mission and its concomitant entitlements.[67]

It is important to bear in mind that the navy's acquiescence to a de facto army-first policy rested on political circumstances in 1906. The navy's dissatisfaction with this agreement ran deep, and given an opportunity, it would likely seek redress. Indeed, in a chiding critique of army policy written in 1907, Satō Tetsutarō, promoted to captain, outlined the direction that a challenge might take. Satō professed to have no quarrel with the idea of continental commitments as such. "There is no doubt that from the vantage point of the development of our nation, Manchuria and Korea are vital," he wrote. However, he questioned the army 's notion of the danger posed by Russia, even in its reassuring appraisal of late 1905. "Unless Russia can at minimum suppress internal disorder, restore national unity, and bring prosperity back to the country, it cannot hope to retain its place among the powers, let alone seek to advance its fortunes," he argued. The motives behind rumored Russian plans for an Amur River extension of the Trans-Siberian Railway lay not in planning a war of revenge but in making up for the fact that they no longer controlled the port of Dairen and had no choice but to channel all their trade through Vladivostok.[68]

If, on the other hand, one accepted the army's assessment of the Russian danger, then "even 50 or 60 divisions would not suffice" to repel an attack. Satō questioned the wisdom of staking claims in Manchuria in the face of such an ominous threat.

From a strategic point of view, we must acknowledge that it would be to our advantage to disengage from (*suteru*) these territories. Personally, I am not in favor of such a radical measure. Unless the circumstances become truly untenable, we should by all means hold onto territories that have already been incorporated into our sphere of influence. On the other hand, the argument that we must stay in Manchuria and Korea regardless of the strategic risks, indeed, that we must even sacrifice the strength of our navy to do so, is not even worthy of consideration.

Given any serious risk, a very circumspect continental policy offered the wisest course. "Our activities in Manchuria should, insofar as possible, be peaceful and internationalist (*sekaiteki*). Rather than seeking to maximize our own gains through various means, we should work to ensure that no crises emerge."[69]

Satō's line of argument demonstrated considerable rhetorical cleverness and boxed the army into a situation that allowed no easy escape. Since Russia, in his view, posed no immediate threat, this eliminated the need for a new military policy that put the army first and imposed constraints on naval expansion. However, if Russia in fact presented a grave danger, as the army contended, Japan should downgrade its commitment and follow a policy akin to neutralization, or at least the kind of involvement Itō would have endorsed. Such circumstances would likewise obviate the need for an army-first defense policy.

This argument, however, represented more than rhetorical skill insofar as it recapitulated, albeit in an exaggerated form, the core elements of the logic underlying the commitment made in 1905. The reports prepared by the staff of the expeditionary army and the survey team had sought to dispel the pessimism in Tokyo generated by assessments of high strategic risk coupled with poor prospects of economic return entailed in a Manchurian venture. The military study reduced the projected risk, and the survey report elevated the appraisal of economic value. The government had committed itself, in other words, on the basis of an acceptable balance between the danger of Russia and the value of Manchuria. The army's ability to make claims based on the new circumstances on the continent, accordingly, rested on the same equilibrium. Any assessment of the Russian threat, along with corollary demands for expanding ground forces, that exceeded the prevailing consensus as to the value of Manchuria might yet jeopardize the venture as a whole, as Yamagata's call for 25 divisions had nearly done earlier.

Satō's critique thus offered a potentially effective line of attack on the army's position. To be sure, conditions in 1906 were such that it remained premature for its application. The balance between the danger of Russia and the value of Manchuria as perceived by a majority of the nation's leaders in 1906 favored the army. Despite rising confidence, few shared Satō's sanguine view of the intentions and capabilities of Japan's recent adversary, and anxieties about a war of revenge ran strong. At the same time, Itō and his sympathizers aside, most leaders held optimistic views of prospects in Manchuria. Having overcome their initial reservations and taken stock of their inheritance, they had every reason to look toward a bright and productive future. However, such attitudes might change, depending on both Russian behavior and progress in Manchuria. Shifts in either or both of these parameters might affect the rather delicate equilibrium on which the army's claims rested and open the door to a navy challenge. In this context, Satō's polemic pointed to the inherent instability of the Imperial Defense Plan as an interservice compact. It also underscored the susceptibility of Manchuria policy to deep entanglement in the politics of interservice competition. Postwar memory would vest in Manchuria much of the meaning of the Russo-Japanese War and its terrible sacrifices. The linking of Japan's commitment in the territory to the conflicting interests of two of the most powerful institutions in the Japanese political world would endow Manchuria with another kind of meaning as well.

Although the particularities of interservice politics may account for the instability of the agreements underlying the Imperial Defense Plan, the bargain also reflects the provisional, expedient, if not jerry-built, quality of many of the arrangements worked out in 1906. The administrative structures created for Manchuria satisfied no one, leaving the door open for incessant wrangling. All agreed on the urgent need for unified leadership in territorial policy, yet the actual compromises only served to institutionalize the entrenched and divided political power of the army and Foreign Ministry in Manchuria, giving each a stronghold. The establishment of the SMR on neutral political ground might seem a wise decision in the context of this rivalry, but the fragmented jurisdiction over the company clearly constituted a formula for trouble. The cumbersome and convoluted system of supervision and policy direction attempted to give every claimant to jurisdiction at least token authority, a solution driven by the logic of bureaucratic politics rather than administrative rationality. It required no great foresight to predict serious conflict in the near future. With the exception of defense policy, programmatic development had produced, at best, a roughhewn agenda. Had clarity of purpose and consensus on aims and strategies constituted preconditions for action, the Manchurian venture would, no doubt, have stalled.

Nonetheless, the fact that Japanese policymakers achieved as much as they did in a relatively short time remains quite remarkable. Although the emphases in this narrative might leave the reader with the impression that Manchuria lay at the center of the Japanese world, the formulation of policy in this area represented only one of a large number of pressing issues on the table in 1906. In foreign affairs, emerging tension with the United States over immigration provided serious cause for concern.[70] Major adjustments in economic and fiscal policy in the aftermath of the war also demanded attention, a task complicated by the growing restiveness and ambition of political parties in the Diet, another trend emerging in the postwar period. While grappling with the problem of the railway in Manchuria, the government simultaneously engaged itself in the process of nationalizing the domestic railway system and coping with the inevitable political battles such a step generated. In fact, Saionji lost his first foreign minister, Katō Takaaki (1860–1926), in part over disputes with the army over Manchuria but also over disagreements about nationalization.[71] Even in the arena of empire-building, issues other than Manchuria demanded attention. Managing the protectorate in Korea occupied much of the energy of imperial statesmen.[72] The nation's leaders had accomplished a great deal in hammering out a working structure and outlining even a rough agenda in less than a year under these conditions. Indeed, it would be fair to say that they had conducted much of this work under the political "field conditions" of postwar dislocation and that, for all the flaws in the designs of 1906, Japan's venture in Manchuria hit the ground running. Symbolizing an efficiency belied by some of the messier aspects of developments in 1906 was the fact that ever since the middle of the war, when the army had retracked captured portions of the CER to accommodate Japanese rolling stock, the trains in southern Manchuria, managed by the army's Field Railway Corps, had not stopped running.

THREE

Managing Manchuria, 1907–1911

The official transfer of the former southern branch of the CER from the army's Field Railway Corps to the SMR on April 1, 1907, marked the end of the extended period of military occupation and the beginning of Japan's management of Manchuria under peacetime conditions. The four years that followed constituted the "shakedown" phase of the venture. During this period, three new tasks came to the fore. First and foremost was strengthening Japan's military position in anticipation of a war of revenge, which required the building of two additional divisions and fine-tuning tactics and strategy, and, most important, the development of the military infrastructure in Manchuria outlined in the plans of 1906. Second was the need to consolidate Japanese claims in the diplomatic arena; this required not only the enforcement of rights stipulated in the Treaties of Portsmouth and Peking but also international recognition of Japan's sphere of interest through bilateral agreements and cumulative diplomatic precedents. Third in order of urgency but a matter of fundamental importance in the long run was securing the financial wherewithal to underwrite the costs of the venture, principally from revenues generated within Manchuria. This endeavor demanded the aggressive management of the SMR as a profit-making business enterprise.

These tasks, in themselves, presented challenge enough. At the same time, however, there were portents of change emerging in the international environment during these four years that the more astute among the nation's political elites might regard as reasons to question the future of the venture. The receding danger of a second war against Russia cast doubt on the need for the army's extensive preparations in Manchuria. Moreover, the inauguration of a dreadnought race among the Great Powers required a broader rethinking of defense priorities. Diplomats encountered greater difficulty than anticipated in pursuing their task. Sino-American cooperation against

Japanese claims in Manchuria was particularly troubling and hinted at an incipient shift in the framework of imperialist diplomacy. The more dedicated and optimistic advocates of an activist policy in the territory saw no need for the nation to change its course. Their opponents, however, would find in some of the developments of this period a basis to strengthen their case for policy reform.

Defense and the Receding Danger of War

Defense preparations during this period proceeded, on the whole, quite smoothly. Insofar as Japan's growing strength and readiness for another war in Manchuria had any direct influence on Russia's policies, the army's planners appear to have outdone themselves. After 1907, Russian leaders seemed anxious to avoid confrontation with Japan and gave little indication of planning for a war of revenge. Indeed, during these years, relations between the two former adversaries improved steadily. By 1911, the army found itself struggling to persuade civilian leaders of the need for continued vigilance, arguing that growing peace and friendship were the product of Japan's military strength.[1]

The army continued to refine its Manchurian operations plans throughout this period. Annually updated versions of these documents available for 1907 through 1910 reveal some significant changes from year to year, but for the most part they outlined the same basic scenario and anticipated a quick, decisive victory. The capture of Harbin formed the principal military objective. So long as the Russians remained dependent on the CER to connect the Trans-Siberian Railway with the Maritime Province, the occupation of this city would divide the Russian Far East, isolating Vladivostok. The army did not anticipate difficulty in holding Harbin against any Russian counterattack coming from western Siberia. Inhospitable conditions in northwest Manchuria, where Russian forces would have to base themselves for such a campaign, would enforce the enemy's dependence on railway transportation for supply. While digging in at Harbin, Japanese forces would launch a secondary attack from northeastern Korea against the Maritime Province. Army planners believed that once Harbin fell, the Russians would have to negotiate, since they could no longer effectively defend their position in the Far East.[2]

Affirming the Manchurian Army's version of the lessons of the Russo-Japanese War, strategic planners saw that the key to military success in a second Manchurian conflict lay in launching a rapid "first strike." With the advantage of short and high-capacity supply lines, the Japanese army could maintain a numerically superior force in Manchuria during the early stages of a conflict. Planners assigned the Kwantung garrison the task of securing the SMR at the outset of hostilities and establishing a forward position north of Mukden to shield the deployment of the main force. Some units, transported by sea, would land in Kwantung; others would move through Korea by rail. The Kwantung Government-General would shed its peacetime "mask" and form the occupation government of the rear areas, which strategists initially defined as the entire region south of Mukden. The army would concentrate its troops behind the line secured by the garrison and then advance north along the SMR and the southern branch of the CER toward Harbin.[3]

These operations plans placed stringent demands on railway construction, and it proved difficult for the SMR to meet the army's specifications during the first few years. Military planners aimed for a deployment rate of one division a day. Stockpiling the bulk of nonperishable supplies in storage facilities in southern Manchuria and drawing on local food sources would ease the pressure on transportation capacity. Nonetheless, the daily movement of 12,000 troops, along with their equipment and essential supplies, from Kwantung and Korea into the Manchurian heartland could not be accomplished without rebuilding the trunk line from Dairen to Ch'angch'un, and eventually, from Antung to Mukden, to accommodate from 40 to 48 trains per day, each carrying 400–ton loads. Construction of such a railway presented both a financial and an engineering challenge. In addition to conversion to standard gauge, military transport requirements included the use of rails weighing 100 pounds per yard rather than the more common 80-pound type, double-tracking to reduce turn-around time, and to allow for high-speed trains, gentle gradients, and wide turning radii. By 1912, these specifications, although only partially fulfilled, had already saddled the SMR with the highest daily operating costs per mile of any railway system in the Japanese empire.[4]

The army also pressed its agenda for the construction of new railway lines during these years. Planners assigned the highest priority to the reconstruction of the temporary light rail running between Antung and Mukden in order to allow the deployment of troops by way of Korea. This project acquired added significance during discussions in 1906 as part of the interservice bargain embodied in the Imperial Defense Plan. The use of this line would, in theory, minimize the army's dependence on the navy to secure the sea routes to Manchuria and allow the navy maximum autonomy in carrying out its own operations plans. Controlling the Strait of Tsushima remained the only demand that army operations placed on the navy. After a lengthy and heated diplomatic dispute with Ch'ing authorities, reconstruction began in 1909 and finished in 1911. The army also pursued its plans for a second Korean line that would link Ch'angch'un to the T'umen River border by way of Kirin. This railway would not only provide an alternative route into Manchuria but also offered a means to redeploy forces between the main front at Harbin and the secondary front in the Maritime Province. The Chinese acquiesced to the building of a rail link between Ch'angch'un and Kirin as a loan concession, meaning that the Chinese would own the railway while granting substantial managerial rights to Japanese creditors. These arrangements placed some nominal limits on Japanese control of the line, but so long as Ch'angch'un remained this line's sole connection to a larger transportation system, it had no alternative but to serve as a branch of the SMR. A portion of the Ch'angch'un–Kirin railway opened to traffic in 1912. Negotiators agreed to defer the issue of extending the line to the Korean border to a later date, although the Chinese agreed to give Japan the right of first refusal on a loan concession should they decide to proceed with such a project.[5]

The army's deployment and supply plans counted on a link between the SMR and the North China Railway Extension as well. Although Chinese plans for this line had originally called for a terminus at Mukden, creating a Peking-Mukden railway, work had stopped at the Liao River town of Hsinmint'un some 60 miles west of the old Manchu capital. During the war, the army had built a temporary connection between Hsinmint'un and Mukden using a two-foot-gauge light rail in order to exploit the North China Extension as a supply route. Military planners sought to ensure the permanent maintenance of this connection and its reconstruction as a standard gauge railway. Initially, they had favored the incorporation of this connecting line as a wholly owned branch of the SMR. The Chinese, however, resisted this idea vigorously. Tokyo's representatives agreed to a compromise in which the Japanese would sell the existing light rail to the Chinese if the latter agreed to rebuild the connection to standard gauge and establish a direct link to the SMR at Mukden. This compromise reveals some significant features of the army's thinking about the military use of railways. Ownership and managerial control remained matters of secondary importance relative to routing, gauge, and connection. The Chinese government owned and operated the North China Railway Extension with some British involvement. The Japanese army nonetheless integrated its use into its war plans. Indeed, from a strategic perspective, any Chinese railway building in Manchuria, as long as it connected with the SMR and was compatible with it, enhanced Japanese military access to the region. As with other facilities in the territory, the army planned not only on mobilizing everything the Japanese controlled but on force-drafting properties owned by the Chinese.[6]

Although railway development remained central to military preparations in Manchuria, the construction of other support facilities in the prospective rear areas emerged as another field of endeavor in this period. The SMR began building harbor facilities at Dairen to military specifications, and in keeping with army plans, the company established a network of hospitals and clinics. It undertook other projects consistent with military objectives, although given their nature as dual-use facilities, it is difficult to determine the degree to which army priorities influenced their implementation. The creation of a large research department within the SMR contributed to the army's desire for good intelligence-gathering operations and supplemented the direct efforts of the Kwantung garrison. The SMR also maintained tree nurseries, a project proposed by the occupation authorities. Warehousing and ancillary transportation ventures and the laying of telephone and telegraph lines, along with infrastructural and public health improvements within Japanese-administered territory, developed apace. In the event of a second war, the Japanese army would be able to mobilize a substantial base of local facilities.[7]

The Kwantung Government-General undertook responsibility for mobilization planning. Significantly, a substantial number of army officers who had served in the Field Railway Corps stayed on in Manchuria as technical staff of the SMR. One member of the company's first team of directors observed in 1907, "At present, the operations of the SMR differ little from those undertaken during the war. . . . It is running in a state of near [wartime] readiness. The attitude of station staff toward passengers, indeed, remains quite soldierly."[8] Continuity of personnel clearly facilitated mobilization, and the employees of the SMR served, in effect, as reservists in the Field Railway Corps. In later years, the army assigned an officer specifically responsible for mobilization planning to the company. Concurrent service in the army and the SMR on the part of some select officers served other purposes as well. The case of Major Satō Yasunosuke (1871–1944), an active duty officer appointed to head the company's Mukden Office in 1909, is an example. The ostensible function of this office was to facilitate business negotiations with regional authorities. According to instructions from the Kwantung garrison, however, Satō's responsibilities clearly included the gathering of intelligence.[9]

On the whole, the army appeared quite certain of its ability to defend Manchuria against Russian attack, and the shifting pattern of deployment outlined in the annual operations plans offers evidence of a steady rise in confidence during this period. The 1907 version designated a point just north of Mukden as the site where the main Japanese force would concentrate before advancing toward Harbin. By 1910, that site had shifted substantially further north, near Ssup'ingkai; this shift reflected an assessment that the army would not encounter a significant Russian threat in the south and could use the territory as a secure staging area. Indeed, as early as 1907, strategic planners appear to have started thinking more in terms of deterrence than of preparing for an inevitable war of revenge. Wrote one staff officer, "The Russians undoubtedly cannot afford to abandon north Manchuria completely from a strategic point of view. However, we can convince them that the defense of the territory would be extremely costly. If so, Japan will be able to maintain a superior position and keep the peace through diplomacy."[10]

The conclusion of a bilateral Russo-Japanese agreement over Manchuria in 1907 that clearly demarcated spheres of interest suggests that Russia had taken stock of Japan's strong position and was seeking to avoid conflict. The boundary ran parallel to the CER somewhat south of the present-day borders of Kirin and Heilungkiang provinces, from the mouth of the T'umen River in the east to a point north of T'aonan in the west (see Map 3.1). The establishment of rather precise borders indicates how seriously both powers took their spheres of interest in Manchuria, but it also points to Russia's growing acceptance of its losses in the region. The 1907 agreement, in fact, marked the beginning of a broader rapprochement between the two former enemies. In a major foreign policy resolution in the following year, the cabinet established cooperation with Russia as a cornerstone of Japan's North-

Map 3.1 Russo-Japanese sphere boundaries in Manchuria, 1907–18 (based on maps in Kajima, *Nihon gaikō shi*, 9: 171; description in third Russo-Japanese accords, 1912, reproduced in ibid., 172–73; Kaneko, *Kindai Nihon ni okeru tai-Manshū tōshi no kenkyū*, 18)

east Asia policy. As discussed below, Russia and Japan would make common cause in 1909 and 1910 against American initiatives to neutralize all railways in Manchuria; this would lead to a second pact between the two powers. It might overstate the case, perhaps, to suggest any warmth between them at this stage, but their relations had unmistakably begun to thaw.[11]

From the army's point of view, the improvement of Russo-Japanese relations testified to the contributions of military strength to securing the peace. Others, however, saw these developments differently, as an indication of an intrinsic decline in the Russian threat and an opportunity to reconsider the scale of Japan's military commitments in Manchuria. The nation's finances remained straitened throughout this period, with austerity budgets imposed repeatedly despite growing demands for spending. Many civilian leaders certainly welcomed the possibility of reducing army expenditures. Pressures from the Diet for cuts were particularly strong. In a speech to the Twenty-Fifth Diet in 1909, Kenseihontō leader Inukai Tsuyoshi (1855–1932) berated the government for pursuing "an armament policy disproportionate to the nation's [financial] strength." Citing Russo-Japanese cooperation over Manchuria and the security of Japan's position in Korea, among other considerations, army expansion plans, he argued, were geared toward strategic conditions that no longer prevailed. Needless to say, the navy also favored a reduction of army appropriations and in fact began pressing the case for a broader reconsideration of armament priorities in 1910.[12]

The navy had accepted the political bargain embodied in the Imperial Defense Plan of 1907 grudgingly. At the time, circumstances militated against a direct challenge to the army's case for primacy. By 1910, however, conditions more favorable to the navy had emerged. The perception of a receding Russian threat contributed substantially to this change in climate. The navy also argued that the technology of naval warfare had advanced dramatically in recent years, as evidenced by the introduction of the "Dreadnought" class of warships by the British in 1906. A new naval arms race between the powers had commenced. The navy pointed out that these circumstances rendered Japanese battleships obsolete and that existing construction plans required substantial revision. The government remained unprepared in 1910 to approve a major new naval construction program, but it did agree to increase appropriations in order to modify the construction of vessels already planned. In response to this measure, the army pointed out that it had agreed to limit its expansion to nineteen divisions only until the nation's finances improved. If the budget contained room to increase defense appropriations, then the army would like funding for two additional divisions. The government, headed once again by Katsura Tarō (July 1908–August 1911), a soldier-statesman expected by his civilian supporters to restrain his own service, declined the request.[13]

In light of these developments, it is not entirely surprising to find the army revising its own rather sanguine assessments about the strategic situation in Northeast Asia and raising the alarm, once again, about the danger of a war of revenge. In an updated assessment of the military balance in the region prepared in May 1911, the Army General Staff warned against complacency about the danger of Russia. Vigilance remained necessary. Russia's eastward advance represented a long historical trend, not a recent or transient phenomenon. The quest for a warm-water port and the push to consolidate the Eurasian scope of its empire had originated with Peter the Great. Moreover, the Russian army had instituted sweeping military reforms during the past few years, correcting many of the shortcomings that had cost it dearly on the battlefields of Manchuria in 1904 and 1905. The Japanese, on the other hand, had let down their guard and stood unprepared for the inevitable rematch.

Japan's prospects for national development have taken a turn for the better since the Russo-Japanese War, but at the same time, people's thoughts have turned toward the frivolous. Extravagance has become popular. We bask in the glory of victory, intoxicated with the prospects of lasting peace before our eyes. . . . We have lost our warlike spirit. Military power has no support today. The shortcomings of diplomacy attract no notice, and we have become careless, unwisely depending on alliances and conventions. No one is looking toward the future, and no one regards arms expansion as an urgent task. Everyone high and low is at ease, lacking any awareness of the danger of a Russian war of revenge. This is precisely the opposite of our spirit before the war. Indeed, the respective attitudes of the Japanese and Russian peoples appear to have reversed entirely, and one can only shudder at the consequences.[14]

Marshal Yamagata Aritomo, one of the last of the elder statesmen still active in political and military affairs and ever the pessimist concerning Russia, took the case before the cabinet in July.

Russia has recovered from the wounds of 1904–5. It has renovated its railways, improved shipping and communications, and promoted large-scale settlement [in the Far East]. The supply of [local] resources is rich, the number of troops stationed in the region has increased, and the weak points of the past have been strengthened. It is not difficult to surmise Russia's intentions. Formerly acknowledged as the world's strongest country, it was defeated by Japan. The grudge born by all Russians high and low knows no limits. It is only natural and inevitable that they would plan to seek revenge against us as soon as possible. Moreover, the acquisition of an ice-free port has been a long-cherished Russian goal. The makeup of Europe does not permit the fulfillment of this goal. Thus, they have no choice today but to seek a facility in the Orient.

Russo-Japanese accords did not imply, he pointed out, receding danger. To interpret them in this manner, in fact, meant falling prey to a Russian trap.

Our agreement with the Russians over Manchuria is effective only while they recover from their wounds. Once this is accomplished, they will not seek to renew this
agreement with us, as I, a supporter of these accords, have frequently warned. I believe you gentlemen are well aware of this. For this reason, while the agreement is in
effect, we must likewise use the time to heal ourselves and prepare to meet the challenge. It is clear that whereas Russia's preparations have progressed steadily, we have
left our army and navy unprepared.[15]

Yamagata's view of what adequate preparations might mean at this time
went further than anything he or others in the army had advocated earlier.
Although his army colleagues eventually persuaded him to moderate his assessment before making a request in 1910, he had apparently favored raising
the already elusive target of 25 standing divisions to 33.[16]

As the debate intensified, army leaders argued that the strategic dangers
not only persisted but had actually increased. The Russians had commenced
the double-tracking of the Trans-Siberian. Their plans also included the
completion of the Amur Railway, which would substantially reduce their
dependence on the CER for access to the Far East. Not only would an
Amur line allow Russia to deploy a much larger force in the region, but it
would eliminate the vulnerability that Japanese army strategy counted on.
Japanese defense plans required revision in order to balance these developments. Moreover, factors other than a revived and stronger Russia contributed to increased dangers. Rising military threats emanated from south of
the Great Wall as well. Army leaders warned that Japan no longer had the
luxury of formulating continental defense plans based on fighting Russia as
the sole adversary. It was increasingly likely that Japanese forces would have to
fight both the Chinese and the Russians simultaneously, and the nation could
not avoid preparing for the contingency of a two-front war. Curiously, however, Yamagata and the general staff arrived at this conclusion about the possibility of fighting the Chinese from diametrically opposing assumptions.[17]

Yamagata viewed China as a growing danger in its own right. He pointed
to a growing trend of national unity and the vigorous military reforms initiated by the Chinese authorities.

No one can truly know what the future holds for China. However, the power and
authority of the central government, it would seem, have not deteriorated as much
as general opinion would have it. Indeed, it may be possible that in the next few
years . . . the political and economic situation in China will stabilize. Moreover, the
Chinese army is no longer what it was in the past. It will be some time before the

Chinese are able to reach their goal of establishing 37 divisions, but they have already organized 13. It is said that these units are disciplined and well trained and not to be taken lightly. The balance of the 37-division plan is partly in place, and a number of additional units are being organized with the effective strength of composite brigades. If China succeeds in fulfilling these military expansion plans, it is inevitable that it will seek to repay us for the humiliation of 1894–95. I would like to believe that we will be able to contain China with only diplomatic means, but this is unlikely.

Yamagata noted that the Chinese army was employing German advisors and that its new leaders had strong German sympathies. Under these circumstances, he warned, Japan would have to assess Chinese military capabilities as well as Berlin's intentions more seriously. The possibility that the nation might confront two vengeful enemies at the same time demanded careful attention.[18]

The general staff, in sharp contrast, saw the danger in China stemming from growing disorder and internal collapse. They saw military action south of the Wall taking the form of a large-scale intervention aimed at restoring order and protecting Japanese and foreign rights.

Any proper evaluation of China's national strength reveals little possibility of that country's posing an autonomous military threat to Japan. However, the prevailing conditions in China give cause for concern. The avarice of the powers looking for opportunities expands day by day. Dissension grows among the people, the court officials are incompetent, and administrative affairs are in disarray. Moreover, antiforeign and revolutionary thought is becoming pervasive. Every important business operation in the country is under foreign control; government revenues stagnate; foreign debt mounts. This situation cannot continue for much longer without jeopardizing order. And once chaos begins, there is no power above to suppress it, and there is no discipline below for self-restraint. Disorder will spread throughout the country. The powers will move to protect their nationals and secure their rights. They will also use this opportunity to expand their claims. This will inevitably produce complex diplomatic problems. The powers, for example, will probably act with self-restraint for the most part. However, we have a special relationship with China, particularly with regard to Manchuria. It will be necessary, therefore, to deploy at least some of our troops. It may, indeed, be difficult to avoid armed confrontation with China. Given this situation, in order to protect our paramount rights, we must be prepared, at any time, to respond appropriately.

The scale of intervention required, in the estimates of staff analysts, amounted to no more than thirteen divisions, well within the army's existing capabilities. The real danger in this situation, however, lay in the possibility of a simultaneous Russian initiative in the north. While Japan was distracted south of the Wall, the Russians would make their move. "Given the current level of our armed forces," they warned, the army would be unable to handle a conflict with more than one adversary except in "extraordinarily favorable circumstances."[19]

Given the political backdrop of a resurgent interservice rivalry, the fact that two radically different assessments pointed to the same conclusion of increased danger and the need for additional infantry divisions renders the underlying arguments suspect. A detailed discussion of this matter is best deferred to an examination of the debate over defense policy in 1912 and 1913, when it escalated into a major political crisis. What is important to note at this stage is that the army's leaders found themselves increasingly hard-pressed after 1910 to make their case about a Russian danger. This difficulty underscores how much conditions, or at least perceptions, had changed since 1905. If the army had sought to make the Japanese people feel secure about a Manchurian commitment, then it had clearly succeeded. A cynic might suggest that it had been too successful.

Railway Diplomacy and Shifting Alignments

Apart from its difficulties with "complacency" in 1910 and 1911, the army faced relatively few obstacles during this period in carrying out its principal responsibility in Manchuria. In contrast, the Foreign Ministry encountered far greater problems in its efforts to consolidate Japan's diplomatic and legal position in the territory, and between 1907 and 1911, Japanese diplomats made what would stand as their greatest and most direct contributions to the development of the venture.[20]

Foreign Ministry officials confronted two major problems in consolidating Japan's position in Manchuria. The enforcement of the terms of the Treaty of Peking, in which the Chinese government had acquiesced to Russo-Japanese arrangements in the Treaty of Portsmouth, presented the most immediate concern. Contentious negotiations in December 1905 had resulted in agreements that left a number of loose ends that the Chinese subsequently exploited to obstruct full implementation. Contested issues included the control of coal mines and, most important, the reconstruction of the Antung–Mukden railway. The Japanese approach entailed some give-and-take bargaining, but for the most part, Japan settled its claims in a straightforward and heavy-handed manner very much in the tradition of gunboat diplomacy. Japanese military police, for example, occupied the disputed mines. Given the fact that a temporary narrow-gauge railway continued to operate between Antung and Mukden and that the task of rebuilding the Dairen–Ch'angch'un trunk preoccupied the SMR and its engineering staff, Tokyo tolerated some Chinese procrastination on the Antung–Mukden question. Patience had run out by 1908, however, and in the following year, the Japanese began purchasing land, stationing guards, and retracking the line unilaterally. These Japanese actions provoked widespread popular protest throughout China, but in the face of Tokyo's intransigence and an ultimatum issued in 1909, Chinese authorities had little choice but to acquiesce. The only consolation they received lay in an agreement that Japanese tenure on the Antung–Mukden line would expire in 1923, the same year in which the lease on Kwantung was scheduled to terminate.[21]

The other major problem, more important in the long run, was to secure Japan's claims to a railway monopoly in southern Manchuria, one foundation of its imperial strategy. This effort required not only the acquiescence of the Chinese but some measure of recognition from the Great Powers. The official basis for a claim to monopoly rights rested on the economic interests of the concessionary railway, which would suffer injury from either the construction of new lines in close proximity to the SMR or the establishment of "hostile" connections to competing transportation systems. In support of this position, Japanese negotiators had included, in a series of agreements supplementary to the Treaty of Peking, the following provision: "The Chinese Government engage, for the purpose of protecting the interest of the South Manchuria Railway, not to construct, prior to the recovery by them of said railway, any main line in the neighborhood of and parallel to that railway, or any branch line which might be prejudicial to the interest of the above mentioned railway."[22] Although this measure would seem to provide sufficient grounds for Japan's claim, it proved inadequate on several counts. For one, the supplementary agreements containing this provision were secret, bilateral protocols that Japan might attempt to enforce on Peking but had no binding force on third parties. Japan had no choice but to seek separate understandings with each of the Great Powers regarding its claims. Although *Spharenpolitik*, the diplomacy of spheres of interest, had established clear precedents for such arrangements during the great scramble for concessions at the turn of the century, at least some of the more influential members of the international community had begun to reconsider their positions. For another, the Chinese had sound, diplomatic grounds to challenge Japanese interpretations of the secret railway protocols. Article IV of the Treaty of Portsmouth stipulated that "Japan and Russia reciprocally engage not to obstruct any general measures common to all countries, which China may take for the development of commerce and industry in Manchuria."[23] China, in other words, had the right to build railways in its own sovereign territory, a matter that might be taken for granted elsewhere in the world but, in an imperialist environment, one necessarily spelled out in a binding treaty. Although this stipulation did not obviate entirely the legitimacy of Japanese demands that purportedly harmful competition be curbed, it placed substantial constraints on any attempt to assert a blanket regional monopoly and forced the Japanese to demonstrate potential injury in fairly specific, economic terms.

Such a demonstration proved challenging. The Japanese construed their sphere of interest in Manchuria as extending from the SMR eastward all the way to the Korean border. The western boundaries remained undefined until 1912, but if we take the Russo-Japanese accord of 1907 as a preliminary indicator, it would seem that the imaginary boundary reached at least as far west as the Chinese frontier outpost of T'aonan in Inner Mongolia. Most railway experts would have found rather implausible the argument that any and all independent lines built within this vast region, apart from those designed specifically to serve as tributaries or "feeders" of the SMR, posed a potential threat to Japanese economic interests. Japanese policymakers, however, cited special circumstances in Manchuria. The widespread use of long-range horse carts, which could carry bulk goods on a commercial basis for distances in excess of 100 miles, created unusual conditions for railway competition in the region. "Feeder" territories could extend as far as 100 miles on either side of a railway, and to build another line within those boundaries could be construed as "prejudicial." A Japanese Finance Ministry report in 1909 noted that "the extent of territory served by Chinese horse carts as opposed to railways in Manchuria is far greater than in other regions. For this reason, parallel lines separated by tens of miles, which under other circumstances might offer little competition, unavoidably generate ferocious rivalry in this territory."[24]

Yet another factor complicating Japan's efforts to secure its monopoly claims lay in a body of prior agreements concerning the Chinese-owned PMR.[25] As a result of negotiations with the British in 1899, the Russians had acquiesced to the construction of this line into Manchuria as far as the Liao River port of Hsinmint'un with the understanding that its extension to Mukden required formal Russian consent. The Japanese inherited this agreement in 1905 and ironically proceeded to undo Russian efforts to limit the challenge posed by the PMR, first by building a connecting line between Hsinmint'un and Mukden and subsequently by agreeing to transfer control of the connector to the Chinese. This decision, however, in no way reflected a lack of appreciation for the principles of railway imperialism. Indeed, the Japanese initially demanded the incorporation of the Hsinmint'un–Mukden line as a wholly owned branch of the SMR proper. As noted, however, strategic concerns demanded some flexibility. Moreover, Japanese policymakers placed a higher priority on resolving the dispute over the Antung–Mukden railway, and Chinese negotiators suggested that they might concede more readily on other issues if Japan would accommodate China's interests in completing the PMR. Unprepared to allow the entire Treaty of Peking to stall over this issue, Japanese diplomats agreed.[26] This concession might have seemed wise at the time, but it also substantially strengthened the prospects for the growth of Chinese railway power in southern Manchuria. It created a transportation system with a harbor outlet at Yingk'ou, operating in direct competition with the SMR for railway traffic between Mukden and the sea. More important, it allowed for a direct connection between Peking and Mukden, Manchuria's political center, nurturing aspirations for further extension of this line to Kirin, an idea that Chinese statesman Li Hung-chang (1823–1901) had envisioned in the 1890s as part of an effort to secure the territory against foreign encroachment (see Map 3.2).

The Japanese sphere of interest in southern Manchuria thus suffered from a soft diplomatic underbelly, and much to the consternation of the Foreign Ministry, the years between 1906 and 1910 saw no shortage of challenges from both the Chinese and the powers. Chinese resistance to foreign encroachment began stiffening significantly during this period. The Russo-Japanese War had stimulated popular nationalism. Ironically, the Japanese emerged as both heroes and villains in Chinese thinking: as representatives of Asia victorious over a Western power, they were a source of inspiration, yet as imperialists at least as rapacious as those of the West, they opened

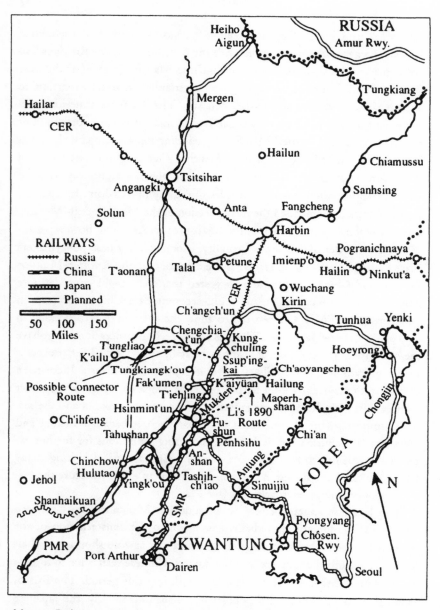

Map 3.2 Railways in Manchuria, 1907–11. Some planned routes are shown based on actual lines built subsequently (based on maps in Tōa keizai chōsakyoku, *Manchoukuo Year Book*, *1934*; SMR, *Eigyō hōkukusho*, *1923*, *1928*, *1930*; DRɪ, looseleaf).

themselves to condemnation. The emergence after 1905 of the so-called Rights Recovery movement, aimed at redeeming foreign railway concessions, represented an early political manifestation of this rising consciousness among students, local elites, and a sector of imperial officialdom.[27]

In addition to mass protests, campaigns to redeem foreign loans, and high-level diplomatic maneuvers, Chinese resistance during this period also took the form of concerted efforts to counter foreign encroachment in Manchuria through competitive initiatives on the ground. Well before the turn of the century, Ch'ing officials had come to recognize the vulnerability of China's position in the lands north of the Great Wall. Their anxieties mounted during the Russo-Japanese War when it became apparent that China stood to lose the territory to one or the other of the contending powers unless it strengthened its hold. They understood the need for aggressive administrative and military reforms, the rationalization of Chinese political institutions, and, at a minimum, the development of a capability to maintain law and order in the territory. The political reorganization of the region in 1907, which placed the "Three Eastern Provinces" (Fengt'ien, formerly Shengking, Kirin, and Heilungkiang) as the Chinese described Manchuria, under a newly created office of a regional governor-general based in Mukden, represented one manifestation of these concerns. The inauguration of a competitive colonization campaign formed another dimension of the emerging pattern of resistance. Regional officials and their backers in Peking understood the kind of game that the Russians and Japanese were playing with railways, banks, and immigration schemes. One official, in fact, compared the SMR to the East India Company.[28]

Chinese leaders sought to resist these imperialist strategies in kind. In one of their early initiatives, they created a government bank (*kuanyinhao*) in Mukden to counter the schemes of Japanese institutions, such as the Yokohama Specie Bank, to expand the position of Japanese yen notes as the major medium of exchange in regional commerce. Land development, improvements in agricultural technology, and the promotion of large-scale Chinese settlement formed major elements of this program as well. Chinese officials targeted control over commerce as a key element in their strategy, aiming, for example, at the development of the port of Yingk'ou as a rival to Japanese-controlled Dairen in Kwantung. China's efforts to build its own railway system in the Three Eastern Provinces, however, was the most important effort, and the PMR provided precisely the wedge it needed to challenge Japan's claim to a railway monopoly through direct competition.[29]

At this time, Chinese railway initiatives in and of themselves probably would not have amounted to a serious threat. The Japanese might well have dealt with resistance on the ground in the same heavy-handed and arbitrary manner with which they had responded to Chinese diplomacy. The attitude of the powers, however, prevented an easy and straightforward resolution of the problem. The Foreign Ministry's efforts to win at least tacit international recognition of Japan's rights, including the claim to a railway monopoly, had scored some early successes. The Russo-Japanese accord of 1907 represented a major achievement, establishing fairly precise boundary lines between a Russian "north Manchuria" and a Japanese "south Manchuria." Tokyo's diplomats had achieved a less explicit, yet nonetheless significant, understanding with France, also concluded in 1907, regarding special rights in Chinese territory contiguous to their respective colonial territories. Japan recognized the paramountcy of French interests in areas of south China adjacent to Indochina, and in return France acknowledged Japan's special claims in Manchuria as a region contiguous to Korea. The British, displeased with Japanese policy in Manchuria, avoided entering into an explicit understanding over Manchuria. Their recognition of Russian claims in 1899, however, had established a promising precedent, and coupled with the renewal of the Anglo-Japanese Alliance in 1905, Tokyo had reason for optimism that no major challenge would emerge from this quarter. The Germans presented some cause for concern, since they leaned toward an Open Door policy in China, despite their own holdings in Shantung, for reasons we will touch on shortly.[30]

The real problem, however, lay with the United States. Since the time of John Hay's (1839–1905) Open Door Notes, U.S. diplomacy had adopted a critical posture toward particularist encroachments in China. This position began to harden in the aftermath of the Russo-Japanese War. The United States' lead in relinquishing railway concessions in 1905 in the face of the Rights Recovery movement had encouraged Chinese efforts. Theodore Roosevelt had expressed displeasure with what he saw as Japanese backsliding on promises of neutralization, but stressing the need for a realistic policy in East Asia, he opposed any active attempt to contest Japanese claims in Manchuria during his administration. Some officials, however, favored an effort to check Japanese expansion and to assert U.S. interests more aggressively. Indeed, American initiatives operating in conjunction with Chinese efforts, at first unofficially but subsequently backed by the full weight of the State Department under the Taft administration, would present the most serious obstacle to the consolidation of Japanese monopoly claims during this era.

The first challenge came in 1907. Hsü Shih-chang (1858–1939), appointed to the newly created post of regional governor-general, and T'ang Shao-i (1860–1938), the American-educated governor of Fengt'ien province, launched a plan to build a branch of the PMR north from Hsinmint'un to the market town of Fak'umen, some 30 miles west of the SMR station of T'iehling (see Map 3.2). The area around Fak'umen and T'iehling was a major soybean-marketing center in the Liao valley, and the SMR and river shippers were already engaged in a fierce competition over freight traffic in this area. Hsü and T'ang's project had the enthusiastic support of Willard Straight (1880–1919), the virulently Japanophobic American consul-general in Mukden, and a British contractor, Pauling and Company. A variant of this plan, only rumored but not implausible, entailed adding a branch of the projected Hsinmint'un–Fak'umen line that would originate at Fak'umen, run east across the SMR to Hailung, a town on the eastern edge of the SMR's commercial service territory, and from there, north to Kirin. If realized, this scheme would reproduce the essentials of Li Hung-chang's railway as well as create a competitive line on the eastern flank of the SMR.[31]

The Hsinmint'un-Fak'umen initiative posed a potentially serious threat, but in this instance, Japanese diplomats managed to present a fairly persuasive case against it. With Fak'umen only 32 miles northwest of T'iehling station, the projected line ran close enough to the SMR to sustain, without exaggeration, Japanese claims of prospective injury. Promoters of the Hsinmint'un–Fak'umen railway attempted to argue that conventional practice in China used a standard of 25 miles of separation in defining injurious competition, but Japanese diplomats responded that the phenomenon of long-distance carting rendered such conventions inapplicable to Manchuria. The Chinese and their supporters also argued that Japanese objections constituted an obstruction of efforts to develop the Fak'umen district in violation of Article IV of the Treaty of Portsmouth. The Japanese had a ready answer to this position as well. If the intent of the railway's promoters was to develop the area around Fak'umen, suggested Tokyo's representatives, the SMR would gladly agree to the construction of a feeder line connecting its Ch'angch'un–Dairen trunk to Fak'umen, which would provide more than adequate access to the region. Such an arrangement, of course, defeated the political purpose of the Fak'umen initiative. Even in the unlikely event that the Japanese chose to forgo any claims to managerial or financial control over a short spur from T'iehling or K'aiyüan to Fak'umen, it would remain entirely subservient to the SMR as a feeder and would only extend the reach of Japanese railway power. Indeed, any line purely tributary to the Ch'angch'un–Dairen trunk, regardless of ownership, would enhance Japanese control over the movement of goods and people in the region while enforcing Chinese dependence.[32] Financial difficulties confronting the project's international backers also facilitated Japanese efforts to thwart this initiative. Straight, moreover, lacked the official support of the State Department. Significantly, the British Foreign Office's refusal to support Pauling and Company seemed to indicate to hopeful Japanese diplomats that the British might tacitly acknowledge Japanese claims. Under the circumstances, the Chinese and their allies had little choice but to abandon the project.[33]

A second railway challenge, initiated two years later, proved substantially more difficult to obstruct. The impetus for this undertaking came from Hsi-liang (1853–1917), appointed governor-general of the Three Eastern Provinces in 1909, and a group of American and British investors, which included E. H. Harriman, Pauling and Company, as well as Willard Straight, this time in the capacity of a private individual heading a financial syndicate. Not long after the failure of the Hsinmint'un–Fak'umen venture, those involved had begun exploring alternatives, such as building a line further west. Such a routing would make it more difficult for Japanese diplomats to argue injurious competition. Although participants in this scheme considered various routes, the plan they favored called for a railway originating at Chinchow station on the PMR and running north to T'aonan. From T'aonan, the line would cross the CER to Tsitsihar and terminate on the Amur River border with Russia at the town of Aigun (see Map 3.2). The strength of this proposal, however, lay not only in the revised routing but also in the backing of the U.S. Department of State. Secretary Philander Knox (1853–1921) saw this undertaking as one way of countering both Russian and Japanese attempts to establish railway monopolies in Manchuria and a key step in a larger effort to push for the full neutralization of all lines in the territory.[34]

Japanese diplomats understood that blocking this project presented a greater challenge than the Hsinmint'un–Fak'umen initiative. The Chinchow–Aigun ran too far west to make a reasonable case against parallel construction. More important, official U.S. involvement precluded any high-handed attempts to scuttle the initiative. Foreign Minister Komura Jūtarō issued a stern warning to the Chinese authorities not to approve the plan and hinted at dire consequences for Sino-Japanese relations. At the same time, however, he also prepared a fallback position. Japan would consent to the plan under two conditions. First, the Japanese would participate fully in the financing, construction, supply, and management of this railway, along with other investor groups. Second, China would grant Japan the right to build a connecting railway between the SMR and the Chinchow–Aigun line. Komura saw this provision as mitigating the potential problems that this project would create for Japanese policy. A connector would permit the Japanese army to intercept the Chinchow–Aigun and prevent its military use against the Japanese position in Manchuria. Indeed, given the logic behind military railway policy, which saw the possibility of mobilizing the Chinese-owned PMR for wartime use, this link to the SMR could turn the Chinchow–Aigun into a strategic asset by extending the shadow of the Japanese military presence deep into the northern and western reaches of the territory. It would also diminish the effectiveness of the offending line as a source of Chinese or American railway power in the region. As we shall see, the SMR developed an aggressive business strategy that could, in theory, attract considerable freight from this projected line by way of the connector. In this way, the Japanese railway could force the Chinchow–Aigun to serve, at least in part, as a feeder drawing traffic from north Manchuria as well as Inner Mongolia.[35]

As it turned out, this fallback position proved unnecessary. The fact that the Chinchow–Aigun venture threatened Russian as well as Japanese interests created an opportunity for the two former adversaries to make common cause. The Russians adamantly opposed this project. Crossing into CER territory constituted offense enough, but taking the line to the Russian border posed a direct and unacceptable threat. Russian diplomats characterized the project as a deliberate political and strategic challenge and protested vigorously to the United States. To the Chinese, they suggested that should Peking ignore these concerns and allow the project to go ahead, Russia would demand compensation in the form of a railway across Mongolia connecting Siberia to North China. The French supported the Russian and Japanese positions. The British had advised Knox earlier against this venture and, once again, declined to support Pauling and Company. As Ian Nish puts it, "If the Americans cared to push through the scheme in the teeth of opposition from Japan and Russia, Britain would remain a spectator."[36]

Against this alignment, the Chinchow–Aigun railway became a dead prospect by the spring of 1910. Not surprisingly, Knox's larger scheme to neutralize Manchuria's railways also fell flat. Ironically, Japanese leaders might have welcomed such an initiative had the Americans placed it on the table before the fateful events of 1904. The Knox neutralization plan, however, came five years and 200,000 casualties too late as a means of allaying Japan's strategic concerns. Both Russia and Japan rejected the proposal, which also failed to win either British or French support. Indeed, the general thrust of Knox's diplomacy, as a number of historians have pointed out, appears to have backfired by giving both the Japanese and the Russians an opportunity to reassert their claims and have them affirmed in an international arena. More important, the combination of the neutralization plan and the Chinchow–Aigun project served to accelerate the rapprochement between Russia and Japan. The 1907 accords had represented an important first step. But whereas the desire to avoid military conflict had provided the main drive behind the first agreement, the defense of common Manchurian interests against the challenge of a third party formed the primary impetus to cooperation in 1909 and 1910. Diplomats negotiated a second Russo-Japanese pact in July 1910 to mark the joint victory. The terms of this agreement underscored the explicit objective of cooperation against developments "of a nature to menace the status quo." Given these circumstances, it hardly comes as a surprise that a growing number of leaders in Japan might begin to think that the possibility of a second war with Russia was receding.[37]

The outcome of the disputes in 1909 and 1910 clearly favored Japan. At the same time, however, success fell short of being complete. Japan had thwarted the U.S. initiative, but it had not won Washington's recognition for its claims, a reason for continued concern. Moreover, despite the fact that France had rallied to the Russian and Japanese cause and that Britain had declined to support the United States, the degree of international support Japan might continue to expect remained uncertain. Mutual interest formed an essential element in maintaining the diplomacy of spheres of interest. Yet in the aftermath of the Russo-Japanese War, the enthusiasm for concession hunting among the Great Powers had noticeably declined. This shift in orientation reflected, in part, rising tensions in Europe, which drew attention from developments in the East. Growing disillusionment with the system of imperial competition contributed as well. The French venture in Yunnan had stalled as a result of technical difficulties. The Germans, who ranked among the hungriest of concession hunters in the late 1890s, had already begun to lose their appetite by 1903. German diplomats and commercial interests grew increasingly concerned that claiming a sphere of interest in Shantung might cost them advantages in other parts of China. Many regarded the territory, poor in comparison to the Yangtze region, as unworthy of the risks, and sentiment in favor of downgrading the commitment had emerged. "Germany only wants the open door in [Shantung]," declared Chancellor Bernhard von Bülow (1848–1929). "Though we secured from the Chinese government certain concrete railway and mining concessions for our entrepreneurs . . . we only did what other powers were doing for their citizens in other parts of China."[38] The rise of Chinese nationalism and the Rights Recovery movement after 1905 no doubt added fuel to incipient disillusionment and changed the cost-benefit calculus of concession hunting. Indeed, this movement raised concerns among Japanese policymakers as well. Itō Hirobumi warned in 1908 that pressing Japanese claims in too heavy-handed a manner in the face of Chinese public opinion might well wind up winning Japan's terms at the cost of a revolution in China. In the aftermath of the Chinchow–Aigun dispute, Komura, well aware of the danger of driving the Chinese into an alliance with the Americans, also saw the need for some moderation in Japan's dealings with China.[39] Growing Chinese resistance demanded either compromise or a stronger, imperialist united front. Russia, ironically, remained the only power on which Japan could count in adopting the latter approach, and if the army's assessment of the nature of Russian friendship was accurate, then Japan's position was rather worrisome.

Nonetheless, in terms of their goals and in view of the difficulties they faced, Japanese diplomats had good reason for satisfaction with their accomplishments at the end of 1910. The shift in attitudes among the powers raised concerns, to be sure, yet the nation's leaders had no reason to doubt the basic soundness of the imperialist system in East Asia. Give-and-take in other areas of mutual interest might help alleviate tension with the problematic Americans. Cooperation over immigration issues, for example, might persuade the United States to allow Japan to have its way in Manchuria, a line of thinking Komura entertained at this time.[40] The trouble brewing in China demanded careful attention, but most Japanese saw the emergent movements not as a genuine national awakening comparable to that which had brought about the Meiji Restoration but as the manifestation of the rising forces of chaos in a moribund Ch'ing empire. The answer to chaos lay not in compromise but in the imposition of law and order with a firm hand.

The Business of the SMR

The consolidation of Japan's position in Manchuria during this period entailed concerted efforts in defense and diplomacy. It also required the establishment of solid economic foundations. In general, modern imperialists demanded financial self-sufficiency of their new acquisitions, and ensuring that their subjects paid for the privilege of being subjugated was one of the principal tasks of imperial administrators. In formal possessions, colonial governments had the fiscal apparatus of the state at their disposal in order to achieve this purpose. In Manchuria, only Kwantung, a small holding with little intrinsic value in its own right, offered such a possibility. The obvious solution, anticipated from the outset, lay in the SMR, which, to borrow Gotō Shinpei's phrase, could function as a "substitute for the state" in extracting the revenues from Manchuria needed to underwrite the venture as a whole.

Financing the SMR itself during these early years presented fewer difficulties than some policymakers, particularly those favoring the Harriman deal, had anticipated. Russian investment represented a major windfall, and although the formal appraisal of transferred properties of the CER at ¥100 million overstated their actual value, the inheritance accounted for over a third of Japanese investment in the territory as a whole before World War I.[41] Although the company had to lay new track, the roadbed remained intact. Construction of the city and harbor at Dairen stood partially complete, and mining at Fushun had already commenced. Full-scale operation of the SMR could begin with a relatively small amount of new investment.[42] The organization of the company as a joint-stock enterprise proved useful in raising funds. The sale of stock to the Japanese public contributed to the effort. Postwar enthusiasm for the Manchurian venture, coupled with the nationalization of domestic railways in 1906, which freed a substantial pool of capital, resulted in an unanticipated response to the initial offer of SMR shares. Prospective investors oversubscribed the issue by a factor of more than a thousand. Policymakers, however, had planned from the outset to rely primarily on loans from abroad, where capital costs remained substantially cheaper.[43] The company's charter allowed borrowing up to twice the level of its authorized capital of ¥200 million. With its obligations guaranteed by the Japanese government, the SMR had relatively little difficulty floating bonds in London to meet most of its needs during this period and raised over ¥130 million yen between 1907 and 1910 through this channel.[44]

Operating the company as a profit-making enterprise generating sufficient revenue to sustain the imperial program as a whole proved far more challenging. During the start-up phase, the SMR's business strategy, as was the case in so many other areas of Japanese activity in Manchuria, followed the Russian lead. Russia's primary reason for building a southern branch for the CER lay in gaining access to Port Arthur. Sergei Witte and his associates, however, also saw better short-term business prospects for railway enterprise in the relatively well-developed Liao River valley of the south than in the thinly populated prairie country of the north. The southern branch could tap the existing demand for commercial transportation generated by the region's thriving soybean trade, which centered on the port of Yingk'ou and relied primarily on the services of the small cargo boats plying the Liao River. Quick profits from this branch, which ran roughly parallel to the Liao for most of its navigable distance, could subsidize the costs of operating the trans-Manchurian trunk in the north. Adopting this strategy with a few modifications, the SMR managed to operate in the black from the start.[45]

The key to success lay in breaking into the existing soy trade, which had a relatively long history in southern Manchuria. By the 1870s, the region enjoyed an expanding commerce in soybeans, bean cake, and soybean oil. At first, China south of the Wall provided the primary market for these products, but after the Sino-Japanese War, the Japanese demand for soy cake as a fertilizer contributed to rapid growth. The soy trade peaked in 1899 but fell on hard times shortly thereafter as a result of the successive disruptions of the Boxer War, the Russian occupation, and the Russo-Japanese War; production did not recover its 1899 level until 1907. During the years that followed, the soybean business in southern Manchuria prospered, fueled by the opening of new markets in Europe.[46]

Until the coming of the railway to Manchuria, boat traffic along the Liao River dominated the shipment of beans from growing regions in the Liao valley and beyond to the port of Yingk'ou. The river was navigable as far north as Chengchiat'un in eastern Inner Mongolia, a port situated about 55 miles west of the SMR's Ssup'ingkai station. The Eastern Liao, the Hun, and the T'aitzu, three tributaries seasonally navigable by small vessels, enhanced its usefulness as a transportation route. Long-range horse carting also increased the reach of this system and allowed the Liao to draw traffic from as far east as Hailung. A network of absentee boat owners from North China, who hired local boat gangs on a seasonal basis, controlled Liao River shipping. Boat gangs, in turn, took on jobs from a variety of shipping agents in the numerous small towns and villages along the river. The shipping business bound itself closely to the Chinese merchant community at Yingk'ou, which maintained strong customary and credit ties with shipping agents, soybean merchants, and landlords upstream. Yingk'ou was also the center of the bean oil industry, which produced residual cake as well as oil. The Liao carried a variety of other goods as well. Grain and timber for local consumption moved between river ports. The trade in cotton goods, sundries, and liquor, which was dominated by suppliers in China proper, moved upstream from Yingk'ou. After Yingk'ou became a treaty port in 1861 and foreign merchants began to take advantage of its new status, imported goods made their appearance as well. As the region's principal cash crop, however, soy provided the engine of Manchurian commerce. As Kaneko Fumio notes, the prosperity of the territory as a whole rested on a "soybean economy."[47]

The SMR's initial efforts to capture the Liao River soy traffic confronted two major problems. One lay in the resilience of the Liao as a competitor. The railway enjoyed a number of substantial advantages, and as the Ishizuka group reported, shippers interviewed at the river port of T'ungkiangk'ou eagerly awaited the reopening of the railway to commercial traffic. Significantly, these prospective clients saw the primary advantages of using the railway not in the costs of transportation, which, in fact, ran somewhat higher, but in terms of speed, reliability, and safety. They emphasized the importance of responding in a timely manner to market prices at Yingk'ou. Agents in the seaport might report a favorable market, but by the time bean shipments reached their destination, the price might have changed significantly. River transportation also suffered seasonal disruptions; it shut down completely during the winter freeze and was curtailed during the summer when water levels fell. Even when the Liao was fully open to traffic, shipping by boat lacked reliability and was subject to a substantial amount of routine damage and loss, compounded by frequent bandit depredations.[48]

At the same time, the Liao had its strong points. As a well-established route regulated by local authorities, merchants accustomed to its use knew what to expect, and not all evinced the open-minded attitude toward railway transportation of those interviewed by Ishizuka's team. Although factors other than price might influence the choice of transportation services, it represented an important consideration. Freight charges as such ran slightly lower by rail than by boat, but additional fees for bagging, loading, and off-loading raised the total cost. The customary ties and long-standing credit relationships binding the network of merchants, boatmen, and shippers constituted even more important factors favoring the river route. The Chinese merchant community based in Yingk'ou dominated the soybean trade throughout southern Manchuria, and their deep ties to the economy of the interior formed a closed system difficult to penetrate through simple market incentives alone. Yamagata probably overstated the case when he described the Liao as a "formidable" adversary. Railway managers, however, could not ignore it. The river might have remained a stronger competitor, in fact, had the Russians not devastated existing shipping facilities during the war in their quest for firewood.[49]

Competition from the PMR posed the second major problem facing the SMR's efforts to break into the soy trade. With its northern terminus in Mukden, the Chinese railway served only a limited transportation watershed in Manchuria, but it nonetheless posed a significant challenge in this start-up phase. The Mukden region, broadly construed, generated a considerable trade in soybeans. SMR stations within 50 miles north or south of city, a rough but reasonable estimate of the area subject to competition between the two railway systems, accounted in 1907 for some 58 percent of the total soy tonnage carried by the Japanese line (38 percent of soy traffic revenue, as measured in ton-miles).[50] Moreover, the PMR enjoyed a larger catchment region than the extent of the rail line itself might suggest, since Chinese merchants often made use of a combination of the Liao and the PMR in shipping goods to Yingk'ou. For example, beans from the northern river port of T'ungkiangk'ou made their way south by boat to Hsinmint'un, where they would be offloaded onto railway cars for the final leg to the seaport. As a result, Japan's successful obstruction of the Hsinmint'un–Fak'umen railway in 1907 failed to suppress entirely the ability of the PMR to draw traffic from northern districts. A combination of the Liao and the PMR, in fact, challenged the SMR for freight at least as far north as the Chengchiat'un-Ssup'ingkai area.[51] Two other factors further strengthened the PMR as a competitor. First, with its seaport terminus at Yingk'ou, the Chinese railway

could take advantage of ties to the local business community and its traditional hold over soy-marketing networks; in this regard it enjoyed the same
strength as the Liao. Newly built Dairen, the SMR's principal outlet, lacked
such relationships. Second, it offered substantially lower rates than the
SMR for shipping beans from Mukden to the sea. PMR charges for a car-
load of beans from Mukden to Yingk'ou ran ¥89 in 1912 in contrast to the
SMR's fee of ¥132 from Mukden to the port of Dairen.[52] In part, this differential resulted from Chinese policies aimed at competing against the Japanese, but it also reflected the substantially shorter distance from Mukden to
the respective seaport outlets of the two lines.

SMR managers had several options in dealing with the PMR. Rate competition certainly presented one possibility, and in fact the company pushed
its rates as low as it could afford. The figures cited above, which reflected
substantial discounts, however, pointed to the inadequacy of such measures.
The main reason company managers avoided further cuts in fees in order to
match the PMR lay in the dangers inherent in rate wars. In general, railway
managers considered rate competition anathema, since it almost invariably
devolved into a mutually destructive race to the bottom of the price schedule. The cost structure of railway enterprises, which also influenced a great
many other decisions, accounts for this tendency. Railways carried very
large, fixed-capital burdens in the form of roadbed, track, and equipment
that had to be paid for regardless of the volume of business. Any revenue
over and above variable costs such as fuel and labor remained desirable, even
if the company operated at a loss, since without that income, it would incur
even greater losses. In an unrelenting rate war, competitors often cut rates
below operating costs to keep paying traffic flowing over their lines.[53]

Alternatively, the SMR might use its own port facilities at Yingk'ou, to
which it maintained a rail connection by way of a spur from Tashihch'iao
station, rather than Dairen as an outlet for soy. Such a step would kill two
birds with one stone. First, since the distance from Mukden to Yingk'ou by
way of the SMR ran 150 miles shorter, it would reduce costs substantially.[54]
Second, it would allow the Japanese to take advantage of Yingk'ou's special
place in soy trade and remove the edge enjoyed by the PMR and the Liao.
However, this approach suffered from several drawbacks. Official Japanese
policy demanded the expansion of railway capacity from Dairen to Mukden
partly for strategic reasons. The government also wanted to promote the development of the Kwantung Leased Territory and had mandated the use of

Dairen as the SMR's principal outlet, although not to the complete exclusion of Yingk'ou, where a substantial Japanese commercial community had established itself. In addition, Dairen offered a far better choice than Yingk'ou for the development of port facilities in the company's own view of long-term business expansion. Its protected waters remained ice-free all year, and its depth accommodated large, ocean-going freighters. Ice rendered Yingk'ou unusable for the three winter months, and its shallowness provided access only to small cargo vessels plying coastal and regional waters. Yingk'ou might suffice for the present, but the future of Manchuria's economic growth lay in the development of Dairen as an international port of call.[55]

In light of these considerations, SMR officials adopted a set of policies aimed at making Dairen an optimally desirable outlet for soy exports. Shippers choosing Dairen over Yingk'ou as a seaport enjoyed several significant advantages that served to offset higher freight charges. Given year-around service, they could ship their goods at times when Yingk'ou remained inaccessible and thus avoid both the costs and risks of stockpiling goods. More important, blue-water freighters serving direct routes between Europe and Asia could call at Dairen, providing bean merchants with direct access to the emerging European market. Greater accessibility would promote the diversification of commerce and open the possibility of establishing regularly scheduled shipping service, ensuring the timely and predictable deliveries vital in the price-sensitive commodity trade. The SMR, in fact, sought to encourage this development by establishing its own maritime shipping division. The attractiveness of Dairen as a port of call, moreover, would eventually invite its use as a regional entrepôt, much like Hong Kong; this, in turn, would promote the development of commodity exchanges and other services of great benefit to those using this outlet. For soybean shippers, not to mention all merchants in the Manchurian trade, Yingk'ou would pale in comparison to Dairen, and the SMR enjoyed a monopoly over access to Dairen.[56]

The creative exploitation of Dairen's superiority as a port alone would go a long way toward enticing even those shippers closely tied to the Yingk'ou business network. The development of attractive, alternative commercial services in the Japanese-controlled port would strengthen its drawing power. Commodity exchanges, banks, insurance agencies, international trading companies, and bonded warehouses would provide bean merchants with access to better prices, wider markets, and new sources of finance, as well as reduce the risks of business. The SMR invited such institutions to Dairen or, when necessary, established its own facilities and pitted the strength of a modern, international commercial network against the traditional system in the soy trade. The inauguration of similar institutions in station towns upstream from Dairen further increased the flow of traffic along the SMR's lines. The establishment of a pooling system for soybean shipments, similar to the arrangements that railways and grain elevator companies in the American Midwest had developed during the late nineteenth century, formed yet another element of the Dairen strategy, although this began only on an experimental basis toward the end of this period. In this system, the SMR graded a bean merchant's shipment and held the goods in common storage, shipping them on the company's own schedule and at its convenience. The merchant received a bill of lading, which he could immediately exchange for beans of the same grade from the company's storage facilities at Dairen or, alternatively, sell the bill as commercial paper and get a quick return. This program would revolutionize the bean trade throughout Manchuria.[57]

The SMR's competitive strategy pitted destinations and associated commercial networks, rather than transportation systems as such, against one another. So long as it offered reasonably competitive costs, the attractions offered by the one and only route to Dairen became irresistible. Indeed, despite its status as a newcomer, the Japanese port quickly took the lead over Yingk'ou in the absolute volume of the soy trade handled. The fact that the demand for soy continued to grow rapidly during these years greatly benefited the SMR, and even Yingk'ou, albeit to a lesser degree, enjoyed gains as a result. Dairen's soy exports grew fourfold between 1907 and 1909, and Yingk'ou's more than doubled. Mitsui Bussan made important inroads in the European market for soy in 1908, and this further improved prospects for the growth of demand. The situation on the supply side, however, was more uncertain and induced SMR managers to begin considering some long-term development strategies.[58]

Given the prevailing level of farming technology, soy cultivation had developed as far as possible in the Liao valley and other areas of southern Manchuria accessible to long-range commercial transportation, and by 1910 the SMR's research analysts had concluded that land suitable for soybean production in the areas south of Mukden had already reached its maximum output. Areas north of Mukden, particularly in the northern reaches of the

SMR's service area such as Kungchuling and Ch'angch'un, offered greater potential, although the latter represented a special case, which we will discuss shortly. In time, however, these outer regions would reach their productive limits as well. Further increases could be achieved only through the introduction of new farming techniques permitting more intensive exploitation of the land. From the perspective of the company's overall income, these prospects raised serious concerns.[59] By 1910, soy products alone had come to account for 47 percent of the railway's gross freight revenues, a substantial share for a single class of agricultural commodity (see Appendix A for statistics on the SMR). More important, soy production drove the growth of the regional commercial economy as a whole and thus affected the business of the railway indirectly as well. Several possible solutions to this problem presented themselves.

One was the active promotion of agricultural development in the regions served by the SMR. The company established agricultural research stations at Liaoyang and Kungchuling in an effort to improve productivity, to disseminate new techniques and experimental seed varieties, and to promote the use of fertilizer. Ishizuka Eizō's team had recommended such measures earlier. The company's agricultural research work also sought new ways to exploit commercially lands unsuitable for soy cultivation, such as stock raising, particularly sheep.[60]

The building of tributary, or feeder, railways offered another solution. With the exception of areas like Kungchuling in the northern reach of the SMR's service area, railways in southern Manchuria had not done a great deal to open new areas to commercial agriculture. For the most part, the SMR and the Liao shared comparable commercial territories. Horse carts continued to carry beans some 150 to 200 miles from Hailung in the east to reach either T'iehling station on the SMR or the nearby river port of T'ungkiangk'ou. The costs of carting across such long distances, although commercially feasible when the price of beans rose high enough, probably provided no more than marginal returns, insufficient to encourage widespread, regular cultivation. The building of railways into these areas would lower transport costs significantly, make bean cultivation more profitable, and encourage expansion. The overall reach of the commercial economy, including trade in textiles and sundries, would also expand as a result. Ishizuka's survey team had recommended feeder lines, particularly on the eastern flank of the SMR.[61] The fact that Chinese authorities planned rail lines on both the eastern and western sides of the Japanese trunk no doubt stimulated interest in feeder development as pre-emptive measures as well. Building new railways, however, lay beyond the purview of SMR managers acting on their own. The pursuit of such an endeavor would require the mobilization of the full resources of the Japanese government, and in this period, the nation's leaders, preoccupied with the task of consolidating what they had already acquired, remained unprepared for such an undertaking. Nonetheless, the company's concerns exerted some pressure to move in this direction in the near future.

Yet another possibility lay in an attempt to reach into the commercial territory of the remaining trunk line of Russia's CER and draw soy traffic from north Manchuria. The SMR's 1910 study on the future of soy production pointed out that although capacity in the south was approaching saturation, the potential in the north remained largely untapped. Indeed, in the not too distant future, north Manchuria would become the true center of soy production in Northeast Asia. Expanding exports of beans, cake, and oil from Vladivostok were signs of this trend. Symptomatic of emerging directions, the SMR's northern terminus of Ch'angch'un had become the single most productive station with respect to soybean shipments, with a large portion of its traffic coming from the north by horse cart (see Table 3.1). The immediate problem confronting any effort to tap this potential, however, lay in working out an agreement with the Russians to allow for connecting soy traffic between the two railway systems. Discussions in 1907 had resulted in accords covering passenger service as well as selected categories of freight. Understandably, however, CER managers showed little interest in sharing the wealth of the rich farmlands in their service area with the SMR, and the Russian railway authorities resisted proposals to extend connecting traffic arrangements to soy and grains. The CER, in fact, had established a special rate schedule for soybeans shipped along the remnant of its southern branch between Ch'angch'un (Kuanchangtzu station) and Harbin. It cost twice as much to ship beans and bean products from Harbin to Ch'angch'un as it did from Ch'angch'un to Harbin. The Russians had apparently adopted a "Vladivostok strategy" comparable to Japan's promotion of Dairen. Repeated negotiations through 1912 failed to produce movement on this issue.[62]

Russian railway policy, however, could only go so far in protecting the CER's soy traffic. Once again, the ubiquitous Manchurian horse cart came

Table 3.1

Soybean and Beancake Shipments from Selected SMR Stations, 1907

Station	Distance from Dairen (mi.)	Tonnage	Ton-mileage	% of total soy ton-mileage
Mukden	248	30,303	7,515,144	7.40
T'iehling	293	44,902	13,156,286	12.95
K'aiyüan	313	22,263	6,968,319	6.86
Ch'angt'u	333	12,014	4,000,662	3.94
Ssup'ingkai	366	16,436	6,015,576	5.92
Kungchuling	399	30,938	12,344,262	12.15
Fanchiat'un	419	7,832	3,281,608	3.23
Mengchiat'un	432	26,216	11,325,312	11.15
Ch'angch'un	438	57,645	25,248,510	24.86
TOTAL (ALL STATIONS)			101,559,262	100.00

NOTE: Ton-mileage calculations assume that all soy products are shipped directly to Dairen.
SOURCES: Calculated from *TKN* 1907, p. 126; mileages from SMR 1, pp. 213–17.

into play. Harbin, about 180 miles north of Ch'angch'un, lay within carting range. Given sufficiently high bean prices, shippers in Harbin might consider using Dairen, bypassing the southern branch of the CER entirely and shipping their goods to Ch'angch'un by cart. South of Harbin, particularly in the areas south of the Sungari River, carting beans to Ch'angch'un presented even fewer difficulties. The SMR's Ch'angch'un station already received a substantial volume of soy through this process. In this context, the potential effectiveness of the Dairen strategy beyond its role in the Liao valley competition became evident. If merchants in Harbin opted for long-distance carting to Ch'angch'un station, the reason, more likely than not, rested in Dairen's advantage as a market destination over Vladivostok. Indeed, Vladivostok suffered from some of the same shortcomings as Yingk'ou with respect to Dairen; it was ice-bound during the winter and was not a regular port of call for international shipping.[63]

Concerns about the future of the soybean economy emerged during this period, but do not appear to have been cause for immediate anxiety. Moreover, although beans and bean products formed crucial elements in the company's business strategy, a wide variety of other commodities contributed to the total volume of its commercial railway traffic. The transportation of miscellaneous goods formed half or more of the company's traffic during this period. The commodities carried included a range of goods produced and consumed in Manchuria, such as timber, fresh meat and fish, kaoliang (Chinese sorghum), and salt from the evaporating fields of Kwantung. Imported goods brought in through Dairen, such as textiles, tobacco, and sundry goods, although a relatively small part of the total volume, played a vital role in balancing outbound traffic with inbound flows. Because of the considerable construction work during this period, materials for the company's own use also constituted a significant component of freight.[64]

The SMR provided passenger service as well, and for the benefit of Japanese and Western travelers, the company maintained lavishly appointed first-class cars, along with the Yamato Hotel network. The SMR also created a special, low-cost, fourth-class category that made use of box cars that would have otherwise returned north empty after discharging their cargoes in Dairen. Fourth-class service aimed primarily at facilitating the movement of "coolie" labor and settlers from North China. As is the case with many long-distance lines, passenger service represented a secondary source of net income. Freight generated the larger part of profits.[65]

The SMR's involvement in the coal business warrants special attention. Coal formed a major component of the freight traffic. Volume grew steadily, and as a single commodity, it stood second only to soy in its contribution to railway revenues, accounting for roughly 10 percent of freight receipts during this period. Its unique importance, however, stemmed from the fact that the SMR owned the Fushun colliery, the principal source of coal for this traffic. The company engaged in mining, hauling, and selling coal, and this allowed for strategies taking advantage of vertical integration. Freight charges made up the larger part of the market price of this commodity, roughly two-thirds of the dockside price at Dairen. The bulk of the company's earnings in the coal business thus came from transportation, a situation that made the SMR a formidable competitor in the East Asian market. By reducing freight charges, it could undersell its competitors by a wide margin when confronted with price wars. Given the particular structure of railway costs, the company might consider steep price reductions, since hauling coal at below cost remained better than not moving it at all.[66]

Some policymakers and business interests regarded the ability of the SMR to undersell in this manner, coupled with the fact that its colliery operations enjoyed low production costs of ¥1.5–2.0 per ton, as a serious threat to Japan's domestic coal industry. A National Railway Board report prepared in 1912 noted complaints from Japanese business interests about the fact that the SMR sold coal at a higher price in Mukden (¥6.80 per ton), roughly twenty miles from the Fushun colliery, than it did in Yokohama (¥6.20 per ton), despite the additional cost of transporting the coal some 270 miles by rail and nearly 1,200 nautical miles by sea. Between 1909 and 1912, the SMR undersold its domestic Japanese competitors in Singapore, an export market of growing importance to Asian coal producers, by a full yen per ton.[67]

Japanese producers depended on export markets in China and Southeast Asia, and they had long worried about the development of a coal-mining industry in China. As early as 1876, Masuda Takashi of Mitsui Bussan, noting the discovery of large fields in North China and Manchuria, had quite frankly recommended a policy of dumping: "We must step up the price war and hinder the development of a coal industry in China. Thus will the demand for our country's coal grow all the more." Ishizuka's survey team had precisely this attitude in mind when it recommended in late 1905 that the Fushun colliery remain in government hands rather than being sold to private interests as some favored. The authors of the report took note of Mitsui's inquiries about Fushun at the time. They suspected that the reason for this interest lay not in developing production but in keeping the Manchurian colliery from threatening Mitsui's own mining interests. The concern proved well founded. During the deliberations of the SMR's Organizing Committee in the summer of 1906, representatives of the coal industry, including Mitsui Mining, called for the complete separation of mining from railway operations and opposed in principle the idea of combined management, despite their own participation in business conglomerates that would later be known as "zaibatsu." The committee rejected this proposal.[68]

The SMR, however, could not entirely ignore the interests of Japanese coal producers. Partly in an effort to address this issue, the company adopted a policy that outlined three priorities for the use of Fushun coal. It gave first preference to internal use, as fuel for powering locomotives and company steamships and for heating offices and station facilities. This category also included the generation of gas and electricity for municipalities under company administration. As a second priority, coal production would meet the general demand within Manchuria, north as well as south, generated by small-scale industry, other railways, and heating and electrical power needs. Exports were the third and lowest level of priority, covering any coal "left over." As it turned out, by 1910, this residual quantity amounted to one-third of total production. Exports would continue to rise and remained a major source of tension between the SMR and Japan's zaibatsu for much of the company's history.[69]

A final way in which the coal business played a significant role in the development of the company's business strategy lay in providing an impetus for diversification. The SMR saw a need not only to diversify traffic and reduce its dependence on soy but also to move into entirely new income-generating operations. Although coal remained subordinate to railway operations during this period, the mining and marketing of this commodity gradually developed into a business in its own right. Its use in generating gas and electrical power and as both fuel and raw material for industry offered promise. Significantly, the company's research facilities began experiments in coal-based chemical production that would bear fruit shortly before and during World War I.[70]

Other sources of diversification emerging during this start-up phase would see fruition in later years. The Dairen strategy, for example, drew the SMR into a variety of supporting business activities in finance, insurance, warehousing, and shipping. The company would spin off its maritime shipping department as a wholly owned subsidiary known as the Dairen Steamship Company in 1915. The large complex of ancillary operations required to maintain railway services in Manchuria, which possessed little modern industry on which the company could draw, provided another important impetus. Circumstances in the territory demanded a high degree of technological self-sufficiency on the part of the SMR. For example, it maintained its own extensive and well-equipped workshops, which not only engaged in repair and maintenance work but also assembled rolling stock. By 1914, these in-house engineering facilities had developed the capacity to manufacture locomotives and began accepting contracts not only for rolling stock from other railways in China but for industrial machinery. The tension between the comparatively high technology of the railway and the rough frontier environment in which it operated forced the company to become, as one Japanese writer put it, a Manchurian "jack of all trades." This orientation would subsequently create the opportunity for fairly wide-ranging diversification.[71]

The problem of operating in a frontier environment had important implications for the SMR's management of the Railway Zone. Policymakers who thought in terms of colonizing the territory placed great importance on this strip of Japanese-administered land deep within the Manchurian heartland. At the same time, however, the Zone also occupied a special place in business administration. In order to build and operate a railway in this environment, the SMR not only needed to bring skilled technicians and workers from Japan but also to keep them in Manchuria. For this reason, management created extensive facilities for its Japanese employees, such as housing complexes, recreational clubs, health clinics, and shops catering to Japanese tastes. Colonization strategies promoting Japanese settlement and the SMR's need to maintain "company towns" thus dovetailed rather neatly.[72]

Profits and Policy

Mutually reinforcing trends between the pursuit of profit and the implementation of imperialist programs emerged in areas other than the building of company towns. Strategies for business growth and for colonization overlapped to a significant degree. Both stressed long-term economic development. The promotion of regional growth, which fueled railway traffic, also expanded possibilities for trade. A Japanese agency guiding this development would facilitate the establishment, to the extent that a watchful international community might allow, of a preferential market for Japanese goods. The building of Dairen and station towns in the interior generated opportunities for Japanese enterprise and employment for settlers. Industrial diversification would expand such opportunities further. The SMR's efforts to broaden its traffic base would lead to new ways to exploit the territory's natural resources. The company's research and development activities, conducted on the one hand for purely business reasons, clearly supported on the other hand the work of "scientific colonization" and mobilization planning.[73]

Competition in the soy business also entailed significantly more than the company's attempts to acquire paying traffic. It represented a struggle between Japanese and Chinese commercial power over the region's economic life blood. Whoever ruled the soy trade would acquire a major influence in shaping the future of the territory. Consider, for example, the fact that both railway charges and the taxes of the region's provincial governments competed for the same margin between the market price of soy beans and the cost of production. Although it is true that a similar case can be made for the relationship between business earnings and tax revenues in general, it is important to bear in mind the particular situation in Manchuria where two entities, a Japanese railway company and the Chinese regional state, operating on comparable scales, contested the same narrow base of agricultural surplus. Taxes and railway revenues, in fact, financed rival programs of colonization.[74]

Competition for traffic also constituted a struggle over the integration and organization of the territory—over whether it would develop along an axis formed by the Liao River valley, with Yingk'ou as its anchor point, or along one defined by the Japanese "railway valley," with its gateway at Dairen. The economics of railway operations gave life to the paper partition of the territory agreed upon by Japan and Russia in the accords of 1907. Essentially ignoring Chinese administrative boundaries, a north Manchuria, dominated by Russia and linked to Vladivostok, and a south Manchuria, dominated by Japan and linked to Dairen, had begun to take shape.

By simply pursuing profit and following the logic of business administration, the SMR accomplished much of what policymakers favoring an imperialist strategy of colonization desired. This confluence underscores the basic capabilities inherent in railways as instruments of territorial power. Intended or not, railways managed as business enterprises have often become major factors in the power structure of a regional community, playing a part in the management of a territory and shaping its future. As noted above, the issue of railways as private enterprises was a major source of political conflict, with battles in the United States fought between populists and big business over the boundaries of public interest and private power. This pattern suggests that the conflict between Japanese encroachment and Chinese resistance in Manchuria involved dynamics that transcended the politics of imperialism. The inherent "colonial" propensities of railway enterprise, moreover, served to deepen the dilemma of would-be moderates on the question of Japanese imperial expansion in the territory. Policymakers of such a persuasion might repudiate the notion of the SMR as a colonial corporation and insist that the company confine itself to the business of running a railway. That business, however, constituted the greater part of the colonization process, and this made it difficult for moderates to escape complicity in the schemes of their more aggressively expansionist colleagues.

Harmony between railway management and colonization and, more broadly, between profits and policy, of course, had limits. In the final analysis, sound business strategy and empire-building operated within different frameworks of logic. Tensions and conflict inevitably emerged, and indeed, during this period we begin to see the formation of fault lines that would become thematic in the history of this venture and repeatedly place company managers at odds with soldiers and diplomats. Early cases of conflict fell into two general categories.

The more straightforward of the two stemmed from specific policy demands that, in the judgment of business managers, lay beyond their ability to underwrite. In general, the company's supervisors in Tokyo agreed that the ability to meet costs without compromising business health defined limits to any policy tasks assigned the SMR. The army's planners, for example, would like to have seen the immediate double-tracking of the line from Dairen to Ch'angch'un. However, they acknowledged the undesirability of placing excessive financial burdens on the company during its start-up period and agreed to wait until the growth of revenues could support such an undertaking. As a result, the initial phase of double-tracking remained restricted to the segment between Dairen and Suchiat'un, the station just south of Mukden from which the branch to Fushun diverged. Heavy coal traffic justified this project in business terms.[75] Not all situations, however, allowed for such clear-cut compromises. Although no policymakers demanded that the company spend resources it did not have, some programmatic initiatives required that the SMR undertake business risks, divert resources from more remunerative areas, or add to its capital burden, thus reducing its profitability. In these situations, there emerged considerable room for dispute, and one such conflict arose over the reconstruction of the Antung–Mukden line.

The army considered the rebuilding of this branch railway as a permanent, standard-gauge line indispensable to its defense plans, and the government as a whole adopted a non-negotiable position in discussions with the Chinese. SMR managers, however, took a rather different stand and argued that, from a business perspective, the project warranted serious reconsideration. In 1908, while negotiations remained in deadlock, they recommended a rerouting of the Korean connection southward, from Antung to Tashihch'iao rather than to Mukden. The terrain along the proposed southern route was more level, in contrast to the mountainous region through which an Antung–Mukden line would pass, and entailed considerably lower construction costs. The Organizing Committee had originally estimated the northern route would run about ¥22 million, but SMR analysts believed that the actual figure was closer to ¥37 million. Moreover, company managers did not expect much traffic between Korea and Manchuria, and this made it difficult to justify such an investment in business terms. As a commercial proposition, an Antung–Tashihch'iao line might not perform any better than a line to Mukden, but at least it represented a substantially lower burden.[76]

The SMR's recommendations faced adamant opposition from the army. Military planners argued that for strategic purposes the further north the connection between Antung and the SMR the better, since it would provide more direct access to the staging areas for a northern campaign. They also pointed out that the more territory encompassed by Japanese railways, the greater the control that could be exercised in the region. Army representatives reminded the SMR that its primary mission was not profits but the national interest. The company scheme also ran into opposition from the Foreign Ministry. In the view of diplomats, who planned on issuing an ultimatum to break the impasse, reopening negotiations for a change of route would only give the Chinese additional opportunities for obstruction.[77]

Faced with a hostile consensus in Tokyo, railway managers had little choice but to comply. Construction began in 1909. It turned out that the building costs ran substantially lower than SMR officials had projected and, at ¥25 million yen, came close to the original estimate. Concerns about low traffic volume, however, remained justified. As a temporary light rail operating between 1907 and 1911, this route steadily lost money. Following the completion of construction in 1911, revenues exceeded operating expenditures but only by a small margin, insufficient to carry its investment burden.[78]

Disputes of this kind over the costs of specific policy initiatives had the potential to become heated. Nonetheless, they remained resolvable insofar as they involved clearly delimited disagreements over costs and business judgments. A second category of conflict between profits and policy, in which the general trend of business strategy ran counter to the fundamental thrust of programmatic goals, proved much more difficult to manage. Such tensions raised deeper questions about the achievability of some of Japan's long-term goals in Manchuria within the boundaries of the SMR's mandate of operating at a profit.

The SMR's labor policies, for example, tended to dampen prospects for any large-scale immigration of Japanese to Manchuria based on the "pull" of employment opportunities. Although not specifically mandated to do so, most policymakers as well as the interested general public expected that, as a quasi-official Japanese corporation, the SMR would preferentially hire Japanese employees. At first, the company appears to have attempted such an approach, but in a major cost-cutting initiative in 1908, it began replacing Japanese workers in lower skill categories with local Chinese. With the exception of technical and managerial posts, company managers targeted the creation of a labor force roughly half Chinese. In view of the large wage differential, this labor policy requires little explanation from an economic perspective. At the time, the average daily wage of a Japanese laborer was ¥0.99, whereas that of a Chinese worker was only ¥0.38. Moreover, in the estimates of managers, Chinese workers had comparable abilities and work discipline. They justified their policies quite frankly in the following terms:

In hiring roughly half our workers from among the Chinese, it is not without some reluctance that we set aside the advice of those who argue that Japanese businesses in Manchuria should, in order to advance our settlement policy, employ mainly Japanese workers. However, it is hardly necessary to point out that business in Manchuria can make good use of Chinese labor, which is generally acknowledged throughout the world for its low price. Our company, moreover, must also consider the fact that our shippers are Chinese, as are many of the others with whom we do business. For these reasons, we must employ a substantial number of Chinese workers. We have, as a result, not only made savings on our payroll costs but also benefited in other ways.

Managers also pointed out that the Russians had attempted, at first, to adopt a Russians-only hiring policy on the CER but had quickly abandoned the effort.[79]

To be sure, any settlement program that relied heavily on the SMR to provide direct employment opportunities suffered from serious weaknesses. Although the company accounted for some 18,000 jobs in 1910, Gotō and other proponents of large-scale settlement thought in terms of half a million or more immigrants within a decade. In view of such goals, direct employment by the SMR could not have contributed more than a small portion of the work opportunities needed to sustain such a population. However, the same reasoning that led company managers to adopt this labor policy would have applied to any prospective Japanese employer in Manchuria, and in

fact, a private enterprise with no special obligation to the Japanese government would have faced fewer constraints in hiring a Chinese workforce.
These circumstances would limit job prospects in Manchuria for Japanese
other than the self-employed (see Appendix B for population statistics).[80]

The SMR's relations with independent Japanese businesses seeking to
establish themselves in Manchuria generated problems as well. Although
policymakers expected the company to assist such ventures, the SMR had
no incentive, from a business perspective, to deal preferentially with Japanese
enterprises. Indeed, its defense of its labor practices underscores the fact that
the Chinese were its most important clients. Chinese merchants shipped
soybeans and, in turn, ordered cotton cloth, matches, and other goods that
the SMR brought in from Dairen. Only at the very top of the distribution
hierarchy, where international connections proved essential, did Japanese
enterprise come to play a special role in the company's strategy. If anything,
the SMR confronted clear disincentives in giving preferential treatment to
Japanese clients and implicitly discriminating against the Chinese.[81]

This orientation toward business relationships also appears to have applied to Western concerns active in Manchuria as well. The complaints of
the Japanese-owned East Asia Tobacco to the Japanese consul at Yingk'ou
about the fact that the SMR's rate policies assisted its chief rival in the region, British American Tobacco, is an illustrative case. The Foreign Ministry's inquiry to the SMR elicited the response that the company offered no
special support to British American. Any shipper working out of Dairen received preferential rates. East Asia Tobacco happened to be based in
Yingk'ou.[82]

Complaints from the Japanese merchant community at Yingk'ou, apparently not uncommon, cast the Dairen strategy in another light. As suggested
earlier, the competition between Dairen and Yingk'ou formed part of a
larger struggle between Japanese and Chinese commercial power in Manchuria. From the perspective of the SMR's business strategy, however, the
fact that the Japanese controlled one port and the Chinese, the other, represented an incidental circumstance. Any one working out of Dairen, whether
Japanese, Chinese, or Westerner, received favorable consideration. Any
commercial enterprise based in Yingk'ou, including Japanese businesses, received discriminatory treatment.[83]

Economic relations with Korea presented another problem. The prospect of creating a regional trade and currency sphere in Northeast Asia by taking advantage of cross-border railway connections formed an important element of Japanese thinking about Manchuria. Although military considerations dominated plans for railway connections between Manchuria and Korea, civilian economic policy also contributed to the government's strong stand on the Antung–Mukden line. Antung lay directly across the Yalu River from Sinuijiu, the northern terminus of the primary Korean trunk line originating at Pusan. Some of the promoters of railway integration, in fact, believed that Korea and the port of Pusan should occupy the role played by Kwantung and Dairen as the anchor of Japan's Manchurian railway system. Not only did Korea represent a more important possession than Kwantung, but connections made through the peninsula offered a more meaningful way of integrating the empire economically. Given the proximity of Pusan to the Japanese ports of Shimonoseki and Moji, some saw the possibility of linking the Japanese, Korean, and Manchurian railway systems into a single transportation system.[84]

Although the issue of a "Pusan strategy" failed to receive active consideration during this period, the anticipated completion of reconstruction work on the Antung–Mukden line in 1911 encouraged discussion of the idea. Predictably, the SMR opposed the scheme. From a business perspective, an attempt to replace Dairen with Pusan presented a number of problems, the most important of which lay in the additional distance. The route from Mukden to Pusan was 500 miles longer than the one to Dairen. Every ton of freight shipped from the Manchurian interior by way of the Korean route would incur an additional 500 miles of railway charges. This added distance, in fact, exceeded the entire 430-mile length of the SMR trunk between Ch'angch'un and Dairen and would effectively double the cost of shipping soybeans from the SMR's northern terminus. Given the fact that railway charges constituted the largest part of the price of Fushun coal, exports out of Pusan could not hope to compete in the Asian market. The SMR's extensive investment in Dairen also provided a motivation for opposition, and as we shall see, the issue would erupt into a major dispute in 1913.[85]

Labor policy, the issue of preferential treatment of Japanese businesses, and the impending problem of a Pusan strategy reflected fundamental incompatibilities in the directions demanded by profits and by policy. As a result, they proved less tractable than more straightforward disputes involving discrete construction and spending decisions. In theory, subsidies or other forms of direct government support might soften the stringent demands of sound business management. However, if the government insisted on maintaining the principle of self-sufficiency and limiting spending to what the SMR could underwrite through its own revenues, business logic imposed clear limits on policy initiatives. Indeed, a firm commitment to such a position would ensure that in the long run, *raison d'affaires* would prevail over *raison d'état* in managing the SMR.

The conflicts between profit and policy emerging during this period would become recurrent themes in the politics of Japanese Manchuria in years to come. At the same time, the gravity of these problems at this stage should not be overstated. Given that these first years constituted a period of shakedown and consolidation, expectations in the area of programmatic achievements remained modest. In defense, the one area in which policy goals carried some urgency, the SMR had met the basic requirements, albeit with some grumbling. Indeed, compliance with military construction specifications, not to mention the building of the Antung–Mukden line, imposed no small burden on a railway enterprise in its start-up phase, creating a substantial excess capacity that, in turn, set the bar for profitability considerably higher as compared to an ordinary commercial railway. All things considered, the SMR's ability to turn a profit in its first year and keep its accounts in the black thereafter represented a significant accomplishment in itself (see Appendix A). The fact that, after a brief grace period, the SMR began paying dividends on government-owned shares in 1909, which likely pleased fiscal conservatives, marked an important milestone. Although the payments remained limited to a modest 2.5 percent, the government owned stock with a face value of ¥100 million, and these dividend payments nearly sufficed to cover the annual deficits, excluding military expenditures, of the Kwantung Government-General. By the end of this period, the Manchurian venture found itself well on the way toward financial self-sufficiency.[86] Policymakers no doubt appreciated the difficulty of the achievement. Ishizuka's team had expressed confidence in 1905 that the railway would pay, but the expectation remained untested until actual operations began. The SMR's accomplishment, indeed, stands out in comparison to the generally weak business performance of railways in China during the early twentieth century. The Russian CER, for example, fared far more poorly during this era than its Japanese offspring.[87]

An attempt to assess the overall profitability of the SMR poses difficult problems. As a percentage of total paid-up capital, including the value of Russian properties turned over to the company, which represented the government's share of investment, clear profits amounted to no more than 3 percent during this period. Corporate accounts separated capital investment according to operating departments: railways, mines, harbors, workshops, and the Zone. Although it is possible to derive estimates based on these data, they lend themselves to misleading interpretations. The railway could not operate without harbors, workshops, or many of the facilities maintained by the department for Zone management, and to calculate railway returns based on this method of breakdown would overstate actual profitability. Nonetheless, many observers came to regard the SMR, with some justification, as one of the most prosperous railway companies in China from early in its history (see Appendix A).[88]

The SMR also quickly acquired a reputation as one of the best-managed and technologically sophisticated railway operations in Asia, a perception that company managers went to considerable lengths to cultivate. A critical letter in 1907 to a Scottish newspaper from a traveler who complained of poor management and unsanitary conditions on the SMR raised serious concerns in the Foreign Ministry.[89] Prestige represented an important consideration in managing Manchuria. The SMR specifically designed the Yamato Hotel network, run at a steady loss, to promote the image of the Japanese bringing high civilization to the rough Manchurian frontier. Natsume Sōseki's account of his 1909 visit to Manchuria points to the extraordinary pride that many Japanese officials in the territory took in introducing the latest technologies to Manchuria. He noted the unmistakably Western facades of the SMR's buildings and the grand scale of its facilities. Sōseki appears to have grown weary of the guided tour and complained that his friend, SMR Governor Nakamura (Gotō Shinpei's successor), "treated [me] as a country bumpkin" (*inakamono atsukai*) on his first visit to the big city. The novelist resolved to stop asking Nakamura about the SMR's works to avoid giving the governor opportunities to boast about the company's feats. Nonetheless Sōseki seems to have been impressed. Like other industrializing peoples of the late nineteenth and early twentieth centuries, the Japanese regarded the railway as a civilizing force. To the people of Meiji Japan, the steam locomotive became a symbol of their own modern transformation.[90] In Manchuria, it emerged as the emblem of their nation's imperial mission.

On the whole, it would be fair to say that the Japanese succeeded resoundingly in their efforts to consolidate the military, legal, and financial machinery of expansion in Manchuria between 1907 and 1911. In each of these spheres of activity, they came to enjoy as secure a position as they might have expected. As railway imperialists and as railway managers, they had performed as well as any of their foreign rivals in China, if not better, despite adverse circumstances. Policymakers had good reason to be satisfied, and these achievements easily overshadowed any incipient problems. The completion of reconstruction work on the Antung–Mukden line in 1911 offered a sense of closure and accomplishment to those who had dedicated themselves to securing Japan's tenure in Manchuria. With the annexation of Korea a year earlier, the Japanese had laid firm foundations for empire in Northeast Asia.

These accomplishments, however, meant only that the imperialists had cleared the decks for a new phase of activity. Indeed, the real work of pursuing programmatic aims that, in the view of many, entailed colonizing Manchuria could begin. During the course of this period, elements in a second agenda were already taking shape. The question of settlement, including the issue of broader land rights in Manchuria, would require serious attention. Immigration disputes with the United States, resolved provisionally with the Gentleman's Agreement of 1908, had heightened interest in this problem. If Japanese found themselves unwelcome in places like the United States, Canada, and "White Australia," where could they go? Foreign Minister Komura saw an answer in Manchuria. In a foreign-policy program laid out in 1908 and articulated in a speech to the Diet in 1909, he promoted his view that Japanese should pull back from attempts to emigrate to Western countries and their colonial possessions and turn instead to opportunities in East Asia. His argument helped spark broad enthusiasm for the idea of settling Manchuria. And if Japanese sought to populate this frontier, to sink roots and stake their futures, then the nation's claims in the territory required further expansion and refinement. Foreign Minister Komura made it clear that Japan's holdings, which treaty agreements guaranteed for only limited terms, would have to be extended in perpetuity at an opportune moment.[91] Japan thus confronted no shortage of new tasks in Manchuria. An imperialist's work was never truly done.

FOUR

The Chinese Revolution, the Taishō Political Crisis, and the Debate over Manchuria, 1911–1914

Had Japanese policy in Manchuria continued uninterrupted along the course charted during the first few years, a major new thrust after 1911 would not have come as a surprise. Indeed, given the final settlement of Korea's status through annexation, imperialists, with appetites far from sated, could direct greater attention to the lands across the Yalu River. Empire-building, however, enjoyed no more than modest progress between 1911 and 1914. The outbreak of revolution in China in October 1911 was one factor that dampened the forward momentum of Japanese expansion in the territory. Although the environment during the early months of the revolution encouraged a large number of plots and schemes, none of them bore fruit. Adventurist pressures, moreover, receded with the establishment of the Chinese Republic in early 1912, which closed the door to easy opportunities.

Another, more important factor slowing the imperialist advance was the rise of dissenting voices within Japan. The Chinese Revolution and the Great Power response had brought to the surface undercurrents in international relations in East Asia that had been increasing in strength since the end of the Russo-Japanese War. To a growing number of Japanese, the imperialist premises that had justified Meiji expansion were no longer as cogent as they had seemed in 1905. Many Foreign Ministry officials, moderate bureaucrats, Diet members, and navy leaders began calling openly for a reexamination of the nation's external policies, particularly toward Manchuria. Those who had been critical of continental expansionism from the start but who had kept their counsel during the early years of the Manchurian venture became less reticent about voicing their objections in this climate. The escalation of interservice competition, which led to a major domestic crisis in late 1912 and early 1913, added intensity to the debate. As the political bargain embodied in the Imperial Defense Plan of 1907 unraveled, arguments about Manchuria became inextricably entangled in the dispute over the relative importance of dreadnoughts and infantry divisions. The death of the Meiji emperor and the inauguration of the Taishō reign in 1912 heightened the sense among many Japanese that a time of great change had come upon them and created a psychological opportunity for advocates of reform in domestic and foreign affairs to press their case.

In the light of subsequent events during World War I, any trend toward moderation in Manchuria emerging during this period might appear transient. Nonetheless, developments between 1911 and 1914 marked the beginning of a longer era in which Japanese imperialism would face growing adversity at home and abroad. Those favoring an activist program of empire-building, however, refused to retreat, as they demonstrated during this period. Instead, recognizing that even the commitment in Manchuria could no longer be taken for granted, they redoubled their efforts to keep the nation on an imperialist course.

Japanese Imperialism and the Chinese Revolution

Developments during the four months of violent upheaval in China between October 1911 and the agreement between Ch'ing loyalists and rebels that created the Chinese Republic in January 1912 would seem to suggest a markedly aggressive turn in Japanese policy. A broad spectrum of Japanese leaders, civilian and military alike, seriously contemplated radical interventionist measures. All agreed that the situation in China was grave. Up to this point, policy calculations regarding Manchuria and China south of the Wall, as well as the larger framework of international relations in East Asia, had assumed the persistence of a stable but weak Ch'ing dynasty. That assumption no longer held. Japanese policymakers also agreed that insofar as possible Japan should manage the outcome to its advantage. Both services gave serious consideration to direct military intervention, if only for the purpose of protecting Japanese nationals and their property. Consensus broke down, however, over the specific course of action to take. Some proposed to support the ruling dynasty, which was likely to collapse without foreign assistance. Others favored backing the rebels, who enjoyed considerable popularity in Japan. Moreover, partition, like it or not, loomed as a possibility, especially if loyalists and rebels found themselves in a stalemate. The Ch'ing dynasty might retain control of the north, and the rebels might gain possession of the south. Given the possibility of such an outcome, the wisest course, yet others argued, entailed cultivating both sides.[1]

As might be predicted, the army emerged as the most vocal proponent of large-scale political and military intervention. In view of its efforts to reaffirm and elaborate on its continental mission, the outbreak of revolution represented a timely development and vindicated warnings emanating from the army earlier that year. The operations plans of the general staff drafted in May had anticipated precisely such an upheaval. Russian involvement in the simultaneous emergence of an independence movement in Outer Mongolia lent further credence to the army's assessment of the strategic situation and confirmed that Japan's old adversary had not abandoned its imperial aspirations in the East.[2] Under these circumstances, the situation in China and Northeast Asia posed a danger that might well warrant pre-emptive action.

At the same time, however, some army officers evinced a strong tendency to see more opportunity than danger in these developments. Turmoil in China offered a once-in-a-century chance to strengthen Japan's influence both north and south of the Wall dramatically. In their view, partition constituted a desirable outcome rather than a threat to Japan's interests. The intelligence division of the Army General Staff played an important part in concocting some of the more audacious schemes along these lines, such as the idea of organizing a Manchurian independence movement in late 1911 and early 1912. As Kitaoka Shin'ichi has demonstrated in his study of the army's continental policies, such thinking reflected an adventurist streak within a sector of the officer corps and ran particularly strong among intelligence officers and others assigned regular postings in China. It also reflected factional strife within the service. Officers of the adventurist persuasion harbored long-standing grievances against the clique politics that influenced promotions, and their complaints on these matters often manifested themselves in criticism leveled against the "soft" continental policies of their seniors. A weak and incompetent China policy, to their thinking, offered evidence that the promotion system in the army favored connections rather than knowledge, experience, and talent.[3]

The window of opportunity for a major interventionist initiative, however, proved relatively small. The government of Prime Minister Saionji Kinmochi, pressed with demands and recommendations from a variety of directions, remained indecisive through the peak months of the upheaval, and by early 1912, rebels and loyalists had arrived at a compromise through British mediation and without any major Japanese contribution. The Ch'ing emperor would abdicate, and a republic would be created, as advocated by the rebels. However, Yüan Shih-k'ai (1859–1916), the leader of the loyalist side, would become the provisional chief executive of the new state, and his allies would retain positions of authority in the new government. These arrangements failed to satisfy either side in China, but they did suit the powers, particularly the British, whose primary concerns lay in maintaining political stability in China and protecting their established rights. By meeting these requirements, the Yüan regime would receive the blessings of the international community.

In Japan, this outcome produced bitter recrimination against the Saionji cabinet for having allowed opportunity to slip through its fingers. Even those who opposed adventurist policies believed that Japan could have played a more active role in the settlement. Some expressed considerable resentment toward Britain for having acted without consulting Tokyo. Nonetheless, although a few radicals still believed that the door to aggressive action remained open, most responsible leaders acknowledged that the time for a major policy coup in either China proper or Manchuria had passed by the spring of 1912. For better or worse, the installation of the Yüan government had restored some semblance of the status quo ante, and leaders in Tokyo settled down to a more sober deliberation of policy.[4]

Moderate Leadership and the Taishō Coalition

For some Japanese leaders, the restoration of order in China and the installation of a government committed to maintaining relations with the Great Powers like those that had prevailed under the Ch'ing dynasty meant that Japan could resume its pre-revolution course in Manchuria. Yüan's regime needed Japan's goodwill and could not easily resist demands for new rights. Although the opportunity for great policy coups had passed, the climate remained ripe for more conventional initiatives in concession hunting. The other powers would likely do the same. Japanese leaders of this persuasion believed that the nation's agenda ought to include at least a revision of existing tenure agreements governing Kwantung and the trunk of the SMR, along with the recently completed Antung–Mukden branch. The lease on Kwantung was scheduled to expire in 1923. The original Russo-Chinese agreement on the CER allowed China to purchase the railway 36 years after the date of completion. This provision remained unmodified in the hand-over to Japan, and this gave China the option of recovering the SMR conces-sion in 1939. As an expedient, Japanese negotiators had agreed to an even earlier date for reversion of the Antung–Mukden line, 1923. The activist trend within leadership circles called for the extension of all leases and ten-ure agreements to 99 years. In addition, this group pressed for new railway and mining rights, provisions to facilitate immigration, such as the right to lease and purchase land outside Kwantung and the Railway Zone, and measures to promote the economic integration of Korea and Manchuria. The army appeared particularly anxious to pursue a forward policy in the territory, no doubt, in part, to assuage disappointment within its ranks over lost opportunities.[5] Concerns about Russia, of course, persisted, regardless of the settlement in China. Russia had de facto placed Outer Mongolia un-der its military protection at the beginning of 1912. This situation required strategic countermeasures, especially in Inner Mongolia.

The Foreign Ministry, in contrast, expressed a strong disinclination to-ward any major initiatives at this time. Some diplomats might have agreed in principle with the goals outlined by imperial activists, but even they stressed the inappropriateness of the timing. The new Chinese government would likely resist further demands from Japan at this point, so soon after the set-tlement of outstanding issues associated with the Treaty of Peking. Yüan himself had little reason to look toward Tokyo with favor, not least because the Japanese had made no real contribution to putting him in power. Pur-suing new concessions under these conditions would require exerting heavy-handed and, perhaps, destabilizing pressure on the recently installed regime at a time when other powers were seeking to shore it up. An aggressive ini-tiative at this time would put Japan at odds with the international commu-nity as a whole.[6]

Japanese diplomats acknowledged that Russia's moves in Outer Mongo-lia required some response. Accordingly, the Foreign Ministry opened talks with St. Petersburg in order to clarify the two nations' positions in Inner Mongolia. Discussions resulted in a third pact, signed in 1912, which ex-tended the demarcation of northern and southern spheres to the meridian of 116.27°, which also formed the western boundary for Japan's Manchurian sphere (see Map 3.1, p. 109). Diplomats warned, however, that this under-standing did not constitute a license for aggressive initiatives within Japan's portion of the territory. In fact, such action would only encourage the perception of the pact in the international community as an act of Russo-Japanese collusion against Chinese sovereignty. The Foreign Ministry also cautioned against comparing Japan's position in Manchuria to Russia's in Outer Mongolia. International treaties recognized Manchuria as a part of China. The situation in Outer Mongolia remained poorly defined, and the powers generally regarded China's status in that territory at best as suzerain.[7]

The Foreign Ministry and others in the government favored a general review of priorities in China at this time. The events of late 1911 and early 1912 pointed to the need for a broader and more comprehensive approach to promoting Japanese interests in China both north and south of the Wall. Japan could not afford to pursue a narrow and inflexible "Manchuria first" policy. Japan had substantial commercial interests in other parts of China. In the economically crucial field of textile exports, for example, markets south of the wall accounted for over 60 percent of Japanese cotton cloth and yarn sales abroad, whereas Manchuria took in only 15 percent. Excessive demands in Manchuria might hurt this trade, just as the Antung-Mukden dispute of 1909 had triggered widespread anti-Japanese boycotts. They would also adversely affect negotiations over rights to exploit vital resources, such as iron ore at the Hanyehp'ing complex in the Yangtze valley on which Japan's emerging iron and steel industry depended. Abe Moritarō (1872–1913), the chief of the Foreign Ministry's Political Affairs Bureau and one of the principal architects of the ministry's China policy during this era, warned that "strident voices raised over Manchuria" might well compromise the nation's interests south of the Wall.[8]

Moreover, new developments had emerged in Great Power relations with China. The powers planned to back the Yüan regime with substantial financial assistance in the form of the so-called Reorganization Loans. Shoring up the regime and helping it consolidate its debts formed the ostensible purpose of this aid. Some of the participants, however, apparently intended to use the loans to exert political leverage over the new government. Discussions included such terms as installing foreign advisors in various government agencies. Foreign Ministry officials urged Japanese participation in the loan plan. With a new game in Great Power competition in China afoot, Japan could not afford to sideline itself. Insofar as initiatives in Manchuria might complicate Japan's relationship with Yüan and the powers, self-restraint seemed advisable.[9]

Other considerations also recommended moderation, at least temporarily. By 1909 and 1910, even hard-line imperialist diplomats like Komura Jūtarō had come to believe that, with the resolution of outstanding items from the Treaty of Peking, Japan might think about letting up its pressure on China for a time and issue fewer and more selective demands. The Great Powers seemed to have toned down their policies in China, and Japan could not continue to run roughshod over mounting Chinese hostility. Tokyo might force Peking to accede to its demands, but whether Chinese leaders responsible for such acquiescence would continue to hold their own against sustained popular outrage remained open to question. In retrospect, Itō Hirobumi's warning in 1908 that excessive Japanese pressure might precipitate revolution seemed prophetic. This is not to suggest that Japanese officials acknowledged their own actions as contributing to the downfall of the Ch'ing or that they regarded Chinese nationalism as anything more than a manifestation of the rising forces of chaos. Recent events, nonetheless, offered food for thought. Advocates for moderation did not openly argue for a retreat from Manchuria; rather, they recommended the postponement of any major steps. In view of the uncertainties prevailing in post-revolution China, their case seemed well grounded.

Cogent or not, the Foreign Ministry's arguments alone could not have pushed Japanese policy in a more cautious direction. They did not persuade the army, which continued to step up its demands for activist initiatives in Manchuria and China proper. Developments in domestic politics, however, significantly strengthened advocates of a moratorium on expansion. A new coalition of the navy, a section of the bureaucracy, and the Seiyūkai, the majority party in the Imperial Diet, dominated two of the three cabinets holding office between August 1911 and April 1914. (The third, headed by Katsura Tarō, proved ephemeral and lasted only three months.) This navy-backed coalition held a decidedly unsympathetic opinion of the army's view of empire and national defense and leaned instead in the direction favored by the Foreign Ministry. Although a detailed discussion of domestic political events during this era lies beyond the scope of this study, the nature of this coalition warrants a brief examination.[10]

The navy's primary goal in thrusting itself into the political arena at this juncture was to advance its warship-construction agenda. Recent developments in naval technology had lent urgency to this campaign, but growing perceptions in Japan of a receding Russian threat had also created an opportune political environment to press the case. During this period, navy leaders escalated their efforts and openly called for a revision of the Imperial Defense Plan of 1907. According to one group of prominent naval strategists in 1913:

Our country's finances will not permit an armament program based on army-navy parity. For this reason, we must emphasize a program that will strengthen our international prestige in the Orient with respect to the Western powers. In other words, we must prioritize naval armament, which is a common factor in the power of France, Germany, and the United States, and give second place to the balance of power on land, which is relevant only to relations with Russia.[11]

Advocates of sea power understood, however, that winning support for their dreadnought program would require not only the persuasive power of strategic reasoning but also greater political skill and activism than they had exercised in the past. Although the army enjoyed good political connections, particularly in the person of Yamagata Aritomo, the navy had nothing comparable. True, the army had also encountered difficulty in making its case for arms expansion in 1910 despite Yamagata's backing and the benefit of having Katsura, one of its own, as prime minister. But the fact that the generals even considered pressing for additional infantry divisions at this point, given both their earlier gains and the shifting strategic circumstances, spoke to a confidence, if not audacity, founded on political strength. Minority party leaders in the Diet who favored the idea of sea power had, in fact, criticized the navy for a lack of backbone in its rivalry with the army. Rectifying this situation required more direct participation in the political process, particularly in the formation of cabinets. By 1911, some officers had begun to consider seriously the possibility of engineering the installation of a pro-navy candidate, if not an admiral, possibly Yamamoto Gonbei, as prime minister.[12]

The idea of a pro-navy cabinet appealed to a group within the civilian bureaucracy, described as the "Satsuma clique" based on their common origin in southern Kyushu. The tradition of clique politics in the Japanese government traced itself back to the Restoration movement that had established the Meiji state, which drew its main leaders and much of its rank and file from the Tokugawa domains of Chōshū and Satsuma. Upon assuming power, men from these two domains formed their own political networks and often granted favorable treatment to members of their own groups in filling desirable posts and granting promotions. Of the two cliques, Chōshū, with Yamagata Aritomo as its patron, emerged as the stronger and acquired a dominant position after the turn of the century. Satsuma bureaucrats, like the navy, felt relegated to second place and sought some means of redress. Significantly, the same domain-based cliques also operated within the armed forces, dividing, to a large extent, along service lines. Generals hailing from Chōshū dominated the army, and admirals from Satsuma occupied a comparable place within the navy. Although Satsuma-clique bureaucrats did not necessarily support the warship-construction program, they shared with their domain brethren in the navy a common desire for political changes that might strengthen their influence. Given clique ties, the likelihood that a pro-navy cabinet might also adopt a more pro-Satsuma attitude in bureaucratic politics provided a basis to make common political cause.[13]

The third partner in the coalition, the Seiyūkai, acted out of more complex motives. Under Hara Takashi's leadership, the party had backed a succession of cabinets between 1906 and 1911, winning both policy concessions and patronage posts as a result of pragmatic bargaining. Criticism of the government's foreign, colonial, and military policies after the Russo-Japanese War had been voiced most actively by opposition politicians, such as Ōishi Masami (1855–1935) and Inukai Tsuyoshi of the Kokumintō (established in 1910 as the successor to the Kenseihontō), the Seiyūkai's principal rival.[14] Although the Seiyūkai usually refrained from attacking the government openly under the strictures of Hara's "politics of compromise," many leading party members, such as Motoda Hajime (1858–1938) and Ōoka Ikuzō (1856–1928) shared these criticisms. The general trend among Diet politicians favored commercial over territorial imperialism, or as Inukai put it, British-style (*Eikoku ryū*) as opposed to French-style (*Futsukoku ryū*) expansionism. For this reason, they tended to look more toward China south of the Wall for advantage rather than Manchuria. They also opposed armament beyond a level they considered reasonable for national defense. Diet members, many of whom leaned toward a navy-first policy, were particularly unreceptive to funding new divisions for the army. At the same time, however, given their general fiscal conservatism and what they regarded as pressing civilian spending priorities, neither were they inclined to support large-scale warship construction at this point. The navy and the Seiyūkai thus might share substantial common ground, but they remained at odds over the crucial question of the dreadnought program.[15]

What ultimately pushed the Seiyūkai toward a more positive alliance with the navy was an internal conflict over party leadership that temporarily pushed Hara Takashi to the sidelines. Although Hara does not appear to have harbored any special sympathy for either armed service, his success in expanding the influence of his party rested on his skill in cutting deals that satisfied the demands of political leaders aligned with the army, such as Yamagata Aritomo and Katsura Tarō. Hara's rivals believed that a partnership with the navy and its bureaucratic allies would not only strengthen their position within the party but might also lead to broader changes in the balance of power in Japanese politics that would open the door to new participants. Saionji Kinmochi, president of the Seiyūkai, supported this approach. Saionji had originally been invited to head the party because of his status as a protégé of the oligarchs and his acceptability to the elder statesmen as a prime-minister candidate. Hara, however, wielded the real leadership within the organization, and the nominal party president had come to resent this arrangement. Under these circumstances, Hara found himself unable to prevent the Seiyūkai from entering into a bargain with the navy and the Satsuma bureaucrats to form a new alignment. A cabinet headed by Saionji and backed by this coalition would adopt a program of sharp fiscal retrenchment in all areas except naval spending. Implicitly, such a policy meant denying the army its new divisions. The opportunity to set this scheme into motion emerged in August 1911 with the resignation of the Katsura cabinet.[16]

The installation of a Saionji government backed by a grouping of political forces inclined toward moderation in imperial affairs contributed, along with the considerations cited earlier, to Japan's indecisive response to the Chinese Revolution. This cabinet certainly had little interest in an aggressive Manchuria policy. Although the army regarded this coalition as an adversary, the government's somewhat vague promise at the end of 1911 to consider funding two divisions in the 1913 budget, which army leaders took as a firm commitment, mitigated tensions for a time. The government's actual proposal for that budget, formulated in late 1912, however, provided substantial funding for the navy's program without including appropriations for new infantry divisions. A furious army minister tendered his resignation, and his service refused to appoint a replacement. Under the Meiji Constitution, no cabinet could hold office without representation from both services. As a result, Saionji's government collapsed in November.[17]

For a brief time, the political situation seemed to turn in the army's favor with the appointment of a cabinet once again headed by Katsura Tarō. However, a hostile Seiyūkai, deeply alienated by the army's actions in bringing down the Saionji government and further angered by Katsura's plans to hold new Diet elections, called for a vote of no confidence and demanded Katsura's resignation. Katsura took the unprecedented step of obtaining an imperial rescript to block the Seiyūkai's move. This initiative backfired and generated widespread outrage at the prime minister, not only for using high-handed tactics but also for dragging the imperial institution through the mud of partisan politics. The Seiyūkai, in cooperation with minority parties, organized massive public demonstrations. Katsura had little choice but to resign after only three months in office. From the army's point of view, the succeeding cabinet, headed this time by none other than Admiral Yamamoto Gonbei, proved even worse than the one it had brought down in late 1912. If the army had found its aspirations frustrated in 1912, for the larger part of 1913 and the early months of 1914, it found itself on the defensive.[18]

Moderate diplomats, of course, welcomed these domestic political developments. With the installation of cabinets receptive to a rational reexamination of policy in Manchuria, an opportunity to seize the initiative had finally arrived. At the same time, diplomats had reason to hope that governments, particularly that of Admiral Yamamoto, with diminished army influence would strengthen the Foreign Ministry's formal control over territorial policy. Compromises defining clear divisions of responsibility had resolved the jurisdictional disputes that had erupted in 1906. In the intervening years, however, the army and, to a certain extent, the SMR had failed, in the view of ministry officials, to live up to these agreements. The army had bypassed official channels and conducted discussions with Chinese authorities that properly belonged under the purview of the Foreign Ministry. This trend increased after the annexation of Korea, with the colonial government, which was dominated by the army, interfering in Manchurian affairs. Japanese diplomats found this kind of activity intolerable, as Abe Moritarō made clear.

Diplomacy must be carried out through diplomatic organs based on national policy. It is unacceptable for some other agency of the same government to interfere in the process. For this reason, the management of foreign affairs must be united under the Foreign Ministry. The Army and Navy ministries as well as their general staffs— indeed, all public officials—have duties defined by the policies of the government. They do not expect interference [from outside bodies]. It is likewise urgent that they comply with the requests of diplomatic agencies in order to ensure the optimum execution of policy.[19]

Not only the promise of a new policy direction but also the logic of bureaucratic politics, then, gave Foreign Ministry officials good reason to embrace the pro-navy coalition.

Manchurian Initiatives Under the Taishō Coalition

The dominance of moderate leadership during this period did not result in a complete halt to new initiatives in Manchuria. Although the navy, the professional diplomats, and their allies opposed any large-scale imperial offensive, they would entertain cautious and restrained steps. Moreover, not even a strengthened navy-centered coalition could ignore army wishes entirely without risking a renewed domestic crisis. Some sort of compromise with advocates of a forward policy in Manchuria made political sense, particularly following the outbreak of a short-lived "second revolution" in China in July 1913, which triggered renewed calls for an adventurist policy. Yet another factor motivated moderates to consider some degree of action in Manchuria. So long as Chinese challenges to Japan's claims persisted, a policy of restraint ran the risk of conveying an impression of a lack of resolve. Foreign Ministry officials might not have wanted to see any major Japanese initiatives at this time, but when it came to defending existing rights, they proved no less determined than hard-line imperial activists. For a combination of these reasons, the Yamamoto government undertook a number of modest steps. Abe Moritarō played a central role in shaping this program of limited, and to a significant extent pre-emptive, expansionism.[20]

Abe and his colleagues entertained the possibility of acquiring new mining claims, particularly in areas adjacent to existing railway lines. The Anshan iron ore field south of Mukden, first explored by SMR geologists in 1909, represented the most important prospect. The development of the nation's iron and steel industry depended on access to ore, one reason why contemporary Japanese policymakers were devoting special attention to the Hanyehp'ing complex in the Yangtze valley. The development of sources of raw materials within the Japanese sphere in Manchuria was an attractive prospect. The Foreign Ministry thus planned to open preliminary discussions regarding rights at Anshan.[21]

Abe also suggested, more tentatively, some ways to promote Japanese immigration in Manchuria. He firmly opposed as unrealistic any attempt to secure unrestricted land rights in the territory. However, as an alternative, Abe suggested the opening of new treaty ports, particularly in Inner Mongolia. The acquisition of special rights to exploit farmland within a limited radius of existing treaty ports and railway towns merited consideration as well. While proposing such ideas, however, Abe stressed the importance of restraint and caution in proceeding with any of these measures. Indeed, his proposals appear more gestures aimed at mollifying advocates of a forward policy in Manchuria than serious attempts at an immigration initiative. Nothing, in fact, came of these proposals before the outbreak of World War I.[22]

Several pilot initiatives in the area of agricultural settlement, however, took shape during this era. In an effort to promote Japanese farming within the Railway Zone, the SMR instituted experimental measures to support immigrants' efforts at rice cultivation. The company provided financial assistance for land purchases, services such as digging wells, and the free use of equipment. SMR agronomists began experimental work with strains of rice that might thrive under Manchurian conditions. In cooperation with the army, company officials also began offering incentives for railway guards completing their term of duty to stay on permanently in Manchuria. The company would grant the household of each former guard a priority claim on up to 60,000 *tsubo* (almost 50 acres) of prime farmland within the Zone. Participants in the program received subsidies for rent and operating expenses. The Kwantung Government-General initiated an experimental venture in agricultural settlement as well. In 1913, authorities selected a site within the Leased Territory they deemed promising and began building paddy fields with the aim of establishing a model rice-farming community. The Government-General planned to complete the groundwork by 1915 and recruit settlers from the home islands. Combining characters from the names of their communities of origin, the first group of residents would call their village "Aikawamura."[23]

The efforts of the SMR and the Government-General, however, represented no more than demonstration projects in agricultural settlement. Total arable land within the Railway Zone amounted to just over 15,000 acres. Even if the company set aside all this acreage for retiring railway guards, it could accommodate a few hundred families at best. As for the Government-General's project, most experts acknowledged that, of all areas in southern Manchuria, the Leased Territory offered the poorest prospects for farming. Whether Aikawamura succeeded or not, it would not provide a viable model for further development in Kwantung itself.[24]

Another undertaking, which received a great deal of attention at the time but remained, in the final analysis, more important in symbol than substance, centered on an attempt to strengthen economic ties among Manchuria, Korea, and Japan. The Foreign Ministry agreed, under pressure from the army and the colonial government in Korea, to negotiate special tariffs for goods crossing the Korean border into Manchuria. Accords signed in May 1913 reduced the frontier tariff by one-third, an arrangement similar to those achieved by the Russians and the French in their respective areas of cross-border trade.[25] In addition, the Government-General of Korea and the National Railway Board, with the reluctant participation of the SMR, implemented an incentive program designed to promote the export of Japanese cotton products by way of Korea into Manchuria. Textile producers in Osaka, for example, could transport their goods to Shimonoseki on Japan's national railway system and transship them to Pusan, where trains running directly to Mukden through the Chōsen (Korea) Railway and the SMR's Antung–Mukden line would carry them into Manchuria. Shippers using this route would receive steep rate discounts from all three railway systems.[26]

With this initiative, the Japanese appeared to have taken a major step toward the goal of creating a railway and customs union in Northeast Asia. It certainly produced a dramatic change in the routing of the targeted category of goods. At Dairen, heretofore the usual port of entry, cotton cloth and yarn bound for destinations in the Manchurian interior declined from almost 17,000 tons in 1913 to 6,661 in 1914. Conversely, the same articles moving from Pusan into Manchuria increased from just under 8,000 tons in 1913 to 17,248 in 1914.[27] However, as a serious effort to redirect the pattern of commercial integration that had taken root in the early years of the venture and bound south Manchuria commercially to Kwantung and Dairen, the scheme offered dubious prospects at best. As noted in the preceding chapter, the plan suffered from inherent economic problems, most notably the greater length and correspondingly higher costs of the Pusan route. The discount program, in effect, partially subsidized the cost of an additional 500 miles. The policy had some prospects for success only if the actual volume of subsidized traffic remained small. Any further effort to increase the use of the Pusan-Mukden route, however, posed serious difficulties, so long as the three railway agencies bore the burden alone. Without a major commitment of resources from the government, this program would not likely move much beyond this limited step.

The opposition of the SMR and vigorous protests from the merchant community in Dairen, which mounted a lobbying effort in Tokyo, probably inflated the significance of this initiative. For some Japanese merchants in Dairen, this shift in the routing of cotton goods posed a major threat to their livelihood. The SMR appears to have reacted more to the possibility of the widening use of this route in the future rather than to the actual measures proposed. In discussions between the three railway agencies, in fact, the SMR's representative had initially agreed to the scheme without objection. Given the underlying economics of the plan, fears about a broader threat to the Dairen strategy appeared largely groundless.[28] So long as the principle of containing demands on the company's resources within the boundaries of profitability remained in place, the government could not persist in any program that seriously undermined the soundness of the SMR's business operations. Apart from revealing the sensitivity of SMR officials to even minor challenges to their strategies, however, these protests illuminate an emerging political alignment of Manchurian "settler" interests, as represented by the company and the Dairen merchant community, against metropolitan policy. Such cleavages, common in the history of modern colonialism, would subsequently play a significant part in the history of Japanese Manchuria.

The token qualities of this imperial integration scheme become even more evident when evaluated in the context of the army's expectations. Consistent with its claims about the growing danger of Russia and the need for two new divisions, the army had argued since early 1911 for the expansion of strategic transportation capacity on the Pusan–Mukden route. This step acquired special importance because the Russians planned to make extensive improvements on their own lines. As a countermeasure, the army wanted both the Chōsen Railway and the Antung–Mukden line double-tracked as soon as possible. Strategic planners regarded the expansion of commercial traffic in peacetime as a way of offsetting the costs of this undertaking.[29] The high volume of coal traffic from Fushun had justified, from a business perspective, the double-tracking of the segment of the SMR trunk between Dairen and Suchiat'un. However, the increased freight in cotton goods would clearly make no more than a negligible contribution toward supporting the expansion of capacity on the Korean route.

The negotiation of new railway rights constituted a more substantive initiative and, in fact, the most significant of Manchurian policy measures undertaken during this period. The Japanese had planned to build a system of feeder lines linking the hinterland to the SMR's trunk line from the beginning. Advocates of colonization envisioned a Manchuria eventually laced with railways connected to nodes of Japanese power. Supporters of a forward policy regarded the possibility of construction into Inner Mongolia with particular interest. The Hsinmint'un–Fak'umen and Chinchow–Aigun projects of the previous decade, both of which had drawn imperialist attention to the area as well as underscored the vulnerability of the Japanese position west of the SMR, provided early inspiration for this idea. The conclusion of the third Russo-Japanese pact, which defined sphere boundaries in the west more clearly than had the first, further stimulated thinking. Building railways offered the best way to solidify claims on paper with power on the ground. Russian moves in Outer Mongolia between 1911 and 1913 highlighted the urgent need for action.

In fact, the army had already surveyed two prospective Inner Mongolian routes in early 1912.[30] One ran from Mukden to T'aonan and was aimed not only at securing Japanese claims in this section of Inner Mongolia and checking a Russian advance from the west but also at providing a second line north from Mukden toward the CER. Such a railway would increase the military transportation capacity available for a campaign in northern Manchuria as well as open the possibility of intercepting, or at least threatening, Russian lines of communication west of Harbin. T'aonan, a Chinese outpost in an area still largely inhabited by ethnic Mongols, formed the northern limit for the construction of such a railway as defined by Russo-Japanese agreements.[31] The other proposed route ran from Mukden to some point in the Jehol region, most likely Ch'ihfeng. This line would strengthen Japanese claims in this part of Inner Mongolia and guard against Russian movement through Outer Mongolia toward North China. The Russians had long planned to build a railway line from the Siberian town of Kiakhta through Urga, the Outer Mongolian capital, to Changchiak'ou (Kalgan), a city west of Peking connected to the capital by rail. In addition to intercepting a Kiakhta–Kalgan line of march, the Jehol railway would play a supplementary role in war plans against China as laid out in 1911 and allow the Japanese army to threaten Peking from the north.[32]

Given the arguments for caution and restraint, a major railway initiative at this juncture would have run against the grain of moderate policies. At the same time, railway building represented a far safer and more restrained form of expansion than the reckless schemes that militant members of the imperial activist camp had favored in 1911 and early 1912. Moreover, political wisdom recommended some form of compensatory response to the army acknowledging at least some of its strategic concerns. What ultimately persuaded Foreign Ministry officials to endorse a new construction program in 1913, however, was the emergence of yet another Chinese initiative. Rumors surfaced in 1912 that Sun Yat-sen (1866–1925), in his capacity as the head of the new republic's central railway agency, planned to build lines in southern Manchuria and eastern Inner Mongolia. The army appears to have conducted surreptitious negotiations with Sun through the offices of Mori Kaku (1882–1932), a Mitsui Bussan executive, a good example of the kind of extra-diplomatic contacts to which the Foreign Ministry took vigorous exception. Further rumors emerged in early 1913, and Japanese diplomats became increasingly concerned when confronted with evidence of the involvement of British and French nationals. Combining the information available, Foreign Ministry officials concluded that the Chinese authorities contemplated two major projects.[33]

One entailed the construction of a railway originating in Mukden and running east to Hailung and then north to the provincial capital of Kirin. This project would create not only a parallel line on the eastern flank of the SMR running through some of the richer soy-growing regions of the territory but also an extension of the PMR to Kirin. The Chinese would thus possess a transportation system linking Peking to Kirin entirely independent of the SMR, breaking Japan's monopoly and fulfilling Li Hung-chang's 1890 scheme. The other, described in the order of planned construction, would originate in Ch'angch'un, the northern terminus of the SMR, and run northwest to Petune (later renamed Fuyu), a port on the Sungari River, and then west to T'aonan. From T'aonan, the line would extend south to Jehol City (Ch'engte). A link between Jehol and Peking would no doubt follow in time. In addition, this railway would connect to the Japanese-financed but Chinese-owned Ch'angch'un–Kirin line, which became partially operational in 1912. This would create a route that would not only cover Inner Mongolia in much the same way as the Chinchow–Aigun project would have done, at least up to T'aonan, but also provide a second system linking Kirin and Peking independent of the SMR[34] (see Map 4.1).

Given the political battle over the Chinchow–Aigun project just a few

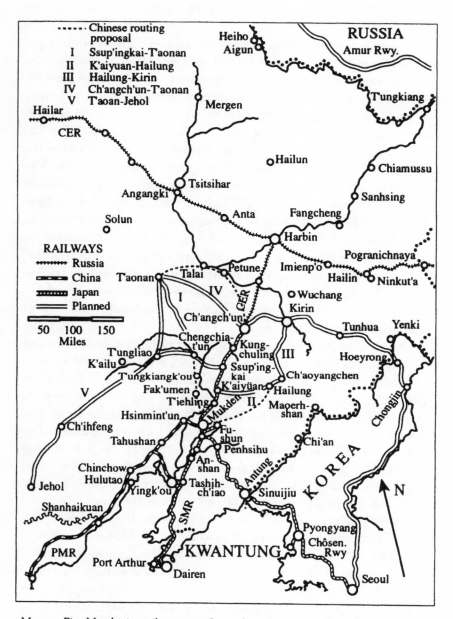

Map 4.1 Five Manchurian railways, 1913. Some planned routes are shown based on actual lines built subsequently. The T'aonan-Jehol route, along with its connector via Cheng-chiat'un, as shown was only one of several possible configurations under consideration at this time (based on maps in Tōa keizai chōsakyoku, *Manchoukuo Year Book, 1934*; SMR, *Eigyō hōkokusho*, 1923, 1928, 1930; DR1, looseleaf).

years earlier, Chinese plans surfacing in 1912 and 1913 represented an unacceptable affront even to moderate Japanese diplomats. At the same time, however, the experience of earlier disputes made it clear that simple obstruction would not offer a viable policy in this case. The Treaty of Portsmouth enjoined Japan and Russia from hindering Chinese efforts at developing their own territory. Moreover, the T'aonan–Jehol segment of the proposed Chinese line in Inner Mongolia ran even further west than the Chinchow–Aigun, forestalling any attempt to invoke the parallel construction clause. Coupled with the desirability of providing the army and other advocates of a forward policy with some measure of satisfaction, these considerations led the Foreign Ministry to adopt a strategy of pre-empting the Chinese initiative. Japan would not attempt to block these plans outright; rather, it would propose an alternative slate of construction projects that would not only serve its own purposes but simultaneously fulfill the purported economic goals of the Chinese schemes.[35]

The Foreign Ministry consulted the army, the SMR, and consular staff in Manchuria as to possible routes that might in some measure accommodate Chinese aims while protecting and advancing Japanese interests. The army pressed for the two lines it had surveyed in 1912, which would provide the access to T'aonan and Jehol desired by both sides. Ochiai Kentarō (1883–1926), the consul general in Mukden, however, advised strongly against the Mukden–Jehol proposal. The route mapped out by army surveyors ran parallel to the PMR for much of its length and would undermine Japan's diplomatic interests in prohibiting parallel railway construction as a matter of general principle. Ochiai also vigorously opposed a line to T'aonan originating in Mukden. In his view, any Chinese-owned railway connecting directly to Mukden, even if financed by Japan, remained objectionable, since it would create the basis for expanding the PMR as a system independent of the SMR. This consideration most certainly applied to the Mukden–Hailung–Kirin line proposed by the Chinese.[36]

SMR officials agreed with Ochiai's concerns and recommended Ssup'ingkai, instead of Mukden, as the point of origin for the line to T'aonan. This routing would take it through Chengchiat'un, the northernmost port on the Liao River and contribute to expanding SMR traffic. Moreover, because the T'aonan area remained relatively undeveloped, the railway would require the existing demand for transportation in the Ssup'ingkai–Chengchiat'un area to sustain it. Soybean traffic from the river port of Chengchiat'un had started moving by horse cart to Ssup'ingkai station in recent years, with active support from the SMR. As an alternative to the Chinese plan for a route from Mukden to Hailung to Kirin, company officials suggested a line to Hailung originating from K'aiyüan station on the SMR instead of Mukden. Both modifications would deny the Chinese access to T'aonan or Hailung without going through the Japanese system. In the SMR's view, a railway from Ch'angch'un to T'aonan offered little advantage at this point but posed no real problems. The Foreign Ministry, however, worried that Chinese plans for running the line through Petune would infringe on the Russian sphere. Diplomats favored a route running well south of the boundary.[37]

On the basis of these consultations, the Foreign Ministry drew up its basic negotiating position. Japan would undertake the construction of five new railways as loan concessions in the following order of priority (see Map 4.1): (1) a line from Ssup'ingkai to T'aonan, which would meet the Chinese goal of accessing T'aonan by rail; (2) a line from K'aiyüan to Hailung, which would presumably satisfying Chinese desires for rail connections to Hailung; (3) a Ch'angch'un–T'aonan line, modified to avoid infringing on Russian interests; (4) an extension from T'aonan to Jehol; and (5) a line from Hailung to Kirin. The T'aonan–Jehol line would include a connector to the SMR at some point south of Ch'angch'un, a provision that not only bore a close resemblance to the intercepting connector proposed by Komura for the Chinchow–Aigun line in his fallback plan of 1910 but would also fulfill, to some degree, the army's interest in a strategic line to Jehol.[38]

Foreign Ministry officials formulated this position with the intention of presenting a moderate and mutually beneficial compromise. Although the Ssup'ingkai–T'aonan and K'aiyüan–Hailung lines would serve as Japanese feeders, they nonetheless provided rail access to these areas consistent with Japanese obligations not to obstruct Chinese development efforts. The Japanese, moreover, agreed to the construction of a railway from Ch'angch'un to T'aonan, a project in which they had little independent interest at this stage.[39] In addition, Abe insisted that loan arrangements for these lines conform to standards set by the powers south of the Wall. He warned that the days when Japan might extract concessions comparable to the Antung–Mukden line, with outright ownership and such amenities as a railway zone, had passed. The Chinese would own and operate all these railways, although the Japanese would hold the managerial rights customarily accruing to creditors for the duration of the loan.[40]

The Chinese, not surprisingly, failed to appreciate the Japanese terms as gestures of self-restraint and generosity. The Chinese goals were to build independent systems with connections at Mukden and to secure Inner Mongolia against Russian and Japanese encroachment. The Japanese demands for rerouting not only defeated these purposes but also created new threats to Chinese sovereignty by providing feeders to the SMR and enhancing the reach of Japanese railway power. Apart from the provision for an "interceptor" link, the Ch'angch'un–T'aonan–Jehol project remained largely intact, but at the price of two injurious railways that received precedence in the order of construction. The building of these lines under the framework of loan concessions, instead of arrangements stipulating full Japanese ownership, offered scant consolation. The Japanese demanded, in effect, that the Chinese borrow money for railways inimical to their own interests. Indeed, in this context, Abe's efforts to make Japan's practice in Manchuria conform to the standards of foreign railway policy south of the Wall appear somewhat misguided. The structure of railway power in these two regions differed substantially. Although the loans might contain similar provisions, most foreign-financed railways south of the Wall represented independent trunk lines connecting major Chinese cities. Upon redemption of the loans, they became fully autonomous Chinese railways. The lines in Manchuria would be tributaries to the SMR rather than independent trunks. Such lines would continue to serve as feeders and extensions of the Japanese system even after the Chinese met their loan obligations and recovered managerial control.[41]

To make matters worse, Abe's intentions notwithstanding, the proposed financial arrangements were far from attractive to the Chinese side. The Ssup'ingkai–T'aonan and K'aiyüan–Hailung were comparatively short lines. Stations along the way would generate much of their business, with relatively little through-traffic moving from terminus to terminus. Since railway operators calculated revenues on the basis of ton-miles, a unit measuring the tonnage multiplied by the distance carried, these lines offered rather poor business prospects. An SMR survey of the K'aiyüan–Hailung route in 1913 confirmed this situation. When interest charges on a Japanese loan for the full construction costs at a market rate of 5 percent were taken into account, the revenues of this line would not cover expenditures. At the same time, the railway would offer substantial benefits to the SMR by expanding the volume of business coming into K'aiyüan station. In general, it made sound business sense for trunk line companies to invest in feeder railways, but the attempt to run feeders as independent enterprises often proved uneconomical.[42] Thus, from a business perspective as well, the Japanese side would gain while the Chinese lost. The package as a whole was a grossly lopsided deal: the agreements required the Chinese to build railways they did not want, to borrow from the Japanese at market rates to do so, and, adding insult to injury, to operate these lines at a loss while the SMR enjoyed a free ride.[43]

Small wonder that Chinese negotiators balked at these terms. Talks dragged on throughout the summer of 1913. The Chinese offered counter-proposals, such as a railway from Mukden to T'aonan, which, ironically, would have provided the Japanese army with precisely what it had initially wanted. In the end, an increasingly frustrated Foreign Ministry resorted to hardball diplomacy in order to achieve an agreement, including warnings about serious repercussions if the Chinese maintained an unreasonable stand, exactly the kind of posture that Japanese diplomats were generally trying to avoid in this period.[44] The two sides finally signed a preliminary understanding, based largely on Japanese terms, in October 1913.[45] The designation of the Yokohama Specie Bank, rather than the SMR, as principal lender was the only adjustment the Chinese managed to win in follow-up talks, based on the argument that the direct involvement of a company regarded as the embodiment of Japanese imperialism in Manchuria would have a damaging impact on public opinion.[46]

Curiously, during the course of these final talks, a brief dispute erupted among Japanese policymakers, in which the army appeared to side with the Chinese. The Foreign Ministry's decision to shift the point of origin of the army's proposed T'aonan railway from Mukden to Ssup'ingkai obviated its intended function as a second line north. The segment on the SMR trunk between Mukden and Ssup'ingkai would continue to create a bottleneck. At the last minute, the army attempted to have Mukden reinstated as the terminus for both the T'aonan and the Hailung lines.[47] An exasperated Yamaza Enjirō (1866–1914), Japan's chief negotiator, demanded the signing of the agreement as negotiated and insisted on leaving any further modifications for subsequent discussion. He added with some sarcasm that "the Chinese side would be more than happy (yorokonde) to accommodate" the army's request.[48]

This dispute over Mukden stemmed from a clash between the logic of a narrowly military railway policy and that of a broader railway imperialism. In strategic terms, since any facilities belonging to the Chinese in peacetime were subject to seizure and use by the Japanese in wartime, this made connections at Mukden desirable. From the perspective of railway imperialism, however, a monopoly remained essential, and this rendered Mukden unacceptable. The army leaders, in fact, found themselves divided on this issue. Tanaka Giichi, one of the chief architects of the Imperial Defense Plan, acknowledged the value of Mukden connections for military purposes but placed more emphasis on the larger goal of preventing the Chinese from developing an independent railway system in Manchuria. In the end, the army chose not to pursue the issue and opted instead to push for the double-tracking of the SMR trunk line to Ssup'ingkai. This measure would resolve the problem of the bottleneck.[49]

In negotiating the so-called Manchuria-Mongolia Five Railways Agreement, Foreign Ministry officials appear to have orchestrated a major imperialist victory in spite of themselves. At the same time, it is important to bear in mind that diplomats approached the problem primarily from a defensive orientation, adopting a pre-emptive strategy that created an opportunity to appease advocates of a more active policy. In addition, however misguided in their practice, they had intended to offer accommodating terms to the Chinese by formulating as "generous" a position as they might, given an established commitment to preserve a Japanese railway monopoly in southern Manchuria. Indeed, having succeeded in pre-empting a Chinese challenge with the signing of the October agreement, diplomats failed, interestingly enough, to mount an aggressive effort to ensure a speedy implementation of the agreement in follow-up negotiations. The Chinese lost little time initiating attempts to stall construction. Discussions over the details of the loan terms dragged on, and little progress had been achieved six months later when the Yamamoto government collapsed. The Chinese, moreover, surreptitiously surveyed the Ch'angch'un–T'aonan route ahead of the others, contrary to the designation of this line as third in priority.[50] Although the Five Railways Agreement provided later governments with the basis for launching a more aggressive policy, the 1913 initiative represented a measure generally consistent with the lukewarm expansionism characteristic of the moderate leadership during these years.

Whither Japanese Manchuria?

Moderates emphasized the need for caution and slowed the pace of expansion in Manchuria but did not openly attempt to reverse established directions. These limited efforts reflected continued ambivalence among this group of leaders about the question of empire as well as a need to compromise with the army and its allies. At the same time, sharper and more forthright criticisms of the Manchurian venture surfaced in a number of influential quarters, some calling for a basic reconsideration of the nation's commitments north of the Wall. These challenges generated a vigorous response from the imperial activist camp. The emergence of this debate, indeed, represents one of the most important developments of this period.

Driven by a range of concerns, criticism of Manchuria policy came from several directions. Some represented broad expressions of disappointment about prospects in Manchuria. Others constituted more narrowly delimited complaints about shortcomings in the conduct of policy. Still others reflected long-standing disagreements with the general trend of expansionism, silenced during the early years of postwar enthusiasm but emerging with the development of a more congenial political atmosphere. Issues one step removed from the merits of Manchuria policy as such informed some of these critical perspectives. Given the polarities of Japanese politics during these years, for example, a challenge to an activist continental policy constituted, at one and the same time, an attack on the army's demands for new appropriations.

A position paper submitted to the Yamamoto cabinet in early 1913 by Matsuoka Yasutake (1846–1923), a member of the House of Peers (not to be confused with the diplomat Matsuoka Yōsuke), offers an illuminating example of criticism. Matsuoka had served as minister of agriculture and commerce in Saionji's first cabinet from 1906 to 1908, when his agency participated actively in some of the economic survey work in Manchuria. Whatever his views at that time, he evinced little enthusiasm about the venture by 1913 and regarded a forward policy in Manchuria as folly. Accepting, at least for the sake of argument, the army's claims about the danger of Russia, he pointed out that Japan could not afford to finance another defense build-up. The debt from the last war remained unretired. Under current political conditions, moreover, aggressive action in Manchuria would likely antagonize China to the point of driving the country into Russian arms. Most important, Manchuria simply did not warrant such risks. It had an inhospitable climate, and the land remained frozen to the depth of three feet for much of the year. The region suffered from a thinly spread, benighted populace beset with endemic banditry. Advocates of a forward policy had made broad claims about the great wealth to be tapped in Manchuria, but its riches had yet to be discovered. The Fushun colliery produced an enormous output, to be sure, but its productivity only hurt Japanese exports by driving down the price of coal throughout East Asia. Immigration had made little progress, and most Japanese who resided in the territory lived off one another.[51]

The opinions of Captain Akiyama Saneyuki, a respected navy staff officer, provide another example, particularly interesting because of the source as well as the sharpness of the critique.[52] Following an inspection tour of southern Manchuria in late 1912, Akiyama offered a number of disparaging observations about the "poor and lax management" of the SMR and, "considering what it does," the excessive staffing of the Kwantung Government-General. His primary thrust, however, lay in his conclusion that the strategy of building Japanese power through railways and other concessions was failing to generate any meaningful benefits for Japan. The opportunities for Japanese to immigrate and pursue productive activities in the territory remained few. The SMR's mines at Fushun and a venture initiated by the Ōkura concern at Penhsihu on the Antung–Mukden line produced at a significant level, but most other mining operations in the region amounted to little more than trial digs. Other than a cement factory here, a flour mill there, the Japanese had promoted little industrial development. The SMR represented one of the few enterprises making money, but it did little to advance Japanese interests otherwise. The company had built roads and schools and brought electricity and other modern amenities to the communities of the Railway Zone. The chief beneficiaries of these projects, however, were not Japanese settlers, but the Chinese, who had begun to move in large numbers to both the Zone and Kwantung. In the Zone, Chinese population growth outstripped the pace of Japanese settlement (see Appendix B).[53]

The fundamental problem, in Akiyama's view, lay in the fact that the Japanese had no opportunity to engage in farming in Manchuria. The principal rewards of Japanese investment in railways and other areas of infrastructural development accrued to those who worked and owned the land. "Manchuria is an agrarian territory and is not ready for industrialization.

And if there is no hope for [Japanese settlers in] agriculture, there is no hope for immigration at all." The lack of rights to own or lease land outside Kwantung, the Zone, and residential sections of the treaty ports, he acknowledged, formed the main obstacle to Japanese farming. Akiyama would seem, then, to be making the case for a forward policy. However, and this is key to his line of argument, he believed the acquisition of such rights under the existing system of international relations with China entirely unrealistic. The Chinese government could not bestow land rights upon the Japanese in Manchuria without granting equivalent privileges to all foreigners throughout the country, and it would never consent to such a measure. Under the circumstances, partition was the only solution to the problem of land in Manchuria, with Japan establishing a protectorate over the territory. Partition, of course, represented neither a desirable nor a feasible step under current international conditions, he noted. Referring to the late foreign minister's proposals, he remarked: "Marquis Komura's argument for 'concentrating emigration in Manchuria' is nothing more than an idle fancy." Akiyama offered a markedly pessimistic assessment overall: "In the main, based on conditions observed during this inspection tour, the further development and management of Manchuria are without prospect."[54]

A report on the SMR prepared by the National Railway Board, released for internal government use in 1913, raised similar concerns, although not with the same degree of pessimism. The report muted its criticism and offered many positive observations about the company's accomplishments. By pointing out problems in management and questioning the ability of the institution to carry out its mission effectively, it did, however, give ammunition to more dedicated critics. The board's inspectors observed that by conventional business standards, the SMR's operations appeared inefficient, its management overstaffed, and its capital construction plans immoderate. The company had built some of its stations to a grand scale disproportionate to the number of passengers served. The report pointed out that the SMR's railway operating costs ran unusually high and were unsurpassed by any other system in the Japanese empire. Costs per mile per day for the company's lines ran at about ¥31, in contrast to ¥25 for the Japanese national system, ¥20 for the Chōsen Railway, and a low of ¥19 for Taiwan.[55]

Like Akiyama, the board's inspectors saw shortcomings in the SMR's efforts to promote immigration as among the more serious problems. The report noted, "One of the most important tasks of the SMR lies in promoting the growth of the Japanese population in Manchuria." Yet, progress remained unimpressive. The SMR had built extensive modern facilities in the Zone, including housing, hospitals, and schools. Station towns were models of urban planning, laid out in grids, and provided with sewers, water, gas, and electricity. Zone residents even enjoyed a form of self-government in company-sponsored municipal councils. Residents paid rents and service fees, but the company subsidized these charges, laying out some ¥770,000 in net expenses annually. Zone residents paid substantially lower school fees than Japanese living in consular jurisdictions and maintaining their own cooperative schools. The Japanese, however, failed to take full advantage of these facilities. Indeed, confirming Akiyama's observations, the report noted that Chinese rather than Japanese settlers were moving in increasing numbers to the Zone and exploiting its educational opportunities. The board's inspectors acknowledged the importance to the long-term development of Manchuria of educating local Chinese and welcomed Chinese children's attendance at Zone schools. However, these projects did not contribute to the growth of Japanese settlement. "Why, despite the fact that the SMR has invested ¥20 million in building all kinds of facilities in the Zone, does this situation persist?"[56]

The board's report cited three major reasons. First, Japanese entrepreneurs could not compete with local Chinese in small-scale business. Accustomed to modest returns and a lower standard of living, Chinese merchants consistently undersold the Japanese. Second, although farming presented a potentially attractive occupation for Japanese settlers, the Zone provided insufficient land for any substantial development. The report underscored the fact that Japanese as yet lacked the right to own or lease land outside areas of their special jurisdiction. Third, although the Zone might offer prospects for industrial development in the future, actual manufacturing opportunities remained limited. Apart from cement manufacture, brick making, oil pressing, flour milling, and cigarette making, the prospects appeared poor. In highlighting the lack of land rights as a barrier to immigration, the report seemed to lend support to those who favored placing the issue on Japan's negotiating agenda. However, like Akiyama, the authors did not consider such a demand within the realm of possibility at this point. They presented a rather pessimistic overall view of immigration possibilities. "Provided that there are no major changes in the international situation, these conditions are likely to persist, regardless of the quality of the SMR's facilities."[57]

On the one hand, the board's assessment absolved SMR managers of responsibility for the lack of progress in promoting settlement. On the other hand, it also pointed to the unproductive nature of the large expenditures and investments the company had made in this field and cast the SMR's work in a decidedly negative light. Coupled with other observations about overstaffing, inefficiency, and the unnecessary scale of construction, the report tended to leave the impression of substantial problems of waste and misspent resources in the SMR's operations. A move to replace the top management of the company at the end of 1913 compounded the sense of a troubled SMR. Although this affair touches on matters beyond the realm of questioning and criticizing Manchuria policy, it offers insight into some of the dynamics of the debate and merits a brief examination.[58]

When offered the portfolio of the minister of posts and communications in Katsura's second government in 1908, Gotō Shinpei had resigned as SMR governor. His vice governor and handpicked successor, Nakamura Zekō (1868–1927), took his place. Like Gotō, Nakamura had served in the administration of colonial Taiwan. The new chief executive's term of appointment nominally expired at the end of 1913, but barring a demonstration of outright incompetence, an extension of his tenure, particularly in view of the need to ensure continuity in management, appeared a matter of course. Unexpectedly, Nakamura failed to gain reappointment, and Nomura Ryūtarō (1859–1943), a National Railway Board official, took his place as governor. Observers might well have construed this step as a vote of no confidence in Nakamura's management. Equally significant, and perhaps indicative of at least one underlying motive for this purge, a Seiyūkai party stalwart received appointment as the new vice governor.[59]

The political maneuvers behind this personnel shuffle remain unclear. Rumors circulating in the press only a few days before the announcement of Nomura's appointment suggested veteran diplomat Ijūin Hikokichi (1864–1924) had won cabinet approval as Nakamura's replacement over the wishes of the army, which favored either retaining the incumbent or installing its own candidate. Other reports hinted at a scheme engineered by Railway Board Governor Tokonami Takejirō (1866–1935) and Hara Takashi, home minister in the Yamamoto cabinet.[60] At least to some degree, the involvement of Hara and the collusion of his ally Tokonami appear quite likely. The politicization of the bureaucracy by securing posts for party members in various ministries and agencies was one of Hara's more effective tactics for expanding party influence in the government. He sought to encourage party affiliation among the ranks of officials as well. Through this process, the once "transcendent" bureaucracy began to forge ties with the majority party in the Diet, with appointments and promotions, in many cases, linked to party affiliation. Hara included among the targets of this strategy the top management posts of semi-official corporations and banks, appointments controlled by the cabinet. Penetrating the SMR would have been a particularly important achievement, since it provided a foothold in a major area of foreign affairs. Moreover, the company's financial self-sufficiency had thus far insulated it from the Diet's power to approve annual government appropriations. A strong party voice in the appointment of senior SMR officers would go a long way toward making the company more accountable.[61] Given the expectation of continuity, however, denying Nakamura reappointment without cause would have proved difficult. Some of the criticism of company performance thus warrants consideration in this light. This is not to suggest that such political machinations lay behind all or even most of the complaints leveled at SMR management. At the same time, it must be acknowledged that the Railway Board did not represent a disinterested source of criticism, any more than did Captain Akiyama of the Navy General Staff.[62]

Although the trend of questioning and criticizing Manchuria policy at this stage appears to have had more than an incidental connection to domestic political rivalries, the arguments themselves stood on their own merits, regardless of ulterior motives. They touched on real problems that, no doubt, struck a chord with those familiar with the situation on the ground; these expressions of dissatisfaction could not be dismissed simply as partisan fabrications. Immigration, for example, had clearly run into difficulty. As of 1913, some 80,000–90,000 Japanese lived in Kwantung, the Railway Zone, and special residential areas (mostly in treaty ports) under consular jurisdiction. (See Appendix B. These figures exclude most ethnic Koreans resident in Manchuria, the majority of whom were Chinese rather than Japanese nationals.)[63] Given that less than a decade had passed, such figures represented a rather significant achievement. However, the numbers had fallen far short of Gotō's goal of settling between a half-million and a million Japanese in Manchuria by 1915. Moreover, the declining proportion of Japanese relative to Chinese living in the Railway Zone troubled those who had hoped to see this area developed as a Japanese enclave. Observations at this time as to the reason for the lack of progress in settlement, of course, did not offer any new insights. At the outset of the venture, Ishizuka's survey group had pointed out potential difficulties. Its optimistic assessment was based not on the expectation that settling Manchuria would be easy but, rather, on the assumption that the government would commit itself to an active policy. Nonetheless, the fact that reports eight years later repeated some of these same observations suggests that policymakers had not taken some of the Ishizuka team's key recommendations to heart.

Akiyama's charge that much of the SMR's work benefited the Chinese more than it did the Japanese also had merit. The problem stemmed from the fundamentals of railway economics. In general, the residents of the service territory, particularly those who owned land in the area, gained the most from railway-linked development. This relationship accounts for the fact that investors often pursued railway enterprise in conjunction with real estate and land ventures. Akiyama pointed out that although the Japanese earned dividends and benefited from trade, they had not properly positioned themselves in the territory to take advantage of their massive investment in transportation. The Chinese enjoyed, perhaps, greater economic returns from the railway in the form of increasingly valuable and productive real estate.

Manchuria's natural resources, too, had proved disappointing, as revealed by more detailed surveys and attempts at commercial exploitation. We have touched on the problem of coal, the territory's most abundant mineral product. Initially, some policymakers thought forestry promising and established such ventures as the quasi-official Yalu River Timber Company in 1906. A more recent army survey, conducted as part of the Kwantung garrison's planning for mobilization, however, offered little cause for optimism. A report completed in 1911 had the following to say about the region's forests and their commercial potential:

It is widely believed that Manchuria is blessed with rich, old-growth forests stretching for thousands of leagues, so dense that one cannot see the sky in broad daylight, and offering a virtually limitless source of high-quality timber. . . . However, the reality is entirely different. If current rates of exploitation continue, the best stands will be gone within ten years. Timber suitable for firewood might survive for yet another ten years of unrestricted cutting, but the supply is clearly not inexhaustible.[64]

Iron deposits in southern Manchuria, particularly at Anshan, presented possibilities, but the mixed quality of the ores, much of it low grade, rendered their value to Japan's iron industry as yet uncertain.[65]

The fact that critiques of Manchuria policy rested on substantive foundations forced the advocates of a forward policy to make a serious effort to address these issues. The postwar honeymoon, during which the value of Manchuria had formed an article of faith, had ended, and the commitment demanded renewed justification. The army and its allies rose to the challenge and presented direct and vigorous rebuttals, including a defense of the SMR.

Lieutenant General Ōshima Ken'ichi (1858–1947), the army's vice chief of staff, offered a sharp and succinct response to Akiyama's views. He reiterated the concept of incremental colonization as the framework for Japan's program in the territory.

In order to absorb a foreign territory, we must gradually expand our rights. With the passage of time, special relationships are created, and in the end, annexation becomes a natural conclusion, leaving no room for the interference of the other powers. For this reason, we first gain treaty ports in Manchuria and promote the freedom of commerce, and we demand for our people the right to settle, work mines, cultivate land, and engage in other industries, increasing our rights step by step.

Ōshima dismissed the navy captain's suggestion that the only way to resolve Japan's problems in Manchuria lay in the establishment of a protectorate as a disingenuous argument amounting to little more than "an artful way of saying 'hands off Manchuria.'" Critics took an excessively narrow and short view of Japan's strategy toward Manchuria and, in the process, obstructed long-term gains.[66]

On the issue of immigration, Ōshima affirmed the idea that a large part of Manchuria's value to Japan lay in "land for agricultural settlement" and saw no reason to retreat from that goal. He believed that the southern part of the territory could readily accommodate as many as 600,000 Japanese farmers in the near future. He agreed with Akiyama that the lack of rights to own or lease land outside the concession areas was a serious obstacle. Unlike the navy officer or the authors of the National Railway Board report, however, Ōshima did not see that pressing the demand for land rights at this time lay beyond the pale of possibility. Akiyama erred in suggesting that nothing short of establishing a protectorate would enable the acquisition of such rights. Contrary to the Foreign Ministry's view, Manchuria, indeed, resembled Outer Mongolia and Tibet; it was a region where a neighboring state with special interests might demand extraordinary privileges without throwing the entire system of Great Power relations with China into an uproar. The real problem lay in the weakness of the Japanese government's resolve. China would concede and the powers would go along if Japan took a firm stand.[67]

Major General Tanaka Giichi offered another rebuttal, updating and sharpening his knowledge of Manchuria during an unexpectedly long stopover en route to Europe at the end of 1913. An attack of amebiasis forced him into a stay at the SMR's Dairen hospital, and he spent several months recovering at the company's hotsprings resort at T'angk'angtzu. During that time, using source materials he had requested from the SMR's Research Section, he drafted an essay entitled "Reflections During My Stay in Manchuria" ("Tai-Man shogan").[68]

Tanaka stood among the ranks of the more uncompromising imperialists within the officer corps and had an orientation bordering on the adventurist. A master strategist as well as a politically astute staff officer, he had played an instrumental role in crafting the interservice pact of 1907 and had, in fact, drafted the first version of the Imperial Defense Plan itself. During the early months of the Chinese Revolution, as well as the second round of unrest in 1913, he had championed active political and military intervention. In general, he found Japan's continental policies in the aftermath of the Russo-Japanese War excessively conservative and criticized them for being limited to cautious steps in Manchuria and for neglecting opportunities south of the Wall. Confronted in 1913 with a challenge from the moderate camp that questioned even this restrained imperialism, however, Tanaka emerged as a vigorous defender of past practice.[69]

Like Ōshima, Tanaka stressed the importance of colonizing Manchuria to Japan's long-term goals and affirmed the feasibility of large-scale agricultural settlement in the territory. In a direct response to Captain Akiyama, he wrote, "Marquis Komura's call to concentrate settlers in Manchuria and Korea was by no means an idle fancy." He acknowledged that recent survey reports had shown much of the arable land in southern Manchuria already occupied, but he pointed out that the relatively low population density left room for doubling if not tripling the current population. "If our own policies are appropriate," he noted, "ensuring that this growth includes Japanese should present no difficulties."[70] Adopting an optimistic view of progress to date, Tanaka noted that, despite the small area open to Japanese residence, 90,000 immigrants had already settled in Kwantung and the Railway Zone. Koreans had also developed rice paddies in the eastern part of the region, in defiance of official Chinese opposition. "Combined with the continued development of transportation facilities in the south Manchurian heartland, the full opening of the territory to [foreign] residence and business activity will result in the rapid growth of the Japanese as well as the Korean population." Moreover, Japan had recently established claims in Inner Mongolia. He suggested that these thinly settled lands had an agricultural potential comparable to the great prairies of north Manchuria.[71]

Although Tanaka emphasized the importance of land and settlement, he also had much to say about the importance of Manchuria's other natural resources.

Japan's domestic resources are limited. From here on, no matter how much we seek to increase our productive capabilities, there is little opportunity for growth apart from manufacturing. People have come to adopt a pessimistic outlook and complain about Japan's poverty. Yet it is intolerable that no one is proposing solutions that will make poor Japan into rich Japan. There is only one way in which to make Japan strong and rich, and that is to use the resources of China. And there is no better way to begin than to develop that unopened treasure house within our sphere of influence known as Manchuria.[72]

He urged increased efforts on the part of the SMR and recommended that the Oriental Development Company, a quasi-official corporation created in 1906 to promote land acquisition and development in Korea, expand its operations beyond the Yalu River border. In general, he strongly favored the coordination of economic as well as administrative policies in Korea and southern Manchuria.[73]

In addition to countering what he considered misapprehensions about the value of Manchuria, Tanaka also chided critics of territorial policy for their short memories and their fickle shifts in attitude.

It is apparently unfashionable these days to invoke our country's historical relationship with south Manchuria, but the fact remains that we have paid ¥2 billion from our national treasury and shed the blood of 230,000 men for this cause. This is something we must not permit ourselves to forget. We must also remember that the reason we have risked the fate of our nation in two great wars during the past twenty years lies in the fact that expansion on the continent provides the key to the survival of our people. How is it, then, that less than ten years have passed, yet many of our countrymen have already lost their will, becoming timid, passive, and uninterested? Indeed, some go so far as to call for the effective abandonment of Manchuria. This is an outrage. Such people are without shame.

In his view, Japan's commitments in the territory had an implicitly moral dimension in addition to economic considerations.[74] This invocation of the blood and iron of the Russo-Japanese War in arguments about Manchuria, along with a revisionist view of the causes and aims of the two wars, would become increasingly commonplace.

Imperial activists outside the army also responded vigorously to those questioning the Manchurian commitment. The SMR had become a focus of direct political attack, and not surprisingly the company's friends and promoters offered an equally forthright defense. Gotō Shinpei, in particular, appeared stung by the cabinet's rejection of Nakamura's reappointment as well as the negative appraisals in the National Railway Board's report, which cast aspersions on the policy line he had initiated during his tenure. He launched a broadside against his critics in a speech to the Miyuki Club of the House of Peers in early 1914.[75]

Gotō took the occasion to outline the importance of an empire to Japan and reiterated his belief in Social Darwinism. Imperialism represented a struggle among nations in which only the fittest could survive and chart an autonomous destiny. Manchuria policy acquired its highest meaning in this context. He described the central issue facing Japan's leaders at this juncture in the following terms:

Before us lie vast prairies several times the size of Japan's territory, presenting us with a great question. Are we to continue our colonial policy, which, since the Meiji era, has been one of advancing the nationalist and imperialist (teikokushugi) cause? If so, the problem of whether these vast prairies will belong to Japan or some other country in the future is one with which we must come to terms today.[76]

Only with a "lofty vision" could one understand the importance of Japan's work in the territory. The benefits of empire did not constitute simple quantities that could be tallied in an accountant's ledger, a point he had made in formulating his program for the SMR in 1906. He rebuked those who complained about excessive costs and the inadequate economic returns of imperial policy as "shallow, narrow, and lowly of vision." Such narrowness characterized much of the criticism leveled at the SMR.

Many believe that Manchurian railway and coal-mining operations can be managed in such a way that all accounts will be in the black, that this can be done without engaging in any unremunerative activities, and that this represents the entirety of the business of the SMR. I do not hesitate to assert that this [attitude] lies at the root of the latent evil that drives our empire from the path of fulfilling its special mission in Manchuria.

This "special mission," in Gotō's view, entailed nothing less than an effort "to create the foundations for the permanent occupation of the territory." Japan's policy in Manchuria, he argued, aimed at gradual absorption through economic and cultural means. *Bunsōteki bubi,* the term he had coined originally to describe the company's role in the army's mobilization plans, took on a new meaning in this context. It defined, in his revised version, a "technology of rulership," a method for peaceful conquest.[77]

The SMR was the principal instrument for this program. Akiyama and the National Railway Board failed to understand the company's essential functions. Railway development formed part of the larger task of bringing modernity to the benighted peoples of Manchuria. The facilities of the Railway Zone helped to forge "bonds of civilization" between the Japanese and the "natives." Altruistic efforts to improve public health and education strengthened Japan's moral authority in Manchuria. Competition with the other powers, he noted, citing U.S. efforts to introduce medical missionaries into the region, represented a cultural struggle as much as a political, economic, and military rivalry.[78]

Gotō did acknowledge one significant deficiency in the SMR's performance. "The only thing I found regrettable in my work," he admitted, "was the failure to meet the goal of settling a half-million Japanese immigrants." He acknowledged, moreover, that slow progress in settlement would ultimately jeopardize Japanese tenure in the territory. "We must not forget that the demand that we relinquish our position in Manchuria will be raised sooner or later. In order to resist this demand, we must quickly settle more than a half-million colonists in the territory." The underlying problem, however, did not arise from any particular shortcoming on the part of management. On the contrary, the real responsibility lay with the obstructionist activities of the Chinese authorities and the failure of Japanese diplomacy to overcome these obstacles. "The key to attracting Japanese capital and settlers to Manchuria is our right to lease and purchase land," he declared. "Without full rights, no real progress can be made."[79]

It is significant that Gotō, along with Ōshima and Tanaka, emphasized Japanese settlement. Akiyama's observations, in particular, appear to have struck a nerve. The benefits of long-term territorial development accrued most directly to the residents of the territory, and if the Japanese were not part of the resident population, they would lose out on the fruits of their own work. Imperialist homesteading, in this way, became linked at a basic level to the problem of realizing the value of Manchuria. To be sure, the promotion of immigration to Manchuria as both ends and means had formed an essential part of Japanese thinking from the beginning. The passage of legislation in California in 1913 targeted against Japanese immigrants appears to have heightened interest in Manchuria at this time.[80] Criticism from moderates and others skeptical of the imperialist program, nonetheless, played a major part in bringing the issue to the top of the activists' agenda.

The specific issue of land rights, moreover, figured prominently in the arguments of all three men. Ōshima, Tanaka, and Gotō asserted in unequivocal terms that the inability of Japanese to own or lease land outside Kwantung and the Railway Zone formed the primary reason for the lack of progress in agricultural settlement. There is no question that this problem posed a serious barrier. At the same time, it is important to bear in mind that Ishizuka's survey group had warned of many other problems facing Japanese attempts at farming in Manchuria.[81] Imperial activists appear to have set these admonitions aside. Gotō, clearly in a position to know better, simply played on popular myths and misconceptions when he invoked the image of vast prairies in Manchuria, which actually lay in the Russian north rather than in the Japanese south.

The emphasis on land rights reflected a larger pattern evident in the attacks and counterattacks of this debate. Advocates of a forward policy acknowledged significant shortcomings in Manchuria. Rather than stopping to reflect on and reconsider national priorities, a response that critics presumably sought to encourage, they called for stepping up Japanese demands. More concessions and broader rights provided solutions to the problems facing the expansionist program. In a sense, these imperial activists took Akiyama's straw-man argument to heart. Although not pushing for immediate partition, they acknowledged that approaches to Manchuria thus far had, indeed, represented inadequate half-measures. Under the circumstances, the proper path for the future lay in pressing forward aggressively. On the whole, it would appear that criticism, rather than promoting moderation, had actually fueled reactive pressures for escalation.

The debate in 1913 and early 1914 reflected increasing polarization over Manchuria. Moderation prevailed in the courses of action pursued during this period as a result of shifts in the political equilibrium in Tokyo, but powerful countercurrents operated beneath the surface and, given an opening, might sweep policy in a more radical direction. The chance came soon enough. The political coalition dominating the government during these years lacked a strong base and had made many enemies. Thwarted at every turn, the army harbored deep resentment. Opposition parties in the Diet also grew increasingly jealous of the Seiyūkai's success. Further efforts by Hara and his colleagues to politicize the bureaucracy generated hostility. Many in Japan's political world felt ready to take advantage of any significant missteps on the part of the Yamamoto government in order to topple it. The opportunity arrived in early 1914 when the navy found itself embroiled in a bribery scandal over a warship contract, the so-called Siemens Affair. Not only did the cabinet resign in disgrace, but the serious damage the navy suffered to its prestige ended its brief period of political ascendancy.

The army and its political friends made a rapid and vigorous comeback. Ōkuma Shigenobu (1838–1922), a veteran politician and founder of the main party lineage in opposition to the Seiyūkai, won their support for the post of prime minister with the promise of new army appropriations. Katō Takaaki, a diplomat of Komura's persuasion, assumed the post of foreign minister. The Seiyūkai found itself in the opposition and forced to table its plans. The new government reduced the navy budget. It also conducted a housecleaning at the SMR, removing the Seiyūkai's appointees and installing a new corporate administration headed by a retired army general. This shift in the political balance also removed the barriers to a more aggressive continental policy and put into positions of power men inclined to action. The changeover proved quite timely. Four months into the tenure of the Ōkuma government, war erupted in Europe, and an era of unprecedented opportunity for Japan in East Asia began.[82]

FIVE

Imperialist Adaptations, 1914–1918

In the view of many historians, World War I represents the highwater mark of Japanese expansion before 1931. There is certainly no question that in issuing the Twenty-One Demands in 1915, Japan adopted a more aggressive posture toward China than it had since the war of 1894–95. The conflict in Europe created a vacuum of power in East Asia and a unique window of opportunity for Japan to pursue its imperial aims relatively free of the constraints imposed by its European rivals. This circumstance encouraged imperial activists to think in terms not of maintaining a dynamic equilibrium in the rivalry over China, as they had in the past, but of making Japan a decisive winner in the game. In light of the policies of the Ōkuma government (April 1914–October 1916), imperialist moderation during the years between 1911 and 1914 would seem to have been no more than a temporary lull. Indeed, Japan's negotiating agenda in 1915 contained numerous elements, such as land rights in Manchuria, that had emerged in the activist response to the criticisms their opponents had raised in 1913.

It would be a mistake, however, to view the entire period of World War I in terms of the Twenty-One Demands. Kitaoka Shin'ichi divides the years between 1914 and 1918 into two distinct phases. The first, coinciding with the tenure of the Ōkuma cabinet, was characterized by a dramatic escalation of concession-hunting and traditional gunboat diplomacy. The second, beginning with the installation of the government of Terauchi Masatake (October 1916–September 1918), however, produced an imperialism of a rather different coloring. By 1916, it had become apparent that the war in Europe, unprecedented in modern times in its combination of intensity and duration, would bring about fundamental changes in the international order. The imperialist system that had defined the framework of Japanese expansionist activity, shaped its purposes, and sanctioned its exercise of power appeared to be in danger of collapse. Terauchi, the army, and a core of civilian imperialists remained dedicated to the cause of continental expansion, but they also recognized the need for fundamental policy reform. Continued growth of the Japanese empire demanded the formulation of strategies adapted to an international environment that would no longer tolerate the high-handed practices of the past. Moreover, although their own faith might be unshaken, committed imperialists would also have to develop new ways of justifying an expansionist course to their fellow Japanese, many of whom were losing their appetite for empire.

In this context, the years between 1911 and 1914 do not represent a pause in the drive for expansion so much as they foreshadow the crisis that Japanese imperialism would confront directly during the second half of World War I. During the years of revolutionary upheaval in China, moderate leaders had attempted to adjust Japan's external policies in a direction compatible with a changing international environment. Activists had resisted such reforms, and their position appeared triumphant for a brief time between 1914 and 1916. After 1916, however, the more farsighted leaders within the expansionist camp awakened to the imminent passing of the age of empire and began working in earnest on their own adaptive strategies.[1]

The Twenty-One Demands and the Failure of Concession Hunting

Most Japanese regarded the outbreak of war between the Great Powers in August 1914 as a European affair. Japan participated on the Allied side on a very limited scale. Honoring its agreement with Britain, it declared war on Germany in August. The Imperial Navy patrolled the Pacific and the Mediterranean throughout much of the conflict, and the army's Twelfth Division, backed by navy units, captured the German leasehold of Tsingtao and occupied the Shantung Railway in November 1914. For the most part, however, Japan sought to limit its entanglements and declined several requests to send ground troops to Europe. Its attention, instead, focused on China and the opportunities the war had created for expansionist activity. Japan carried out its operations in Shantung in the name of the Allied cause, but the principal interest of most of the nation's leaders lay in the chance to take over the German position in the province rather than in delivering a strategically important blow against the enemy.[2]

Opportunities for Japan in China did not end with Shantung, however. The war demanded the full attention of the European powers, and they had no choice but to withdraw from any substantive activity in the East. This situation, in turn, offered Japan the possibility of moving well beyond the normal constraints on imperialist behavior imposed by the balance of Great Power interests. Such freedom remained far from complete, to be sure, particularly since the United States did not enter the war until 1917 and maintained a watchful eye on Japanese opportunism. On the other hand, Japan could count on the tolerance, however grudging, of Western allies in need of friends in the East. European withdrawal also weakened the government of Yüan Shih-k'ai, which had depended on collective Great Power support during the upheaval of the revolutionary era. Abandoned, in effect, by many of its most important friends and beset with internal difficulties, the Chinese Republic found itself in a poor position to resist Japanese pressures. Overall, conditions for a concerted imperialist push on the part of Japan had never been better and, in the view of many in Tokyo, might never be so favorable again. Differences between those favoring aggressive activism and those calling for restraint remained, but what might be described as the "baseline" consensus among Japanese leaders had shifted in favor of imperial activism. Even those who had firmly opposed any major initiatives during the revolutionary period had little choice but to concede that the time for action had arrived. It is this environment that inspired the Twenty-One Demands.[3]

Presented to the Chinese government following the capture of Tsingtao and incorporated into a series of treaties and agreements signed on May 7, 1915, these demands were a motley collection of measures, organized into five groups. One group, dealing with the Hanyehp'ing mining complex, the principal source of raw materials for Japan's iron and steel industry, aimed at resolving issues outstanding from negotiations in 1913. Another called on China to promise not to lease or cede any coastal territory to another power and, in effect, extended the non-alienation agreement on Fukien to all the republic's littoral provinces. Yet another, designated "Group V," included such miscellaneous items as railway concessions in Fukien and the freedom of Japanese missionaries to proselytize. It also called for the standardization of the weapons used by the armed forces of the two countries and, perhaps most important, the installation of Japanese advisors in key positions in the central government. Those in Tokyo of a more moderate persuasion had grave reservations about the last two elements in Group V. Indeed, Foreign

Minister Katō Takaaki himself, under activist pressure, had included these measures with some reluctance. Group V also drew sharp criticism from British and U.S. representatives, who had indicated a willingness, albeit grudging, to tolerate other elements of the Japanese initiative. All things considered, Katō decided to withdraw them as formal demands and reframed them as "desiderata" for specific discussion at a future time.[4]

Among the Twenty-One Demands, those dealing with Shantung and Manchuria formed the most important and substantive elements. Group I called on China to sanction the transfer of all German claims in Shantung to Japan following a final peace settlement. It also contained provisions for a new branch line for the Shantung Railway that would connect the main trunk to either Lungk'ou or Chefoo on the north coast and for additional treaty ports in the province. Chinese acquiescence to these terms represented a major breakthrough for Japan's imperialist diplomacy. Although the downgrading of Group V put initiatives in Fukien, once again, on hold, Japan's acquisition of a sphere of interest south of the Wall opened a new imperialist front and qualitatively broadened its expansionist activities.[5]

The prospect of managing a sphere in Shantung inevitably diminished the centrality of Manchuria in Japan's imperial policies. At the same time, the lessening of attention remained relative. In absolute terms, those elements of the Twenty-One Demands pertaining to Manchuria, designated Group II, substantially strengthened Japan's position in the territory. They extended the lease on Kwantung to 99 years from the original date, allowing Japan to hold the territory until 1997. A similar extension of reversion dates on the SMR and its Antung–Mukden branch to 99 years guaranteed Japanese possession of the trunk line until 2002 and the Antung–Mukden branch until 2007. Group II also included a long list of iron and coal mines to be opened to Japanese exploitation. Of the iron mines, Anshan represented the most important by far, and the SMR almost immediately began implementing plans to start a small-scale ironworks. As the former head of Japan's state-owned Yawata Ironworks, General Nakamura Yūjirō (1852–1928), the new governor of the SMR, had good credentials to lead such a venture.[6] Among coal mines, the Hsinch'iu mine in Jehol presented itself as the most promising, with reserves rumored to be comparable to those at Fushun. No railway line served Hsinch'iu, however, and its full-scale commercial exploitation could not proceed without new transportation facilities.[7] Although this initiative contained no new Manchurian railway concessions, one clause in Group II gave Japan the right of first refusal on any railway loans made in southern Manchuria and constituted a bilateral recognition of Japan's claim to a railway monopoly. Another clause in this group called for a "fundamental revision" in the loan arrangements governing the Ch'angch'un–Kirin railway, a step that would lead in 1917 to the placement of the line under the SMR's contract management.[8]

The most important achievement of imperialist diplomacy in Manchuria, however, lay in the acquisition of rights to lease land on a long-term and renewable basis. Although Tokyo's negotiators failed to win terms for outright ownership or to extend the scope of lease rights to Inner Mongolia, the agreement reached on this issue fulfilled Japan's essential concerns and removed what Gotō Shinpei and others had postulated as the principal barrier to further imperialist progress in the territory. This diplomatic coup had far-reaching ramifications. Enjoying extraterritorial privileges, Japanese settlers would be immune from Chinese courts and police and fall under the authority of consular officials. These arrangements implied the establishment, on a scale dependent on how many Japanese settled in the territory, of a dual system of law and administration in Manchuria, one for Japanese, the other for Chinese. Taken to a logical conclusion, this dualism would lay the foundations for a quasi-colonial condominium in the territory. Indeed, should certain districts come to be settled by a Japanese majority, they would become virtual Japanese possessions, and consular authorities, the equivalent of colonial officials. Such an outcome, of course, was precisely what advocates of colonization hoped to achieve.[9]

Katō's accomplishments in high diplomacy, however, formed only the first step in this new round of expansion. Agreements in 1915 served to open doors, but the real work of empire-building lay in the exercise of concessionary rights, and there remained many obstacles yet to confront. Realizing in practice the gains Japan had acquired on paper would require much effort as well as a clear set of policies. Some officials, responsible for the front-line implementation of a program based on Japan's new rights, worried that diplomatic success might lead to complacency about the hard road ahead and took the occasion to remind Tokyo that the task of chewing what Japan had bitten off presented major difficulties.

The views of SMR Governor Nakamura Yūjirō represent this admonitory line well. In a lengthy memorandum prepared in June 1915, he underscored the need for a clear Manchuria policy.

How will we, in practice, make use of the rights we have acquired? A number of opinions have been raised in public discussion, but thus far, I have heard nothing that resembles a full-dressed plan of action. Indeed, there have been little more than desultory efforts to induce a few footloose spirits with a little money in their pockets to cross the plains of Manchuria. After the fall of Tsingtao last year, the newly occupied territories were deluged with what might be called a "flood tide of the empty-handed"; with nothing to do, these people were in short order reduced to poverty. Should this disgraceful state of affairs be reproduced in Manchuria, there is reason to fear damage to our national prestige and credibility. It is clear that in the future, anyone in the least bit interested in engaging in the task of developing Manchuria, whether through mining, agriculture, or animal husbandry, must be furnished with substantial capital and operate on a large scale if he expects to succeed. Moreover, he will be all the more blessed economically if he can make skillful use of Chinese workers, whose strong points lie in their willingness to accept the lowest standards of living and to tolerate the extremes of the climate.[10]

On agricultural immigration in particular, he warned:

The settlement of Japanese farmers to engage in cultivation in Manchuria is vital to the establishment of our national power in the region. However, the popular notion that agricultural settlers without capital can, with their labor alone, compete with the Chinese is mistaken. . . . We must strictly avoid encouraging the immigration of tenant farmers.[11]

Nakamura had good reason to emphasize the need to clarify settlement policy. The polemics of 1913 tended to place the blame for slow progress on the lack of rights and the weakness of Japanese diplomatic resolve. Experts acquainted with conditions in the territory and the problems facing large-scale immigration certainly knew better.

Experiments in agricultural settlement launched before the war in Kwantung and the Railway Zone, in fact, lent support to Nakamura's point. Although unlikely to have figured directly into the governor's assessment in June, preliminary results available by the end of 1915 offered little cause for encouragement. The Kwantung Government-General had completed basic construction work at Aikawamura, the model rice-farming village, in April 1915. The crude and inhospitable conditions encountered by the first group of families recruited for the project on their arrival, however, so discouraged many that they turned around and went home without even attempting to establish themselves. Only two families remained at the end of the year. No doubt this development represented a major embarrassment for the Government-General. The SMR's project for settling former railway guards fared somewhat better, not least because the candidates had direct knowledge of the conditions in the territory from the outset. In 1914, five households took up the offer. In 1915, seven more joined the undertaking, and most enjoyed some success at commercial farming. Their achievements, however, rested heavily on SMR support, including low-interest loans and a dramatic 80 percent discount on rents. A subsequent analysis pointed out that these farm ventures could not have survived without this help. Land rights, then, clearly failed to provide the panacea promised by advocates of a forward policy in 1913. Given the difficulty in promoting Japanese farming in areas under the full protection of Japanese colonial power, the barriers to making a success of homesteading in the Manchurian hinterland appeared all the more formidable.[12]

The problems inherent in settling large numbers of Japanese in Manchuria, land rights aside, represented one stumbling block facing Japanese policymakers in the attempt to take advantage of their diplomatic breakthrough. Another serious problem was the difficulty of raising foreign capital for Japanese imperial ventures during the early years of the war. Historians who have emphasized the financial aspects of Japanese imperialism have pointed out that Japan exported relatively little of its own capital during the early years of expansion and relied, instead, on borrowing abroad.[13] The outbreak of war in Europe virtually choked off this source, and progress on a variety of projects, particularly on outstanding railway concessions, came to a virtual halt. The inability to raise funds, indeed, explains, in part, why railways did not figure more prominently in the Twenty-One Demands. A push to conclude formal contracts on the lines negotiated in 1913 would seem a natural element in an initiative containing numerous other efforts at cleaning up unfinished business. The inaccessibility of funds, however, precluded any major thrust in this area.

The status of the Ssup'ingkai–T'aonan railway, the first priority among the five concessions negotiated in 1913, illustrates this problem. Talks on this project had progressed at a snail's pace during the first few months of the Ōkuma cabinet. Following the outbreak of the war, Katō decided to suspend further discussion because of potential difficulties in financing the project even if negotiations succeeded.[14] The incongruity of stalled progress on railways in Manchuria in the midst of Japan's great imperialist push, however, seems to have troubled Katō. Probably concerned that the failure

to press forward on existing concessions might cast doubt on Japan's determination to follow through its new rights, the foreign minister sought to reopen talks shortly after the conclusion of the 1915 agreements. The problem
of capital, however, forced him to modify plans for implementation. Although claims regarding the five railways remained unchanged, the Foreign
Ministry would, for the time being, limit its efforts to negotiate a contract
for the construction of a short, 55-mile segment of the Ssup'ingkai–T'aonan
line running to the river port of Chengchiat'un. This step represented a token initiative entailing no more than a small fraction of the hundreds of
miles of railways agreed upon in 1913.[15] Economic prosperity during the second half of the war would relieve these financial constraints dramatically,
but in 1915 funds remained extremely tight and imposed a low ceiling on
what Japan could do in China, regardless of political opportunities.

Japanese negotiators successfully concluded talks on the Ssup'ingkai–
Chengchiat'un railway in December 1915, with construction slated to begin immediately. Discussions had proved strenuous and frustrating; it had taken a
full six months to reach agreement over a very short line. Japan's chief representative in these talks, Odagiri Masunosuke (1868–1934) of the Yokohama
Specie Bank, noted that the Chinese side had thrown every conceivable obstacle in the way of resolution and examined each word in the contract mi-
croscopically.[16] Such behavior underscored yet another kind of problem
facing policy implementation in the aftermath of the Twenty-One Demands. Japanese efforts to enforce the Treaty of Peking after 1905 had made
it clear that if defeated at the level of high diplomacy, the Chinese possessed
many inner lines of defense to which they could retreat and carry out an effective resistance. Japanese diplomats no doubt anticipated a grueling and
possibly protracted effort to break through such barriers to the exercise of
the rights won in 1915. The Chinese did not disappoint them. For example,
consuls in Manchuria maintained a close eye on local compliance with the
recent agreement allowing Japanese to lease land. They began to see the direction that obstruction would take in a number of early test cases. Local officials told those seeking leases that they had no instructions from the central government authorizing such privileges. Evidence emerged of Chinese
officials explicitly ordering landlords not to rent or lease property to Japanese. Consuls in Mukden and Ch'angch'un reported in late 1915 that local
authorities "have not significantly changed their attitude since the signing of
the agreement."[17]

Although Japanese policymakers had anticipated obstructionism of this kind, Odagiri, who had been involved in talks on Manchurian railways since 1913, believed that Chinese recalcitrance had worsened since the spring of 1915. Indeed, he thought this trend was related to the popular outrage in China following the Twenty-One Demands, which he found rather surprising in its scale and ferocity.[18] The Chinese popular response to the Antung–Mukden railway affair in 1909 had foreshadowed such reactions, but the groundswell of anger in 1915 had little precedent. An anti-Japanese boycott movement began in March while negotiations were continuing, organized in part by Chinese students returning from Japan, and spread fairly quickly throughout the country. The Japanese ultimatum on May 7 led to an escalation of protest that drew the Chinese business community into the movement. The boycott quickly transformed itself into an active "buy Chinese" campaign. Business leaders also launched a popular fundraising campaign to support the expansion of the nation's arsenals and the build-up of its armed forces. In addition to mass rallies, protests entailed occasional violence as well, including attacks on Japanese businesses and residents. In Hankow, the protest erupted into a minor riot in the Japanese quarter. Yüan at first appeared to comply with Japanese demands to suppress such activity, but at the same time, he seemed to gain strength from the movement. Public anger was aimed directly at Japan rather than at the Peking government for yielding to the ultimatum. Officials in Tokyo, as well as their representatives stationed in China, suspected the Yüan regime of sponsoring the anti-Japanese campaign.[19]

Few Japanese at this time took Chinese nationalism any more seriously than they had earlier. Political unrest was seen as a reflection of the same benighted factionalism that had enfeebled Korea in the late nineteenth century and necessitated Japanese intervention. Outrage at Japan resulted from misunderstanding and deliberate misconstruction by officials with an interest in manipulating popular opinion for their own gains.[20] Nonetheless, the groundswell of Chinese resistance at all levels, regardless of its fundamental nature, could not be ignored.

Two major trends in thinking about how to deal with the mounting anti-Japanese movement emerged in the second half of 1915. One called for moderation, a softening of attitudes toward China, and the introduction of more give-and-take in negotiations. Odagiri's views, articulated in a lengthy report on the course of the Ssup'ingkai–Chengchiat'un railway talks submitted in

December 1915, represented this trend. In his assessment, further pressure on China would only increase resistance. Although he nominally affirmed the Twenty-One Demands as a positive and necessary step, he expressed his criticism of the approach in no uncertain terms. He warned:

If we are to continue the kind of aggressive, menacing, and coercive attitudes we have adopted in the past few years, we invite the anger and indignation of China's government and the majority of its people. Needless to say, this will obstruct the development of our economic and business interests. If, on the contrary, we wish to develop our economic and business interests, we must approach this government and its people by upholding principles of peace, magnanimity, and compassion in our relations.

Odagiri saw the need to turn a new leaf in Sino-Japanese relations. At the same time, his view of reform essentially entailed a shift to the use of what Mao Tse-tung would have described as "sugarcoated bullets." Judicious bribery, in his view, represented the best way of demonstrating "magnanimity" in railway negotiations.[21] Even among those inclined toward greater imperial activism, some appeared to have shared this perspective. Before the opening of negotiations over the Twenty-One Demands, Lieutenant General Ōshima Ken'ichi had recommended that bargaining contain some element of reciprocity. "What we seek from China is by no means small. If we wish to succeed in our negotiations, we cannot avoid offering the Chinese something in return." He frankly recommended a policy of alternating carrots with sticks. "Under a long period of political degeneration, China has lost its proper values as a nation. Selfishness and shortsightedness dominate. If Japan is to lead and assist China under these conditions, it will be necessary to apply both force and gentle persuasion, severity and leniency, in alternating doses." His remarks also underscore the fact that the call for a milder approach had little to do with respect for Chinese nationalism.[22]

The other trend called for the use of the iron fist in response to intransigence. According to this view, Foreign Minister Katō had adopted an excessively conciliatory position from the beginning, and backing-down on Group V had demonstrated Japan's lack of resolve. Major General Machida Keiu (1865–1939), military attaché to the Japanese legation in Peking, had argued for a hard-line position from the beginning of the talks. He had warned in 1914, "The Chinese have never been a people who can be won over with kindness. . . . The only thing that influences the Chinese is power. I am certain that if Japan acts in this instance with great resolve and manifests its strength with the backing of armed force, the fulfillment of our demands will not be a difficult matter."[23] From this perspective, softening Japan's stance in the face of resistance in the second half of 1915 represented precisely the wrong approach to take. Officers in the Army General Staff with adventurist leanings, like Lieutenant General Tanaka Giichi, favored stern measures against Yüan.[24]

In the end, the Ōkuma government not only decided on a hard-line approach but concluded that the most productive course was to topple the Yüan regime.[25] Several factors account for the turn of policy in this extreme direction. One was Katō Takaaki's resignation as foreign minister in July 1915. Blamed for the response in China, Katō found himself attacked from both ends of the political spectrum, by one group for going too far and by the other for not having gone far enough. Moreover, he had alienated Yamagata Aritomo, who continued to exert influence behind the scenes, by failing to consult with him adequately in the declaration of war against Germany, the formulation of the Twenty-One Demands, and the subsequent negotiations. Under the circumstances, Katō felt it wise to remove himself from the spotlight for the time being and leave the follow-up work to others. Within the context of the times, Katō had represented a moderating force in China policy, and his resignation removed that influence.[26]

A series of initiatives on Yüan's part constituted another factor. The Chinese president had come to favor the idea of abolishing the republic established in 1912, restoring the monarchy, and installing himself as emperor. Seeing in the nationalist upsurge an opportunity to rally support to his cause, he stepped up this effort in 1915 following the conclusion of Sino-Japanese negotiations. His monarchical ambitions, however, triggered violent opposition, beginning with an armed revolt in Yunnan. Advocates of an adventurist approach to policy in China, as they had in 1911 and 1913, saw this development as a chance to make even greater gains and possibly push the situation toward partition.[27]

The perception that Yüan planned to enlist the support of the Great Powers against Japan, however, was probably decisive in persuading the Ōkuma cabinet of the need for drastic steps. The Allies had been pressing the Chinese government to drop its neutrality in the conflict, to break relations with Germany, and to support the war effort by providing material assistance. The Japanese government, as we shall see, sponsored such a move only a year later, but at this time Tokyo saw Yüan's favorable response to

Allied overtures as a ploy to pit the Great Powers against Japan. Although Britain and the United States had expressed their displeasure with the Twenty-One Demands in 1915, they had not, as anticipated, offered active support to China or substantive opposition to Japan. As a member of the alliance, however, China would enjoy a major change in status. Sino-Japanese disputes could potentially become a matter of concern for the Allies and invite intervention. Moreover, China would find itself in a good position to obstruct the postwar confirmation of Japanese gains, particularly in the matter of transferring German rights in Shantung.[28]

The combination of these considerations led the Ōkuma government to adopt a policy of deposing Yüan. In the early months of 1916, it authorized covert action to foment unrest in China and tap anti-monarchical sentiment where possible. These operations included the initiation of another Manchurian independence movement, which enlisted the support of a dissident Mongol prince. Toppling Yüan rather than severing Manchuria from China proper, however, was the primary aim of this gambit, and the government in Tokyo called off the action once the embattled Chinese president agreed to back down. Yüan died of illness on June 5, 1916. In his place, the relatively weak figure of Li Yüan-hung (1864–1928) assumed the presidency. Insofar as Li seemed to pose no threat to Japan's interests, Tokyo found him acceptable. The Japanese believed, in any event, that they had taught Chinese political leaders an important lesson in the consequences of thwarting their wishes.[29]

The death of Yüan Shih-k'ai marked the beginning of an era of prolonged instability and disorder in China that would last for more than a decade. The late president's associates in the Peiyang Army, which had formed the strongest military force in China since the twilight years of the Ch'ing and the principal prop of the republican government, began competing for power. Military leaders and associated civilian officials splintered into a confusing array of regional cliques of so-called warlords. Among them, a former bandit turned local official by the name of Chang Tso-lin (1873–1928) moved quickly to establish a base in Manchuria. In Peking, Yüan's prime minister and former Peiyang Army general, Tuan Ch'i-jui (1865–1936), continued in this post under President Li and appeared the best positioned among the contenders. No one, however, seemed quite strong enough to fill Yüan's shoes. Yüan's regime, to be sure, had lacked real strength, and he had failed to rein in the centrifugal forces unleashed in 1911. The Ōkuma government, however, clearly bore great responsibility for triggering the collapse of a political center in China, a development that, in the long run, proved far more injurious to China than the Twenty-One Demands themselves. Ōkuma and his colleagues, moreover, appeared not to have a clear follow-up plan to their scheme of overthrowing Yüan. No doubt, a dramatically weakened Chinese government was favored by some of those who engineered the campaign. Chaos offered opportunities to move toward partition or to establish a virtual protectorate over China. On the other hand, disorder and instability might well prove counterproductive to Japanese interests. Imperialists had always favored a weak but stable Chinese government as essential to the system of concession hunting. In any event, what the Ōkuma cabinet might have done, given time, remains a matter of speculation since its resignation some four months after the death of Yüan bequeathed the problem of a follow-up policy in China to its successor.

Imperial Policies of the "Korean Clique"

Okuma's decision to step down stemmed more from domestic considerations than from developments in China. The question of China policy, however, did have a considerable influence on the choice of his successor. Ōkuma had hoped to resign in favor of Katō Takaaki and lobbied for his appointment in 1916. Katō, however, had alienated leaders across a broad spectrum in his handling of the initiative in 1915. Yamagata, feeling particularly aggrieved at Katō's failure to consult him on key policy issues, firmly opposed such a succession and put forward his protégé General Terauchi Masatake as a candidate. In the elder statesman's estimate, Terauchi would not only carry out an effective and responsible China policy but also transcend the petty bickering of party politics plaguing national leadership. Yamagata managed to win a consensus for this choice.[30]

The next two years under Terauchi would witness policies in Manchuria and China proper that departed significantly from those of the Ōkuma government. A number of factors contributed to this change. From the outset, the new prime minister committed himself to rectifying what he regarded as the errors of his predecessor. A veteran army leader who had enjoyed an unprecedented tenure as service minister between 1904 and 1911, Terauchi came to office with impeccable imperialist credentials. He had most recently held office as Korea's first governor-general, earning a reputation for brutal and iron-fisted administration, and had provided much of the impetus behind the Manchuria-Korea integration scheme of 1913. At the same time, he firmly opposed adventurism and had sharply criticized the campaign against Yüan Shih-k'ai in 1916. Indeed, dissidents within the army, who had taken heart with the rise of a more militant China policy since the outbreak of the war, regarded Terauchi as an adversary, not only because of what they regarded as his "soft" stance on empire but also because of his perpetuation of clique politics during his tenure as army minister. By the same token, the new prime minister enjoyed support among civilian policymakers favoring moderation in China, who looked to him to curb extremist tendencies within his own service.[31]

Terauchi's opposition to adventurism, however, reflected mainstream army views, and dissident charges notwithstanding, his position on issues of empire and national defense hardly warranted characterization as "soft." Moreover, as an officer who had dedicated much of his career to the development of his service, he would show little hesitation in using his position to promote the institutional interests of the army. Those hoping for any substantive moderation would find themselves deeply disappointed. Terauchi's ties to colonial Korea further strengthened the imperialist complexion of his administration. He brought with him two associates from his stint as governor-general who would serve as his key aides in the management of China policy during his tenure. Shōda Kazue (1868–1948), the governor of the Bank of Chōsen, Korea's central bank, received appointment as finance minister. Nishihara Kamezō (1873–1954), a one-time employee of the same bank and an active colonial business promoter who had helped organize cotton traders in support of the Pusan–Mukden scheme, would act as Terauchi's personal representative in negotiations with Chinese authorities during this period.[32] Detractors described the China policy team of Terauchi, Shōda, and Nishihara as the "Korean clique."

Political developments in China also deeply influenced the making of policy during this period. A dangerous rift between north and south began to take shape, and Tuan Ch'i-jui's prospects as China's aspiring strongman grew increasingly dim. Although Tuan had shown no pro-Japanese tendencies during Yüan's tenure, the new situation demanded that he find helpful foreign friends, and Japan appeared the logical candidate. This circumstance created an opportunity for Japan to improve relations with China and to adopt a superficially softer stance without running the danger of appearing irresolute. Moderates favored a decisive shift to the use of carrots in the pursuit of policy goals in China under the guise of rendering friendly support to the "legitimate" government of the country. Others saw greater possibilities and entertained the notion of managing Tuan as a Japanese client.[33]

Yet another factor of major importance to the policies of this period was a dramatic improvement in Japan's financial situation. By the middle of the war, unprecedented prosperity had come to East Asia. The withdrawal of Western competition coupled with war demand had triggered a business boom in both China and Japan. Investment capital became more widely available, and Japanese enterprise began moving into areas of heavy industry at home and manufacturing in China it had been unable to enter before. The revenues of the Japanese government also improved substantially, nearly doubling from ¥709 million in 1915 to ¥1.4 billion in 1918. The stringent conditions that had forced Katō to struggle to finance the Ssup'ingkai–Chengchiat'un line no longer prevailed. For the first time, Japan found itself in a position to use its own financial resources as leverage in China policy, one reason why Shōda, as finance minister, would enjoy an unusually powerful voice in this field.[34]

Finally, developments in the European war had a major impact on Terauchi's policies. The conflict remained unresolved by the end of 1916, and its outcome was uncertain. It had already lasted far longer than analysts in Japan had expected, and it would likely produce more far-reaching changes in the balance of power globally, and most certainly in East Asia, than anticipated.[35] Beset with domestic difficulties as well as a flagging effort on the Eastern Front, Russia found itself in serious trouble by 1916, and in the spring of 1917 it would face revolution. Leaders in Tokyo recognized that plans based on earlier assumptions about the postwar situation demanded major revision. The European conflict also helped shaped policy for a different reason. Japanese military observers began drawing lessons from the war in Europe, on the battlefield as well as the home front, that demanded a basic rethinking of defense policy.[36] This re-examination would have a profound and lasting influence on the army's view of the relationship between empire and national defense.

Emerging opportunities and needs, along with the proclivities of Terauchi and his colleagues during this era, produced a large and complex body of imperial policies. They encompassed renewed efforts to create an integrated economy in Northeast Asia, structural reforms aimed at strengthening army authority in Manchuria, and the opening of a new expansionist front in north Manchuria and Siberia. They also included a massive foreign aid program for the Tuan regime, along with some tentative steps in a new program for imperial autarky.

The concern with economic integration between Manchuria and Korea clearly reflected the influence of the Terauchi government's colonial ties on the policies of this period. The three railway agencies continued the discount schedule on the Pusan–Mukden route initiated in 1913 and expanded the program in 1916 to cover a spectrum of goods beyond cotton, including imports as well as exports. For the most part, however, the items covered by the expanded policy remained low-volume, high-value goods. Predictably, the new discounts provoked protests from Dairen-based interests. In 1917, the Terauchi government took integration one step further by placing the Chōsen Railway under the management of the SMR on a contractual basis. The SMR assumed full responsibility for the operation and maintenance of the Korean railway system. Under this arrangement, the SMR would absorb losses suffered by the Korean system but share net earnings with the colonial government. These terms provided considerable relief to authorities in Seoul, given the financial troubles plaguing their railway, and demonstrated the value of having former colleagues in high places in Tokyo. The fact that a Manchuria-based Japanese corporation took over the management of a state-owned railway in colonial Korea also speaks to the unique status of the SMR.[37]

Driven in part by the overall expansion of trade between Japan, Manchuria, and Korea resulting from the war boom, railway traffic along the Pusan–Mukden route grew noticeably during this period. The discount policy continued to influence the movement of cotton goods, allowing Pusan to hold the dominant position it had acquired over Dairen in this field in 1913. In 1914, textile distributors shipped 17,248 tons by way of the Pusan route as opposed to 6,661 through Dairen. In 1917, Pusan had lost some relative ground, but absolute growth remained impressive: 24,343 tons moved by way of Pusan and 10,451 by Dairen. The expansion of bilateral trade between Manchuria and Korea, as opposed to Japanese trade with Manchuria routed through Korea, represented a particularly significant development. Manchurian exports to Korea increased in value from about ¥3.3 million in 1914 to ¥18.3 million in 1919. Imports from Korea increased from ¥2.6 million to ¥5.3 million in the same period. Traffic along the Antung–Mukden line expanded steadily, from one million tons in 1914 to 2.3 million in 1919, a rate of growth better than that of the main line before 1918.[38]

Changing traffic patterns offered promise, but achievements fell substantially short of goals. Although the Pusan route performed substantially better, the Dairen route retained its dominance over the main areas of commercial transportation. Growth, in other words, had not altered the fundamental economic problems inherent in the attempt to pursue a "Pusan strategy." Contract management of the Korean system by the SMR did little to resolve these problems. In fact, although the SMR assumed managerial responsibility, providing personnel, capital, and technology, it continued to operate the Manchurian and Korean railways as separate systems, with discrete administrative and accounting structures. The Chōsen Railway and the Government-General of Korea clearly benefited from this measure, and insofar as providing such assistance constituted a policy goal, these arrangements succeeded. As steps toward a genuine railway union, however, they proved less significant than they might seem.[39]

The SMR's takeover of the Korean railway system, however, held symbolic importance for advocates of integration. Terauchi, in fact, appears to have seen this measure at least partially in such terms. Ever since the initiation of the Pusan–Mukden scheme in 1913, Terauchi had pressed for administrative as well as economic union. He supported the long-standing idea of merging the Kwantung and Korean governments-general, which, given the relative responsibilities and power of the two entities, would have meant the effective subordination of Kwantung to Seoul. The idea had made little headway before Terauchi's ascension to the post of prime minister as a result of the vehement opposition of the Foreign Ministry. Merger of the two agencies would have constituted a violation of the bargain struck in 1906, which required the maintenance of the Kwantung Government-General as an agency of relatively modest influence under the supervision of the army but subject to the direction of the Foreign Ministry as well. Placing its functions under a much more powerful colonial government in which the army enjoyed less compromised control would mean, for all intents and purposes, the further expansion of army authority in Manchuria. Terauchi wanted to reintroduce this scheme under his cabinet, but he hesitated because of a likely adverse international reaction. He told his successor in Korea, General Hasegawa Yoshimichi (1850–1924), that the administrative integration of railways represented a step in the right direction and would have to substitute for more comprehensive action for the time being.[40]

One other element of note in the effort to advance the program of integration lay in the aggressive initiatives of the Bank of Chōsen to expand its operations into Manchuria. The process began in 1913 but accelerated markedly during the war under Shōda, first as the bank's governor and subsequently as finance minister. Korea's central bank sought to establish itself as a major issuer of currency in Manchuria, and its gold yen notes gained popularity. The Bank of Chōsen moved into Manchurian railway and business loans as well, and working in conjunction with the Japan Industrial Bank and the Bank of Taiwan, displaced the Yokohama Specie Bank as the main player in this field. Another Korea-based colonial institution, the Oriental Development Company, also advanced into Manchuria and established several branches in the territory in 1917. Financing the growth of Japanese business enterprise formed its principal objective.[41]

The significance of these developments to the larger goal of regional integration, however, warrant some caution in interpretation. The expansion of the Bank of Chōsen, for example, did not necessarily imply closer economic ties between Korea and Manchuria. The Korean bank's initiatives in the territory formed part of a broad program of diversification. Pursuing opportunities created by the war boom, it also expanded its activities in the home islands and in China proper, as did the Bank of Taiwan. In this respect, the Bank of Chōsen was becoming more cosmopolitan and not dedicating special attention to bilateral economic integration. The same might be said for the Oriental Development Company.[42]

Terauchi's sponsorship of imperial integration policies reflected his continued interest in Korean affairs, but it also pointed to his role as a patron of army interests. The creation of a railway union had formed a central element of the army's agenda in 1913. Structural reforms in Manchurian administration instituted in 1917 offered further indications of this aspect of the government's political complexion. In a significant, albeit short-lived, triumph for the army in its institutional rivalry with the Foreign Ministry, reforms under Terauchi placed consular officials in Manchuria under the immediate supervision of the Kwantung Government-General. The concurrent appointment of SMR Governor Nakamura Yūjirō as governor-general of Kwantung constituted a further step toward unifying Manchuria policy under army control. This measure gave Nakamura extraordinary powers over the Leased Territory, the SMR, and the consular apparatus. Unification of

Manchurian administration along these lines would not outlast the Terauchi government and would not re-merge until 1932. Nonetheless, the army's political victory was significant and highlights once again the value of friends in high places.[43]

Integration and structural reform constituted what might be described as the pet projects of the "Korean clique." Policies formulated in response to developments in Russia and its position in East Asia occupied a more important place among the initiatives of this period. In view of the army's dire warnings about growing Russian military strength during the debates of 1911–13, Japan's traditional nemesis and recent friend had revealed surprising weakness in the first two years of the war in Europe. By 1916, Russia faced serious difficulty in the fight against Germany as well as the possibility of revolution at home. By the following year, the Allies had grown sufficiently worried to press Japan for ground troops to shore up the Eastern Front. Tokyo steadfastly declined such involvement and, reflecting a familiar pattern, looked instead toward the opportunities that an enfeebled Russia might create for Japan in East Asia.[44]

The opening of talks between Russia and Japan over the possible sale of the branch of the CER running between Ch'angch'un and Harbin offered the first indication of what such opportunities might entail. Although Japanese leaders declined the invitation to send troops to Europe, they offered other forms of material assistance, such as munitions shipments, and a railway deal entered consideration as part of a reciprocal bargain. That the Russians would even consider such a measure represented a major development and signaled the possibility of a fundamental change in its commitments in the East. The sale of the CER's southern branch would make north Manchuria strategically untenable, something that Japanese military analysts had pointed out when unfounded rumors of such a prospect first circulated in 1907. Japanese strategy as developed since 1905 focused on the seizure of Harbin as the decisive moment of a war against Russia. From a military perspective, then, this deal would essentially give the Japanese army Harbin without firing a shot.[45]

As talks progressed, however, it became clear that the Russians would not concede their position entirely. They tentatively agreed to the sale of half of the line, a segment stretching from Ch'angch'un to T'aolaichao station on the banks of the Sungari River. The river marked at this location the boundary of Russia's and Japan's respective spheres of influence as established in the 1907 accords, and this segment of the CER had always represented a "violation" of the demarcation line. Russian resistance to giving up more than that portion of the line extending south of the sphere border indicated that they intended to maintain their traditional claims.[46] Although this agreement still represented a major gain for Japan, particularly for the ability of the SMR to compete for northern traffic, it came as a letdown to many imperial activists. Further disappointments awaited. The outbreak of revolution in March 1917 disrupted the Russo-Japanese talks. The Kerensky government, which took power as a result of the upheaval, proved as anxious for assistance as its predecessor and agreed to the sale, only to fall in November to an uprising staged by the Bolsheviks. The installation of a "red" government that Japan remained unprepared to recognize put an end to the idea of a railway agreement in the immediate future.[47]

The collapse of imperial Russia itself had earthshaking significance for Japan and overshadowed any disappointment about the failure of the railway scheme. Concern that the European war would spread to the East shaped one immediate reaction to this event. The Bolsheviks had made peace with Germany, and many Japanese analysts believed German domination of Russia likely. Such an eventuality might well force Japan to increase its role in the conflict. Perceptions of unparalleled opportunity for Japanese expansion in the fall of this once-great empire of the north, however, informed another response. In the view of some army leaders, the notion of buying a segment of the CER paled before the prospect of seizing the whole of north Manchuria by armed force. Moreover, such an initiative might readily include sections of the Russian Far East as well. Both anxiety and opportunity thus appear to have played a part in Japan's decision to participate in an Allied intervention in Siberia launched in July 1918. Japan joined the United States, Britain, and France in a 28,000-member expeditionary force to which it contributed 12,000 troops. Three months later, Japan sent an additional 73,000 troops into Eastern Siberia. This action represented the largest mobilization and deployment of Japanese armed forces since the Russo-Japanese War.[48]

The story of the Siberian Expedition has received detailed treatment in English and requires no repetition here. The principal consequences of this undertaking, which lasted until 1922, will be considered in the next chapter. What is important to note at this point is that a vacuum of power had emerged in Northeast Asia. The attempt to fill that space before another power, including the Bolsheviks themselves, seized the opportunity would become a central concern of Japanese imperial policy for the next decade. With the demise of old Russia, the agreement of 1907 no longer limited the frontiers of Japanese Manchuria, and at least in the imperialist imagination, that realm had come to encompass the vast prairies of the north.

The emergence of a power vacuum in north Manchuria and Siberia might be regarded as an extreme manifestation of the kind of opportunity that had shaped Japanese expansion in China since the beginning of the war. In this particular case, however, the elimination of Russia, at least in the form of the Great Power that the Japanese had confronted in 1904, constituted a permanent rather than a temporary change in the dynamics of competition in the East. This development marked the close of an era in the history of Japanese expansionism in which Russia as adversary and more recently, as accomplice, had occupied a central place in the calculations of imperial policy. It also contributed to a perception emerging among Japanese leaders that this unexpectedly protracted and destructive war in Europe had begun to change the world in unforeseen ways and removed many of the certainties that had underpinned Japanese policy in East Asia since the turn of the century. This war would likely produce a much more profound shift in the international balance of power than originally anticipated. Russia would no longer be an element in the equilibrium, nor would Germany, assuming an Allied victory, and Britain and France might prove too exhausted to resume a major role in East Asia in the foreseeable future. The logic of opportunism prevailing during the first half of the war would have deemed such a situation an advantage to Japan, giving it more time to pursue an aggressive policy in China. By 1917 and 1918, however, that logic had lost some of its cogency.

The workings of the imperialist system that had enabled Japan to acquire concessionary rights, which, in turn, formed the foundations of its power in Manchuria, depended heavily on the mutual recognition of these claims by expansionist states with similar interests. The imperialist community had presented a united front against Chinese resistance as well as the attempts of interlopers, such as the United States, to change the rules of the game. This system had already shown signs of weakening during the years after the Russo-Japanese War. The enthusiasm for concession hunting had declined among the Great Powers as a result of tensions in Europe, rising Chinese resistance, and disappointment with the actual benefits growing out of this approach. At the same time, the United States had become more actively critical of Great Power practices in China and was trying to put teeth in the principle of the Open Door as well as extending a sympathetic hand toward Chinese nationalism. In response, Russia and Japan had closed ranks, but they became increasingly isolated from their fellows and dependent on one another as active practitioners of the traditional imperialist game. In postwar Asia, Japan could no longer count on the Russian partnership, let alone the weaker support of France and Britain. The United States, the country least sympathetic to Japanese interests, appeared the one Western state likely to emerge from this war with its strength intact. By 1917, it required no great foresight to realize that Japan might find itself standing alone in confronting a hostile Chinese-American diplomatic combination after the war. Under these circumstances, the question of how Japan would secure and defend its wartime gains, once the conflict came to an end, became a major concern for the Terauchi cabinet.[49]

New Strategies: The Nishihara Loans

The prospect of a sea change in the imperialist order, coupled with the problem of escalating Chinese resistance, triggered a series of bold policy initiatives on the part of the Terauchi government during its last year in office, commonly known under the rubric of the "Nishihara Loans." Between September 1917 and September 1918, Japan poured an unprecedented ¥140 million into the coffers of the Chinese government, specifically to the benefit of Tuan Ch'i-jui and his circle, an undertaking made possible by wartime prosperity. Loans negotiated by Nishihara Kamezō, as Terauchi's personal representative, included ¥20 million for military reforms, ¥20 million for the reorganization of the Communications Bank, another ¥20 million for the development of telephone and telegraph service, ¥30 million for mining and forestry in north Manchuria, and ¥50 million for railways in Manchuria and Shantung. The total would have run even higher had Terauchi and his associates had their way. Nishihara discussed with Tuan's representatives the possibility of remitting Japan's share of the Boxer Indemnity for the purpose of promoting agricultural development, along with an additional low-interest loan of ¥100 million, in order to underwrite China's nationalization of iron mining and manufacturing operations in the country. Opposition from within Japan's government and the business community blocked these efforts. Nonetheless, the scale of financial agreements concluded during this single year remains remarkable.[50]

These loans had multiple policy targets, and the schemes they served operated at several levels. The Terauchi government linked the military reform loans, for example, to a plan to sponsor China's entry into the war on the Allied side. Ironically, preventing precisely such participation had been one motive for the Ōkuma government to overthrow Yüan. The Terauchi cabinet, however, saw an advantage in pre-empting U.S. sponsorship of Chinese war participation and thus ingratiating Japan with the Allies. Military aid, of course, would also support Tuan against his adversaries in the impending civil war in China and cultivate friendly ties with the Peking government.[51]

The ¥50 million in railway loans or, more precisely, advances against larger, prospective loan contracts constituted measures of a rather different character. In effect, they were "bribes" aimed at facilitating Chinese acquiescence to Japanese railway demands along the lines that Odagiri had recommended, an attempt to "purchase" concessions rather than to extract them under duress in the tradition of gunboat diplomacy. Shōda Kazue believed strongly that the lack of reciprocity in past railway agreements had formed a major source of Chinese resistance and obstruction, and he undertook a review of negotiations on the Ssup'ingkai–Chengchiat'un line shortly after taking office. He found Japanese terms excessively one-sided and onerous, injurious to the "spirit of Sino-Japanese friendship." In order to make any serious progress, he believed it important to "set aside the problematic baggage of the past, give consideration to Chinese wishes, and demonstrate [Japan's] sincerity."[52] Offering more lenient loan terms formed one aspect of the approach he favored, but perhaps more than anything else, he believed that generous advances, which the Chinese side could use for whatever purposes they might deem appropriate, would underscore Japanese goodwill.[53]

This tactic appeared to prove itself in the conclusion of a preliminary agreement for the construction of the Kirin–Hoeryong railway in June 1918. The army as well as other advocates of Manchuria-Korea integration had long sought the extension of the Ch'angch'un–Kirin line to the Korean border and eventually on to the port of Chongjin. The Chinese had acquiesced to its construction in principle in a 1909 agreement, but this understanding left the scheduling of construction to Chinese discretion. The Chinese appeared to have no intention of initiating the project in the foreseeable future, if ever. Such reluctance hardly came as a surprise. China had little interest in strengthening Japanese access to the region, which, with its large ethnic Korean population, remained vulnerable to schemes for annexation. Nor did the Chinese have anything to gain by creating a rail link to a Korean port, which would only facilitate Japanese military access and establish yet another foreign outlet for Manchurian commerce. Political and strategic problems aside, this railway represented an extremely unattractive financial proposition to the Chinese. Because of the mountainous terrain, construction costs would run inordinately high, and given the relative underdevelopment of the region, the railway promised little in the way of commercial return for the foreseeable future. An SMR survey conducted in early 1918 estimated that this 262-mile stretch of rail would cost some ¥50 million to build. An average of ¥190,000 per mile made the prospective Kirin-Hoeryong route the most expensive of all lines completed or planned in Manchuria to date. By comparison, estimates for the K'aiyüan–Hailung line in the 1913 group of concessions ran at ¥77,000 per mile and the Ssup'ingkai–Chengchiat'un at ¥91,000. Even the SMR's Antung–Mukden line, which had elicited strong objections from company management, had entailed lower costs of ¥141,000 per mile. SMR estimates for the Kirin-Hoeryong's annual net income during its early years ran to ¥2,281,000, but after deducting interest payments on the loan, calculated at an optimistic 5 percent, the railway would run a net annual deficit of approximately a quarter-million yen. The Chinese, then, confronted the prospect of building an enormously costly railway that would serve only Japanese purposes, injure their own security and sovereignty, turn over to the Japanese all its net revenue, and, on top of this, force them to dip into their own pockets to make up for the shortfall. It would be difficult to imagine a railway project in Manchuria for which the Chinese would have shown less enthusiasm.[54]

Nishihara, nonetheless, managed to persuade China's Ministry of Transportation to agree to the project. He offered, as Shōda favored, lenient loan terms. He used the model of the Anglo-German T'ientsin–P'uk'ou contract of 1908, in which the Chinese side had managed to acquire unprecedentedly favorable terms. Local taxes would serve as collateral rather than the property or revenues of the railway, ensuring that the Chinese would not lose control of the line even if they defaulted. Moreover, the chief engineer, as opposed to the larger complement of personnel written into most other contracts, was the only foreign staff required. Foreign observers had criticized the T'ientsin–P'uk'ou loan at the time for its "undue leniency and insufficient care for the safety of foreign investors."[55] The decisive factor in Nishihara's success, however, lay in the offer of a ¥10 million advance to the

Chinese against a prospective ¥50 million loan. Given the desperation of the Tuan regime for funds, its representatives were unlikely to have looked much beyond this provision before setting their seals to the agreement.[56] Nishihara and Tuan's people worked out similar arrangements in September for two railway concessions in Shantung, for a ¥20 million advance, and for the outstanding lines in Manchuria from the 1913 agreement for yet another ¥20 million.[57] Nishihara thus appeared to have achieved, in the space of a few short months, what other negotiators had failed to do over the course of five years, and in the case of the Kirin–Hoeryong, a decade. Carrots offered a clear way to overcome Chinese obstreperousness.

Nishihara limited the scheme of "buying" concessions, however, to railway loans. The main purpose behind the remaining ¥70 million earmarked for the Communications Bank, the telephone and telegraph project, and mining and forestry in north Manchuria lay elsewhere. Although developing communications and natural resources constituted matters of interest in their own right to the Japanese, Terauchi's government appears to have used these particular loans to funnel aid to the Tuan regime; the nominal projects simply served as a means to "launder" political funds. Based on inter-power accords at the time of the Reorganization Loans to the Yüan government in 1913, all "administrative loans" fell under the jurisdiction of a six-member consortium, an arrangement designed to preclude the efforts of any one power to exert undue financial influence over the Chinese government. The agreement excluded "industrial loans," however, and Nishihara used this provision to circumvent consortium rules for precisely the purpose of establishing influence over the Peking regime. These loans would cement Japan's ties with Tuan and his circle and establish the would-be Chinese strongman as a Japanese client, dependent on Tokyo's financial largesse and, accordingly, willing to do its bidding. The military loan and, as a secondary function, the railway loans, would serve this purpose as well. Although couched in the language of bilateral cooperation and, for some Japanese leaders, pan-Asian solidarity, working through client rulers represented a well-established practice in modern imperialism, one that might serve as prelude to the creation of a protectorate. Attempts to reduce the Korean monarchy to client status had formed a component of Japanese strategies on the peninsula at least until 1895. Some had favored such an approach for China as well. Yamagata and Terauchi had, indeed, advocated "cooperation" with

Yüan at the outset of the war and had viewed Group V of the Twenty-One Demands as a step in this direction.[58]

Both the opportunity and need for a client-management strategy in China had become more apparent by 1917 than at the start of the war. The Chinese backlash to the Twenty-One Demands had demonstrated the limited efficacy of traditional gunboat diplomacy, and given the likely outcome of the war, the Japanese could no longer count on imperialist solidarity to support and legitimize their claims. Tuan, the strongest contender for national leadership, faced both numerous rivals and the possibility of civil war and appeared to be a far better candidate for client-ruler than Yüan Shih-k'ai. Cooperation with a dependent Tuan, propped up by Japanese funds and indirect military support, would at least mitigate, if not largely resolve, the problem of Chinese resistance to Japanese encroachment. It would also eliminate the need for Great Power support of Japanese claims in Manchuria and Shantung. Under the framework of bilateral Sino-Japanese cooperation, the Chinese themselves would sanction those claims and foreclose the opportunity for U.S. diplomatic intervention.

The scheme underlying the aborted iron-nationalization loan, although closely related to this emerging strategy of bilateral cooperation, represented yet another dimension to the Nishihara Loans and in some ways signaled an even greater departure from traditional imperialist approaches. This project was part of a larger proposal, which also included plans for a joint Sino-Japanese venture for the development of cotton and wool production in China, along with a Japanese-sponsored effort to nationalize China's railway system.[59] Nishihara's plans, not surprisingly, excluded existing Japanese mining concessions, such as those at Anshan and Penhsihu. Nonetheless, taken at face value, Japanese political support for the nationalization of the Chinese iron-mining and -manufacturing industry, let alone a willingness to underwrite its costs, would seem to represent a dramatic reversal of past positions. Indeed, with the aim of protecting existing as well as prospective concessionary rights, Japanese diplomats, in cooperation with representatives of the Western powers, had taken a firm stand against Yüan Shih-k'ai's attempts to place all of China's iron resources under national control in 1914.[60] Given the likelihood that similar measures on the part of the Chinese to reassert sovereign control over their natural resources would follow the nationalization of the iron industry, Nishihara's proposal implied a break with traditional concepts of imperialist rights, a readiness to abandon the framework of proprietary concessions that had formed the foundations of Japan's expansionist strategies since the beginning of the century. Indeed, Nishihara, an advocate of pan-Asian solidarity and economic cooperation, as well as Finance Minister Shōda, who shared similar views, called for reforms in China policy precisely along these lines. In a memorandum to the cabinet in the summer of 1917, Shōda expanded his critique of railway loans to encompass Japan's overall economic relations with China.

In the past, we have, for the most part, considered securing our own advantage to be the most urgent concern in our economic relations with China. In our investments in China, for example, we have sought to maximize our gains while minimizing those accruing to the Chinese. Not only has this situation led to frequent disputes, but we have succumbed to the error of absorbing ourselves in pursuing immediate advantage while losing sight of the larger picture. Regrettably, this has invited misunderstanding and suspicion on the part of the Chinese people.[61]

The iron-loan proposal would seem to represent an effort to introduce a genuine element of reciprocity in economic relations, to launch what might be described as a Sino-Japanese "alliance for progress."

Not surprisingly, however, Japan's generous offer of foreign aid did not come without strings attached. The Japanese loan would finance the establishment of a national ironworks, with the facility itself as collateral. A Japanese chief engineer would head technical operations. The ironworks would produce for export as well as for domestic demand and, on the basis of a special contract, would guarantee Japan sufficient output to meet its requirements.[62] Nishihara's plan, then, involved, among other things, a straightforward, pragmatic bargain. China would gain at least nominal sovereignty over its iron resources and an end to foreign concession hunting in this field, including Japanese encroachments. Japan would gain, in effect, secure and privileged access to all of China's iron reserves. Placed in the larger context of the emerging strategy of "bilateral cooperation" with the Tuan regime, the arrangement offered Japan other advantages. It could appease Chinese nationalist sentiment, while actually accelerating economic encroachment. Nationalization, moreover, would pre-empt foreign competition. To be sure, Japanese business would also have to forgo the opportunity of acquiring proprietary concessions, but from a broader perspective of national policy, the tradeoff seemed worth the cost. Even the most successful concession-hunting campaign could never have brought more than a small fraction of China's iron resources under Japanese control. Under Nishihara's scheme, Japan would become a silent partner in China's iron industry as a whole.

Taken to its logical conclusion, this approach had far-reaching ramifications for Japanese imperial policy. It could be applied, as Nishihara envisioned, to the development of agricultural resources, which would have been difficult, although not impossible, as the SMR had demonstrated in Manchuria, to manage through traditional techniques. It also offered useful applications in railway policy. Rather than seeking concessions on a piecemeal basis, Japan might direct the development of China's national network through special arrangements with the Chinese Ministry of Transportation. Applied at the broadest level, this strategy might well allow Japan to abandon concession hunting altogether. The reform of China policy represented not a retreat from the nation's broader imperialist commitments but, rather, a shift from encroachment at the "retail" level, so to speak, to the "wholesale."[63]

Nishihara's iron scheme represented an innovative approach to imperial expansion, an adaptation to growing Chinese resistance and the inimical environment anticipated in the postwar period. At the same time, a new set of concerns played a central part in motivating this initiative. The Japanese had sought secure access to China's iron resources since the founding of the Yawata Ironworks in 1898. The attempt to exert control on the vast scale made possible by "cooperation," however, constituted more than a simple extension of this goal, inflated by imperialist greed and megalomania. Indeed, although Nishihara offered many pragmatic and ideological reasons in defense of his proposals for managing Chinese resources, his primary justification rested on growing concerns about economic self-sufficiency. The nation's future security, in his view, would depend on its ability to sustain an autarkic sphere in East Asia. This understanding, in turn, stemmed from the lessons that Japanese military analysts had drawn from their observations of the European war during the tenure of the Terauchi cabinet. Ultimately, the inability of Terauchi and his team to persuade the government as a whole of the urgency of this problem accounted for the failure of the iron scheme.[64] Nonetheless, in the years to come, the quest for self-sufficiency would become a dominant factor shaping the course of Japanese expansion and merits special consideration here.

New Aims: Autarky

By the beginning of the Terauchi cabinet, the war in Europe had entered its third year. Most Japanese military analysts had expected the conflict to be brutal, extremely costly, and, for those very reasons, of short duration. Based on their own experience during the Russo-Japanese War, they believed that the belligerent powers could not sustain an unrestrained armed conflict involving the mobilization of all the resources at their disposal for any significant length of time. They predicted that the Europeans would exhaust themselves in a year or, at most, eighteen months. Contrary to such expectations, more than two years had passed, and no clear resolution seemed in sight. The fighting in Europe appeared to have taken the form of a protracted total war, a contradiction in terms in traditional Japanese military thinking. Somehow, the belligerents had managed to continue their efforts and replace the enormous volume of material being consumed by tapping resources normally unavailable. A new kind of warfare had emerged in which economic struggle played as important a role as the conflict on the front lines.[65]

The most influential study on the lessons of the European war economy conducted during this period was a book-length work by Major Koiso Kuniaki (1880–1950), entitled *Teikoku kokubō shigen* (The empire's national defense resources) and released for internal circulation within the army in August 1917. Koiso was a somewhat unlikely source of expertise in this field. His specialty at this time lay neither in mobilization planning nor in industrial procurement but, rather, in covert operations in China. His leadership of the second Manchurian independence gambit during the anti-Yüan campaign of 1916 had been his most notable activity up to this time. Koiso's knowledge of Europe, moreover, came at third hand. He drew much of his source material from a translation prepared by his brother, also a staff officer, of a German work on industrial mobilization. Nonetheless, Koiso's study was widely read and gave him a reputation that, no doubt, played an important part in redirecting his career.[66] He would subsequently become one of the Japanese army's chief experts on industrial mobilization planning, credentials that would take him to Manchoukuo during its formative years in the 1930s and, ultimately, to the post of prime minister during World War II.

The idea that, in the new kind of warfare emerging in Europe, "victory or defeat [would] likely be decided by the economic struggle" was the central theme in Koiso's study. The systems that the belligerent powers had devised for industrial mobilization had clearly contributed to their success in allocating the resources necessary to sustain a protracted conflict. Although Japan had acquired considerable experience in this field during the war against Russia, mobilization in Europe operated on a qualitatively different scale. Countries engaged in this conflict had created new relationships between government and business and had designed special control agencies capable of managing national economies in far more effective and efficient ways than had previously been seen. The ability of these military-industrial systems to convert rapidly from peacetime to wartime production and to divert substantial capital, raw materials, and labor from the civilian to the defense sector without generating a paralyzing economic crisis impressed Japanese observers. Koiso framed the equivalent problem for Japan in terms of mobilizing nine million men and four million horses, a hypothetical scenario on which he based his analysis. Without extensive preparation, the diversion of these resources alone, not to mention additional requirements for food and fodder, equipment, and munitions, would cripple the Japanese economy.[67] It was essential to create a legal framework for mobilization and to promote systematic cooperation between government and business in the development of strategic industries.

In Koiso's view, however, the single most valuable lesson of the war in Europe was the importance of self-sufficiency in industrial production, raw materials, and foodstuffs. The belligerent powers understood that the military stamina of their adversaries rested on their economic strength, and mutual efforts to undermine that foundation had become essential elements of the conflict. Both sides sought to strangle their opponents through the use of naval blockades or submarine warfare. Koiso believed that Germany had gained the upper hand in this struggle. The Allies, he noted, had initially expected the sustained blockade to lead to the collapse of the German economy within nine months. Germany frustrated such expectations, however, by pursuing a program aimed at self-sufficiency within the territory under its military control. German scientists had developed synthetics to substitute for raw materials no longer available from abroad. Occupied territories fed Germany. They also provided fuel, lead, and explosives as well as additional industrial plant and labor. Britain, in contrast, fared poorly as a result of what Koiso regarded as misplaced confidence in the supremacy of sea power. Not only had the vaunted Royal Navy failed to paralyze the

German economy, but it had also proved itself incapable of protecting Britain's own economic lifeline. German submarines had devastated British shipping, and even the Strait of Dover no longer remained secure. Food shortages in Britain had become serious. Koiso drew clear conclusions from these observations: "The triumph in protracted war where a quick and decisive victory is not possible belongs to the country that can manage a self-sufficient economy."[68]

This lesson, illustrated by a negative model in Britain and a positive one in Germany, had profound relevance to Japan. A great many manufactured products, particularly producer goods, and the larger part of the nation's industrial raw materials came from abroad. A dangerous tendency of importing food, particularly rice, had also emerged. If, indeed, Japan mobilized nine million men and four million horses for war, Koiso believed that despite the opinion of experts at the time that Japan suffered from a surplus labor problem in agriculture, severe food shortages would develop. He also pointed out that if the great British navy could not secure vital sea lanes against enemy submarines, "Japan's weak naval power" had no hope of doing so. Accordingly, Koiso argued that "as an absolute condition for the survival of our nation, we must do everything possible, using whatever means available, to prepare in peacetime for wartime economic self-sufficiency." This effort demanded, of course, improving agricultural productivity and eliminating dependence on imported manufactured goods. Only the expansion and diversification of exports could create a capacity in excess of domestic consumption needs that, in turn, would facilitate conversion to military use. The effort would also require a program of stockpiling, although unless restricted to absolutely essential materials, such measures would incur prohibitive costs. These steps alone, however, would not overcome the nation's fundamental weakness. Even with Taiwan, Korea, and Karafuto (southern Sakhalin), Japan lacked an adequate resource base. Land ultimately formed the limiting factor in food production, and even if the country expanded its industrial plant, raw materials and fuel would remain problems.[69]

The solution in Koiso's view, and here his background becomes relevant, lay in China. Like Germany, Japan could achieve wartime self-sufficiency by exploiting neighboring countries, through the voluntary cooperation of their inhabitants if possible, but through occupation and coercion if necessary. One way or another, China would form part of the resource base subject to Japan's war mobilization policies. To survive a protracted conflict of the kind being waged in Europe, Japan would have no alternative. In order to lay the political and economic groundwork for such a program, to ensure the accessibility and availability of resources, and to remove any possible impediments to wartime exploitation, peacetime policies toward China had to be revised. Koiso outlined a number of major tasks entailed in achieving these goals.[70]

China's borders encompassed a natural bounty sufficient to provide for most of what Japan needed. It could produce rice, wheat, beans, and meat in abundance, and it possessed large amounts of land suitable for the cultivation of cotton and the raising of sheep. Koiso also noted China's potential to become one of the world's leading producers of iron, coal, and tin, and its vast reserves of other ores were more than adequate to meet both countries' needs. Oil was a possible area of deficiency. Shensi had one producing field, and the French saw promise in Yunnan. Koiso also believed that Jehol might have oil reserves. American geologists had surveyed the area and concluded the region offered no commercially viable prospects, but Koiso found these reports suspect in view of the Americans' interest in protecting their own oil industry. Japanese geologists ought to conduct an independent study.[71] Despite this potential, however, the current output of China's farms and mines remained dismally low. The Chinese had done little to develop their natural endowment because of their short-sighted view of economic matters. The country's leadership lacked the spirit of *fukoku kyōhei* (national power and prosperity) that had driven Japan during the Meiji period. China imported goods that it had the resources to produce on its own. It also allowed foreigners to "drain" its wealth by granting numerous concessions. (Japan, of course, represented a special case whose concerns were distinct from other foreigners.) If this situation continued unchanged, China clearly could not fulfill its function as Japan's wartime resource base, and any attempt to redress the problem after the outbreak of war would come too late. These conditions demanded the promotion of development, while peace still prevailed.[72]

Such an effort would necessarily begin with improvements in transportation. Relative to the size of the country, China's railway network remained poorly developed and left much of its land and natural resources commercially inaccessible. The oil field in Shensi provided a case in point. Because of the lack of railway connections, transportation costs rendered the price of domestic oil nearly prohibitive; as a result, the operation had tapped only one of four wells. Coal, iron, and other mineral resources would remain largely untouched without low-cost transportation, as would arable land not yet opened to cultivation. Railways occupied a crucial place in Koiso's scheme for another reason as well. The inability of the Imperial Navy to guarantee Japanese control of the sea lanes between Japan and China was a working assumption in his study. All materials would move by railway through Manchuria and into Korea; this gave new importance to the Pusan–Mukden route. Although the strait separating Pusan from Moji or Shimonoseki was relatively narrow, Koiso sought to eliminate dependence on the navy's ability to control even these waters. He recommended, in all seriousness, the construction of a tunnel to connect the peninsula to Kyushu.[73]

Railway construction would be only the beginning of aggressive development efforts in China. To meet Japanese wartime requirements, Chinese peacetime output in key materials would have to exceed substantially the combined total of China's domestic consumption and ordinary commercial exports to Japan. This consideration demanded the growth of exports aimed at diversified markets that could be reallocated in wartime. In agriculture, Manchurian soybean production offered a good example that should be emulated in the production of rice, wheat, meat, leather, cotton, and wool. Tin was one mineral already exported in quantities sufficient for diversion to Japan's needs in wartime. Coal production warranted expansion. China had barely developed its vast iron reserves, and only the establishment of a modern Chinese iron industry could remedy this state of affairs.[74]

Koiso recognized the difficulty of meeting such high expectations. Given appropriate assistance, guidance, and encouragement, however, he believed the task manageable. He suggested a number of specific approaches. The establishment of a domestic flour-milling industry in China would encourage wheat cultivation on a broad scale with possibilities for export. A similar approach might be taken in the promotion of cotton cultivation. A strong domestic spinning industry with a growing demand for raw cotton would encourage farmers to start planting. A woolens industry would do the same for sheep raising. The overall scope and scale of the problem, however, required proportionally dramatic approaches, and Koiso believed that China could not fulfill its projected role in Japan's plans unless the two countries entered into a program of systematic, bilateral economic cooperation.[75]

Koiso offered a rough sketch of what such an economic alliance would entail. In general, China would supply the necessary land, natural resources, and labor, and Japan would provide capital and technology. Along the lines envisioned in Group V of the Twenty-One Demands, China would employ Japanese economic and financial advisors in key organs of government. Special joint agencies would manage the development of agriculture. Direct business investment in China would shift from its current emphasis on exclusive Japanese proprietorship to cooperative enterprise. Joint Sino-Japanese ventures would become the norm.[76] Most important, the two countries would form a customs union. Koiso believed that China could overcome its dependence on imports only with tariff increases and called on Japan to drop its opposition to revising the unequal treaties. Following the revisions, a special bilateral tariff agreement would establish an East Asian common market. All these measures would also contribute to diminishing foreign economic influence in China, something Koiso regarded as essential to the success of this scheme. Although Koiso appears to have taken the importance of this step for granted, subsequent tracts on strategic autarky would argue that foreign ownership of Chinese resources would create a serious impediment to mobilization.[77]

In Koiso's thinking, true economic cooperation would also demand basic changes in Japanese attitudes toward the pursuit of its economic interests in China. Given the dichotomy of economic principles operating in war and peace, the program would require, in some instances, the sacrifice of Japanese advantage as determined by peacetime standards. The development of a Chinese coal industry would certainly curtail Japanese exports, just as Fushun had challenged the coal-mining industry in Kyushu and Hokkaido. A Chinese spinning industry would likewise eat into the market of home producers. China's importance to Japan's wartime self-sufficiency, however, warranted such sacrifices; the Japanese had to think in broader and more far-sighted terms than they had in the past.[78]

Bilateral cooperation as such was neither an original strategy nor one that required autarky to justify. Although the problem of wartime self-sufficiency clearly informed the policies favored by Nishihara and Shōda, so, too, did concerns about mounting Chinese resistance and the uncertain future of the imperialist system in Asia. Nonetheless, Koiso's arguments offered the most cogent reason for the superiority of this approach over concession hunting as a means of controlling China's resources. Traditional proprietary rights, even under the most favorable of conditions, would simply not suffice. Only a wholesale exploitation of the region's raw materials, land, and labor could sustain a Japanese war economy.

Koiso's ideas were a substantially new contribution to the development of aims and purposes in Japanese imperialism. Clearly, many of his schemes had affinities with existing concepts and practices. The notion of developing Manchuria's resources for wartime mobilization dated back to the Manchurian Army's plan of 1905. Taken as a whole, however, the concept of strategic autarky represented a radical departure from the ways in which the Japanese had looked at the question of empire in the past. It posited a new purpose for expansion absent from earlier considerations. Self-sufficiency, on the order Koiso envisioned, had little in common with older concerns about trade protection, economic integration, and the balance of payments. Prior to World War I, defense planners did not regard it as essential, as remarks by the managers of the Osaka Arsenal during the Russo-Japanese War illustrate.

Our people naturally desire self-sufficiency in weapons production, for military reasons as well as those of national prestige. As our national strength develops, we expect to fulfill this goal. Yet, true self-sufficiency requires not only enormous resources but also international markets. To attempt self-sufficiency in weaponry at this time would be highly disadvantageous to our national economy and is, in fact, militarily unnecessary. Currently, we are relying on supplies from Europe and the United States and are truly self-sufficient in no more than two or three items.[79]

The quest for autarky within a compact and defensible geographic perimeter also introduced a new standard for appraising the economic value of China's resources. All things being equal, Australian wool surpassed that produced by Manchurian sheep in quality, as did American cotton compared with the short-fiber Chinese variety. Anshan ores were low in iron content, and the cost of producing iron from them would be high. Under wartime conditions, however, these same resources would become invaluable and essential to Japan's economic survival.

Perhaps one of the most radical implications of these ideas for Japanese imperialism lay in a basic shift in the relationship between empire and national defense. In traditional military thinking, imperial holdings enhanced security by creating buffer zones and forward bases or by preventing an adversary from gaining the advantage of strategic geography. In addition, empire, whatever the reason for acquisition, generated defense commitments, whether against foreign threats or native rebellion. The army had used

Manchuria as a base against Russia and China and, at the same time, secured Japanese interests in the territory. Strategic autarky introduced a new element into the picture. Empire was more than an outer wall on which soldiers stood watch—it was the lifeline of a nation under siege. If soldiers had to abandon the outposts, they could always fall back to inner lines of defense and attempt to hold out. If they lost their source of economic sustenance, however, defeat became only a matter of time. On Koiso's premises, empire constituted an absolute requirement for national survival in a protracted war, not a relative question entailing degrees of security. Moreover, this new concept no longer bound the strategic value of empire to a particular war scenario or prospective adversary. Manchuria's importance to Japan's defense stood independent of any threat posed by Russia in Northeast Asia. It would remain essential to national security even in a war fought against the United States in the Western Pacific, the Philippines, and Guam.

Significantly, this view of empire and national defense defined a new mission for the army, since the task of securing Japan's economic defense perimeter on the continent would inevitably fall to the nation's ground forces. In a conflict with the United States, sea power would provide the first line of defense, but the ultimate outcome of the war would depend on the army's control of China. Taken to its logical conclusion, the fundamental importance of strategic autarky provided a cogent argument for an army-first policy. Indeed, Koiso's work contained a frank and unmistakable anti-navy bias. His use of Britain as a negative example, his assumption that the Japanese fleet could not control even the Strait of Tsushima, and his emphasis on the devastating impact of submarines implied that the value of sea power had greatly diminished in the new kind of warfare emerging in Europe.[80]

The emergence of a new role for the army as the guardian of Japan's economic defense perimeter represented an extraordinarily timely development. The collapse of imperial Russia in 1917 had raised fundamental questions about the army's future role. The Russian menace had provided the principal justification for its growth as a world-class fighting force, for its claims to the nation's resources, and for its status with respect to the navy. To be sure, army leaders had started rethinking the question of mission well before the outbreak of the revolution in Russia and had emphasized the importance of intervention in China. The beginnings of this shift, in fact, may be traced back to 1911. The Twenty-One Demands and the anti-Yüan campaign no doubt strengthened the idea. In 1916, Lieutenant General Tanaka Giichi, appointed vice chief of staff the previous year, began a draft revision of the Imperial Defense Plan that stressed the role of the army in defending and advancing Japanese interests in China, and implicitly downgraded the significance of fighting Russia.[81] Koiso's ideas, however, added a new argument for redirecting the army's strategic attention to China, one far more cogent than the conventional tasks of protecting Japanese interests against the forces of chaos and bullying the Chinese government.

Not surprisingly, Koiso's work generated considerable enthusiasm among his colleagues. Others had prepared similar studies. Military planners also drafted proposals for new mobilization laws, lobbied for the expansion of the iron and steel industry, and pursued research to develop substitutes for imported raw materials. Politically, the notion of an economic defense perimeter on the continent offered special attractions at this time in view of the reopening of the interservice debate over appropriations.[82] The concept of strategic autarky, however, failed to win universal support among army leaders. Although it would appear that most senior officers gave lip service to the idea of seeking wartime control of China's resources, some disagreed with the fundamental premise of a protracted total war underlying Koiso's analysis. Deeply invested in the idea that victory or defeat in war rested on managing the conflict toward a decisive engagement, as Japan had done in 1905, critics believed it fundamentally mistaken to think in terms of protracted wars. The lessons of the Russo-Japanese War emphasized the importance of striking first, moving quickly, and securing the "high ground" before the enemy had a chance to bring its superior manpower and material resources to bear. This represented the only kind of war that Japan, as a small and relatively poor country, should think about fighting. Chief of Staff Uehara Yūsaku, a long-time political adversary of Terauchi, stood among the most influential in this group.[83]

Civilians had a generally mixed reaction to these ideas but, on the whole, leaned toward skepticism. On the one hand, they found the underlying concerns about Japanese economic vulnerability in wartime difficult to dismiss. Although Japan had generally prospered as a result of Europe's embroilment in war, it had also began to suffer shortages, particularly in steel. In 1917, the problem became acute, a condition many Japanese described as "steel starvation," when the United States restricted exports to conserve material for its own war effort. In response, the SMR expanded its iron and steel program at Anshan from a small pilot project into an ambitious scheme aimed at eventually producing one million tons of pig iron annually. The Terauchi government managed to pass two pieces of legislation relevant to the management of a war economy: a general mobilization law and a law aimed at the promotion of a domestic truck industry. The cabinet also instructed the SMR to begin a program to breed army horses.[84]

The limits of commitment to the cause of strategic autarky, however, became clear when the cabinet faced Nishihara's proposal for the ¥100 million iron loan to China. Those skeptical of the concept of autarky might humor its advocates with legislation aimed at meeting a remote contingency or with token projects such as horse breeding in Manchuria, but they balked at endorsing a plan with such a staggering price tag. For policymakers receptive but not fully convinced, the costs no doubt pushed them toward the camp of the skeptics. The Foreign Ministry launched an active campaign against the idea, and Terauchi and his colleagues had no choice but to abandon the plan shortly before the government resigned in September 1918.[85]

The Fall of the Terauchi Government

The idea of strategic autarky would gain more support over the next few years, partly as a result of more active army lobbying. In 1918, the concept was new, its ramifications were far-reaching, and the dubious reception it received was understandable. The defeat of the iron initiative, however, reflected more than skepticism about the need for self-sufficiency; it was also a result of mounting opposition within Japanese leadership circles toward the China policies of Terauchi and his associates. The business community and its supporters in the Foreign Ministry objected to the iron scheme, in part, because it disrupted negotiations in progress over mining concessions and undermined future business opportunity. Not only the scale of the iron proposal but the general handling of loans to China under the Terauchi government also troubled fiscal conservatives. Nishihara had left the very large advances given to Tuan unsecured under the assumption that the two sides would sign loan contracts with adequate provisions for collateral in the immediate future. Critics regarded the practice of handing over money before the conclusion of final contracts as grossly irresponsible. For many policymakers of a moderate persuasion, the proposed iron loan was the last straw in a succession of actions they believed ill considered. In their view, the whole idea of bilateral cooperation advocated by Terauchi and his team became problematic when taken beyond the level of modest measures aimed at securing Chinese goodwill. A few gratuities here and there, along with some softening of loan terms, were reasonable measures. They saw the attempt to revise the fundamental basis of Sino-Japanese political and economic relations, however, as foolhardy, pointless, and counterproductive. Hara Takashi, the Seiyūkai leader, who had been brought into a special consultative role under the Terauchi government in a forum known as the Foreign Policy Research Council (Gaikō chōsakai), reflected this view in his diary in 1917.

Although it is not to be publicized at home, let alone abroad, from the point of view of our national interest, it is of no account whether China actually becomes civilized, rich or strong. In view of the Chinese national character, it is extremely dubious whether she would adopt a friendly attitude toward our country, were she actually to become rich and strong. . . . We should advise the Chinese to unify their country, but if they fail, it is of no matter to us. The point is that we should avoid antagonizing them and causing them to have ill feelings toward us.[86]

The Foreign Ministry, moreover, had grown particularly unhappy with the Terauchi government's policy, not only because the increasingly frank client relationship formed with Tuan would create serious complications with the powers but also because Nishihara had pursued his negotiations without reference to official diplomatic channels. Yoshizawa Kenkichi (1874–1965), acting minister to China, wrote a blistering critique of Nishihara's activities shortly after the resignation of the government.[87]

Terauchi and his associates also faced opposition and criticism from those who ought to have stood firmly within their camp. Governor Nakamura of the SMR resented Nishihara's intrusion into railway negotiations. He considered the preliminary contracts regarding Manchurian railways as highly inadequate. He also objected to Nishihara's arrangements that designated a consortium consisting of the Bank of Chōsen, the Bank of Taiwan, and the Industrial Bank of Japan, rather than the SMR, as the principal Japanese party to the loan agreement.[88] A particularly serious blow to the iron scheme as well as the broader framework of Terauchi policy, however, came from Gotō Shinpei. Gotō had originally joined the Terauchi cabinet as home minister and governor of the National Railway Board. He received appointment as foreign minister in April 1918 with the expectation that he would serve as a loyal member of the prime minister's team. He had expressed some disagreement from the start, however, over Nishihara's activities, and he openly broke with the "Korean clique" over the iron issue. Although there appear to have been a number of reasons for his stand, as an imperial activist, Gotō remained wedded to the traditional approach of concession hunting and opposed any measures that would undermine what he saw as the foundations of Japanese expansionism.[89]

Overall, the Terauchi government seems to have lacked the kind of political support it needed to push through its programs. It had no strong base. The imperial activist camp lacked unity, and the prime minister enjoyed less than solid support within the army as a result of long-standing factional divisions stemming from his tenure as army minister, during which he alienated many key leaders such as Chief of Staff Uehara. Although he intended his government to "transcend" party interests, he could not avoid negotiations with the Diet, one upshot of which entailed the creation of the Foreign Policy Research Council, an advisory body but one that nonetheless gave those party leaders granted seats, including Inukai Tsuyoshi, one of the army's more persistent critics, an unprecedented voice in foreign affairs. His growing dependence on the Seiyūkai's Hara for support represented another consequence of his need to work with the Diet.[90]

The enormous scale of Japan's contribution to the Siberian expedition generated popular opposition, and this, too, added to the government's troubles. The Rice Riots of 1918, however, delivered the fatal blow to the Terauchi cabinet. Between July and September, a popular movement protesting high rice prices resulting from wartime inflation spread throughout the country. The movement added other political and economic grievances to the problem of rice prices and further fueled public anger. Serious outbreaks of rioting occurred in some localities. The government used army troops in addition to civilian police to suppress the disorders. This action severely damaged the army's prestige and, combined with the unpopularity of the Siberian Expedition and a general rise in anti-military sentiment following the end of the war, would lead to a low point in the army's popularity from which it would take years to recover.[91] The Terauchi government resigned in September. Hara Takashi, with Yamagata's grudging approval, received the emperor's charge to form a new cabinet.

Coincidentally, Tuan Ch'i-jui, while retaining his post as the commander of the Japanese-financed War Participation Army, resigned as the prime minister of the Chinese republic in the same month. Significantly, he left office before concluding formal contracts on those railway loans for which he had received hefty advances. For those dubious about bilateral cooperation to begin with, these developments only confirmed their worst fears. The Terauchi government would be vilified for years to come, and the Nishihara Loans became virtually synonymous in some quarters with irresponsible foreign lending practices. For others, however, Terauchi left an important legacy that would serve the imperialist cause very well in the difficult years ahead. The goal of strategic autarky and the methodology of client management, both areas in which Terauchi failed to achieve desired results but opened the doors of possibility, would form the foundations of a reformed imperialism emerging in the 1920s.

Terauchi, ironically, also played an important part in paving the way for moderate leadership in foreign affairs. He redirected imperialist impulses heading in a decidedly adventurist direction in the last years of the Ōkuma government into new channels, and although he and his closest associates advocated ideas no less audacious in their own right and no less imperialist in their purposes, they evinced considerable responsiveness to many of the same concerns exercising moderates. The tactical shift from sticks to carrots alone represented an important contribution in this direction. Perhaps more important, in attempting to initiate reforms in basic expansionist strategy, his government helped to prepare imperial activists for changes to come. Bilateral cooperation, more than anything else, constituted a pioneering effort to come to grips with the fact that the days of gunboat diplomacy were numbered and that the world that Japanese imperialists had learned to navigate during the decade after the Russo-Japanese War faced radical change.

SIX

The Politics of
Imperialist Compromise, 1918–1922

The years following the end of World War I were lean times for Japanese imperialism. Under the twin pressures of the "new diplomacy" championed by the United States and a maturing nationalist movement in China, Japan had little choice but to relinquish many of its wartime gains south of the Wall, including its sphere in Shantung. It managed to retain its old core of concessionary rights in Manchuria but only at the price of agreeing to a "freeze" on all further expansionist endeavors in the territory. That the Japanese chose not to resist more vigorously than they did suggests that their commitment to the type of wartime imperialism exemplified by the Twenty-One Demands was not as deep as it might have seemed. Japanese acquiescence also points to the fact that moderates and activists alike had prepared themselves during the second half of the war for the possibility of a retreat.

To be sure, the pressures exerted by American diplomacy and Chinese nationalism on Japan's position in China between 1918 and 1922 were greater than most Japanese leaders, including moderates, had expected. Some of the demands made on Japan were regarded as excessive even by those who had long championed restraint in China and cooperation with the powers. It is important to bear in mind that, by the standards of a post-colonial age, mainstream Japanese moderates were imperialists. Indeed, the same might be said of the architects of the new diplomacy in the West. Leaders such as Itō Hirobumi, Abe Moritarō, Yamamoto Gonbei, Odagiri Masunosuke, Inukai Tsuyoshi, and Hara Takashi harbored no ideological antipathy toward expansionism. Although some within the moderate camp might favor a liberalization of colonial policy, few gave serious thought to restoring Taiwan to China or to granting Korea independence. They supported the unequal treaty system in China, defended commercial rights and privileges acquired under that system, and had no qualms, in principle, about dispatching troops to suppress Chinese strikes against Japanese textile factories. Nonetheless, they did oppose the aggressive program of the army, which, in their view, needlessly antagonized China and the powers, drove Japan against international currents, and sacrificed rational economic interests in an elusive quest for territorial gains. Apart from the need to compromise with the army, their past willingness to entertain any measures beyond a relatively mild commercial imperialism had rested largely on the premise that Japan's security and prosperity depended on active participation in the Great Power rivalries that had dominated international relations in East Asia since the late nineteenth century. If the old order had truly come to an end, as the new diplomacy seemed to promise, the nation had no reason to persist in an aggressively expansionist policy. With a few adjustments, Japan might "graciously" relinquish some of its more recent claims in China. On balance, then, moderates found the idea of accommodating the new order palatable, and the declining influence of the army made such a policy politically feasible.

Imperial activists were, to say the least, deeply dissatisfied with this turn of events. In their view, the rules may have changed but the imperialist game continued, and it was a dangerous folly to think otherwise. Many were particularly loath to forgo what they saw as an opportunity in north Manchuria following the demise of imperial Russia. At the same time, however, most members of this camp were realists, and they had been conditioned by Terauchi's experiments in imperialist reform to think about empire-building in innovative ways. Embracing the new program of autarky with growing enthusiasm, they argued that securing a hegemonic position in East Asia had become all the more urgent in the postwar environment. A strategic retreat might be unavoidable for the time being, but Japan's future depended on finding effective ways to pursue its imperial agenda, at least in Manchuria, despite external constraints. Some activists favored a program of development in depth and the exploitation of Japan's existing rights in the territory with greater intensity and efficiency, but most believed that such steps were inadequate. The army and its allies, however, were in a poor political position to pursue even a modest forward policy at this time, and any further advance in Manchuria might have been stalled indefinitely had it not been for an unexpected overture from Chang Tso-lin. Chang had established himself as the de facto ruler of the Three Eastern Provinces as political turmoil in China escalated into civil war, and his request for Japanese aid provided a fortuitous opening for a new expansionist initiative. Cooperation with Chang in Manchuria along the lines that the Terauchi government had attempted with Tuan in China as a whole seemed to offer the best hope for the survival of a Japanese Manchuria in this "post-imperialist" era.

Moderate Ascendancy and the Decline of Army Power

The appointment of Hara Takashi, president of the Seiyūkai, to succeed General Terauchi in September 1918 is one of the great milestones in Japanese political history and marks the beginning of a brief era of parliamentary rule. More important for the present discussion, this event signaled a major shift in the balance of competing forces in matters of imperial policy. Moderate leaders found themselves on a much stronger footing than they had during their brief ascendancy between 1911 and 1914. Although this shift owed much to the growing currency of moderate views in the Diet as well as the nation's political elites at large, of equal if not greater importance was the concomitant decline of army power. The army's political influence had reached its peak in the years immediately following the Russo-Japanese War but began eroding shortly thereafter. Symptoms of decline had already begun to surface by 1910. Although the army enjoyed restored standing during World War I, the recovery was short-lived. The use of troops to suppress the Rice Riots ravaged the army's prestige. The nascent postwar climate of pacifism, liberalism, and anti-militarism sweeping the world further damaged its position. General Ugaki Kazunari, superintendent of the War College, expressed deep anxieties about the future of the military in Japan at the end of 1918. In his view, the army, in particular, faced grim prospects as a result of the "emerging spirit of the times" and its disregard for national defense.[1]

At a deeper level, however, the root of the army's problem lay in the collapse of imperial Russia. Although the service had been moving toward a diversification of its mission since 1911, its claims to pride of place within the defense establishment and, as a corollary, within overall national leadership rested in the cogency of a war scenario in which Japan would, once again, fight Russia in Manchuria. But with the Russian state in virtual collapse after 1917, the prospects of such a conflict appeared reduced, at least for the foreseeable future, to a remote possibility. Army leaders argued that the

Siberian Expedition was a logical extension of Japan's traditional northern defense strategy, a permutation of the Russian war scenario. In the long run, this undertaking would settle the situation in the Russian Far East in Japan's favor and ensure once and for all that no threat would emerge from that direction. In the short run, military operations in the north would check the spread of the "forces of chaos" generated by turmoil in Russia and pre-empt any effort by the powers, particularly the United States, to take advantage of the situation to the detriment of Japanese interests. The Siberian venture, however, proved highly unpopular among civilian leaders as well as the general public. Few outside the army saw the need for this massive and costly deployment of armed force, and this attitude only added to the army's political difficulties.[2] In effect, rather than buttressing the army's position, action in Siberia had become a liability and represented a net drain on its dwindling stock of political capital.

Acutely aware of this dilemma and egged on by the resurgence of a navy challenge, army leaders began working toward a fundamental revision of their mission after 1918. The idea of strategic autarky articulated by Major Koiso Kuniaki in 1917 formed a pivotal element in these efforts. To be sure, the argument for establishing an economic defense perimeter on the continent had already gained considerable influence in some quarters. At the time, however, it had represented one among many elements underpinning the army's view of empire and national defense. After 1918, it came to shoulder the larger part of the burden. Operational plans of the type we have examined for the years after the Russo-Japanese War are unavailable for this period. Indirect evidence, however, suggests that scenarios in which the army would occupy Chinese territory from Manchuria south to the Yangtze valley for the explicit purpose of securing the raw materials, foodstuffs, and industrial facilities required to sustain Japan's wartime economy had become major features of strategic planning by the beginning of the 1920s. Significantly, the army insisted that this new mission would require the same fully mobilized force strength of 40 divisions originally designed to meet the Russian threat.[3]

The proliferation of studies of strategic autarky between 1918 and 1922 provide additional evidence that army leaders had taken up the cause with energy and enthusiasm during this period. One document, for example, reframed the mission of the army in Siberia in terms of securing raw material sources unavailable in China and underscored the advantages of creating a compact economic defense perimeter in Northeast Asia immune from foreign naval attack. Others explored, in far greater detail than provided in Koiso's preliminary work, the availability and accessibility of Chinese raw materials.[4] Indeed, a more disciplined and systematic attempt to quantify Japan's raw material needs and to assess China's ability to meet those requirements characterized the new work. The most sophisticated studies postulated various degrees of self-sufficiency that might be sustained, depending on the scope of the economic defense perimeter. The sphere of autarky almost always encompassed Manchuria as its core element, but in the variations considered, the perimeter might entail an expansion north to Siberia, west to Mongolia, or south to the Yangtze valley. Most interestingly, they looked at alternative schemes for managing continental resources depending on China's standing with respect to Japan: allied, neutral, or hostile.[5]

Civilian leaders, however, remained skeptical. The steel embargo in 1917 had caused some alarm, but with the conclusion of the war civilian anxieties seemed to have receded rather quickly. Pacifistic trends, reinforced by the belief that the end of the conflict in Europe might, indeed, bring an era of lasting peace, along with pronouncements by Western statesmen such as Woodrow Wilson (1856–1924) in favor of liberalizing trade, further diminished the credibility of autarkic schemes advocated by the army. As a concession to army pressure, however, the government established an independent National Census Board (Kokuzei in) in 1920; a major part of its mission was to facilitate military-economic planning. To the consternation of army planners, however, the government collapsed the agency's functions into the Ministry of Agriculture and Commerce in 1922. This development implicitly downgraded efforts in strategic economic planning. It not only indicated a lack of commitment to the scheme on the part of civilians but testified to the diminished political clout of the army.[6]

In time, the army would succeed in making a more persuasive case about strategic autarky, and as Soviet power began to emerge later in the 1920s, it would revive a variant of the old Russian war scenario. During the immediate postwar years, however, its arguments had limited currency, and civilian leaders found themselves in a good position to shed their traditional deference to the claims of national defense and take a more assertive approach in matters of foreign policy. These circumstances enabled Hara Takashi, allied with the Foreign Ministry, to steer a reformist course during this era. Hara himself espoused a moderate imperialism, of a traditional orientation, committed to competitive engagement in the international arena but stressing the need for caution and restraint. He favored an active pursuit of Japan's commercial interests in China but remained generally skeptical of the kind of colonial schemes in Manchuria outlined by Gotō. Hara held China's national aspirations in profound contempt and appears to have had few reservations about exploiting a neighbor's disabilities and misfortunes. At the same time, he placed a high priority in foreign policy on maintaining harmonious relations with the powers, particularly with the United States, an emphasis that, all else aside, dictated moderation in external affairs.[7] Above all, Hara was a pragmatist, quick to compromise, a quality key to his success as a politician who had brought his party to power after more than a decade of endeavor. This orientation would serve the prime minister well in managing the tasks he faced in the international arena during his tenure.[8]

At the time he took office, Hara, like Terauchi, understood the need to reform foreign policy, to grapple with the problem of mounting Chinese resistance to Japan and to come to terms with the emergence of the United States as the paramount Western power in East Asia at the end of the war. Lacking the complex agenda and the hard-line imperialist commitments of his predecessor, however, he adopted a more simple and straightforward approach. If the Japanese engaged in some give-and-take bargaining with the powers, offered some reasonable compromises, and worked to mollify Chinese feelings, they could steer the postwar situation to their advantage. In this context, his efforts leading up to the peace conference at Versailles centered on undoing what he considered the excesses of the Ōkuma and Terauchi governments and on recasting China policy in a more restrained and flexible mold.[9]

Among his immediate concerns in late 1918, he regarded containing the scope of the Siberian Expedition, which he had opposed from the start, as the most urgent. Inheriting a policy not of his making, he sought to limit the damage and, above all, prevent escalation. The problem lay not only in the expedition's excessive costs but also in the risk of friction with the United States and in the danger of adventurism on the part of the army in the field. In managing this situation, he saw developing a good working relationship with his army minister, Tanaka Giichi, as vital, and he recognized the need to make compromises in order to win the general's cooperation. Tanaka himself, of course, had a long history of imperialist militancy and had actively supported the Siberian venture. He had, however, mellowed over the

years. A realist, he understood that with the end of the war, the days of un-
bridled opportunity had come to a close.[10]

The need to dismantle the remnants of the program of bilateral cooperation established under Terauchi was a close second in Hara's list of priorities. As we have seen, Hara placed little stock in the efficacy of his predecessor's approach, and, more important, he saw the scheme as injurious to the
nation's relations with the powers. Japan needed to reaffirm its commitment
to multilateralism in its dealings with China. Although Hara achieved a significant measure of success in this regard, the attempt to make a clean break
proved rather difficult. For one, the army resisted the idea of cutting off bilateral aid to the Chinese government entirely, and Hara had little choice
but to offer some concessions, particularly to Yamagata Aritomo, who still
harbored hopes for Sino-Japanese cooperation. The fact that Tuan Ch'i-jui,
although no longer prime minister, still headed the so-called Frontier Defense Army (War Participation Army), the military force financed by the
Japanese loan in 1918, further complicated matters. This relationship imposed on Japan a continuing obligation and responsibility as well.[11]

A third emphasis in the initial policy framework of the Hara government
lay in retrenchment in Manchuria. Reforms in Manchuria policy also encompassed issues of bureaucratic prerogative. Hara committed himself to asserting the primacy of civilian leadership in foreign affairs, a goal that entailed dismantling the structural arrangements devised by the Terauchi
government. Indeed, in this effort, Hara appeared less compromising than in
other areas. Going beyond a simple restoration of the institutional status
quo ante in Manchuria, his administration abolished the Kwantung Government-General and replaced it with a separate garrison command, known
as the Kwantung Army, and a purely civilian authority for governing the
Leased Territory proper, described as the Kwantung Administration (Kantōchō). These reforms limited the jurisdiction of the garrison commander to
strictly military affairs, a significant step in diminishing army influence in
Manchuria that would have seemed inconceivable only a few years earlier.[12]

Changes at the SMR offered further indications of the enhanced influence of moderate leaders. In 1918, the Hara government reappointed as chief
executive Nomura Ryūtarō, who had briefly held the position in 1913–14.
This move strengthened the practice of linking company appointments to
changes of cabinet and of transforming high offices in the SMR into party
patronage posts.[13] The downgrading of the title of the chief executive from

"governor" (*sōsai*) to "president" (*shachō*) also represented an important, albeit symbolic, shift. *Shachō* is conventionally translated into English as "president," and it normally refers to the head of an ordinary business organization. The change in nomenclature clearly implied that the government regarded the SMR as a business enterprise. In view of Gotō Shinpei's early efforts to upgrade the position as much as possible, the change in title reflected the orientation toward Manchuria of the moderates, who favored rational economic management and generally opposed schemes for colonization. Indeed, during this period, the SMR's public relations work underwent a marked reorientation, and a concerted attempt was made to shed the institution's image as a colonial company. Consider the complaints of the author of a promotional work on Manchuria, published in English by the Bank of Chōsen in 1920:

Of the nature of the company, the author has heard people compare it, not so often nowadays as at the time of its establishment,—and take delight in so comparing it—with the East India companies established by England, Holland, France and other European countries in the course of the seventeenth and eighteenth centuries. But nothing is further from the truth. Those East India companies, ostensibly trading corporations, were in fact political organizations with even military powers conferred upon them by their respective Governments, whereas the South Manchuria Railway Company is an economic institution, pure and simple, in both name and reality.[14]

The greatest challenge facing Hara's government in the arena of foreign policy, of course, were the negotiations at Versailles that began in January 1919. A straightforward pragmatism characterized his initial approach in this matter as well. He expected some hard bargaining over Shantung, the most important issue on the table from the Japanese perspective. At the same time, however, Hara and his colleagues remained confident that, with some judicious bargaining, the Japanese position would prevail. Britain and France had given their assurances of support for Japanese claims during the war, although with considerable reluctance on Britain's part. Japan would retrocede the leasehold at Tsingtao, a step that would, it was hoped, mitigate Chinese ill-feeling. Significantly, the Terauchi government had made last-minute concessions to China in the process of negotiating for two branch railway lines in Shantung as part of the Nishihara Loans. Japan would station no troops in the province, Chinese authorities would take over the policing of the Shantung Railway, and the Shantung Railway itself would operate as a joint Sino-Japanese venture. Loan advances for the branch lines had cemented the deal. Although Hara had little use for Terauchi's overall approach, some of the initiatives of his predecessor lent themselves to moderate adaptations and might prove quite helpful. Japan went to Versailles, then, with a significantly softened position and what seemed a like solid body of international commitments, in addition to the agreement extracted from China in 1915.[15]

The American Challenge and Japan's Retreat in Manchuria

If Japanese leaders had expected smooth progress at the peace talks, however, they found themselves sorely disappointed. The experience at Versailles, in fact, awakened the Hara government to the full magnitude of the transformation emerging in Great Power diplomacy. As if a bad omen, Chinese nationalists organized a mass demonstration in Tsingtao, some 40,000 strong, two days before the peace conference took up the issue of Shantung. As the discussion opened, President Wilson proposed that rather than transferring rights in Shantung to Japan directly, the conference turn over all German territories and holdings to the Allies as a group and determine their final disposition subsequently. Chinese representatives argued that their own declaration of war on Germany had voided any Japanese claims and that the peace conference had no business making what China construed as a punitive settlement against the interests of a member of the alliance. Lloyd George acknowledged Britain's obligation to support Japan but expressed a preference for the American approach. The Americans warned that they questioned the validity of treaties, like those associated with the Twenty-One Demands, signed under duress. Japanese delegates countered that such a stance might force them to withdraw from the talks. In the end, Japan succeeded in making its case but only after offering guarantees regarding the stationing of troops, the transfer of police powers, and the joint management of the railway as promised earlier.[16] When news of the decision in Paris reached China, it triggered a massive protest movement that began in Peking on May 4, organized largely by students, and spread to major cities in China.[17] The outrage in China and the scale of the protests were in themselves cause for concern to the Japanese government, and combined with the very reluctant acquiescence of the powers to the Shantung transfer, they also underscored the unpopularity of Japan's position, the danger of isolation, and the enormous difficulties that lay ahead for Japan in the pursuit of its policies in China.[18]

The dispute over Shantung, moreover, marked only the beginning of a broader U.S. initiative launched at Versailles. President Wilson had previously enunciated principles lofty and global in scope, calling for disarmament, an end to traditional power politics, the creation of a system of collective security embodied in the League of Nations, the promotion of more open economic relations among countries, and a moratorium on further territorial expansion. As applied to East Asia, Wilson's "new diplomacy" demanded an end to the particularistic competition over China that had erupted at the close of the preceding century, the abolition of spheres of influence, the strict enforcement of Open Door principles, a sympathetic view of China's national aspirations, and the gradual dismantling of the unequal treaty system. Although framed in broad terms, this initiative inevitably entailed a very direct and specific challenge to Japanese claims. With Russia out of the picture, Germany defeated, France in no condition to pursue imperial adventures in China, and Britain generally supportive of the American position, Japan remained the only power active in China whose behavior demanded rectification at this point. Indeed, from the perspective of American diplomats at Versailles, the construction of a new international order in East Asia meant, first and foremost, a policy of rolling back Japan's wartime gains in China, in Manchuria as well as Shantung.[19]

The most important element in the U.S. challenge took the form of a proposal to establish a new, multilateral banking consortium with jurisdiction over all major foreign loans to China. American diplomats envisioned creating a successor to the international body established in 1913 on the occasion of the Reorganization Loans. Ensuring multilateralism in lending to China and preventing any one power from using financial leverage to influence the Yüan regime had formed the principal mission of the original consortium. However, it had excluded from its jurisdiction "industrial loans," which encompassed specific economic ventures such as mining and the all-important category of railway concessions. Nishihara had used this loophole to launder foreign aid funds to Tuan. The new proposal, which the United States had first floated in the summer of 1918, aimed not only to close this loophole but also to prevent, once and for all, the use of railways as a means for foreign powers to establish particularistic claims in China. The specific terms, discussed in nonbinding talks at Versailles in May 1919 by representatives of the United States, Britain, France, and Japan, called for the consortium, and this body alone, to undertake all future railway loans to China. Moreover, in a process described as "pooling," member powers would surrender to the consortium all existing options and concessions, excepting those governing operating lines, such as the Ch'angch'un–Kirin, and construction projects "upon which substantial progress had been made," like the Ssup'ingkai–T'aonan.[20] These terms would have a major impact on Japanese claims. Although the Shantung Railway, the SMR and its branches, and the two lines mentioned above would remain outside the consortium's jurisdiction, Japan would have no choice but to surrender all other railway concessions acquired since 1913 and affirmed during the war.

More than any other development, this proposal made it clear that the Hara government had erred in its initial expectation that a simple softening of Japanese imperial policy would constitute an adjustment sufficient to accommodate the demands of the postwar era. Japan's leaders had seriously underestimated the nature of the changes in the wind. The Americans, backed by the British and reinforced by a mobilized Chinese public opinion, had apparently decided to force a Japanese retreat in China not only by challenging its wartime gains but also by attacking the very foundations of imperialist rights. The target remained restricted to loan-based railway concessions at this point, but it required little imagination to see an extension of the challenge, in a not too distant future, to the SMR itself.[21]

To be sure, Wilson's ideas for a new order appealed to many Japanese. Liberal intellectuals and journalists, influenced by the postwar spirit that Ugaki had decried, endorsed the proposed reforms in principle. So, too, did some veteran diplomats, such as Makino Nobuaki (1861–1948), head of the Japanese delegation in Paris and foreign minister under the Yamamoto government in 1913–14. Younger Foreign Ministry officials, particularly those with extensive Western experience, also sympathized with these ideas. Shidehara Kijūrō (1872–1951), a rising career diplomat who had served as ambassador to the United States, best represented this group.[22] Few Japanese leaders, even those expressing a general affinity for the thrust of Wilsonian reforms, however, could embrace, without reservation, the practical implications of the new diplomacy for Japan's position in Manchuria and Shantung.

For those with strong, expansionist inclinations, the U.S. initiative amounted to little more than Knox policy warmed over, another iteration of imperialism, American style. In the view of Konoe Fumimaro (1891–1945), a young official of aristocratic lineage who served on the staff of Japan's delegation to Versailles, Wilsonian precepts, stripped of their moral pretensions, represented an effort on the part of strong powers, which had largely completed their empire-building endeavors, to deny newcomers such as Japan a share of the global wealth and a rightful place in the world. The new diplomacy demanded that Japan cease active encroachments in China, the only area open to Japanese expansion, yet none of the other powers had offered to surrender its existing holdings in Africa and Asia.[23] To Konoe and others of like mind, the expression "What's mine is mine and what's yours is negotiable" aptly summarized the attitude of Western reformers. Indeed, the U.S. position seemed quite blatant in this regard. The well-known discussions in 1917 between Foreign Minister Ishii Kikujirō (1866–1945) and Secretary of State Robert Lansing (1868–1928) had contributed to the popularization of the idea that Japanese imperialism in China bore many similarities to the practice of the Monroe Doctrine, much to the dismay of the Americans who firmly rejected such comparisons. From the Japanese perspective, however, it appeared that the United States, which had occupied Haiti and had intervened with impunity elsewhere in the Western hemisphere, had little basis for taking the moral high ground in criticizing Japan in China. As General Ugaki Kazunari pointedly remarked in his diary in 1920,

The United States has a tendency to ostracize and oppress those who do not share its own national ideals and values. This is the way of the conqueror and not of the king and is based on a belief in its own omnipotence. In particular, it often interprets the Monroe Doctrine in a self-serving manner, as it if were a synonym for righteousness. In this attitude, we may discern the United States' internal contradictions and its hypocrisy. It is to be pitied.[24]

Regardless of the nature of American motives, whether idealistic or reflective of a self-interested imperialism, the initiative posed a serious challenge for Japan. Confronted with an unfriendly array of forces and lacking any solid allies, Foreign Ministry officials, not surprisingly, favored some form of accommodation. Harmony with the powers, in their view, took priority over Japan's specific interests in China. Debuchi Katsuji (1878–1947), who, as acting ambassador to the United States, played an important role in talks with the U.S. State Department over the consortium issue, emerged as one of the most articulate spokesmen for this position.

In Debuchi's view, Japan had little choice but to join the consortium, given the postwar balance of power in Asia. The option of resisting the

United States' policy initiatives in collusion with the likes of Russia, as Japan had in the case of the Knox plan a decade earlier, no longer existed. France and Britain had endorsed the international body. If Japan chose to stand up to the United States, it would do so alone, with little likelihood of a favorable outcome. Stubbornly remaining outside a working consortium, moreover, would only injure the nation's economic interests, surrendering the advantage to the member-powers. Japan could not hope to hold its own against the combined financial strength of Britain, France, and the United States as investors in China. Self-imposed exclusion from the body would also diminish Japan's political influence. Membership, in contrast, would enable Japan to check American activity, which, if unrestrained by a collective international body, might prove even more inimical to Japanese interests.[25]

Debuchi also argued that the practice of maintaining spheres of interest no longer gave Japan an obvious advantage. The country had developed its economic strength significantly over the past decade, particularly during the recent war, and could manage quite well in commercial competition on a level playing field. Indeed, even without claims to a privileged sphere, Japan's established position and its "special knowledge" of China gave the nation an edge over other powers. Moreover, the consortium as proposed could do little to challenge Japan's paramount position in Manchuria. Kwantung, the Railway Zone, and the SMR remained outside the jurisdiction of the international body, and these holdings would provide more than an adequate basis for Japan to pursue its goals in the territory. According to Debuchi, "With the South Manchuria Railway and the gateway of Dairen firmly in our hands, the foundations of our economic development program are quite secure. Even if our five Manchurian railways [the four lines of 1918 and the Kirin–Hoeryong] are turned over to the new consortium as joint ventures . . . I do not believe that our plans will suffer a significant setback."[26]

Debuchi pointed out that, in any event, the political climate in China made further progress on outstanding railway projects, or any other concessionary demands, for that matter, extremely unlikely. The efforts of the Hara government to follow up on some of the concessions negotiated by its predecessors confirmed this assessment. Diplomats had failed in their efforts to enforce land rights. Although talks had produced some movement toward completing the Ssup'ingkai–T'aonan line and building a western branch of this line from Chengchiat'un to T'ungliao, other projects remained stalled. With the departure of Tuan from the premiership and the new mood emerging in Chinese public opinion, opposition on the part of officials who might otherwise have leaned toward "cooperation" had stiffened. The Foreign Ministry's efforts to negotiate a formal contract on the Kirin-Hoeryong railway had proven fruitless thus far. Officially, Chinese representatives resisted the demand that they honor the agreements struck with Nishihara on the grounds that Japan had hardened its contract terms relative to what it had offered in 1918. The Hara government, indeed, was demanding greater stringency than originally promised in an effort to introduce greater security for Japanese loans. Given the postwar climate in China that vilified the officials who had negotiated with Nishihara as traitors, however, it is unlikely that loan terms alone formed the principal obstacle. Under the circumstances, Debuchi questioned whether relinquishing concessionary rights meant giving away anything of substance.[27]

Debuchi's economic and geopolitical assessment of the postwar situation presented a strong case for accommodating the American initiative, but in the final analysis, the single most important argument he offered lay in the arena of national defense. The need for a forward base against Russia had provided one of the more cogent reasons for maintaining a sphere of influence in Manchuria. With the collapse of Japan's mortal adversary, however, that need had clearly dissipated.

It cannot be imagined that in the future, [Russia] will be able to wield a large army, invade Manchuria, and threaten Korea. Given this change in conditions, the military and political significance of our management of Manchuria is no longer the same. Therefore, I believe it is only reasonable to adjust our plans, at least to some extent, for managing railways and other facilities in accordance with these new conditions.[28]

In a sense, the entire moderate position rested on this assessment. Other arguments held little import so long as the army could persist in its traditional claims. With the old logic of empire and national defense in tatters, the new yet to gather significant momentum, and the political prestige of the army at a historical nadir, moderates might, for the first time, strike at the foundations of the activist position.

Debuchi's arguments no doubt fell on many receptive ears within Japanese leadership circles. Still, however sound his line of reasoning, he was asking a great deal of his colleagues, particularly from members of the imperial activist camp. To accept this approach meant undoing the work of the past decade and giving up virtually everything won since 1908, a retreat difficult to consider even for some moderates. Activists certainly found good reason to question many of Debuchi's assessments. Japanese participation in the consortium might check American economic dominance to some degree, but the disproportionate financial strength of the United States would nonetheless make this international body a creature of Washington and open the door to American domination throughout China, including Manchuria. To Army Minister Tanaka, the U.S. initiative constituted nothing less than a reprise of the 1910 scheme.[29] Moreover, not all shared Debuchi's confidence in Japan's economic capabilities. The war boom notwithstanding, traditional imperialists like Gotō continued to argue at the end of the war that the strength of the West in East Asia lay in its capital resources, whereas Japan's rested in its military power. The nation's policy ought to draw on its inherent strengths rather than allow the contest to shift to ground where Japan remained weak.[30] Ugaki made a similar point in early 1919: "Britain and America seek, through the League of Nations, to tie down the military power of other states while nibbling away at them through the use of their long suit, capitalism. There doesn't seem to be much difference between military conquest and capitalistic nibbling."[31]

The army, of course, rejected Debuchi's arguments about the strategic value of Manchuria and its railways. Although the Russian state might not have constituted a plausible threat in 1919, the future remained uncertain. Moreover, given the revolutionary disorder in Siberia and the danger of chaos spreading to Manchuria, as well as the possibility of another power exploiting the circumstances to entrench itself in the region, Japan could not afford to adopt a sanguine view of the situation in Northeast Asia. Most important, those advocating Japan's support of the consortium proposal ignored the new economics of national defense. International control over China's railways and the development of its natural resources would hinder the army's program for strategic autarky. The other powers would hardly cooperate willingly in Japan's efforts to secure raw materials and economic facilities that would enhance its military capabilities.[32]

Although activists had ample reason to object to Debuchi's ideas, some aspects of the moderate position proved difficult to refute. As the diplomat had argued, the postwar balance of power in East Asia militated against a Japanese effort to resist the American initiative. Ugaki himself remarked at the end of 1918, "For the foreseeable future, the world will be an Anglo-American realm (*tenka*)."[33] Terauchi's policy, which had anticipated U.S.

dominance in the postwar world, had sought to circumvent through bilateral cooperation, rather than challenge directly, the pressures that the United States might bring to bear against Japan. Konoe and those who shared his views might rail against American hypocrisy, but their own assessment that Versailles reflected imperialist *realpolitik*, rather than idealism, recommended a pragmatic response to the demands of the new order.[34] Power, exercised righteously or otherwise, deserved respect. In this context, activists and moderates not only spoke the same language but also could find considerable common ground. Accommodating the Americans posed not a black-and-white question but one of degree, and here emerged room for compromise.

This compromise took the form of an attempt to exempt Manchuria from the jurisdiction of the consortium. Japan would endorse the U.S. proposal with this proviso.[35] Although far from allaying many of the activists' concerns, this step would go a long way toward minimizing Japanese losses and preserving the core of the nation's imperial claims. The notion of excluding the lands north of the Wall from international agreements concerning China had ample precedent. During negotiations over the formation of the 1913 loan consortium, Russia and Japan had insisted on removing the territory from the consortium's jurisdiction. In discussing the 1919 proposal, some policymakers initially argued in favor of exempting not only Manchuria but also Shantung. Others, however, believed too many exclusions would jeopardize negotiations over Manchuria. In order to make a credible claim to participation in good faith, Japan would have to offer some loan concessions to the consortium pool, and most policymakers considered the two branch railways in Shantung negotiated by Nishihara in 1918 the least objectionable candidates.[36] The Shantung Railway itself remained outside the scope of the proposed body and Japan's claims were relatively secure, but the willingness of many in the government to surrender these branch lines suggested a readiness to retreat from that province all together.

Joining the consortium under these terms represented, on the one hand, a significant retreat on the part of Japan's imperialists, who had so recently come to think in terms of dominion over China as a whole. On the other hand, it also constituted a rather audacious proposal, an attempt to formulate an implicit "two-China policy." In one China, south of the Wall, the financial body would operate without constraint, and the writ of the new order proposed by the Americans would operate in full force. In the other, north of the Wall, although nominally part of the same sovereign country, different international rules would apply, the consortium would have no jurisdiction, and the principles of the old imperial order would remain in place. Hara did not necessarily accept the full implications of this dualistic policy, but he did consider a bargain centered on Manchurian exclusion worth the attempt. Uncertain as to whether the powers would entertain such a proposal, however, he instructed Japanese representatives to avoid taking an intransigent position on the issue. In his view, Japan would have to join the consortium in one form or another.[37]

Flexibility proved essential, since the United States and Britain rejected out of hand Japan's attempt to remove Manchuria entirely from the jurisdiction of the proposed body. American representatives objected, in particular, to the implication that the lands north of the Wall constituted a region distinct from the rest of China.[38] As a fallback position, Japanese negotiators sought to enumerate specific concessions that would remain outside consortium control. The initial list encompassed all railway rights and options negotiated with Chinese representatives through 1918, including those on which actual work had yet to begin. The British and the Americans remained unmoved, regarding the Japanese list of exemptions as tantamount to complete exclusion. In the face of such resistance, Tokyo's representatives saw little hope of reaching an agreement without more substantive compromise on their part, and they chose the T'aonan–Jehol line as their sacrifice.[39]

Surrendering this line to the consortium would weaken Japan's position in Inner Mongolia. Moreover, insofar as the Jehol railway constituted a partial recapitulation of the old Chinchow–Aigun project, the Japanese side would, in effect, be granting Philander Knox a belated victory. At the same time, relinquishing Japan's claim to the T'aonan–Jehol line represented the least undesirable of the options facing the nation's diplomats. Any other choice would have brought the consortium deep into the heartland of Japanese Manchuria. Moreover, policymakers had in mind some steps that might make this concession more palatable. The interceptor strategy against the Chinchow–Aigun outlined by Komura in 1910 might help mitigate any problems caused by consortium control of the Jehol line. The Chengchiat'un–T'ungliao branch of the Ssup'ingkai–T'aonan line, already under discussion with the Chinese, would serve this purpose well.[40] Japanese diplomats anticipated getting the T'ungliao project past the scrutiny of its Western negotiating partners by arguing that a branch of a railway exempted from consortium jurisdiction would share the same status.[41] As a second measure aimed at reducing any injury that a consortium-controlled T'aonan–Jehol railway might cause, Japan would insist that any extension of this line north to Tsitsihar be subject to its approval.[42] Such a claim would preclude a full revival of the Chinchow–Aigun scheme and, more important, preserve Japanese options to construct a northward extension of its own Ssup'ingkai–T'aonan line to Tsitsihar. Both the SMR and the army had indicated a strong interest in building this extension, given the opportunity created by the collapse of Russia and an effective end to the boundary agreements of 1907 and 1912.[43]

American and British negotiators responded more favorably to this modified bargaining position. Provided a surrender of the Jehol railway, they would go along with the remainder of Tokyo's desired exemptions. Japanese claims to a "veto" over a T'aonan–Tsitsihar connection, however, remained unacceptable as a matter of principle. Japan could rest assured that the consortium would not act in a manner injurious to its legitimate interests, but guarantees of the type it sought ran against the spirit of undertaking as a whole.[44] Having little choice, the Japanese yielded on this issue. In the end, in May 1920 they formally consented to join the body with the understanding that four railway concessions would be excluded from its jurisdiction: the Ch'angch'un–T'aonan, the K'aiyüan–Hailung–Kirin (originally two lines in the 1913 agreement), the Kirin–Hoeryong, and the Ssup'ingkai–T'aonan. Japan turned over to the consortium the rights to the T'aonan–Jehol line, its seaport connector, and the two Shantung loan concessions.[45]

The exclusion of these Manchurian railways were the decisive factor in determining Japan's attitude toward the international body, but other issues came under dispute as well. The most important among these, ultimately left unsettled, concerned the status of the CER. The British and the Americans insisted that any loans to the CER fell under the jurisdiction of the new group. Japanese representatives firmly resisted this claim, arguing that the nature of the railway differed fundamentally from the loan concessions falling within the scope of the consortium's activities.[46]

Although the official Japanese position certainly had merit, it is also important to bear in mind that the Japanese had sought, since 1916, to acquire some measure of control over the Russian railway for themselves. These efforts had not ceased and clearly contributed to Japan's concerns about the Anglo-American position. The army and its allies had produced a plethora of schemes to achieve control of the CER in the aftermath of the Bolshevik

Revolution. They had initially attempted to ally themselves with the White Russian director of the railway company and subsequently shifted to a plan to have Tuan seize the line using his Frontier Defense Army. The Allied intervention in Siberia, however, thwarted such overt efforts. The participating powers pointedly denied the Japanese army jurisdiction over the CER and assigned it instead to take control of the Amur and Ussuri segments of the Trans-Siberian Railway. In 1919, an Inter-Allied Technical Board, directed by an American engineer by the name of John Stevens, assumed temporary management of the CER. This development only fueled the army's suspicions about American intentions. The future status of this railway remained in flux. In keeping with its anti-imperialist posture, the Soviet government had at first renounced any claims. The Chinese government, however, had aligned itself with White Russian interests in its efforts to recover the railway. The parent company of the CER, the Russo-Asiatic Bank, had reorganized itself in exile, with offices in Paris and Peking, and continued to assert its claims. These developments, among others, induced the Soviet government to reverse its position. Under these circumstances, Japan found it difficult to adopt a clear and straightforward approach to the problem, although a number of options remained under consideration. These schemes generally involved some kind of large-scale loan to the CER that would provide an opening for Japanese managerial rights. The Japanese aimed at acquiring control over the entire railway as a maximum goal. At a minimum, they sought to induce CER managers to retrack the Harbin–Ch'angch'un branch to standard gauge, to make it compatible with the SMR. Consortium claims to jurisdiction over a loan to the CER would jeopardize such plans and aggravate an already complicated situation.[47]

For its own reasons, the SMR shared the army's interest in the CER in particular and expansion in north Manchuria in general. The company had enjoyed an enormous windfall during the war as the CER curtailed its commercial operations. The Russian government had mobilized this line to serve military transportation requirements and had allocated much of its rolling stock to other parts of the Russian railway system. As a result, commercial traffic, which would otherwise have moved through Vladivostok, shifted south by way of the SMR to Dairen. In 1913, some 225,000 tons of soy products had reached the SMR's Ch'angch'un station from CER territory, carried primarily by horse carts. By 1917, that figure had leaped to 489,000 tons. The significance of this development bears emphasis. North Manchurian freight represented fully 36 percent of the soy tonnage carried by the SMR. Moreover, traffic from north Manchuria reaching Dairen traveled the full length of the trunk line, and with charges calculated as a product of tonnage multiplied by mileage, it represented some of the most valuable business of the Japanese railway (see Table 6.1).[48] Company analysts had predicted in 1910 that the future of soy production belonged to the north. It appeared, at least during the war, that the SMR would share in that future. From a perspective of business strategy, managers clearly needed to find some means of sustaining the SMR's wartime gains. Miyazaki Masayoshi (1873–1954), the SMR's resident Russia expert, outlined the company's concerns succinctly in 1918:

Since the Russian Revolution, the CER has lost its military significance with respect to Japan, and for internal and external reasons, it may be said that the economic life-blood of this railway is now flowing south to the SMR. This situation, however, cannot be regarded as a permanent change. With the collapse of Russia, the railway's military importance is unlikely to revive in the near future. However, it is probable that its economic function as an advantaged challenger to the SMR will recover quite quickly. So long as it remains possible for a third country to take over the line and so long as Japan lacks any special rights with regard to the railway, the SMR must anticipate a resumption of competitive pressure from the CER. Japan must adopt a policy of utilizing opportunities currently available to reduce the advantages enjoyed by the CER and achieve a balance of power.[49]

An active north Manchuria policy thus constituted not only a matter of strategic necessity and imperial opportunity but also an urgent demand stemming from *raison d'affaires*.

Japanese and Western negotiators had failed to reach agreement on the consortium's jurisdiction over loans to the CER by late 1920. Hara had no desire to allow this issue to confound the agreement as a whole, yet neither could he concede, given the weight of army and SMR interests. Further compromises on railway issues, particularly regarding north Manchuria, might well make his efforts to persuade the army to disengage from Siberia all the more difficult. In the end, negotiators left the matter unresolved. The final document took note of the Anglo-American position as well as the fact that Japanese delegates lacked authorization from their government to commit themselves on this question. American claims and the failure of the Japanese government to maintain a firm stand on the issue, no doubt,

Table 6.1
Soy Traffic Patterns on the SMR, 1913 and 1920

Station	Distance (miles)	1913 Ton-miles	%[a]	1920 Ton-miles	%
Liaoyang	208	4,281,472	1.4	6,111,040	0.7
Mukden	248	2,692,288	0.9	2,898,624	0.3
Hsint'aitzu	276	3,425,712	1.1	8,437,044	1.0
T'iehling	293	18,980,833	6.3	16,488,575	2.0
K'aiyüan	313	65,073,952	21.7	109,020,404	13.1
Ch'angt'u	333	3,812,517	1.3	4,860,135	0.6
Shuangmiaotzu	348	5,031,036	1.7	4,693,824	0.6
Ssup'ingkai	366	15,863,538	5.3	25,436,634	3.1
Ssup'ingkai Line	366	n/a	n/a	4,460,442	0.5
Kuochiatien	382	9,240,198	3.1	9,451,062	1.1
Kungchuling	399	37,820,811	12.6	44,485,707	5.4
Fanchiat'un	419	12,981,877	4.3	53,588,675	6.5
Ch'angch'un[b]	438	91,144,734	30.4	339,067,188	40.8
CER Connection	438	7,220,430	2.4	164,809,326	19.9
TOTAL		277,569,398	92.5	793,358,181	95.6

NOTE: The distance is calculated from Dairen. Ton-mile calculations are estimates only, based on the assumption that all soy shipped out was destined for Dairen.
[a] Percentage of SMR's total soybean and beancake traffic (ton-mileage), excluding the Antung–Mukden line. The Antung–Mukden line carried a relatively small volume of soy products; a maximum estimate for 1913 is 1 million ton-miles and for 1920, 5 million ton-miles.
[b] Includes feeder-line traffic from the Ch'angch'un–Kirin line.
SOURCES: Calculated from *TKN* 1913, pp. 232–36; *TKN* 1920, pp. 276–83.

troubled the army and its allies. Coupled with indications that the consortium would assert its rights to jurisdiction over such projects as the T'aonan–Tsitsihar railway, prospects for Japanese expansion into north Manchuria, which had appeared so bright in 1917, seemed to have dimmed. At the same time, however, the army and SMR could find some consolation in the fact that no final agreement had been reached on this issue. Talks had not definitively closed the door, and that residual glimmer represented, perhaps, the best they might have hoped for under the circumstances.

Given the potential for domestic as well as international crisis inherent in any challenge to Japan's position in Manchuria, the overall outcome of the negotiations no doubt pleased the Hara government. The consortium agreement, loose ends and all, constituted a viable internal as well as external modus vivendi that satisfied the Great Powers while winning at least grudging acceptance from imperial activists at home. The government's official assessment of this agreement, contained in a cabinet resolution on Manchuria hammered out in the spring of 1921 at the Eastern Conference, a comprehensive review of East Asia policy that is discussed below, represented an exercise in the ambidextrous "politics of compromise." A counterpoint of activist and moderate voices runs throughout the text.

On the one hand, it reaffirmed Japan's commitments in Manchuria and underscored recent successes in defending its position in the territory. "That Manchuria, which borders on our national territory, bears a profound and intimate relationship to our national defense and the economic survival of our people requires no explanation today," it stated in the preamble. "With these two concerns informing our aims, the core of our policy in Manchuria is to transplant our power into the territory." The resolution went on to review past problems encountered in the effort to win recognition for Japanese claims, citing challenges from the powers going back to the years immediately following the Russo-Japanese War. In this regard, it noted that the consortium agreement constituted a highly positive development and offered "a guarantee of our special position" and "the first clear recognition" from the international community of Japan's claims in the territory. Fleshing out the implications of the new inter-power understanding, the resolution outlined a two-China framework for future policy and justified Manchurian exceptionalism in the following terms:

Our argument for the so-called exclusion of Manchuria is based on the deep and particular relationship between Manchuria and our empire in terms of national defense and the economic survival of our people. Therefore, we cannot regard our enterprises and investments from a purely economic standpoint. Accordingly, there will be times when we will find it difficult to act in unison with the powers.[50]

On the other hand, the same resolution also emphasized the fact that the consortium agreement imposed significant limitations on Japanese activity in the territory.

At the same time, we must emphasize and firmly assert that none of this means we intend to monopolize economic benefits within a particular geographic zone, to preserve and expand a so-called sphere of influence, or to violate the principle of preserving China's independence and territorial integrity.[51]

Lest there be any confusion as to the boundaries of permissible activity, the resolution offered clarification in three admonitory points:

1. We will, of course, endeavor to preserve and exercise our existing privileges and special status, and we will, in the future, continue to secure such rights and claims as required by national defense and the economic survival of our people. However, given trends in the world at this time, [changes in] international relations, and the movement for national self-determination, even such urgent and reasonable demands are apt to be misunderstood as evidence of aggressive trends, damaging our international standing and compounding our difficulties. We must, therefore, exercise the utmost discretion, along with mature deliberation, in pursuing these goals.

2. Although we will uphold and exercise our existing rights, we must also be aware from the outset that our relationship with the China loan consortium, which has been established with our government's approval, will impose certain limitations. For example, we may continue to insist, with respect to the Chinese, upon the efficacy of our claims, as established in the Sino-Japanese accords of 1915 [the Twenty-One Demands], to the right of first refusal on all railway loans in south Manchuria and the placement of advisors [in regional administration], but we cannot do so in their entirety with respect to member-states of the loan consortium.

3. Given the principle of cooperation fundamental to the mission of the loan consortium, which our government has recognized, and the principle of the Open Door and equal opportunity in China, it would be inadvisable to pursue a policy of exclusion and monopoly so long as our defense and the economic survival of our people are not threatened. Such activity will only win the suspicion and antagonism of the powers. Moreover, it will retard the economic development of Manchuria and, in the final analysis, result in self-inflicted injury to our own interests.[52]

The attempt at balance in this document and, in particular, the effort to cast the consortium agreement in positive, imperialist terms are unmistakable. Nonetheless, the Eastern Conference resolution marked a historic setback for the activist camp. Indeed, it would not be unreasonable to suggest that Hara and his moderate colleagues found the Anglo-American initiative a convenient instrument to restrain the army and its allies since it allowed them to shift to an external villain responsibility for a course of action they generally favored. From the perspective of would-be hard-liners, the outcome could have been worse, an understanding accounting for their acquiescence. Japan had managed to defend some of its outstanding concessionary rights and had kept its options open for building the Kirin–Hoeryong, the K'aiyüan–Hailung–Kirin, and the Ch'angch'un–T'aonan railways. But by the provisions of the agreement of May 1920, these lines, along with the Ssup'ingkai–T'aonan and a branch from Chengchiat'un to T'ungliao, would form the last elements of a Japanese-controlled network in Manchuria.

At the same time, the significance of this setback must be kept in perspective. Traditional approaches to expansion in China faced obstacles from sources other than the new diplomacy of the Great Powers, and imperial activists themselves had called their efficacy into question well before the end of World War I. Even if Japan had won the full exclusion of Manchuria, the Chinese indicated no willingness to grant any further concessions, and in the new climate of the May Fourth movement, any attempt to return to the old practices of gunboat diplomacy, the attitude of the powers notwithstanding, would probably produce violent confrontation without substantive progress. Indeed, barring a sea change in Sino-Japanese relations, the fate of even those lines Japan had managed to exempt from consortium jurisdiction remained very much in doubt. In this respect, despite anxious handwringing about the future of Manchuria by imperial activists, the U.S. consortium initiative was little more than an attempt to place a diplomatic padlock on gates rusted shut for some time.

Alternative Strategies: Industrial Manchuria

The fact that the more farsighted among advocates of aggressive expansion had begun to acknowledge the obsolescence of concession hunting during the Terauchi period may have pre-empted the explosive potential inherent in the consortium issue. Imperialist *realpolitik* and the diminished influence of the army clearly contributed as well, but in this instance, as in others, the abortive reforms of the Terauchi government seemed to have helped Hara and the moderates bank the fires of wartime imperialism, wean activists from old ways and expectations, and thus soften the disappointments of the postwar era. There is no doubt that imperialist frustrations ran deep, approaching perhaps the level of "impotent rage" that John Young ascribes to army leaders during this era, yet such sentiments appear to have been directed less at Hara than at larger developments beyond the control of the Japanese government.[53]

At the same time, however, it would be a mistake to conclude that activists had resigned themselves to the apparent dead end confronting their cause at the beginning of the 1920s. Imperialists were nothing if not creative, and the historical strength of Japanese expansion lay in its adaptive qualities, in its ability to make the best of existing circumstances. This era offers evidence of this adaptive process at work in the emergence of a relatively quiet, alternative strain of imperialist thinking about Manchuria. Denied the opportunity to expand in breadth by a combination of the new diplomacy and an invigorated Chinese nationalism, Japan might turn, instead, toward an approach of building empire in depth, of better exploiting its existing rights rather than attempting to acquire new concessions. One of the more intriguing possibilities along these lines lay in the idea of developing Kwantung and the Railway Zone into an urbanized, industrial Japanese enclave in Manchuria. At this stage, the notion of an "industrial Manchuria" remained more a broad vision than a coherent strategy, and it would not emerge until the 1930s as a dominant element in Japanese policy. However, as an important aspect of Japanese adaptations to the environment of this era, it warrants examination in some detail.

The idea of emphasizing empire-building in depth first emerged during the war. The reforms of Terauchi, Shōda, and Nishihara represented one approach to breaking the stalemate confronting traditional concession-hunting strategies. Governor Nakamura of the SMR proposed another direction. Like others involved in the front-line implementation of imperial policy in Manchuria, he understood that measures such as those contained in the Twenty-One Demands did not constitute the panacea that some claimed. Nakamura believed that visions of an agrarian Japanese Manchuria suffered from unrealistic expectations, and such ventures as specialty farming or modern ranching aside, the main hope for tapping the latent value of the territory rested in strengthening the Japanese position in modern commerce and industry. Development in these areas offered the most effective means to exploit Manchuria's resources as well as the most promising way to promote Japanese settlement. He foresaw a division of labor in the territory in which the Chinese would do most of the basic farming, while the Japanese controlled trade, banking, manufacturing, and transportation. Nakamura stressed, in particular, the importance of manufacturing that made use of local raw materials and energy sources. He had no reason to oppose the further expansion of rights, but in the immediate future the best prospects for improving Japan's position in the territory rested in a more intensive exploitation of Kwantung and the Railway Zone that would result in the construction of an industrial and urban Manchuria nestled in the railway valley of the SMR.[54]

When Nakamura articulated this idea in 1915, it seemed, no doubt, a long shot. The subsequent war boom and developments in Manchuria, however, lent cogency to the concept. The years between 1916 and the onset of a recession in 1921 constituted a period of unprecedented economic prosperity for Japan, one in which Japanese industry took advantage of the opportunity of diminished European competition to move into areas of production not seriously contemplated before. Wartime circumstances tolerated high prices and relatively low quality, allowing many Japanese enterprises to achieve breakthroughs. The same conditions also facilitated the spread of the industrial boom to Manchuria. What might have appeared, at best, marginal opportunities before the war became newly attractive. As Kaneko Fumio has described in considerable detail, Japanese investment in Manchuria leaped between 1916 and 1920 and resulted in the establishment of 482 new companies with paid-up capital of ¥135 million. This contrasts sharply with the mere 44 companies with a combined capital of ¥20 million set up in Manchuria during the entire decade after 1905, excluding the SMR itself. The manufacturing sector experienced particularly rapid expansion—161 new companies with a total paid-up capital of ¥43.5 million. Between 1905 and 1915, only nine manufacturing companies with a combined capital of ¥3.2 million had taken root in the territory. A deep and prolonged recession followed the war boom, and many enterprises foundered in the home islands and Manchuria alike. But as in Japan proper, new industries in Manchuria had acquired a foothold and, given strenuous rationalization, a chance to survive. Possibilities not considered before opened themselves to active exploration.[55]

The SMR's Anshan Ironworks formed the heart of this nascent vision of an industrial Japanese Manchuria. Governor Nakamura's modest plans in 1915 had called for no more than a small-scale pilot project. Anshan possessed huge ore reserves, estimated as high as 900 million tons, but the proportion of accessible, high-grade ores appeared relatively small. This was one reason for a fairly conservative approach to exploiting this resource. Nakamura and his advisors understood that a large-scale commercially viable venture had to await development of ore-enrichment techniques. The iron and steel crisis in Japan, however, induced company managers to upgrade their program dramatically, and they initiated a plan to produce one million tons of pig iron and 800,000 tons of crude steel annually. The achievement of such targets would have made Anshan the largest producer of iron and steel in the empire. Koiso attached great importance to this venture in his 1917 study. Indeed, in civilian as well as military economic thinking, the success of Anshan alone would have represented a vast elevation of the value of Manchuria. This undertaking held significant symbolic meaning as well. The locomotive had served as an icon of modernity in Meiji. Iron and steel likewise stood for industrial Japan and a new vision for Manchuria.[56]

Fushun coal stood second only to Anshan iron in importance to promoting the industrialization of Japanese Manchuria. Production costs ran extremely low, and if used at nearby plants, it had great potential as a raw material and as an inexpensive source of fuel for energy-intensive industries. SMR managers had pioneered its use as a raw material for chemical manufacture in 1912 with the trial production of ammonium sulfate using Mond gas generators. Ammonium sulfate was not only a chemical fertilizer of growing importance in Japan but a key precursor in the production of a variety of explosives. Anshan's coking ovens, using Fushun coal, produced byproducts that could also be used to manufacture munitions. Other coal derivatives were used in the production of pharmaceuticals, paints, and dyes. The SMR's Central Research Laboratory directed considerable effort to the development of a commercial paint industry in Manchuria that would exploit these derivatives as well as readily available soybean oil as a base. A few small paint companies had started operations in the territory by 1920 as a result. The dry distillation of coal formed another area of SMR research. Trials led to the production of briquettes for use as a household fuel, along with the development of a creosote substitute suitable for preserving railway ties and mining timbers. The navy, which sought secure sources of liquid fuel, expressed interest in experiments in this field, as well as in the possibility of exploiting the oil shales found in large quantities at Fushun.[57]

The potential of Fushun coal as a cheap fuel for energy-intensive industries found several important applications in this period as well. One lay in supplying the needs of the ironworks. The fact that a number of Japanese industries appear to have considered relocating to Manchuria as a result of low energy costs, however, promised even broader uses. Denki kagaku kōgyō (Electrochemical industries), in cooperation with the SMR, for example, set up an electrochemical plant for the production of ammonium sulfate. When the price of ammonium sulfate plunged shortly after the start of operations in 1919, Denki kagaku pulled out. Although this particular venture failed, the idea of electrochemical industries remained an area of interest to the SMR, and its efforts in this field would continue throughout the 1920s. The ceramics industry proved more immediately successful in taking advantage of cheap coal as a fuel source, supported by the availability of rich deposits of limestone, dolomite, and silica within the Kwantung Leased Territory. The SMR's Central Research Laboratory explored a variety of ceramics projects, such as plans to manufacture crystal and plate glass and to produce firebrick for use at Anshan.[58]

Iron and steel, chemicals, and energy-intensive ventures represented the most attention-catching and novel elements of this new thrust in Manchuria, but developments in more conventional areas of light industry, such as textiles, also played an important part in the industrialization scheme. Hemp cloth mills had made an appearance early on to meet the demand for bags for packing beans. Japanese cotton textile makers, following the pattern found elsewhere in China, began to locate plants in Manchuria during this period. Japanese textile production in this region, however, also had special significance for strategic economic policy as part of an effort to promote the production of local raw materials. Developing wool resources formed a major impetus behind the founding of Manchurian Woolens in 1918. Cotton textile manufacturing would similarly encourage the cultivation of local cotton.[59]

A variety of other modern industries took root as well. A sugar refinery started operations in Mukden in 1916 with the intention of using locally grown beets. South Manchuria Sugar became the largest Japanese-owned enterprise in the territory apart from the SMR. A Japanese company established a bean oil factory in Dairen in 1918, using a benzene extraction technique developed by the SMR's Central Research Laboratory and machinery built by the company's Shahok'ou Railway Workshop. In addition to exploiting coal byproducts, pharmaceutical makers made use of local licorice and barium salts. Machinery production offered another promising possibility. Many small workshops that made parts and did repair work for the SMR and other large enterprises sprouted throughout Kwantung and the Zone during this period. The SMR's Shahok'ou facilities offered a model of development for moving from repair and parts production into broader manufacturing ventures. It had produced its first locomotive in 1914 and began expanding its manufacture of rolling stock during the war. It also built machinery for other industries, such as the oil mill, and played a major role in supplying Anshan's needs.[60]

Although the idea of an "industrial Manchuria" remained no more than a rough vision during this period, it began to acquire some coherence by 1920 as a Manchurian "industrial policy" of sorts emerged under the direction of the SMR and the Kwantung Administration. The program in Manchuria had affinities with efforts to manage economic development in the home islands, but it also had distinctly imperial roots in the practice of scientific colonization. The Central Research Laboratory, the brainchild of Ishizuka Eizō, who had originally established the facility under the Kwantung Government-General during his stint as civil administrator, served as one of its most important agents. It also represented a distinctly imperial policy in discouraging the development, with a few exceptions, of industries that would compete with home interests. The SMR and the Kwantung Administration chose fields of enterprise that might optimally exploit the special advantages offered in Manchuria by making use of its raw materials and low energy and labor costs. Strategic economic considerations were major criteria as well. Targeted areas of enterprise received subsidies, breaks on land use, favorable railway rates, and supportive regulations where applicable.[61]

The SMR played a special role in industrialization and increasingly redefined its role as a development agency. The company functioned as what some have described as an "industrial organizer" by pulling together in a vertical combination various operations needed to make a particular field of production commercially viable, much as the zaibatsu and general trading companies had done in the home islands. Industrial organizers coordinated the supply of raw materials and energy, the manufacturing process, transportation, distribution, and, in many cases, finance.[62] As a diversified railway company with industrial subsidiaries, the SMR found itself in a particularly good position to fulfill this role. Like the zaibatsu, the SMR would also contribute decisively to the rationalization of Manchurian industry following the collapse of the boom. The company's stamina, which rested on the continued prosperity of its railway business, helped sustain ventures that might otherwise have gone under. The Anshan Ironworks provides a good example. Iron and steel prices collapsed in 1920 as production recovered worldwide. The SMR's production costs ran substantially higher than the market price, and it had no choice but to scale back its plans. It did not abandon the effort, however. Relying on the company's deep pockets, Anshan continued to operate while, at the same time, its technologists worked on new ore-enrichment techniques.[63] Another special function of the SMR in promoting industrialization, again similar to what the zaibatsu and general trading companies did in the home islands, lay in facilitating the flow of capital. It could borrow at much lower costs than smaller independent companies and channel those funds into investment in Manchuria. The fact that in 1920, the Diet allowed the SMR to more than double its authorized capital from ¥200 to ¥440 million yen, strengthened its capabilities in this field. The government maintained its half-share of ownership by taking over the company's outstanding foreign debt.[64]

The emerging role of the SMR as an industrial-policy agency was an extension of its older function in promoting territorial development, but it must also be understood as an outgrowth of business strategy. Efforts to find new uses of coal, to employ existing facilities more efficiently, and to diversify sources of income, all of which sought to improve the company's performance as an economic enterprise, were responsible for the initial thrust into industry. The subsequent incorporation of these initiatives into a larger policy framework during this period offers a good example of adaptive rationalization in the formulation of programmatic goals, a pattern we have seen since the beginning of the venture. It also highlights the importance of the cumulative effects of Japanese activity in broadening the horizons of possibility in Manchuria.

The industrialization of areas under Japanese jurisdiction served an important function in its own right as a part of an emerging vision of Manchuria's future, but it also had significant ramifications for immigration policy. Nakamura had suggested in 1915 that urban settlement, driven by expanding employment opportunities in manufacturing and modern services, offered a much more realistic approach than agrarian homesteading. This argument appeared to be validated by developments during the war boom. The ethnic Japanese population in the Leased Territory and the Railway Zone leaped from 85,000 in 1915 to 137,000 in 1920.[65] Of the immigrant population in 1920, excluding those born in Manchuria, fully half had arrived in the past three years. By 1920, settler numbers in Manchuria approached those in Taiwan, which had 166,000 ethnic Japanese residents, and more than a respectable third of Korea's 347,000. Other encouraging indications emerged. People immigrated to Manchuria with their families, planning for a long-term stay if not intending to settle permanently. Sex ratios approached parity, and the natural growth rate of the population was comparable to that of

Table 6.2
Age and Gender Distribution of the Japanese
Population in Manchuria, 1920

Age	Total	Female		Male	
		Number	%	Number	%
5 and under	20,526	10,129	49.35	10,397	50.65
6 to 10	14,287	6,930	48.51	7,357	51.49
11 to 15	10,115	4,793	47.39	5,322	52.61
16 to 20	15,967	7,349	46.03	8,618	53.97
21 to 25	29,149	10,734	36.82	18,415	63.18
26 to 30	21,759	9,868	45.35	11,891	54.65
31 to 35	18,886	7,834	41.48	11,052	58.52
36 to 40	15,415	5,604	36.35	9,811	63.65
41 to 46	10,230	3,523	34.44	6,707	65.56
46 to 50	5,727	1,969	34.38	3,758	65.62
51 to 55	3,238	1,209	37.34	2,029	62.66
56 to 60	1,693	787	46.49	906	53.51
61 to 65	1,095	618	56.44	477	43.56
65 to 70	687	467	67.98	220	32.02
71 and older	614	439	71.50	175	28.50
TOTAL	169,388	72,253	42.66	97,135	57.34

NOTE: These figures include residents from outlying consular jurisdictions such as Harbin, Kirin, and Tsitsihar.
SOURCE: SMR, Chōsaka (Kudō Takeo), *Waga kuni jinkō mondai to Manmō*, pp. 97–98.

the home islands. The growing number of Japanese children resident in the Railway Zone, in fact, began straining the SMR's school system. Settlement had started, at long last, to make serious headway, even without land rights (see Table 6.2 and Appendix B).[66]

This nascent vision of an urban and industrial Japanese Manchuria had potentially broad appeal. It represented an approach to empire-building that moderates could endorse and, indeed, seemed quite consistent with what Debuchi had in mind. At the same time, it offered a program that would fulfill at least some of the purposes dear to imperial activists, not only in the new arena of strategic autarky but in the older agenda in which *Lebensraum* had occupied a prominent place. To be sure, it promised only modest gains in comparison to the grand ambitions of wartime imperialism, yet the approach already appeared to have produced more tangible evidence of progress than either the Twenty-One Demands or the Nishihara Loans had provided. In themselves, the possibilities of building an industrial enclave hardly compensated for larger disappointments, but they nonetheless offered a source of encouragement in an era of multiple setbacks. How this vision might have evolved in subsequent years, had it become the dominant adaptation of Japanese imperialism to the new order, poses an intriguing problem for contrafactual speculation. We might well have seen Kwantung emerge as the Hong Kong of Northeast Asia, and the railway valley of the SMR become one of the great industrial corridors of the region.

As it turns out, however, an unanticipated development in late 1920, which presented far more attractive prospects for the revival of Japan's imperialist fortunes in the territory, overshadowed the significance of "industrial Manchuria" as an adaptive strategy. An unsolicited overture for a partnership from a regional Chinese military leader by the name of Chang Tso-lin offered Japan's empire builders an opportunity that made alternatives pale in comparison. At least for a time, Chang would prove a godsend for an embattled Japanese imperialism.

Chang Tso-lin: Deus ex Machina

Ironically, the circumstances that produced Chang Tso-lin's initiative seemed, at first, yet another setback for the imperial activist camp. Elements in the army continued to favor some form of "cooperation" with Tuan Ch'i-jui and his associates, a group that had come to be known as the Anfu Club, with the implicit aim of fishing for advantage in the troubled waters of a politically fragmented China. In the summer of 1920, a civil war between competing factions erupted. The rival Chihli Clique roundly defeated Tuan's group, dashing any lingering Japanese hopes based on their erstwhile client. Chang and his so-called Fengt'ien Clique, originally allied with Tuan, had switched sides and played an instrumental role in ensuring the outcome.[67]

Chang Tso-lin's official title in 1920 was "inspector-general of the Three Eastern Provinces," a position that made him, in effect, an autonomous ruler in the region. He had begun his ascent in Chinese politics as a bandit leader turned soldier and subsequently rose to regional officialdom, a transformation reflective of the environment in Manchuria in the late Ch'ing and early Republican years. Mobility in the rough frontier society of the wild Northeast, coupled with the decline of traditional authority, made Chang's career possible. By 1918, he had emerged as the foremost Chinese power in the region, representative of a new kind of figure in Chinese politics commonly described as a warlord. The Japanese had dealt with him earlier. During the anti-Yüan campaign of 1916, they had considered him as a possible collaborator. By late in the war, he had allied himself with Tuan's group. On the whole, however, the Japanese and Chang Tso-lin had looked on each other with ambivalence. In fact, the Manchurian warlord seemed a rather improbable source for a friendly overture, since he had made his debut as a national figure by turning on Tuan. However, his new involvement in national politics as the leader of the rising Fengt'ien Clique and the vicissitudes of warlord politics drove him to seek a relationship with Japan. Chang harbored ambitions for controlling the central government himself, and anticipating conflict with Chihli leaders, his recent allies, he wanted a strong foreign friend at his back, one that might be willing to supply him with guns and money. In making his overture, he offered himself as the "new Tuan" and suggested a number of ways in which he might help Japan in exchange for material and political support.[68]

Chang's overture piqued Japanese interest for the clear reason that it opened the door to the possibility of reviving some form of bilateral cooperation, if only in a limited, Manchurian venue. Given an opportunity, a strategy of client management offered an obvious solution to the impasse facing the expansionist program in Manchuria. At minimum, greasing the palms of officials in a quasi-autonomous government in Mukden could overcome resistance to the exercise of existing rights, including long-stalled railway projects, and possibly even facilitate progress on the question of land rights. It might even be possible to work out some arrangement over the CER, involving, perhaps, a joint effort to settle the status of the railway to mutual advantage, an undertaking to which Chang had alluded in his initial approach.[69] As a maximum goal, the Japanese might nurture a relationship with the Manchurian leader along the lines that Terauchi and his colleagues had envisioned for Tuan, an alliance and partnership that would develop Manchuria according to Japanese designs and bypass the obstacles presented by both the new order and Chinese nationalism. If Chang proved suitable as a client, the horizons of imperialist possibility in the territory might expand more than ever before.

The fact that active empire-building in Manchuria, apart from the development of Kwantung and the Railway Zone, had reached a virtual dead end by 1920 no doubt made those traditional imperialists who had opposed bilateral cooperation under Terauchi more receptive to the idea. Still, significant skepticism remained within the activist camp, not so much about managing clients as a general strategy as about Chang Tso-lin as the client. Chang's decisive contribution to the Anfu Club's defeat did little to endear him to those who had placed their hopes on Tuan. The Anfu-Chihli war, in fact, underscored the degree to which the Chinese political world had fragmented and recommended caution. Any client-management approach might not be advisable at this time.

Although some of the army's China experts expressed strong support for Chang, many uncharacteristically urged a policy of neutrality. The Kwantung Army staff pointed out the need to approach the Manchurian leader with caution. His words might be pro-Japanese, but his actions in the past cast doubt on his professions of friendship. Chang had previously obstructed Japanese mining ventures and had even convened a meeting of local officials to discuss ways in which to prevent the Japanese from exercising land rights. Perhaps the greatest concern among those skeptical about Chang, however, was that the warlord's overture most likely stemmed from his desire to enlist Japanese support for his ambitions south of the Wall. Even those who favored working with the inspector-general saw the relationship limited to the Three Eastern Provinces, where his power was firmly established and at least partly legitimate. The notion of installing another client president or prime minister to exert control over China as a whole remained beyond their consideration at this point. Tuan, who had been in a much better position to consolidate his control over the country in 1918 had failed, and most believed that Chang had no serious chance of doing better.[70] Moreover, for the same reasons that imperial activists felt compelled to agree to a compromise over the consortium issue, they believed that, at least for the time being, their initiatives would be best focused north of the Wall.

Still, given the grim prospects facing Japanese expansion at this time, the possibility of working with Chang proved difficult to dismiss. Proponents of a partnership pointed out that support for Chang as ruler of Manchuria could be distinguished from endorsing him as a candidate for national leadership in Peking. Japan would aid him in the management of the Three Eastern Provinces, dealing with him exclusively as a regional power, and disavow involvement with his adventures south of the Wall. Major General Satō Yasunosuke, whom we previously encountered as a major and head of the SMR's Mukden Office (see Chapter 3), strongly recommended the formulation of a policy based on such distinctions. The army had assigned Satō, a veteran Manchuria expert personally acquainted with Chang, to talk with the warlord and assess his intentions. Precisely what a policy of supporting Chang in Manchuria while maintaining neutrality south of the Wall might look like in practice remained unclear. Satō's recommendation appears, nonetheless, to have helped overcome resistance. Army Minister Tanaka Giichi, who had known Chang since the Russo-Japanese War, gave the idea his blessing.[71]

Upon hearing Satō's recommendations and Tanaka's endorsement, Prime Minister Hara appeared receptive. Such a response might seem somewhat surprising, given Hara's moderate inclinations and his disdain for the idea of cooperation during the Terauchi government. Hara's propensity to compromise in politics offers part of the explanation. At this juncture, any reasonable measure that the army and its supporters desired deserved a serious hearing, particularly since Hara needed Tanaka's help to get the army out of Siberia.[72] More important, however, a working relationship with Chang did not necessarily imply bilateral cooperation of the sort Hara had opposed before. Exercised on a limited scale and for specific purposes, playing factions against one another, exchanging favors, and engaging in political horse trading were practices that the prime minister found acceptable. As Hara put it, "The truth is that Chang wants Japan's backing to expand his power. For our part, we must treat Chang well if we want to develop our position in the Three Eastern Provinces. As a matter of happenstance, the interests of both sides are in harmony at this point."[73] That he saw the mutual back-scratching as a short-term and limited expedient is evident from other remarks about the Manchurian leader in his diary. Hara noted, for example, the usefulness of Chang in allowing the Japanese army to conduct punitive raids across the T'umen River against Korean guerrillas, a problem that had become increasingly serious since the suppression of the March First movement, the 1919 uprising in Korea. Chang suggested that he would probably have to protest officially to satisfy public opinion, but he would otherwise look the other way if Japanese troops crossed the border.[74] At the same time, Hara warned, "I believe that given today's situation it is necessary to form ties with Chang from the perspective of protecting ourselves in our rule of Korea and the management of Manchuria. . . . However, to raise his expectations excessively and disappoint him later would not be wise."[75]

Perhaps the most persuasive reason for moderates such as Hara to consider some form of ties with Chang, however, lay in the simple fact that Japan needed a responsible party to deal with in Manchuria, whether in efforts to punish Korean "outlaws" or to discuss outstanding railway concessions such as the Kirin–Hoeryong line. Given the disintegration of central authority in China, it had become rather pointless to talk to Peking about matters in Manchuria over which Chang exercised real power.

The Eastern Conference of May 1921 took up the issue of forging a relationship with Chang Tso-lin. The formulation of an overall body of policies governing China and Siberia in anticipation of further discussions among the powers about the situation in Asia formed the primary purpose of this gathering, which included representatives not only of all the ministries involved in the management of East Asian affairs but also of key agencies in the field. Hara wanted to press for a concrete commitment and timetable for the army to withdraw from Siberia. In addition, he sought a clear resolution of the Shantung problem. A growing consensus among policymakers favored moving beyond the surrender of the two concession railways to the consortium and abandoning claims to a sphere of interest in the province altogether. Although Japan would retain mining rights, it would withdraw all troops and sell the Shantung Railway to China for an appropriate price. Hara also sought an affirmation of the consortium decision as part of a more comprehensive policy. In a broad sense, this meeting, if successful, would ratify a general imperialist retreat in East Asia, which moderates believed essential for Japan's adaptation to the new order. Although all parties had accepted the overall direction of these policies, grudgingly in some instances, Hara sought an explicit understanding with respect to the entire package on the table. This context strengthens the impression that Hara's willingness to go along with a policy of working with Chang Tso-lin involved an element of political compromise, an implicit bargain that would allow imperial activists to accept the basic thrust of his program.[76]

The resolution on Chang Tso-lin worked out at this conference, however, made it clear that Hara and the moderates had in mind a relationship rather different from what activists envisioned. Two distinct interpretations appear to coexist in the final document. It represents a work of studied dualism and political counterpoint, much like the consortium resolution examined above:

1. The thrust of the empire's assistance to Chang is not directed to Chang as an individual but to the holder of real power in Manchuria for the purposes of securing our special position in the territory.

For this reason, the empire is prepared to render such assistance to anyone who comes to occupy the same status in Manchuria as Chang, to cooperate with him, and to work for mutual benefit.

2. Once we have withdrawn our troops from Siberia, we will be confronted with a large number of problems requiring negotiation and settlement with China, including Manchuria policy, the administration and maintenance of law and order in Korea, and border issues involving China, Japan, and Russia. It is also clear that Chang is the person we must deal with directly on the Chinese side at this time. In order to achieve the above objectives, we must induce Chang to deal with us in a friendly manner. For this purpose, we must be prepared to render such assistance that will prevent Chang from losing his base in Manchuria.

3. So long as the Great Power agreement on an arms embargo on China remains in force, we cannot, in the final analysis, fulfill Chang's desire for arms. However, it is permissible to have him establish an arsenal and create the basis to supply himself.

4. Although the imperial government will not be parsimonious in giving consideration to provisional financial assistance, it is extremely important that such assistance should, insofar as possible, take the form of economic loans, particularly through investment in joint ventures, in order to avoid the jealousy and suspicion of both the powers and the central Chinese government. In regard to this matter, Inspector-General Chang should also understand that if both sides work to realize the possibility of "coexistence and coprosperity" through the mutually beneficial promotion of new as well as established joint ventures in land development, mining, forestry, and other promising areas, Sino-Japanese cooperation will result in an improvement of the finances of the Three Eastern Provinces as a matter of course.

5. If our policy regarding the CER is to be achieved, there are a large number of matters on which we must come to an understanding with Chang Tso-lin, particularly with regard to the retracking [to standard gauge] of the southern branch of the railway. We must explain to him that there are three major advantages, administrative, economic, and military, to be gained from this measure: (1) transportation connections between north and south Manchuria, both under Inspector-General Chang's control, will be improved; (2) in particular, it will be possible to realize direct connections with the PMR and unify the network; (3) the deployment of troops north and south will be facilitated. Loans to the CER may be extended through Chang, and his influence can be used to move the CER authorities to undertake the retracking project.[77]

The first two clauses point to the influence of the moderate view of a pragmatic and limited working relationship. They underscore the fact that Japan extended cooperation not to Chang himself but to the office of Manchurian ruler. They also specified the areas in which Japan desired cooperation, matters that, under other circumstances, Tokyo would have handled through official talks in Peking. At the same time, the contribution of the client-management line also appears unmistakable. Some of the measures outlined in Clauses 3 and 4, in particular, bear a close resemblance to the Nishihara Loans. Joint ventures and economic cooperation would circumvent the limitations imposed by the consortium agreement, the same kind of subterfuge as the "industrial loans" that Nishihara had used to launder aid money. Clause 5 on the CER could fit both interpretations, although it was weighted toward bilateral cooperation, which carried the implication of a partnership in a joint northern policy. The first clause could also be read in a way consistent with client management. Although moderates might interpret it as calling for impartial support of the office of Manchurian ruler, others could draw rather different conclusions. It implied not so much that Japan would offer its cooperation to whomever occupied that post but, rather, that cooperation with Japan formed a necessary condition for ruling Manchuria.

The dualism embedded in this policy toward Chang would have serious ramifications in the future. The phenomenon of divergent purposes being pursued through a common course of action, however, hardly represented a new pattern in Manchuria policy. In the original program worked out in 1906, some saw the SMR as an instrument of colonial power, and others saw it, or at least tried to see it, as a more straightforward economic undertaking. In a similar fashion, one group of policymakers saw Chang Tso-lin as a client-candidate, a partner in the management of Manchuria, and the other chose to regard him simply as a clerk who happened to be minding the store.

Although moderates could rationalize this relationship in terms consistent with their outlook, there is no question that the decision to support Chang represented a victory for imperial activists. Precisely how far this partnership would go, how pliable the Manchurian leader would be, and whether he would work out at all as a client had yet to be determined. Nonetheless, Chang Tso-lin offered at least the possibility of lifting the state of diplomatic siege confronting Japanese imperialism at this juncture. He held the key to a back door through which Japanese power might enter

Manchuria, allowing an end run around the guardians of the new order watching the front gates. If he proved a good client, he would also help Japan overcome the stubborn resistance of his countrymen and break the stalemate that had frustrated traditional expansionist strategies. If there remained any hope for a continuation of active empire-building in Manchuria, it lay in the hand of friendship extended by this wily, illiterate, former bandit leader.

In this context, it is tempting to adapt an old aphorism and suggest that if Chang had not invented himself as a Japanese client, the Japanese would have invented him. However, it would not be an accurate suggestion. The decision to establish some sort of relationship with the inspector-general was, in the final analysis, an opportunistic response to Chang's initiative. Imperial activists, let alone moderates, had not sought such an arrangement on their own. It is not clear, in any event, how they might have gone about "inventing Chang," short of heavy-handed bribery or threats of military intervention, and it is unlikely that moderates would have gone along with a scheme entirely of Japanese making. Intervention of this sort would have gone against everything that Hara and his allies sought to accomplish. An opportunity falling into Tokyo's lap, however, was a different matter. Just as the inheritance of a turnkey project in railway imperialism in 1905 had led Japanese policymakers into a course of expansionism more ambitious than they might have considered otherwise, Chang Tso-lin's overture allowed them to contemplate a more audacious course in 1921 than the balance of views and of influence among leadership circles would have ordinarily allowed.

Insofar as Hara saw acquiescing to a relationship with Chang Tso-lin as a sop to the army and its allies, it must have seemed a small price to pay at the time. The prime minister and his colleagues had pressed for a large step back from expansionist commitments that had preoccupied a generation of national leaders. The Eastern Conference ratified withdrawal from Shantung and Siberia and Japan's membership in the loan consortium. Thus, the Japanese delegation to the multipower conference in Washington, which opened in November 1921, could concede most of what the United States demanded. Deputy Foreign Minister Shidehara Kijūrō took the opportunity of the conference to announce Japan's decision to evacuate Siberia. Japan would also agree to sell the Shantung Railway to China, in addition to retroceding Tsingtao. In addition, Tokyo became a signatory to a system of treaties that formally inaugurated the new order in East Asia and committed it-self to uphold the Open Door, to respect the territorial integrity and sover-eignty of China, and to renounce all claims to spheres of interest. Japan promised, sincerely in most respects, to behave as a good international citizen in China south of the Wall.[78]

In retrospect, of course, the price of Japan's entry into the Washington system proved enormously high. The relationship with Chang Tso-lin would provide the foundations for the reconstruction of an aggressive Japanese expansionism in Manchuria. In the history of Japanese imperialism as a journey on the road to the Pacific War, historians have often sought to identify missed opportunities for halting or diverting that march toward catastrophe. If ever there was a time when the basic direction of Japanese activity in East Asia might have been changed and the momentum of imperialism decisively checked, it was during these early postwar years. The prestige of aggressive imperialists in Japan never stood lower, and the standing of moderate reformers in foreign affairs, never higher. Conditions in Japan and in the world at large would not be as favorable again for a generation to come.

SEVEN

The New Diplomacy
and the New Imperialism, 1921–1925

The Eastern Conference of 1921 established a framework for the coexistence of continued expansionism in Manchuria alongside adherence to the new order in China proper. In the years that followed, policymakers on both sides of the imperialist divide fleshed out this dualism in practice. In China south of Wall, Japan sought to fulfill commitments made at Washington to the principles of the Open Door, multilateralism, and respect for legitimate Chinese national aspirations as conscientiously as any of the other powers. As foreign minister between 1924 and 1927, Shidehara Kijūrō emerged as the exemplar of the new diplomacy in Japan. A rather different pattern unfolded north of the Wall, as imperial activists labored to cultivate Chang Tso-lin as a client ruler and launched a new spate of railway building in north Manchuria in a pre-emptive strategy against the Soviet Union. Under the inspired leadership of SMR director Matsuoka Yōsuke (1880–1946) and backed by the weakened but still considerable political muscle of the army, empire-building in Manchuria made impressive strides, all the more remarkable given the inimical nature of the international and domestic political environment.

Defense and Diplomacy, 1921–1923

For those seeking to guide the nation into the fold of the new international order, the conclusion of the Washington Treaties in February 1922 represented a major triumph and gave the advocates of foreign-policy reform in Japan unprecedented influence. Japan's acquiescence to U.S. terms had generated substantial criticism in the Diet during the 1921–22 session, but Prime Minister Takahashi Korekiyo (1854–1936), who succeeded Hara Takashi, continued to enjoy the support of a Seiyūkai majority. Much of the opposition, targeted against naval arms limitations in particular, came from the Seiyūkai's principal rival, the Kenseikai (a descendant of the Dōshikai), which proved more than ready to adhere to the new course in foreign and defense policy when given a chance at power in the summer of 1924. Moving beyond the traditional moderation and pragmatism that had informed Hara Takashi's policies, a growing number of national leaders, particularly in the Foreign Ministry, came to embrace the principles of the new diplomacy. A succession of governments of moderate inclination in foreign affairs between 1921 and 1927, with the exception of the short-lived (January–June 1924) cabinet of Kiyoura Keigo (1850–1942) supported the efforts of diplomats in moving the country on a fresh course. Significantly, admirals headed two of the first post-Washington cabinets, a further sign of the historic shift in the balance of political power in Tokyo against the army and the imperialist camp. The passing of Marshal Yamagata Aritomo in the same month as the closing of the Washington Conference symbolized these changes in policy direction as well as the fortunes of the principal players and marked the final close to a long era.[1]

Apart from the Washington Conference itself, the most important development defining the reformist trends of the early 1920s was perhaps a fundamental change in national defense policy. Interservice negotiations produced a revised Imperial Defense Plan, promulgated in 1923, that designated the United States as Japan's principal hypothetical adversary and postulated a conflict in the Western Pacific as the scenario defining new armament priorities. As a result, the navy acquired formal precedence over the army for the first time. The revised plan, however, did not signify the emergence of ominous new tensions with the United States. The accords at Washington, which, in addition to understandings regarding China, entailed substantial naval arms reductions on the part of the United States, Britain, and Japan, actually eased tensions. The primary significance of the revision, in fact, lay in the adaptation of the nation's defense policy to the collapse of Russia as a great power and, given the withdrawal from Siberia, the diminished likelihood of a land war in Northeast Asia. The United States had traditionally occupied the number-two position on Japan's list of hypothetical adversaries, and in this respect, its elevation in standing resulted from default. The change, nonetheless, had significant ramifications. The army had little choice but to give into pressures for cuts in troop strength in 1923. It received a major boost to its flagging prestige as a result of its relief work during the Great Kantō Earthquake of September 1923. Ugaki Kazunari warned his colleagues, however, not to over-estimate the depth of popular gratitude and assume that the fortunes of their service had fundamentally changed. Opinion among the general public and among members of the Diet continued to favor the reduction of ground forces. Indeed, two years later, the army reluctantly acquiesced to the outright elimination of four infantry divisions. By the middle of the decade, then, the Imperial Japanese Army had lost nearly all the force-level gains achieved since the war against Russia.[2]

Proponents of disarmament and the new diplomacy, however, had not achieved an unalloyed victory. They had purchased their ability to move the country in a new direction at the price of a commitment to tolerate contin-ued empire-building in Manchuria. Although suffering from a diminished base of political support and a vastly reduced arena of activity, the imperialist cause remained very much alive during the years after the Washington Conference. Indeed, activists and, in particular, the army redoubled their efforts north of the Wall in order to make the most of the limited freedom of action granted them. For the most part, moderates had envisioned the compromise struck at the Eastern Conference as a "containment" policy en-tailing little more than a maintenance of the status quo in southern Man-churia. Activists, however, saw the former Russian dominion in the north-ern part of the territory, particularly after the army's withdrawal from Siberia, as fair game within the context of the bargain and one of the few ar-eas where the possibility for new gains remained open. The 1921 resolution on Chang Tso-lin, in fact, had specified the acquisition of some measure of control over the CER as one of the reasons for seeking cooperation with the regional regime.

The army, which pushed the idea of strategic autarky with renewed vigor in an effort to underscore the continued importance of maintaining a capacity for armed continental intervention, adapted its program to the opportunities and constraints of the new era by defining a more compact economic defense perimeter in Northeast Asia. Major General Hata Eitarō (1872–1930), chief of the Army Ministry's Military Affairs Bureau wrote in early 1924:

The establishment during peacetime of the facilities necessary to develop China's rich resources, principally in Manchuria, followed by north China, in order to sup-plement wartime insufficiencies, particularly in the vital areas of iron, coal, raw cot-ton, and wool, is an urgent matter for national defense.

At present, the variety and quantity of resources for which we must look to China in order to supplement our [projected] insufficiencies in meeting military as well as civilian demand during wartime are enormous. This material must come not only from Manchuria and north China but also from as far south as the Yangtze valley. This means, in turn, that our sphere of military operations must likewise extend as far south as the Yangtze valley. Such an expanded sphere of operations is undesirable and will increase the difficulty of acquiring the necessary resources. For this reason, we must exert our efforts toward developing the natural wealth and promoting the expanded production of vital resources in Manchuria and north China and thus achieve what may be described as "self-sufficiency" within this sphere.[3]

The limited geographic scope demanded, of course, a more intensive management of the territory within the perimeter. As Hata argued, "We must exert our best efforts toward opening a path for our advance into north Manchuria, where our facilities have been poorly developed in the past, making use of our incomparable political and geographic status."[4]

Army leaders regarded an initiative in the north as particularly urgent because the favorable conditions would not last. At the time of the Eastern Conference, activists still hoped that Japan might assert some form of control over the CER through a loan agreement or at least have the CER's Harbin–Ch'angch'un branch rebuilt to the same gauge as the SMR. Prospects for such a settlement, however, had faded. Although the Allies had withdrawn their control, the status of the CER remained in limbo. A White Russian staff, nominally working under the presidency of the Chinese official in charge of policing the CER Zone, continued to manage the line. This highly anomalous and unstable situation could not persist indefinitely, and in fact, Soviet authorities had begun to formally reassert their claims to the railway in 1922 and 1923.[5] By the end of 1923 and early 1924, many observers regarded the full recovery of the railway by the Soviet Union only a matter of time and had ruled out the possibility of a negotiated Japanese acquisition. In March 1924, the Soviets signed a preliminary accord on the status of the CER with the Peking government, and parallel accords were concluded with Chang's regime in September. Although these developments represented, on the one hand, a serious setback, they strengthened, on the other, the argument for swift, pre-emptive action. The emergence of even a weak Soviet presence in Manchuria, moreover, lent credibility to war scenarios involving a continental menace from the north and allowed the army to dust off its old war plans against Russia and adapt them to the new threat.[6]

The prospects for cooperation with Chang Tso-lin, which, based on the compromise of May 1921, would have provided an avenue for the continued pursuit of expansionist goals in Manchuria, were mixed. The relationship had gotten off to a rather poor start. Immediately after the Eastern Conference, Chang, supported by some in the army as well as sympathetic diplomats who argued that the Manchurian leader was seeking only to defend himself in his home territory, began pressing for arms. Citing the international arms embargo against China and underscoring the need to keep Japan's ties with local leaders within the boundaries of international rules, the Foreign Ministry successfully resisted such pressures.[7] Restraint proved wise, given that Chang and his Fengt'ien Clique were, in fact, preparing for war against their erstwhile allies in Wu Pei-fu's Chihli Clique in a bid to strengthen their power south of the Wall. A preoccupation with dreams of southern conquest and a lack of forthright help from Tokyo, in turn, left Chang rather unreceptive to discussing Japanese desiderata in Manchuria.

Conditions for pursuing the relationship deteriorated further with the opening of hostilities between the Fengt'ien and Chihli cliques in the spring of 1922. Chang appealed for Japanese help, and once again, some activists, particularly civilian and military officials stationed in Manchuria, strongly endorsed the idea. Tokyo, however, remained cool, given that the war involved Chang's aims in China proper and the fighting took place south of the Wall. Most mainstream leaders, whether moderates or activists, agreed that aid under such circumstances would be inappropriate and affirmed the understanding established at the Eastern Conference that Japan would support Chang's power in Manchuria but not his aspirations in Peking. On the other hand, the Japanese presence clearly dissuaded the Chihli forces from pursuing the Fengt'ien army north of the Wall and thus contributed indirectly to Chang's survival. Since the Japanese had withheld direct aid at his hour of greatest need, however, the warlord did not feel beholden to Japan. This circumstance underscored a fundamental problem in this relationship from Chang's point of view. The Japanese offered him assistance in managing the lands north of the Wall, where he saw no need for help, while refusing to aid him in his campaigns in the south, the cause for which he had sought Tokyo's support in the first place.[8]

Chang's defeat and his retreat to his home base, nonetheless, created better conditions for a policy of cooperation. He seemed ready to settle down and devote his energies to putting his own house in order. His declaration of the independence of the Three Eastern Provinces from China proper represented a particularly promising development. This measure did not necessarily indicate actual separatist intentions. Many warlords made such pronouncements as an expression of opposition to Peking and as a challenge to the legitimacy of the sitting government. Even so, it pointed to an orientation more compatible with Japanese interests and opened the door to discussion.[9]

Other developments in 1923 and early 1924 contributed to an increasingly favorable climate for an activist initiative. Nationalism continued to spread throughout China and among people from all walks of life. Moreover, radical trends had gained strength, as represented by a reorganized Kuomintang under Soviet influence and the newly formed Communist Party. Even the warlord-backed Peking government, regarded by radicals as an enemy of the nationalist cause, adopted a tough posture toward foreign imperialism. Although growing Chinese resistance had earlier lent support to arguments for moderation, the emergence of what seemed an intemperate and escalating counterattack against interests that most Japanese regarded as legitimate might well provoke a backlash. This appears to have happened in 1923. In March of that year, Peking repudiated all Sino-Japanese treaties based on the Twenty-One Demands and called for the immediate retrocession of the Kwantung Leased Territory and the Antung–Mukden line, the leases for which expired that year according to the original agreements. Tokyo's rejection of the initiative triggered a massive, nationwide boycott of Japanese goods. Although the movement died down in September, partly out of sympathy for Japan's plight in the aftermath of the Great Kantō Earthquake, it had served, nonetheless, to put Manchuria in the limelight once again, to rekindle an imperialist spirit among many Japanese, and to force even moderates to affirm Japan's core commitments in the territory.[10]

Events unfolding on the other side of the world also exerted an indirect yet profound influence. In 1923, the U.S. Congress began consideration of a comprehensive immigration reform bill that would abrogate the face-saving Gentleman's Agreement of 1908, which had allowed the Japanese to restrict migration to the United States on a voluntary basis. The new law would virtually exclude all further Japanese immigration. Not only did news of this development lead to tensions in Japanese-American relations and tarnish the idealistic claims of the new diplomacy, but given the historic linkage between the problem of emigration to the West and the quest for *Lebensraum* in the East, a resurgent interest in settlement in Manchuria was hardly a surprise.[11] To be sure, neither the level of revived concern about Manchuria nor the degree of disillusionment with the Washington system, outside the activist camp, should be overstated at this juncture. Nonetheless, even a minor shift in opinion, after five difficult years, undoubtedly gave those favoring an expansionist policy encouragement.

Chinese Railway Initiatives

Ironically, the initiative that set Japanese imperial activism into renewed motion came from the Chinese side in the form of two sets of railway proposals, which Yoshii Ken'ichi has described in a pioneering article.[12] The first came from Wang Yung-chiang (1871–1927), civil governor of Fengt'ien province and Chang Tso-lin's principal economic advisor. In early 1923, Wang approached the SMR and expressed the desire of his government and a group of local investors to build a railway from Mukden to Hailung with an eventual extension to Kirin city. He requested that the Japanese drop their long-standing opposition to Mukden connections for new railways and that they set aside their claims to the K'aiyüan–Hailung concession, which would largely duplicate the same route. He assured SMR representatives that his group intended to build and finance the Mukden–Hailung entirely on its own without recourse to foreign loans. In exchange, the Chinese side would allow the construction of a railway from T'aonan to Tsitsihar, which would serve as an extension of the recently completed Ssup'ingkai–T'aonan feeder (provisionally open to traffic in November 1922) to the CER.[13] And in November 1923, the provincial government in Kirin offered a proposal for the construction of two lines. One would run from Kirin city east to Tunhua, and the other, from Ch'angch'un west to Fuyu (Petune) on the Sungari River (see Map 7.1). The Kirin authorities understood that these routes represented portions of two Japanese concession lines, the Kirin–Hoeryong and Ch'angch'un–T'aonan, respectively. Implicitly requesting the Japanese to set aside any previous financial and diplomatic obligations, they proposed to pursue these projects as new provincial undertakings with financial assistance from the SMR.[14]

The Chinese railway proposals of 1923 formed part of a larger program of construction undertaken nominally by local governments and investor

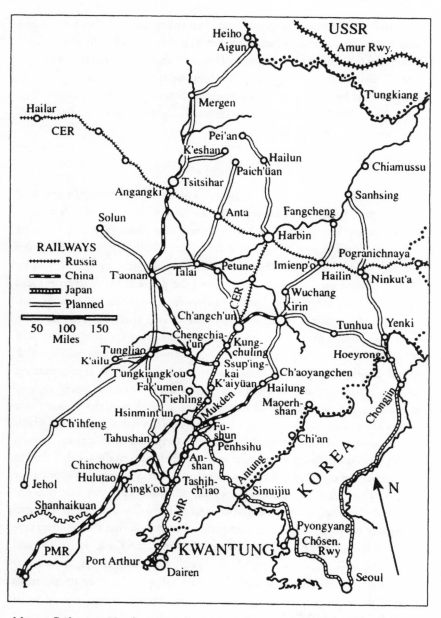

Map 7.1 Railways in Manchuria, 1926. Some planned routes are shown based on actual lines built subsequently (based on maps in Tōa keizai chōsakyoku, *Manchoukuo Year Book, 1934*; SMR, *Eigyō hōkokusho, 1923, 1928, 1930*; DRI, looseleaf).

groups with Chang's support. Regional authorities had evinced a strong interest in railway building since the beginning of the decade, but the timing of these particular schemes appeared linked to Chang's seizure and partition of the PMR north of the Great Wall following his defeat in the Fengt'ien-Chihli War of 1922. The Manchurian regime asserted sole control of the railway from Shanhaikuan to Mukden and retreating Fengt'ien forces had taken possession of the larger portion of the PMR's rolling stock. Chang and his colleagues' attempt to exploit this prize to maximum advantage inspired schemes for large-scale development. The Mukden–Hailung line would serve as an extension of the PMR and eventually connect to Kirin city. Wang apparently planned to extend the line even further north, from Kirin to Hailin station on the CER. A Kirin–Tunhua line would function as an eastern branch of this Mukden–Kirin–Hailin trunk, and a combination of the Ch'angch'un–Fuyu and the existing Ch'angch'un–Kirin would form a branch to the west. These developments would substantially expand the transportation watershed of the PMR. The T'aonan–Tsitsihar, although offered as concession to the Japanese, also served a second purpose in creating a Chinese trunk line in Inner Mongolia. In 1921, the PMR had initiated the construction of a short eighteen-mile spur from Tahushan station just north of Chinchow to Chang Tso-lin's Pataohao coal mine. The Chinese side apparently planned to extend this spur north to T'ungliao and, subsequently, directly to T'aonan. A T'aonan–Tsitsihar line would complete the link between the PMR and the CER. Even without a direct connection between T'ungliao and T'aonan, traffic might be routed from T'ungliao to Chengchiat'un along the Japanese-financed line and thence to T'aonan by way of the Ssup'ingkai–T'aonan railway. In either case, the Chinese would acquire a route from Tahushan to Tsitsihar entirely independent of the SMR. As a vital supplement to this scheme, Chang revived plans to build a port at Hulutao, first proposed under Hsi-liang's administration in 1910, which would provide the PMR with an ice-free alternative to Yingk'ou. Upon completion of this grand program, Chinese Manchuria would be served by two major trunk lines running on either side of the SMR, penetrating deep into the territory of the CER, and connected to an ice-free port with the potential to compete with Dairen. In 1924, Chang would organize a "Transportation Commission of the Three Eastern Provinces" (Tung-san-sheng chiao-t'ung wei-yüan-hui) to coordinate the effort.[15]

No informed observer could fail to recognize at least the commercial aspects of the challenge to the Japanese system inherent in the envisioned network. In approaching the SMR for understanding and assistance, Chinese railway promoters appeared to go out of their way to allay Japanese anxieties. They offered assurances that their plans did not constitute hostile initiatives but rested entirely on legitimate economic interests and concerns with regional development. Allowing the building of a T'aonan–Tsitsihar line not only provided material compensation for any possible losses due to competition but was an earnest of good faith. True to their claims, financial motivations no doubt played a prominent part. Chang's military organization, along with the civil administration in the provinces, found themselves perennially short of revenue, a problem exacerbated by the cost of the 1922 war. One solution, commonly exploited by warlords throughout China, lay in tapping railway revenues.[16] The PMR offered a good start, and its extension would allow the Chinese side to share in the great wealth that the SMR had thus far monopolized (see Table 7.1). Although new railways would take time to build and begin generating income, land sales along prospective routes offered more immediate returns. Moreover, among the projected lines, the Mukden–Hailung, which would tap the same rich source of soy traffic feeding both K'aiyüan station on the SMR trunk and its Fushun branch, promised quick success.[17]

At same time, Chinese railway schemes contained an undeniably adversarial element. Apolitical commercial competition, which the Japanese might be expected to tolerate to some degree on the basis of give-and-take bargaining, readily shaded into economic nationalism, given the climate of the times and the slow but steady spread of new ideological influences north of the Wall. Indeed, as the local Chinese elite began moving beyond its traditional bases in commercial agriculture and small-scale merchant enterprise into modern sectors of the economy, the old symbiosis with Japanese interests broke down. A desire among the Manchurian Chinese business community to strengthen its position with respect to the Japanese could readily lead to a desire for railway autonomy. Wang Yung-chiang, who favored an active development policy and enjoyed considerable support among the local business elite, held moderate nationalist leanings. Within limits, he sought to strengthen the Chinese position in the territory against Japanese encroachment through economic and cultural means. His founding of the

Table 7.1
Revenues of Fengt'ien Province and the SMR Compared, 1918–24
(*1,000 yüan, yen*)

	Fengt'ien revenues			SMR net railway revenues
	Yüan	Exchange yüan/yen	yen	
1918	15,622	0.97	¥16,105	¥27,955
1919	15,759	0.93	16,945	36,531
1920	15,801	1.00	15,801	48,557
1921	17,332	1.39	12,469	45,031
1922	18,492	1.35	13,698	53,644
1923	18,991	1.39	13,663	56,482
1924	22,521	1.38	16,320	56,008

SOURCES: Based on data in Nishimura Shigeo, *Chūgoku kindai tōhoku chiiki shi kenkyū*, pp. 148, 154; SMR2, pp. 1340–41.

University of the Northeast (Tung-pei ta-hsüeh), an institution designed to train Chinese technical personnel, is one example of such activity. Another more overt example lay in his sponsorship of the "educational rights recovery movement" in 1924, which was aimed at asserting control over the schooling of Chinese children residing in communities of the Railway Zone. This campaign represented a modest attempt to weaken Japan's colonial authority in the Zone. Wang's nationalism, however, fell short of supporting the political reunification of China at this juncture and, as an advocate of regional autonomy, he actively opposed Chang Tso-lin's efforts to extend his power south of the Wall. This attitude, along with his dedication to economic development, led many Japanese to regard him in a positive light, despite his adversarial tendencies.[18]

Chang Tso-lin himself harbored little sympathy for modern nationalism, and his brutal suppression of the May Fourth movement in his territory won him favor with many Japanese officials. He might adopt a nationalistic posture as a political expedient, given that no Chinese leader in the 1920s could maintain credibility without some lip service to patriotism. He certainly had little interest in provoking a confrontation with Japan over railway construction at this point, and his motivations probably lay primarily in financial gain. At the same time, however, railway autonomy served to strengthen his hold over the Three Eastern Provinces by facilitating both administration and military control. And although he might vacillate in his posture toward the CER, he shared with the Japanese a desire to weaken the Soviet presence in the north. Moreover, Chang cherished his independence. He sought Japanese aid in his campaign south of the Wall, but he had made himself master of Manchuria on his own and had every intention of maintaining that situation. An appreciation of the advantages of creating an autonomous network that would allow him to administer, pacify, and develop his territory without reliance on the Japanese required no higher nationalist consciousness, only a basic grasp of the nature of railway power.[19]

Well aware of the broader sweep of Chinese railway plans, the Japanese reacted with deep ambivalence when approached by Wang and subsequently by the Kirin authorities. The proposal held almost irresistible attractions because it promised an unanticipated opening in a vital policy area where progress had virtually stood still for a full decade. Of the five lines negotiated in 1913, only one, the Ssup'ingkai–T'aonan, had been completed, and that modest achievement had entailed nine years of fitful construction, punctuated by a succession of disputes and renegotiations, along with no small sum in bribes. In 1918, Nishihara had paid out ¥20 million in advances against prospective loans on modified versions of the remaining four, along with another ¥10 million for the Kirin–Hoeryong, but repeated talks had not produced a single, signed contract, let alone a start to construction. One new line, the Chengchiat'un–T'ungliao branch of the Ssup'ingkai–T'aonan, provided the single point of light in this otherwise dismal record, but the prospects for further progress appeared grim.

In this context, the proposal from the Chinese side offered cause for optimism, precisely the kind of advantage that many activists saw in a policy of Sino-Japanese cooperation in Manchuria. Chang Tso-lin finally appeared ready to prove his worth. The army found proposals for the T'aonan–Tsitsihar railway particularly compelling. The line held enormous strategic importance and would be an effective instrument to pre-empt the rise of Soviet power and extend Japanese influence in north Manchuria. It allowed for the interception of the CER west of Harbin, a prospect as effective as a direct route to the "capital" of Russian Manchuria itself. With the virtual possession of Tsitsihar, the Japanese would control the gateway to the north Manchurian plain, and this, in turn, would force any invading Soviet army to base itself in the inhospitable Hsing'an mountain range.[20]

Given the need to compete with the CER for agricultural traffic, the SMR, too, had strong interests in this project and had conducted a preliminary survey of this route in 1920. Company managers would have preferred a negotiated agreement with the CER as opposed to the construction of invasive feeders. In fact, the two railway companies had worked out a bargain on rates and quotas in a series of talks beginning in 1920, but as the Japanese feared, the failure of the CER management, operating a bankrupt line, to hold up its end of the deal undermined the agreement in a variety of ways. By 1923, the SMR had begun to consider aggressive countermeasures, and the impending Soviet takeover only strengthened its commitment.[21]

As for the Kirin government's proposal, the Kirin–Tunhua and Ch'angch'un–Fuyu lines offered the possibility of fulfilling two long-delayed projects. In particular, the Kirin–Tunhua, although stopping well short of the Korean border, represented a breakthrough on a railway scheme that the Chinese had adamantly opposed since 1905, and it presented an opportunity extremely difficult to overlook.

Attractive though these prospects might be, however, the Chinese proposals presented cause for serious reservations as well. The construction of a T'aonan–Tsitsihar railway would allow the Japanese to penetrate north Manchuria, but it would also open the door to involvement of the international consortium, given the failure of Japanese negotiators to exclude this line in 1920. Thus far, the international body had initiated no activity in the territory, and it might make sense to let sleeping dogs lie. The Kirin–Tunhua and Ch'angch'un–Fuyu lines posed a different kind of problem. Each represented segments of concession lines negotiated with the government of Tuan Ch'i-jui in 1918 that carried large outstanding debts from Nishihara's advances. The current regime in Peking, held responsible by the Japanese government for the agreements concluded with Tuan, lacked both the will and, given the political autonomy of Three Eastern Provinces, the ability to honor these obligations. Chang and the Kirin government were clearly not offering to redress any existing diplomatic or financial claims; rather, they were proposing an entirely new set of local understandings concerning railways that happened to coincide with Japanese concessions. To consent to such an arrangement would imply that Japan might not hold the regional authorities in Manchuria responsible for all agreements concluded with Peking. This would set a dangerous precedent. Insofar as the Mukden–Hailung line could be treated as a substitute for the K'aiyüan–Hailung concession, as implicit in Wang's initiative, this venture posed a similar problem. The current proposals from the Chinese side would thus permit the construction of desired railways, but it would also require setting aside hard-won diplomatic victories, writing off some ¥30 million in debt, and reopening talks on an entirely new basis.[22] Many policy-makers questioned the value of such a tradeoff.

A more fundamental problem, going beyond the specific construction projects under consideration, lay in the prospect of opening the door to significant Chinese railway competition. Insofar as all the planned lines in the Chinese program connected to the SMR at some point, any difficulties posed from the perspective of the company's business interests would likely prove manageable. The commercial magnetism of Dairen would transform almost any connecting railway into a partial feeder of the SMR, even given the option of direct and independent access to Hulutao. Some segments of the SMR would, no doubt, lose traffic to the Chinese system, but in the long run, given the promise of commercial growth stimulated by new railway construction, the total business of the company would likely increase. In any event, so long as competition remained on a purely commercial footing, rational business negotiations would settle any major conflicts.

Quite apart from business considerations, however, permitting the construction of an autonomous Chinese network would end the SMR's near-monopoly over modern transportation in southern Manchuria and undermine the traditional foundations of Japanese power in the territory. The Mukden–Hailung–Kirin scheme had formed the centerpiece of Chinese countermeasures against Japanese railway imperialism since 1905. Japanese diplomats had made the prohibition of Mukden connections for any new railways a point of principle in 1913 and persuaded the army to concede its strategic preferences in order to prevent the construction of an independent system linked to the PMR. A T'aonan–Tsitsihar connected to the PMR by way of a Tahushan–T'ungliao–T'aonan line was nothing other than a variant of the Chinchow–Aigun railway. Allowing the construction of the kind of system planned by the Chinese might not irrevocably injure the SMR as an economic enterprise, but it would surely compromise its effectiveness as an instrument of railway imperialism.[23]

At the same time, much had changed in Manchuria and the wider world since the heyday of "conquest by railway." No foreign powers appeared to stand behind the Chinese initiatives of 1923 as they had in 1907, 1910, and, at least from the perspective of Japanese suspicions, 1913. In these earlier situations, foreign collusion had been the primary source of anxiety. Moreover, Chang and his associates did not appear to be mounting an anti-Japanese offensive and had legitimate economic reasons for undertaking their program. The pioneers of imperialist cooperation, such as Shōda, Nishihara, and Koiso, had argued for introducing more genuine give-and-take in economic relationships, including some substantive sacrifices on the Japanese side. Under these circumstances, the Chinese proposals could not be dismissed out of hand as they might have been in 1913. Still, Chang Tso-lin had proved himself a mercurial figure, and his favorable orientation toward Japan might not last. Moreover, given the vicissitudes of warlord politics, his tenure was far from secure. Agreements undertaken in the spirit of cooperation with a friendly regime in Mukden today might provide a hostile successor administration with powerful weapons against Japan in Manchuria.

Even setting such considerations aside, advocates of Sino-Japanese cooperation during World War I had never given serious thought to surrendering existing Japanese rights. Nishihara had intended his approach to apply to future undertakings with established concessions protected by an implicit, imperialist grandfather clause. His scheme to support China's nationalization of its iron industry, for example, exempted such holdings as Anshan. The juxtaposition of the two resolutions on Manchuria at the Eastern Conference also underscored this qualification. One called for a new era of Sino-Japanese cooperation in the development of Manchuria, anticipating the launching of a host of joint ventures with Chang Tso-lin. The other touted the exclusion of existing Japanese railway rights in the territory from the consortium agreement of 1920 as a signal triumph of Japanese diplomacy. Overall, then, the Chinese railway proposals created a serious dilemma for Japanese policy with little precedent for resolution. In this context, a decisively important contribution toward charting a clear course came from a young SMR director by the name of Matsuoka Yōsuke.

Matsuoka Yōsuke and the "New Imperialism"

Matsuoka is best known as the diplomat who led the Japanese delegation out of the League of Nations in 1933 and who, as foreign minister in 1940, concluded the Axis Pact. His activities in Manchuria during the 1920s, however, represented a vital phase of his career; it was during this period that he first rose to prominence in national policymaking and earned notice in army and imperial activist circles. An enigmatic figure in many respects, his ideas did not fit easily into established pigeonholes. He started his career as a professional diplomat, and his first major post was acting consul-general in Shanghai during the Russo-Japanese War. In 1907, he received appointment as the chief of external affairs of the Kwantung Government-General, a position controlled at the time by the Foreign Ministry. He served as the ministry's commercial attaché in Siberia during the early phases of the Allied Intervention and joined the Japanese delegation to Versailles in 1919 as a junior member. It was at the peace conference that Matsuoka decided to leave the Foreign Ministry. Under the new order, he foresaw an era in which diplomacy would become an arena for faceless bureaucrats following established rules and regulations rather than one in which a strong leader might exercise energetic and creative statesmanship. Aspiring to higher goals, he saw little future in remaining in this career track. Working for the SMR offered better prospects, a steppingstone that might do for him what it had done for Gotō Shinpei. In 1921, he accepted an appointment as a member of the board of directors responsible for railway negotiations. As a career strategy, the move proved timely. He assumed his duties during the tenure of a relatively inactive president and at a juncture when the post of vice president remained unfilled. Indeed, during his first few years as a director, he is said to have functioned, for most intents and purposes, as the company's acting chief executive.[24]

Matsuoka had other reasons for departing the Foreign Ministry and joining the SMR. As a dedicated imperialist, his dissatisfaction with the new diplomacy stemmed not only from its limited opportunities for creative leadership but also from its basic content. His view of international relations remained rooted in the politics of power and saw the "Yamato people" locked in a historic, Social Darwinian struggle for survival against the "Anglo-Saxon" world.[25] In that struggle, the key to success lay in empire-building. Like most imperialists at this time, Matsuoka regarded Manchuria as the primary focus of Japan's expansionist efforts. In his view, the final status of the "Three Eastern Provinces" remained open to adjustment. He considered Chinese claims to the territory historically shallow, ambiguous at best during the Ch'ing era and formally asserted only after what he regarded as an arbitrary annexation of these lands by the Chinese Republic in 1912. By virtue of the Russo-Japanese War, Japan held stronger claims. "The Japanese people risked their nation, shed their blood, and borrowed considerable money to restore to the Chinese the very land they had virtually given away to the Russians. From this perspective Japan has greater right to a say in Manchuria than does China." To Matsuoka, however, securing the territory represented a matter more of need than of right. Only through the control of this land could Japan resolve its problems in the areas of food supply, population growth, industrial raw materials, export markets, and, of course, national defense, including wartime economic security. Foreshadowing his later characterization of this territory as Japan's "lifeline," he wrote in 1926, "The day when Japan must retreat from Manchuria is the day when the Yamato nation relinquishes its right to exist."[26]

Matsuoka emphasized the singular importance of Manchuria in somewhat stronger terms than many of his activist colleagues. He believed that Japan should desist from any major attempts at asserting influence in China south of the Wall, at least for the foreseeable future. The problem loomed too large and the circumstances were too complex to manage to the nation's advantage. Indeed, deepening the conceptual partition entailed in the "two-China" orientation of the Eastern Conference policies of 1921, he saw Manchuria not so much as part of a larger "China question" as such but as the central element of a Northeast Asian policy framework that encompassed Korea, Manchuria as a whole, and even the Soviet Far East. The Japanese, he believed, ought to think in terms of a geographically compact empire in this region rather than to disperse their energies far and wide, a perspective that meshed well with the army's concept of a more limited economic defense perimeter.[27] He also shared with the army a view of the urgency of pre-emptive initiatives against the return of Russian power.

During the next twenty to thirty years, Russia will probably make significant and decisive strides toward full recovery, and it is not hard to predict that a strong Russia . . . will once again pursue an expansionist positive policy in the Far East. Unless we exert the full strength of our country toward accelerating the development of Manchuria's railway network and deeply root our power in the territory before that development comes to pass, we may not be able to meet their challenge.[28]

Such circumstances demanded, in particular, steps to assert Japanese power in north Manchuria during this window of opportunity.

Matsuoka distinguished himself most clearly from mainstream activists at this time, however, in his call for a decisive shift in the strategies of power employed in Manchuria. Railway imperialism and, more broadly, schemes for colonization had served the cause of empire-building well during the early years, but they had proved decreasingly effective with the rise of Chinese nationalism. They no longer offered a viable approach under the constraints of the new order. Japan should place its emphasis, instead, on a strategy of client management. Rather than relying on direct, proprietary control of the territory's vital facilities, land, and resources, the Japanese should exercise power in Manchuria through partnership with a compliant native administration, which, of course, would play a subordinate role in the relationship. Matsuoka's idea of client rule went well beyond an opportunistic policy of taking advantage of Chang Tso-lin's current amenability to cooperation. Chang might change his mind, and equally likely, he might lose his position through war or rebellion. A client relationship could provide an enduring basis for imperial power in Manchuria only if the Japanese government committed itself to maintaining, on a permanent basis and by whatever means necessary, a stable, pro-Japanese regime in the Three Eastern Provinces. A friendly and cooperative government in Mukden, whether headed by Chang or a successor, would receive financial, political, and covert military support and, if need be, protection from external invasion by the likes of Wu Pei-fu. Tokyo and Mukden, moreover, would make common cause against the Soviet Union in the north. At the same time, Japan would simply refuse to tolerate the emergence of a hostile regime by making clear its readiness to depose an administration that incurred its displeasure. Matsuoka described this aggressive and resolute policy of enforcing cooperation upon any prospective Mukden government with the term daikanshō, literally meaning "big intervention."[29] Taken to its logical conclusion, daikanshō implied the establishment of a protectorate-like arrangement over the Three Eastern Provinces.

As an experienced diplomat, the SMR director understood that a formal extension of Japanese protection over Manchuria would never pass muster with either the international community or moderate leaders at home. In practice, the partnership would rest on a firm but quiet understanding on both sides. At the same time, however, he believed that he could justify intervention and enforce cooperation in terms at least nominally defensible in the international arena by invoking ideas associated with the so-called Asian Monroe Doctrine. Matsuoka affirmed the nation's right and responsibility, as a neighboring country with major strategic and economic interests in the region, to take whatever action was necessary in order to maintain peace and stability in Manchuria. Japan could not stand by while the Three Eastern Provinces fell victim to invasion or internal upheaval. Chaos would not only threaten the SMR and other business ventures, along with the Railway Zone, Kwantung, and the Japanese resident community, but would directly endanger the security of Korea. Significantly, the SMR director adopted a rather broad interpretation of the possible conditions that might warrant action, which included not only war and rebellion but also gross administrative mismanagement. He cited, for example, financial disruptions caused by the uncontrolled printing of inconvertible paper notes as a cause for a vigorous Japanese response. By extension, virtually any line of action inimical to Japanese interests might be construed as a pretext for intervention. In effect, Matsuoka equated a regional government committed to peace and stability with a pro-Japanese regime.[30]

This shift in strategies of territorial control paved the way for a further departure in Matsuoka's ideas from mainstream thinking: the possibility of decoupling railway policy from the task of sustaining imperialist power. The logic of colonization, with its emphasis on proprietary concessions, would no longer constrain railway construction, business investment, or resource management as it had in the past. With a regional government firmly in Japan's grasp, imperial policymakers could freely follow the dictates of economic and strategic rationality in pursuing their programs. Under such circumstances, Mukden connections, desirable for strategic purposes but precluded by the demands of railway imperialism, would become permissible. Indeed, the elimination of proprietary control as a precondition for investment or financial aid would enable a sweeping liberalization of railway policy and allow the Japanese to lend their support to any activities, including Chinese initiatives, that contributed to the development of Manchuria as a whole. A general improvement in the economic and cultural conditions in the territory would clearly serve Japan's broader imperial interests, even if the Chinese might benefit more directly in the short run. A prosperous Chinese Manchuria meant greater opportunity for Japan in the future, more access to natural resources, larger export markets, and broader economic foundations for wartime self-sufficiency. The slogan, *Manmō no tame no Manmō*, loosely translated as the "[development of] Manchuria for Manchuria's sake" encapsulates the SMR director's revisionist orientation toward economic policy.[31]

Matsuoka pushed the idea of imperialist cooperation well beyond the boundaries constraining the thinking of most of his contemporaries. The prevailing view among activist circles tended to regard the relationship with

Chang Tso-lin as an expedient to acquire new railway, land, and mining concessions that used such time-honored tools as bribery, gunrunning, and palace intrigue. The SMR director sharply criticized such practices, commonly associated with Japanese army advisors to other Chinese warlords, as an opportunistic and shortsighted form of meddling that generated suspicion and distrust without producing lasting gains.[32] In the new course of action he advocated, partnership with the regional state served as a comprehensive alternative, and not a supplement, to older strategies of colonization and railway imperialism. Matsuoka did not rule out the use, within limits, of bribery, along with other "carrots and sticks," in managing a client ruler if need be. In fact, he considered Chang Tso-lin far from ideal as a candidate, a rather venal and benighted figure even among the general run of Chinese warlords who would, no doubt, require the employment of such methods to move him in the desired direction. The purpose of bribery or pandering, nonetheless, lay not in "buying" concessions from Chang but in asserting Japanese control over territorial administration as a whole.[33]

Indeed, in the long run, Matsuoka saw Sino-Japanese cooperation in Manchuria resting on a more high-minded foundation, enforced by mutual interests in securing peace and prosperity in the Three Eastern Provinces and in defending the region from common external threats. The rising influence of "enlightened" Chinese leaders such as Wang Yung-chiang represented an encouraging development in this regard. The people of Manchuria desired nothing more fervently than protection from the kind of civil disorder plaguing China south of the Wall and an opportunity to pursue their livelihood in a stable environment, as expressed in the slogan, *pao ching an min* (secure the borders, pacify the people). Moreover, reiterating the perspectives articulated by Shōda Kazue, Matsuoka underscored the need to introduce a genuine mutuality to economic cooperation and to break with the one-sided pursuit of Japanese advantage characteristic of the concession-hunting orientation of the past. Harsh if not usurious loan terms, demands for intrusive Japanese managerial rights, and an inflexible insistence on the sanctity of the SMR's monopoly had placed major obstacles in the way of railway development during the past decade and a half. The Japanese could hardly expect the Chinese to welcome construction projects that disregarded their legitimate economic interests. Such an approach to development, he suggested, was tantamount to "climbing trees to catch fish." Recent initiatives illuminated the surging Chinese interest in railway building in Manchuria. Rather than impede such activity by invoking treaty rights, the Japanese ought to offer active encouragement by providing real financial assistance and technical support and might even consider setting aside outstanding concessionary claims in the name of cooperation.[34]

Matsuoka argued that the era of inter-imperialist rivalry over spheres of interest had passed, and along with it, the need to worry about the political elements of railway competition embodied in concessionary rights. In principle, even foreign investment in Manchuria no longer presented cause for major concern. "The petty idea that we must exclude the Americans from the development of Manchuria, that we must link up with the Russians and block the British, is not only untenable today, but seriously mistaken," he wrote. "Whoever comes to Manchuria today, regardless of their nationality, comes to a region where Japan occupies a secure place. There is not the slightest need for anxiety. Regardless of whom we choose to work with in the development of the territory, those who stand to benefit the most from any progress are the Japanese and the Chinese."[35] Taken at face value, these remarks bear a close resemblance to Debuchi Katsuji's views in the debate over the consortium in 1919 and suggest that Matsuoka favored the Open Door. His confidence in the security of Japan's position in Manchuria, however, stemmed not from a faith in the virtues of the invisible hand but from the empire's ability to assert firm control over the regional state.

Matsuoka called for a decisive break with the old concession-hunting strategy; nevertheless his commitment to liberalization had definite limits. His suggestions about foreign investment, for example, served to illustrate a larger point of principle, but in practice he appears to have favored avoiding the complications of consortium involvement in railway building insofar as possible. As we shall see, the army, which, in all other respects, came to embrace the SMR director's views, insisted on obstructing foreign engagement in Manchuria by all means available. Moreover, Matsuoka's willingness to modify or even set aside outstanding railway concessions did not imply a readiness to compromise treaty rights governing the SMR, the Railway Zone, or the Kwantung Leased Territory. Like Shōda, Nishihara, Koiso, and other imperial revisionists before him, he saw such matters as lying beyond the pale of negotiation. And although he opposed an inflexible insistence on protecting the SMR's transportation monopoly, he regarded the company's business interests as legitimate concerns requiring respectful consideration from the Chinese side. Such reservations suggest that Matsuoka sought to preserve some measure of traditional power on the ground as a possible hedge against problems with the client relationship. Retaining a core of Japan's colonial presence, in any event, would prove useful in the implementation of a policy of daikanshō by providing not only a credible pretext for intervention but also the ready means to do so as well. At the same time, however, Matsuoka did not see the SMR's role in terms of a simple back-up strategy. Under the new framework of cooperation, it would serve an expanded role as the principal economic agency for the Japanese side and work in partnership with the Mukden regime in promoting development. The Chinese side might have the will to transform Manchuria, but it lacked the technical knowledge and resources to do so. The SMR would provide vital assistance in this context and carry out much of the actual reconstruction work on behalf of its partners.[36]

In view of the developments in imperialist thinking since World War I, neither the political nor the economic aspects of Matsuoka's ideas entailed genuinely original concepts. His primary contribution lay not so much in adding new substance to the concepts worked out during the Terauchi cabinet and at the Eastern Conference as in removing the ambiguities and hedges characteristic of earlier schemes. He promoted the notion of imperialist cooperation as a comprehensive substitute for older strategies with greater conviction and confidence than had his predecessors. His framework divorced power from program, and in separating the problems of territorial control from those of development, his approach would eliminate many of the constraints that had long held back imperialist progress. This separation, in turn, produced a jarring and heterodox juxtaposition of a hard-line interventionism worthy of the army's adventurist faction during the Chinese revolutionary period, on the one hand, with an economic liberalism that would have warmed the hearts of Foreign Ministry reformers, on the other. For this reason, Matsuoka encountered considerable difficulty in persuading his activist colleagues, let alone moderates, to embrace his views in full. His formulations, nonetheless, offered an effective adaptation of imperialist strategy to the opportunities and constraints of the 1920s, representing a countervailing force to the "new diplomacy" that might well be described in this context as a "new imperialist" synthesis.[37]

The Railway Bargain of 1924

The Chinese railway initiatives of 1923 presented Matsuoka with an opportunity to put his ideas into practice. Inspired in particular by Wang's offer of a bargain involving the Mukden–Hailung and T'aonan–Tsitsihar, he submitted a proposal to the Foreign Ministry to open negotiations using a radical new approach. The SMR director recommended the handling of all future railway projects of interest to Japan, regardless of their actual provenance or history, as new, local Chinese initiatives. This nominal framework, or *tatemae*, would apply not only to the T'aonan–Tsitsihar line but also to the Mukden–Hailung, Kirin–Tunhua, and Ch'angch'un–Fuyu lines. Japan would set aside, although not formally surrender, its concessionary rights to the K'aiyüan–Hailung–Kirin, the Kirin–Hoeryong, and the Ch'angch'un–T'aonan routes. The local authorities would, in turn, agree to build on their own terms either these railways as originally designed in whole or in part or lines serving equivalent functions, with some allowance for route modifications. The Japanese side would consider the Mukden–Hailung railway a modified, functional equivalent of the K'aiyüan–Hailung portion of the Japanese concession line and would not invoke any outstanding diplomatic or financial claims regarding the Kirin–Tunhua or Ch'angch'un–Fuyu lines. If requested, the Japanese would also render financial and technical assistance for all these ventures without reference to any past loan agreements or outstanding obligations. The SMR, rather than the original syndicate of the Chōsen, Taiwan, and Japan Industrial banks organized under the Nishihara Loans, would be designated the sole Japanese party to any financial arrangements. Moreover, aid would take the form of short-term construction contracts with the SMR rather than long-term loans of the traditional type and be payable on completion of the work, with the possibility of an extended grace period. The SMR might even provide subsidies during the start-up years when these lines would likely operate at a loss. The Chinese would be offered the option, if they chose to defer payment, of long-term loans with the SMR under terms as generous as possible. The Chinese would be under no obligation to seek Japanese participation and would be free to build and finance any project entirely on their own, an approach that Wang favored for the Mukden–Hailung. If the Chinese sought foreign assistance, however, it was understood that Japan would have the right of first refusal.[38]

Matsuoka had both principled and pragmatic reasons for adopting this novel approach to negotiations. The conceptualization of all these lines as Chinese undertakings and the discussion of terms on a clean slate clearly reflected the SMR director's perspectives on cooperative development. All new railway initiatives would follow this pattern, and the formulation that allowed the Chinese to build "functional equivalents" of Japanese concession lines on their own terms represented a transitional measure that put old claims on a new footing. To be sure, Matsuoka did not favor renouncing existing rights entirely. This reservation represented, no doubt, a hedge against the breakdown of cooperation as well as a negotiating stance that allowed the Japanese side to demonstrate magnanimity. As we shall consider shortly, however, his primary concern in reserving established rights lay in diplomacy with Peking and the powers. The idea of channeling all financial and technical assistance through SMR construction contracts also stemmed from his ideas about reforming railway policy. This arrangement would allow the Japanese side to offer optimally favorable terms. All the railways under consideration and most of those likely to be built in the future not only served Japanese policy goals but also directly benefited the SMR as feeders. From a business perspective, the company would likely have built them on its own if given the opportunity and recoup most of its investment from increased traffic revenues on the trunk line. Under these circumstances, the SMR, unlike an independent contractor or financial agency, had no need to undertake construction or financing as paying propositions. Indeed, given the fact that it would earn a substantial return from feeder traffic, the company might well discount even further construction costs to the Chinese side. The indefinite extension of a grace period for repayment would not cause undue hardship to the SMR and minimize the need for long-term loans.[39]

In addition to the logic of cooperative development, Matsuoka's scheme also offered a number of pragmatic, tactical advantages. For one, conceptualizing all these railway projects as local initiatives without reference to outstanding concessions resolved the problem of the Nishihara Loans and set aside any residual claims of the Peking government to authority over railway agreements in Manchuria. These lines represented new undertakings and financial arrangements. Matsuoka did not suggest that the Japanese side forgive the ¥30 million in advances by any means, but he recommended their settlement on a separate basis in conjunction with other issues under discussion with the central government. Old baggage could not be permitted to impede railway construction in Manchuria.[40] A second tactical benefit this scheme offered lay in the possibility of circumventing the consortium's claims to participate in railway loans. The Japanese would invoke the exclusion provisions of the 1920 agreement on any railways they construed as functional equivalents of existing concessionary rights, one reason why Matsuoka favored reserving these claims. Exclusion, however, would not apply to loans for entirely new lines, such as the T'aonan–Tsitsihar, along with many others that the Japanese would seek in the future. At the same time, the T'aonan–Tsitsihar would only become a matter of concern to the consortium if the Chinese chose to take out a long-term loan. If the SMR's involvement remained at the level of a construction contract, the international body would have no basis for interference at all.[41]

The Foreign Ministry official charged with responding to Matsuoka's proposal was none other than Debuchi Katsuji, recently appointed chief of the Asia Bureau. His overall reaction in discussions at the end of the year appeared rather cool. Foreseeing serious problems with the CER and the Soviets, Debuchi expressed his particular unhappiness with the idea of building a T'aonan–Tsitsihar line. He suggested delaying this project for a more suitable occasion and concentrating on outstanding concession lines instead. Debuchi's emphasis on the Kirin–Tunhua and Ch'angch'un–Fuyu lines did not reflect real enthusiasm for pursuing these older projects. As we have seen, he had favored surrendering them to the consortium in 1919, and all things considered, he might have preferred a moratorium on railway building in Manchuria at this point. Debuchi's successors would, in fact, subsequently emphasize the importance of resolving outstanding loan concessions as a tactic to forestall those new railway initiatives in north Manchuria they considered similarly problematic.[42]

Far from discouraged by the Foreign Ministry's response, Matsuoka continued to pursue his scheme during the first few months of 1924 and enlisted the support, among others, of the army.[43] In an effort to present Tokyo with a more concrete proposal, he initiated follow-up talks with Wang Yung-chiang under the authority of Mukden Consul-General Funatsu Tatsuichirō (1873–1947), an advocate of cooperation with Chang Tso-lin. As a result, by the late spring of 1924, Matsuoka had obtained a preliminary understanding with the Chinese for the construction of the T'aonan–Tsitsihar, Kirin–Tunhua, Ch'angch'un–Fuyu, and the Mukden–Hailung railways along the lines he had proposed to Debuchi in late 1923. Subsequent negotiations would reveal that Wang Yung-chiang and his colleagues did not entirely share Matsuoka's interpretation of the agreement. The Chinese side believed that the bargain entailed only a one-for-one exchange of the Mukden–Hailung line for the T'aonan–Tsitsihar. This gap in understanding would cause considerable difficulty in the not-too-distant future. For Matsuoka, however, the arrangement, as he interpreted it, provided sufficient basis to submit a more concrete proposal to Tokyo.[44]

The SMR director's initiative enjoyed a more positive reception in the spring of 1924 than it had at the end of the previous year, not only because it rested on more solid ground but also because the government had changed hands in January. Admiral Yamamoto's cabinet gave way to one headed by Kiyoura Keigo, an old Yamagata ally, backed by a faction in the House of Peers more receptive to a positive policy in China. As one of its first actions, the new government called for an interministerial conference to review the situation in China. Significantly, Shōda Kazue, returned once again as finance minister, spearheaded this initiative. Although this conference produced no new policy line as such, it affirmed and clarified the basic direction outlined at the Eastern Conference of 1921, including the dualistic framework of cooperation with Chang Tso-lin north of the Wall coupled with a commitment to the Washington system in China proper. In particular, it emphasized the importance of taking advantage of the relationship with Chang and pursuing a more active policy in Manchuria, especially in the north. The army expressed its enthusiasm for the T'aonan–Tsitsihar project and proposed a number of other northern railway ventures as well. Reiterating his opposition to the Tsitsihar line, Debuchi presented his reservations about an excessively close relationship with Chang and any course of action that might complicate relations with the Soviet Union. He also warned against reviving the failed policies of the Terauchi period. These views, however, represented a minority position at this conference. The Kiyoura government heartily endorsed Matsuoka's scheme. At the same time, it became evident by the late spring of 1924 that the cabinet's days were numbered. Mounting party opposition to this attempt at restoring "transcendent" government gathered public support. Acknowledging that it would be inappropriate for a "lame-duck" cabinet to launch a major initiative in foreign affairs, it resolved to defer any action and hand over its work to the incoming administration in the form of recommendations.[45]

Intervention, Escalation, and the "Invisible War"
in North Manchuria

A three-party coalition of the Kenseikai, the Seiyūkai, and the Kakushin kurabu, a group led by Inukai Tsuyoshi, formed a new government that took office in June 1924. Katō Takaaki, president of the Kenseikai, assumed the post of prime minister. The appointment of the man widely regarded as the architect of the Twenty-One Demands caused considerable consternation in political circles in China, and even Chang Tso-lin appears to have braced himself for an aggressive new policy. Many Chinese expected Japan to issue "forty-two demands." Contrary to such expectations, however, the Katō cabinet committed itself to a policy of moderation. Katō had never been quite as uncompromising an imperialist as his reputation, earned during his stint as foreign minister during World War I, suggested, and his views toward China had softened since that time. The Kenseikai had been sharply critical of the Washington treaties in late 1921 and early 1922, but as Bannō Junji points out, it had long been common practice in Japanese politics for opposition parties to adopt a hard-line, nationalistic posture in foreign affairs only to moderate their positions on assuming power. The selection of Shidehara Kijūrō as foreign minister, a man more dedicated to the new diplomacy than any other official of comparable stature in Japan, made the orientation of the Katō government clear.[46]

What Shidehara would have done in Manchuria had he received a clean policy slate is something about which we can only speculate. From the perspective of a diplomat espousing the principles of the new order, the basic framework established at the Eastern Conference represented compromise enough. All things being equal, he would, no doubt, have preferred to minimize new activity in the territory. However, the previous cabinet had handed him a nearly finished agreement, and he possessed no stronger grounds for objecting than had Debuchi. Nothing in the proposed arrangements, taken at face value, violated the principles of the new diplomacy, and although the expansionist and anti-Soviet implications of the railway program may have presented cause for concern, the SMR's *raison d'affaires* offered a mitigating basis to justify the policy. Shidehara thus agreed in August to carry through the plan based on further details worked out during the summer.[47]

No doubt pleased that his project had been accepted by the new administration, Matsuoka was at the same time anxious that Katō and Shidehara understand its full ramifications. In a letter to the prime minister, he underscored the fact that this railway agreement rested on a recognition of Chang Tso-lin as a Japanese ally deserving appropriate support and that the building of the T'aonan–Tsitsihar railway committed Japan to what would, in effect, amount to an "invisible Russo-Japanese War" (mukei no Nichi-Ro sensō).[48] Matsuoka had good reason for concern, since Shidehara agreed with neither of these premises. He would go along with this particular initiative, but he had no intention of dealing with Chang as an ally or partner, nor had he any interest in waging a cold war against the Soviet Union over railway development. Indeed, the limits of coexistence between Matsuoka's new imperialism and Shidehara's new diplomacy defined themselves sharply not long after this seemingly harmonious start as the result of a crisis precipitated by Chang Tso-lin's embroilment in a second war against the Chihli Clique in the autumn of 1924.

Chang's engagement in yet another conflict highlighted the inherent flaw in Japanese policy papered over in the Eastern Conference of 1921 with the theoretical distinction drawn between support for Chang in Manchuria on the one hand and his aspirations south of the Wall on the other.[49] This neat dichotomy posed major problems in practice. Whatever made Chang Tso-lin stronger, richer, and more secure in Manchuria only gave him a greater ability to pursue his ambitions in the south. Japanese policymakers deluded themselves if they actually believed, for example, that Chang would use munitions produced at the Mukden Arsenal only for the defense of the Three Eastern Provinces and not for wars fought elsewhere. The very fact that Japan insisted on maintaining "order and stability" in Manchuria, that it would defend with force its citizens and their property in the event of a war spreading north of the Wall, constituted a form of passive intervention on Chang's behalf. Chang Tso-lin enjoyed a secure base under Japanese protection; he could attack his adversaries while simultaneously securing himself from a counterattack by any enemy not prepared to confront Japan. In this second Fengt'ien-Chihli War, Chang compounded the dilemma facing Japanese policymakers by getting himself into serious military difficulty in short order. Not long after the start of hostilities, the two sides found themselves deadlocked at Shanhaikuan, the gateway to Manchuria, with the Fengt'ien army facing the possibility of defeat.[50]

The army and Matsuoka favored active and direct intervention in support of Chang, since the circumstances clearly presented both the opportunity and the need to demonstrate Japan's commitment to a policy of *daikanshō*. The government in Tokyo opposed taking sides in a Chinese civil war. Shidehara would authorize action only if he saw a threat to Japanese nationals and their property. To get around this impasse, the army and the SMR colluded to bribe one of the Chihli group's key allies, Feng Yü-hsiang (1880–1948), to persuade him to withdraw from the fight and, instead, to occupy Peking. Feng's actions threatened the rear of the Chihli army and forced it to disengage from Shanhaikuan. Chang Tso-lin was saved from destruction.[51]

As Gavan McCormack and others have pointed out, Shidehara's position, even in the absence of the army-SMR scheme, might well have stayed a Chihli invasion and rescued Chang.[52] Nonetheless, it is important not to obscure the real differences between the new diplomats and new imperialists over the handling of this affair. The second Fengt'ien-Chihli War pointed not only to the difficulty of trying to distinguish support for Chang north and south of the Wall but also to the tension between the two interpretations of the relationship with the Manchurian strongman embedded in the Eastern Conference resolution. Shidehara's refusal to commit the government to forthright intervention, which, in Matsuoka's view, formed an essential ingredient for the long-term success of his policy, deeply dissatisfied the activist camp. Without a commitment to *daikanshō*, economic cooperation in itself, which Shidehara and his allies might happily endorse, held little meaning. An official posture of noninterference sent problematic messages to Chang and others in the Chinese political world. The fact that the army and the SMR had little choice but to resort to subterfuge in order to aid Chang is indicative of the limits on the influence enjoyed by the advocates of the new imperialism.

These deeper problems aside, supporters of the Matsuoka line could construe the outcome itself as a net success for their policies. Chang had survived as a result of Japanese intervention, which constituted an achievement in its own right and also a development that would strengthen Japanese leverage over the warlord by placing him deeper in Japan's debt. In this context, the future of the new strategy seemed bright, and the year that followed saw a marked rise of expectations among imperial activists.

Progress on the T'aonan–Tsitsihar railway offered particular encouragement. Construction commenced shortly after the conclusion of the war.

SMR analysts expressed optimism about the value of this line as a feeder capable of drawing substantial traffic from north Manchuria. It would put considerable competitive pressure on the CER, which, as of the end of 1924, had come under firm Soviet control. Since the new Russian general manager was disinclined to bargain with the SMR over quotas and rates, the construction of this railway proved timely. The SMR offered a rather skeptical preliminary analysis of the T'aonan–Tsitsihar's business prospects, however, and projected losses for the first few years. Consistent with Matsuoka's recommendations, one report called for financial aid to the line, since the SMR would reap substantial benefit from feeder traffic.[53]

Matsuoka also talked to the Kirin government and Chang's representatives about the Ch'angch'un–Fuyu and Kirin–Tunhua lines. As mentioned above, it became fairly clear during follow-up talks, however, that the two sides had different understandings of the agreement reached in August 1924. The Chinese saw the arrangements governing the T'aonan–Tsitsihar and Mukden–Hailung lines as a one-for-one exchange, and if the Japanese wanted the Chinese side to proceed with two additional lines, it expected something more in compensation. Chinese representatives suggested that a substantially padded loan might do nicely. The two sides suspended talks temporarily in the late spring of 1925 as popular reaction to the May 30 incident in Shanghai, in which British police shot and killed a number of demonstrators, spread to Manchuria. Japanese negotiators let up their pressure in hopes that the sentiment would die down. Resumed bargaining eventually achieved agreement on the Kirin–Tunhua railway by the end of the year, and this accomplishment, despite tortuous progress, was seen as a positive sign by the Japanese.[54]

Important developments in Chang's relationship with Soviet authorities in north Manchuria reinforced optimism and took the edge off any disappointments about problems with regard to the Ch'angch'un–Fuyu and Kirin–Tunhua lines. Chang's government had worked out a modus vivendi with the Soviets in 1924 that gave Soviet-appointed officials a dominant position in the management of the CER. He had softened his stance partly in an effort to avoid trouble in the rear while confronting the Chihli group in the south. Driven back once again to his base in the Three Eastern Provinces, he adopted a less accommodating position and began pressuring the Soviets for greater Chinese control over the railway. By mid-1925, he had assumed an openly threatening posture. This circumstance certainly pleased those in Japan favoring an anti-Soviet alliance between Tokyo and Mukden.[55] Indeed, during that summer, those in the army inclined toward adventurism, such as the Kwantung garrison's chief of staff, Major General Saitō Hisashi (1877–1953), called for supporting Chang in an armed bid to take over the CER. Saitō's views may be regarded as a radical version of "cooperation." Central army authorities, however, under the relatively moderate leadership of Army Minister Ugaki Kazunari, warned against such initiatives. In Ugaki's view, Japan planned to engage the Soviets in an "invisible war" waged with railways and not through direct military confrontation. Encouraging Chang to take precipitous action would jeopardize the railway program.[56]

Although central army authorities opposed adventurist schemes, Chang's attitude toward the Soviets offered an unprecedented opportunity to strengthen the Japanese position in north Manchuria. To this end, the general staff outlined a program of northern railway expansion in November 1925 that went much further than anything Matsuoka or Hata had outlined the previous year. The army organized its new list of railway desiderata into a two-phase construction program.[57] The foremost project in the first phase was a railway from T'aonan to Solun in Inner Mongolia, the initial segment of a line that would eventually extend to Manchouli, the western border town where the CER joined the Chita branch of the Trans-Siberian Railway. Strengthening the army's operational capabilities against the Soviet Union by building a line paralleling the CER formed one objective of this venture. The projected T'aonan–Manchouli railway would form the western segment of a grand trunk linking the Ch'angch'un–T'aonan, the Ch'angch'un–Kirin, and the Kirin–Hoeryong lines, with connections to the Korean port of Chongjin (see Map 7.1). The army also sought to improve access to economic resources in Inner Mongolia and the eastern portions of Outer Mongolia. The railway would pass through lands suitable for stock raising, which the SMR would promote through the establishment of agricultural stations, and would also intersect a traditional trade route for Mongolian products moving to market at T'ientsin.[58]

In addition to the T'aonan–Solun project, the army's first-phase list also included a railway that would branch off from the projected Ch'angch'un–T'aonan line at Fuyu and run north to Anta station on the CER. This line would intercept the CER west of Harbin and, at the same time, tap one of the more productive agricultural regions of the north. (Unknown to Japanese policymakers at the time, a short distance to the west of Anta lay one of the largest oil fields in East Asia.) A railway extending north from the Korean border town of Hoeryong to Yenki to Ninkut'a, then on to Hailin station on the CER, occupied third place on the priority list. This line would intercept the CER in the east, allowing the army to sever connections between Manchuria and the Maritime Province. The second-phase program included railways on the north side of the CER, from Anta to Paich'üan, from Hailin to Sanhsing, from Tsitsihar to Mergen, from Kirin to Wuch'ang to Imienp'o to Fangcheng, from Harbin to Hailun, and a further extension of the Chengchiat'un–T'ungliao branch of the Ssup'ingkai–T'aonan to K'ailu and on to Linhsi. The army's plans, once completed, would hardwire north Manchuria and Inner Mongolia for military operations and rapid occupation and make the region as a whole untenable for the Soviet Union by the time it built up its military strength.[59] It would also make the region economically accessible and promote development as demanded by the program for wartime self-sufficiency. All of Manchuria would be incorporated into Japan's economic defense perimeter.

The general staff proposal bore clear marks of the influence of Matsuoka's ideas about cooperative railway development. All new construction in the north would nominally take the form of Chinese-sponsored ventures of the kind defined in the SMR director's plan, rather than Japanese loan concessions. Indeed, army planners coined the term "Chinese-style railways" (Shina-shiki tetsudō) to describe them. Chinese state ownership and managerial control of these lines would allow the Japanese to fend off Soviet protests as well as preclude foreign involvement. "In order to prevent the penetration of the influence of other countries into Manchuria, it would be to our advantage to have all future railways constructed under Chinese ownership. We must be alert with regard to privately built railways, which may serve as proxies for foreign powers."[60]

The army proposal also insisted on limiting Japanese involvement in the building of these "Chinese-style railways" to the SMR. "Given that our railway policy in Manchuria necessarily purports to be an economic policy on the surface, the South Manchuria Railway Company must be our principal agent." The pretext of business competition against the CER would play an important part in refuting Soviet charges of Japanese military designs. The general staff, in fact, recommended the deliberate obstruction of any talks between the SMR and CER aimed at mitigating competition. "Negotiations involving Japan, Russia, and China over Manchuria railways as proposed by the Russians are aimed at eliminating railway competition. However, this will result in the determination of natural spheres of influence, which carries the danger of undermining China's sovereignty. We must either oppose the opening of such a conference or, should it be convened, block any resolution." This recommendation is noteworthy not only in calling for the sabotage of railway talks but, more interestingly, in presenting the army as the defender of Chinese sovereignty and an opponent of imperialist spheres of influence, an extraordinary transformation made possible by its growing faith in the partnership with Chang Tso-lin.[61]

The outbreak of imperialist railway fever in 1925 gripped SMR managers as well as military planners. In the fall of that year, company officials laid out a visionary, four-phase, twenty-year scheme aimed at the eventual construction of 5,500 miles of new track. The pace of expansion would begin at a rate of 161 miles a year during the first phase, from 1926 to 1928; accelerate to 230 miles annually in the second phase, from 1928 to 1933; to 300 miles in the third, from 1933 to 1937; and to 347 miles in the fourth, from 1938 to 1944. The list of railways coincided to a large degree with that of the army but included a number of additional lines as well. This breathtaking program of accelerated construction appears rather unrealistic, given the snail's pace of development of the preceding twenty years. Nonetheless, it illuminates the ebullient optimism and high expectations taking shape in the summer and fall of 1925.[62]

The army and the SMR found themselves allies in this prospective northern campaign. The SMR's business interests in expanding a feeder network into CER territory, moreover, served a particularly important purpose in providing, as the general staff proposal noted, an economic "cover" for this activity. Camouflage proved useful for internal political reasons as well. Shidehara and his supporters put little stock in the military logic underlying the construction program and, in fact, tended to regard the army's schemes as unnecessarily provocative. They found it more difficult, however, to deny the claims of the SMR and its need to compete actively with the CER. Supporting Japanese enterprise abroad, after all, formed one of the major functions of the "economic diplomacy" of the Foreign Ministry. In initial discussions with Debuchi in 1923, Matsuoka had invoked the SMR's *raison d'affaires* as a major justification for his plans.[63] Although diplomats would certainly not have given in to company demands uncritically, appeals to business rationality softened and limited their opposition.

The convergence of army and SMR interests in railway policy at this time, however, had limits. For example, all things being equal, the SMR would have preferred a stable pact with the CER, based on negotiated quotas and rates, as opposed to continued competition through building feeders and other aggressive methods. Some company officials also worried about the potential impact of some of the projected railways on the SMR's business interests. Ironically, the Kirin–Hoeryong railway, which had figured prominently in Japanese policy for nearly two decades, was one of the principal sources of anxiety. Because of its well-established position in Japan's official policy agenda, company managers remained cautious about expressing their opposition publicly.[64] Studies of this railway conducted in the mid-1920s, however, gave cause for concern. When completed, the Kirin–Hoeryong line might well draw substantial amounts of north Manchurian traffic coming into Ch'angch'un eastward to Korea and the port of Chongjin. The route from Ch'angch'un to Chongjin, in fact, was substantially shorter than that from Ch'angch'un to Dairen and thus posed a much greater threat to the Dairen strategy than the Pusan route ever had.[65]

In addition, not all SMR officials shared Matsuoka's sanguine view of the prospects of Chinese railway competition. Many of his colleagues believed that the 1924 agreement allowing the construction of the Mukden–Hailung line would open the floodgates to a series of similar projects. Fellow director Ōkura Kinmochi (1882–1968) warned him of a public announcement in a leading Chinese railway journal in 1925 of the PMR's plans to build a railway north from Tahushan station to T'ungliao. Matsuoka reportedly dismissed the announcement by suggesting that such a project had little possibility for realization.[66] Although he may indeed have resorted to such an argument in fending off the objections of his associates, his assessment would seem difficult to accept at face value. The segment from Tahushan to Pataohao had been completed in 1922, and underwriting the larger venture lay well within the capabilities of a relatively healthy PMR. At the same time, allowing the Chinese to build this line would have been entirely consistent with Matsuoka's views.

Some SMR officials even questioned the wisdom of the northern campaign itself. In April 1924, the company's Tokyo office sent a query to Matsuoka about the T'aonan–Tsitsihar project noting that this line formed part of a plan "to weaken Russian power [in Manchuria] as much as possible." However, "the diminution of Russian power means the inevitable growth of Chinese power," observed the author. "The Chinese will make the same demands on the SMR as they have made on the CER. Will this not be disadvantageous to our company?" This line of questioning suggested that old ways of thinking, emphasizing inter-imperialist alliances against the Chinese, persisted in some quarters. Matsuoka explained in his reply, "Our motive is to prevent future Russian penetration [of Manchuria]. For this purpose, we must make use of opportunities to cooperate with a weak China."[67] In other instances, too, Matsuoka found himself at pains to explain his views to his fellow directors and the company president, who had broad doubts about the new directions emerging in Manchuria policy.[68] These circumstances point, on the one hand, to Matsuoka's role in leading the SMR during this period. On the other hand, they suggest that the adherence of the company to the program of northern expansion and Sino-Japanese cooperation depended heavily on the influence of one man.

A second crisis over intervention in Manchuria in late 1925 underscored the fact that this new expansionist trend continued to face resistance within Japanese leadership circles. In this instance, Chang Tso-lin found himself confronted by a revolt from within the ranks of his own followers led by Kuo Sung-ling (1883–1925), a professionally trained soldier with revolutionary nationalist sympathies and alleged ties to the Kuomintang. Matsuoka, the army, and most Japanese officials in Manchuria, along with the settler community, favored active intervention on Chang's behalf. Shidehara and the government in Tokyo firmly opposed any action beyond securing the Railway Zone against the spread of fighting. Shidehara made it clear that although Japan had an obligation to protect its citizens, it had no interest in the outcome of this internal conflict in Manchuria and that he found Kuo no more or less acceptable than Chang as a regional ruler. For Matsuoka, *daikanshō* demanded resolute support for Chang. Maintaining order and stability, in his view, clearly went beyond defending the Railway Zone and required a commitment to preserve the framework of cooperation being built around Chang, which Kuo's actions threatened to disrupt. Although Kuo sought to assure Japan that he would respect existing Japanese rights, such assurances proved insufficient for the new imperialists. Faced with a hard position in Tokyo, however, Chang's Japanese supporters once again had little choice but to resort to subterfuge in rendering assistance. In this case, the Kwantung Army interpreted its orders loosely and took a more active role in protecting the Railway Zone than intended by the government. Japanese troops denied Kuo's forces free movement and permission to cross the SMR. The forbidden Railway Zone thus became a Japanese anvil against which Chang's loyalist troops hammered their opponents.[69]

Internal disagreement and the under-the-table methods notwithstanding, Japanese action had, once more, rescued Chang Tso-lin. Advocates of imperialist cooperation underscored this point to the Manchurian leader in their subsequent talks and suggested that the time had come for him to demonstrate his gratitude in a more expansive manner. Indeed, by the end of 1925, frustration with what they increasingly perceived as unacceptably slow progress mounted even among the strongest supporters of this policy line. In retrospect, Chang had proven less forthcoming than expected, and cooperation, in the balance, had been rather one-sided, with the Japanese rendering assistance without getting a fair return. In part, dissatisfaction emerged as an inevitable product of the unreasonably high expectations that had mushroomed in the summer and fall of 1925. Disillusionment, however, ran deeper in some quarters and reflected a growing sense that Chang Tso-lin might prove fundamentally unsuitable as a client in the long run. Significantly, Matsuoka himself began arriving at such conclusions even before the Kuo rebellion. During the course of difficult negotiations over the Kirin–Tunhua line, he expressed his views in a letter to a colleague in October 1925. Ironically, Matsuoka compared Chang negatively to Feng Yü-hsiang, who had gravitated toward the Soviet Union and had thus made himself persona non grata with Japan.

I have discreetly been studying conditions in various areas while in Peking during the past four months, and what has impressed me, in particular, is the earnestness and haste with which Feng Yü-hsiang has undertaken the development of his northwestern territories. Moreover, he has been taking the initiative in all directions in order to realize the construction of railways, the foundations of such development, even approaching me during the last two years. Recently, in fact, an influential figure in Feng's camp came to me with a request [for assistance]. Given my relationship with Commander in Chief Chang, I could offer only a superficially friendly attitude and had no intention of responding favorably to such a request, but I must admire this man [Feng] who is undertaking such a lofty enterprise with enthusiasm, who has a thorough understanding of the importance of railways, who refuses to take a single *ri* in commissions, who will do what is necessary to build railways even a single *sen* more cheaply, and who seeks to repay the principal of [railway] loans as quickly as possible. The difference between his attitude toward railways and that of

Commander in Chief Chang is enormous. Unless Mr. Chang engages in some self-reflection, he will have cause for regret.

Although it is obvious that the extension of railways in Manchuria is of advantage to Japan, in reality the main beneficiaries will be Commander in Chief Chang and the Three Eastern Provinces. Over the past four years, I have discussed this with him repeatedly, and each time he has presented an attitude of understanding. Yet in reality it would appear that he does not understand. The most important assistance that the SMR, indeed Japan, has rendered Mr. Chang, in fact, lies in railway building.[70]

Matsuoka's suggestion that Chang would have cause for regret could be taken as an ominous warning. In his view, Japanese support accrued to the institution of Manchurian strongman, not to any individual. *Daikanshō* implied a resolute support of Japanese friends and an equally firm commitment to prevent enemies of Japan from acquiring a position of power in Manchuria. If Chang Tso-lin failed to "reflect" and mend his ways, Japan might well have to find someone more suitable.

Yet what might seem to be clear and straightforward in the theoretical framework of Matsuoka's strategy posed serious practical problems on two counts. One lay simply in the fact that the Japanese government, with its foreign policy under the control of Shidehara, had shown itself unwilling to intervene, as the second Fengt'ien-Chihli War and the Kuo affair made clear. A government unprepared to render assistance to a friendly leader would likewise desist from taking resolute action against an unfriendly one. The other, more serious problem, which had nothing to do with Shidehara and represented a fundamental flaw in Matsuoka's scheme, rested in the difficulty of finding an appropriate replacement for Chang. Army Minister Ugaki summarized the dilemma succinctly in a diary entry in December 1925.

A strong supporter of imperialist cooperation, Ugaki had played an instrumental role in moving the army behind this position. As of the fall of 1925, he remained enthusiastic about its prospects. During the months that followed, however, he grew increasingly disillusioned and developed an intense dislike for Chang and even described him as a greedy and faithless bandit. He compared him unfavorably to Kuo Sung-ling and regretted deeply that political realities had forced Japan to back Chang against a man whom he found personally admirable. Unfortunately, for all Chang's shortcomings and despicable qualities, the Japanese had little recourse but to continue their support.

Chang's power in north Manchuria is not something he has acquired over night. Rather, it is the crystallization of a decade and more of effort. Whoever replaces Chang in Mukden will, I believe, require some time before his influence reaches north. Today, we are making steady efforts to expand into north Manchuria through the power of Chang. With the departure of Chang, we will, for a time, lose this advantage. Moreover, the heads of Kirin and Heilungkiang provinces will naturally challenge the new center at Mukden and engage in rivalry. Should this happen, just as Feng Yu-hsiang has, to preserve himself, turned to the power of Red Russia and has been in turn used, it is possible that a second or third Feng may appear in north Manchuria allowing the power of Red Russia to penetrate. This will clearly obstruct our development. In other words, the overthrow and destruction of Chang is disadvantageous for our north Manchuria policy.[71]

Ugaki subscribed to the principle of *daikanshō* and agreed that replacing Chang posed no problem in theory. At this point, however, no one other than Chang had the ability to govern the Three Eastern Provinces as a unified political entity and to facilitate Japan's north Manchurian advance.

By the end of 1925, the new imperialism confronted a number of major challenges that it had finessed rather than overcome, and the difficulties that lay ahead in dealing with an obstreperous Chang, on the one hand, and an uncooperative Shidehara, on the other, cast shadows over the high optimism of the summer. Placed in a larger context, however, these problems should not obscure the fact that Matsuoka and his allies had managed to chart what seemed a clear course around the obstacles imposed by Chinese nationalism and the new international order; they had, moreover, circumvented internal opposition in Tokyo as well. Although the great northern railway campaign remained as yet little more than lines penciled on a map of CER territory, the construction of the T'aonan–Tsitsihar line constituted an important first step and, in itself, a breakthrough that could not be taken for granted. Despite its numerous shortcomings, cooperation with Chang Tso-lin offered the best hope for Japanese empire-building efforts in this period. Activists had good reason, then, to look to the future with far more confidence than they had during the dark days of the Hara cabinet.

Industrial Manchuria: Mixed Results

The effort to build new railways by managing Chang Tso-lin as a client did not represent the only activity of note in Manchuria during the mid-1920s. The new imperialism aimed at the development of Japanese power in breadth, at pre-empting the growth of Soviet influence, and at extending the scope of Japan's economic defense perimeter. The pursuit of a strategy of development in depth, emphasizing the Railway Zone and Kwantung, continued as well. Although the preoccupation with north Manchuria and Chang Tso-lin overshadowed this secondary line of expansion, the developments of this era demand a brief examination.[72]

The attempt to build an industrial and urban Japanese Manchuria in Kwantung and the Railway Zone had met with a mixture of successes and failures by the middle of the decade. The most significant achievement, without question, lay in the development of the Anshan Ironworks. Even as this venture struggled with heavy losses in the first few years of the decade, it steadily increased its output. By 1923, it produced 18 percent of the pig iron used for steel production in Japan and 13 percent of that used for casting. In 1923, SMR scientists achieved a breakthrough in ore-enrichment technology. "Reduction roasting," which magnetized iron compounds and permitted the application of magnetic enrichment techniques, allowed the company to make economical use of the abundant, low-grade ores available at Anshan. Encouraged by this development, the SMR renewed its commitment to large-scale production, investing an additional ¥11 million in the project between 1923 and 1925. Difficulties remained, however, and the venture continued to demand considerable internal subsidy.[73] In an effort to improve its prospects, the SMR sought to have its Anshan operations classified under Japanese industrial policy as a "domestic" producer, which would exempt its output from tariffs and make it eligible for subsidies. Significantly, in lobbying for this measure, SMR officials invoked the blood and iron of the Russo-Japanese War in their arguments.

One needs no reminder that South Manchuria is a land acquired through the sacrifice of many tens of thousands of our countrymen twenty years ago. In spirit, it is a land which is, in the final analysis, inseparable from our country. Yet, the moment we turn to economic affairs, it is treated as a place entirely separate from Japan. Indeed, it has been treated to this day as a foreign country.[74]

The SMR managed to win its desired classification because of the particular importance of iron and steel. In general, however, economic policymakers in the home islands, concerned about competition between Manchurian and domestic producers, continued to oppose unrestricted development of the territory.[75]

The SMR and its partners in private industry made significant progress in a number of other areas as well. Their continuing work with various methods of ammonium sulfate production resulted in a growing volume of commercial output. Experiments in glass making conducted by the Central Research Laboratory formed the basis for a joint venture between the SMR and Asahi Glass in 1924 to produce plate and crystal glass.[76] This undertaking placed Manchuria on the leading edge of Japanese efforts in this field. In an important new development, the SMR began working on a pilot project in shale-oil production in 1923. Large deposits of oil-bearing rock overlay much of the coal at Fushun and had to be removed in any case for open-pit mining. Company scientists sent samples to Scotland for evaluation, and positive results stimulated interest on the part of both armed services. The army, navy, and SMR began discussing plans for experimental production in 1925, but the effort bogged down in questions of financing. Skeptical about the commercial prospects for shale oil, the SMR wanted a program of continuing subsidies. Army and navy representatives, however, argued that for any industry to be of use to the armed forces in wartime, it needed to prove its commercial viability in peacetime. The SMR's establishment of a small experimental plant in 1925 kept the possibilities for further development in this field open.[77]

Although Manchurian industrialization included some prominent areas of success, the overall business situation in the territory provided less reason for optimism. The dramatic growth among larger, joint-stock enterprises that began during the war boom had come to a halt, and excluding the SMR and its wholly owned subsidiaries, capital investment in large-scale enterprise had actually declined. This trend reflected, in part, the general slowdown in East Asian economies after 1920 and the winnowing of weak and speculative ventures set up during the war. It also stemmed from the limited opportunities within Kwantung and the Railway Zone. Promising areas of activity such as iron and steel or coal-based chemicals required enormous amounts of capital, the ability to work with cutting-edge technologies, and a long time horizon for investment. Few enterprises, apart from the SMR itself, had the capacity and will to assume the burden of pursuing such ventures in Manchuria. Low profits made it difficult to attract new private capital from Japan. Even the larger joint-stock corporations based in the territory paid, on average, dividends at only half the rate of their domestic counterparts between

1918 and 1926. Total Japanese investment in Manchuria, apart from the SMR, continued to rise, but most of the growth took the form of an increasing number of small companies. In manufacturing, for example, nearly 63 percent of incorporated enterprises were capitalized at less than ¥100,000 in 1926. In commerce, an even smaller scale prevailed, with 82 percent of incorporated enterprises below that threshold, and nearly half with capital of less than ¥10,000. The size of individual firms does not, in itself, constitute a measure of business health or of their contribution to the economy as a whole. However, other indications emerged during the mid-1920s that Japanese small business faced difficulty from inadequate capitalization, problems in securing commercial loans, and stiff competition from Chinese enterprise, which demonstrated rapid growth in small-scale manufacturing and commerce in Kwantung and the Railway Zone[78] (see Table 7.2).

Not unexpectedly, economic difficulties had a negative impact on the progress of immigration, and by the mid-1920s, clear signs of distress in the settler community in Kwantung and the Railway Zone had appeared. Opportunities for employment in modern industry failed to materialize, revealing a fallacy inherent in the notion of promoting immigration through industrialization. One of the main attractions of Manchuria for Japanese business lay in low labor costs, and manufacturing firms locating in this territory tended to hire a predominantly Chinese workforce. According to a study by Nishimura Shigeo, Japanese workers constituted only 13.4 percent of factory labor in Kwantung and the Railway Zone. They earned an average daily wage of ¥2.56 in contrast to ¥0.66 paid to Chinese workers. The same tendency held in the SMR's operations at Fushun, Anshan, and Shahok'ou.[79] This preference for Chinese labor meant that the principal opportunities available to Japanese, apart from jobs as managers, technicians, and skilled workers in the larger firms, remained employment in small business or individual enterprise. According to census data, either self-employment or work in very small, unincorporated firms provided sustenance for a large proportion of the settler community. According to 1920 figures, some 5,600 respondents, somewhat more than a quarter of those employed in manufacturing, and 7,600, a third of all employed in commerce, described themselves as heads of firms. Comparable data are not available for 1925, but the pattern of employment appears similar.[80] Given the fact that most small Japanese enterprises engaged in head-to-head competition

Table 7.2
Occupational Distribution in Japanese Manchuria, 1925
(%)

Occupation	Kwantung	Railway Zone*	Other areas	Total
Agriculture	1.05%	1.48%	0.18%	1.22%
Marine products	0.77	0.02	0.03	0.39
Mining	0.15	9.57	0.21	4.63
Manufacturing	26.91	16.96	6.66	21.37
Commerce	20.27	24.32	53.29	23.51
Transportation	17.26	24.27	2.18	19.99
Professions and public service	24.83	14.96	22.14	20.03
Others	4.47	4.37	5.63	4.47
Domestics	1.16	1.21	3.25	1.27
Unemployed	3.13	2.84	6.43	3.12
TOTAL	100.00	100.00	100.00	100.00

*Includes residents of consular jurisdictions along the SMR.
SOURCE: SMR, Chōsaka, Waga kuni jinkō mondai to Manmō, pp. 137–38

with their Chinese counterparts to exploit the same opportunities with similar levels of skill, distress in this sector came as no surprise. The Japanese, in fact, appeared to be losing relative ground in all areas of employment. As of 1925, ethnic Japanese constituted less than 15 percent of the total workforce in Kwantung and the Railway Zone, with downward projections for the future.[81]

Settlers sought relief from their difficulties by appealing to the government and the SMR for assistance. Their demands included low-interest loans, official protection from Chinese competition, and the reinvestment in Kwantung and the Railway Zone of SMR dividends paid to the government. One particular demand, that the SMR abolish its consumer cooperative, which, settlers charged, deprived them of business, indicated the marginal position of many in the Japanese community. Employees of the SMR and their dependents at this time accounted for nearly one-third of the total Japanese population in the territory and thus represented a significant market for Japanese specialty goods.[82] At the same time, this settler demand suggests that a significant portion of Japanese business activity in Manchuria operated within a narrow ethnic enclave economy. As one contemptuous critic had noted a decade earlier, the Japanese in the territory "lived off one another."[83]

The government considered some relief measures, such as creating a special loan fund available through the Bank of Chōsen and other selected lenders.[84] The SMR also responded by reorganizing, although not abolishing, its consumer cooperative.[85] On the whole, however, neither company officials nor government authorities did much more than offer sympathy. Official attention in the development of Kwantung and the Railway Zone focused on such major endeavors as Anshan, and this left small business, for the most part, to its own devices. The SMR, on which the burden of relief efforts might have been expected to fall, found itself in a poor position to offer much in the way of material resources. By the mid-1920s, the company had overextended itself financially, as a result not only of industrial investment but also of capital improvements in the Railway Zone. Arguably, the company had already done a great deal for the settler community by building infrastructure and expanding its school system. The SMR's railway business performed well, but expenditures in other areas were rising, and net revenues remained relatively flat during the middle of the decade; the SMR faced declining profitability with respect to its total assets (see Appendix A).

The limited commitment on the part of the government and the SMR to settler relief also indicated shifting priorities. Although the idea of promoting Japanese settlement in Manchuria continued to occupy a place of nominal importance among policy goals, it no longer enjoyed a high priority in practice. Traditional moderates had never demonstrated any great enthusiasm for the idea, nor did the new diplomats of the 1920s. Advocates of colonization, such as Gotō Shinpei, had provided the strongest support. Although some remained dedicated to breathing life into the moribund land rights agreement of 1915, cooperation had displaced colonization in the thinking of leading activists.

Matsuoka Yōsuke's view of land rights testifies to this shift. In a letter to Shidehara in December 1925, in which Matsuoka made the case for active intervention on Chang's behalf against Kuo Sung-ling, he acknowledged that the Manchurian leader's compliance with Japanese wishes had been less than ideal. However, "with the exception of minor and abstract problems (for example, the matter of land-lease rights), Mr. Chang has generally given us his support, as is well known."[86] Matsuoka parenthetically relegated what had been one of the main goals of traditional Japanese policy in Manchuria to the category of "minor and abstract problems."

Although leadership attitudes toward settlement had thus changed substantially by the middle of the 1920s, popular views of Manchuria had not made the same transition. Ideas about a "bountiful Manchuria" and the promise of *Lebensraum* continued to dominate public expectations, the result of years of effective imperialist education. Some SMR officials appeared troubled by this gap between the new policy directions and popular perceptions. Unrealistic expectations would, at minimum, make the company vulnerable to criticism for failing to live up to its promises, as had happened a decade earlier. A series of pamphlets that began to appear in 1924, entitled "What Should We Expect from Manchuria?" ("Manmō yori nani o kitai subeki ka"), suggests an effort at public re-education. The opening lines of this pamphlet address the problem bluntly: "What should Japan expect in economic terms from Manchuria? What capabilities does Manchuria have to provide Japan with natural resources? As soon as people open their mouths, they speak of the bottomless bounty of Manchuria, but is this, in fact, the case?"[87]

The thrust of the work offered a restrained optimism about the territory's natural resources, but it also stressed the importance of patience and the need for long-term development. It cautioned implicitly against expectations of quick successes in business, of individuals arriving empty-handed and making their fortunes in Manchuria. The pamphlet frankly dismissed the prospect of agricultural settlement with the exception of those planning to pursue large-scale mechanized farming or specialties such as cultivating fruit. It essentially repeated arguments made by experts in the field since 1905, but did so more sharply. Significantly, it took on the issue of land rights directly. "Even if, in the future, the question of land-lease rights were to be resolved . . . is it, in fact, possible for our people to compete directly and successfully with Chinese farmers in agricultural enterprise?" With the exceptions of mechanized and specialized farming, the author of this tract answered with an unequivocal no. He cited statistics about annual farming costs and income, pointing out that Japanese farmers would not stand a chance of competing with Chinese counterparts on a level playing field. He added that difficulties of adjusting to the harsh climate and unfamiliar environment would severely "handicap" (transliterated English in the original) Japanese farmers' efforts from the start. He cautioned that Japanese immigration to Manchuria was "essentially different from Japanese immigration to America." Subsequent editions of this pamphlet stressed this point even more strongly, with the opening paragraph warning against the expectation of Japanese homesteading in the territory.[88]

By the middle of the 1920s, most policymakers understood that no easy fixes could resolve the problems facing industrial Manchuria and the efforts to promote settlement, whether urban or rural. Difficulties stemmed from the rise of Chinese economic competition and the limitations inherent in the kinds of business opportunities the Japanese sought to pursue. The lack of rights clearly did not constitute the fundamental problem, as had been argued in 1913 and 1915. Nor did blame rest on the new order, Chinese resistance, or a soft government in Tokyo. Clear signs had emerged that Japan was beginning to lose the struggle on the ground in its strongholds of Kwantung and the Railway Zone, where it retained near-colonial rights. Even with a firm legal basis, a strategy of defensive entrenchment and development in depth no longer was the workable option it might have seemed in the early 1920s. Such an assessment only strengthened the convictions of those advocating cooperation with Chang Tso-lin that their way offered the only viable course for empire-building. However difficult this approach might be, the alternative was an inevitable decline of Japanese Manchuria.

EIGHT

Troubled Partnership, 1926–1928

If the architects of the new imperialism in Manchuria were confident that they had placed their strategies on the right track at the end of 1925, developments in the spring of the following year began eroding their confidence rather quickly. Chang Tso-lin launched yet another concerted campaign to extend his power south of the Wall. Bolstered by his initial success and his alliance with a group of northern warlords, he began demonstrating an increasingly recalcitrant and, in many instances, an openly defiant attitude toward Japan. Japanese leaders across the political spectrum agreed that the time had come to adopt a firm, no-nonsense attitude toward the obstreperous warlord. The new imperialists had thus far favored the use of carrots in managing their client but were not averse to using sticks to remind Chang of his dependence on Japan and to induce cooperative behavior. The new diplomats, for their part, also favored a tough stance, and saw in this turn of events not only a need to stop Chang from complicating the situation south of the Wall but also an opportunity to rein in the army's policy of northern expansion. At the same time, a vocal and growing minority among leadership circles lent their support to a hard-line approach for yet another reason. These officials had never placed much stock in Matsuoka Yōsuke's strategies and called for the reassertion of a more traditional imperialism. In their eyes, Chang's behavior offered clear evidence of the bankruptcy of both imperialist and liberal reformers, and a crackdown in Manchuria, long overdue, provided an opening to push for a return to the principles of gunboat diplomacy.

The adoption of a hard line, not surprisingly, failed to improve relations. Tensions increased, degenerating into a state of open antagonism by the spring of 1927. In this climate of mounting frustration, disillusionment, and criticism coming from all directions, the government of Tanaka Giichi (April 1927–July 1929) agreed to a comprehensive review of policy in China both north and south of the Wall and called a second Eastern Conference in early summer. Although Tanaka's promises to carry out a "positive policy" in Manchuria raised expectations among imperial activist circles, the Eastern Conference, in fact, produced little in the way of new lines of action. Tanaka sought to give cooperation with Chang Tso-lin another chance and maintain the course charted by Matsuoka and the army in 1924–25. The fact that Chang had suffered major reversals in his southern campaign in the spring of 1927 offered encouraging prospects for a restoration of imperialist cooperation, and matters seemed to be moving, albeit haltingly, in the desired direction during the year that followed. Just when the effort appeared on the verge of success in June 1928, however, it collapsed, the result of Chang's assassination in a conspiracy led by a disaffected Kwantung Army officer.

Inflation, Railway Disputes, and the Deterioration of Relations with Chang Tso-lin

Developments south of the Wall contributed substantially to the deterioration of relations between Chang and the Japanese in 1926 and early 1927. Chang Tso-lin continued to embroil himself in the struggle for the Chinese heartland. He allied himself with his former enemy, Wu Pei-fu of the Chihli Clique, a development that marked the beginnings of a broader warlord coalition aimed at resisting the Northern Expedition of the Nationalist-Communist alliance, launched in the summer of 1926. Japan's leaders had yet to arrive at a consensus regarding the Kuomintang (Nationalist Party). A minority favored supporting Chang and the northern coalition against the revolutionary southern alliance. Most mainstream leaders, military as well as civilian, however, agreed that whatever final position they might adopt toward the Northern Expedition, Chang's proper place remained in Manchuria. The need to separate policies north and south of the Wall became more urgent than ever, and Tokyo issued increasingly strident warnings to the Manchurian warlord throughout the year. Rather than heed these admonitions, however, Chang cooled toward Japan as a result. Facing the greatest challenge and opportunity of his career at this juncture, he would have welcomed help, but in its absence, he found little reason to cultivate the Japanese. Indeed, by 1926 he seems to have started looking elsewhere for support. Japan's view of Chang as a regional strongman in the Three Eastern Provinces and Chang's view of Japan as an underwriter of his bid to become master of all China had stood at odds since the beginning of the relationship.

Both sides appear to have submerged this contradiction in wishful thinking over the years. By 1926, however, the stakes had grown too high to set these differences aside, and the result was increasingly open tension.[1]

Although the impending civil war in China presented a major cause of friction, factors particular to Manchuria also came to the fore in 1926 and early 1927. Mounting conflict over Chang's fiscal and economic policies figured prominently. Financial pressures had already induced the Chang regime to adopt increasingly active measures in the Three Eastern Provinces after 1922 to raise revenues, and with escalating engagement in the south, the need for funds grew all the more desperate in 1926. As one step, Chang declared his intention to collect a 2.5 percent customs surcharge in Manchuria. The powers had discussed the possibility of allowing the Chinese government this surcharge as a step toward tariff autonomy in 1925 but had not come to a final decision. Offering a model that Chang hoped to emulate, the Kuomintang regime in the south had begun collecting this charge unilaterally. Tokyo might consider some flexibility over this matter but remained rather unhappy with the prospect.[2] Another scheme entailed the implementation of a soy monopsony in the Three Eastern Provinces. Chang granted provincial banks and officially designated merchant houses special rights to purchase the region's soy crop in an attempt to generate hard-currency earnings. Japanese trading companies such as Mitsui Bussan protested vigorously. A company report in 1926 made the following observations:

In the past, purchasing in the interior has been much more advantageous than buying in markets like Dairen, but this year, the practice has proven entirely profitless. This is due to the dominance of official merchants. . . . If we were to ask who is the biggest buyer in the Manchurian hinterlands, it is not international traders . . . it is Chang Tso-lin who has obstructed this company's purchasing, setting up publicly financed bean wholesalers to compete in this trade.

Interestingly, Mitsui Bussan had harsh words for the SMR's soy-trading subsidiary, International Transport (Kokusai unsō), whose allegedly unfair practices contributed to the difficulties faced by private business.[3] Indeed, the SMR itself appeared ready to come to terms with the soy monopsony and negotiated special, mutually advantageous deals with official merchants to ship their goods south rather than to Vladivostok. Once again, it appeared that the SMR's interests ran counter to those of the home business community and that the Japanese side lacked unity on this issue.[4]

The problem of rampant inflation in Manchuria, however, generated far greater concern and led to a consensus among the Japanese, moderates and activists alike, on the need for vigorous countermeasures. Official banks had accelerated their printing of inconvertible paper currency for use in the Three Eastern Provinces, which allowed the regime to save hard currency for expenditures south of the Wall. Measured against the Bank of Chōsen gold notes, which, after World War I had become the dominant currency of Japanese Manchuria, 1.00 Fengt'ien paper yüan had exchanged for ¥1.00 in 1920. The yüan, as a silver-standard currency, declined in value as the result of falling silver prices during the early 1920s but held a level roughly between ¥0.74 and ¥0.71 between 1921 and 1925. The yen value of Fengt'ien currency fell markedly in 1925 to ¥0.59, plummeted in 1926 to ¥0.27, and crashed to ¥0.10 the following year. The problem, as the Japanese saw it, lay not only in the injury that inflation caused to trade and other business activity but also in the threat it posed to stability in the region. Uncontrolled printing of paper money represented a source of potential political and social unrest in Manchuria and was reflective of the kind of maladministration that had contributed to the recent revolt against Chang.[5] Matsuoka considered fiscal irresponsibility a justification for *daikanshō* precisely because of the threat of such disorder.

Escalating disputes over railways formed yet another source of conflict during this period, partly related to economic tensions, but with broader and more complex ramifications. All major players on the Japanese side expressed deep dissatisfaction with Chang's work in this arena, but their complaints often came from diametrically opposed directions, putting the Mukden regime in a lose-lose position. The army and other adherents of Matsuoka-style cooperation, for example, found stalled progress on the plans they had outlined in 1925 unacceptable. The problem, in this case, clearly stemmed from inflated expectations, already unrealistic by the middle of 1925 and buoyed to further heights in the wake of the intervention against Kuo Sung-ling. Japanese representatives had proposed the grand schemes outlined by the SMR and the Army General Staff in 1925 to Chang through various channels, but discussions had not resulted in an agreement. The only firm commitment achieved thus far remained the understanding of August 1924, which entailed the construction of the T'aonan-Tsitsihar, Kirin-Tunhua, and Ch'angch'un-Fuyu (revised in 1925 with a terminus at Talai, a short distance west of Fuyu on the opposite bank of the Sungari; hereafter

described as the Ch'angch'un–Talai) railways. Of these, the T'aonan–
Tsitsihar (actually, T'aonan to Angangki station on the CER just south of
Tsitsihar) line had opened to traffic by the summer of 1926, and work had
commenced on the Kirin–Tunhua, slated for operation in 1927. As yet, there
was no contract for construction of the Ch'angch'un–Talai line, although
intermittent talks continued. A Foreign Ministry report in July 1926 concluded that the railway program had proved quite successful in light of past
experience.[6] Expectations, however, remained all important. Many in the
army believed that, if for no other reason than to express his gratitude for
services rendered during the Kuo rebellion, Chang owed Japan more forthright cooperation. They regarded the failure to move on the northern railway program, let alone old, outstanding projects like the Ch'angch'un–Talai,
as intolerable.[7]

Chang himself had contributed to unrealistic Japanese expectations in his
efforts to solicit military and financial aid, and he continued to do so in 1926,
seemingly toying with army hopes. The danger inherent in this game became
evident in the case of a T'aonan–Solun railway proposal briefly considered
during the spring and summer of 1926. Because it illustrates the broader dynamics of railway disputes during this period, it warrants examination in
some detail.

In April and May 1926, Chang made several overtures to Mukden Consul-General Yoshida Shigeru (1878–1967), who had replaced Funatsu Tatsuichirō in 1925, and to SMR Director Ōkura Kinmochi, who took over
Matsuoka's responsibilities for railway negotiations after the latter's resignation in March. Chang indicated his willingness to support the construction
of a railway from T'aonan west to the frontier settlement of Solun in Inner
Mongolia if the Japanese would lend him ¥20–40 million.[8] Chang clearly
aimed for a Nishihara-style advance, a major part of which he intended to
use for purposes other than building the railway. The estimated cost of the
line ran no more than ¥8–10 million. Chang's advisor Machino Takema
(1875–1968), a colonel in the Japanese army reserve but serving the warlord in
the capacity of a private citizen, highlighted this aspect of the proposal quite
frankly. Suggesting a more specific figure of ¥30 million, Machino explained
that ¥10 million would go for railway construction, ¥10 million for Chang's
general use, and the remaining ¥10 million for currency stabilization, a
measure that Japan had been pressing on Chang. Machino sought to
sweeten the deal, on his own initiative, by hinting that the Chinese authori-

ties might grant special land rights in the Solun district if a satisfactory loan agreement could be worked out.[9]

The prospect of a Solun line tantalized the army. In a recommendation to the Foreign Ministry in July, the general staff urged action on what it considered one of the most valuable of strategic railways in the north and a "major guarantor of peace between Japan and Russia." This new opportunity also seems to have softened the army's attitude toward Chang and revived its optimism about a policy of cooperation.

Today, as in the past, north Manchuria is the source of tension between Japan and Russia. The problem stems from the fact that neither country has a decisive advantage over the other. Should Japan establish a firm and unchallengeable position [in the territory], a weak Soviet Russia would be forced to reconsider its ambitions. Russo-Japanese tensions would thus dissipate in due course. In concrete terms, the most effective method for establishing our power in the north lies in the pursuit of our railway policy. It is difficult to find any approach comparable in its effectiveness. At present, Soviet Russia fears us. Chang Tso-lin himself bears an implacable antipathy toward the Russians, and his rising star has forced them into unmistakable retreat. Chang's hard-line position and his clear willingness to cooperate with us against the Russians presents us with an excellent opportunity to carry out our policy in north Manchuria. Indeed, the fact that the Russians lack the ability to do anything to obstruct our railway plans has already been demonstrated in the case of the T'aonan–Tsitsihar project.[10]

If Chang was seeking to mollify the Japanese army, he calculated well in choosing this railway as a means. From a business perspective, the proposal initially intrigued the SMR because of its value in providing feeder traffic for the Ssup'ingkai–T'aonan line and in tapping into the Mongolian trade. The associated demand for massive financial assistance, however, proved problematic and ultimately caused the scheme to fall flat. Company officials balked at the size of the loan. Based on Machino's numbers, the proposed Solun railway loan would amount to three times the actual construction cost. By contrast, financial arrangements for Nishihara's Kirin–Hoeryong had run only 20 percent above actual costs. Since the railway would carry the burden of repaying the total loan, the proportion of padding represented a major consideration. SMR officials appear to have estimated 25 percent as the upper limit for such overruns, a figure that Finance Minister Shōda used as a guide in 1918. The Solun line could not possibly shoulder a ¥30 million debt. Ōkura suggested in his discussions with Machino that although the

company might manage a ¥2.5 million "advance" to Chang, any such arrangement would require the explicit approval of the Japanese government.
Machino acknowledged the problem, but he also offered the following clarification, lest there be any misunderstanding about what his employer
sought: "Chang doesn't want the railway. What he wants is ¥10 million. This
is why he's latched on to the railway. Under any other circumstances, he'd
say 'no' to the project."[11] Once that point had been made clear, pursuit of the
scheme reached an impasse. Given the experience with the Nishihara Loans,
Tokyo would hardly consider any funding of Chang at such a level, let alone
offer a major portion of the sum without strings attached. Chang had thus
managed to do little more than tempt the army while holding the prize out
of reach. The episode served only to nurture further ill-will and underscore
Chang's venality without demonstrating his redeeming usefulness as an ally.

Even if Chang had presented more reasonable terms, however, the Foreign Ministry's vigorous opposition would have made any effort to consum-
mate the Solun project extremely difficult. Indeed, for the moderates and
new diplomats, the Solun railway epitomized a Manchuria policy that had
gotten out of hand. As they had feared, the T'aonan–Tsitsihar project had
caused friction with the Soviet Union. If the initiative stopped at this point,
the problem remained manageable, but if the army meant to pursue in earnest an "invisible war" against the Soviet Union, as reflected in the railway
program laid out in 1925, extremely serious complications could result. From
the perspective of the diplomats, the Soviet Union presented a negligible
threat at this point. The only danger came from Japanese provocations. As
Kimura Eiichi (1879–1947), the new chief of the Asia Bureau, noted in the
summer of 1926:

All the recent military plans concerning North Manchuria have been based on operational plans that treat Russia as the hypothetical adversary. I believe that anticipating another Russo-Japanese war in this day and age is rather fanciful. Even if the
Russians were to attack south, they would do so from the direction of the Uriankai-
Maimaich'eng region [Outer Mongolia]. Moreover, as has become clear through our
earlier disputes over the southern branch of the CER, Russia has yet to prepare a
plan for war with Japan as an adversary. I have deep reservations about Japan initiating a military build-up against the Russians and attempting to drive them from
north Manchuria at a time when Russia is not making war preparations.

Kimura committed himself to checking if not reversing this course insofar as
possible, and the T'aonan–Solun railway, which he regarded as the most

dangerous of the proposed northern projects, was where he decided to draw the line.[12]

Kimura, however, could not confront the army directly over its strategic plans. As a civilian diplomat, disputing army assessments lay outside his official competence. Instead, he chose to approach the problem obliquely by placing the onus of responsibility for the project squarely on Chang Tso-lin and berating him for even considering it.

In the final analysis, given the location of this railway, its value cannot be realized unless it is extended beyond the Hsing'an Range to the Hailar region. In any event, it is doubtful whether the revenues of this line, once operating, will meet expenses. At the same time, it must be said that given the current financial and economic conditions in the Three Eastern Provinces, this plan for a large-scale and, moreover, unproductive railway is rather reckless. There are, in fact, many other pending lines, such as the Ch'angch'un–Talai, which local people and officials desire and are more economically significant. That the Mukden authorities ignore such railways and instead want to spend vast sums to build the T'aonan–Solun, which has no urgency, raises doubts about their motives. The main objectives of this plan are undoubtedly military and political.

Kimura added that padding loans violated standing Japanese policy and that if Chang wanted aid, he should approach the appropriate authorities directly. The government would gladly extend assistance in restoring financial stability to the Three Eastern Provinces. The position paper concluded, "Should the Mukden authorities seek to pursue this matter in the future, we must take the opportunity to press forward those railway lines we have planned for previously."[13]

This critique of Chang's initiative seems rather disingenuous on a number of counts. The Solun line constituted an undertaking no more or less financially irresponsible or economically unproductive than other railways on Japan's list of desiderata. Managed as an autonomous business unit, the T'aonan–Solun route would, indeed, have difficulty making ends meet during its first few years of operation. Most of the new railways planned in Manchuria, however, suffered from the same problem, including the recently completed T'aonan–Tsitsihar line, projected to lose some ¥27,000 during its first year of operation. According to SMR studies, the Ch'angch'un–Talai and Kirin–Hoeryong lines offered equally poor, if not worse, financial prospects in the short run. If Chang's pursuit of the Solun project at a time of fiscal crisis for the Three Eastern Provinces reflected irresponsibility, following the Foreign Ministry's advice would only compound his misbehavior.[14] Kimura's call to place first priority on outstanding railway proposals, as opposed to new projects, represented the same expedient that Debuchi had used in 1923 to discourage Matsuoka's plans for a T'aonan–Tsitsihar line. The central fiction in this critique, however, lay in his assertion that Chang alone had initiated the idea of a Solun line, which brazenly ignored the interest of the Imperial Japanese Army. Unable to launch a frontal attack on the position of their own colleagues in the military, diplomats appear to have selected Chang as the target in their efforts to obstruct the program of northern expansion.

The Solun issue highlights the fact that moderates and activists demanded, from the start, different, if not contradictory, behavior from the Manchurian warlord. Pleasing the activists meant alienating the moderates, and vice versa. Chang no doubt found this dilemma familiar. He had expressed his frustration in 1922, when ties remained in a formative phase: "Unfortunately, I am at present unable to figure out what Japanese policy is toward me. If it is that Chang should be helped, then help me. If it is that he should not be helped, then please let that meaning be made clear."[15] Five years later, the contradictions in Japanese policy had, if anything, deepened, and Chang could hardly be blamed for seeking to wash his hands of the Japanese altogether.

The eruption of a dispute over two independent Chinese railway initiatives further complicated the increasingly troubled relationship with Chang in the second half of 1926. In August, the PMR began construction of the Tahushan–T'ungliao line, a project planned since 1922 and officially announced in 1925. Since the undertaking entailed no foreign loans, the Chinese proceeded without consulting Japan, an act that elicited vigorous objections from Tokyo. In November, the government of Kirin and local investors, with Chang's support, initiated the building of a railway that would link the provincial capital to the Mukden–Hailung line; this represented the second phase of Wang Yung-chiang's 1923 plan to complete the long-anticipated rail corridor between Peking and Kirin. Again, since this venture involved no foreign borrowing, the Chinese began work without seeking Japanese permission. This, in turn, triggered another round of diplomatic protests authorized by Foreign Minister Shidehara. A major row over such construction initiatives would have been entirely predictable ten years earlier. In view of the recent trends in Japanese railway policy, however, the nature of the underlying conflict requires closer examination.

There is little question that the Japanese side had tacitly accepted the pursuit of both lines under Matsuoka's leadership. Although the agreement of August 1924 did not grant the Chinese explicit permission to build a railway from Kirin to Hailung, Matsuoka's formula of allowing the construction of "functional equivalents" of Japanese concession lines and the army's notion of "Chinese-style" railways clearly implied approval. Indeed, the draft resolution on the original Mukden–Hailung deal presented to the Katō cabinet in the summer of 1924 had taken into account the extension to Kirin and had minimized any negative ramifications.

Once the Mukden–Hailung line is completed, it is not difficult to anticipate the Peking–Mukden railway's acquiring a portion of its traffic. . . . However, in considering the larger picture: (1) the South Manchuria Railway Company's direct losses would be limited to a level posing no serious problem; and (2) even with the future extension of the Mukden–Hailung to Kirin and points north, there is no reason to fear a negative impact on our fundamental commitment to preserving the South Manchuria Railway as the [region's principal] transportation artery. Given these two points, we must acknowledge that a new understanding with the authorities of the Three Eastern Provinces as proposed here will create no cause for concern.[16]

The Chinese had certainly made no secret of their intentions to pursue a Tahushan–T'ungliao line. When the PMR had officially announced its plans a year earlier, Matsuoka had chosen not to raise objections, a silence readily understood as assent.

The economic "liberalism" of Matsuoka and his colleagues, however, rested on the premise of reciprocity, and Chang Tso-lin had clearly failed to hold up his end of the bargain. The Mukden authorities needed reminding of the two-way nature of cooperation. A threat to block both of these construction plans would serve this purpose quite effectively. Old treaty provisions prohibiting parallel construction, along with outstanding claims to the Kirin–Hailung route, provided solid legal grounds for obstruction and weakened any objections that moderates might raise. Matsuoka had advocated the suspension of such traditional rights in the name of cooperation but had not favored renouncing them entirely, a hedge that proved convenient under the present circumstances. Invoking these claims did not signal an abandonment of the strategies of the new imperialism and a reversion to the old ways by any means. Frustrating the construction of these two railways would certainly do nothing, in itself, to advance the goals of the activist camp. However, a hard-line posture would demonstrate Japan's readiness to use sticks as well as carrots in enforcing cooperation and make it clear that Chinese obstreperousness would be met in kind. Tokyo would withdraw its objections once Chang showed a readiness to work with the Japanese in good faith by complying, at minimum, with the 1924 agreement.[17]

Foreign Minister Shidehara's reasons for authorizing formal protests over both Chinese initiatives appear to have been less straightforward. He certainly had no objection in principle to the liberalization of railway policy, and as a pre-eminent champion of the new diplomacy, trotting out the secret protocols of the Treaty of Peking that prohibited parallel construction would seem entirely out of political character. Nor did he have any interest in facilitating the client-management strategy whether by means of carrots or sticks. Moreover, in Shidehara's China policy, which gave preponderant weight to the nation's commercial interests, regions south of the Wall were far more important to Japan than Manchuria. In 1926, for example, the Three Eastern Provinces took in less than 7 percent of Japan's vital cotton exports to China. Manchuria's overall place in Japan's foreign trade remained relatively small, accounting for no more than 7.5 percent of total Japanese exports and 7.7 percent of total imports (1928). At the same time, however, Chang's recent behavior, if left unchallenged, created problematic precedents. Irresponsible fiscal policies, unilateral tariff revisions, and disregard for treaty rights could not be tolerated anywhere in China without undermining the basic framework of foreign economic relations with that country. Tariff increases were open to discussion and old treaty rights might well warrant fundamental revision, but reforms had to be negotiated and carried out in an orderly manner. The result, otherwise, would be diplomatic chaos. In this context, the railway issue provided an expedient and lawful form of leverage to discipline Chang.[18]

A second consideration likely contributing to Shidehara's position at this time stemmed from domestic politics. Shidehara had taken office in 1924 in a three-party coalition government that included the Kenseikai, with which the foreign minister affiliated himself, as well as the Seiyūkai. A single-party Kenseikai government had assumed power in August 1925, forcing the Seiyūkai into opposition. Seeking to exploit mounting public concern about the Northern Expedition and the impact of turmoil in China on Japanese interests, the Seiyūkai began launching strident attacks on government policy in

China, criticizing, in particular, Shidehara's "soft" diplomacy. The end of 1926 and the beginning of 1927 witnessed an escalation in the opposition's campaign and a hardening of public opinion in favor of a get-tough policy, fueled by incidents in central China in which fighting between the northern and the southern armies had placed Japanese residents at risk.[19] Purportedly lenient attitudes toward Chang Tso-lin came under attack as well, a factor that, no doubt, encouraged Shidehara to adopt an uncharacteristically hardline posture in Manchuria.

A third consideration may well have been thinking similar to Kimura Eiichi's in dealing with the Solun railway problem. Protesting Chang's railway schemes offered a means to forestall the army's campaign in north Manchuria. A more cynical interpretation might suggest that Shidehara would have gladly allowed all further railway construction to bog down over this dispute if it precluded such dangerous plans as the Solun project. At the very least, withholding permission to build the Tahushan–T'ungliao and Kirin-Hailung lines until the Chinese side agreed to start building the relatively benign Ch'angch'un-Talai and to complete the long-awaited Kirin-Hoeryong would likely delay any new initiatives for some time. Shidehara and the army might agree on tactics, then, but with opposite outcomes in mind.

Shidehara as well as the advocates of imperialist cooperation saw these protests as bargaining chips that they would withdraw once Chang complied with Japanese demands. Encouraged by the emergence of this seemingly hard line, however, some Japanese officials began calling for a more basic reconsideration of the liberalizing trends of the past few years. Consul-General Yoshida, for example, unlike his immediate predecessor, had little sympathy for Matsuoka's policies. As we shall discuss subsequently, Yoshida represented an unreconstructed imperialism of the old school that emphasized concession-hunting, treaty rights, and gunboat diplomacy. He had little patience with what he considered pandering to Chang Tso-lin and had taken the lead in urging the foreign minister to stand firm on the issue of railway competition.[20] Significantly, a number of SMR officials had also come to favor a revision of liberal railway policies. By 1926, many company managers were openly expressing concern about the threat of competition and joined Yoshida in urging Shidehara to adopt a firm stand against parallel construction and in defense of traditional rights. This development in the SMR's orientation appears to have resulted not so much from the emergence of any new appreciation of Chinese plans but from Matsuoka

Yōsuke's resignation as a member of the Board of Directors in March 1926. Matsuoka had played an instrumental role in aligning the company with the army in support of the new imperialism. In the absence of his leadership, SMR officials seem to have reverted, by default, to a more narrow business orientation in which considerations of traffic acquisition and profitability dominated.

Matsuoka's decision to leave the company after five years of service did not stem from fundamental disillusionment with the policy course he had initiated during his tenure. He had accomplished a great deal from a nominally minor position in the decision-making hierarchy, but the limitations he faced as a second-tier company official, no doubt, proved frustrating. During his early years at the SMR, he had enjoyed considerable freedom of action and de facto authority while working under a relatively inactive president and a vacant vice presidency. However, the appointment of a new cabinet in the summer of 1924 had, along with installing Shidehara as foreign minister, brought in a new team of top managers, both of whom tended to sympathize with Shidehara's policies. Matsuoka managed to exert his influence throughout 1924 and 1925, but the climate within the company became increasingly inimical to his views.[21] As an aspiring statesman as well as a dedicated imperialist, Matsuoka appears to have concluded in early 1926 that the usefulness of an SMR directorship as a vehicle for both his cause and his career had come to an end. Although he left the company in March, he remained actively interested in territorial affairs and offered advice, both solicited and unsolicited.[22] Moreover, he would return to Manchuria after a relatively brief hiatus of eighteen months, when the Tanaka cabinet appointed him the SMR's new vice president.

An indication of a new orientation toward railway policy surfacing after Matsuoka's departure may be found in a study prepared by Takeuchi Toraji, a member of the SMR research staff, in 1926.[23] Takeuchi warned that the Chinese aimed to build an independent railway network in Manchuria capable of competing with the SMR and doing the company considerable damage. If they succeeded in their current plans, they would possess two trunk lines on either side of the SMR connected to the ice-free port of Hulutao.[24] He raised the alarm, in particular, about the Kirin–Hailung line and the completion of an independent connection between Mukden and Kirin. He criticized implicitly the shortsightedness of Matsuoka's policy in allowing the Chinese to build the Mukden–Hailung railway in the first place. In his view, Matsuoka and others who had supported the bargain in 1924 had seriously underestimated the threat of this line. True, the losses suffered in the short term from the Mukden–Hailung route alone might not be great, but that assessment stemmed from assumptions unlikely to hold true in the long run. There was no guarantee, he warned, that the larger portion of traffic from Hailung would be off-loaded at Mukden and transferred to the SMR for shipment to Dairen. On the contrary, Chinese shippers might well choose to transfer most of their goods at Mukden to the PMR for shipment to Yingk'ou. With the construction of Hulutao, such routing would become increasingly attractive. As a consequence, most of the traffic in soy and other goods from the productive Hailung region, which accounted for a major part of the business enjoyed by K'aiyüan, the second most prosperous of the company's stations, might bypass the SMR entirely.[25] The problem could only become worse with the connection of the Mukden–Hailung to Kirin. Not only would such a line compete for traffic currently reaching the northern segment of the SMR, but it might well suborn the Ch'angch'un–Kirin and Kirin–Tunhua railways into becoming its own feeders.

Takeuchi outlined a somewhat extreme position in his study, particularly in his criticism of the Mukden–Hailung project, an issue that represented water under the bridge by 1926. Not all of his colleagues shared his anxieties, at least to the same degree, and one of them would chide Takeuchi for his alarmism in a follow-up report on the Mukden–Hailung.[26] Indeed, somewhat unusual in reports of this type, the preface disavowed any official endorsement of the contents and noted that "the opinions contained in this study are those of the author Takeuchi Toraji and not necessarily those of the company."[27]

The SMR's concerns do not appear to have had a major bearing on Shidehara's diplomacy at this juncture, other than offering a convenient pretext for protest. Had the Foreign Ministry taken Takeuchi's warnings to heart, it would not have considered withdrawing its complaints in exchange for Chang's compliance on other matters. It is important to bear in mind that although company officials might voice vigorous objections to the Tahushan–T'ungliao and the Kirin–Hailung lines as competitive threats, they had also projected equally dire scenarios involving the Japanese-sponsored Kirin–Hoeryong railway. If Chang Tso-lin's railway-building program threatened the SMR's interests, so, too, did long-standing plans endorsed by the Japanese Foreign Ministry. Tokyo was clearly not prepared to accept *raison d'affaires* as an inflexible element of policy.[28]

The SMR's position notwithstanding, Japanese leaders initiated their protests to Chang Tso-lin with the aim of facilitating negotiations on other issues, not with the intention of engaging in a major dispute over railway competition as such. They miscalculated rather seriously, however, if they had expected Chang to respond favorably to pressure tactics of this kind. In reacting to the Tahushan protest, the Chinese leader replied curtly, and rather brazenly in the face of physical evidence, that no immediate plans for construction existed and that if an effort were made in the future, it would not, in any event, be a matter for Japan's concern. He reminded the Japanese that they had long pressed him to undertake more aggressive efforts to develop his territory and that they should be pleased if he chose to build more railways.[29] Chang's willingness to defy Tokyo's protests and pursue these projects reflected, in part, his cooling attitude at this juncture. If Japan would not aid him in his fight in the south, then it had nothing to offer him of real value at this point. The danger of appearing a Japanese client, moreover, offset any fear of harder pressures. Nationalist sentiment in Manchuria continued to grow, foreshadowed by the educational rights recovery movement of 1924. Popular response in Manchuria to the May 30 incident in 1925 proved sufficiently strong to disrupt railway discussions that year.[30] Chang's campaign in the south and his role in leading the warlord coalition also increased incentives for him to minimize his identification with Japan, particularly since his enemies portrayed him as a Japanese puppet. Chang Tso-lin, then, seemed to have little to lose and something to gain by defiance. As a result, the shift in Japanese tactics from carrots to sticks only contributed to the further deterioration of the relationship. Chang's intransigence, moreover, became an issue in its own right, since it was seen as an injury to the empire's prestige and a matter demanding redress.

Relations reached a new low in May 1927, with the outbreak of an incident in the Korean border region of eastern Manchuria. For some time, the Japanese had demanded the right to establish a subconsulate at Maoerhshan on the Chinese side of the Yalu River, a district, like Chientao, heavily settled by ethnic Koreans. The Chinese authorities had steadfastly refused permission. In line with the trend toward a get-tough policy, the Japanese resolved to press the issue by unilaterally selecting a site and dispatching a consular appointee and his staff to set up an office in the district. Unexpectedly, an angry group of local residents, apparently supported by Chinese police, greeted Japanese officials and forced them to retreat. Adding insult to injury, local protesters burned the designated site of the subconsulate. The Japanese Foreign Ministry demanded an apology and permission to go ahead with the establishment of an office. Neither was forthcoming.[31] Preoccupied with his "southern expedition" against the Nationalist-Communist alliance, Chang gave the "Japanese problem" in Manchuria a lower priority. To many Japanese officials, this incident represented the last straw. The humiliation required a swift and appropriate response. Indeed, for a growing number of leaders, moderate and activist alike, the time had also come not only to re-evaluate the desirability of a continued relationship with Chang Tso-lin but to rethink Japanese policy in Manchuria at a fundamental level.

The Second Eastern Conference and Critiques of Manchuria Policy

In April 1927, the task of managing the impending crisis with Chang passed from the Kenseikai government and Foreign Minister Shidehara to a new government formed by the Seiyūkai and headed by General Tanaka Giichi. This change of administration resulted, in part, from the Seiyūkai's success in attacking the sitting cabinet on China policy, blaming the "soft and weak" diplomacy of Shidehara for Japanese setbacks and humiliations, and promising instead a new, "positive policy." As one of its first acts, the Tanaka cabinet initiated an armed intervention in Shantung for the ostensible purpose of protecting Japanese subjects and their property from the spreading civil war and seemed well on its way to fulfilling its promises. Although the Seiyūkai presented an unmistakably militant posture more assertive of Japanese interests both north and south of the Wall than that of the previous government, its so-called positive policy was long on nationalistic posturing but short on real content and did not offer a coherent, overall program. Despite its self-styled label, it remained largely negative in orientation and attacked Shidehara's purported shortcomings without offering alternative solutions. What new directions the government would take appeared rather unclear in its first few months. Given the past practice of parties in opposition moderating their hard-line postures on achieving power, it remained far from certain that Tanaka would continue on a relentless course of showing the flag in China.[32]

General Tanaka, who chose to serve as his own foreign minister, was a veteran imperialist well aware of the complexity of the problems he confronted in both Manchuria and China south of the Wall. Circumstances demanded a systematic approach. He also recognized the need to build some degree of consensus among the contending groups within Japan, although given the growing polarization among leadership circles since the middle of the 1920s, to which his own fire-breathing rhetoric had contributed, the possibilities seemed bleak. In an attempt to lay the groundwork for a broad policy initiative, he called for a meeting of the heads of all agencies concerned with China policy in June. Consciously modeling this convocation after Hara's efforts in 1921, he described it as an "Eastern Conference" in the hopes of producing a similar overarching policy framework through debate and compromise. As a preliminary step, he called for an airing of views on China and Manchuria and actively solicited opinions, an invitation apparently accepted with enthusiasm as evidenced by the plethora of position papers generated. Three opinions calling for reform in Manchuria, representing the major lines critical of the status quo and reflecting the mounting frustration with Chang Tso-lin, warrant special consideration.[33]

Major General Saitō Hisashi, the Kwantung Army chief of staff, whose views on Chang and the CER we encountered in Chapter 7, offered the most straightforward and concrete proposal for reform. Saitō criticized past Japanese policy toward Chang in Manchuria for its excessive equivocation. The reluctance to make full use of the client relationship had led to missed opportunities. He reiterated his argument that Japan should induce Chang to seize the CER and thus settle the northern problem once and for all. At the same time, mixed signals from Tokyo and the lack of a resolute stand encouraged Chang to misbehave. All recent problems in Manchuria stemmed from the Japanese government's failure to lay down clearly what it expected from the warlord. In order to rectify this error, he recommended four measures to introduce a more formal structure to the relationship.

1. A position of chief administrator of the Three Eastern Provinces shall be established, and that administrator will declare the region autonomous.

2. A new agreement concerning the management of existing railways and the construction of new lines shall be concluded.

3. Land development, mining, and stock raising, along with commerce and industry, shall be promoted through the principle of Sino-Japanese coexistence and coprosperity.

4. Japanese advisors shall be appointed as required for the purpose of reorganizing the administration of the Three Eastern Provinces, and in particular, its finances.

Japanese advisors shall be placed in the central administration [of the Three Eastern Provinces] as well as in each province as required for the purposes of military reform.

The garrison chief of staff asserted that Japan should tolerate no further nonsense from regional authorities. "Chang must accept the above demands. If he should refuse, a suitable candidate approved by the empire must be selected and installed as the chief administrator of the Three Eastern Provinces." Invoking the spirit of *daikanshō*, Saitō added, "We must resolve to drive out those who resist the implementation of our policies in Manchuria, and if necessary, we must be prepared to use armed force."[34] The general called, in effect, for an arrangement that fell little short of a protectorate in Manchuria. Although the idea represented a radical escalation of Japan's imperial encroachments in the territory, it must also be understood as an extension of the policies formulated by Matsuoka and the army during the middle of the decade.

Kimura Eiichi, who continued in his post as chief of the Asia Bureau and who, with Shidehara's departure, served as senior spokesman for the new diplomacy at this conference, launched a second line of criticism. Kimura's views also represented an extension of an earlier position and took to a logical conclusion the approach he had adopted in 1926 during the Solun affair. Chang Tso-lin, in his view, rather than providing solutions to Japan's problems in Manchuria, was their principal source. The true threat of disorder in the territory came, not from the Nationalists, the Communists, or Soviet agents, but from Chang himself, who, through misrule of the lands under his control both north and south of the Wall, had managed to make himself the most unpopular military dictator in all of China. Shifting the blame once again, the Asia Bureau chief pointed out that Chang had maneuvered Japan into rescuing him from his enemies. Indeed, the warlord had managed to drag the Japanese, against their interests, into his own fights with the Russians and the Nationalists. Kimura reiterated in no uncertain terms that the responsibility for the recent deterioration of relations with the Soviet Union lay entirely with Chang, pointedly ignoring the contributions of the Imperial Japanese Army to this state of affairs. In his view, the best course of action for Japan lay in breaking relations with Chang entirely and letting him twist in the wind. The withdrawal of Japanese support would inevitably result in his overthrow, whether through revolt from within his own regime or defeat at the hands of the Nationalists. Either way, his removal from the scene constituted a development that Japan ought to welcome.

Going beyond a call to abandon Chang Tso-lin, Kimura also favored an end to the two-China framework established at the first Eastern Conference, which had allowed for the coexistence of a new imperialism north of the Wall and a new diplomacy in the south. He presented a number of scenarios as to what the situation in Manchuria might look like after Chang's political demise, but whatever the outcome, he believed that Japan should no longer afford the regional government of the Three Eastern Provinces special treatment. Urging reconciliation between any post-Chang Manchurian regime and the Nationalists would best serve Japanese interests.[35]

Yoshida Shigeru, the irascible consul-general in Mukden, presented a third line of criticism. Yoshida, like Kimura, called for the wholesale revision of the policy framework in which cooperation with Chang had occupied a central place, but his attack came from a decidedly imperialist direction. In his thinking, recent efforts at client management in Manchuria constituted no more than petty attempts at pandering to Chang in the hopes of winning favors, a line of action unworthy of a great imperial power. Japan should stand on its treaty rights in the territory and not trouble itself about the goodwill of the local authorities. Japan required of Chang Tso-lin nothing more nor less than his respect for the legitimate claims and power of the empire. As far as Yoshida was concerned, official protests over railway competition in the second half of 1926 represented steps in the right direction, but he believed that Japan should not waver in its opposition to these "unlawful" railways and should not offer any bargains. From the beginning, he had pressed for following up verbal protests with hard, material sanctions. He proposed that the SMR deny Chang military transportation services, refuse to carry materials bound for construction of the Kirin–Hailung railway, and prohibit PMR trains from crossing the Railway Zone at Mukden, a measure that would prevent them from reaching their home terminus at Shenyang Station to the east of the Japanese railway line. He also recommended the armed occupation of the Mukden Arsenal, a facility vital to Chang's war effort.[36]

Although pandering to Chang represented the most serious failing in recent years, Japan had gone astray in other respects, too, according to

Yoshida. Implicitly criticizing the notion of "developing Manchuria for Manchuria's sake," he argued that the policy of economic cooperation had promoted Chinese interests without generating reciprocal benefits for Japan. In his view, railway building in north Manchuria and Inner Mongolia offered great opportunities for the Chinese, who could settle and farm the prairies, but Japan's principal advantage lay in the development of better communications links with Korea. In addition, overshadowed by railway expansion, the issue of land rights had been set aside for too long. Japan had not repudiated these rights in Washington, and they remained at the heart of Japanese interests in the territory.[37]

Yoshida's colleague and the consul-general in Harbin, Amau Eiji (1887–1968), generally supported these views. Amau believed that the root of all Japan's troubles lay in relying on Chang Tso-lin and pursuing an illusory policy of cooperation. Japan's treaty rights, including those pertaining to land, formed the foundations of its position in Manchuria, not its relationship with the local ruler. He also disagreed with the entire program of northern railway expansion. Reflecting a traditional view of imperialist spheres, he argued that the SMR and CER had common interests in defending themselves against Chinese challenges and that the Japanese side had allied itself with the wrong party. Encouraging Chang to build railways into the north would only cause difficulties for Japan, a problem already evidenced by the Tahushan–T'ungliao and Kirin–Hailung initiatives.[38]

Both Yoshida and Amau, whose perspectives were shared in more militant form by Mori Kaku, Seiyūkai leader and parliamentary vice minister for foreign affairs, clearly represented an older strain of expansionist thinking in Japan. That such ideas should endure, given their deep roots in the Japanese national experience, is not entirely surprising. They found little opportunity for active expression during the years following World War I, and indeed, according to the very precepts of power politics inherent in this orientation, the realities of the postwar Anglo-American hegemony demanded that Japanese empire-building efforts assume a low profile. By the late 1920s, however, the international environment had begun moving in a direction favoring the old ways. Multilateralism seemed to be breaking down in the face of revolutionary nationalism, and the Washington order to be falling into disarray. The British, indeed, had recently invited the Japanese to join them in a display of gunboats on the Yangtze.[39] Under these circumstances, a bold assertion of "imperialist right" arguably offered the sole source of stability for the

Japanese position anywhere in China, and showing the flag, the only meaningful way to protect the empire's entitlements.

The influence of this line of thinking remained limited at this time. Its
antipathy toward northern railway policy placed it at odds with the army's
goals and could thus expect little support from that all-important quarter.
At the same time, it represented more than an isolated view. Their official
functions as consuls-general bore more than an incidental relationship to the
positions that Yoshida and Amau took. Their concern with defending treaty
rights reflected their responsibility to look after the interests of Japanese
residents and business enterprise in the territory. As noted above, the settler
community had suffered growing distress since the middle of the decade,
and with the escalation of economic nationalism in Manchuria, even those
institutions at the top of the economic food chain, like Mitsui Bussan, faced
difficulty. Kodama Hideo (1876–1947), chief administrator of Kwantung,
observed that the Japanese resident community in Manchuria looked toward
the Tanaka government for more active political support.[40] We might consider those officials of the SMR who were critical of Matsuoka's policies and
anxious about Chinese railway building supporters of this position as well.

Trends in public opinion, promoted in large part by the Seiyūkai's "positive policy" campaign, which continued under Mori's leadership in preparation for the 1928 elections, further encouraged the revival of old-fashioned
imperialism.[41] Although the positive policy offered little in the way of a coherent program in itself, it played on popular notions about empire by emphasizing trade, business opportunity, and, above all, land and *Lebensraum*.
Repeated efforts by the SMR to offer more realistic assessments of opportunities for settlement, as represented by the pamphlet "What Should We
Expect from Manchuria," testify to the difficulty of transforming traditional
ways of thinking. Matsuoka, too, made an attempt at educating the public
about the new imperialism in his 1926 essay "Manchuria in Motion," yet readers not thoroughly immersed in the problems of imperial strategy likely found
that discordant mixture of expansionist ideas and quasi-liberal economic
views rather difficult to grasp. The Seiyūkai's appeals to the more tangible
values of the old imperialism and its invocation of the image of Japanese rights
trampled under foot, in contrast, proved far more accessible.[42]

Yoshida, Kimura, and Saitō separately articulated positions that clearly
revealed the depth of frustration among leadership circles with existing policy in Manchuria. Yoshida and Kimura shared a common antipathy toward

Chang Tso-lin, and Saitō's opinion implied a very limited patience with the warlord's recent behavior. At the same time, critics of the status quo proceeded from radically different assumptions and advocated reforms that would move policy in incompatible directions. Yoshida and Saitō might agree on the need for severe, material sanctions against Chang as a means of rectifying his behavior, but the responses they sought were contradictory. The possibility of forging any meaningful consensus encompassing the demands of the Kwantung Army for more resolute client management, the militant version of the new diplomacy represented by Kimura, and the revived traditional imperialism of Yoshida appeared slim at best.

Calls for radical reform at this conference, to be sure, failed to drown out entirely voices favoring staying the course with Chang. General Honjō Shigeru (1876–1945), military attaché in Peking and a former advisor to the Mukden regime, believed any attempt to abandon Chang and the policy of cooperation seriously mistaken. Significantly, Yoshizawa Kenkichi, minister to Peking, offered a particularly strong case for rendering continued support to Chang. Proceeding from the perspective of a moderate diplomat who emphasized the importance of stability in Manchuria, Yoshizawa, in effect, affirmed some of the basic assessments articulated by Ugaki and Matsuoka in 1925. Chang Tso-lin remained the one regional leader capable of holding the Three Eastern Provinces together as a political unit. His rule in Manchuria resulted from a long history of base building, and no successor could be expected to maintain the same degree of control. No civilian candidate could manage the regional military elite, and no one military leader enjoyed sufficient support among his colleagues to emerge supreme. Manchuria without Chang would likely splinter into rival factions. Whatever his faults, the current officeholder offered the best prospects for maintaining some semblance of stability and order in the region, and Yoshizawa regarded casual talk of replacing him or tolerating his removal irresponsible.[43]

Tanaka's Attempt to Restore the Partnership

No doubt, the airing of views at the Eastern Conference proved useful to Tanaka by illuminating the sea of contending opinion on China policy he would have to navigate. Some historians have suggested that Tanaka, easily influenced by those around him, lacked firm commitments of his own and that the conflicting perspectives expressed at this meeting contributed to an essentially incoherent policy during his tenure.[44] However, the fickle qualities of his leadership have, perhaps, been overstated. Admittedly, the morass of political maneuvers and compromises in which the prime minister embroiled himself obscure what he sought to accomplish during his first year of tenure. Tanaka could not simply set aside the wishes of his political constituents, his advisors, and the powerful professional bureaucracies involved in the making of foreign policy. Nonetheless, he appears to have brought a well-defined agenda to office. If we consider his history, the positions he adopted at the Eastern Conference, and the actions he authorized during the months that followed, a clearer picture of his strategy and programmatic aims emerges.

As a dyed-in-the-wool expansionist, Tanaka had dedicated his professional life to the cause of empire and national defense. By the middle of the 1920s, however, the image of the uncompromising imperial extremist that his reputation and his own attacks on Shidehara would seem to suggest had come to depart significantly from the reality. He had long since shed the adventurist leanings of his early years and had exercised a restraining influence on his colleagues as army minister under the Hara government. Tanaka had thrown his political weight behind cooperation with Chang Tso-lin at the time, and the dual policy of the first Eastern Conference was, at least in part, his handiwork. During his last few years as an active duty officer before retiring and joining the Seiyūkai in 1925, he had emerged as the army's gray eminence and was responsible in large measure for steering that institution along a comparatively moderate course. He had backed Army Ministers Yamanashi Hanzō (1864–1944) and Ugaki in their respective efforts at arms reduction, a position that did not sit well with some of his colleagues.[45] Given this background, it is reasonable to surmise that his sympathies lay with the "new imperialism" of Ugaki and Matsuoka, at least through the mid-1920s.

Indications that this orientation persisted, despite his hard-line rhetoric as president of the Seiyūkai, appeared during the early months of his government. For example, anticipating a new "positive" policy in Manchuria with the change of cabinet in April 1927, Yoshida Shigeru immediately proposed a series of tough sanctions against Chang that would strike at his material interests. Belying expectations, however, Tanaka made it clear that protests over railway construction would remain verbal at this point.[46]

Tanaka's request for advice from both Yoshizawa and Yoshida regarding Japan's policies toward Chang Tso-lin in June, shortly before the opening of the conference, offer a more important measure of his thinking. At this juncture, Tanaka saw the virtual inevitability of a Nationalist victory throughout China south of the Wall, despite Chiang Kai-shek's (1888–1975) bloody anti-communist coup in April and continuing conflicts within the Kuomintang coalition. He believed that the Nationalists, at least on the surface, appeared to represent the "popular will" and the aspirations of the "vast majority" of the Chinese people. He argued that any lingering communist influence within the Nationalist camp would not deter the powers from granting at least tacit recognition to Kuomintang rule over territory under their control. After offering this observation, which implied that Japan, too, would have little choice but to go along, he noted: "The fate of Chang Tso-lin, given the circumstances above, will have a profound impact on the political situation in the Three Eastern Provinces, and given our intimate interest in the Manchurian problem, it is vital that we determine an attitude and a policy toward the relationship between the southern regime and the Fengt'ien Clique." He then proceeded to outline three possible scenarios and asked the diplomats for their opinions as to how Japan ought to respond.[47]

In the first scenario, Chang would suffer complete defeat in fighting south of the Wall, his career ending in death or exile. He asked whether any successor might emerge from within his regime with "a relatively modern outlook, open to coming to terms with the southerners, and capable of wielding both civil and military authority" in Manchuria. By "coming to terms," Tanaka meant a peace settlement conceding North China to the Nationalists while preserving the autonomy of the Three Eastern Provinces. In the second scenario, Chang, realizing the difficulties of his circumstances, would retreat to Manchuria with his army intact and organize a defense of the territory to block a Nationalist invasion, most likely at Shanhaikuan. He observed that this situation would create circumstances similar to those produced by the two wars fought against the Chihli Clique in 1922 and 1924 in which Japan had intervened on Chang's behalf. Alternatively, even without an open military confrontation at Shanhaikuan, he suggested that the Nationalists might engage in a campaign of assassination and subversion against the Chang regime and deliberately foment disorder in the territory. What would be an appropriate Japanese response? he asked. In the third scenario, Chang would decide to resist for a time in the Peking-T'ientsin region but, facing defeat, would return to his home base badly weakened. What should Japan do if the Nationalist army pursued him north of the Wall, spreading civil war to the area? What should Japan do if Chang's weakened position led to rebellion within the Fengt'ien Clique, as had happened in 1925 with Kuo Sung-ling?[48]

In soliciting their opinions, Tanaka urged the diplomats to offer frank advice without hesitation, yet it is difficult to escape the impression that the prime minister was asking questions to which he had already crafted his own answers and merely sought confirmation of his own views. In describing the first scenario, he expressed his skepticism about the likelihood of a viable successor to Chang and noted that the emergence of a suitable candidate would be rather "unexpected." His listing of the necessary credentials, indeed, virtually ruled out the possibility from the outset. "Modern thinkers" like Wang Yung-chiang, and military leaders open to a peace settlement with the Nationalists, like Chang's lieutenant, Yang Yu-t'ing (1885–1929), certainly existed within the Fengt'ien Clique. None, however, possessed those qualities as well as the ability to wield both civil and military powers in the territory. Neither modern thinking nor openness to a peace settlement characterized Chang Tso-lin, but the old warlord had, at least, managed to maintain law and order in the Three Eastern Provinces. As for the second scenario, Tanaka's reference to the precedents set by the two wars against Chihli and the fact that Japan had so recently intervened in Shantung to protect Japanese subjects against the spread of civil war almost precluded any answer other than an affirmation of Japan's obligation to assist Chang in a defensive fight at Shanhaikuan. The only acceptable response to the question about a Nationalist assassination or subversion campaign, of course, was that Japan could not tolerate such activity. A similar answer applied to the third scenario as well. Yoshizawa responded with the "correct" answers: no, Chang could not be easily replaced, and yes, Japan must prevent the spread of disorder north of the wall, whether by open invasion or subversion.[49] Yoshida, characteristically undeterred by the orientation of this inquiry, rejected Tanaka's basic premise that the future of Chang had great bearing on Japanese interests. He responded, "I hope that the imperial government will neither rely on Chang nor look to Wu, but stand on our superior and independent position and have confidence in the strength of our own people in their efforts to develop our position in Manchuria."[50]

That Tanaka had committed himself to restoring a cooperative relationship with Chang Tso-lin and to supporting his rule in Manchuria became quite clear by the end of the Eastern Conference. In a broad policy statement purportedly incorporating the advice offered at this meeting, he articulated three broad points regarding Manchuria.

> Given that Manchuria (*Manmō*) ... has a profound bearing on our national defense interests and in providing for the livelihood of our people, it warrants special consideration. We cannot but shoulder our responsibilities as neighbors to preserve order and promote development in this region as a place where both local people and foreigners (*naigaijin*) may live in peace. Moreover, with the aim of accelerating the peaceful development of this territory, we must encourage the economic activities of local people and foreigners alike in the spirit of the Open Door and equal opportunity. Our efforts to protect our rights and resolve outstanding issues must be pursued within this framework as well.
>
> It would be the best of all policies if the people of the Three Eastern Provinces were to stabilize the political situation in the territory through their own efforts. The empire should be prepared to render appropriate assistance to [any] powerholder in the Three Eastern Provinces who is willing to respect our special position and who sincerely works toward establishing political stability.
>
> Should the waves of chaos spread to Manchuria and cause disorder, should we have reason to fear that our special position and our rights are in jeopardy, we must be ready to defend ourselves, regardless of the source of the threat. We must not shrink from the obligation to preserve the status of this land as one where local people and foreigners alike may develop and live in peace.[51]

Tanaka's characterization of Manchuria as a territory with special bearing on Japan's defense and national livelihood reaffirmed the basic formulation of the first Eastern Conference and represented, for all intents and purposes, a code phrase for a two-China policy. As for a commitment to the principles of "the Open Door and equal opportunity," its inclusion might be taken at face value had the author of this paper been Shidehara. At the same time, Tanaka's endorsement of the idea was by no means insincere, given the affinities between the Open Door and the economic quasi-liberalism associated with imperialist cooperation of the Matsuoka strain. Japan's long-term interest lay in the overall development of the territory, and the question of the ownership of investment capital remained a secondary concern. It also reflected the view that Japan's power in Manchuria rested not on proprietary control of territorial resources and facilities but on the political and military relationships outlined in the second and third paragraphs. Indeed, the admonition that the Open Door constrained the defense of traditional rights implicitly warned advocates of the Yoshida line not to expect aggressive concession hunting of the old type. The reference to maintaining law and order in both the first and third paragraphs constituted an unmistakable assertion of the policy of *daikanshō*, as a brief explanatory note on this point appended to the document made clear: Japan would intervene, without hesitation, in the case of internal rebellion, a Soviet incursion, or a Nationalist military thrust north of the Wall.[52]

The second paragraph regarding support for a regional "powerholder" contained some ambiguity, and Tanaka himself appears to have felt the need for clarification, because he appended a lengthy note:

This clause addresses the issue of respecting the so-called public will. In other words, we must encourage and promote the success of efforts on the part of any ruler of the Three Eastern Provinces who, sharing our own views, is prepared to promote economic development, preserve law and order, maintain political stability, and uphold the principles of the Open Door and equal opportunity, whoever he might be. Although this clause has not been inserted for the purpose of supporting Chang Tso-lin, should Chang return to the Three Eastern Provinces and carry out a policy of *pao ching an min* (secure the borders and pacify the people), he must, of course, be supported. Naturally, if another should come to rule the Three Eastern Provinces and pursue policies consistent with our position, we must also be prepared to give him support. This clause is meant, then, neither as support for Chang Tso-lin nor as a call to depose him. We must adopt an autonomous position in determining our course of action.[53]

Tanaka hedged his support for Chang, but given the political atmosphere of the conference, his position represented an unmistakable endorsement of continued efforts to work with the current powerholder.

The policy direction that the prime minister defined at the end of the conference disappointed many in both the moderate and the activist camps, particularly those who sought an end to the relationship with Chang, one way or another. In an effort to mollify opposition, Tanaka agreed to consider the use of hard sanctions of the sort Yoshida and, for reasons of its own, the Kwantung Army had favored should the warlord persist in his intransigence.[54] He also included a number of modest programmatic proposals in his policy statement with the aim of appeasing some of his critics. As a gesture to Foreign Ministry officials worried about the army's anti-Soviet railway schemes in north Manchuria, he gave first priority in Japan's construction agenda to outstanding projects such as the Kirin–Hoeryong and the Ch'angch'un–Talai, rather than the problematic Solun line.[55]

To the traditional imperialists, represented by Yoshida, Tanaka offered some measures in the arena of land rights. The prime minister believed it inappropriate at this time to attempt a full-scale push for the fulfillment of the 1915 accords; he recommended, instead, a limited, "experimental" initiative that would pave the way for a more active policy in the future. He would authorize negotiations with the Chinese for a modest expansion of the perimeters of existing treaty ports, together with the establishment of new ones along recently completed and projected railway lines. Such steps would substantially increase opportunities for a direct Japanese presence in these areas. In exchange, the Japanese side would modify its claims to extraterritoriality in any new and expanded concession. "The experiment conducted through these new treaty ports will persuade Chinese officials that there is no great danger in allowing Japanese the right to lease land," noted Tanaka. "On the contrary, it will be of advantage to the Chinese side. This will facilitate the conclusion of a treaty in the future granting the right to lease land throughout all of Manchuria."[56]

The incorporation into this policy statement of measures aimed at appeasing his opponents no doubt contributed to the perception of the prime minister as a man easily swayed by the opinions of others. Yet the evidence suggests that these steps represented nothing more than gestures that did little to compromise his commitment to a policy of imperialist cooperation in Manchuria. Although he conceded railway-construction priorities to the Foreign Ministry, for example, he made it clear that he intended to pursue the Solun line at the earliest opportunity, rather than relegating it to an indefinite future as Kimura and his colleagues would have preferred.[57] Tanaka's agreement to carry out an experimental land-rights project likewise constituted a token measure, one bearing a remarkable similarity to Abe Moritarō's proposal of 1913. Indeed, in offering to modify claims to extraterritoriality, he appears to have deliberately designed the initiative to allay Chinese concerns about Japanese colonization schemes, an approach more consistent with the views of a new imperialist than those of an advocate of traditional strategies. Tanaka made no concessions to Yoshida and the traditionalists on the issue of railway competition. Affirming the negotiability of the two disputed lines as well as Matsuoka's approach to bargaining, he instructed that protests on the Kirin–Hailung line be withdrawn if the Chinese side consented to Japan's construction agenda. Tanaka subsequently

ordered Japanese negotiators to rescind protests over the Tahushan–
T'ungliao line as well, upon the successful conclusion of a broader railway
agreement.[58]

As for the use of hard sanctions against a recalcitrant Chang Tso-lin, the
prime minister made it clear that he intended to employ such methods as a
last resort. Significantly, Consul-General Yoshida chose to interpret this
conditional approval of sanctions as a call to action and began making preparations, in conjunction with the Kwantung Army, to carry them out. Tanaka put a halt to this activity and indicated that Yoshida did not have
authorization to go beyond making threats at this stage. As a result, Yoshida
and Mori, along with some of the more impatient officers in the Kwantung
Army, grew increasingly disenchanted with the imperialist soldier-statesman
who had come to office promising a positive policy.[59]

Over the next nine months, in fact, Tanaka would demonstrate a rather
remarkable patience toward Chang and continue to resist increasingly strident calls for action from Yoshida, Mori, and the Kwantung Army. Chang,
for his part, showed no inclination toward a rapprochement with the Japanese. Quite the contrary, in response to the hard-line posturing emanating
from Tokyo at the time of the Eastern Conference, he dug in his heels and
adopted an increasingly antagonistic stance, tolerating, if not actually promoting, openly anti-Japanese activities in Manchuria. Holding court in Peking on what appeared to be a permanent basis, Chang also made it clear
that he had no intention of retreating north of the Wall.[60]

Withholding permission for hard sanctions against Chang cost Tanaka
considerable political capital, but he had good reasons for a policy of inaction. As the analysis laid out in his June discussions with Yoshizawa and
Yoshida implied, the prime minister believed that Chang's days as a power
in north China were numbered. The Fengti'en Army and what remained of
the warlord coalition had already come close to defeat at the hands of the
Northern Expedition in the spring. Chang had won respite only as a result
of trouble within the Nationalist coalition that had stalled the offensive, and
despite his recent defiance and anti-Japanese bravado, he lived on borrowed
time. Sooner or later the full thrust of the Nationalist campaign would resume. When Chang finally came to appreciate his peril, he would begin to
change his attitude and withdraw north of the Wall with his forces intact. If
not, the Nationalists would force him to retreat, with only Japan to prevent
his annihilation. Given this understanding, Chang Tso-lin would finally be-

gin to behave as befit a regional client ruler and concentrate on the development and pacification of his territory in cooperation with the Japanese. In addition, the Kuomintang would more than likely allow Chang to retain control in Manchuria if he abandoned his aspirations south of the Wall. Tanaka seemed fairly confident that once that the Nationalists subjugated North China, they would not risk confrontation with Japan in a direct military push into Manchuria. In short, this scenario would lead to a resolution of all past difficulties with Chang Tso-lin and simultaneously set the stage for a long-term accommodation with the Nationalists as well. With such prospects on the horizon, the political costs of playing a waiting game must have seemed worthwhile.[61]

Although the thrust of his policy entailed waiting, Tanaka did not remain entirely passive in the months following the Eastern Conference. Using both official and unofficial channels, he probed for an opportunity to open talks with Chang that would, if nothing else, serve to mitigate criticism of his policy. One approach entailed informal diplomacy through the SMR. In keeping with what had become established practice with each change of cabinet, the Seiyūkai government chose to replace the top officers of the company. Tanaka appointed veteran imperialist Matsuoka Yōsuke as vice president, a choice reflecting his policy orientation, but for the chief executive's job, he selected Seiyūkai secretary Yamamoto Jōtarō (1886–1935), a trusted personal ally in the rough-and-tumble of party politics. He asked the company president to begin testing Chang Tso-lin's receptiveness to reopening railway negotiations. With little experience in diplomacy or Manchurian affairs, however, Yamamoto apparently exceeded his instructions and attempted to conclude a series of formal accords. Following face-to-face talks with the warlord in October, the company president believed he had won not only Chang's consent to build five new railways but also a sweeping agreement for bilateral economic cooperation, along with a mutual defense pact placing the Three Eastern Provinces under virtual Japanese protection. Not surprisingly, it turned out that Chang had agreed to none of these measures, as Yoshizawa Kenkichi, minister to Peking, quickly discovered in follow-up talks. Yamamoto's well-intentioned amateur diplomacy failed to yield any positive results and actually hurt Tanaka's efforts to mitigate frustration with Chang among his colleagues by raising expectations and dashing them almost immediately. It also damaged Tanaka's standing with a Foreign Ministry angered by his resort to private channels of negotiation.[62]

Tanaka agreed to leave further efforts to initiate railway talks with Chang to Yoshizawa, but the diplomat enjoyed no better success than Yamamoto through the beginning of 1928. Chang, preoccupied with concerns other than his "Japanese problem," seemed to harden his stance. In early 1928, Tanaka gave into pressure to impose some measured sanctions against Chang and restricted the movement of PMR trains across the SMR Railway Zone, but the action appeared to have little effect.[63]

Although these efforts to persuade Chang to negotiate proved unproductive, Tanaka did find reason for encouragement in exchanges with the Nationalists at the end of 1927 and the beginning of 1928. In talks with Chiang Kai-shek in November and follow-up discussions with one of his aides in January 1928, Tanaka arrived at a tacit understanding that the Nationalists would not attempt a military push into Manchuria if Japan would agree not to obstruct their efforts to establish control over the Peking area. An optimistic reading of this understanding on Tanaka's part suggested that the Nationalists had agreed to conditions that would make his scheme for maintaining Chang as a Japanese client in Manchuria possible.[64] Such an interpretation undoubtedly allowed the prime minister to maintain a course of patient restraint during the first part of 1928 and wait for military developments in China south of the Wall to run their course.

When the Northern Expedition resumed in full force in the spring and Nationalist troops once again pushed into Shantung, however, Tanaka's program nearly unraveled. The prime minister dispatched a second expeditionary force to the province with the aim of protecting Japanese subjects from the fighting at the end of April, but on May 3, Chinese and Japanese troops engaged in a major clash at Tsinan. Intermittent fighting lasted until May 11. The Tsinan incident resulted in a serious deterioration of relations between Tokyo and the Kuomintang, although senior leaders on both sides actively sought to avoid further escalation. Hoping, nonetheless, that his earlier understanding with Chiang might still hold, Tanaka proceeded to issue a warning on May 16 to both the Nationalists and to Chang Tso-lin that Japan would not tolerate an extension of the fighting north of the Wall. The Kwantung Army would disarm combatant forces of either side crossing the line at Shanhaikuan. Fortunately for Tanaka, in spite of the crisis at Tsinan, Chiang indicated a willingness to refrain from a drive into Manchuria so long as Chang Tso-lin would withdraw. What remained for the Japanese side, then, was to persuade Chang to retreat in good order.[65]

At first, Chang misinterpreted the meaning of the Tsinan affair and believed that Japan had finally decided to back him in his fight against his enemies. Accordingly, he responded favorably to yet another overture to open railway negotiations from SMR President Yamamoto and agreed to build the Ch'angch'un-Talai, to complete the Kirin–Hoeryong by linking Tunhua to the Korean border, and to discuss other lines. In subsequent talks with Minister Yoshizawa, it became clear to Chang, however, that the Japanese had not conducted their operations in Shantung on his behalf. The diplomat informed the Chinese leader of his options. If Chang would withdraw north of the Wall immediately and in good order, Japanese troops would not disarm him. If he waited until he was forced to retreat with Kuomintang forces in hot pursuit, the Kwantung Army would disarm both sides. Bitterly disappointed at the limits of Japanese help, Chang initially resisted. However, recognizing the futility of further fighting and advised by all of his key aides to withdraw, he began preparations for an orderly retreat to Manchuria. On June 3, 1928, he boarded a special PMR train that would take him from Peking back to Mukden.[66]

With Chang's agreement to withdraw, Tanaka's strategy appeared to have succeeded, and the prime minister had good reason for optimism. Should matters proceed without further incident, the long impasse with Chang would come to an end. Moreover, if Tanaka could overcome the bad blood generated by the Tsinan affair, he would have in hand a stable policy framework for China as a whole. Patience and a persistent commitment to the policy of cooperation in Manchuria seemed to have paid off. Despite the difficulties that Tanaka had faced when he first took office and the readiness of many leaders across the political spectrum to abandon Chang during the previous summer, the policy goals that Japan had pursued since the beginning of the decade appeared closer to full realization than ever before.

Viewed in context and at this historical moment, the generally negative appraisal of the so-called Tanaka diplomacy, shared by contemporary observers and historians alike, warrants re-examination. The characterization of Tanaka's program as fickle, aimless, and inconsistent does not take into account what the prime minister sought to achieve. Past work has attempted to analyze the policies of this period in terms of a simple bipolarity that places the new diplomacy of Shidehara at one end and a traditional imperialism, most faithfully represented during this era by Yoshida and Mori, at the other. This framework provides no room for the category of expansionist policy defined in this study as the "new imperialism." If we view Tanaka Giichi as a leader of this persuasion, his aims appear more coherent, his efforts, more effective, and his commitments, far stronger than prevailing interpretations have allowed. None of this is to suggest that Tanaka's approaches lacked serious flaws, but given the fact that he attempted to carry out a course of action that had become increasingly unpopular and that offered rather slim chances of success, his accomplishments as an imperialist statesman deserve more recognition than they have received.

An understanding of Tanaka's policies as an expression of the new imperialism in Manchuria may also help shed additional light on the long-standing debate over the relationship between Shidehara and Tanaka diplomacy.[67] The Eastern Conference of 1921 established a dualism in Japanese policy, a two-China framework that allowed for the coexistence of both expansion and adherence to the new order. Shidehara, albeit reluctantly, accepted that framework. The new diplomacy would dominate policies south of the Wall at the expense of tolerating a "new imperialism" in the north. Tanaka likewise accepted that framework. It allowed him to pursue the nation's vital imperial interests in Manchuria at the cost of acquiescing to the new diplomacy and the accommodation of Chinese nationalism south of the Wall. The two men represented very different outlooks on China and visions for the future of Japan, as many scholars have pointed out. Both, however, shared a common commitment to the historic compromise struck in 1921. Shidehara's policy represented dualism with a new diplomat at the helm, and Tanaka's, the same two-China approach under the paramount leadership of a new imperialist.

The Assassination of Chang Tso-lin

To be fair, historical memory cannot be faulted excessively for overlooking Tanaka's achievements, because they proved short-lived, his triumph no more than momentary. As Chang Tso-lin's train approached Shenyang Station on June 4, passing under the SMR railway bridge outside Mukden, an explosion ripped through his railway car, killing him and one of his aides. The assassination of Chang was the work of a group of Kwantung Army officers headed by Colonel Kōmoto Daisaku (1883–1955), senior staff officer, thinly disguised as the act of Kuomintang agents. The initiative enjoyed widespread sympathy within the Japanese garrison and, some historians have suggested, the foreknowledge of superior officers. Although the leadership of the Kwantung Army had favored tightening the client relationship with Chang in 1927, their patience had worn thin, and they would have happily seen him replaced with a more suitable candidate. Developments since that time had given them little reason to look more favorably upon Chang, and by the spring of 1928, they had come to favor forcing him to step down. Indeed, Kwantung Army officers had initially proposed the idea of disarming the combatants, should they cross the Manchurian border, with the aim of creating an opportunity to depose Chang. They welcomed the news of the cabinet's decision in favor of armed mediation in the middle of May and began making preparations to confront Chang's forces at either Chinchow or Shanhaikuan. The garrison's leaders, however, had anticipated instructions to disarm the Fengt'ien Army regardless of circumstances and not the conditional terms conveyed by Yoshizawa to Chang. Clarification from Tokyo prohibited intervention if Chang retreated in good order. The garrison command made repeated remonstrances to its superiors, but in the end, it called off preparations and sent the troops back to their barracks. It was at this point that Kōmoto and a number of associates put a contingency plan they had prepared into action.[68]

Colonel Kōmoto, like many of his colleagues, had become thoroughly disgusted with Chang and the comparatively moderate policies adopted at the Eastern Conference. He had committed himself to resolve this problem, on his own if need be, for some time. He outlined his views and plans to a friend, Colonel Isogai Rensuke (1886–1967), in a letter in April 1928.

Given the increasing high-handedness of the Chinese side in Manchuria, there are, if we face the facts, too many things that are difficult to overlook. It can't be denied that Japanese army cliques bear some responsibility for encouraging the Chinese to become presumptuous.

Resolving the Manchurian problem isn't something that anyone can do using reason. Resorting to such ploys as exchanging favors is no good. There is no road other than armed force. Of course, it is essential that anyone who uses force choose his pretext and his battle standard carefully.

At this point, given the slightest cause, we should deal them a great blow and force them to change their attitude toward Japan.

We seem to have started to do this over the railway problem recently, but the government was unable to overcome internal opposition and adopted the useless approach of economic retaliation. Right now, they're having the SMR block the movement of freight cars in and out of Mukden city, but it's having no effect. On the contrary, the Chinese side is instigating strikes of cart drivers at Mukden station, obstructing communication lines between Ch'angch'un and Harbin, and the like, creating difficulties for the Japanese side.

It's inevitable that the Japanese side is going to lose any economic struggle, since Manchurian enterprises depend on Chinese labor. This is clear from the past example of Hong Kong versus Canton. For this reason, this method is only going to make our side howl.

We ought to put an end to this bankrupt policy. It's no good unless we apply military pressure. . . .

. . . Chang's intolerable behavior after the Chang-Kuo war is such that it can't be put into words. Those Japanese who were convinced that, by granting favors, they could reap rewards have been duped.

Cash transactions over this and that are no good. From here on, we should understand that we need to look toward a general settlement of accounts for the past twenty years. If we don't, we won't be able to settle the Manchurian problem.

What does it matter if Chang Tso-lin and a few others are left to die? This time, and this time for sure, I'm going to do it. Even if they try to stop me, no matter what, I'm going to do it.

The "it" Kōmoto referred to was, of course, the assassination of Chang.[69]

This letter gives clear insight into why the colonel believed such action necessary. It described the line followed by Matsuoka, Ugaki, and Tanaka as a policy of petty transactions, quid-pro-quo bargains in which the crafty Chinese leader had repeatedly duped the Japanese. Getting rid of Chang would remove the foundations of this "bankrupt" policy. At the same time, the letter also made it clear that Kōmoto rejected any return to the ways of the old imperialism. Any attempt to compete with the Chinese for control of the territory through "economic methods," as he described them, would prove futile. He painted a grim, overall picture of the situation. The new imperialism was a policy of dupes; the old, a contest that the Japanese could not win. Killing Chang, creating upheaval, and thus broadening the horizons of possibility offered the only way for Japan to settle "accounts."

Kōmoto's views reflected mounting frustration and disappointment with the developments of recent years. Yet it would be a mistake to see his motivation solely in terms of policy disagreements and the incipient crisis of the times. His letter to Isogai also hinted at a personal orientation that helps explain his action. Kōmoto was a disaffected officer with deep contempt for his superiors. One indication of his attitude lay in his characterization of the policy of cooperation with Chang as the work of Japanese "military cliques" (*gunbatsu*)—a pejorative term that clearly implied unprofessional and self-serving behavior. Another is found in his preliminary greetings to Isogai in which he offered commiseration for their mutual frustrations in dealing with superior officers and suggested his readiness to leave the army. "There is no reason to stick with such devotion to the military life forever. We ought to forget it and go into some other line of work. Indeed, this might give our superiors something to reflect on as well." He added, "I have had plenty of experience with the arbitrary and selfish criticism of superiors, and I no longer pay it any mind." Kōmoto seems to have had a somewhat troubled career; reputed to be bright and capable, but also headstrong, he was unable to work well with others and was in disfavor with his seniors. He came from a prosperous family and had acquired a reputation as a playboy with a taste for the good life.[70] He also admitted an attraction to violence, which he conveyed in this same letter. "I like upheaval," he wrote. More revealing was his remark toward the end of this note: "What I hope for, no more and no less, is a bloodletting in Manchuria. I believe this is the key to the fundamental resolution of the problem."[71] This view appears to be that of a man who preferred direct action for its own sake and not necessarily because it offered the best solution to the problem. Combined with his dissent over China policy and his disaffection with the army hierarchy and its cliques, this affinity for direct action appears consistent with a profile common to members of the radical adventurist trend in the army, an old pattern going back to the 1911 Revolution.

Kōmoto directed his attack against Chang Tso-lin, but his real target, in the final analysis, was Tanaka Giichi. Reflecting the classic mentality of the terrorist, the colonel had hoped, by killing Chang, to destroy the foundations of a policy he opposed and, simultaneously, to force a reluctant government into action. Political disorder would likely follow, along with anti-Japanese rioting, and even some provocative response from the Nationalists. The Tanaka cabinet would then have no choice but to intervene in the name of law, order, and stability. Following the logic of "in for a penny, in for a pound," such intervention would, in turn, open the door to further positive measures.[72]

If Kōmoto had anticipated such a scenario, however, he must have found the manner in which events unfolded after the death of Chang deeply disappointing. Although Japanese responsibility for the murder was an open secret, the Chinese side in Manchuria as well as south of the Wall exercised great restraint and took pains to avoid any activity that would provide a pretext for an armed Japanese response. Popular anti-Japanese movements, which had run strong in the territory's major cities during Chang's last year, appeared to bank their fires as well. As a result, Chinese Manchuria remained surprisingly calm, as if an unfortunate railway accident, rather than an act of Japanese terrorism, had taken the life of its longtime leader. Even if the government in Tokyo had been eager to take military action, the situation in the territory did not offer a suitable opportunity. Given a cabinet disinclined, in any event, to adopt aggressive measures, let alone undertake an armed intervention, no precipitous response materialized.[73]

Kōmoto thus failed to achieve his positive aim of inciting Japanese military action, but he had largely succeeded in the pursuit of his negative goals. The colonel had demolished Tanaka's scheme as thoroughly as Chang's railway car. There seemed little possibility of restoring, even partially, the policy framework in place since the beginning of the decade. In principle, as Japanese policymakers had repeatedly asserted since the first Eastern Conference of 1921, cooperation would be extended to or enforced on, depending on whether one subscribed to the new diplomats' or the new imperialists' interpretation, the institution of Manchurian strongman, rather than the individual who happened to hold the office. Yet in practice, as Ugaki had bemoaned in 1925 and as Yoshizawa had reasserted in 1927, Chang was not easy to replace. The viability of a relatively restrained two-China policy based on managing a Manchurian client ruler had depended heavily on the particular qualities and credentials of Chang Tso-lin as an individual. Removing the man who had been the linchpin of Japan's Manchuria policy since the beginning of the decade could only have a shattering impact and left the future dangerously uncertain.

NINE

The Sino-Japanese Railway War and the Manchurian Crisis, 1928–1931

The assassination of Chang Tso-lin marked the collapse of the strategy of bilateral cooperation that had sustained Japanese empire-building efforts in Manchuria throughout much of the decade. During his second year in office, Tanaka Giichi made a last, desperate attempt to establish a client relationship with Chang Hsüeh-liang (1898–2001), the old warlord's son and successor. Nothing came of the effort, other than discrediting the prime minister's policies in the eyes of his critics, before a bitter dispute over the question of punishing Chang's killers forced the cabinet to resign in the summer of 1929. Shidehara once again took the reins of foreign-policy leadership in the administration that followed, and not surprisingly, empire-building made few gains during the next two years.

In the meantime, frustration mounted within the activist camp. Developments of the recent past had persuaded many, especially in the army, that no viable imperialist middle ground remained between retreat on the one hand and a decisive settlement through armed intervention, on the other. The call for a military solution, aimed at either the installation of a hand-picked and abjectly dependent client ruler or the outright occupation and annexation of the territory, came to enjoy a level of support that Kōmoto Daisaku's initiative had lacked in 1928. The intensification of the competition between Chinese railways and the SMR contributed significantly to creating a suitable pretext for action and cultivating within popular opinion the perception of a Japanese Manchuria under siege. The onset of the depression in 1930 further enhanced the climate for carrying out a radical solution and strengthened the claims of imperialism while discrediting the new diplomacy. Sensing that the circumstances favoring bold action had become ripe, the Kwantung garrison seized the initiative on September 18, 1931, and, in defiance of home authorities, launched the conquest of Northeast China.

Tanaka Giichi and Chang Hsüeh-liang

The assassination of Chang Tso-lin left Tanaka disconsolate. He had little choice, however, but to forge ahead and to maintain the pretense that Chang's demise did nothing to change Japan's course in Manchuria. Official policy sought to restore as completely and as quickly as possible cooperative relations with the successor regime in Mukden. By the end of June 1928, it appeared likely that Chang Tso-lin's son Hsüeh-liang would head that regime. Aware of the younger Chang's nationalist sympathies as well as the discussion in the provincial assemblies of rapprochement with the recently established Kuomintang government in Nanking, Japanese army and diplomatic officials warned the new regional regime that their expectations remained unchanged. Tokyo considered all agreements reached with the late Chang Tso-lin fully valid, continued to regard the Three Eastern Provinces as a special region of vital national interest, and would look with extreme disfavor on any overtures to the Kuomintang. In a conversation in July, Lieutenant General Muraoka Chōtarō (1891–1930), commander of the Kwantung Army, offered a frank admonition to Chang Hsüeh-liang against working with Nanking. "For a decade and more, your honored father, Tso-lin, stood for cooperation with Japan and thus brought about the prosperity that the Three Eastern Provinces enjoy today. Yet you, sir, even before the completion of your father's funeral ceremonies, are prepared to surrender to his enemies and bring ruin to the Three Eastern Provinces."[1]

If young Chang felt outrage at being berated so brazenly by the commander of the soldiers who, as he was quite aware, had murdered his "honored father," he kept such feelings to himself in his dealings with Japanese officials during the first few months after the assassination. Indeed, despite the circumstances, he displayed an unexpectedly benign, if not openly friendly, attitude toward Japan, as Mukden Consul-General Hayashi Kyūjirō (1882–1964), who had succeeded Yoshida in the post in March, discovered in exploratory talks with Chang Hsüeh-liang and his supporters in June and July. Hayashi reported that the new regime favored retaining an autonomous status for the Three Eastern Provinces and remained, contrary to Japanese fears, suspicious of Nanking. More important, young Chang indicated a desire for Japanese support, and promised to honor all agreements made with his father, including contracts for the construction of the Kirin–Hoeryong and Ch'angch'un–Talai lines signed in May with Yamamoto Jō-tarō. Chang Hsüeh-liang even suggested that he might consider discussing land rights with the Japanese if they, in turn, would negotiate the issue of extraterritoriality. No doubt Hayashi found this attitude surprising. At the same time, the consul-general persuaded himself of the sincerity of Chang's stance: the young leader faced challenges from within his father's old clique as well as pressure from Nanking to submit to central authority and welcomed Japanese assistance under the circumstances.[2]

For Prime Minister Tanaka, Hayashi's appraisal of Chang Hsüeh-liang came as a godsend. He seized the opportunity to resuscitate his shattered schemes with an almost reckless enthusiasm and in mid-July outlined a grand plan for negotiating a series of new cooperative agreements. Japan would protect the Manchurian regime from both the Soviet Union and the Chinese Nationalists, gradually surrender claims to extraterritoriality in exchange for the right of Japanese to lease land, and provide financial and technical assistance to the new regime. Chang Hsüeh-liang, in return, would permit unrestricted access to the territory's natural resources and, above all, proceed without delay in implementing all outstanding railway projects. Tanaka even drew up a new list of railway desiderata that this new and strengthened client relationship would make possible.[3]

Although Hayashi's appraisals might have provided some reason for hope, Tanaka's ebullient optimism and expectations, less than six weeks after the devastating setback of June 4, seem excessive. The experience of the past few years, which, from Japan's perspective, entailed a string of broken promises and disappointments, might have warranted a more skeptical attitude. General Ugaki Kazunari, who had lost faith in the client-management approach he had supported since the middle of the decade, certainly regarded the prime minister's plans as ill-advised. "For the time being, we should not rely on the Chinese or place emphasis on dealing with them," he wrote in September. "In the current game, in which Tso-lin is no longer a player, it is essential that we act in accordance with developments unfolding in the environment."[4] Apparently reluctant to look a gift horse in the mouth, however, Hayashi and Tanaka seemed to have ignored, or rationalized away, numerous indications surfacing during the late summer and fall of 1928 that cast doubt on the sincerity of Chang's friendly overtures. Despite a professed interest in cooperation, for example, the new regime repeatedly found reasons to delay further talks with the Japanese about railways or any other matters of substance.[5]

In retrospect, it seems quite clear that Chang Hsüeh-liang had no intention of becoming a Japanese client, that he had "hooked" Hayashi and Tanaka and had played them like a skillful angler. Young Chang certainly intended to safeguard his Manchurian patrimony, and he harbored suspicions about Chiang Kai-shek. His position during the first six months of his tenure remained insecure, subject to challenge by such powerful figures as Yang Yu-t'ing, his late father's chief lieutenant. At the same time, as a member of the generation that had launched the May Fourth movement, modern nationalism had shaped his outlook. Kuo Sung-ling had taught him at the military academy in Mukden, where young Chang developed a sympathy for Kuomintang ideas. Although he doubtless had differences with Chiang, he saw himself as a Chinese patriot dedicated to the unification of his country and, unlike his father, did not demand that unity be achieved under his rule. Given this orientation, Chang Hsüeh-liang could not have but adopted an adversarial view of Japan. Moreover, whatever the degree of personal affection between father and son, family pride and honor made it difficult for him to overlook the fact that Japanese soldiers had killed his father.[6]

As his own position improved, Chang presented an increasingly cool attitude toward the Japanese during the months following his initial talks with Hayashi. By late fall, negotiations with Nanking for a formal framework of national unification had produced arrangements satisfactory to both sides: the Mukden regime would be reorganized as the Northeast Political Council (Tung-pei cheng-wu wei-yüan-hui), with Jehol as a fourth province under its jurisdiction, and would enjoy considerable autonomy. By the beginning of 1929, Chang Hsüeh-liang had eliminated the most dangerous rivals from among his late father's followers. Having secured himself, young Chang quickly dropped his mask of cooperation, a change of attitude that even Hayashi could no longer overlook after talks in January. The consul-general arrived at the inescapable conclusion that the Japanese had been duped and that the time had come to show the flag. Like his predecessor, Hayashi began calling for hard-line sanctions against Mukden.[7]

However, doubtless demoralized and his reservoir of optimism run dry, Tanaka refused to authorize any action throughout the remainder of his administration.[8] Persistent international suspicion of Japanese responsibility for Chang Tso-lin's assassination, along with lingering tensions with the Nationalists over the Tsinan incident, made aggressive moves inadvisable. Negotiations with Nanking over revising the unequal treaties assumed growing importance as the other powers prepared to come to terms with the Nationalists. The prime minister also faced serious political difficulties at home. In addition to attacks by the Minseitō (the Kenseiaki renamed) on his China policy, the question of an inquiry into the assassination and punishment for the perpetrators had come to the fore, with the emperor's chief advisor, Saionji Kinmochi, pursuing the matter with considerable vigor. In the end, the problem of punishing Kōmoto and his fellow conspirators led to the government's downfall. Pressured by Saionji and other critics to take stern action on the one hand and encountering resistance from the army on the other, Tanaka found himself in a nearly impossible situation. The embattled soldier-politician resigned in July, and Hamaguchi Osachi (1871–1930), heading a Minseitō cabinet, took his place. Under the new government, Shidehara Kijūrō once again assumed the post of foreign minister.[9]

Shidehara's primary concern during his second ministry centered on negotiating treaty revisions with Nanking. These talks presented enormous difficulties in themselves, and the foreign minister had every reason to avoid further trouble over Manchuria. At the same time, he could not ignore the situation in the territory. Indeed, given the likelihood that any settlement with Nanking would require some significant concessions from the Japanese side regarding its rights in China, he could not hope for solid support among leadership circles at home without addressing the concerns of imperial activists and pressing for some measure of special consideration for Manchuria. A dualist compromise of some sort continued to form an essential condition for the success of Shidehara diplomacy. What he might do at this point to satisfy the army and its political allies while remaining within the boundaries of flexibility dictated by his own goals and principles, however, remained unclear. Shidehara thus failed to take any significant steps during the first year of his second term beyond the requisite posturing about protecting Japanese rights, the affirmation of a general commitment to improve relations with Chang Hsüeh-liang, and a few desultory attempts to reopen railway talks.[10] Such inaction, which activists found maddeningly predictable on the part of the master of "weak-kneed" diplomacy, only increased their frustration. Given what seemed the abject failure of all other alternatives, a growing number of dedicated imperialists had arrived at the conclusion that only direct, military action would break the deadlock in Manchuria.

The Collapse of an Imperialist Middle Ground

The idea of a forceful resolution of the "Manchurian problem" had already gathered significant momentum in some quarters by the time of Tanaka's Eastern Conference. Saitō Hisashi's proposal in 1927, the Kwantung Army's eagerness to disarm Chang in the spring of 1928, and substantial sympathy within a sector of the officer corps for Kōmoto's actions that summer offered clear indications of this trend. For those already inclined toward armed intervention, the events unfolding since June 1928 only served to strengthen their convictions.[11] Support, moreover, had broadened, the result not only of the demonstrated futility of attempts to establish a client relationship with Chang Hsüeh-liang but also of an emerging respect, in adversarial terms to be sure, for Chinese nationalism.

Imperialist strategies had long taken Chinese resistance into account as a major factor, particularly since the Twenty-One Demands of 1915. At the same time, most Japanese leaders across the spectrum generally regarded Chinese political behavior as driven by xenophobia, the benighted traditional politics of clan and clique, youthful political faddism, or transitory reactions to one perceived outrage or another.[12] According to the experts, true nationalism ran against the grain of Chinese character, which was individualistic, self-serving, venal, and spineless. What passed for patriotic sentiment among the general public seldom produced more than occasional outbursts and became dangerous only when combined with either official collusion or foreign interference. Under the proper circumstances, an artfully managed mixture of bribes and threats could readily overcome resistance at high levels, and compliant officials would then deal with the recalcitrance of their own people. Even the bilateral cooperation approach of Nishihara and Matsuoka was ultimately based on these premises. Although advocates of this line might consider making substantial concessions to Chinese economic interests in the name of reciprocity, the very idea of managing client rulers rested on a fundamental contempt for Chinese national aspirations.[13]

By the late 1920s, however, cumulative experience had transformed old attitudes, and many imperial activists began to appreciate the fact that China's quest for modern nationhood constituted a historic and enduring force that could no longer be dismissed. One indication of this emerging shift in awareness appeared, ominously, in an analysis of the prospects of a Sino-Japanese war prepared by the Army General Staff in late 1927. The authors of this paper argued that Chinese resistance to Japanese expansion represented more than a transient and tractable phenomenon that could be tamed through the application of carrots and sticks. Just as national destiny impelled the Japanese to seek empire in Manchuria, the logic of their own development as a people drove the Chinese to resist such encroachment. These historical trajectories made the erosion of Japan's traditional rights under Chinese pressure, as well as the failure of attempts at establishing stable client relationships, inevitable. Sooner or later, a Sino-Japanese collision would result. At that point, wrote the authors, "we will have arrived at the crossroads of our empire's survival, and we will have no choice but to resolutely take up arms."[14] General Minami Jirō (1874–1957), who would occupy the post of army minister during the fateful summer of 1931, concurred with this basic assessment of Chinese nationalism. In a speech delivered in August, appropriately regarded by the contemporary Japanese press as a call to arms, he argued that the rights recovery movement and the economic nationalism sweeping Manchuria had broad foundations and constituted developments, he warned, that "must in all certainty be recognized not as temporary but permanent phenomena."[15]

Later observers have sometimes attributed the violent confrontation in East Asia that began in the 1930s to the failure of Japan's more militant expansionists to recognize the realities of China's national awakening. Yet it would seem that, on the contrary, it was precisely contemptuous Japanese assessments of Chinese nationalism that had informed the more moderate or restrained forms of encroachment defining a middle ground of expansionist policy. Once imperial activists came to accept the fact that bribery, gunboat diplomacy, or the cultivation of client rulers could no longer manage Chinese resistance effectively, they found their options reduced to the extremes of ignominious retreat or a violent push forward.

Certainly not all leaders within the imperialist camp agreed that Japan faced such stark choices as of 1929 and 1930. General Ugaki, who served as army minister in the Hamaguchi cabinet until replaced by Minami in April 1931, warned against aggressive action for the time being. He saw a strategic retreat from the grand aspirations of the mid-1920s and an effective abandonment of the northern campaign unavoidable. In time, Japan might create the circumstances for the resumption of a more active policy, but the use of force under the current climate in China would entail serious risks and might make matters worse. "We may well be able to resolve the Manchurian problem to a certain extent relying on our power alone," he wrote in his diary in September 1928, "but at the same time, we will only alienate the Chinese further, driving them into the arms of the powers." In Ugaki's estimate, the wisest course of action lay in an effort to maintain Japan's position in the territory based on those traditional rights it had managed to preserve, to affirm their validity in diplomacy, and defend them vigorously on the ground.[16] Shortly after his reappointment, he wrote, "Regardless of what anyone may say, we absolutely cannot concede our existing position in Manchuria. So long as I am in office, and indeed, regardless of who may succeed me, there is absolutely no chance that we will consider such matters as a revision of the Twenty-One Demands, the retrocession of the Leased Territory, or the return of the SMR."[17]

The army minister's emphasis on defensive measures in Manchuria did not preclude some hope for modest progress. He saw possibilities in the development in depth of Kwantung and the Railway Zone, with renewed attention to the troubled, secondary strategy of "industrial Manchuria" pursued since the beginning of the decade. Aware of the difficulties, he called for the improvement of facilities in Kwantung and the Railway Zone, increased support for the settler community, and the expansion of private business investment. Ugaki also highlighted the need to reform the SMR's policies. Success in this approach demanded that the company assume responsibility for a broader scope of public-interest activities, render more direct support to other institutions and business interests, and break with its narrow, profit-making orientation. He implicitly criticized the policies of SMR President Yamamoto, who, in an effort to rechannel resources toward industrial development during his tenure, had cut back on new Zone facilities, reduced subsidies, and raised what amounted to company taxes on Zone residents.[18]

The idea of circling the wagons in the traditional heartland of Japanese Manchuria understandably offered little attraction for those of Ugaki's colleagues who believed that a continued program of active expansion in Manchuria remained vital to the nation's security and economic future. Moreover, even had they found Ugaki's drastically reduced goals acceptable, the prospects of preserving the status quo appeared dubious without the implementation of measures more aggressive than the army minister contemplated at this juncture. Maintaining Japan's established position was not simply a matter of defending treaty claims, which a determined government might accomplish. The real problem lay in the fact that the Japanese had gradually been losing the contest on the ground, a situation that the enforcement of rights alone could not change. As Kōmoto had warned, the Japanese stood little chance of success in competing with the Chinese for a place in Manchuria using peaceful means. The difficulties faced by Japanese business enterprises and the settler community, apparent by 1926, had worsened by the end of the decade with no real prospects for improvement in sight.

One study of business investment, prepared in 1928 by Mikami Yasumi of the SMR Research Section, offered a rather pessimistic view of the future of Japanese economic activity in the territory.[19] Mikami undertook an extensive review of more than 1,200 Japanese corporate enterprises in Manchuria and concluded that the business community not only faced trouble in the short term but also confronted the likelihood of long-term decline. He noted the impressive volume of total investments on paper, which exceeded ¥1.4 billion. However, excluding the SMR, which contributed half of this figure, moribund companies that had suspended operations or stood on the verge of doing so accounted for much of the remainder. Apart from the SMR, capital invested in what he regarded as healthy companies with reasonable prospects for the future amounted to only about ¥100 million. Mikami acknowledged that many factors contributed to this state of affairs, including the general economic environment of the 1920s. The process of winnowing unsound enterprises created during the war boom still continued. He also pointed to poor management practices on the part of Japanese entrepreneurs looking for quick returns. Obstruction of a variety of sorts by Chinese officials played a significant role as well. The fact that opportunities for Japanese business in the territory remained too constrained to allow for healthy and sustained growth, however, constituted the fundamental problem. There were limits to what could be accomplished so long as Kwantung or the Railway Zone remained isolated enclaves of Japanese business opportunity. Mikami argued that "it is a mistake in the first place to expect the kind of economic development we are aiming for in such a small strip of territory." There is little question that he regarded "industrial Manchuria" as a failed strategy. The only hope, in his view, lay in winning full access for

Japanese enterprise throughout Manchuria, and such a situation would not materialize without basic political changes in the territory.[20]

Significantly, Yamamoto Jōtarō seems to have arrived at the same conclusions as Mikami toward the end of his tenure as SMR president in 1929. He had started out quite enthusiastic about the prospects of an "industrial Manchuria" strategy, and his political alignment with General Tanaka notwithstanding, he believed that Japan's future in the territory rested on a policy of development in depth rather than breadth. Unlike his patron or SMR Vice President Matsuoka Yōsuke, he does not appear to have held firm convictions regarding cooperation with Chang Tso-lin or, ironically, the northern railway policy he attempted to negotiate. In undertaking his mission in backdoor diplomacy, Yamamoto seems to have served Tanaka's policy goals out of loyalty rather than political agreement. His background, apart from his work in the Imperial Diet, lay in business management, including an early career as a Mitsui Bussan executive and subsequent participation in the founding of numerous ventures in Korea and China.[21]

As SMR president, he devoted much of his energy to reorganizing the business structure of the company and instituted a sweeping rationalization program that substantially improved profitability and won him the sobriquet "father of the SMR's revival." He also focused more attention than his predecessors on heavy industrial projects. At the beginning of his tenure, he outlined a grand program for the accelerated development of three, major ventures: the Anshan Ironworks, which he hoped to spin off as an independent subsidiary to be known as "Shōwa Steel"; the full-scale exploitation of Fushun's oil-shale resources in cooperation with the navy; and finally, the commercialization of ammonium sulfate production. In order to finance investment in these areas, he sought to reduce what he regarded as unproductive expenditures in the Railway Zone, a step that earned him Ugaki's criticism despite their broader, common goals.[22]

The assassination of Chang Tso-lin appears to have had a profoundly demoralizing impact on the company president. Yamamoto remarked shortly after the incident, "All that I have worked for has gone up in smoke."[23] He continued to follow through on his projects with a show of determined optimism, including his plans to transform the Anshan iron and steel venture. However, he revised his scheme in a manner that suggested a sea change in his outlook. In 1929, he presented the government with an extraordinary proposal to transfer most of the plant and equipment at Anshan to Sinuijiu in Korea, just across the Yalu River from Antung. The company would transport ore by rail from Manchuria to Korea. He offered a variety of reasons for this move, which included tax benefits. He also argued that given the strategic importance of the steel venture, its relocation in uncontested Japanese colonial territory would provide for greater security. He pointed out further that employing Korean as opposed to Chinese labor would offer the advantage of keeping wage expenditures within the family of the Japanese empire. Shipping ore by rail would, in principle, entail significant additional costs, he acknowledged, but the Antung–Mukden branch of the SMR had long suffered from the problem of excess capacity. The company could, therefore, offer transportation services at extremely low cost without incurring new losses. In general, he regarded the location of the iron and steel works in Chinese territory, which made operations susceptible to political strikes, official harassment, and other pressures, highly disadvantageous. A move across the border presented Shōwa Steel with the best chances of success.[24]

Although Yamamoto limited this argument to the iron and steel venture, the underlying logic could readily be extended to other activities. Most major business enterprises faced vulnerabilities similar to those cited for Shōwa Steel and would reap the same purported benefits of relocating their plants to Korea while drawing raw materials from Manchuria. The proposal also held great symbolic significance. The idea of moving the flagship venture of industrial Manchuria across the Yalu signaled a general retreat and indicated an unmistakable lack of confidence in the future of Japan's position in the territory. Aware of these sweeping implications, the Hamaguchi government rejected the proposal. Ugaki pointedly opposed relocation. While declining to comment on the economics of the scheme, he criticized the strategic argument as entirely groundless.[25] Yamamoto's plan may have been too extreme at this juncture to win support among mainstream policymakers. Nonetheless, the fact that the president of the SMR even contemplated, in all seriousness, an economic "evacuation" of Japanese Manchuria pointed to the deep pessimism emerging in some quarters.

The outlook for the settler community, not surprisingly, was also bleak. A study of the demographics of Japanese Manchuria by Kudō Takeo of the SMR Research Section outlined the problems in considerable detail. Prepared in 1928, Kudō's work bore the title "Manchuria and Our Country's Population Problem" ("Waga kuni jinkō mondai to Manmō"), which might suggest a treatise promoting the cause of *Lebensraum* in Manchuria. Contrary to such expectations, however, the author had come to the unequivocal conclusion that the territory held little promise for large-scale Japanese settlement of any kind. Kudō went beyond the argument, already accepted by most experts, as to the impracticality of promoting widespread agricultural immigration. He concluded that even a limited program of colonization centered on Kwantung and the Railway Zone would not succeed in the long run. Kudō reviewed the history of immigration, demographic changes, and employment patterns within the areas of direct Japanese jurisdiction and pointed to the persistent problems that Japanese settlers faced, most of which had become evident by 1926. Escalating competition with Chinese moving into Kwantung and the Zone and the lack of secure employment opportunities posed particularly serious difficulties. These conditions had pushed a significant part of the Japanese settler community into small-scale commerce and workshop manufacturing, areas facing the greatest economic distress. The situation had worsened in recent years and appeared unresponsive to straightforward relief measures.[26]

Kudō cited "two fundamental factors," among many others, that hindered permanent settlement. Echoing Mikami's view, he saw "the wide range of restrictions on Japanese activity in the territory" as one obstacle. Yet Kudō saw little hope for change. "We cannot expect that the Chinese authorities, given today's feverish climate of national rights recovery, will open all of Manchuria to our people." The other problem appeared yet more intractable and would remain even with the removal of political restrictions. "In the final analysis," he concluded, "the Japanese cannot hold their own in competition with the Chinese." Short of barring the Chinese from certain fields of business enterprise and employment in Kwantung and the Railway Zone or excluding them altogether in an attempt "to establish an entirely autonomous community," no effective way of overcoming this difficulty presented itself. Exclusionary measures, in Kudō's view, lay beyond the pale of possibility. "To consider seriously restricting Chinese economic activity within Chinese territory is something we cannot even dream about," he remarked. Basic economics rendered any effort to create an insular, self-sufficient Japanese community in Manchuria unrealistic. "The employment of high-priced labor and the buying and selling of high-priced goods in a land offering low-wage labor and cheap commodities, no matter how important such efforts might be from the perspective of national policy, cannot be sustained for any long period of time."[27]

Significantly, a growing sector of the settler community considered the situation intolerable and favored radical solutions. By the late 1920s, many Japanese living in Kwantung and in the Railway Zone, in particular, had come to see themselves as an endangered minority besieged by an overwhelming majority of increasingly hostile "natives." Chang Tso-lin's suppression of anti-Japanese demonstrations in the mid-1920s may have satisfied high policymakers in Tokyo, but growing expressions of nationalism in the territory continued to generate anxiety among Japanese settlers. The resumption of demonstrations during Chang Tso-lin's final years and the openly nationalistic stance of his son's regime only accentuated their concerns. Chinese competition, which threatened their precarious livelihood, added an economic dimension to their self-image as embattled colonists. A petition submitted to Prime Minister Tanaka in 1929 enumerated their woes.

We Japanese and Korean residents have been pioneers in the development of Manchuria. Battling a [hostile] natural environment, we have, through our hard work and long struggle, gradually established a foothold. Yet, prevented from expanding our endeavors, externally by the oppression of the Chinese authorities and their failure to enforce law and order, internally by the monopolistic, profit-seeking policies of the SMR and the unregulated, high-interest lending policies of financial institutions, we are beset with misfortune and being driven day by day toward extremity.[28]

Foreign Minister Shidehara seemed to confirm their view of an indifferent, if not unsympathetic, home government in remarks to the Diet in early 1931. He blamed the settlers themselves for their troubles and suggested that the primary source of "stagnation in Manchuria" stemmed from the fact that Japanese residents had "adopted an attitude of superiority toward the Chinese and a spirit of dependence on the Japanese government."[29]

Militant settlers, best represented by an organization known as the Manchurian Youth League, founded in 1928, saw the solution to their plight in the armed overthrow of the Chang Hsüeh-liang regime and the establishment, in its place, of a sovereign Manchurian state severed from China and linked to Japan. The idea of an independent Manchuria, favored by some during the Revolution of 1911 and a possibility inherent in the two-China policy of the advocates of imperialist cooperation, represented nothing new in itself. Settler support for this solution, however, stemmed from their particular position and experience and reflected their sense of alienation from the motherland.[30] Sata Kōjirō, head of the SMR Research Section, adapted some of the more radical ideas favored by elements in the settler community into two alternative proposals for the territory's future: the formation of a monarchy headed by P'u-i (1906–67), the last of the Ch'ing rulers, who had abdicated in 1912; or the creation of a Manchurian republic based on principles of popular sovereignty and ethnic pluralism.[31]

As we shall see, the settlers' vision of an independent Manchuria would eventually come to pass, although not in quite the manner they foresaw nor in the form they desired. At this time, it represented a scheme somewhat off the beaten track. Army leaders certainly found some of these ideas intriguing, and the existence of a firm base of support for military action within the Japanese community in the territory proved heartening. Most mainstream imperial activists favoring an armed resolution of the situation in Manchuria, however, looked toward either the overthrow of Chang Hsüeh-liang and his replacement with a suitable client or the outright seizure and eventual annexation of the territory. Those supporting the replacement of the Chang regime with a pro-Japanese regional administration represented the more moderate of the two positions and saw the need for some restraint in order to avoid a frank and irreparable breach with Nanking and the Washington powers. The client relationship they envisioned at this time, however, probably resembled the arrangements described in the Kwantung Army's proposal for a quasi-protectorate in 1927, in which Mukden would retain only nominal ties to China proper, with Japanese control over the client government far more structured and tightly managed than anything considered in the mid-1920s. General Minami seems to have preferred this option.[32] Those who favored outright conquest either disregarded the international consequences or had concluded that the benefits of military action in Manchuria would outweigh the costs. A wariness toward any kind of client management after the experiences of the past few years, even given more structured safeguards such as Saitō Hisashi had proposed in 1927, no doubt informed their views as well. Indeed, by 1929, the leaders of the Kwantung garrison had moved one step beyond Saitō's Eastern Conference proposal and come to favor outright seizure.[33]

By 1930, army leaders had begun giving serious consideration to military action in the near future. The general staff, in its famous situational analysis for the year 1931, prepared in the fall of 1930, laid out three graded options to be pursued in sequence. The first was to continue the attempt to improve relations with Chang Hsüeh-liang and to reopen railway talks, a nominal endorsement of Shidehara policy. The second, in the likely event of the failure of these efforts, called for the overthrow of the current regime and the installation of a new regional government willing to adopt a more appropriate attitude toward Japan. The third, contingent on opportunity, involved the outright occupation, partition, and eventual annexation of Manchuria.[34] By this point, the first option represented no more than a pro forma concession to political propriety or, perhaps more accurately, an effort to give the foreign minister sufficient rope to hang himself. Whether through the second or third option, the army had clearly committed itself to carrying out a military solution. Only the questions of timing, opportunity, and as Kōmoto had put it, the selection of an appropriate "battle standard," remained unsettled.

The Sino-Japanese Railway War, 1929–31

A dramatic escalation of Sino-Japanese railway competition in 1930 and 1931 contributed significantly to resolving these issues.[35] Chinese authorities in Manchuria had taken an active interest in regional railway building since the early 1920s. Upon his succession, Chang Hsüeh-liang adopted a particularly vigorous program for the improvement and expansion of transportation facilities. Financial considerations continued to fuel this effort, but a broader and self-conscious commitment to an economic nationalist agenda in Manchuria emerged as a pronounced feature of the policies of the new regime. The need to strengthen his control and centralize his authority also motivated the younger Chang, and the building of an integrated Chinese railway network throughout the four provinces of the Northeast provided an effective way of binding his realm together. The formation of an agency known as the Northeast Transportation Commission (Tung-pei chiao-t'ung wei-yüan-hui; NTC) in 1928 reflected the new government's dedication to a policy of railway nationalism. Two major tasks constituted the agency's mission.[36]

One entailed organizing all existing Chinese-owned lines in Manchuria into a unified, independent network. The designated railways included the PMR, the Mukden–Hailung, and the Kirin–Hailung (completed in 1929), all under essentially complete Chinese administrative control, as well as the T'aonan–Tsitsihar and Kirin–Tunhua, built under Matsuoka's scheme of construction contracts. Although these were initially conceived as autonomous Chinese lines, regional authorities had exercised their option for long-term borrowing in an effort to secure padded loans. Under the liberalized framework of Japanese policy in the mid-1920s, however, the Chinese side retained considerable managerial authority. In addition, the NTC's integration plans also targeted the Ssup'ingkai–T'aonan, a traditional loan concession line over which the Japanese, as creditors, enjoyed substantial managerial rights. The NTC planned to "suborn" this railway, which since 1922 had been an SMR feeder, to serve as part of a Chinese system. At present, all these lines fell under the management of separate railway bureaus with their own sets of policies. The NTC sought to forge from these disparate agencies a working business alliance capable of competing against the Japanese network. The negotiation of uniform rates, standard insurance arrangements, and connecting traffic agreements formed the first step in this process. The ultimate aim lay in the creation of an autonomous Chinese railway system capable of moving goods directly from Ch'angch'un, Kirin, or Tunhua by way of the Kirin–Hailung–Mukden trunk, or from Tsitsihar, points north, and even Ssup'ingkai, by way of an Inner Mongolian route (Tsitsihar–T'aonan–Chengchiat'un–T'ungliao–Tahushan) to the PMR's seaport outlet at Yingk'ou[37] (see Map 9.1).

The construction of new railways formed the other major responsibility of the NTC. Significantly, plans for a group of lines in the north corresponded closely to what the Japanese had attempted to negotiate with Chang Tso-lin in the mid-1920s and with Chang Hsüeh-liang during the brief and illusory honeymoon of the summer of 1928. It included lines from Tsitsihar to K'eshan to Mergen (started in 1927); from T'aoan (just north of T'aonan) to Solun to Manchouli (1930); from Kirin to Wuch'ang to T'ungkiang (1930); and from Yenki to Ninkut'a to Hailin. Railways running from T'ungliao to T'aonan, which would complete a direct link between Tsitsihar and Tahushan and bypass the Chengchiat'un–T'ungliao route, and from T'aonan to Harbin constituted a western group. T'aonan (or T'aoan) would serve as a major regional junction of the Chinese network. On the eastern side of the SMR, Ch'aoyangchen, a town north of Hailung on the Kirin–Hailung line, would form another a key junction, and from there, railways would radiate south to Antung and northeast to Yenki. In addition, rumors of a line from Chengchiat'un to Ch'angch'un circulated widely.[38] The reactivation of plans for an ice-free harbor at Hulutao, which

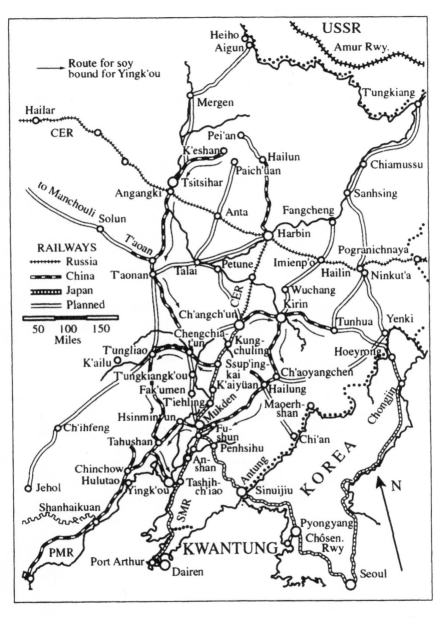

Map 9.1 Railways in Manchuria, 1931. Some planned routes are shown based on actual lines built subsequently (based on maps in Tōa keizai chōsakyoku, *Manchoukuo Year Book, 1934*; SMR, *Eigyō hōkokusho, 1923, 1928, 1930*; DR1, looseleaf; Matsuoka, *Ugoku Manmō*).

would eventually replace the problematic port facilities at Yingk'ou, formed an integral element of the program. The NTC, in fact, finalized arrangements with a Dutch contractor in 1930 to build the port.[39]

Although the NTC anticipated the building of a large number of new railways throughout Manchuria, its agenda gave clear priority to the northern lines. This emphasis emerged as the result of a brief but hard-fought Sino-Soviet war in the late summer of 1929. Chang Hsüeh-liang had begun exerting pressure on the Soviet position in north Manchuria in May by ordering the closing of offices in the CER Zone and expelling Soviet officials on the charge of communist agitation. The action stemmed, in part, from Chang's goal of strengthening Chinese sovereignty within his dominions, an effort directed at the Soviets as well as the Japanese. Indeed, in the short run, he may have regarded the Soviets as the easier target. The deterioration of relations between Nanking and the Soviet Union, however, dictated the particular timing of the initiative. With the blessing and encouragement of the authorities in Nanking, Chang launched his challenge with some confidence, expecting the Soviets to back down in the face of a Chinese show of force. Tensions became serious by midsummer, and by August, they had erupted into full-scale hostilities. The Chinese badly underestimated both Soviet will and capabilities and suffered a thorough defeat. In negotiations in November, Chang had little choice but to restore the status quo ante.[40] However, he had no intention of letting the issue rest and saw in railway construction the possibility of accomplishing what he had failed to do through armed force. The fact that Chang's northern lines reproduced much of what the Japanese Army General Staff had sought in 1925 was thus no coincidence.

Had imperial activists in Japan had any hope of Chang Hsüeh-liang's redemption, his belligerent attitude toward the Soviet Union and his strategic northern railway program, on balance, should have been cause for celebration. In waging war against the Soviets over the CER, young Chang had done precisely what Major General Saitō of the Kwantung Army had wanted of his father. Construction starts on the Tsitsihar–K'eshan, Kirin–Wuch'ang, and, above all, the T'aoan–Solun represented a genuine breakthrough in military railway policy that had eluded Matsuoka and Tanaka despite their best efforts. The NTC's attempts to build a competing system in the southern part of the territory posed some serious problems, to be sure, but Japanese policymakers had anticipated this development since the railway agreement of August 1924. Advocates of cooperative development had been prepared to tolerate not only a considerable degree of Chinese railway autonomy in Manchuria but also a measure of controlled competition as part of a larger bargain. The Japanese had formally objected to the building of the Tahushan–T'ungliao and Kirin–Hailung lines, which formed critical components of the NTC's rival system in the south, but intended from the start to rescind their protests as part of a negotiating ploy.

The fact that imperial activists no longer saw any prospects in restoring a client relationship with the existing Manchurian regime, however, fundamentally changed the calculus of Japan's response to these developments. Nothing short of Chang Hsüeh-liang's removal would provide a satisfactory solution. Chang's war against the Soviet Union failed to rekindle any interest in an alliance, a clear indication of how far Japanese army attitudes had already shifted by the summer of 1929. The general staff called for neutral observation and sought to use the war as an opportunity to learn about Chinese and Soviet military capabilities, but it made no effort to exploit the occasion politically or to render the Chinese side even covert support. Significantly, the Kwantung Army command instructed subordinate units to stand down and avoid moves that the belligerents might construe as taking sides. Garrison leaders advocated more stringent neutrality measures regarding military transportation on the SMR than did civilian diplomats.[41] Indeed, cooperation with the Chinese was the last thing on the mind of Lieutenant Colonel Ishiwara Kanji (1889–1949), the Kwantung Army's chief of operations. He and a group of fellow staff officers toured north Manchuria during the summer of 1929 in the midst of the Sino-Soviet crisis for the ostensible purpose of studying anti-Soviet war plans. His real goal, however, was to hone his strategy for war against the Chang regime. It was during this tour that Ishiwara revealed his program for a conquest of Manchuria that he would carry out two years later.[42]

Chang's northern construction program, likewise, did nothing to improve his standing with the Japanese army. Quite the contrary, imperial activists chose to portray Chinese railway policy in its entirety as an intolerable threat to the nation's vital interests in Manchuria. Indeed, reversing not only its recent enthusiastic endorsement of Chinese-style railways but also long-standing policies that tolerated parallel construction so long as it offered strategic advantage, the army informed Foreign Minister Shidehara in November 1930 that it considered Chinese railway competition the most serious problem confronting Japan in Manchuria.[43]

The army and its allies evidently intended to use the railway question to build the case for intervention, and they appear to have orchestrated a major public relations campaign aimed at mobilizing opinion against Chang Hsüeh-liang and cultivating a siege mentality in popular discourse about Manchuria. Major urban newspapers embraced the issue during the second half of 1930. Indeed, Yoshii Ken'ichi suggests that military sources fed receptive journalists with inflammatory reports. Early articles treated the problem of Chinese railway building in a relatively low-key manner, with headlines such as "Chinese Pressuring SMR." Treatment subsequently escalated into attacks on government policy: "Outwitted by the Chinese— Manchurian Railway Policy in a Corner." Journalists accused the SMR and the Foreign Ministry of adopting "do-nothing, strike-out" policies. By December, they began sounding the alarm: "Our Manchuria Policy: On the Verge of Collapse." Articles charged that Chang intended to build an "iron ring" (*hōi mō*) around the SMR and planned to drive the Japanese railway into the "jaws of death." Newspapers commonly employed the language of war, describing the NTC's "siege" (*hōi kōgeki*) of the SMR. One report adopted the title "The Advance in Ch'inhuangtao [a harbor site alternative to Hulutao]: General Assault on Dairen and the SMR." Even the relatively staid *Tōkyō Asahi* commented, "Not only has the SMR, the anchor of our country's special position in Manchuria, fallen into a state of paralysis, but our nation's Manchuria policy has arrived at the point where it confronts the likelihood of total failure."[44]

The quality of coverage, marked by considerable misinformation and outlandish claims, points to a lack of independent journalistic inquiry and reinforces Yoshii's view of an orchestrated campaign. Articles displayed little consistency in identifying which Chinese railways posed a mortal threat to the SMR and almost no explanation of why. One, entitled "Construction Plans for Three Railways Threaten the SMR" and citing "reports from reliable sources," listed the Fushun–Kaip'ing, the Tsitsihar–K'eshan, and the Tunhua–Ilan (Sanhsing) lines.[45] The first, although not appearing on any official list, was clearly a route paralleling a portion of the Dairen–Mukden segment of the SMR trunk. The other two, however, driving deep into CER territory, not only formed elements of the army's 1925 program but also had no conceivable negative impact on the SMR. If anything, they would only enhance the flow of northern traffic to the company's lines. Another article a week later presented two other railways as the most serious threats: the

T'ungliao–T'aonan and a northern extension of the T'aonan–Tsitsihar to the "Nonni River plain." The first represented a long-standing concern taken into account in the liberalized policies of the mid-1920s, and the second, once again, a demand of the Japanese army. Reports included rumors, dismissed by SMR analysts as unfounded, of British, German, and American involvement and made no mention of the recent history of Japanese railway policy.[46]

Interestingly enough, Matsuoka Yōsuke, who, after leaving the SMR in 1929, had embarked upon a new phase in his political career as a member of the Imperial Diet, emerged as one of the leading proponents of a militant response to the Chinese railway challenge. Few of those listening to the position he outlined in a radio address on the Manchurian problem in May 1931 would have guessed that, only a few years earlier, this bellicose politician had taken the lead in advocating the "liberalization" of Japanese railway policy in the name of cooperation. At the close of his speech, he declared:

The Chinese are building railways to encircle and, in effect, drive the SMR to destruction. They are exerting their energies toward extinguishing Japanese power in Manchuria in other ways as well. This is the true shape of our diplomatic situation. As I've explained, Manchuria is truly our nation's lifeline. To demand that our people withdraw from this country is to deny the Yamato nation the right to exist.

Matsuoka had little need to spell out the inevitable conclusion: Chang's policies warranted resistance by all available means.[47]

The hue and cry over Chinese competition as a mortal threat to Japan seems reminiscent of the nation's Manchuria policy of 1913. The rhetoric of the old railway imperialism might have carried some credibility had a significant segment of the activist camp called, at this juncture, for a return to a traditionalist approach to managing Manchuria based on concessionary rights. By 1930, however, few informed imperialists other than General Ugaki retained any faith in the viability of such strategies. Indeed, even as the army pressed Shidehara on the urgency of responding to the railway challenge, it had already committed itself to military action. For the majority of activists, Chang Hsüeh-liang posed the real problem, the principal obstacle in the way of resolving the deadlock in Manchuria, and the alarm raised over the "iron ring" constituted nothing more than a pretext, pure and simple, to move against him. Indeed, the *Tōkyō Asahi* reported ominously at the end of December, "Military watching Manchurian railway negotiations

closely—general staff will harden position if Chinese side continues in its in-
sincerity."[48]

For the purpose of mobilizing public opinion, the issue of railway competition proved highly useful, and it is unlikely that the army and its allies
could have fabricated a more appropriate "battle standard." It posed a readily
understandable problem, one susceptible to presentation using the imagery
of a wartime siege that justified a military response. The propaganda campaign fell on receptive ears, given the Japanese public's exposure to a steady
diet of "positive policy" rhetoric since Tanaka's Eastern Conference. As
General Ugaki noted in his diary in 1929:

There is but one thing for which I am prepared to thank the diplomacy of the Seiyūkai government, which otherwise deserves thorough condemnation for having
done nothing other than sowing the seeds of trouble. And that is, it has nurtured
profound awareness of the fact that our expansion in Manchuria is the absolute and
indispensable minimum condition for the existence of our nation. . . . Although the
costs of their "positive policy" may have outweighed the benefits . . . I must acknowledge that the hearts and minds of our people have been permeated with an understanding of the relationship between Manchuria and the survival of our country.[49]

The fanning of public outrage offered the additional advantage of putting
enormous pressure on Shidehara to act decisively, which remained, to be
sure, highly unlikely, or to face attack for surrendering Japanese Manchuria
to the Chinese.

The exploitation of this issue as a pretext for aggressive action does not
imply that the concerns about injury to the SMR lacked substance. Most
SMR managers and analysts saw some cause for worry. Tolerance of competition in the policies of the mid-1920s, which had never enjoyed unani-
mous support among company officials, rested on the premise of a larger
framework of a client relationship with the Manchurian ruler. Under these
circumstances, cooperative bargaining over rates and connection agreements,
or even quotas, would control and mitigate business conflict. In contrast, an
open-ended and antagonistic competition, particularly where political rather
than economically rational objectives motivated Chinese railway policies,
presented the possibility of significant damage to company interests. For example, an NTC willing to take massive losses in order to exert pressure on
the SMR might well provoke a devastating rate war.[50] The fact that silver
prices relative to gold had been falling dramatically compounded the threat

Table 9.1

SMR Freight Revenues by Commodity, 1927–30

Commodity	1927	1928	1929	1930
Soybeans and cake	¥27,949,474	¥30,196,329	¥35,724,331	¥23,079,726
Other commercial	31,755,839	30,619,574	27,933,596	21,857,264
TOTAL COMMERCIAL	59,705,313	60,815,903	63,657,927	44,936,990
Internal coal*	33,191,022	35,516,795	35,725,863	31,790,289
Other internal	1,144,484	1,405,449	1,705,684	1,209,409
INTERNAL TOTAL	34,335,506	36,922,244	37,431,547	32,999,698
GRAND TOTAL	94,040,819	97,738,147	101,089,474	77,936,688
% soy	29.7%	30.9%	35.3%	29.6%
% other commercial	33.8	31.3	27.6	28.0
% internal coal	35.3	36.3	35.3	40.8
% internal other	1.2	1.4	1.7	1.6

*From SMR mines.

SOURCE: SMR3, p. 524.

of such a tactic. The SMR levied its freight charges in gold yen, whereas the Chinese lines used the silver standard, which magnified the discounts offered by the latter.[51] The threat of aggressive Chinese competition, moreover, emerged at a time when the company found itself in a poor position to absorb business injury. The onset of the world depression in 1930 had a severe impact on its revenues. Freight receipts plunged by more than 20 percent that year, and total net income fell by more than half (see Appendix A).[52]

The SMR's real difficulties compounded anxiety and lent credibility to the propaganda campaign.[53] However, the actual effect of Chinese railway policies on the company's business position, as of late 1930 and early 1931, remained marginal. Freight volume fell in all categories of traffic and not only in those areas, such as soybeans, subject to Chinese competition (see Table 9.1). Moreover, a windfall gain in 1929, when the partial shutdown of the CER during the Sino-Soviet conflict diverted a large volume of northern freight to the SMR, exaggerated the overall decline in traffic.[54]

The volume of freight lost by SMR seaports to the PMR's Yingk'ou outlet provided a more accurate measure of the real impact of Chinese rail-

Table 9.2
Soy Traffic from Chinese Railways Reaching PMR–Yingk'ou (Hopei)
Versus SMR Seaports, 1930–31
(*tons*)

Chinese railway	PMR–Yingk'ou	% PMR	SMR ports	% SMR
Tsitsihar–K'eshan	13,650	5%	245,970	95%
Kirin–Tunhua/ –Ch'angch'un	11,060	3	370,074	97
Ssup'ingkai–Angangki	73,855	66	38,392	34
Ssup'ingkai Station	9,180	18	41,441	82
Mukden–Hailung	87,890	26	248,082	74

SOURCE: SMR, Chōsaka, *Manshū Shinagawa tetsudō ensen chihō ni okeru daizu no demawari zōka jijō oyobi sono taisaku an,* pp. 13–14.

way policy. All freight arriving at Dairen or the SMR's facilities at Yingk'ou, regardless of origin, constituted traffic feeding the SMR trunk at some point along the line, but only those goods reaching PMR–Yingk'ou represented traffic routed entirely on the Chinese system. Statistics on this traffic for early 1931 indicated minor losses (see Table 9.2). With the exception of traffic generated by stations along the Ssup'ingkai–T'aonan–Angangki (Tsitsihar) route, most of the soy shipped initially on Chinese railways eventually fed the SMR and arrived at Dairen or SMR–Yingk'ou. Even the Mukden–Hailung line served primarily as an SMR feeder for soy traffic and not as an extension of the PMR. The so-called iron ring, in other words, continued to function as a branch system of the SMR, contrary to both the intentions of the NTC and the claims of Japanese propagandists.

Successful railway management, of course, necessarily took stock of the long view, and in this context, SMR officials could not afford complacency. The Chinese lines would probably improve the quality of their service, and local shippers would gradually gain confidence in the NTC's network. The disadvantages of using Yingk'ou as an outlet would disappear, moreover, on completion of construction at Hulutao. In the way of countermeasures to such eventualities, some company analysts proposed creative business strategies. One idea, initially suggested at the end of 1928 by Hirano Hiroshi of the SMR Research Section, called for the adoption of a "Mukden strategy." This scheme entailed the transfer of many of the commercial and financial institutions that had made Dairen such an advantageous destination to Mukden, transforming the regional capital into the prime market venue for Manchurian soy. This "recentering" of the soy trade would encourage bean merchants to ship their goods to Mukden in order to take advantage of the market rather than commit themselves in advance to either Dairen, Yingk'ou, or Hulutao. The SMR would then have the opportunity to compete for beans arriving in Mukden on Chinese lines. This strategy would also actively discourage bean shippers from using the Inner Mongolian trunk (Tsitsihar–T'aonan–T'ungliao–Tahushan), which would bypass Mukden altogether.[55]

Company analysts proposed a variety of other business countermeasures as well.[56] Given the viable options, most SMR officials, while deeply concerned, do not appear to have taken alarm. Some, like Yamamoto Jōtarō, adopted a rather sanguine view. Shortly before his resignation in the summer of 1929, when the problem of competition began to escalate, he remarked, "We often hear a variety of speculations and criticisms expressing anxiety about injury inflicted [on the SMR] from competing Chinese railways and the recent opening of the Kirin–Hailung line. However, there is absolutely no reason for us to fear competing railways."[57] His successor, Sengoku Mitsugu (1857–1931), a former head of the National Railway Board and a Minseitō appointee, regarded the situation unfolding under his watch as more serious, but he believed, nonetheless, in reaching a mutually satisfactory resolution through reasoned compromise. The company's railway department concurred, warning of the futility of maintaining adversarial relations with the Chinese system. "The SMR operates within Chinese territory. The vast majority of our customers, passengers as well as shippers, are Chinese. Moreover, the goods carried by our lines are produced in territory under Chinese sovereignty. Given these circumstances, an attempt to carry on a protracted fight with Chinese railways is unlikely to benefit the SMR."[58] The more militant among imperial activists, no doubt, regarded such an approach as defeatist. Much like Yamamoto's proposal to move the SMR's ironworks to Korea, it seemed to concede the future of Manchuria to the Chinese. At the same time, however, it represented an orientation consistent with rational railway management, which almost always chose a negotiated peace over destructive competition.

Not surprisingly, the Japanese home press directed much criticism at Sengoku and the SMR. The company returned fire and attempted to counter inflammatory coverage of the railway war in Manchuria. As reported in *Tōkyō Asahi*, Sengoku pointed out that the SMR's difficulties stemmed primarily from the depression and not Chinese railway competition. Moreover, he suggested that Japan could not properly prevent the Chinese from building railways in their own country.[59] Significantly, the *Manshū nippō*, Japanese Manchuria's leading newspaper, published by a subsidiary of the SMR, carried very few articles dealing with railway competition during the height of the campaign at home. Those pieces touching on the problem sought to downplay its significance. In an interview article entitled "Cooperation with Chinese Railways Is Good," Sengoku suggested that newspaper coverage in Japan suffered from gross exaggeration and misinformation. There was no crisis and thus no need for vigorous countermeasures. Other articles reinforced the same point: "Prospects for SMR Revenues Next Year Not Bad—Impact of Chinese Railways Minimal"; "Railways in Regions Outside the SMR's Reach Are Fine—Work for the Development of Manchuria Through Sino-Japanese Cooperation."[60]

Confident that he could resolve the problem through business negotiations so long as high politics were kept out of the discussion, Sengoku had asked Foreign Minister Shidehara for authority to conduct talks with the NTC in the spring of 1930. Shidehara might have been expected to endorse this approach, which conformed to his commitment to peaceful "economic diplomacy" in China. However, as Ogata Yōichi has described in his study of railway negotiations during this period, the foreign minister rejected Sengoku's proposal and instead chose to pursue a two-layered, if not two-faced, approach to the dispute.[61]

The public aspect of Shidehara's policy entailed an uncharacteristically hard-line posture. In policy statements drafted in November and December 1930, the foreign minister echoed the same fierce rhetoric employed by the home newspapers and condemned Chinese plans to "encircle" the SMR and drive the company into the "jaws of death." He declared that Japan would not tolerate any Chinese railway construction posing a mortal challenge (*shimeiteki eikyō*) to the SMR and would obstruct such projects using "all available means" (*arayuru shudan*). Shidehara also called for the pursuit of a "positive policy" in which he would seek the prompt reopening of discussions over outstanding railway projects such as the Ch'angch'un–T'aonan and Kirin–Hoeryong.[62]

Beneath the surface of this tough talk, however, lay an actual negotiating position far more accommodating and flexible. Shidehara appears to have limited his classification of railways posing "mortal threats" to only the most egregiously injurious and rather improbable of lines, rumored but yet to be built, such as a Chengchiat'un–Ch'angch'un connection, rather than the working system that the NTC had already cobbled together from existing railways.[63] He regarded all others as open to discussion and favored an approach to bargaining likely not very different from what Sengoku had in mind. Moreover, he offered to revise all outstanding railway loans in favor of the Chinese side, including a renegotiation of the contract management arrangement for the Ch'angch'un–Kirin line established in the Twenty-One Demands. His view of reopening discussions on outstanding Japanese railway projects likewise demonstrated flexibility and a desire to conciliate. Ironically, Shidehara expressed his willingness to accept the NTC's initiation of the T'aoan–Solun line, a project that he had long opposed, as a positive step toward fulfillment of Japan's requirements. He suggested further that the Japanese side would drop its long-standing protests over the Kirin–Hailung and Tahushan–T'ungliao railways in exchange for no more than an agreement from Chang Hsüeh-liang to open negotiations over the Ch'angch'un–T'aonan and Kirin–Hoeryong lines. In contrast to past policy, he did not demand that the Chinese sign loan contracts, let alone begin construction, as a condition for rescinding these protests; rather his only condition was that they consent to engage in serious talks.[64]

These rather "soft" terms make it fairly clear that Shidehara had not undergone a sudden change of heart on Manchurian railway questions and that his overall approach represented a political maneuver aimed at defusing the issue. In an era of parliamentary rule and an expanded franchise, not even the most thoroughly professional of diplomats could afford to ignore such a groundswell of public opinion as that generated by agitation over railway competition, and he no doubt found the adoption of hard-line rhetoric for domestic consumption politically unavoidable. At the same time, he presented lenient bargaining terms aimed at persuading the Chinese side to offer some concessions, if only modest, that would demonstrate the efficacy of peaceful diplomacy in resolving these kinds of disputes. There is certainly no reason to believe that Shidehara included the dispatch of troops under his rubric of "all available means."[65] The foreign minister, however, clearly undertook a dangerous gamble in adopting this ploy. By characterizing Chinese actions as intolerable and employing the rhetoric of railway war, he gave legitimacy to the claims of activists and, implicitly, their demands for an appropriate response should the Chinese persist.[66] In order to avoid playing into the hands of militants, he needed at least a token of compliance from Chang Hsüeh-liang. The fact that Kimura Eiichi, whom he had recommended to fill Matsuoka's old post in the SMR directorate, would take charge of the direct talks in Mukden, offered some hope for reasonable, give-and-take discussions.[67]

Unfortunately for Shidehara, Chang Hsüeh-liang and his associates failed to see the need for any conciliatory gesture. Chang found himself preoccupied with new responsibilities in North China, which he had acquired in the aftermath of a civil war that had erupted in March 1930 and remained unsettled until October. His advisors also believed that Shidehara was playing domestic politics with the railway issue and saw no urgency for a change in their policy.[68] The foreign minister thus lost his gamble. The army and its allies had no interest in resolving the issue peacefully at this point, and from the beginning Shidehara's approach had little hope for success beyond mollifying public opinion and weakening a pretext for armed intervention. The failure to elicit even a token response from Chang Hsüeh-liang thoroughly discredited his policy of peaceful engagement, called attention to the intransigence of the Chinese side, and most important, gave credence to the notion of a grave crisis in Manchuria.

To make matters worse, the transparency of his strategy left him open to questions about his sincerity. During the opening session of the Fifty-Ninth Diet in January 1931, which took up the issue of Manchuria at length, Matsuoka leveled a withering attack on Shidehara.

It has been a year and a half since the establishment of the current cabinet. And what has the current cabinet done during that time? During the last year and a half, our agencies in the field, foremost among them the SMR, have engaged in no formal negotiations, other than an occasional exchange of official greetings. During this year and a half, what we have seen is, in fact, the thorough implementation, without reservation, of Foreign Minister Shidehara's principles of absolute inaction and passivity in Manchuria. Indeed, it is only when the views of our press begin to harden a bit or when a Diet session approaches, that suddenly Kasumigaseki [the Foreign Ministry] holds meetings and makes announcements as if negotiations over the Manchurian problem were about to begin on a grand scale. As soon as the Diet session opens, on the next day or the day after that, SMR Director Kimura is dispatched to Mukden. This is a transparent deception aimed at the Diet and domestic politics. Does [the foreign minister] believe that such an approach, lacking all sincerity and integrity, will resolve the crucial problems outstanding? Does Foreign Minister Shidehara believe that one meeting between SMR Director Kimura and Chang Hsüeh-liang will immediately create an opening to resolve all these problems? Under today's conditions, that simply won't do. Even the Chinese side publicly disparages this approach as a tactic aimed at the Diet.[69]

The railway problem continued to fester during the first half of 1931, and no progress was made, despite the persistent efforts of Kimura and Shidehara. Other incidents during the summer added to mounting tensions and intensified the perception of a Japan humiliated and besieged in Manchuria.[70] The Wanpaoshan affair in July created a new focus for agitation. The incident began as a relatively minor dispute between Chinese and Korean farmers over water rights but subsequently escalated into violent anti-Chinese riots in Korea, which took the lives of as many as 190 ethnic Chinese. *Tōkyō Asahi* reported the emergence of a "crisis on both sides of the Yalu River."[71] In August, the Chinese troops shot and killed Nakamura Shintarō, an army officer on a reconnaissance mission in north Manchuria, providing yet another focus for Japanese outrage. One newspaper article characterized the killing as "an atrocity rare even in wartime and an extreme humiliation for the government." A photograph of Captain Nakamura's distraught young widow with their infant child in her arms accompanied the report.[72]

The Making of a Radical Synthesis

The emerging sense of siege in Manchuria in 1930 and 1931 alone might have provided a sufficiently conducive environment for military action, but a fortuitous concatenation of domestic and international crises imparted further momentum in that direction. One of these parallel developments was a bitter political battle between the armed services and the Hamaguchi cabinet over a new disarmament initiative. The global spread of the depression, which compounded the serious economic slump in Japan that had begun as the result of a banking crisis in 1927, provided the second source of crisis. Neither of these developments had any intrinsic connection to the other or to the situation in Manchuria, but in combination, they created a fateful synergy in which resolution of the Manchurian question acquired magnified importance and was inextricably linked to a host of political and economic difficulties facing the country at this juncture. Among those already clamoring for action, this triple crisis produced a radical conceptual synthesis in which Manchuria became the pivotal element in schemes for resolving a much larger body of national problems.

The naval disarmament talks in London in 1930, at which Japanese negotiators agreed to further limitations on warship construction, provided the trigger for a furious dispute between the armed forces and the civilian government. Many in the navy believed that the agreement would seriously impair the nation's security and guarantee Anglo-American dominance. These talks did not directly affect ground force levels, and had warship numbers remained an isolated matter, the army might not have challenged the government's action. Driven by both an inclination toward the new diplomacy and domestic financial considerations, however, the Hamaguchi government favored broad arms reductions, and army leaders felt compelled to resist the general trend. Their response included the launching of a public awareness campaign aimed at the "popularization of national defense thought." The fact that civilian officials had agreed to impose restrictions on naval construction against the wishes of the admirals also led to a conflict over the command prerogatives of the armed forces and raised the question of whether civilians had the authority to decide, as a matter of defense as opposed to fiscal policy, the force levels for either the army or the navy without the explicit agreement of military leaders. The issue thus escalated into a constitutional problem, which brought into question the institutional claims of the armed forces for a final say in matters of national defense.[73]

This dispute, narrowly defined, had no direct bearing on the problem of Manchuria, but given the long-standing linkage of empire, national defense, and the institutional interests of the army, a cross-infection of these matters emerged almost as a matter of course. The army already felt embattled. The decade of the 1920s saw not only a precipitous fall in its prestige but also two successive arms reductions that had reduced the nation's ground forces to seventeen, pared-down standing divisions, the lowest level since the immediate aftermath of the Russo-Japanese War. In the eyes of army leaders, the very notion of further reductions clearly pointed to a government that took the issue of national security far too lightly. The fact that the same government had also adopted a policy of virtual inaction in Manchuria since taking office only confirmed that assessment. Although the connecting logic had changed over the years, a firm stand on Manchuria remained one and the same as a commitment to a strong defense in the thinking of most army leaders. Within the army, anger at the civilian government spilled over into enmity for General Ugaki, who had agreed to the elimination of four divisions in 1925, an action that had significantly diminished his moderating influence on questions of empire. The dispute, in effect, created a dynamic in which the Hamaguchi government, challenging the army on the issue of force levels and institutional prerogatives, induced the army to counterattack not only in the arena of military policy but in Manchuria as well.[74]

Some army officers took their understanding of the linkage between Manchuria and the Hamaguchi government's policies even further. The problem of a government soft on defense as well as empire went beyond the particular orientation of Hamaguchi, Shidehara, and their Minseitō associates; it was a failing rooted in the Japanese political system as a whole. In their eyes, the quality of national political leadership had degenerated since the rise of party cabinets, which had led to endemic corruption, the narrow pursuit of sectional interests, and the subordination of matters of national security and foreign policy to party strategies in parliamentary elections. The parties, in turn, found themselves beholden to the self-serving, cosmopolitan big business community that financed them. The Manchurian stalemate represented a symptom of a deeper crisis, and only an attack on the roots of the problem could resolve the impasse. The Sakurakai, an organization of middle-echelon officers who dedicated themselves to both fundamental political change at home and empire abroad and who refused to rule out a coup d'état in order to achieve those ends, exemplified this line of analysis. Few senior leaders may have shared the revolutionary orientation of these officers, but they harbored considerable sympathy for basic elements of their view.[75]

The onset of full-blown depression in 1930 had an even broader impact on how Japanese, officials and the general public alike, perceived the problem of empire. The global economic crisis did more than any imperialist polemic to discredit the claims of the new diplomacy. Favorable views of the post-imperialist order of the 1920s rested on assumptions of relatively free trade and the expectation that the reformed international system would allow a country like Japan to thrive without vast reserves of land and natural resources or captive markets associated with old notions of empire. Not only had that system failed to deliver on its promises, but the Great Powers themselves were moving toward autarky, transforming their colonial empires into closed economic blocs as countermeasures to the depression. Those who had warned against faith in the promises of Wilsonian diplomacy appeared vindicated. Under these circumstances, critics found little difficulty in making the case that adherence to the Washington system, already frayed by the breakdown of inter-power cooperation in the face of Chinese nationalism, had proved seriously mistaken. Equally important, the economic crisis and associated developments gave renewed cogency to the cause of empire as a positive solution to the nation's problems. The notion that Manchuria formed Japan's lifeline came to enjoy more credibility than ever in 1930 and 1931.[76]

Such perceptions linked the depression and Manchuria as problem and solution in a fairly straightforward manner, but the two issues also became subject to a similar kind of synthesis seen in the ideas of the Sakurakai. The same wrongheaded liberals, soft on Manchuria and dangerously complacent about defense, had placed their faith in an economic system that had demonstrated itself fundamentally dysfunctional, domestically as well as internationally. Corruption, self-interest, and an economic ideology that, in fact, encouraged selfishness stemmed from common roots in the existing political and economic system in Japan. Solving any one aspect of the problem required an attack at its source. Indeed, even if one's first and foremost concern remained Manchuria, the matter could never be settled without a fundamental renovation of Japan's established order. In this line of thinking, the distress of small shopkeepers, of the unemployed and marginally employed in the cities, and of farmers in the hard-hit Tōhoku region became tied to the problem of Manchuria.[77] Such a radical analysis had potential popular appeal. It not only spoke to the immediate concerns of a troubled and anxious people but also drew upon a long history of "imperial democracy." Throughout the industrial world, the depression had generated a populist response and an attack on the established order. Circumstance and history in Japan led that response in a decidedly expansionist direction.[78]

The synergistic effects of the disarmament and economic crises raised the stakes in Manchuria. They encouraged, among advocates of military solutions, a willingness to take greater risks than they might have considered under other circumstances. In the international arena, there appeared to be more to gain and less to lose than ever before, and the domestic political climate seemed to ensure broad support.

The Manchurian Incident

In June 1931, a special joint conference of section chiefs from the Army Ministry and general staff outlined a proposed course of action.

Item: We must work closely with our Foreign Ministry officials in turning around the anti-Japanese orientation of the Chang Hsüeh-liang regime in Manchuria. The central army authorities must endeavor to restrain and provide leadership to the Kwantung Army so as to avoid any regrettable developments.

Item: If, despite such efforts, anti-Japanese activities continue to expand, military action will likely be unavoidable.

Item: In order to resolve the Manchurian problem, it is essential that our position be understood both domestically and internationally. Through the cabinet, the army minister must endeavor to thoroughly acquaint his fellow ministers with the situation in the territory.

Item: The task of informing the general public and, in particular, the press of the situation in Manchuria will fall principally to the Military Affairs Bureau, with the cooperation of the Intelligence Department.

Item: The Military Affairs Bureau of the Army Ministry and the Intelligence Department of the Army General Staff will communicate with the appropriate parties within the Foreign Ministry to inform the interested powers of the state of anti-Japanese activities in Manchuria. Should we be faced with the need for military action, we must have in place a meticulous plan to ensure that the powers will understand our resolve and will not exert unjust pressure against us, and any action must receive prior sanction of superior authorities in order to ensure its smooth execution. . . .

Item: The task of preparing domestic and international opinion will require approximately one year, that is, until next spring, and we hope this will proceed smoothly.

Item: The leadership of the Kwantung Army must clearly understand the policy of the central authorities. For the next year, they must exercise self-restraint and forbearance and avoid being drawn into any confrontations precipitated by anti-Japanese activities. If such confrontations occur, they must act to contain them and not allow them to escalate.[79]

The deliberate efforts of the army and its allies to inflate the problem of railway competition into a major crisis during the preceding year as well as the campaign to "popularize national defense thought" were consistent with the emphasis in this document on the need for careful preparation of both public and official attitudes. It also represented, within the spectrum of opinion among those favoring military solutions, the relatively cautious position of Army Minister Minami.

The document also contained a frank admonition to the Kwantung Army not to act without explicit authorization. The concern proved well founded. Under the direction of Lieutenant Colonel Ishiwara Kanji, the garrison staff had engaged in planning for a military initiative in Manchuria since the summer of 1929. Ishiwara, whose career Mark Peattie has explored at length, was a maverick officer with unorthodox ideas about empire and national defense. He viewed his mission in Manchuria in the broader context of a historically inevitable "final war" between Japan and the United States. A military conflict on the continent, moreover, would create favorable conditions for sweeping political and economic reform at home. Like other army leaders, he regarded the resources of Manchuria as vital for national security. Unlike Koiso Kuniaki, who thought in terms of a program of strategic autarky informed by the lessons of World War I, Ishiwara, drawing upon the experience of the Russo-Japanese War and his historical study of the strategies of Frederick the Great and Napoleon Bonaparte, saw the problem within the framework of an enlarged policy of "field procurement." The peculiarities of his visions, however, are not immediately germane to understanding his plans for action. The idea of seizing Manchuria by force certainly enjoyed support far beyond Ishiwara and his followers. Ishiwara's special contribution rested in his audacity, charisma, and, most important, his role as a master strategist and tactician. Through careful preparation over the course of two years, he outlined plans in which the Kwantung Army, a relatively small unit little more than a single division strong, might conquer the territory with a minimum of reinforcement. If necessary, he believed it possible to accomplish the task without the support of the home authorities.[80]

By the summer of 1931, Ishiwara and his colleagues had persuaded themselves that the time had come to set a military solution into motion. They had no intention of exercising the kind of "self-restraint and forbearance" that central authorities had called for. Increasingly impatient and concerned that a more cautious senior leadership might allow opportunity to slip through their fingers through procrastination or, in the worst case, change their minds altogether, officers of the Manchurian garrison decided to take matters into their own hands. They had confidence that once hostilities began, the military authorities in Tokyo would have no choice but to support the troops in the field and that the civilian government would soon follow suit. During the night of September 18, 1931, Japanese military engineers set off a small explosion on the SMR tracks north of Mukden to support the fiction of a Chinese attack. In a well-orchestrated plan, Kwantung Army troops responded swiftly, occupying Mukden by the morning of the following day. The occupation of major urban centers along the SMR quickly ensued, and on September 21, Japanese forces moved against Kirin. As the garrison expanded its operations, troops from Korea provided reinforcement. Lieutenant Colonel Ishiwara and his colleagues defied repeated instructions to desist from further action and, through a variety of subterfuges, managed to evade other efforts by the home authorities to contain the conflict. In October, the Kwantung Army launched an air attack on Chinchow, the site of Chang Hsüeh-liang's government in retreat, an operation, as one historian has noted, aimed as much at Shidehara as at Chang.[81] By November, just two months after the start of the campaign, Japanese troops had probed Tsitsihar in the north and were poised to attack Chang's remaining forces in the vicinity of Chinchow. Although occupation of the territory fell short of complete as of the beginning of the new year, concentrated as it was in the major urban centers of the south, the military situation had been all but decided. Adopting a policy of nonresistance in an effort to avoid provocation while awaiting diplomatic intervention, Chang Hsueh-liang's forces had withdrawn south of the Great Wall. The majority of Chang's senior officials remained loyal, but a number of defections strengthened the Japanese position. As the Soviet Union's disinclination to intervene became clear, the Kwantung Army's confidence increased. In the spring of 1932, Japanese troops expanded their occupation to the north, investing Harbin in April. Thereafter, apart from one major flare-up of fighting in Jehol in early 1933, the principal military actions consisted of mop-up operations and efforts to suppress guerrilla resistance.[82]

Military and civil authorities in Tokyo initially opposed the Kwantung Army's actions, and during the first few weeks of the affair, they pursued vigorous efforts to halt operations. For Foreign Minister Shidehara, the events in Manchuria were nothing short of catastrophic. For Army Minister Minami, they represented precisely the kind of precipitous and irresponsible behavior he had feared from the garrison and had explicitly warned against earlier in the summer. The Kwantung Army, however, steadfastly refused to stand down. Its leaders asserted the autonomy of field command in military emergencies and discovered a string of pretexts to continue offensive action. The defiance of the Manchurian garrison, compounded by the collusion of the Korean Army, created an extraordinary problem for the home government. The failure of even the Army General Staff to secure the compliance of its soldiers in the field left the authorities in Tokyo with few options. To treat Ishiwara and his colleagues as mutineers and deal with them as such or to admit to the world that the Japanese government had lost control of its own armed forces lay beyond the pale of consideration for most policymakers.

Making matters worse, military-civil unity in Tokyo proved short-lived, as army authorities began eyeing the garrison's action with increasing favor. General Minami and other senior army leaders clearly did not oppose military action in Manchuria in principle, given their own plans for the spring of 1932. They based their initial opposition to Kwantung Army operations on a number of specific reservations, which dissipated rather quickly as the conquest progressed. As noted, the Soviets showed no evidence of a readiness to intervene. The garrison's striking successes, moreover, pointed to a quick and decisive victory. An unexpectedly enthusiastic public response proved particularly encouraging.[83] These circumstances precipitated an opportunistic conversion among the more cautious army leaders in Tokyo. For similar reasons, such conversions spread well beyond the army. Defections in the civilian government led to the fall of the Minseitō cabinet in December and put an end to Shidehara's diplomatic career. Consistent with its posture of recent years, the new Seiyūkai government adopted a position more sympathetic to action in Manchuria. Prime Minister Inukai Tsuyoshi, whose views on empire and national defense had shifted significantly by the time he assumed the Seiyūkai's presidency in 1929, retained enough of his old orientation to express grave reservations about developments in the territory. Voices of restraint in the government, however, had lost much of their strength. By the end of the year, moreover, even moderates had come to the conclusion that, like it or not, events had passed the point of no return and that the restoration of the status quo ante was no longer realistic. By the beginning of 1932, the government in Tokyo signaled its readiness to acknowledge the seizure and partition of Manchuria as a *fait accompli*. Many leaders wholeheartedly endorsed this direction as a positive development. Others acquiesced with great reluctance and dedicated themselves to containing the damage already done to Japan's international position and to forestalling further recklessness. Regardless of underlying attitudes, however, the Japanese government had committed the nation to following the Kwantung Army's lead.[84]

Ishiwara and his colleagues had initially aimed for a sequence of occupation, partition, and annexation. Shortly after the launching of military action, however, they began to rethink the goal of a straightforward colonial settlement and to entertain the idea of establishing an independent Manchurian state completely severed from China and under Japanese control. Garrison leaders vacillated on this point through the end of 1931, but by early 1932 they had fully committed themselves to the new scheme. Setting up a provisional committee of local collaborators as a front in February, they declared the independence of the four provinces of Fengt'ien, Kirin, Heilungkiang, and Jehol. On March 1, they proclaimed the founding of the sovereign state of Manchoukuo. At first, the desire to circumvent Tokyo's opposition had been their primary reason for adopting this independence gambit. However transparent the pretext might be, presenting developments in Manchuria as the work of an indigenous separatist movement created obstacles to intervention on the part of home authorities and their attempts to restore control.[85] As leaders in Tokyo reconciled themselves to the inevitability of conquest, however, the home government itself began to see advantages to the scheme in mitigating the criticism of the international community. As one Foreign Ministry official pointed out, claims of Manchurian independence would not deceive anyone, but given an assumption that the powers remained reluctant to intervene, the international community might welcome a pretext for avoiding open confrontation.[86] The idea, to borrow a phrase from the lexicon of late twentieth-century American diplomacy, was to hide the Japanese conquest behind a blind of "plausible deniability." The home government thus came to accept the formula of independence. Japan formally recognized Manchoukuo in September 1932, one year after initiation of hostilities, and quite fittingly, given the circumstances, appointed the commander of the Kwantung Army as its first ambassador to the new state.[87]

To an astute observer of East Asian affairs at the turn of the decade, a Sino-Japanese collision over Manchuria would hardly have come as a surprise. Without deeper knowledge of trends within the Japanese military, however, few could have foreseen the scope and scale of Japanese aggression. Even less predictable were the precipitous collapse of moderate leadership by the end of 1931 and the acceptance of the conquest as a *fait accompli* by the government as a whole by the beginning of the new year. During the early months of the Manchurian war, the powers had, indeed, muted their criticism of Japanese action in the expectation that Shidehara and his colleagues would bring matters under control. The political tactics of the Kwantung Army and its ability to hold the authorities in Tokyo virtually hostage to its defiant actions offer a partial explanation for the abject failure of efforts at restraint. Manchuria had provided Ishiwara and his colleagues a place to stand and a lever long enough to move the empire. At a deeper level, the paralysis of moderate political leadership owed much to the depression and its contribution to discrediting their policies. Standing up to the army would have demanded not only great courage but also a political strength they no longer enjoyed. As Akira Iriye has argued, the impact of the depression represented the culmination of a long erosion of the position of those advocating Japan's adherence to the post-imperialist order.[88]

An understanding of the dualism of Japan's policies toward China north and south of the Wall during this decade suggests yet another line of explanation. Moderates and the new diplomats had proved themselves either unwilling or unable to call for a clean break in Manchuria and to pursue a forthright policy of disengagement. Such a line of action would have presented enormous political difficulties, to be sure, yet not even Shidehara appears to have made a concerted attempt in this direction. His disinclination to follow Sengoku's advice and his adoption of a belligerent posture during the railway war highlights a reluctance to take a firm stand on Manchuria consistent with his convictions. The Hamaguchi government's rejection of Yamamoto's scheme for a gradual retreat points to a similar attitude. This orientation did not emerge anew with the tense climate after 1928. Shidehara had opted to tolerate the railway schemes of Matsuoka and the army in 1924, despite grave misgivings, and endorsed an agreement that opened the door to the new imperialism. Throughout the 1920s, moderates saw the need to avoid forcing the issue, to compromise with activist demands, and to resign themselves to some measure of continued expansion in Manchuria. They directed their primary energies in this policy arena to limiting injury to Japan's international position stemming from activist initiatives. The first Eastern Conference established this basic pattern. If Hara and his colleagues found themselves unable to press for full disengagement at the height of moderate power in the early 1920s, we could hardly expect their political successors to behave with greater boldness at the nadir of their influence a decade later. Their acquiescence to the Kwantung Army's *fait accompli* in 1931, along with their subsequent efforts to adapt national policy to the realities of Manchoukuo and contain the corollary damage caused by aggression, in a sense, represented an extension of what they had been doing for much of the decade.

Conclusion

Much of the literature dealing with Japanese imperialism in the 1930s tends to highlight its radical, if not revolutionary, qualities. There would certainly seem ample reason for such an emphasis. In foreign policy, the conquest put an end to Tokyo's long-standing commitment to multilateralism in China and, more broadly, led to a definitive rejection of the principles of the new diplomacy, a breach symbolized by Japan's withdrawal from the League of Nations in 1933. In the aftermath of the Manchurian Incident, the nation launched itself on a course of defiant autonomy in its external affairs and isolated itself from the international community. Japanese policymakers undertook a new course in the arena of defense as well, reversing the decade-long efforts at arms reduction and repudiating the idea of collective security in favor of a program of "peace through strength." Rearmament, alongside economic recovery, emerged as a national priority. In the political world at home, the nation's elites, with considerable support from a broader public, turned away from the liberalizing trends of the 1920s and looked increasingly toward the army and the bureaucracy for leadership in this time of crisis. This development, in turn, led to a concomitant erosion of parliamentary power and a dramatic decline in the influence of moderates in domestic as well as in foreign affairs. These changes were mirrored in the ideological sphere by the gradual spread of the radical synthesis of the turn of the decade from the margins of the army officer corps to the mainstream of military-bureaucratic leadership.[1]

A bird's-eye view of developments in occupied Manchuria also appears to underscore a fundamental break with the past. The Japanese army proceeded to destroy systematically the existing Chinese regional state and replace it with a political organization of its own design. Although Manchoukuo remained, in law, outside Japan's colonial empire, its administrators reported to the staff of the Kwantung Army. Its head of state, P'u-i, hand-picked by the Japanese and lacking any roots or base of power in Chinese Manchuria, signed a series of treaties establishing what amounted to a pro-tectorate relationship. Controlled from within and without, the new state enjoyed little more sovereignty in practice than did Korea or Taiwan.[2] The crossing of the Rubicon between informal and formal empire in itself marked a basic departure from patterns that had prevailed for a quarter-century. Some have argued that Manchoukuo represented a significant in-novation in strategies for controlling foreign territory and foreshadowed the creation of the Greater East Asian Coprosperity Sphere.[3]

Contemporary observers as well as later writers have characterized Man-churia during the 1930s as a great imperialist "experiment."[4] The notion would seem particularly apt for Japan's economic policies in the territory. Scholars have directed their attention, in particular, to the program of heavy industrialization, which outlined breathtaking production targets for iron and steel, chemicals, precision engineering, liquid fuels, and even automobile manufacturing. Economic historian Hara Akira has noted that this attempt at the heavy industrialization of a dependent territory represented a unique undertaking in colonialism worldwide.[5] An emphasis on state planning was perhaps the most striking aspect of the program, which, many scholars have argued, provided important lessons for subsequent economic policy in the home islands. Manchoukuo's experiment in the creation of a managed econ-omy culminated in the adoption of a formal five-year plan in 1937.[6] This commitment to create a new order in Manchuria was reflected in a radical turn in the ideology of empire, which came to be characterized by a discor-dant mixture of revolutionary and reactionary utopianism that incorporated an "imperial socialism" of the strain associated with Takahashi Kamekichi (1894–1977) as well as Confucian ethics and moral economy.[7] As Louise Young has pointed out, social imperialism also occupied an important place in the management of Japan's "brave new empire." Partly in an effort to re-lieve agrarian distress at home, policymakers set into motion a mass immi-gration scheme focused on north Manchuria, which SMR publicists de-scribed as a "covered wagon movement" aimed at settling the region's vast prairies.[8]

These trends at home as well as in Manchuria have led some historians to argue that the 1930s witnessed the emergence of a new kind of imperialism that had more in common with Italian Fascism and German National Socialism, along with their inherent propensity toward external aggression, than with older patterns of empire-building originating in the late nineteenth century. Whatever the validity of a "Japanese fascism," it is clear that the depression triggered social, political, and economic upheaval throughout the industrial world and created both the opportunity and the need for radical countermeasures everywhere, including the United States. That Japan might also undertake drastic solutions to resolve its crisis should hardly come as a surprise. Indeed, given the centrality of empire to the nation's development, we might well expect a Japanese "new deal" to entail a major imperialist component.[9]

There is no denying that the events of the 1930s lend themselves to interpretation in revolutionary terms. At the same time, however, an understanding of the history of empire-building in the territory suggests that we should view the construction of Manchoukuo, along with some of the broader policy changes unfolding in the aftermath of the Manchurian Incident, as the denouement of an older story as much as the beginning of a new. Examined in the light of the record of pre-conquest Japanese Manchuria, much of what we see emerging during this decade seems rather familiar, recognizable as logical extensions of patterns, trends, and policies established well before 1931.

The foreign and defense policies of the 1930s, for example, were a clear departure from those pursued in the recent past, yet the general line taking form in the aftermath of the Manchurian Incident represented nothing new in itself; rather, it was the unfettered expression of a course of action long favored by the expansionist camp. The army and its allies had regarded the Washington system as nothing more than imperialism, American style. In their view, the quest for empire and the politics of power had never lost their relevance. A strong defense provided the best guarantee of peace, and only fools, lulled into complacency by high-minded promises, placed their faith in treaties and collective security agreements. Their grudging acquiescence to the policies of the 1920s rested on a recognition of realities in the international sphere as well as domestic politics. Even so, they had forced moderates to compromise and to tolerate an energetic, albeit truncated, expansionist program in Manchuria in exchange for adherence to the rules of the new order south of the Wall. The Manchurian Incident, along with its strategic and diplomatic consequences, which shattered the framework of compromise and paralyzed the moderates, cleared the way for a triumph of the activist line. In this context, any contrasts drawn between the 1920s and 1930s, and between the old imperialism and the new diplomacy, must bear in mind that Japan's leadership as a whole had never embraced the postwar order fully. The change, indeed, is better understood as a shift in the equilibrium of an existing dualism rather than a revolutionary break.

As I argued in the preceding chapter, the momentum for conquest had been building for some time, as a vanishing imperialist middle ground left policymakers only the stark choices of complete retreat and outright seizure. The colonial proclivities inherent in Japanese interests in Manchuria from the beginning, however, point to deeper, historical tendencies pushing expansion toward formal empire. Informal methods permitted under the rules of Great Power engagement in China provided a poor match for an imperialism oriented toward national defense, *Lebensraum*, and long-term economic development. External constraints as well as internal opposition, however, precluded colonial solutions before 1931, and activist leaders had devised a series of innovative substitutes that pushed steadily toward the threshold of direct rule. I suggested at the beginning of this study that, given these proclivities, an understanding of the Manchurian Incident requires us to ask why a final settlement took so long to achieve. In large part, the answer lies in the fertile imagination of a long line of imperialist statesmen such as Gotō Shinpei, Kodama Gentarō, Nishihara Kamezō, Matsuoka Yōsuke, and Tanaka Giichi. On the one hand, these men personified the relentless energy driving expansionism forward and may thus be regarded as the architects of Japanese Manchuria. On the other hand, their creativity in reconciling the conflicting demands of expansion and maintaining harmony with the powers made a circumscribed imperialism possible. Matsuoka's ingenuity, for example, allowed Japan to have both empire in Manchuria and membership in the Washington system at the same time during the 1920s. Tanaka attempted to preserve that balance during his troubled tenure.

The legacy of pre-conquest Japanese Manchuria in the economic programs of Manchoukuo appears even more direct. For the most part, the radical policies of the 1930s represented an acceleration and expansion of an older agenda and resulted from the elimination of obstacles impeding imperialist progress before 1931. Significantly, although the pace of such undertakings as railway building picked up markedly, economic planners devoted almost all their efforts until 1936 toward clearing the backlog of unfinished construction projects dating back to the first decade of the venture.[10] The promotion of Japanese settlement in Manchuria had formed a key element of policy since 1913, and many activists had argued that the primary barrier to success lay in Chinese obstruction. Conquest finally removed that impediment. Indeed, what is surprising is not that Japanese planners in Manchoukuo initiated a major push for Japanese immigration but that their initiatives remained rather modest before 1937, and their achievements, even more so. Between 1932 and 1936, the resident Japanese population in the territory doubled, yet the larger part of the growth occurred in the Railway Zone and Kwantung, where Japanese had long enjoyed established property rights.[11] In 1932, policymakers launched an experimental program for settling some 3,000 Japanese farmers in the north in five successive waves. Even this project, however, ran into serious difficulty when forced land sales provoked a Chinese peasant uprising in northern Kirin.[12] Conquest clearly failed to remove all obstacles in the quest for *Lebensraum* in Manchuria.

The idea of autarky, as a possible solution to the nation's economic crisis during the 1930s, received greater attention from a broader range of policymakers than ever before, but the drive for self-sufficiency had clearly formed the centerpiece of Japanese Manchuria's development program since the end of World War I.[13] Interestingly enough, Koiso Kuniaki, appointed chief of staff of the Kwantung Army in August 1932, played an instrumental role in managing economic policy during the first few years of Manchoukuo.[14] As for the emphasis on heavy industry, often regarded as a hallmark of the 1930s, it is unmistakably rooted in the "industrial Manchuria" program of the 1920s. The SMR had initiated the vast majority of the projects at the core of Manchoukuo's industrial sector, including defense-related production, long before the founding of the new state.

Indeed, during Manchoukuo's early years, the SMR not only retained managerial control over these industries but also served provisionally as the central planning agency of the new state, a logical extension of the role it had played in the territory from the time of its founding. Although the SMR was gradually displaced by new economic policy organs, Manchuria's experiment in "imperial socialism" before the inauguration of the five-year plan in 1937 constituted, in essence, an expanded version of the SMR's long-established practice of "industrial organizing."[15] Alfred Chandler has suggested some intriguing affinities between corporate capitalism and planned economies in his seminal work on the rise of the modern business corporation. He notes that in large, multi-unit business organizations, managerial bureaucracies came to employ administrative methods to coordinate the flow of materials, funds, and information across a diversified set of inter-locking economic operations. What he describes as "managerial capitalism" emerged when "administrative coordination took the place of market mechanisms in coordinating the activities of the economy and allocating its resources."[16] The link between "managerial capitalism" and "managed" econ-omies may seem somewhat far-fetched in the American historical context, but the connection appears considerably more plausible in Japanese Man-churia. In a situation in which a single, highly-diversified, quasi-official cor-poration dominated the modern sector of the territorial economy, it is not surprising to find a blurring of the boundaries between business strategy and economic planning. Significantly, the staff of the SMR found little difficulty in recasting the practice of business administration and the mission of the company itself in terms of the "imperial socialism" of the 1930s. In the tradi-tion of colonial economic planning, the company had long opposed a laissez-faire policy toward business investment and warned that uncontrolled pri-vate enterprise would hinder the development of the territory's resources. Ishizuka Eizō's survey team in 1905 had accused Mitsui of seeking control of the Fushun colliery in order to suppress competitive production. It is only fitting, then, that some of the more radical attacks on the evils of free-enterprise capitalism in Manchoukuo emanated from the SMR itself.[17]

If the Manchurian economic experiment of the 1930s had significant precedents in the earlier work of the SMR, in a broader sense, much of the brave-new-world ethos of Manchoukuo might also be traced to pre-conquest roots. A self-conscious imperial utopianism appears to have in-formed Japanese thinking about the venture from early on. The grandiose scale of the SMR's stations, the conspicuous displays of engineering skill throughout its facilities, and the lavish attention paid to urban development in the Railway Zone, for which Gotō Shinpei's critics took him to task in 1913, reflected a general concern among imperialists with their "civilizing mis-sion" as well as a particular mindset that Richard Samuels describes as "techno-nationalism." Great buildings and bright new machines impressed the "natives" with the empire's power and presented to the West Japan's cre-dentials as a worthy colonizer. Audacious undertakings, however, also mir-rored the spirit of the railway age, its visions of the future, and its faith in the transformative power of modern technology. Raymond Betts suggests that the dreams of some of the more ambitious railway builders of the late nineteenth and early twentieth century and the imaginative writings of Jules Verne had much in common. The same spirit was exemplified in the images of Japanese Manchuria that the SMR's publicists sought to cultivate: late-model locomotives hauling sleek trains across the Manchurian plain, steel trestles spanning the Yalu River, and the towering smokestacks of the Anshan Ironworks. The Railway Zone, in particular, served as a showcase of what might be described as a "techo-imperialist" vision. One promotional tract published in 1920, for example, describes the visit of an imaginary tourist to the Zone in terms that suggest the Disneyesque atmosphere of an imperialist theme park, with its promise of a glimpse into the future of a Japanese Manchuria under the benevolent corporate rule of the SMR.[18]

In noting programmatic continuities, I do not wish to minimize the dramatic changes in the scale, scope, and pace of implementation. Accelerating development by eliminating political obstacles, after all, had formed the primary purpose of the conquest. Nor am I overlooking the introduction of substantively new elements in the policy agenda after 1931. The establishment of uncontested Japanese control over the territory vastly broadened the horizons of possibility and created opportunities to do things that, as Kudō Takeo put it in his pessimistic 1928 study, the Japanese could never "even dream about" before. Moreover, the depression not only recast autarky from a purely strategic program to a countermeasure against the economic crisis but also imbued immigration policy with a decidedly social-imperialist coloring. Although Japan's isolation and insecurity were self-inflicted, they nonetheless added urgency to the Manchurian program as a whole.

Yet even in the emergence of these new elements we may find a dynamic continuity. The revision of programmatic aims in response to changing needs and opportunities in the environment had characterized policymaking in Manchuria from the beginning, and it would come as a surprise if such innovation suddenly ceased in 1931. In addition, we have noted the importance of contingency planning in the outlook of Japan's imperialists and their appraisal of the value of empire as a hedge against an uncertain future. In the 1930s, albeit partly as a result of Japan's own doing, that future had arrived, and Manchuria's role as the nation's lifeline found itself put to the test.

Manchoukuo represented the culmination of a long history of empire-building. The trajectory of development, however, followed a decidedly nonlinear course. Indeed, a knowledge of the starting conditions and the initial vectors of late Meiji imperialism alone would hardly suffice to extrapolate the outcome 25 years later. Manchoukuo represented no more than one obscure and narrow branch in a highly ramified tree of historical possibility arising from the roots of the Russo-Japanese War. At the same time, the evolutionary progression I have attempted to reconstruct in this book, however convoluted, traced a pattern far from haphazard. It is possible to discern from within the process of development a logic of incremental, cumulative, and adaptive change worth reviewing in summary fashion here.

Manchuria first entered Japanese imperialist considerations as a target of opportunity. There is no doubt as to the dedication of Meiji leaders to the cause of expansion and the place of empire in their visions of the nation's future. Yet if any direction for expansion beyond the acquisition of Korea made itself evident before the summer of 1904, it pointed southward toward Fukien and not toward the lands across the Yalu River. The Japanese held pressing strategic interests in Manchuria, but the settlement they envisioned, even after the opening of hostilities with Russia, centered on neutralization rather than occupation. The abrupt reversal of commitments to the Open Door and the redirection of expansionist attention from south to north were an opportunistic response to an unexpected degree of military success. Meiji imperialism was an art of the possible, and Manchuria became desirable in the autumn of 1905, not because of its intrinsic qualities, which remained unchanged, but because it had fallen within Japanese reach.

As in Taiwan a decade earlier, the Japanese had no fixed, predefined goals for exploiting their Manchurian acquisitions. They formulated their policies through a process of retrofitting productive goals and purposes to a course of action determined largely by circumstance, a pattern I have described as "adaptive." The Japanese found themselves taking possession of a leased territory on the tip of the Liaotung Peninsula and operating a railway running from Port Arthur to Ch'angch'un, not because these concessions best suited their own needs and capabilities, but because they had inherited them from the Russians. As a result, policy formulation in 1905 demanded not an open-ended deliberation of "Whither Japanese imperialism?" but a consideration of the more pragmatic and immediate problem of what to do with a railway in Manchuria. In a sense, the effort to find worthy answers to this question formed the driving force behind the development of Japanese policy in the decades that followed.

During an era in which belief in the omnipotence of the railway ran as deep as faith in the value of empire, neither this question nor the range of possible answers proved as narrowly circumscribed as they might seem. The versatility of this technology as an instrument capable of transforming Manchuria according to Japanese will could serve a wide variety of schemes, from the modestly commercial to the audaciously colonial. The nature of the territory further broadened the horizons of imperial possibility. As a rough frontier land, relatively undeveloped and underpopulated, yet vast and rich in natural resources, Manchuria offered the Japanese opportunities akin to what Americans had found in the great expanses west of the Mississippi. These same conditions might have disappointed those primarily interested in short-term commercial gains, but for dedicated imperialists who saw empire as an investment in the future, the untapped potential in a realm as close to a wilderness as they might find in East Asia made the venture particularly attractive.

This adaptive imperialism generated a number of corollaries important to understanding the evolutionary dynamics shaping Japanese Manchuria. It encouraged a diversity of strategic, economic, and geopolitical schemes for exploiting the territory. Manchuria provided a bulwark against Russian and Chinese threats as well as the forces of chaos endangering peace in Asia. It simultaneously offered a lucrative trade in soybeans and coal and, in time, would provide a valuable source of industrial raw materials along with a market for Japanese manufactured goods. Through the integration of Manchuria with Korea and the home islands by means of a customs, currency, and railway union, Japan might eventually construct a protected economic sphere in Northeast Asia. If nothing else, even passively holding a claim in the territory would ensure Japan a place at the table in bargaining over the future of China. The versatility of uses permitted the coexistence of different views of empire and appraisals of the value of Manchuria; it offered something for everyone and thus broadened support for the venture. At the same time, a process of exploration that allowed for the regular discovery of new utilities also made possible the constant renewal of purpose, a periodic "reinvention" of Japanese imperialism in Manchuria. Reinvention, in turn, goes a long way toward explaining both the persistence of the empire-building process and the gradual escalation of encroachments over the course of a quarter-century.

We must not take the tenacity of Japan's undertaking in Manchuria for granted. Although the span of time might seem unimpressive, the quarter-century between the Russo-Japanese War and the Manchurian Incident

constituted an era of enormous upheaval in the international environment
and of rapid transformation in Japan. Moreover, as a result of the opposition
of the powers and mounting resistance on the part of the Chinese, the costs
of empire-building rose steadily over the years. Nonetheless, the Japanese
persisted. A variety of factors contributed to this seemingly immovable
commitment. The memory of the Russo-Japanese War certainly provided a
powerful binding force. Japan experienced the most terrible armed conflict
in its modern history before 1937 and its first total war in the confrontation
with Russia. Japanese from all walks of life came to vest the meaning of that
struggle in Manchuria, a prize acquired at a horrific cost in blood and gold.
Redeeming that sacrifice, one way or another, became an obligation that the
nation's leaders, moderates included, found difficult to set aside. Memory
alone, however, could not have exerted an abiding influence on national policy had the idea of empire, at least to the activist camp, failed to retain its
fundamental cogency. In this context, we should bear in mind the deep historical impact of imperialism on the construction of the Japanese worldview
from the beginning of the Meiji era. Japan was introduced to the principles
of international relations at gunpoint, and the values of the age of empire
shaped the thinking of a generation of political leaders and intellectuals. And
as is often the case in cultural and linguistic borrowing by peoples living on
the periphery of dominant civilizations, received wisdom may persist unmodified among the borrowers long after those same ideas have been abandoned at the source.

It would be a mistake, however, to regard this sustained Japanese faith in
empire as a static imperialist fundamentalism immune to the influence of
new ideas. The nation's experience in the twentieth century did much to re-
inforce the object lessons of the mid-nineteenth. For all the high-minded
discourse of the 1920s, which implied that the size of a nation's territorial
endowment mattered little in a world dedicated to peace and free trade, no
Great Power had actually liberated its colonies. Many Japanese understandably regarded the claims of the new diplomacy with skepticism and
viewed American criticisms of imperialism as a case of the rich preaching the
virtues of poverty to the poor. American immigration policy served as a persistent reminder that the Japanese remained unwelcome in much of the
world, a circumstance that simultaneously undermined the claims of inter-
nationalism while strengthening expansionist arguments for Lebensraum. For
those who had struggled to keep the imperialist faith in the lean years fol-

lowing World War I, the events of the turn of the decade came as a vindication. Global depression and the rise of protectionism belied the promise of prosperity through cooperation and economic liberalism. Claims as to the virtues of imperialist abstinence rang hollow as the Great Powers exploited the advantages of empire to defend themselves against the onslaught of economic crisis. Activists regarded these developments not as a betrayal but as a confirmation of their beliefs and an occasion to reproach their liberal and moderate colleagues with a resounding "I told you so."

Although war memory and the enduring strength of imperialist values formed a conceptual bedrock anchoring Japan's venture in Manchuria, the contributions of these factors to persistence are easily overstated. In the final analysis, the resilience of the Japanese commitment in the face of adverse pressures lay not so much in the permanence of its foundations as in its adaptability. The sustained relevance of empire-building in a world undergoing rapid transformation resulted more from the constant renewal of meaning and purpose, from periodic wholesale reinvention, than from a rigid defiance of change. Policy developments in 1913 offer a good example of creative imperialist revisionism. Revolution in China, changing strategic circumstances, shifting policies among the Great Powers, and disappointing results from the first five years of the venture led moderates and their allies in the navy to question the wisdom of the nation's single-minded devotion to expansion in Manchuria. Activists answered the challenge by introducing a new threat assessment of a two-front war against both China and Russia, which weaned defense policy away from the exclusively anti-Russian orientation of the early postwar years. In the economic sphere, they acknowledged the marginality of commercial returns but called for a greater emphasis on long-term development and the economic integration of Manchuria and Korea. Most important, they advocated the recentering of Japanese policy on the aim of *Lebensraum*. The need for territory suitable for mass settlement, underscored by a new wave of anti-Japanese legislation in California, defined a basis for Japan to act toward Manchuria in a way different from its approaches to other regions of China and to adopt an orientation at variance with the practices of the powers.

Imperialists undertook their most comprehensive and historically significant effort at reinvention, however, at the end of World War I, when they introduced the idea of an economic defense perimeter. The timing of this initiative proved crucial. Fundamental changes in the framework of international diplomacy, national defense, and relations with the Chinese rendered older policies geared toward the opportunities and needs of the age of empire largely irrelevant or impractical. The emergence of strategic autarky as a new programmatic aim at this juncture rewired the connection between empire and national defense, cast the economic value of Manchuria in an entirely new light, and presented the nation with an expansionist purpose worthy of enormous cost and risk. The survival of Japanese Manchuria into the 1920s thus owed much to the innovative work of Koiso Kuniaki, Nishihara Kamezō, and Shōda Kazue.

The adaptive qualities of Japanese imperialism in Manchuria help to explain not only persistence in the face of mounting pressures for disengagement but also the tendency toward escalation over time. From the outset, efforts at rationalization pointed toward uses of the territory better served by formal rather than informal methods of management and produced such schemes as colonization in which a gradual expansion of control formed an inherent element. Other factors, however, also contributed to a steady increase in the level of encroachment as well as rising expectations of benefit. The cumulative effects of successive initiatives and their subsequent rationalization into new policy lines played an important part in driving this trend. Japanese activity dramatically changed the environment in Manchuria over the years, and much of that transformation resulted, to be sure, from deliberate effort. Development also broadened the horizons of possibility, however, and created opportunities not originally foreseen. The emergence of an "industrial Manchuria" strategy offers a case in point. Most policymakers would have dismissed the notion of transplanting smokestack industries to a rough frontier land as running counter to the conventional economic wisdom of modern imperialism. Yet partly as a by-product of the SMR's need for comprehensive technological support facilities and partly as a result of the scientific colonization work of the company's research organization, industrial foundations began to emerge. Company planners subsequently nurtured these seeds into a new and systematic way of exploiting the territory. Koiso Kuniaki also drew inspiration for at least some elements of his scheme for strategic autarky from projects that the SMR had put into place for entirely different reasons. Plans for an ironworks at Anshan, for crossbreeding sheep, and for introducing new strains of cotton and rice antedated World War I. Koiso harnessed these projects to greater and unanticipated uses in his program for an economic defense perimeter.

The adaptive qualities of Japanese imperialism fueled escalation in yet another manner. Many of the initiatives launched in Manchuria over the course of two and a half decades fell wide of their mark, and no small number ended in abject failure. For moderates, the lack of demonstrable success in realizing the territory's promise provided an argument for downgrading the nation's commitments. Activists, however, regarded failure not as an indication of the intrinsic impracticality of their aims but as the result of Chinese obstruction and the inadequacy of Japanese control in Manchuria. The solution, in their view, rested in demands for additional rights and concessions and an intensification of pressure on the Chinese. The debates of 1913 provide an example of this dynamic at work. Moderates initiated their critique of policy by emphasizing the meager quality of achievements to date in an effort to curb further expansionist initiatives. Yet activists responded with a call for more aggressive action and pointed out that the shortcomings in efforts to promote Japanese settlement, for example, stemmed from Chinese refusals to grant land rights. The remedy for this problem, along with other difficulties encountered in the expansionist program, lay in an escalation of Japanese demands on a broad front. The momentum generated by this activist response provided the drive behind the Twenty-One Demands of 1915. Arguments along these lines might appear as a convenient excuse for the failure of imperialism to deliver on its promises. Moderates, no doubt, saw activist logic as a call to throw good money after bad. At the same time, the colonial proclivities inherent in Japanese policy aims suggest a rational connection between failure and escalation as well. For activists, whose patience with the halfway measures of informal empire ran thin to begin with, criticism provided precisely the justification they needed to push policy toward the colonial threshold. Under these circumstances, the line of attack adopted by moderates in 1913 proved entirely counterproductive. Indeed, toward the end of the 1920s, nothing lent more weight to the case for conquest than the mounting evidence of the thorough bankruptcy of a restrained imperialism.

Closely related to the dialectic of frustration and escalation was the propensity of activists to raise their expectations and inflate their promises as the costs of expansion began to rise. In response to mounting pressures for disengagement, they adapted their policy aims in a manner that justified a continued commitment. The debates of 1913, once again, offer a good example. Concerns unique to Japan and vital to the nation's future, such as the need for living space, warranted a policy that defied international trends and risked open confrontation with the Chinese. Strategic autarky likewise reflected this pattern of escalation. Only a life-and-death matter of national defense could have provided sufficient motive to stand against the combined onslaught of a maturing Chinese nationalism and the forces of the new order. Not surprisingly, activists made even greater promises, embodied in the radical synthesis emerging with the onset of the depression, to justify the conquest in 1931. This pattern of argument, which steadily and deliberately raised anticipated benefits to offset growing costs, might offer a better case for speciousness than the logic of frustration and escalation. We must temper such an interpretation, however, with an understanding of the open-endedness of the adaptive pattern in imperial policymaking. The venture began without predetermined goals and, accordingly, lacked a clear framework for evaluating success and failure. Activists never defined a ceiling in their appraisal of Manchuria's value, and the absence of such limits rendered impossible any meaningful cost-benefit analysis. In their eyes, Manchuria represented an imperial cornucopia, and if the claims they made to justify its possession seemed endless, such was the nature of the bounty of empire. Only the most narrow-minded and shortsighted of "bean counters," whom Gotō Shinpei roundly chastised in his 1914 speech, would seek to set a fixed value on Manchuria based on the returns it offered at the moment.

The propensity toward reinvention and the open-endedness of the commitment presented Japanese critics of Manchuria policy with an elusive, constantly moving target. Moderates thus found themselves persistently disadvantaged in their competition with the activists. This problem, however, was only one manifestation of a deck stacked against advocates of restraint by the unique and compelling opportunities that Japan encountered in Manchuria. At the outset of the venture, for example, the Russian legacy pushed Japanese policymakers into a more aggressive course of action than they would have considered had they started from a clean slate. Itō Hirobumi's arguments for a limited, commercial use of the railway proved unpersuasive in the face of the far greater possibilities inherent in the apparatus designed by Russian imperialists. Special conditions in Manchuria further encouraged the pursuit of more audacious schemes, such as colonization, than even activists might have contemplated elsewhere in China. The opportunities of World War I delivered a major blow to opponents of aggressive expansion, who seemed to be gaining the upper hand between 1911 and 1914. Moderate ascendancy in Manchurian affairs after the war was checked by the fortuitous appearance of Chang Tso-lin in 1920. His offer of a partnership provided the basis for a framework of continued expansion in the territory that activists, at the low ebb of their political fortunes, could never have established on their own. The growing dominance of leaders of a moderate persuasion in most other areas of national affairs notwithstanding, opportunity and circumstance repeatedly undermined their efforts to rein in activist initiatives in Manchuria.

This dynamic is essential to understanding the nature of Taishō imperialism, a problem raised at the beginning of this study. To be sure, opportunity had played a central role throughout the history of Japanese imperialism. Empire-building in the Meiji era proceeded along the path of least resistance rather than that of an autonomous strategic or economic logic. Shōwa imperialism was no less opportunistic in its own way. Depression, the breakdown of the international order, and a deepening domestic crisis provided strong justifications for bold action in Manchuria. Yet it is questionable whether the pressing problems cited by the army and its allies would have led to imperialist solutions in the absence of a long history of empire-building in Manchuria. The legacy of the SMR contributed to the developments of the early 1930s in much the same way as Japan's inheritance from Russia had fueled the audacity of the expansionist course launched in 1905. There is, however, a significant difference in the relative importance of opportunity in shaping the imperialisms of the Meiji, Taishō, and Shōwa eras. The Meiji environment predisposed the nation's political elites to look for fortuitous openings and to take advantage of them wherever they might appear. The same might be said of the early Shōwa climate. Such predisposing factors, in contrast, although not entirely absent, were markedly weaker during the Taishō years. Opportunity thus played a correspondingly greater role by amplifying comparatively feeble expansionist pressures into an unexpectedly vigorous imperialism in Manchuria.

This is not to suggest, by any means, that moderates were simply victims of circumstance and activists, its beneficiaries. It would be an error to minimize the role of political leaders as autonomous actors, ultimately responsible for their choices, in shaping the course of events. The outcome of competition between moderate and activist camps, indeed, owed much to the strength of their respective commitments and political skills. In the case of the moderates, weak influence over developments in Manchuria may be at-

tributed in no small measure to their own ambivalence toward expansionism
and the fact that their convictions about policy directions were usually not
strong enough to risk a major political confrontation with the army and its
allies. Given the link between Manchuria and the perennial rivalry over
military appropriations during the early years of the venture, the navy had
perhaps the strongest motives for adopting a firm stance. Interservice bargains, such as the Imperial Defense Plan of 1907, however, mitigated its opposition to continental expansion to a certain degree. After 1922, international arms limitations agreements, rather than the competing demands of
the army on the defense budget, formed the primary barrier to warship construction and diminished the weight of Manchuria in the navy's political
calculations.

Hara Takashi was, perhaps, typical of civilian moderates. He had no
compunctions about the use of gunboats in the pursuit of national policy
aims and exploiting the weaknesses of Japan's Asian neighbors. His objections to activist schemes stemmed from pragmatic concerns about the army's
adventurist proclivities, the cost-benefit balance of aggressive expansion, and
the risks of alienating Britain and the United States. Inukai Tsuyoshi's opposition to the army and its view of empire stemmed from deeper ideological
roots, but he certainly could not be described as an "anti-imperialist" in the
sense that such a label might be applied to the liberal journalist Ishibashi
Tanzan (1884–1973) or the pan-Asian idealist Miyazaki Tōten (1871–1922),
let alone leaders of the radical left, such as Noro Eitarō (1900–1934). As for
Shidehara Kijūrō, the depth of his support for the new diplomacy might set
him apart from the general run of moderates, but it was so muted by compromise in practice as to obscure his principles. In this context, it may be
said that tensions between moderates and activists stemmed from differences of degree rather than kind. Some historians, indeed, see few meaningful distinctions between the policies of Hara and of the army.[19]

I would not dispute the fact that many of the debates described in this
study were essentially family squabbles within Japan's governing elite rather
than deeper conflicts rooted in class, culture, or ideology. The ambivalence
of the moderates and the relatively small gap that separated them from the
activist camp made them susceptible to opportunism during World War I
and led them to endorse the Twenty-One Demands. In the long run, weak
convictions softened their resistance to expansion in Manchuria and left
them waging rearguard actions against army excesses rather than seizing the

policy initiative. At the same time, however, it would be a mistake to belittle the distinctions between leadership groups excessively. Differences of degree often dictate the choice between war and peace. Hara, not to mention leaders of Shidehara's persuasion, would have gladly abandoned Manchuria in an effort to avoid armed conflict.

Ambivalent attitudes diminished moderate influence in Manchuria, but so, too, did ineffectual and inconsistent leadership. Despite the general antipathy among major parties in the Diet toward army policies in Manchuria, for example, the tactics of political rivalry often led the opposition party to launch strident and sometimes damaging attacks on the moderate policies of the government in power. Hara's judgment in engineering the historic compromise of the first Eastern Conference, which opened the door to renewed initiatives in Manchuria at a time when the possibility of disengagement seemed greater than ever before, is certainly questionable. Even given the necessity of compromise, Shidehara demonstrated a striking lack of political skill in his handling of Manchurian affairs on a number of critical occasions, particularly during the railway war. At a broader level, the failure of civilian moderates and navy leaders to build a stronger alliance, largely the result of divisions over appropriations and arms limitation treaties, would seem to represent a major opportunity lost. At the crucial juncture of 1930, the Hamaguchi government managed to alienate both services at once and gave them reason, in fact, to make common cause.

Whereas conviction and leadership were factors that weakened moderate influence, they contributed significantly to activist success. The dedication and talent of men like Komura Jūtarō, Gotō Shinpei, and Matsuoka Yōsuke proved invaluable. Most important, however, was the extraordinary role of the Imperial Japanese Army, which clearly provided the driving force behind the venture from 1905 on. The singular devotion of Japan's professional soldiers to the Manchurian cause owes much, certainly, to the strategic importance of the territory as a bulwark against Russia and the forces of chaos; as a staging area for offensive action in China, Mongolia, and Siberia; and in the 1920s, as a pivotal continental asset within Japan's extended economic defense perimeter. At the same time, however, the army's near-obsession with Manchuria did not rest entirely on professional military concerns; it also included a broader dedication to imperial expansion as a national endeavor. In the initial debate over the Harriman initiative in 1905, staff officers not only stressed the economic value of the territory but downplayed the immediate danger of a Russian war of revenge in order to avoid frightening a hesitant civilian leadership away from a commitment. A similar logic may be discerned in the debates of 1913, when General Tanaka, for example, underscored the Russian threat but, at the same time, drew attention to the wealth and opportunity of Manchuria as a great treasure house that made any strategic risks worthwhile. Indeed, it is important to bear in mind that prior to the introduction of strategic autarky as a policy aim, critics of Manchuria policy could make a reasonable case for withdrawing from the territory as a means of reducing Japan's exposure to regional military threats. Army leaders, however, found the notion of sacrificing imperial claims as a way of managing the problem of national defense unacceptable. The army's imperialism, then, demands an explanation that goes beyond strategic considerations as such.

One line of interpretation looks toward the army's institutional interests for an answer. As we have seen, the continued expansion of the nation's ground forces after the development of an effective naval defense in the 1890s rested on the need for a continental expeditionary force. The interservice disputes between 1896 and 1903 underscored the linkage between continental intervention and the growth of the army. The prospect of war with Russia over Korea drove the augmentation of standing force levels from seven to thirteen infantry divisions. New postwar commitments on the continent, in turn, sustained a further expansion toward a target of 25. The army saw Manchuria as providing decisive justification for that growth, even at the expense of naval construction, as evident in the debates of 1913. The end of World War I and the demise of the traditional imperialist system, accompanied by the collapse of Russian power, called this entire framework into question. The demand for arms reduction ran strong at home and abroad. Although the army proved unable to resist such pressure entirely, the emergence of strategic autarky as a policy goal offered rescue from much more drastic cuts. The army, then, stood not only as the principal advocate of expansion in Manchuria but also as a major institutional beneficiary, its claims to appropriations and its place in the defense establishment intimately bound to sustained engagement in the territory.[20]

The fact that a group advocates a course of action from which it benefits materially does not necessarily imply self-interest as a motivation. It only offers a framework of plausibility for the argument. In fact, I would not suggest that institutional interest constituted a primary, let alone the sole, explanation for the army's attitudes. Without other cogent reasons for expansion and broad support for the Manchurian cause, it would not have been possible to make a case for empire and its corollary military commitments. Nor would I argue that the army's use of Manchuria to justify its share of defense appropriations and its assertion of parity with the navy represented a cynical political ploy. Although some arguments might appear specious, on the whole, there is no basis to doubt the sincerity of Japan's soldier-statesmen in their claims about empire and national defense. Students of organizational behavior have long pointed out that institutional self-interest is commonly subsumed within an ideology that justifies organizational growth in the service of a higher purpose and enjoys the genuine belief of its proponents.[21] Such ideological commitments make this line of argument difficult to support with conclusive evidence. Nonetheless, the pattern of army growth and its relationship to Manchuria provides a compelling if circumstantial case, and the hypothesis offers some measure of predictability. Push the army on issues of appropriations, and it would almost invariably push back in Manchuria.

An examination of this hypothesis with the depth it deserves lies well beyond the scope of this study and demands a direct inquiry into the institutional history of the army. The question of self-interest, however, should not obscure the more fundamental reality of the intimate relationship between Manchuria and the Imperial Japanese Army. Soldiers proved instrumental in determining the course of events in the territory. Manchuria, in turn, shaped the development of their institution. The Imperial Army as a world-class military organization took form in the crucible of the Russo-Japanese War, and in a sense, it never lost its identity as the force that defeated the Russians at the Yalu River, Port Arthur, and Mukden. Its principal mission, thereafter, entailed replaying variants of that same war. In this respect, it would not be unreasonable to describe the army itself as a "Manchurian" institution. The relationship between the army and Japanese Manchuria, indeed, offers an example of a broader phenomenon we have touched on throughout the narrative, although not as explicitly as we might, and one worth highlighting as a final, summary observation.

The story recounted in the preceding pages has been told, for the most part, in terms of how Japan shaped Manchuria, but as I suggested at the beginning of this book, one of the reasons why the subject is of such significance to a broader understanding of modern Japanese history lies in the profound impact of Manchuria on Japan. That impact is unmistakable in the 1930s. Events in the territory turned the nation upside down and triggered a revolution in foreign policy that fundamentally transformed Japan's relations with China and with the community of Great Powers. It also precipitated a shift in the balance of power at home and catalyzed the emergence of a new direction for the nation as a whole. The timing of these developments, simultaneous with the world depression and the escalating challenge of revolutionary Chinese nationalism, might encourage us, with some justification, to see them as the outcome of the peculiar concatenation of crises emerging at the turn of the decade. At the same time, they must also be understood in terms of the enormous weight exerted on national affairs by Manchuria itself. The events of the 1930s did not mark the first time that developments in the territory turned the Japanese world on its head. A quarter-century earlier, Japan's initial commitment to the venture had led to a revolution in the nation's relationship with China and the powers, shifts in the balance of power at home, and the rise of a new trend in leadership.

Although the influence of Manchuria in the intervening years might appear less dramatic, it remained, nonetheless, profound. Throughout the quarter-century following the end of the Russo-Japanese War, this expansionist venture formed the pivotal element in Japan's relationship with the outside world, defined friends and enemies in the West, and dictated the terms of its all-important ties with China. The Manchurian venture represents a case of the "tail wagging the dog" on a grand scale.[22] An appreciation of the intertwined histories of the army and Japanese Manchuria underscores this pattern. Frederick Jackson Turner wrote, "The peculiarity of American institutions is, the fact that they have been compelled to adapt themselves to the changes of an expanding people."[23] The same might be said of Japanese institutions and of the imperial frontier on the development of the nation. In this respect, there is little question that the making of Japanese Manchuria formed a major part of the story of modern Japan.

Appendixes

APPENDIX A

Selected SMR Statistics

Table A1

Composition of SMR Freight Revenues, 1907–32

Year	Soy[a]	% soy	SMR coal	% SMR coal	Total freight
1907[b]	¥2,253,297	37.3%	¥246,894	4.1%	¥6,045,716
1908[b]	5,341,788	57.4	750,335	8.1	9,311,811
1909[b]	5,330,014	48.6	1,217,564	11.1	10,959,594
1910	5,467,554	47.0	1,484,676	12.8	11,641,529
1911	5,212,039	41.8	1,956,745	15.7	12,471,415
1912	5,055,898	36.3	3,030,142	21.8	13,913,341
1913	5,399,358	33.4	4,420,337	27.4	16,159,171
1914	7,420,941	42.3	4,200,335	23.9	17,550,150
1915	6,861,996	39.8	3,907,355	22.6	17,260,655
1916	7,364,156	37.0	3,955,945	19.9	19,882,476
1917	8,326,300	35.0	4,116,781	17.3	23,793,056
1918	10,812,422	35.6	6,309,150	20.8	30,377,682
1919	18,980,517	41.0	8,134,575	17.6	46,305,759
1920	22,694,099	35.6	13,223,860	20.8	63,687,030
1921	19,750,050	33.1	14,350,251	24.1	59,615,835
1922	21,138,588	30.4	20,190,704	29.0	69,518,111
1923	25,392,809	35.0	23,537,379	32.4	72,582,757
1924	24,517,740	31.8	26,794,218	34.7	77,019,368
1925	22,402,267	27.8	28,187,333	35.0	80,535,820
1926	25,088,239	28.0	31,168,095	34.8	89,513,059
1927	27,949,474	29.7	33,191,022	35.3	94,040,819
1928	30,196,329	30.9	35,516,795	36.3	97,738,147
1929	35,724,331	35.3	35,725,863	35.3	101,089,474
1930	23,079,726	29.6	31,790,289	40.8	77,936,688
1931	31,301,010	44.1	26,487,339	37.4	70,897,756
1932	36,062,563	42.4	25,123,257	29.5	85,022,315

[a]Includes soybeans, bean cake, and bean oil.
[b]A breakdown of traffic composition is not available for the SMR as a whole before 1910. Data for 1907–9 are based on traffic on the main trunk only and exclude goods carried by the Antung–Mukden line.
SOURCES: SMR1, 342–43; SMR2, 349; SMR3, 524.

Table A2
Net Revenues by Source, Selected Years, 1907–31

Category	1907	1911	1916
Railways	¥3,667,272	¥10,617,934	¥19,379,409
Ships	n/a	−147,539	213,662
Harbors	12,342	96,789	364,241
Mines	553,005	2,178,102	2,076,688
Ironworks	n/a	n/a	n/a
Electricity	−36,316	184,278	589,119
Gasworks	n/a	53,197	125,708
Hotels	−30,827	−46,771	−7,084
Zone facilities	−130,212	−615,120	−1,267,560
General overhead	−1,397,631	−1,640,495	−3,299,866
Miscellaneous	472,408	−1,590,010	−1,396,292
Interest income	n/a	786,711	131,508
Debt service	−1,093,456	−6,067,319	−6,925,097
Misc. interest payments	n/a	n/a	n/a
Chosen Railway	n/a	n/a	n/a
TOTAL NET REVENUE[a]	2,016,585	3,667,428	10,107,608
	1921	1926	1931
Railways	¥45,031,416	¥61,971,944	¥48,185,482
Ships	−254,923	n/a	n/a
Harbors	668,656	994,499	1,288,724
Mines	3,295,921	5,488,880	16,938
Ironworks	−2,873,726	−3,806,594	−2,980,040
Electricity	813,771	271,164	n/a
Gasworks	289,920	n/a	n/a
Hotels	−219,159	−336,809	−96,757
Zone facilities	−6,431,539	−12,567,163	−10,877,411
General overhead	n/a	n/a	−18,803,513
Miscellaneous	2,395,465	−1,113,969	n/a
Interest income	3,819,491	5,887,353	4,997,275
Debt service	−10,584,861	−16,674,302	−25,421,749
Misc. interest payments	−2,682,987	−3,790,502	n/a
Chosen Railway	303,218	n/a	n/a
TOTAL NET REVENUE[a]	31,386,139	34,157,884	−3,401,380

NOTE: n/a = not applicable or not available. The SMR spun off its gasworks in 1924 and most of its electricity-generating operations in 1925. Since categories as well as methods changed, not all the data are comparable across the years. Figures for 1931, for example, are based on major accounting reforms introduced under Yamamoto Jōtarō between 1927 and 1929.

[a]Categories of income and expenditure not recorded in this table are included in the total.

SOURCES: SMR1, 936–43; SMR2, 1325–48; SMR3, 2749–65.

Table A3
Cumulative Investment by Sector, Selected Years, 1906–31

Division	Inheritance[a]	1911	1916
Railways	¥24,848,783	¥92,607,522	¥102,888,856
Workshops	132,972	5,815,865	6,919,084
Ships	n/a	2,812,434	3,144,034
Harbors	6,117,527	13,133,636	21,761,738
Mines	45,730,936	54,727,777	65,716,586
Ironworks	n/a	n/a	n/a
Electric	349,553	4,742,522	5,455,851
Gas	3,592	987,218	1,466,569
Hotels	13,539	1,088,212	2,057,875
Zone	3,067,627	9,478,374	16,407,008
Miscellaneous	7,558,669	17,887,019	20,899,833
TOTAL	87,823,198	203,280,579	246,717,434

	1921	1926	1931
Railways	¥178,847,524	¥225,039,369	¥278,697,598
Workshops	11,304,109	11,984,115	n/a
Ships	3,301,689	4,322,011	n/a
Harbors	34,709,990	49,783,232	85,145,771
Mines	115,636,241	129,127,155	115,799,474
Ironworks	33,905,767	45,902,286	29,233,501
Electric	13,607,787	n/a	n/a
Gas	3,449,941	n/a	n/a
Hotels	2,317,195	2,766,774	4,532,437
Zone	35,995,380	75,360,801	184,368,715
Miscellaneous	41,368,145	49,638,057	60,895,532
TOTAL	474,443,768	593,923,800	758,673,028

NOTES: n/a = not applicable or not available. Because of major accounting reforms introduced under Yamamoto Jōtarō, the figures for 1931 are not entirely comparable with those for other years. In 1927 alone, for example, ¥113,988,926 in nominal assets were written off (SMR3, 2725).
[a]The value of assets transferred from the Russians as estimated by the SMR Organizing Committee in 1906.
SOURCES: From SMR2, 1325–26; SMR3, 2726–33.

APPENDIX B

Population Statistics, Japanese Manchuria

Table B1

Distribution of the Japanese Population in Manchuria, 1909–26

Year	Kwantung	Railway Zone	Consular[a]	Total	% female
1909	32,102	21,804	11,995	65,901	41.50%
1910	36,668	25,266	12,337	74,271	43.57
1911	41,214	25,550	12,237	79,001	44.48
1912	45,317	27,852	12,168	85,337	44.87
1913	47,354	29,833	13,110	90,297	45.40
1914	48,990	32,739	12,978	94,707	45.47
1915	50,176	34,396	12,490	97,062	45.77
1916	52,591	37,572	12,862	103,025	46.33
1917	55,523	42,674	13,381	111,578	46.05
1918	60,024	50,712	13,619	124,355	45.74
1919	65,397	60,348	13,989	139,734	45.57
1920	73,894	61,576	17,317	152,787	45.80
1921	77,038	64,734	16,361	158,133	46.52
1922	82,131	65,684	15,772	163,587	47.48
1923	86,300	76,198	6,718	169,216	47.40
1924	86,498	81,109	6,289	173,896	47.99
1925	90,542	83,620	5,987	180,149	48.29
1926	93,187	86,137	5,960	185,284	48.33

NOTES: The sudden drop in the population of consular jurisdictions in 1923 was due to the incorporation of treaty-port districts in Yingk'ou and Antung into the Railway Zone. The number of Japanese living in Manchuria outside the three categories in this table (including Harbin and Kirin, for example) was relatively small, ranging from about 2,500 in 1911 to a stable high of just under 8,000 during the 1920s (SMR, Chōsaka, *Waga kuni jinkō mondai to Manmō*, 68–69). I have used this narrower set of data because it provides a breakdown by sex.

[a] These data include only those consular jurisdictions located along the SMR proper, usually adjacent to the Zone.

SOURCE: SMR, Chōsaka, *Waga kuni jinkō mondai to Manmō*, 103–4.

Table B2
Composition of the Population of the SMR Railway Zone by Nationality, 1907–32

Year	Japanese	Chinese	Total[a]	% Japanese
1907	17,943	8,902	26,852	66.82%
1908	21,270	16,416	37,724	56.38
1909	22,310	20,469	42,798	52.13
1910	32,494	26,854	59,362	54.74
1911	30,426	33,435	63,865	47.64
1912	32,976	40,732	73,741	44.72
1913	35,663	48,859	84,575	42.17
1914	38,155	51,619	89,920	42.43
1915	40,158	59,744	100,066	40.13
1916	43,841	65,623	109,653	39.98
1917	n/a	n/a	n/a	n/a
1918	50,414	79,048	129,697	38.87
1919	59,148	92,382	151,715	38.99
1920	71,643	103,043	174,945	40.95
1921	72,521	108,634	181,514	39.95
1922	74,499	108,315	183,137	40.68
1923	75,549	123,457	199,823	37.81
1924	97,339	177,800	276,534	35.20
1925	100,143	193,501	295,122	33.93
1926	102,045	199,899	303,629	33.61
1927	101,617	212,864	316,229	32.13
1928	108,032	237,008	348,867	30.97
1929	119,450	247,252	368,671	32.40
1930	127,529	254,593	383,927	33.22
1931	133,399	233,189	368,074	36.24
1932	157,509	238,140	397,004	39.67

NOTES: In 1924, the SMR shifted its census schedule from March to December. Data from 1917 are not available in the company histories. The figures for Japanese explicitly include Koreans after 1927. They are presumably included in earlier data as well. There were 8,913 Koreans resident in the Zone in 1927, 11,383 in 1928, 13,877 in 1929, 16,015 in 1930, 20,937 in 1931, and 28,166 in 1932 (SMR3, 2085).
[a] Includes a small number of non-Japanese foreigners.
SOURCES: SMR1, 720; SMR2, 1074; SMR3, 2085.

Reference Matter

Notes

Complete author names, titles, and publication data for items cited here in short form may be found in the Works Cited, pp. 481–505. For the abbreviations used here, see pp. xvii–xviii.

Introduction

1. David Landes ("Some Thoughts on the Nature of Economic Imperialism," 499) considers the existence of market constraints as one criterion for determining whether an international economic relationship can be described as imperialist.

2. Peattie, "Introduction," 10.

3. For a representative sampling of recent studies of Japanese imperialism, see Myers and Peattie, *The Japanese Colonial Empire*; Duus, Myers, and Peattie, *The Japanese Informal Empire in China*; and idem, *The Japanese Wartime Empire*. See also Beasley, *Japanese Imperialism*; Conroy, *The Japanese Seizure of Korea*; Duus, *The Abacus and the Sword*; Eckert, *Offspring of Empire*; Park, *Colonial Industrialization and Labor in Korea*; Peattie, *Nan'yō*; Nahm, *Korea Under Japanese Colonial Rule*; P. Tsurumi, *Japanese Colonial Education in Taiwan*.

4. For a discussion of informal imperialism, see Duus, "Introduction." For an attempt at a highly structured definition of "informal empire" in China, see Osterhammel, "Semi-Colonialism and Informal Empire in Twentieth Century China."

5. For comparison between the SMR and the English and Dutch East India companies, see Miura, *Mantetsu to Higashi Indo kaisha*.

6. Yoshiaki, *Conspiracy at Mukden*; Ogata, *Defiance in Manchuria*; Peattie, *Ishiwara Kanji and Japan's Confrontation with the West*; Crowley, *Japan's Quest for Autonomy*. See also Thorne, *The Limits of Foreign Policy*; Weland, "The Japanese Army in Manchuria."

7. See, e.g., Berger, *Parties Out of Power*.

8. Johnson, *MITI and the Japanese Miracle*; Young, *Japan's Total Empire*. See also Coox, *Nomonhan*; Egler, "Japanese Mass Organizations in Manchuria"; Jones, *Manchuria Since 1931*; Kinney, *Japanese Investment in Manchurian Manufacturing, Mining, Transportation and Communications*; Myers, *The Japanese Economic Development of*

Manchuria; Schumpeter and Allen, *The Industrialization of Japan and Manchukuo*; K. C. Sun and Huenemann, *The Economic Development of Manchuria in the First Half of the Twentieth Century*; Wilson, "The 'New Paradise.'"

9. Iriye, *After Imperialism*; idem, *Pacific Estrangement*. Other diplomatic histories that deal at length with Manchuria are Bamba, *Japanese Diplomacy in a Dilemma*; Hunt, *Frontier Defense and the Open Door*; Vevier, *The United States and China*; Morton, *Tanaka Giichi and Japan's China Policy*; Tang, *Russian and Soviet Policy in Manchuria and Outer Mongolia*. Some prewar studies of note are Clyde, *International Rivalries in Manchuria*; and C. W. Young, *The International Relations of Manchuria*.

10. Remer, *Foreign Investments in China*, 426, 470. See also Hou, *Foreign Investments in China*.

11. McCormack, *Chang Tso-lin in Northeast China*. See also Fogel, "Introduction"; and Myers, "Japanese Imperialism in Manchuria." Beasley, *Japanese Imperialism*, is one of the few studies that provides a long view of the history of Japanese expansion, although it does not focus specifically on Manchuria. Humphreys, *The Way of the Heavenly Sword*, devotes a chapter to Manchurian developments toward the end of the 1920s. Some prewar studies of note are C. W. Young, *Japanese Jurisdiction on the South Manchuria Railway Areas*; and Kingman, *Effects of Chinese Nationalism on Manchurian Railway Development*.

12. This study shares the chronological framework as well as the broad concerns of Hirano, *The Japanese in Manchuria*"; and Bix, "Japanese Imperialism and Manchuria." These two dissertations, however, concentrate heavily on early developments and offer a relatively brief treatment of subsequent events.

13. Studies of the Manchurian Incident and Manchoukuo in Japanese are extensive. For works on the Manchurian Incident, see, e.g., Eguchi, "Manshū jihen kenkyū no saikentō"; idem, *Nihon teikokushugi shiron*; Fujiwara and Imai, *Jūgonen sensō shi*; Inoue Kiyoshi, "Manshū shinryaku"; Rekishigaku kenkyūkai, *Taiheiyō sensō shi*; Seki, "Manshū jihen zenshi"; Shimada, *Kantōgun*; and Usui, *Manshū jihen*. On Manchoukuo, see, e.g., Manshūshi kenkyūkai, *Nihon teikokushugika no Manshū*; Yamamoto Yūzō, *Manshūkoku no kenkyū*; and Yamamuro, *Kimera*. For topical treatments, see, e.g., Asada Kyōji, *Nihon teikokushugi to kyū shokuminchi jinushisei*; Hara Akira, "'Manshū' ni okeru keizai tōsei saku no tenkai"; Kobayashi Hideo, "1930 nendai 'Manshū kōgyōka' seisaku no tenkai katei"; idem, *Nihon kabushikigaisha o tsukutta otoko*; Koshizawa, *Manshūkoku no shuto keikaku*; Okabe, "Manshū nōgyō imin seisaku no tenkai"; Sakamoto, "Mitsui bussan to 'Manshū'-Chūgoku shijō"; Shimizu, "Tai-Man kikō no hensen"; Suzuki Kunio, "'Manshūkoku' ni okeru Mitsui zaibatsu"; Takahashi Yasutaka, "Minami Manshū tetsudō kabushikigaisha no kaiso keikaku ni tsuite"; and Tanaka Ryūichi, "Manshūkoku chigai hōken teppai to Mantetsu."

14. Kitaoka, *Nihon rikugun to tairiku seisaku*. See also Tsunoda, *Manshū mondai to kokubō hōshin*.

15. Kaneko, *Kindai Nihon ni okeru tai-Manshū tōshi no kenkyū*.

16. Andō Hikotarō, *Mantetsu*. Kobayashi Hideo, *Kindai Nihon to Mantetsu*, the most recent work focused on the SMR, was published after the completion of my manuscript. See also Andō Minoru, "Mantetsu kaisha no sōritsu ni tsuite"; Harada, *Mantetsu*; Ishida, "Shokuminchi kaihatsu shutai to shite no Mantetsu"; Kobayashi Hideo, *Mantetsu*; Suzuki Takashi, "Minami Manshū tetsudō kabushikigaisha (Mantetsu) no sōritsu katei"; and Uda, "Nihon shihonshugi no Manshū keiei." In Chinese, see Su Ch'ung-min, *Man-t'ieh shih*. There are also works about the SMR's vast research organization, some of which have been written by former staff members; see, e.g., Hara Kakuten, *Mantetsu chōsabu to Ajia*; Itō, *Life Along the South Manchuria Railway*; Kusayanagi, *Jitsuroku Mantetsu chōsabu*; Yamada, *Mantetsu chōsabu*; Ishidō Kiyotomo et al., *Jūgonen sensō to Mantetsu chōsabu*. Kobayashi Hideo, *Mantetsu*, focuses on the research organization as well.

17. Examples of topical studies are Ogata Yōichi, "Tōhoku kōtsū iinkai to iwayuru 'Mantetsu hōi tetsudō mō keikaku'"; idem, "Dai niji 'Shidehara gaikō' to 'Manmō' tetsudō kōshō"; and Yoshii, "Dai ichiji taisen go no "'Manshū' tetsudō mondai" on railway policy; Shibata, "Nihon no tai-Manshū tsūka kin'yū seisaku no keisei to sono kinō no jittai" on currency policy; Nagura, *Nihon tekkōgyō shi no kenkyū*; and Sakurai, "Minami Manshū tetsudō no keiei to zaibatsu" on iron and steel policy; Kobayashi Michihiko, "Nichi-Ro sengo no Manshū gunji rūto mondai"; idem, "'Teikoku kokubō hōshin' saikō"; and Muroyama, "'Teikoku kokubō hōshin' no seitei" on military policy. See also Manshikai, *Manshū kaihatsu yonjūnen shi*. Useful bibliographies are Kaneko, "1970 nendai ni okeru 'Manshū' kenkyū no genjō"; Suzuki Takashi, "'Manshū' kenkyū no genjō to kadai"; and Takahashi Yasutaka, "Minami Manshū tetsudō kabushikigaisha (Mantetsu) shi kenkyū."

18. Most Japanese-language studies tend to focus either on political, economic, or military affairs, with relatively little overlap. Kitaoka, *Nihon rikugun to tairiku seisaku*, is a significant exception.

19. SMR, Chōsaka, *Manmō ni okeru Nihon no tōshi jōtai*, 118.

20. Davis and Wilburn, *Railway Imperialism*, offers a basis for comparison.

21. For a study of the economics of foreign railways in China, see Huenemann, *The Dragon and the Iron Horse*.

22. Maier, *Recasting Bourgeois Europe*, 3.

23. For a succinct analysis of Meiji imperialism, see Jansen, "Japanese Imperialism"; and Duus, *The Abacus and the Sword*, 1–25. The collection of essays in Morley, *Dilemmas of Growth*, offers a variety of perspectives on Shōwa imperialism. Duus and Okimoto, "Fascism and the History of Prewar Japan," reviews some of the main lines of the argument linking Germany, Italy, and Japan in the 1930s.

24. The term "greater Taishō," encompassing 1900–1930, comes from Minichiello, "Introduction," 1. Other studies have used a similar framework, e.g., Silber-

man and Hartoonian, *Japan in Crisis*. On the army in the 1920s, see Humphreys, *The Way of the Heavenly Sword*; and Imai, "Taishō ki ni okeru gunbu no seijiteki chii."

25. Landes, "Some Thoughts on the Nature of Economic Imperialism"; Headrick, *The Tools of Empire*. Among works I have used for background are Owen and Sutcliffe, *Studies in the Theory of Imperialism*; and Mommsen, *Theories of Imperialism*.

26. Mannheim, *Man and Society in an Age of Reconstruction*, 53–55.

27. The term "rational shopping" is borrowed from Westney, *Imitation and Innovation*, 5.

28. Betts, *Uncertain Dimensions*, 91–96.

29. Chandler, *The Visible Hand*, 473–74.

30. This is Headrick's thesis in *Tools of Empire*.

31. The term "imperial frontier" as a reference to Manchuria is borrowed from Peattie, *Ishiwara Kanji and Japan's Confrontation with the West*, 101.

32. For a history of the Foreign Ministry's activities in China, see Brooks, "China Experts in the Gaimushō"; see also idem, "The Japanese Foreign Ministry and China Affairs."

33. Notable exceptions include Presseisen, *Before Aggression*; Humphreys, *The Way of the Heavenly Sword*; and Cook, "The Japanese Officer Corps."

34. Among the few English-language works on this institution published after World War II are Fogel, "Introduction"; and Myers, "Japanese Imperialism in Manchuria."

35. For an English-language catalog of these materials, see J. Young, *The Research Activities of the South Manchuria Railway Company*. For a more comprehensive bibliography, see Ajia keizai kenkyūjo, *Kyū shokuminchi kankei kankōbutsu sōgō mokuroku*.

36. L. Young, *Japan's Total Empire*, 5–10.

37. Gordon, *Labor and Imperial Democracy in Japan*.

38. On the importance of studying both encroachment and resistance in order to achieve a broader understanding of the imperialist process, see Asada Kyōji, "Nihon shokumin shi kenkyū no genjō to mondai ten"; and idem, "Nihon shokumin shi kenkyū no kadai to hōhō."

Chapter 1

1. I use the term "Manchuria" rather than the more cumbersome "Manchuria-Mongolia" as a translation of *Manmō* throughout this book. Even when the Japanese used the technically narrower term *Manshū* during the early years of the venture, they included, for all intents and purposes, sections of eastern Mongolia. The traditional eastern boundary of Mongol lands was marked by the Outer Palisade, which ran from Ch'angt'u northeast toward the Sungari River. By this definition, a significant portion of the route of the SMR as well as the terminus of Ch'angch'un, lay on the Mongolian side of the palisade. Significantly, even Chinese provincial bounda-

ries by the turn of the century ignored this division. Both Shengking and Kirin incorporated territory on the Mongolian side. In this context, the term *Manmō*, in itself, did not necessarily represent a more inclusive geographic concept than *Manshū*.

2. For background, R. H. G. Lee, *The Manchurian Frontier in Ch'ing History*; see also Lattimore, *Manchuria: Cradle of Conflict*, 31–78.

3. Jansen, "Japanese Imperialism"; Duus, *Abacus and the Sword*, 1–25.

4. Langer, *Diplomacy of Imperialism*, 75.

5. Beasley, *Japanese Imperialism*, 27–40. For a study of a key "enlightenment" thinker's attitudes toward imperialism, see Craig, "Fukuzawa Yukichi."

6. Jansen, "Modernization and Foreign Policy in Meiji Japan." On Yamagata, see Hackett, *Yamagata Aritomo in the Rise of Modern Japan*.

7. Conroy, *The Japanese Seizure of Korea*, 76–220; Duus, *Abacus and the Sword*, 29–65; Oh, "Sino-Japanese Rivalry in Korea"; Lone, *Japan's First Modern War*, 12–17. On the activities of Mitsui Bussan in China, see Yamamura Mutsuo, "Nihon teikoku-shugi seiritsu katei ni okeru Mitsui bussan no hatten," esp. 32–34.

8. On the "line of interest," see Yamagata Aritomo, "Gaikō seiryaku ron," 3/1890, in *YAI*, 196–200.

9. See Chapter 2.

10. Yamagata, "Gunji ikensho," 1/1888, in *YAI*, 174–85; idem, "Gaikō seiryaku ron," in *YAI*, 197. On the history of the Trans-Siberian Railway, see Marks, *Road to Power*, esp. 28–93.

11. Yamagata, "Gaikō seiryaku ron," in *YAI*, 198–99. Duus, *Abacus and the Sword*, 64.

12. On the causes of the Sino-Japanese War, see Lone, *Japan's First Modern War*, 12–29; Beasley, *Japanese Imperialism*, 41–49; and Fujimura, "Nisshin sensō," 11–21. For Foreign Minister Mutsu Munemitsu's account, recorded in 1895, see Mutsu, *Kenkenroku*, 5–65.

13. Herbert Bix ("Japanese Imperialism and Manchuria," 11–12) suggests that the Japanese army had linked possession of Liaotung to the problem of securing Korea since the early 1880s. There is little question that some officers thought in these terms. However, it is questionable how seriously such ideas were taken by senior leaders before 1894.

14. On the diplomatic settlement in Korea, see Lone, *Japan's First Modern War*, 17–24, 30–40; Beasley, *Japanese Imperialism*, 49–54; Duus, *Abacus and the Sword*, 66–102; and Mutsu, *Kenkenroku*, 91–105. On the seizure of Taiwan, see Chen, "Japan's Decision to Annex Taiwan." On the Triple Intervention, see Langer, *Diplomacy of Imperialism*, 186–89; Lone, *Japan's First Modern War*, 171–77; Mutsu, *Kenkenroku*, 203–55; Suzuki Takashi, *Nihon teikokushugi to Manshū*, 1: 9–11; and Fujimura, "Nisshin sensō," 32–34.

15. Peattie, "Attitudes Toward Colonialism," 82–85; Chang Han-yu and Myers, "Japanese Colonial Development Policy in Taiwan"; Gotō, "The Administration of

Formosa (Taiwan)"; Kobayashi Hideo, "Gotō Shimpei to Mantetsu chōsabu," 10–13.

16. Langer, *Diplomacy of Imperialism*, 385–412; Beasley, *Japanese Imperialism*, 69–70. The terms "sphere of interest" and "sphere of influence" are sometimes used interchangeably. "Sphere of interest," however, usually refers to pre-emptive claims with respect to rival powers whereas "sphere of influence" often implies a significant measure of power on the ground. For a discussion of the distinction, see Willoughby, *Foreign Rights and Interests in China*, 270–73. A similar distinction may be found in the Japanese terms *rieki ken* (sphere of interest) and *seiryoku ken* (sphere of influence). I use the term "sphere of influence" when translating *seiryoku ken* from the Japanese or when I am referring to a region over which Japan exercised a significant degree of power.

17. E-tu Zen Sun, *Chinese Railways and British Interests*, 3–18, 27–50; Schrecker, *Imperialism and Chinese Nationalism*, 19–42, 59–85; Huenemann, *The Dragon and the Iron Horse*, 47–64. See also Mie Rucheng, *Teikokushugi to Chūgoku no tetsudō*.

18. Gaimushō, *Komura gaikō shi*, 213.

19. Suzuki Takashi, *Nihon teikokushugi to Manshū*, 1: 19–20. For an account of the Amoy scheme, see Jansen, *The Japanese and Sun Yatsen*, 96–104.

20. Romanov, *Russia in Manchuria*, 62–93; Nish, *Origins of the Russo-Japanese War*, 32–34, 41–44, 60–63; Tsunoda, *Manshū mondai to kokubō hōshin*, 22–26; Inoue Yūichi, *Higashi Ajia tetsudō kokusai kankei shi*, 102–26; Duus, *Abacus and the Sword*, 116–26. For a dated but nonetheless useful and historiographically important study of the Russo-Japanese War, see is Shinobu and Nakayama, *Nichi-Ro sensō shi no kenkyū*.

21. Kobayashi Michihiko, "'Teikoku kokubō hōshin' saikō," 39–40.

22. Duus, *Abacus and the Sword*, 171–79; Nish, *Origins of the Russo-Japanese War*, 97–100; Tsunoda, *Manshū mondai to kokubō hōshin*, 30–35, 44–48; Suzuki Takashi, *Nihon teikokushugi to Manshū*, 1: 35–51.

23. Nish, *Origins of the Russo-Japanese War*, 44–48; Tsunoda, *Manshū mondai to kokubō hōshin*, 102–23.

24. Nish, *Origins of the Russo-Japanese War*, 50–60; Tsunoda, *Manshū mondai to kokubō hōshin*, 178–99. On American aims, see Michael Hunt, *Frontier Defense and the Open Door*, 20–38.

25. Tsunoda, *Manshū mondai to kokubō hōshin*, 123–50, 163–70; Gaimushō, *Komura gaikō shi*, 277–80. For a comprehensive treatment of the alliance, see Nish, *The Anglo-Japanese Alliance*.

26. This generational difference is noted in Okamoto, *The Japanese Oligarchy and the Russo-Japanese War*, 30–31; Jansen, "Changing Japanese Attitudes Toward Modernization," 73; and Kitaoka, *Gotō Shinpei*, 76.

27. Okamoto, *The Japanese Oligarchy and the Russo-Japanese War*, 72–73. Tsunoda, *Manshū mondai to kokubō hōshin*, 150–60.

28. Tani, *Kimitsu Nichi-Ro senshi*, 82–85. Tani, executed in China by the Nationalist government in 1947 for his role in the Rape of Nanking as commander of the Sixth Division, was an instructor at the War College in the 1920s (see biographical notes by Inaba Masao, in ibid., 4–9). This book is a reproduction of his lecture notes, used in an elite officers' course in 1925.

29. Tani, *Kimitsu Nichi-Ro senshi*, 88–89. For Komura's views of Manchuria, see Gaimushō, *Komura gaikō shi*, 278.

30. Muroyama, "'Teikoku kokubō hōshin' no seitei," 1195–98; Tsunoda, *Manshū mondai to kokubō hōshin*, 160–62.

31. Nish, *Origins of the Russo-Japanese War*, 192–257.

32. Tsunoda, *Manshū mondai to kokubō hōshin*, 238–39; Okamoto, *The Japanese Oligarchy and the Russo-Japanese War*, 101. Significantly, General Fukushima Yasumasa, who would subsequently adopt a militantly expansionist position on Manchuria, continued to argue for neutralization during the early months of the war, recommending that the CER be placed "under international ownership and made open to all investors regardless of nationality" (Ōta, *Fukushima shōgun iseki*, 269–70).

33. General background on the course of the war is drawn from *DR*1, 100–27. See also, Okamoto, *The Japanese Oligarchy and the Russo-Japanese War*, 101–12. General Alexei Nikolaevitch Kuropatkin (*The Russian Army and the Japanese War*, 257, 263), the Russian army commander, explained Japan's easy victories during the early part of the war by pointing out that "the burden and heat of the campaign was borne by five East Siberian Rifle Divisions" prior to the summer of 1904. Reinforcements by railway arrived in "driblets." The Russians were, in other words, badly outnumbered, as Japanese military strategists had anticipated.

34. By "existing rights," Komura refers to ordinary commercial rights that Japan and other powers might claim anywhere in China.

35. For the full text of the document, see *NGN*, 1: 228–31. All three excerpts are from this document.

36. Tsunoda, *Manshū mondai to kokubō hōshin*, 238–39, 244–47; Teramoto Yasutoshi, "Manshū kokusai chūritsuka an to Komura gaikō." On the annexationist expectations of occupation authorities, see, e.g., a report on Japanese military administration in Kaip'ing prepared in May 1905: "Shinkoku Gaihei chōsa jikō," in *NGB, Nichi-Ro sensō*, 5: 426–507. The *NGB* collection of Foreign Ministry documents will be cited as *NGB* with subject, as in this case or, more commonly, year and volume (series and part if appropriate).

37. Tsunoda, *Manshū mondai to kokubō hōshin*, 246–51; Tani, *Kimitsu Nichi-Ro senshi*, 367–68; Okamoto, *The Japanese Oligarchy and the Russo-Japanese War*, 110–11.

38. *DR*1, 123–27.

39. Okamoto, *The Japanese Oligarchy and the Russo-Japanese War*, 117–18.

40. Yamagata, "Sengo keiei ikensho," 8/1905, in *YAI*, 287–88.

41. Kobayashi Michihiko, "'Teikoku kokubō hōshin' saikō," 48–49.

42. Yamagata, "Sengo keiei ikensho," in YAI, 278–79.

43. Suzuki Takashi, Nihon teikokushugi to Manshū, 1: 70–76.

44. Claude M. MacDonald to the Marquess of Landsdowne, 11/22/06, in Gooch et al., British Documents on the Origins of the War, 64–65.

45. On the role of Kuhn Loeb and some of the general financial considerations associated with this affair, see Best, "Financing a Foreign War"; and Nomura, "Jē-kobu Shifu to Takahashi Korekiyo."

46. George Kennan, E. H. Harriman's Far Eastern Plans, 22. On Inoue's views on the advantages of a joint venture, see Inoue Kaoru kō denki hensankai, Segai Inoue kō den, 103.

47. "Katsura-Hariman kan Manshū tetsudō ni kansuru yobi kyōtei oboegaki," in NGN, 1: 249. Communications Minister Ōura Kanetake (1850–1915) is said to have represented the single dissenting voice in the cabinet (Kagawa, Ōura Kanetake den, 86–91).

48. Metaphors involving food do not translate well across cultures. The "aroma of the eel" is meant to have very positive connotations.

49. For a discussion of the historiography of the Harriman affair, see R. Chang, "The Failure of the Katsura-Harriman Agreement"; and Kawai Toshizō, "Hariman Mantetsu baishū keikaku zasetsu no kokusaiteki haikei." See also Nagao Sakurō, Shokuminchi tetsudō no sekai keizaiteki oyobi sekai seisakuteki kenkyū, 283.

50. Honda Kumatarō (Tamashii no gaikō, 226–27), Komura's secretary, claimed that the ambassador plenipotentiary had drafted a comprehensive Manchurian policy proposal during his voyage home from the United States.

51. Manshūgun, Sōshireibu, Waga rikugun sengo keiei ni kanshi sankō to subeki ippan no yōken, undated, Miyazaki shiryō, item 40, held at Bōeichō bōei kenkyūjo tosho-kan. 24 leaves, bound, mimeographed. Based on references within the document and the fact that the Manchurian Army was decommissioned in November, Kobayashi Michihiko ("'Teikoku kokubō hōshin' saikō") believes that this document was prepared sometime between September and November 1905. Kobayashi's article was responsible for directing me to this source, hereafter designated as Miyazaki 40. Other sources in this collection will be designated likewise using the appropriate item number. Leaf numbers provided in direct references to this document (apart from quotations drawn from Kobayashi's article) are based on counting the title leaf as "leaf 1." Kantō totokufu, Minseibu, Manshū sangyō chōsa shiryō, 8 unnumbered volumes (1906), hereafter cited as MSCS(C) for the volume on commerce and manufacturing, MSCS(A) for agriculture, and MSCS(M) for mining. Hirano Ken'ichirō ("Manshū sangyō chōsa ni tsuite") introduced this source. As a general reference on lesser-known civilian officials, I have used Hata, Senzenki Nihon kanryōsei no seido, soshiki, jinji.

52. Miyazaki 40, leaves 6–10, 15.

53. Ibid., leaf 8. According to his biographers, Tanaka Giichi, then a major assigned to the operations section of the Army General Staff, is alleged to have "cooked" transportation capacity data for the Trans-Siberian in 1903 in order to arrive at lower estimates. This deliberate distortion was supposedly a way of strengthening the government's commitment to war. The evidence offered is anecdotal (Tanaka Giichi denki kankōkai, *Tanaka Giichi denki*, 229–42). As a general reference on army officers, their career records, and pronounciation of personal names, I have used Nihon kindai shiryō kenkyūkai, *Nihon riku kai gun no seido, soshiki, jinji*.

54. Miyazaki 40, leaves 7–8, 15. Interestingly, the assessment of Russian military shortcomings during the war provided in retrospect by General Kuropatkin (*The Russian Army and the Japanese War*) seems to support the Manchurian Army's assessment. He laments, "If, at the beginning of the war we had only one more military train a day, we would have had present at the battle of Liao-yang the First Army Corps and Sixth Siberian Corps, and with these sixty extra battalions must certainly have defeated the enemy." Between May and October 1904, the Russians suffered 100,000 casualties but were able to replace only 21,000 of these. Kuropatkin attributes this problem directly to inadequate railway capacity (259). He describes the general problem of railway capacity in much the same terms anticipated by Japanese army planners (243–68). Historical studies of the Russo-Japanese War tend to confirm the Manchurian Army's assessment. The strength of the Eleventh Division, a unit closely followed in Ōe Shinobu's (*Nichi-Ro sensō no gunjishiteki kenkyū*, 78, 224.) seminal study, fell below 75 percent in September 1904 following the Battle of Liaoyang and never recovered. After the battle of Mukden, its effective strength was down to 50 percent. At the same time, however, total Japanese troop strength increased throughout the war, surpassing the 300,000 mark of full mobilization and reaching 900,000 toward the end of the conflict. These problems are also discussed in Tani, *Kimitsu Nichi-Ro senshi*, 424–84.

55. Miyazaki 40, leaves 4–6.

56. Ibid., leaves 7–8. Kobayashi Michihiko, "'Teikoku kokubō hōshin' saikō," 49–52.

57. Miyazaki 40, leaves 6–7, 14–15, 19.

58. Iguchi to Manchurian Army Commander in Chief Ōyama, 7/15/05, NGB, *Nichi-Ro sensō*, 3: 355–56.

59. Nishikawa to all quartermasters, 7/21/05, in MGS, 1049. The compilation of MGS was begun in the immediate aftermath of the war by the occupation authorities (Kantō sōtokufu). The work was subsquently transferred to the Army Ministry. Completion was delayed for a variety of reasons until World War I. Most documents appear to be reproduced in full with a minimum of commentary. Document titles and addressees of correspondence will not be cited unless specially warranted.

60. Iguchi to Ōyama, 8/18/05, in MGS, 1049–50.

61. Ishizuka to Nishikawa, 10/17/05, in *MSG*, 1054–56. On Ishizuka's Taiwan background, see Hirano, "Manshū sangyō chōsa ni tsuite," 431–32. Ishizuka would subsequently serve as the civil administrator of the Kwantung Government-General and, at the height of his career in 1929, colonial governor of Taiwan.

62. MSCS(C), 121–28, 201–32.

63. Ibid., 208–13, 221, 214–16.

64. Okamoto Shumpei (*Japanese Oligarchy and the Russo-Japanese War*, 229) suggests that the government's attitude toward the Hibiya Riots reflected a general insensitivity toward public opinion in oligarchic decisionmaking.

65. Andō Hikotarō, *Mantetsu*, 37.

66. Bureaucratic competition is discussed in Chapter 2. Big business remained ambivalent about Manchuria for some time. Although businesses were enthusiastic about purchasing stock in the SMR, they were reluctant to initiate any undertakings on their own before World War I (see Kaneko, *Kindai Nihon ni okeru tai-Manshū tōshi no kenkyū*, 54). On Mitsui Bussan's complex interests in Manchuria, see Yamamura Mutsuo, "Nihon teikokushugi seiritsu katei ni okeru Mitsui bussan no hatten," 35–45.

67. Conroy, "Meiji Imperialism," 140; Duus, "The Takeoff Point of Japanese Imperialism."

68. Iriye, *Pacific Estrangement*, 104.

69. Ōe, *Nichi-Ro sensō no gunjishiteki kenkyū*, 131.

70. An example of a commemorative record from Nagano prefecture is Kamiminochi gunyakusho, *Meiji sanjūshichi-hachinen Kamiminochishi shi*. On the empress's role, see Nolte and Hastings, "The Meiji State's Policy Toward Women, 1890–1910," 159–60. Marwick ("Problems and Consequences of Organizing Society for Total War") provides a theoretical overview. For a discussion of popular movements and imperialism in the context of the Hibiya Riots, see Bix, "Japanese Imperialism and Manchuria," 35–42; Gordon, *Labor and Imperial Democracy in Japan*, 23–25, 26–79; and Nakamura Masanori et al., "Nihon teikokushugi to jinmin."

71. Duus, "The Takeoff Point of Japanese Imperialism," 157.

72. Tsunoda, *Manshū mondai to kokubō hōshin*, 688–89.

73. See Chapter 2.

74. Such arguments were offered by members of the Imperial Diet opposing arms expansion in early 1906. For example, see Ōishi Masami's interpellation in the budget committee session of the 22nd Diet, 1/26/06, in *Teikoku gikai shūgiin iinkai giroku, Meiji hen* 33: 13.

75. Hata, *Taiheiyō kokusai kankei shi*, 37–38, 42.

76. Beasley, *Japanese Imperialism*, 56.

77. Bannō, *Taishō seihen*, 28.

78. Najita, *Hara Kei in the Politics of Compromise*, 12–30; Duus, *Party Rivalry and Political Change in Taishō Japan*, 6–49.

79. Najita, *Hara Kei in the Politics of Compromise*, 32–79. See also Ōishi Masami's interpellation in the budget committee session of the 22nd Diet, 1/26/06, in *Teikoku gikai shūgiin iinkai giroku*, Meiji hen 33: 13; and Katō Masanosuke's interpellation, 1/26/06, in ibid., 18–21.

80. See Chapters 3 and 4.

Chapter 2

1. I first encountered a systematic use of this expression in Ronald Robinson's characterization of this phenomenon in his introduction to Davis and Wilburn, *Railway Imperialism*, 3. The underlying idea, however, is well established. "In these decades of imperialism," writes Ian Nish (*Origins of the Russo-Japanese War*, 18), "railways were a means of one country expanding its territory." The nature of railway power, however, is often taken for granted and subject to different interpretations.

2. This discussion is based on Pratt, *The Rise of Rail-Power in War and Conquest, 1833–1914*, esp. 1–20; and an 1888 Japanese Army General Staff study of the military uses of railways, Sanbō honbu, *Tetsudō ron*.

3. The literature on railways and economic development is voluminous. The following have been particularly useful to this study: A. Johnson and Supple, *Boston Capitalists and Western Railroads*; Gourvish, *Railways and the British Economy*; Mercer, *Railroads and Land Grant Policy*; and Chandler, *The Visible Hand*. On the politics of railways, see Kerr, *Railroad Politics*; and Benson, *Merchants, Farmers and Railroads*.

4. Anderson, *Imagined Communities*, 9–36.

5. Ericson, *The Sound of the Whistle*, 92–94; see also idem, "The Engine of Change."

6. Marks, *Road to Power*, 13–27; Roman, "Railway Imperialism in Canada."

7. Betts, *Uncertain Dimensions*, 77–90. On railways in German Africa, see Gann, "Economic Development in Germany's African Empire"; and in French Africa, Thompson and Adloff, "French Economic Policy in Tropical Africa." See also Davis and Wilburn, *Railway Imperialism*; Nagao, *Shokuminchi tetsudō*; and Izawa, *Kaitaku tetsudō ron*.

8. See Chapter 1, note 17. See also Hunter, "Japanese Government Policy, Business Opinion and the Seoul-Pusan Railway"; and Davis, "Railway Imperialism in China."

9. Huenemann, *Dragon and the Iron Horse*, 57.

10. Marks, *Road to Power*, 35–45, 141–69, 196–219; see also Romanov, *Russia in Manchuria*, 62–93. Theodore von Laue (*Sergei Witte and the Industrialization of Russia*, 149–57) stresses the restrained quality of Witte's aspirations in Manchuria relative

to those of other Russian leaders. Commenting on plans for the CER, Laue (p. 154) notes, "If this was imperialism it was of a particularly subtle and patient variety."

11. Eckstein et al., "The Economic Development of Manchuria." For an interesting turn-of-the-century travelogue, see Hosie, *Manchuria, Its People, Resources and Recent History.*

12. For background, see R. H. G. Lee, *The Manchurian Frontier in Ch'ing History.* On the idea of "reservoir," see Lattimore, *Manchuria: Cradle of Conflict,* 31–78. On Ch'angch'un, see Koshizawa, *Manshūkoku no shuto keikaku,* 33–34.

13. Lattimore, *Manchuria: Cradle of Conflict,* 3.

14. After a period of 80 years, the railway would pass to Chinese ownership gratis.

15. For general background on the operations, organization, and legal status of the CER, see Chinese Eastern Railroad, Printing Office, *North Manchuria and the Chinese Eastern Railway.* The construction contract and statutes governing the CER are reproduced in MacMurray, *Treaties and Agreements with and Concerning China,* 1: 74–77, 84–91.

16. CER Printing Office, *North Manchuria and the Chinese Eastern Railway,* 42. See also MacMurray, *Treaties and Agreements,* 1: 89, concerning the authority of the Trans-Amur Guards and the governor-general of the Amur region.

17. MacMurray, *Treaties and Agreements,* 1: 76, 88–90. On the history of urban planning in Manchuria, Japanese as well as Russian, see Koshizawa, *Shokuminchi Manshū no toshi keikaku;* and idem, *Harupin no toshi keikaku.* See also Fogel, "Integrating into Chinese Society," 48.

18. For an overview of these companies in the British empire, see Griffiths, *A License to Trade.* See also Miura, *Mantetsu to Higashi Indo kaisha.* Gotō Shinpei, the first governor of the SMR, who favored this analogy for political reasons as well as a means of articulating his concept of colonization, engaged in extensive studies of European colonial companies (see note 53 to this chapter). On the relationship between railway enterprise and real estate, see Johnson and Supple, *Boston Capitalists and Western Railroads,* 107–26, 149–55. Japan's urban railways also offer good examples of this dialectic. Many began as suburban real estate ventures in which railway transportation played a supportive part; see Wakuda Yasuo, *Nihon no shitetsu;* Nihon keieishi kenkyūjo, *Hanshin denki tetsudō hachijūnen shi;* Noda et al., *Tōkyō-Yokohama dentetsu enkakushi.*

19. MacMurray, *Treaties and Agreements,* 1: 328, 335.

20. Tsurumi Yūsuke, *Gotō Shinpei,* 649–91.

21. Miyazaki 40, leaf 6; Sanbō honbu, "Meiji yonjūnendo Nihon teikoku rikugun sakusen keikaku" (3/1907). The earliest year for which complete operations plans in Manchuria have survived is 1907. Partial plans for 1906 are available in Rikugunshō, *Meiji gunjishi,* 1563–64. A comparison of information provided in Tani, *Kimitsu Nichi-*

Ro senshi, 365, on plans being discussed in April 1905 with the 1906 and 1907 plans indicates that the basic strategy and tactics involved are the same.

22. Miyazaki 40, leaves 6–7, 15, 19; Tani, *Kimitsu Nichi-Ro senshi*, 365, 367–68; Kobayashi Michihiko, "'Teikoku kokubō hōshin' saikō," 50–51. For a comprehensive plan drafted slightly after the events under consideration, see Sanbō honbu, *Man-Kan kōtsū kikan jūbi kansei no kyūmu*, Miyazaki shiryō, item 23 (no date; references within the text allow for a fairly certain dating of 1907); cited hereafter as Miyazaki 23.

23. These plans are outlined in a document prepared in early 1906 by the occupation authorities and reproduced in Ōyama, "Shiryō shōkai." Earlier planning work during the war along these lines is documented in *MGS*, e.g., 916–28 (on transportation other than railways). For a broader look at the army's occupation policies and its international ramifications, see Satō Saburō, "Nichi-Ro sensō ni okeru Manshū senryōchi ni taisuru Nihon no gunsei ni tsuite."

24. Ōyama, "Shiryō shōkai," 120–25. Manchuria, and through Manchurian commercial connections, North China had supplied a substantial portion of the food, fodder, and firewood used by the army. Local sources provided 90 percent of all fresh meat and 60 percent of all meat products consumed. Army quartermasters purchased more than half of the total animal fodder from Chinese merchants and farmers (Ōe, *Nichi-Ro sensō no gunjishiteki kenkyū*, 485–87). An afforestation campaign was launched by the occupation authorities in April 1905 (*MGS*, 1164–71). On the Russian practice of breaking up boats for firewood, see SMR, Chōsaka, *Ryōga no suiun*, 16. On the problem of horses, see Tani, *Kimitsu Nichi-Ro senshi*, 375–77; and Ōe, *Nichi-Ro sensō no gunjishiteki kenkyū*, 449–53. On proposals for stock raising, see *MGS*, 1132–38.

25. Gunseichō, "Roji jidai ni okeru [Dalny] setsuryaku," 5/1905, in NGB *Nichi-Ro sensō*, 3: 522.

26. The importance of local procurement for the Russian side as well during the Russo-Japanese War is underscored in Kuropatkin, *The Russian Army and the Japanese War*, 265. The Manchurian Army credited its adversaries for making better use of local resources than anticipated, which allowed them to deploy larger forces than Japanese intelligence had estimated based on railway capacity alone (Miyazaki 40, leaf 8).

27. Kodama is quoted in Andō Hikotarō, *Mantetsu*, 31. The Manchurian Army cautioned in 1905 that all these schemes would have to be managed "under the watchful eyes of the powers" (Miyazaki 40, leaf 23). On Gotō's use of the phrase *bunsōteki bubi*, see Tsurumi Yūsuke, *Gotō Shinpei*, 818–21; and Kitaoka, *Gotō Shinpei*, 94.

28. The idea of establishing a regional agricultural institute in Mukden contained in the Ishizuka report of 1905 offers a good example of this orientation; see *MSCS(C)*, 208–10.

29. Andō Hikotarō, *Mantetsu*, 38–39; Shukuri, *Kodama Gentarō*, 672. For the views of the army and the Ishizuka group, see *MGS*, 962; *MSCS*(C), 221, 231–32.

30. *MSCS*(C), 208–9. On the land grab in Korea, see Duus, *Abacus and the Sword*, 364–96. For an example of the kind of reports informing Japanese views of Manchuria's land, see Ogoshi, *Manshū ryokōki*, 65–74. Sōseki's observations (*Man-Kan tokoro dokoro*, 292–93) were made from a hilltop in Kwantung during a visit to Manchuria at the invitation of his friend Nakamura Zekō, who at the time, occupied the post of governor of the SMR.

31. *MSCS*(C), 211–13, 221.

32. Kaneko, *Kindai Nihon ni okeru tai-Manshū tōshi no kenkyū*, 37–44.

33. Gaimushō, *Komura gaikō shi*, 213; Beasley, *Japanese Imperialism*, 71.

34. *MGS*, 1254, 1258.

35. Ericson, *Sound of the Whistle*, 283–84.

36. Kaneko, *Kindai Nihon ni okeru tai-Manshū tōshi no kenkyū*, 132–137.

37. *SMR*1, 110. These ideas are similar to those promoted by General Iguchi and other officers involved in the occupation administration; see Iguchi to Manchurian Army Commander in Chief Ōyama, 7/15/05, in *NGB Nichi-Ro sensō*, 3: 355–56; "Shinkoku Gaihei chōsa jikō," 5/1905, in *NGB Nichi-Ro sensō*, 5: 426–507. The army's ideas are discussed in the context of conflict with the Foreign Ministry in Teramoto Yasutoshi, "Nichi-Ro sensō go no tai-Man seisaku o meguru Gaimushō to rikugun no tairitsu."

38. *MSCS*(C), 208–09.

39. Currency and banking schemes, in particular, lent themselves to this direction. One Finance Ministry official, for example, envisioned the establishment of a quasi-official, Japanese sponsored regional development bank along with the imposition of an advisory staff on the Chinese governor-general in Mukden (Kaneko, *Kindai Nihon ni okeru tai-Manshū tōshi no kenkyū*, 135).

40. Duus, *Abacus and the Sword*, 95–200.

41. Kurihara, "Nichi-Ro sengo ni okeru Manshū zango sochi mondai to Hagiwara shodai Hōten sōryōji"; Tsunoda, *Manshū mondai to kokubō hōshin*, 308–32. The text of the conference transcript used in this study is from Hirazuka, *Itō Hirobumi hiroku*, 391–408.

42. Hirazuka, *Itō Hirobumi hiroku*, 404–5, 407–8.

43. Ibid., 396.

44. See, e.g., Najita, *Hara Kei in the Politics of Compromise*, 18–19.

45. Lensen, *The Damned Inheritance*.

46. Hirazuka, *Itō Hirobumi hiroku*, 398–99.

47. Andō Hikotarō, *Mantetsu*, 38–39; Shukuri, *Kodama*, 672; *MGS*, 962; *MSCS*(C), 221, 231–32.

48. On the integration of Japanese administrative agencies in Korea and Manchu-

ria, see Miyazaki 40, leaf 24. On the army and railway gauge, see Inoue Yūichi, *Higashi Ajia tetsudō kokusai kankei shi*, 138–51. By 1906, strategic planning assumed the maintenance of a permanent garrison in Kwantung; see note 21 to this chapter. For some of the factors delaying Russian evacuation, as well as the army's armament plans in 1906, see Kobayashi Michihiko, "'Teikoku kokubō hōshin' saikō," 44, 48–52.

49. Kurihara, "Kantō totokufu mondai teiyō." For the charter and table of organization of the government-general, see ibid., 240–52.

50. The Foreign Ministry's line of argument is summarized in Home Minister Hara Takashi's diary, *Hara Takashi nikki*, 6/8/1906 entry, 2 (supplement): 346. The idea of placing consular officials in Manchuria under army supervision was proposed during the war (*MGS*, 962). On Kodama's argument, see Hirazuka, *Itō Hirobumi hiroku*, 407–8.

51. SMR1, 15–21, 67–73; Andō Hikotarō, *Mantetsu*, 41–43. In principle, subscription to company stock was also open to the Chinese government and citizens, but there were no takers.

52. SMR1, 109; Kitaoka, *Gotō Shinpei*, 85.

53. Gotō compares the SMR to colonial companies on a number of occasions, but his most comprehensive discussion is contained in *Minami Manshū keiei ron* (1907), in *Gotō Shinpei monjo*, Item 8.12, unpaginated. See also SMR1, 105–6; Andō Hikotarō, *Mantetsu*, 33–34, 38; Tsurumi Yūsuke, *Gotō Shinpei*, 683–84, 737–50; and Harada Katsumasa, *Mantetsu*, 75–77. For Gotō's role in creating the SMR's research organization, see Kobayashi Hideo, "Gotō Shinpei to Mantetsu chōsabu."

54. Kaneko Fumio, "1920 nendai ni okeru Nihon teikokushugi to 'Manshū,'" 151.

55. Tsurumi Yūsuke, *Gotō Shinpei*, 772–73, 1023–24. On the Kenseihontō's position, see Katō Masanosuke's interpellation, 1/26/06, *Teikoku gikai shūgiin iinkai giroku, Meiji hen*, 33: 18–21.

56. Background for the discussion that follows is drawn from Muroyama, "'Teikoku kokubō hōshin' no seitei," 1195–216; Tsunoda, *Manshū mondai to kokubō hōshin*, 505–715; DR1, 129–75; and Hata, *Taiheiyō kokusai kankei shi*, 168–71.

57. For a discussion of early coastal defense plans, see Takada, "Kokubō hōshin seitei izen no rikugun nendo sakusen keikaku." The Army General Staff underscored the importance of expanding the national railway network and thus the role of the army in national defense by citing the continued weakness of the Japanese navy (Sanbō honbu, *Tetsudō ron*, 6–7). See also Presseisen, *Before Aggression*, 118–25; and Evans and Peattie, *Kaigun*, 22–25.

58. DR1, 29–32.

59. On Satō and his early career, see Evans and Peattie, *Kaigun*, 133–51.

60. Indications of this sharpening rivalry and the army's elaboration of its continental mission may be found in Yamagata Aritomo, "Gunbi kakujū ikensho," 4/15/1895, in *YAI*, 228–239. For a discussion of Satō's views, see DK1, 103–7. A later

version of his work has been republished in full; see Satō Tetsutarō, *Teikoku kokubō shiron*.

61. Ugaki, *Ugaki Kazunari nikki*, 22–23.

62. DR1, 63–64; Muroyama, "'Teikoku kokubō hōshin' no seitei," 1196–98. Kobayashi Michihiko ("'Teikoku kokubō hōshin' saikō," 36–48) argues that Japan, in fact, pursued a navy-first armament policy during the interwar period and that postwar armament plans actually represent a restoration of balance. He suggests that many scholars have overstated the sharpness of interservice conflict during the period immediately following the Russo-Japanese War.

63. Miyazaki 40, leaves 8–9.

64. Ibid.

65. Muroyama, "'Teikoku kokubō hōshin' no seitei," 1210–11. On the domestic political climate favoring continental expansion at this time, see Bannō, *Taishō seihen*, 21–38.

66. For the full text of this document, see Shimanuki, "Nichi-Ro sengo igo ni okeru kokubō hōshin, shoyō heiryoku, yōhei kōryō no hensen," quoted passage from p. 3; and in *DK1*, 112–20.

67. The nature of the Imperial Defense Plan as a political compromise containing elements contrary to the doctrines of both services is underscored in Evans and Peattie, *Kaigun*, 146–50.

68. *DK1*, 106–7.

69. *DK1*, 107.

70. Iriye, *Pacific Estrangement*, 132–35.

71. Ericson, *Sound of the Whistle*, 245–309; on Katō, see ibid., 280–82.

72. Duus, *Abacus and the Sword*, 201–41.

Chapter 3

1. Hata, *Taiheiyō kokusai kankei shi*, 53–54.

2. Sanbō honbu, operational plans in Manchuria for the years 1907–10, held at Bōeichō, Bōei kenkyūjo toshokan. See also DR1, 129–79.

3. Sanbō honbu, "Kantō totoku ni atauru Meiji yonjūnendo sakusen keikaku kunrei" (3/1907).

4. Miyazaki 23, leaves 1–7. Specific numbers for capacity and load targets are derived from an Army General Staff document prepared in 1911 and may be somewhat higher than the actual targets set in earlier years; see Sanbō honbu, *Futatabi waga kuni rikugun sentō nōryoku o zōka sezarubekarazaru yuen o ronji*, (5/1911), appendix 2 (Miyazaki 48). See also Tani, *Kimitsu Nichi-Ro senshi*, 360–61; and Kobayashi Michihiko, "Nichi-Ro sengo no Manshū gunji yusō rūto mondai." For cost comparison, See Tetsudōin, Kantokukyoku, *Mantetsu shisatsu hōkokusho*, 25–26.

5. On the Antung–Mukden line and the Imperial Defense Plan, see Shimanuki, "Nichi-Ro sensō igo ni okeru kokubō hōshin," 6, for the text; Muroyama, "'Teikoku kokubō hōshin' no seitei," 1210–11; and Kobayashi Michihiko, "'Teikoku kokubō hōshin' saikō," 83. On military plans for the Ch'angch'un–Kirin line, in addition to Miyazaki 40, see Sanbō honbu, *Man-Kan tetsudō keiei ni kansuru ikensho* (9/1909), Item 5 (Miyazaki 41); and Miyazaki 23, leaves 21–22. A cabinet decision, on Aug. 13, 1909, regarding the Ch'angch'un–Kirin and its extension to Hoeryong on the Korean border is reproduced in *NGN*1, 318–23.

6. Tani, *Kimitsu Nichi-Ro senshi*, 362–64.

7. *SMR*1, 690–815; Kantōchō, *Kantōchō shisei nijūnen shi*, 330–90, 478–569.

8. Andō Hikotarō, *Mantetsu*, 11.

9. The official functions of this office are described in *SMR*1, 89–90. The appointment of Satō to head this office in 1909 is also noted (91), although his status and rank are not mentioned. A later army document discusses Satō's responsibilities along with those of another officer attached to the SMR to facilitate mobilization; see Army vice minister to SMR governor, 2/3/14, in *MDN*, 1914, vol. 2, jinken. Satō appears to have been employed earlier by the SMR in another capacity. A letter of introduction from Gotō to Itō Hirobumi in 1907 describes "Army Major Satō Yasunosuke" as a "member of our company's research staff" (Tsurumi Yūsuke, *Gotō Shinpei*, 979–80).

10. Sanbō honbu, operational plans in Manchuria for the years 1907–10, at Bōeichō, Bōei kenkyūjo toshokan. Staff planners designated Ch'angch'un as the concentration point in 1911 (Miyazaki 48, appendix 2). The quotation is from Miyazaki 23, leaves 4–5.

11. See cabinet resolution "Nichi-Ro dai ikkai kyōyaku," 7/30/07, *NGN*1, 280–82, for the text of the 1907 pact; and cabinet resolution "Tai-gai seisaku hōshin," 9/25/08, *NGN*1, 306, for the 1908 decision.

12. Hata, *Taiheiyō kokusai kankei shi*, 53–54; Inukai, "Gaikō no konpon o ayamaru gunbi keikaku," 39–40.

13. Kitaoka, *Nihon rikugun to tairiku seisaku*, 68–69. Also see Evans and Peattie, *Kaigun*, 159–67.

14. Miyazaki 48, leaf 3.

15. Yamagata Aritomo, "Tai-Ro keikai ron," 7/31/11, in *YAI*, 334–36.

16. Kitaoka, *Nihon rikugun to tairiku seisaku*, 70.

17. Miyazaki 48, leaf 4.

18. Yamagata Aritomo, "Tai-Ro keikai ron," 7/31/11, in *YAI*, 335.

19. Shimanuki, "Nichi-Ro sensō igo ni okeru kokubō hōshin," 13. Shimanuki reproduces a portion of Sanbō honbu, *Tai-Shin sakusen keikaku* (5/1911), Miyazaki 47.

20. For an overview of regional diplomacy during this period, see Iriye, *Pacific*

Estrangement; Hunt, *Frontier Defense and the Open Door*; Vevier, *The United States and China*; and Nish, *Alliance in Decline*, 3–59.

21. For background on Sino-Japanese diplomacy related to the Treaty of Peking, see Baba Akira, "Nichi-Ro sengo ni okeru dai ichiji Saionji naikaku no tai-Man seisaku to Shinkoku," 67–73; Inoue Yūichi, *Higashi Ajia tetsudō kokusai kankei shi*, 155–79; Tsunoda, *Manshū mondai to kokubō hōshin*, 344–48, 434–35. The basic outline of Japanese policy can be found in a cabinet resolution, "Manshū ni kansuru tai-Shin shomondai kaiketsu hōshin kettei ni kansuru ken," 9/25/08, *NGNi*, 309–12. On the Antung–Mukden issue, see cabinet resolution "An-Pō tetsudō kaichiku narabini Kitsu-Chō tetsudō shakkan saimoku ni kansuru ken," 6/22/09, *NGNi*, 317–18.

22. For the English text of the "secret protocol," see MacMurray, *Treaties and Agreements*, I: 554.

23. Article IV of the Treaty of Portsmouth; see ibid., 523.

24. Quoted in Kaneko, "Sōgyōki no Minami Manshū tetsudō," 190. The phenomenon of long-range carting is described in early Japanese studies conducted by the occupation authorities during the Russo-Japanese War and by Ishizuka's survey teams; see *MGS*, 916–24, 938–42; and *MSCS(C)*, 101–11. For estimates of commercial ranges, as found in a 1910 study of the SMR's tributary regions, see SMR, Chōsaka, *Minami Manshū keizai chōsa shiryō*.

25. The PMR involved British financing as well as technical support. The British, however, had no claim to a mortgage on this line, and the employment of Claude Kinder, the British chief engineer, had antedated any loans. It was not a concession line in the same sense as others, and more than any other major railway at this time, it could be considered a Chinese-controlled venture. On the history of the PMR, see Inoue Yūichi, *Higashi Ajia tetsudō kokusai kankei shi*, 14–72; SMR, Chōsaka, *Manmō tetsudō no shakai oyobi keizai ni oyoboseru eikyō*, 40–41; and Huenemann, *The Dragon and the Iron Horse*, 55–58, 72.

26. On diplomacy associated with the Hsinmint'un–Mukden line, see Baba, "Nichi-Ro sengo ni okeru dai ichiji Saionji naikaku no tai-Man seisaku to Shinkoku," 62–67; Inoue Yūichi, *Higashi Ajia tetsudō kokusai kankei shi*, 185–214.

27. On the rights recovery movement, see En-han Lee, *China's Quest for Railway Autonomy*; on the impact of the Russo-Japanese War on Chinese nationalism, see ibid., 33–35.

28. Hsi-liang, the second governor-general of the Three Eastern Provinces (Bix, "Japanese Imperialism and Manchuria," 109).

29. On Chinese policy in Manchuria during this period, see Nishimura Shigeo, *Chūgoku kindai tōhoku chiiki shi kenkyū*, 39–67; R. H. G. Lee, *The Manchurian Frontier*, 138–74; Hirano, "The Japanese in Manchuria," 61–73; Bix, "Japanese Imperialism and Manchuria," 179–93. On currency policy, see Kaneko, *Kindai Nihon ni okeru tai-Manshū tōshi no kenkyū*, 123–71. For an overview of railway policy, see Kaneko,

"Sōgyōki no Minami Manshū tetsudō," 191–92; and E-tu Zen Sun, *Chinese Railways and British Interests*, 142–47.

30. In addition to the English-language works on diplomacy of this era cited above, see Tsunoda, *Manshū mondai to kokubō hōshin*, 358–428. For the text of the Franco-Japanese understanding, see MacMurray, *Treaties and Agreements*, 1: 640. On American concessions and the rights recovery movement, see En-han Lee, *China's Quest for Railway Autonomy*, 50–84.

31. For general background on this affair, see Vevier, *The United States and China*, 35–56; Baba, "Nichi-Ro sengo ni okeru dai ichiji Saionji naikaku no tai-Man seisaku to Shinkoku," 72–74; Tsunoda, *Manshū mondai to kokubō hōshin*, 368–78; Inoue Yū-ichi, *Higashi Ajia tetsudō kokusai kankei shi*, 216–28; and E-tu Zen Sun, *Chinese Railways and British Interests*, 143–48. On the economic importance of the Fak'umen and T'iehling lines, see SMR, Chōsaka, *Minami Manshū keizai chōsa shiryō*, 4: 113–38. On the possibility of extending this line from Fak'umen to T'iehling to Hailung and then to Kirin, see Kantō totokufu, Rikugun, Keiribu, *Manshū ippan shi*, 4: 306.

32. In this context, the term "railway monopoly" as applied in Japanese Manchuria should be qualified to mean trunk-line monopoly. Although the Japanese sought to avoid the creation of an independent Chinese railway system in the region, they welcomed the construction of dependent tributary lines. This policy would become clear in 1913; see Chapter 4.

33. Inoue Yūichi, *Higashi Ajia tetsudō kokusai kankei shi*, 228–36. For Gotō's role in this affair, see Tsurumi Yūsuke, *Gotō Shinpei*, 1054–55.

34. For background, see Vevier, *The United States and China*, 88–170; Hunt, *Frontier Defense and the Open Door*, 188–229; Tsunoda, *Manshū mondai to kokubō hōshin*, 446–79; Inoue Yūichi, *Higashi Ajia tetsudō kokusai kankei shi*, 246–57; E-tu Zen Sun, *Chinese Railways and British Interests*, 148–54.

35. Cabinet resolution, "Kin-Ai tetsudō ni kansuru ken," 3/2/10, in NGN1, 330–32; Tsunoda, *Manshū mondai to kokubō hōshin*, 480–81. Inoue Yūichi, *Higashi Ajia tetsudō kokusai kankei shi*, 257–65. The idea of an "interceptor" railway would recur with later Chinese and foreign initiatives to build a T'aonan-Jehol railway; see Chapter 4.

36. "Beikoku no Manshū tetsudō chūritsu teigi oyobi kaitō," in NGN1, 327–30; Tsunoda, *Manshū mondai to kokubō hōshin*, 480–83; Inoue Yūichi, *Higashi Ajia tetsudō kokusai kankei shi*, 265–74; E-tu Zen Sun, *Chinese Railways and British Interests*, 154–64; Nish, *Alliance in Decline*, 30.

37. Nish, *Alliance in Decline*, 31–32; cabinet resolution, "Dai nikai Nichi-Ro kyōyaku ni kansuru ken," 3/1910, NGN1, 332–36. For the English text of the 1910 Russo-Japanese accords, see MacMurray, *Treaties and Agreements*, 1: 803–4.

38. Schrecker, *Imperialism and Chinese Nationalism*, 140–43.

39. Tsunoda, *Manshū mondai to kokubō hōshin*, 444, 494–96. Komura acknowledges the difficulty of securing new concessions and the need for caution in response to an interpellation in the 27th Diet (12/23/10–3/23/11); see *Teikokugikai shūgiin iinkai giroku, Meiji hen*, 62: 26.

40. Gaimushō, *Komura gaikō shi*, 754.

41. Actually valued at ¥88 million. The company's cumulative investment as of 1914 was ¥240 million (SMR2, 1326).

42. Total new investment in 1907 totaled ¥14 million (SMR1, 932).

43. Paid up capital from privately owned shares amounted to only ¥2 million before 1912 (SMR1, 925).

44. In an effort to appease American sentiment, Saionji ordered the SMR to try to make arrangements in New York with Kuhn Loeb (Saionji to Foreign Minister Hayashi, 11/13/06, NGB 1906, 1: 649–50). These efforts were unsuccessful. On financing the SMR, see Andō Hikotarō, *Mantetsu*, 48–63; Kaneko, "Sōgyōki no Minami Manshū tetsudō," 177–79; Ericson, *The Sound of the Whistle*, 363–64.

45. MSCS(C), 101–2. The analytical framework for this discussion of SMR startup strategies draws on A. Johnson and Supple, *Boston Capitalists and Western Railroads*, 8–10, 329, 343–44.

46. Kaneko, *Kindai Nihon ni okeru tai-Manshū tōshi no kenkyū*, 45–49. Yamamoto Jōtarō made an early study of the Manchurian bean trade during the Sino-Japanese War. At the time, Yamamoto was a young clerk working for Mitsui Bussan. He would become the president of the SMR in 1927 (Yamamoto Jōtarō denki hensankai, *Yamamoto Jōtarō ronsaku*, 366–488). My understanding of the SMR's early strategy owes much to Kaneko, "Sōgyōki no Minami Manshū tetsudō," 80–90. See also Su, *Man-t'ieh shih*, 90–184.

47. MGS, 1045–48; MSCS(C), 111–25; SMR, Chōsaka, *Ryōga no suiun*, 22–25. Kaneko, *Kindai Nihon ni okeru tai-Manshū tōshi no kenkyū*, 45.

48. MSCS(C), 210–11, 221–28.

49. SMR, Tetsudōbu, Unyuka, *Kamotsu chōsa hōkoku isan*, 11–16, 24–25; SMR, Chōsaka, *Ryōga no suiun*, 30–31; SMR, Chōsaka, *Minami Manshū keizai chōsa shiryō*, 3: 1–36.

50. Estimates based on actual soy traffic reaching SMR stations between Liaoyang and T'iehling in 1907 (soy data from TKN, 1907, 126; mileages from SMR1, 213–17). Railways charge by the ton-mile, a unit calculated by multiplying tonnage by distance traveled.

51. On general traffic patterns, see MSCS(C), 222–24. On cooperation between river and railway, SMR. Chōsaka, *Minami Manshū keizai chōsa shiryō*, 4: 8–12.

52. SMR, Chōsaka, *Manshū Shinagawa tetsudō ensen chihō ni okeru daizu no demawari zōka jijō oyobi sono taiō saku*, 40.

53. On the general problem of rate competition for railways, see Chandler, *The Visible Hand*, 134.

54. The actual discount rate cited in the text reflects a policy of equalizing rates between soy shipped from Mukden to SMR-Yingk'ou and Dairen. This means that the use of Yingk'ou would not have necessarily resulted in yet lower charges. However, it would have allowed the company more leeway to cut its rates by reducing operating costs.

55. Kaneko, *Kindai Nihon ni okeru tai-Manshū tōshi no kenkyū*, 111–14.

56. In addition to ibid., see *MSCS(C)*, 1–3; and SMR, Chōsaka, *Ryōga no suiun*, 2–3.

57. Kaneko, "Sōgyōki no Minami Manshū tetsudō," 187–89. On the pooling system, see Tetsudōin, Kantokukyoku, *Mantetsu shisatsu hōkokusho*, 76. On special facilities, amenities, and services, see SMR1, 375–86 (shipping), 755–61 (urban development), 352–62 (warehousing and insurance), and 893–97 (commercial services). On American practices, see Chandler, *The Visible Hand*, 210–13.

58. Kaneko, *Kindai Nihon ni okeru tai-Manshū tōshi no kenkyū*, 41, 45–46.

59. SMR, Chōsaka, "Manshū ni okeru daizu," 21–22.

60. *MSCS(C)*, 208–10; SMR1, 878–93. Similar efforts were made by the Atchison, Topeka and Santa Fe in Kansas during the 1870s (A. Johnson and Supple, *Boston Capitalists and Western Railroads*, 293–98). See also Su, *Man-t'ieh shih*, 295–335.

61. On traffic patterns, see SMR, Tetsudōbu, Un'yuka, *Kamotsu chōsa hōkoku isan*, 4–7; and SMR, Chōsaka, *Minami Manshū keizai chōsa shiryō*, 5: 3–7, 92–93, 71–73. For feeder recommendations, see *MSCS(C)*, 221.

62. Kaneko, *Kindai Nihon ni okeru tai-Manshū tōshi no kenkyū*, 41; Kaneko, "Sōgyōki no Minami Manshū tetsudō," 193–94; SMR1, 343–47.

63. A chart showing carting ranges may be found in SMR, Tetsudōbu, Unyuka, *Kamotsu chōsa hōkoku isan*. Early studies of border-region traffic are available (see SMR, Chōsaka, *Minami Manshū keizai shiryō*, vol. 5), but the most comprehensive study available (prepared in 1916) and used for background here is SMR, Chōsaka, *Tō-Shin tetsudō nanbu sen chihō keizai chōsa shiryō*.

64. Statistical tables offer a detailed breakdown of commodities carried; see, e.g., *TKN*, 1907, 127–31.

65. For passenger service, see SMR1, 300–7; for information on discounts, see ibid., 307. On special provisions for "coolie" transport, see SMR, *Eigyō hōkokusho*, no. 8 (1910), 18. Gross revenues from passenger service in 1908 were ¥2,784,353, compared to gross freight revenue of ¥9,311,810 (SMR, *Eigyō hōkokusho*, no. 4 [1908], 51; no. 5 [1908], 50).

66. *MSCS(M)*, 143–44.

67. Tetsudōin, Kantokukyoku, *Mantetsu shisatsu hōkokusho*, 61–63. For Singapore coal prices, see SMR, Chōsaka, *Bujun tan no hanro*, 58.

68. Masuda is quoted in Kasuga, "Kan'ei Miike tankō to Mitsui bussan," 211–12. For the survey group's recommendations, see *MSCS(C)*, 219–21. On the deliberations of the Organizing Committee, see Andō Hikotarō, *Mantetsu*, 45–46. Mitsui Bussan had also protested a plan for the SMR to move directly into the soybean trade (ibid., 45–46).

69. SMR1, 603–26.

70. Ibid., 629–43.

71. Ibid., 369–70, 375–86; Hoshino, *Economic History of Manchuria*, 123.

72. Tetsudōin, Kantokukyoku, *Mantetsu shisatsu hōkokusho*, 70–72; SMR1, 691–897.

73. Much of the concern with business development in the report of the Ishizuka survey of 1905 is directed at the problem of promoting settlement (*MSCS[C]*, 211–16, 230–31). For research institutions, including the Central Research Laboratory, see SMR1, 897–908.

74. An edict from the government-general of the Three Eastern Provinces raising taxes on soy production describes soybeans as the "foundation" of the regional economy and cites the importance of these taxes for regional defense (reproduced in SMR, Chōsaka, *Ryōga no suiun*, 39–40). In 1918, the revenues of Fengt'ien provinces amounted to some ¥16 million as opposed to ¥22 million in net income for the SMR (see Table 7.1, p. 277).

75. Miyazaki 23, leaf 24. Army planners argued that the development of a coal trade with north Manchuria would justify the double tracking of the entire length of the line (ibid.).

76. Rikugunshō, Kōheika, "An-Pō tetsudō kaichiku ni kansuru ken," 3/1908, in *MDN* 1908, vol. 2, yōsai tetsudō 1, 3, 5; Miyazaki 23, leaf 30.

77. Rikugunshō, Kōheika, "An-Pō tetsudō kaichiku ni kansuru ken," 3/1908, in *MDN* 1908, vol. 2, yōsai tetsudō 1–11.

78. Revenue figures from SMR1, 342–43, 931.

79. Ibid., 135–38. The company did not act on its own in this instance but had the support of the Finance Ministry (Andō Hikotarō, *Mantetsu*, 112–13). The wage data are from 1917.

80. SMR1, 132.

81. For example, Chinese were allowed to participate in the self-governing residents' councils established within the SMR's railway towns (Tetsudōin, Kantoku-kyoku, *Mantetsu shisatsu hōkokusho*, 75).

82. Japanese consul in Niuchuang to foreign minister, 9/12/12, Gaimushō microfilm, S61921, 1774–83.

83. Matsumoto Toshirō (*Shinryaku to kaihatsu*, 36–37) points out that Japanese economic activity in Kwantung and the Railway Zone constituted more an element of the regional Chinese economy than an imperial extension of Japan's.

84. This issue is discussed at greater length in Chapter 4, but for background on early Japanese thinking about this issue, see Hashitani Hiroshi, "Chōsen tetsudō no Mantetsu e no itaku keiei o megutte"; Kitaoka, *Nihon rikugun to tairiku seisaku*, 34–44; and Inoue Yūichi, *Higashi Ajia tetsudō kokusai kankei shi*, 105–28.

85. Based on estimated ton-mile charges derived from SMR revenue tables (SMR1, 342–43), a ton of Fushun coal would have carried total freight charges of ¥1.88 arriving at dockside in Dairen. The same ton of coal arriving in Pusan would have been charged ¥5.66. A ton of soy from Ch'angch'un would have cost ¥8.60 to ship to Dairen by rail, but ¥19.00 to Pusan. Charges for coal transportation reflect special discounts of roughly half the actual cost, which was closer to ¥4.00 from Fushun to Dairen (two-thirds of the dockside price). Until 1919, SMR coal sold for a near-uniform price throughout southern Manchuria, independent of transportation costs from Fushun (SMR 2, 706–7). The figure of ¥0.0075 per ton-mile used to calculate coal charges is an estimate of the average effective rate, derived from calculations of revenue and average ton-mileage. This estimate is confirmed by the Railway Board's figure of ¥0.008 in 1913 (Tetsudōin, Kantokukyoku, *Mantetsu shisatsu hōkokusho*, 25).

86. Subsidies to the government-general ran approximately ¥3 million annually during the first several years (Kantōchō, *Kantōchō shisei nijūnen shi*, 94–95; Remer, *Foreign Investments in China*, 444–45).

87. The CER registered net losses through 1909, averaging some 12.5 million rubles annually ([SMR], *Chū-Tō tetsuro un'yu tōkei*, 92). On the generally poor financial performance of Chinese railways, see Huenemann, *The Dragon and the Iron Horse*, 176–218.

88. Nominal rates of return between 20 and 40 percent are sometimes cited. Such figures are calculated on the basis of a narrow definition of railway investment, which excludes not only ancillary operations such as docks and harbors but also workshops and general overhead capital. In some calculations, Russian investment is also excluded; see, e.g., Huenemann, *The Dragon and the Iron Horse*, 190–91. These calculations may be useful for certain comparative and analytical purposes, but they do not reflect the real profitability of the SMR as an integrated railway enterprise.

89. London consul-general to Foreign Minister Hayashi, 3/1/07, in NGB, 1907, 2: 299–300.

90. For Gotō's argument for building high-class hotels, see Tsurumi Yūsuke, *Gotō Shinpei*, 795–96; see also Peattie, "Attitudes Toward Colonialism," 88. For Sōseki's observations, see *Man-Kan tokorodokoro*, 209–10, 215, 218–19. On the symbolism of Meiji railways, see Ericson, "The Engine of Change," 37–41.

91. Cabinet resolution, "Tai-gai seisaku kettei hōshin no ken," 9/25/08, in NGN1, 308; Gaimushō, *Komura gaikō shi*, 754.

Chapter 4

1. Much of the following discussion is based on Usui Katsumi, *Nihon to Chūgoku*, 1–40; and Kitaoka, *Nihon rikugun to tairiku seisaku*, 89–102. See also Jansen, *The Japanese and Sun Yatsen*, 131–74; and Ikei, "Japan's Response to the Chinese Revolution of 1911."

2. Tang, *Russian and Soviet Policy in Manchuria and Outer Mongolia*, 82–84, 299–305; Lattimore, *The Mongols of Manchuria*, 119–22.

3. Kitaoka, *Nihon rikugun to tairiku seisaku*, 74–86. On the Manchurian independence initiative, see Jansen, *The Japanese and Sun Yatsen*, 137–40; and Kurihara Ken, "Dai ichiji, dai niji Manmō dokuritsu undō to Koike Gaimushō, Seimukyokuchō no ishoku."

4. Kitaoka, *Nihon rikugun to tairiku seisaku*, 96–98.

5. Ibid., 97–100.

6. A tug of war between activist and moderate trends is apparent in the government's initial response to the revolution; see Cabinet resolution, 10/27/11, in NGN1, 305–9.

7. Cabinet resolution, 1/1912, appendix to resolution, 6/26/12, in NGN1, 363. Abe Moritarō ("Shina ni kansuru gaikō seisaku kōryō," 1913, in *NGN1*, 373) was quite explicit in making the distinction between Manchuria on the one hand and Mongolia and Tibet on the other.

8. Cotton trade figures are based on 1914 data (Kaneko, *Kindai Nihon ni okeru tai-Manshū tōshi no kenkyū*, 43). For Abe's views, see Abe Moritarō, "Shina ni kansuru gaikō seisaku kōryō," 1913, in NGN1, 373.

9. Usui, *Nihon to Chūgoku*, 22–31.

10. Much of the background for the discussion that follows is based on Bannō, *Taishō seihen*. Bannō's view differs from English-language scholarship on the so-called Taishō Political Crisis in his emphasis on problems of defense appropriations and the formation of a navy-Seiyūkai alliance. See also Kitaoka, *Nihon rikugun to tairiku seisaku*, 126–42; and Tsunoda, *Manshū mondai to kokubō hōshin*, 775–804.

11. DR1, 183–87.

12. Bannō, *Taishō seihen*, 71–79. Yamagata had supported a balanced development between the two services during the early years but began leaning more decisively toward the army after the Russo-Japanese War.

13. Bannō, *Taishō seihen*, 79–97. Although clique politics continued to play a significant role well into the early 1920s, their overall importance should not be overstated. Itō and Yamagata, for example, were both Chōshū men, yet became archrivals. Army generals from Satsuma, like Uehara Yūsaku, might cooperate with Satsuma-clique bureaucrats on some matters but remained army partisans and were

no closer to Satsuma admirals than Chōshū generals. On the Uehara faction within the army, see Kitaoka, *Nihon rikugun to tairiku seisaku*, 74–86, 126–42.

14. See Ōishi interpellation, 1/25/10, 26th Diet, *Teikokugikai shūgiin iinkai giroku, Meiji hen*, 55: 40–42; Inukai, "Rikugun kakuchō to gunsei kaikaku" (1910).

15. Motoda interpellation, 1/23/11, 27th Diet, *Teikokugikai shūgiin iinkai giroku, Meiji hen*, 62, 18–20; Ōoka interpellation, 1/23/11, 27th Diet, *Teikokugikai shūgiin iinkai giroku, Meiji hen*, 62: 23–26. Significantly, Motoda's and Ōoka's criticisms were raised during a period when relations between the Katsura government and the Seiyūkai had soured. Negotiations concluded three days later on January 26, 1911, healed the breach (Bannō, *Taishō seihen*, 61–66). For Inukai's view of British and French expansionist "styles," which correspond closely to historians' analytical categories of informal and formal imperialism, see Inukai, "Taiheiyō mondai no shōrai" (1910), 247.

16. Bannō, *Taishō seihen*, 79–97.

17. Ibid., 97–120.

18. Ibid., 121–41. Kitaoka, *Nihon rikugun to tairiku seisaku*, 143–60.

19. Abe Moritarō, "Shina ni kansuru gaikō seisaku kōryō," 1913, in *NGNi*, 375–76.

20. Kurihara, "Abe Gaimushō, Seimukyokuchō ansatsu jiken to tai-Chūgoku (Manmō) mondai," 96–97. For the full text of Abe's program, see Abe Moritarō, "Shina ni kansuru gaikō seisaku no kōryō," 1913, in *NGNi*, 369–76. Based on references in the document and the date of Abe's assassination, the draft was probably completed sometime between April and September 1913, most likely in the spring. Beasley (*Japanese Imperialism*, 108) sees Abe's program as foreshadowing the Twenty-One Demands.

21. For a series of memoranda on these negotiations conducted in the spring and early summer of 1914, see *NGB*, 1915, 2: 505–10.

22. Abe Moritarō, "Shina ni kansuru gaikō seisaku no kōryō," 1913, in *NGNi*, 372.

23. On the SMR's efforts, see *SMRi*, 890–92. On Aikawamura, see Kantōchō, *Kantōchō shisei nijūnen shi*, 662–64; and SMR, Chōsaka, *Waga kuni jinkō mondai to Manmō*, 162–63.

24. On arable land in the Railway Zone, see *SMRi*, 735–36; in Kwantung, see Kantōchō, *Kantōchō shisei nijūnen shi*, 480. In 1906, 164,00 acres were under cultivation in Kwantung.

25. "Sen-Man kokkyō kan kamotsu kanzei keigen torikime," 5/29/13, in *NGNi*, 376–77.

26. Kitaoka, *Nihon rikugun to tairiku seisaku*, 103–9; Kaneko, "Sōgyōki no Minami Manshū tetsudō," 195–97. Kitaoka offers the most comprehensive analysis of political aspects. Kaneko's treatment emphasizes the economic policy aspects. See also Hashitani Hiroshi, "Chōsen tetsudō no Mantetsu e no itaku kei'ei o megutte"; and Motoyama Minoru, "Sansen renraku mondai no rekishiteki kōsatsu."

27. *TKN*, 1913, 244, 248; 1914, 256, 257.

28. In addition to Kaneko, "Sōgyōki no Minami Manshū tetsudō," see Ishimoto et al., *Sansen mondai undō keika hōkoku*. This report, prepared by a Dairen merchants' lobbying group, deals with the dispute that broke out in 1916 over the expansion of the discount program initiated in 1913. The basic issues, however, are much the same. Aioi Yoshitarō (1867–1930), a leading member of the Dairen business community and head of a labor contract company, spearheaded the campaign; for a biography, see Shinozaki Yoshirō, *Manshū to Aioi Yoshitarō*.

29. On the army's schemes to strengthen the Pusan–Mukden route, see Miyazaki 48; Yamagata Aritomo, "Man-Sen tetsudō keiei hōsaku," 6/1911, in *YAI*, 323–33; and Kitaoka, *Nihon rikugun to tairiku seisaku*, 103–11. At the beginning of 1913, the army began conducting deployment maneuvers on the Pusan–Mukden railway route (Rikugun, Un'yubu, "Tetsudō senpaku gunji yusō ni kansuru jikken jisshi no ken," in *MDN*, 1914, vol. 4, un'yu tsūshin 1).

30. Instructions to Major Nanbo Teiji and Major Seki Shōichi, 2/10/12, *Mitsu dai nikki*, in source appendix in Kurihara, *Tai Manmō seisaku shi no ichimen*, 295. Army plans are fleshed out in Rikugunshō, Gunmukyoku, Gunjika, "Tōnan tetsudō ni kansuru ken," 1/1914, in *MDN*, 1914, vol. 4, un'yu tsūshin 3; Army Chief of Staff Hasegawa Yoshimichi to Army Vice Minister Kusunose Sachihiko, "Shina ni oite gunjijō waga kibō suru tetsudō mō," 3/16/14, in *MDN*, 1914, vol. 4, un'yu tsūshin 4.

31. On T'aonan and Chinese settlement in Eastern Inner Mongolia, see Lattimore, *The Mongols of Manchuria*, 211–13.

32. DR1, 166–67.

33. The following dispatches provide an outline of these projects as the Japanese became aware of them (all page references are to *NGB*, 1913, vol. 2): Minister to China Ijūin to Foreign Minister Katō, 2/7/13, 658–59; Ijūin to Katō, 2/8/13, 657; a second dispatch, same correspondents and dates, 659–60; Mukden Consul-General Ochiai to Katō, 2/19/13, 661; Ijūin to Foreign Minister Makino, 2/26/13, 661–62; Makino to Ijūin and Ochiai, 3/12/13, 667.

34. The T'aonan–Jehol line was clearly a modification of the Chinchow–Aigun project. According to a 1911 report of the Kwantung Garrison, Fengt'ien provincial authorities endorsed plans for a Mukden–Hailung railway in 1910 (Kantō totokufu, Rikugun, Keiribu, *Manshū ippan shi*, 4: 307).

35. Ijūin Hikokichi, minister to China, believed at first that Japan would have no alternative but to relinquish its monopoly claims and allow Sino-foreign railway initiatives in Manchuria (Ijūin to Foreign Minister Katō, 2/8/13, in *NGB*, 1913, 2: 659). He was strongly opposed by Ochiai. Abe Moritarō ("Shina ni kansuru gaikō seisaku no kōryō," 1913, NGN1, 372) appears to have favored at least a pre-emptive initiative on the railway to T'aonan.

36. Ochiai to Makino, 3/19/13, in *NGB*, 1913, 2: 669–71.

37. Abe to Nakamura, 3/12/13, and Nakamura to Abe, 3/26/13, in *NGB*, 1913, 2: 667 and 671–72. For the SMR's assessment of traffic prospects for a feeder line from Hailung, see SMR, Chōsaka, *Minami Manshū keizai chōsa shiryō*, 3: 37–116. On a revised routing for the Ch'angch'un–T'aonan line, see Makino to Minister to China Yamaza, 8/18/13 and 8/22/13, in *NGB*, 1913, 2: 681 and 690.

38. Yamaza to Makino, 9/10/13, and Ochiai to Makino, 9/21/13, in *NGB*, 1913, 2: 692–93 and 693–95. The connector line would eventually take the form of a branch of the Ssup'ingkai–T'aonan originating at Chengchiat'un and terminating at T'ungliao (Payintala), through which a T'aonan–Jehol line would likely pass.

39. The army had originally proposed a bargain with Sun Yatsen in which the Japanese would support construction of the Ch'angch'un–T'aonan line in exchange for its own proposals; see Takagi Rikurō (Asahi shōkai) to Abe Moritarō and Mori Kaku (Mitsui Bussan), 2/1/13, in *NGB*, 1913, 2: 650–58; attachment, Army General Staff recommendations, ibid., 651; and attachment, Mori memorandum, also supporting a concession on this point, ibid., 651.

40. Abe Moritarō, "Shina ni kansuru gaikō seisaku no kōryō," 1913, in *NGN1*, 371–72. In Huenemann's (*The Dragon and the Iron Horse*, 58–59) analytical scheme of foreign railway concessions, "colonial" concessions involved effective foreign ownership and managerial control, along with ancillary rights. The SMR, the Russian CER, the German Shantung Railway, and the French Yunnan Railway were the only lines of this type. "Financial concessions" were lines nominally owned by Chinese interests but built using foreign capital. Most loan contracts had provisions for considerable managerial control.

41. Abe seems to have been looking at the Anglo-German T'ientsin–P'uk'ou loan of 1908 as representative of the trend toward more lenient terms. The T'ientsin–P'uk'ou, however, was clearly an example of an independent trunk line. On this particular loan, see Huenemann, *The Dragon and the Iron Horse*, 72.

42. Consider the fact that one ton of soy shipped from Hailung to K'aiyüan would earn this feeder line 124 ton-miles in freight charges. That same ton, continuing on to Dairen, would earn the SMR 313 ton-miles, over two and a half times the feeder's revenue.

43. SMR, Tetsudōbu, Kōmuka, *Kaigen–Chōyōzan kan yotei tetsudō senro tōsa hōkokusho* (Senchō dai 6 gō, survey of 12/1913, published 1919), 18–23; 33–37.

44. For example, Yamaza Enjirō, who replaced Ijūin as minister to China, linked a favorable outcome on the railway question to settling the Nanking incident of 1913. Three Japanese had been killed by Chinese troops entering the city on September 1. Yamaza hinted ominously that the Japanese people were far from satisfied with the situation (Yamaza to Makino, 9/10/13, in *NGB*, 1913, 2: 692–93).

45. Ibid.; "Manmō tetsudō shakkan shūchiku ni kansuru kōbun kōkan," 10/5/13, in *NGN1*, 378.

46. Cabinet resolution, 12/20/13, in *NGB*, 1913, 2: 722.

47. Although the railway to Hailung was not part of the army's original agenda laid out in 1912, Hailung was of considerable military significance, since it was the site of a battle during the Russo-Japanese War. Operational plans for 1910 called for the deployment of three divisions at this town (Sanbō honbu, "Meiji yonjūsannendo Nihon teikoku rikugun sakusen keikaku," 1909).

48. Makino to Yamaza, 10/3/13, and Yamaza to Makino, 10/7/13, in *NGB*, 1913, 2: 705–6 and 709–10.

49. Rikugunshō, Gunmukyoku, Gunjika, "Tōnan tetsudō ni kansuru ken," 1/1914, in *MDN*, 1914, vol. 4, un'yu tsūshin 3

50. Odagiri Masunosuke, "Shi-Tei tetsudō shakkan kōshō shimatsu hōkoku-sho," 12/20/15, in *NGB*, 1915, 2: 450–70. Odagiri was an official of the Yokohama Specie Bank.

51. Matsuoka Yasutake, "Tai-Manmō saku," 2/1913, in Yamamoto Jirō, *Terauchi Masatake kankei monjo*, 699–706. Domestic coal producers complained that Fushun had already forced down the market price in T'ientsin by 35 percent (Mitsui bunko, "Mitsui bussan kabushikigaisha torishimariyaku kaigiroku," 423).

52. On Akiyama's career and contributions as a naval strategist, see Evans and Peattie, *Kaigun*, 69–74.

53. "Akiyama Saneyuki danwa, Minami Manshū keiei hōshin; fu, dō danwa Ōshima Kenichi iyaku," ca. early 1913, in Yamamoto Jirō, *Terauchi Masatake kankei monjo*, 713–15. (No date is provided for the document in this collection. The estimate is based on the ranks and titles of Akiyama and Ōshima. Akiyama, referred to as "captain" in this document, was promoted to rear admiral in February 1913. Ōshima, referred to as "vice chief of staff," held the position from April 1912 to April 1914. The document, in any event, is well within the range of the period under consideration.)

54. Ibid., 715.

55. Tetsudōin, Kantokukyoku, *Mantetsu shisatsu hōkokusho*, 25–26, 85–91.

56. Ibid., 70–79.

57. Ibid., 78.

58. Harada, *Mantetsu*, 83–84; Katō, "Hara Takashi to Mantetsu," 42–46; Kobayashi Hideo, *Mantetsu*, 664–67. See also Kitaoka, *Nihon rikugun to tairiku seisaku*, 120–21.

59. Nomura actually had solid credentials to occupy this post. Not only was he a National Railway Board official with a technical background, but he had also been responsible for leading a survey team that mapped the Antung–Mukden railway route during the Russo-Japanese War (Sashūkai, *Nomura Ryūtarō den*, 172–217). The new vice governor was Itō Ōhachi, a Diet member from Nagano Prefecture (Harada, *Mantetsu*, 84).

60. *Manshū nichi nichi*, 12/17/13, 12/18/13, 12/19/13. Tokonami, a career bureaucrat, hailed from Satsuma and had joined the Seiyūkai in 1913.

61. Several weeks before the official announcement of management changes, Hara Takashi recorded in his diary his intention to place a Seiyūkai man in the office of vice governor and to discuss a suitable candidate for governor with Tokonami (Harada, *Mantetsu*, 84).

62. At a banquet held for the new SMR appointees, Hara stressed the need for reforming company management and reducing unnecessary expenditures (ibid.). General Tanaka Giichi bitterly criticized this move as being entirely groundless (Tanaka Giichi denki kankōkai, *Tanaka Giichi denki*, 549). According to the *Manshū nichi nichi*, 12/20/13, the House of Peers attacked the appointment as a party maneuver. Newspapers in Japan raised questions and criticisms as well; see, e.g., *Osaka Mainichi*, 12/20/13, in Meiji Taishō Shōwa shinbun kenkyūkai, *Shinbun shūsei Taishō hen nenshi*, vol. for 1912, 224–25; *Tōkyō Asahi shinbun*, 2/19/14.

63. The total ethnic Korean population in Manchuria at this time was at least a quarter of a million. The vast majority of Koreans in this territory lived and owned property in areas normally closed to foreign residence (principally in the border region known as Chientao). This was tolerated by the Chinese government with the understanding that these people were Chinese nationals. Japanese diplomats attempted to contest this status on a number of occasions. See Inoue Manabu, "Nihon teikokushugi to Kantō mondai"; and Brooks, "Peopling the Japanese Empire."

64. Kantō totokufu, Rikugun, Keiribu, *Manshū ippan shi*, 1: 242–43.

65. Nagura Bunji, *Nihon tekkōgyō shi no kenkyū*, 267–68.

66. "Akiyama Saneyuki danwa," in Yamamoto Jirō, *Terauchi Masatake kankei monjo*, 716.

67. Ibid., 716–17.

68. Tanaka Giichi denki kankōkai, *Tanaka Giichi denki*, 547. "Tai Man shogan," ca. 12/1913–3/1914 is reproduced in full in ibid., 547–84.

69. In his effort to encourage policymakers to look beyond Manchuria and develop a vigorous continental policy, Tanaka included some rather disparaging remarks about the territory in the preface to his 1906 draft of what would become the Imperial Defense Plan. "The climate of this territory and its economic conditions are clearly such that they offer little advantage to our people. . . . As is well known, South China, in contrast, is rich in resources, with fertile land that is blessed by heaven. In climate and in its accessibility, it cannot be compared with Manchuria" (quoted in Tsunoda, *Manshū mondai to kokubō hōshin*, 688–89). Given the context, it would be difficult to accept this view at face value; it suggests rhetorical overkill more than anything else. Interestingly, Tanaka had good things to say about Manchuria's climate in 1913: "According to some, Manchuria offers little prospect for the growth of Japanese settlement because the winters are intensely cold and unrelent-

ing in severity. This is nothing more than uninformed conjecture. Although the cold winds are strong, they do not create difficulties for earning a livelihood. On the contrary, the climate is refreshing and invigorates the spirit" (Tanaka Giichi denki kankōkai, *Tanaka Giichi denki*, 551–52). The idea of Manchuria providing an "invigorating" environment appears in other writings about the territory. One author even suggested that settlement in Manchuria would lead to the development of a hardy new breed of Japanese; see *Manshū nichi nichi*, 4/6/13.

70. Tanaka Giichi denki kankōkai, *Tanaka Giichi denki*, 551–52.

71. Ibid., 552, 558–59. Similar views about the settlement problem appear in *Manshū nichi nichi* 5/13/13.

72. Tanaka Giichi denki kankōkai, *Tanaka Giichi denki*, 554.

73. For a discussion of the Oriental Development Company, see Moskowitz, "The Creation of the Oriental Development Company."

74. Tanaka Giichi denki kankōkai, *Tanaka Giichi denki*, 554–55.

75. Gotō, "Shokumin seisaku ippan," in idem, *Shokumin seisaku ippan*, 43–136.

76. Ibid., 134. The phrase in which he uses the term "teikokushugi" reads as follows: "Shitagatte tōsei no kokuminshugi ni kuwauru ni teikokushugi o motte shinkō suru to iu kenchi kara Meiji jidai yori keizoku no shokumin seisaku ni doryoku sen to suru naraba."

77. Ibid., 104, 114, 120, 122–23.

78. Ibid., 103–5.

79. Ibid., 113, 116.

80. *Manshū nichi nichi*, 4/15/13, 5/13/13.

81. In their full report in 1906, they had offered the following appraisal: "Our survey has found that the quantity of arable land not already in use is extremely small. Moreover, there are good reasons why such land is not cultivated. Some areas are subject to flooding; others are inaccessible because of the mountainous terrain. Indeed, one's first impression upon entering Manchuria is the extent to which the hills and plains have been cultivated. There is virtually no land that can truly be described as empty" (*MSCS*[A], 231–32).

82. On the negotiations leading to the formation of the Ōkuma Cabinet, see Bannō, *Taishō seihen*, 178–213.

Chapter 5

1. The analytical framework of this chapter owes much to Kitaoka, *Nihon rikugun to tairiku seisaku*, 163–234. For a different line of interpretation of the impact of the war on Japanese imperialism, see Dickinson, *War and National Reinvention*.

2. See Nish, *Japanese Foreign Policy*, esp. 93–96 and 83–104 for a profile of Katō's policy; idem, *Alliance in Decline*, 115–31. See also Dickinson, *War and National Reinvention*, 33–85.

3. Background on events leading to the Twenty-One Demands is drawn from Usui, *Nihon to Chūgoku*, 41–60; Kitaoka, *Nihon rikugun to tairiku seisaku*, 63–171; and Chi, *China Diplomacy*, 1–27. Influential Japanese who actively opposed the initiative itself were in a distinct minority; see Okamoto, "Ishibashi Tanzan and the Twenty-One Demands," 184–98. For more on Ishibashi's anti-imperialist position, see Nolte, *Liberalism in Modern Japan*, 147–65. See also Dickinson, *War and National Reinvention*, 84–116.

4. Usui, *Nihon to Chūgoku*, 61–83; Kitaoka, *Nihon rikugun to tairiku seisaku*, 171–75; Chi, *China Diplomacy*, 28–61. For the English text of the Demands, see MacMurray, *Treaties and Agreements*, 2: 1231–34; for the series of Sino-Japanese agreements signed in May, see ibid., 1216–30.

5. One of the more detailed proposals for the development of Shantung, explicitly taking advantage of the close communications between the region and Manchuria, was prepared by Shirani Takeshi, the chief civil administrator of the Kwantung Government-General, "Seitō kanpu no sai yōkyū subeki jikō ni kanshi iken gushin no ken," 10/1914, in *NGB*, 1914, 2: 925–27. On the German economic experience in Shantung, see Schrecker, *Imperialism and Chinese Nationalism*, 210–48.

6. Nakamura, a retired army general, was appointed by the Ōkuma government to replace Seiyūkai appointee Nomura Ryūtarō. This move, heartily approved by the army, was ostensibly aimed at forestalling the practice of changing SMR management with every cabinet, but in fact, it strengthened the precedent set by the Yamamoto government. For Hara Takashi's account of the events leading to the undoing of his 1913 initiative, see *Hara Takashi Nikki*, various entries, 6/1914–7/1914, 4: 74, 79–80, 81–82, 84, 85–87; see also Harada, *Mantetsu*, 105.

7. For background on the Hsinch'iu mine and an assessment of early Chinese plans to build a railway connection to the PMR and to use the mine to challenge Fushun, see Kantō totokufu, Rikugun, Keiribu, *Manshū ippan shi*, 4: 297–301.

8. The Japanese initially sought to build the Ch'angch'un–Kirin line as a wholly owned branch of the SMR. As part of the same compromise involving the Hsinmint'un–Mukden line, they agreed to a loan concession instead. For a record of initial negotiations, see *NGB*, 1907, 2: 336–76. Construction was delayed, according to Japanese sources, by Chinese obstruction as well as the revolution of 1911–12. Although the line became operational in 1912, it was plagued by serious problems, which provided a pretext for this move. For background, see SMR, Chōsaka, *Mammō tetsudō no shakai oyobi keizai ni oyoboseru eikyō, zenpen* (1931), 47–49. For a broader analysis of this line, see SMR, Un'yubu, *Ekizei ippan: Kitsu–Chō no bu* (1916).

9. Japanese policymakers had attempted to create a precedent for this arrangement in 1909 by claiming jurisdiction over all ethnic Koreans residing in the section of southeastern Manchuria known as Chientao. The Chinese refused to acknowledge these claims. On the Chientao issue and the status of Koreans in the region

during this period, see Inoue Manabu, "Nihon teikokushugi to Kantō mondai." Katō's position on this question seems to have been considerably more moderate. He did not fully expect the Chinese to acquiesce to Japanese demands for land-lease rights and had prepared a fallback position that was little different from what Abe had outlined in 1913; see Katō to Hioki, 12/3/14, in NGN1, 383.

10. Nakamura to Ōkuma, 6/22/15, in NGB, 1915, 2: 965.

11. Ibid., 967.

12. Kantōchō, *Kantōchō shisei nijūnen shi*, 662–64; SMR, Chōsaka, *Waga kuni jinkō mondai to Manmō*, 162–63; SMR1, 890–92.

13. Jon Halliday (*Political History of Japanese Capitalism*, 100), for example, describes the financial aspects of Japanese expansion as "imperialism without capital."

14. Katō to Hioki, 12/18/14, in NGB, 1914, 2: 85–86.

15. Katō to Hioki, 6/15/15 and 6/29/15, in NGB, 1915, 2: 431 and 432–35.

16. Odagiri Masunosuke, "Shi-Tei tetsudō shakkan kōshō shimatsu hōkokusho," 12/20/15, in NGB, 1915, 2: 450–70.

17. Ochiai (Mukden consul-general) to Ōkuma, 9/1/15, and Ishii (foreign minister) to Obata (acting minister to Peking), 10/26/15, in NGB, 1915, 2: 999–1003 and 1011–14. See also Usui Katsumi, "Nan-Man Tō-Mō jōyaku no seiritsu zengo," 126–36.

18. Odagiri Masunosuke, "Shi-Tei tetsudō shakkan kōshō shimatsu hōkokusho," 12/20/15, in NGB, 1915, 2: 468–70.

19. Usui, *Nihon to Chūgoku*, 85–87.

20. Good examples of this attitude are found in the recommendations of Ōshima Ken'ichi (army vice minister) and Major General Machida Keiu (military attaché in Peking) in 1914; see NGB, 1914, 2: 903–9 and 914–19.

21. Odagiri Masunosuke, "Shi-Tei tetsudō shakkan kōshō shimatsu hōkokusho," 12/20/15, in NGB, 1915, 2: 466, 468–70.

22. Ōshima Ken'ichi, 8/24/14, in NGB, 1914, 2: 907.

23. Machida Keiu, 9/21/14, in NGB, 1914, 2: 917.

24. Kitaoka, *Nihon rikugun to tairiku seisaku*, 173–78.

25. On the campaign to topple Yüan, see ibid., 181–90.

26. Ibid., 181–82; Nish, *Japanese Foreign Policy*, 103–4. See also Dickinson, *War and National Reinvention*, 117–53.

27. Chi, *China Diplomacy*, 62–80; Kurihara Ken, "Dai ichiji, dai niji Manmō dokuritsu undō to Koike Gaimushō, Seimukyokuchō no jishoku," 145–61; E. P. Young, *The Presidency of Yüan Shih-k'ai*, 210–40.

28. Usui, *Nihon to Chūgoku*, 93–95.

29. Ibid., 99–102.

30. Duus, *Party Rivalry and Political Change in Taishō Japan*, 86–97; Lebra, *Ōkuma Shigenobu*, 123–30.

31. Kitaoka, *Nihon rikugun to tairiku seisaku,* 190–93, 196–200. See also Dickinson, *War and National Reinvention,* 154–203.

32. Kaneko, "Sōgyōki no Minami Manshū tetsudō," 196.

33. Tuan had actually advised Yüan to reject the Japanese ultimatum over the Twenty-One Demands in 1915 (E. P. Young, *The Presidency of Yüan Shih-k'ai,* 191; Kitaoka, *Nihon rikugun to tairiku seisaku,* 200–212).

34. Japan's gold reserves rose from ¥342 million in December 1914 to ¥2.178 billion in December 1920 (Allen, *Short Economic History of Modern Japan,* 102).

35. Lieutenant General Ōshima (*NGB,* 1914, 2: 905), for example, argued in August 1914 that advances in military technology had made warfare so destructive that none of the belligerents would likely aim for total victory. All sides, he predicted, would come to a relatively hasty, negotiated settlement, which made it all the more urgent for Japan to move quickly.

36. Bōeichō, Bōeikenshūsho, Senshishitsu, *Rikugun gunju dōin,* 15–32.

37. On railway policy, see Hashitani, "Chōsen tetsudō no Mantetsu e no itaku keiei o megutte," 159–78; Kaneko, *Kindai Nihon ni okeru tai-Manshū tōshi no kenkyū,* 235–42; and Kitaoka, *Nihon rikugun to tairiku seisaku,* 235–46. See also Chōsen sōtokufu, Tetsudōkyoku, *Chōsen tetsudō yonjūnen ryakushi,* 90–95. For an example of a report provided by a Dairen lobbying group, see Ishimoto Kantarō et al., *Sansen mondai undō keika hōkoku.*

38. On trade, see Kaneko, *Kindai Nihon ni okeru tai-Manshū tōshi no kenkyū,* 181. Traffic statistics calculated from SMR1, 721; and TKN 1914, 256, 260; 1917, 281, 285, 286, 290.

39. Hashitani, "Chōsen tetsudō no Mantetsu e no itaku keiei o megutte," 165–71.

40. Ibid., 164–65, 167. Interestingly, the idea of contract management as a substitute for full administrative integration of the two territories appears in one of the Chōsen Railway's official histories; see Chōsen sōtokufu, Tetsudōkyoku, *Chōsen tetsudō yonjūnen ryakushi,* 90–92.

41. Kaneko, *Kindai Nihon ni okeru tai-Manshū tōshi no kenkyū,* 252–60.

42. During the war, the Bank of Chōsen also opened branches in Tsingtao, Shanghai, T'ientsin, Tsinan, Kobe, Shimonoseki, Vladivostok, Khabarovsk, Chita, London, and New York (Kaneko, *Kindai Nihon ni okeru tai-Manshū tōshi no kenkyū,* 254–56, 288–92).

43. For a series of documents relevant to these reforms, see source appendix in Kurihara, *Tai-Man seisaku shi no ichimen,* 264–74. See also Kitaoka, *Nihon rikugun to tairiku seisaku,* 262–75.

44. Morley, *The Japanese Thrust into Siberia,* 28–31.

45. Seki and Fujii, "Nihon teikokushugi to Higashi Ajia," 525. On the 1907 assessment of the Army General Staff, see Miyazaki 23, leaves 4–5.

46. See NGB, 1917, 1: 117–28, for a series of documents pertaining to these nego-tiations between January and May 1917. Japanese negotiators were prepared to offer up to ¥25 million for this segment, along with a subscription to ¥200 million in Rus-sian government bonds and an agreement to fill Russian orders for heavy artillery and other munitions.

47. Kaneko, *Kindai Nihon ni okeru tai-Manshū tōshi no kenkyū*, 244.

48. On the launching of the Siberian Expedition, see Morley, *The Japanese Thrust into Siberia*. See also Seki and Fujii, "Nihon teikokushugi to Higashi Ajia," 517–24.

49. See Kitaoka, *Nihon rikugun to tairiku seisaku*, 196–214. See also Beasley, *Japanese Imperialism*, 117–21.

50. Scholars differ as to what loans to include under the category of the Nishihara Loans. Some exclude the military loans. Others include an additional ¥5 million to the Communications Bank. The classification used here follows Suzuki Takeo, "Kaidai," in idem, *Nishihara shakkan shiryō kenkyū*, 3–67. For an overview of the Nishihara Loans, see also Kitaoka, *Nihon rikugun to tairiku seisaku*, 215–34; Ōmori, "Nishihara shakkan ni tsuite"; Nochi and Ōmori, "Dai ichiji taisenki no Nihon no tai-Chūgoku shakkan," 51–87; and Baba Akira, *Nitchū kankei to gaisei kikō no kenkyū*, 3–37.

51. On the issue of war participation, see, in addition to Kitaoka, *Nihon rikugun to tairiku seisaku*, Usui, *Nihon to Chūgoku*, 105–12.

52. Shōda to Inoue (governor of the Yokohama Specie Bank), 5/12/17, in NGB, 1917, 2: 518–19; Shōda to Sugi (secretary, Finance Ministry), 6/4/1918, in NGB, 1918, 2: 824.

53. These "bribes" would be added to the actual cost of railway construction. The requirement that the railway repay these advances out of the proceeds of the con-struction loan added significantly to the financial burden of the venture. Shōda be-lieved, however, that most railway projects could carry a burden of some 20 percent above construction costs without creating serious difficulties (Shōda to Sugi, 6/4/1918, in NGB, 1918, 2: 824).

54. For data on the Kirin–Hoeryong line, see SMR, Sōmubu, Kōmukyoku, Sekkeika, *Kitsurin–Kainei kan kōki tetsudō yotei senro chōsasho*, 30–31. For the K'aiyüan–Hailung line, see SMR, Tetsudōbu, Kōmuka, *Kaigen–Chōyōzan kan yotei tetsudō senro tōsa hōkokusho*, 33–37. For the SMR, calculated from SMR1, 932; and SMR2, 1325.

55. Quoted in Huenemann, *The Dragon and the Iron Horse*, 72.

56. For Nishihara's report on this agreement and some cautionary notes, see Nishihara to Sugi, 6/4/18, in NGB, 1918, 2: 822–23.

57. The 1918 agreement on Manchurian railways specified four lines: the Ch'angch'un–T'aonan, the T'aonan–Jehol, the K'aiyüan–Kirin, which represented a merger of the K'aiyüan–Hailung and Hailung–Kirin lines from the 1913 agreement, and an unspecified spur to connect the T'aonan–Jehol railway to a seaport, most

likely Hulutao. This spur may have been designed as a pre-emptive measure to control the use of the T'aonan–Jehol railway as a competitor to the SMR. The original demand for a connector between the T'aonan–Jehol and the SMR does not appear in this agreement. A line that would serve such a purpose, running from Chengchiat'un to T'ungliao (Payintala) was being discussed under a separate set of negotiations (*NGN*1, 466–68). Kitaoka (*Nihon rikugun to tairiku seisaku*, 228) points out that loan advances for these four railways along with the two in Shantung were initiated as a last minute substitute for the failed iron loan scheme.

58. Kitaoka, *Nihon rikugun to tairiku seisaku*, 163–68.

59. Nishihara, "Nisshi ryōkoku shinzen ni kanshi kyōyaku shisetsu ni taisuru ryōkoku seifu daihyō oboegaki," 4/13/18, in Suzuki Takeo, *Nishihara shakkan shiryō kenkyū*, 184–85.

60. See, e.g., Hioki to Katō, 12/20/14, in *NGB*, 1914, 2: 428–29.

61. Shōda quoted in Suzuki Takeo, "Kaidai," in idem, *Nishihara shakkan shiryō kenkyū*, 9.

62. Nishihara, "Nisshi ryōkoku shinzen ni kanshi kyōyaku shisetsu ni taisuru ryōkoku seifu daihyō oboegaki," 4/13/18, in Suzuki Takeo, *Nishihara shakkan shiryō kenkyū*, 184.

63. As evidenced by Manchurian railway negotiations, the Terauchi government considered Manchuria and Shantung to be special cases outside the framework of this emerging policy of cooperation. This principle is implicit in the Terauchi government's early outlines of China policy; see cabinet resolutions, "Tai-Shi hōshin," 1/9/17 and 7/20/17, in Suzuki Takeo, *Nishihara shakkan shiryō kenkyū*, 119–20.

64. Shōda underscores autarky as the principal justification for the Nishihara loans as a whole in an essay written in defense of his policies shortly after the resignation of the Terauchi government; see Shōda, "Kiku no newake," in Suzuki Takeo, *Nishihara shakkan shiryō kenkyū*, 287–342, esp. 287–92.

65. For an overview of this issue in English, see Michael Barnhart, *Japan Prepares for Total War*, 22–49. Barnhart only briefly touches on developments during the era under consideration here. In Japanese, see Rekishigaku kenkyūkai, *Taiheiyō sensō shi*, vol. 1, *Manshū jihen*, 75–84; and Bōeichō, Bōeikenshūsho, Senshishitsu, *Rikugun gunju dōin*, 1: 33–88.

66. Bōeichō, Bōeikenshūsho, Senshishitsu, *Rikugun gunju dōin*, 1: 37–40.

67. *TKS*, 1, 32–38. Koiso's numbers take into account a surplus labor force in the countryside of over 10 million, the drafting of over 2 million horses, each of which is counted as the labor-equivalent of four people, and a shift of 1.5 million workers from agriculture to industry.

68. Ibid., 5–9.

69. Ibid., 13–17.

70. Ibid., 10–12.

71. Ibid., 98–142.

72. Ibid., 142–47.

73. Ibid., 17–22, 264–67.

74. Ibid., 117–19, 125–26, 146.

75. Ibid., 152–62. Koiso specifically cites the work of the SMR in the area of sheep hybridization. Mitsui Bussan and other Japanese trading companies often set up processing and manufacturing plants in China as a means of securing raw material supplies for broader distribution; see Yamamura Mutsuo, "Nihon teikokushugi seiritsu katei ni okeru Mitsui bussan no hatten," 33.

76. TKS, 149–60.

77. Ibid., 146–48.

78. Ibid., 149, 160.

79. Quoted in Ōe, *Nichi-Ro sensō no gunjishiteki kenkyū*, 420.

80. TKS, 5–9.

81. The first revision of the Imperial Defense Plan (1918) has not been found. An early draft version prepared by Tanaka (11/12/16) is reproduced in Yamaguchi Toshiaki, "Hamaomote Matasuke bunsho," 233–34. See also Saitō Seiji, "Kokubō hōshin dai ichiji kaitei no haikei."

82. Bōeichō, Bōeikenshūsho, Senshishitsu, *Rikugun gunju dōin*, 1: 44–66; Dingman, *Power in the Pacific*, 54–63.

83. Humphreys, "Crisis and Reaction," 85–90.

84. On the problem of steel and civilian responses to the resource problem, see Matsumoto, "Nihon teikokushugi no shigen mondai." On horse breeding, see Army Ministry, "Manmō bahiki kairō hōshin," 8/4/19, in MDN, 1921, vol. 6, basei 6. This particular memorandum provides detailed specifications for the horse-breeding program. The original instructions were issued to the SMR by the cabinet in 1918.

85. Kitaoka, *Nihon rikugun to tairiku seisaku*, 225–28; Ōmori, "Nishihara shakkan ni tsuite," 44; Baba, *Nitchū kankei to gaisei kikō no kenkyū*, 10–37.

86. Quoted in J. Young, "The Hara Cabinet and Chang Tso-lin," 140–41.

87. Yoshizawa to Foreign Minister Uchida Yasuya, 10/10/18, in NGB, 1918, pt. 2, 2: 934–40.

88. Nakamura memorandum, 11/26/18, in NGB, 1918, pt. 2, 2: 958. Previous loan agreements had designated the Yokohama Specie Bank as the principal party for the Japanese side as a result of Chinese objections to SMR participation. Nakamura wanted to establish the company's central role in railway loans.

89. Kitaoka, *Gotō Shinpei*, 161–86.

90. On politics within the army under the Terauchi cabinet, see Kitaoka, *Nihon rikugun to tairiku seisaku*, 311–30. For an example of the role of the Foreign Policy Research Council, see Morley, *The Japanese Thrust into Siberia*, 269–83.

91. See Lewis, *Rioters and Citizens*, 251.

Chapter 6

1. Ugaki, *Ugaki Kazunari nikki*, undated 1918 entry, 187.

2. Kobayashi Yukio, "Tai-So seisaku no suii to Manmō mondai," 172–82; Lewis, *Rioters and Citizens*, 251.

3. Indications that the army was planning for such a scenario may be found in Sanbō honbu, *Senji sōheiryoku kettei ni kansuru kaigi gijiroku*, 10/13/20, Miyazaki shiryō, item 60. This is a transcript of a conference between the Army Ministry and general staff dealing with the question of setting force levels for the future. The standard for this determination appears to have been the number of divisions required to extend Japanese control from Manchuria in the north to Hank'ou in the south. Additional indications are offered in Hayashi Yasakichi, Military Attaché, Beijing Legation, report, "Kita Shina kōryaku sakusen ni tsuite," 2/21/23, in *MDN*, 1923, vol. 5, gaikō 34. This document envisions a war against China in terms of Japan's effort to secure an autarkic sphere. Army mobilization plans up to this point called for roughly doubling the number of peacetime divisions during a full-scale war.

4. On Siberia, see Chōsengun, Sanbōbu, "Shiberiya no fugen ni tsuite," 1/27/20, in *MDN*, 1920, vol. 4, tosho 19. On China, there is a series of strategic resources studies conducted by the T'ientsin (Boxer Protocol) Garrison contained in a report from the garrison command to Army Minister Tanaka in 1919: "Gunju hin chōsa no ken hōkoku," 4/14/19, in *MDN*, 1919, vol. 2, chōtatsu 3.

5. Sanbō honbu dai 2 bu, "Shina shigen riyō ni kansuru kansatsu," 5/17/1922, in *MDN*, 1923, vol. 5, item 14. Even army leaders dubious of the idea in principle were not averse to using autarky as a justification for expansionist policies; see, e.g., Chief of Staff Uehara Yūsaku to Army Minister Ōshima Ken'ichi, "Shina ni taishi teikoku no kibō suru riken tetsudō mō ni kansuru ken, shōkai," 10/13/17, in *MDN*, 1920, vol. 4, senpaku kōtsū 4.

6. Barnhart, *Japan Prepares for Total War*, 24.

7. This emphasis had less to do with ideological sympathies for U.S. policy than with the realities of power and economic relationships. That Hara saw Japan's relations with the United States in terms of power politics was clear in his view of China policy on the eve of the Twenty-One Demands. Key to success in China, he argued, lay in preventing the Chinese from exploiting friction between Japan and the United States. If ties between the two Great Powers remained amicable, Japan could achieve its objectives in China as a matter of course (Hara Takashi, *Hara Takashi nikki*, 9/29/14 and 9/30/14 entries, 5: 49–51).

8. Hara as a master of compromise is a theme central to Najita's book, *Hara Kei in the Politics of Compromise*, from which I have borrowed the title of this chapter.

9. For an overview of the diplomacy of the Hara government, see Mitani,

"'Tenkanki' (1918–1921) no gaikō shidō." See also Dickinson, *War and National Reinvention*, 204–37.

10. Bannō Junji, *Kindai Nihon no gaikō to seiji*, 98–99. See also Kitaoka, *Nihon rikugun to tairiku seisaku*, 228–32.

11. In addition to Mitani, "'Tenkanki' (1918–1921) no gaikō shidō," see Suzuki Takashi, *Nihon teikokushugi to Manshū*, 1: 329–32.

12. Kurihara, "Kantō totokufu mondai teiyō," 57–59, 275–84; Suzuki Takashi, *Nihon teikokushugi to Manshū*, 1: 334–40, Imai Seiichi, "Taishō ki ni okeru gunbu no seijiteki chii," 1250–57.

13. Harada, *Mantetsu*, 103–4; a major corruption scandal in 1921 rocked Nomura's administration and damaged the company's reputation, generating further criticism of the practice of patronage appointments (ibid., 104–9). See also Katō, "Hara Takashi to Mantetsu," 50–56; and Kobayashi Hideo, *Mantetsu*, 67–69.

14. Hoshino, *Economic History of Manchuria*, 91–92.

15. Usui, *Nihon to Chūgoku*, 137–40; Suzuki Takashi, *Nihon teikokushugi to Manshū*, 1: 338–40.

16. Usui, *Nihon to Chūgoku*, 146–50.

17. Ibid., 153–62; see also Chow, *The May Fourth Movement* (1960).

18. Characteristic of Japanese perceptions of Chinese nationalism at this time, General Ugaki (*Ugaki Kazunari nikki*, undated 1919 entry, 202) attributed the May Fourth movement to the machinations of "Anglo-American schemers."

19. On U.S. and British policies, see Iriye, *After Imperialism*, 1–22; Nish, *Alliance in Decline*, 263–87; and Levin, *Woodrow Wilson and World Politics*, 236–45.

20. For the English text of the 5/11/19 resolution, see *NGB*, 1919, pt. 2, 1: 239.

21. For an overview of the loan consortium problem, see Usui, *Nihon to Chūgoku*, 162–72.

22. Iriye, "The Failure of Economic Expansion," 239–50.

23. Oka, *Konoe Fumimaro*, 10–15.

24. Ugaki, *Ugaki Kazunari nikki*, undated 1920 entry, 324 (the diary does not provide specific dates for this period; this entry comes from a section written between April and July 1920).

25. Debuchi to Foreign Minister Uchida, 6/29/19, in *NGB*, 1919, pt. 2, 1: 297–301.

26. Ibid., 299. Nishihara's renegotiation of the 1913 Manchurian railway agreement resulted in four lines: the Ch'angch'un–T'aonan, the T'aonan–Jehol, the K'aiyüan–Hailung–Kirin (consolidating the two separate lines of 1913), and a seaport connector for the T'aonan–Jehol. The Ssup'ingkai–T'aonan was excluded because construction was already in progress.

27. Ibid., 300. On the Ssup'ingkai–T'aonan and its Chengchiat'un–T'ungliao branch, see *NGB*, 1918, pt. 2, 1: 516–19. For a record of the grueling negotiations over the Kirin–Hoeryong line in 1919, see *NGB*, 1919, pt. 2, 1: 745–888. For the Chinese

representatives' protest over the new Japanese government's changed terms, see transcript of session, 2/10/19, in ibid., 741. On talks over the four Manchurian railways renegotiated by Nishihara in 1918, see NGB, 1919, pt. 2, 1: 889–938.

28. Debuchi to Uchida, 6/29/19, in NGB, 1919, pt. 2, 1: 299.

29. Army Minister Tanaka to Foreign Minister Uchida, 2/8/19, in NGB, 1919, pt. 2, 1: 616–17.

30. Kobayashi Yukio, "Tai-So seisaku no suii to Manmō mondai (1917–1927)," 168.

31. Quoted in Ikei, "Ugaki Kazushige's View of China and His China Policy," 209.

32. Foreign ownership as an impediment to mobilizing Chinese natural resources during wartime is discussed in Sanbō honbu, Dai 2 bu, "Shina shigen riyō ni kansuru kansatsu," 5/17/22, in MDN, 1923, vol. 5, item 14, 8.

33. Ugaki, *Ugaki Kazunari nikki*, late Dec. 1918 entry, 187.

34. Dower, *Empire and Aftermath*, 47.

35. Uchida to Finance Minister Takahashi, 5/6/19, in NGB, 1919, pt. 2, 1: 234–37; cabinet resolution, 5/20/19, in NGB, 1919, pt. 2, 1: 244–45.

36. Minister to China Obata to Uchida, 6/11/19, in NGB, 1919, pt. 2, 1: 280.

37. Usui, *Nihon to Chūgoku*, 167; Hara Takashi, *Hara Takashi nikki*, 8/13/19 entry, 5: 128–29.

38. Memorandum to the British government, 2/27/20, in NGB, 1920, pt. 2, 1: 191–92 (English text). An identical memorandum dated the following day was forwarded to the U.S. government; see ibid., 198–201. For the U.S. State Department's reply of 3/16/20, see ibid., 231, 232.

39. Japanese reply to U.S. State Department, 3/30/20, in NGB, 1920, pt. 2, 1: 243–45.

40. Chengchiat'un Consul Iwamura to Foreign Minister Gotō, 9/1918, in NGB, 1918, pt. 2, 1: 516–19. The use of this line as an "interceptor" for the T'aonan–Jehol had been incorporated into railway plans in 1913 as well.

41. Uchida to Obata, 2/28/21, in NGB, 1921, 2: 412–17.

42. Japanese reply to U.S. State Department, 3/30/20, in NGB, 1920, pt. 2, 1: 244–45.

43. SMR, Gijutsubu, Senroka, *Tōnan–Chichiharu kan tetsudō yotei senro tōsasho* (survey of 1919), esp. 12–17.

44. British reply, 4/28/20, in NGB, 1920, pt. 2, 1: 282–84; U.S. reply, 4/29/20, 277–79.

45. Hara (*Hara Takashi nikki*, 5/4/20 entry, 5: 235–36) argued that Japan should accept these Anglo-American assurances and not seek formal guarantees in the form of further railway exclusions. For the formal Japanese acquiescence, 5/5/1920, see NGB, 1920, pt. 2, 1: 290–92; for the cabinet resolution on the final position, 9/3/1920, see NGB, 1920, pt. 2, 1: 357–62.

46. For a series of memoranda and dispatches on this problem, dated 10/14/20, see NGB, 1920, pt. 2, 1: 397–404.

47. Discussion of options and various strategy proposals regarding the CER may be found in NGB, 1920, pt. 3, vol. 2: chief of staff, Vladivostok Army, to army vice chief of staff, 2/10/20, 1151–53; Foreign Minister Uchida to Harbin consul-general, 3/23/20, 1175–76; Army Ministry to Foreign Ministry, 5/3/20, 1182–83; Uchida to Shidehara (ambassador to United States), 8/2/20, 1202; SMR to Foreign Ministry, 10/5/20, 1210–12; Army Ministry to Foreign Ministry, 10/9/20, 1213–20.

48. Calculated from TKN, 1917, 276; and SMR, Chōsaka, Tō-Shin tetsudō nanbu ensen chihō keizai chōsa shiryō, 64–65, 71–73.

49. SMR, Chōsaka, Jikyoku to Tō-Shin tetsudō (written Oct. 1918, published 1919). Miyazaki would play a central role in economic planning in Manchuria and in the empire as a whole during the 1930s; see Kobayashi Hideo, Nihon kabushikigaisha o tsukutta otoko (1995).

50. Cabinet resolution, "Manmō ni taisuru seisaku," 5/13/21, in NGN1, 523.

51. Ibid., 523.

52. Ibid., 524.

53. J. Young, "The Hara Cabinet and Chang Tso-lin," 129.

54. Nakamura proposal for cabinet discussion, 6/22/15, in NGB, 1915, 2: 694–70.

55. Kaneko, Kindai Nihon ni okeru tai-Manshū tōshi no kenkyū, 191–201; figures are calculated from data in SMR, Chōsaka, Manmō ni okeru Nihon no tōshi jōtai, 85.

56. SMR1, 629; SMR2, 739–53, 56–59. In 1920, for example, Japan produced 521,000 tons of pig iron domestically, of which the state-owned Yawata Ironworks accounted for 243,000 tons (Yonekura, The Japanese Iron and Steel Industry, 89).

57. SMR2, 759–63, 783–98; Kantōchō, Kantōchō shisei nijūnen shi, 580–84, 605–7.

58. SMR2, 765–74, 891–95, 1044–49; Kantōchō, Kantōchō shisei nijūnen shi, 610–15.

59. Kantōchō, Kantōchō shisei nijūnen shi, 585–92.

60. Ibid., 596–98, 603–5, 608; SMR2, 387–92. On Shahok'ou, see SMR, Shakakō kōjō gaikyō. On the research activities of the SMR during the 1920s, see Okabe, "1920 nendai no Mantetsu to Mantetsu chōsabu."

61. SMR2, 865–72. Nakamura (proposal, 6/22/15, in NGB, 1915, 2: 965–66) underscores the economic policy role of the Central Research Laboratory.

62. On the idea of "industrial organizers," see Togai, "Saisho ni shutsugen shita sōgoshōsha," 81–82; and Morikawa, "Sōgōshōsha no seiritsu to ronri," 44. See also K. Yamamura, "General Trading Companies."

63. Nagura, Nippon tekkōgyō shi no kenkyū, 266–72; Yonekura, The Japanese Iron and Steel Industry, 104–06.

64. Kaneko Fumio, "1920 nendai ni okeru Nihon teikokushugi to 'Manshū,'" pt. 1, 172–79.

65. The term "ethnic Japanese" is used to distinguish this group from ethnic Koreans residing in Kwantung and the Railway Zone, who were included as "Japanese" in some statistics. These figures do not include residents of consular jurisdictions.

66. SMR, Chōsaka, *Waga kuni jinkō mondai to Manmō*, 25–26, 68–69, 93–111; SMR2, 1137–44.

67. McCormack, *Chang Tso-lin in Northeast China*, 49–58.

68. Ibid., 15–56; Hayashi, "Chō Sakurin gunbatsu no keisei katei to Nihon no taiō," 122–34.

69. J. Young, "The Hara Cabinet and Chang Tso-lin," 134–36.

70. Ibid., 128–31; Hayashi Masakazu, "Chō Sakurin gunbatsu no keisei katei to Nihon no taiō," 134–42; J. Young, "The Hara Cabinet and Chang Tso-lin," 128–31.

71. J. Young, "The Hara Cabinet and Chang Tso-lin," 133–34; McCormack, *Chang Tso-lin in Northeast China*, 56–58.

72. Morton, *Tanaka Giichi and Japan's China Policy*, 40–45.

73. Hara Takashi, *Hara Takashi nikki*, 11/24/20 entry, 5: 315.

74. Ibid., 11/11/20 entry, 5: 310.

75. Ibid., 11/19/20 entry, 5: 313.

76. Amamiya, "Shiberiya tettai katei to tōhō kaigi"; McCormack, *Chang Tso-lin in Northeast China*, 58–62.

77. Cabinet resolution, "Chō Sakurin ni taisuru taido ni kansuru ken," 5/17/21, NGN1, 524–25.

78. See Asada Sadao, "Washinton kaigi to Nihon no taiō."

Chapter 7

1. For a perspective on this period in diplomatic history, see Iriye, "The Failure of Economic Expansion"; and Asada Sadao, "Washinton kaigi to Nihon no taiō." For a sampling of criticism during the 45th Diet (1921–22), see *Teikoku gikai shūgiin iinkai giroku, Taishō hen*, 31: Matsushita Teiji (Kōshin kurabu) interpellation, 1/27/22, 14–16, and 1/30/22, 31–32; Nagai Ryūtarō (Kenseikai) interpellation, 1/27/22, 39–46; Kawasaki Katsu (Kenseikai) interpellation, 2/2/22, 112–14; Mochizuki Shōtarō (Kenseikai) interpellation, 2/2/22, 118–23. The predominantly pro-navy orientation of this criticism suggests that it should not be construed as being in sympathy with the army's orientation toward Manchuria. The Kenseikai's disagreements with the government's moderate positions were not as large as they might seem from the strident tone of the attacks.

2. DR1, 44–60; Shimanuki Takeji, "Dai ichiji taisen igo no kokubō hōshin, shoyō heiryoku, yōhei kōryō." See also Humphreys, *The Way of the Heavenly Sword*, 60–107; and Dingman, *Power in the Pacific*, 122–35. For Ugaki's remarks, see Ugaki, *Ugaki Kazunari nikki*, undated 1923 entry, 448.

3. Hata Eitarō position paper, 3/14/24, in NGB, 1924, 2: 774.

4. Hata's notes, 4/4/1924, in NGB, 1924, 2: 800.

5. Lensen, Damned Inheritance, 8–13; for Japanese reports, see various dispatches, Aug.–Nov. 1923, in NGB, 1923, 1: 529–48.

6. For a contemporary assessment of emerging Soviet power in north Manchuria, see Hashimoto Kingoro (Captain), "Tō-Shi ensen ni okeru Rōnō Rokoku no seiryoku," 1/14/24, in MDN, 1925, vol. 5, gaikoku jōhō Shina 10. See also paper by Hata, 3/14/1924, in NGB, 1924, 2: 774–75; and GSS, 32: xxii. Matsunawa Zensaburō ("Ro-Shi kyōtei ni itaru Tō-Shi tetsudō no riken kaishū to Nihon no taiō") suggests that the Sino-Soviet accords of 1924 raised concerns within the Japanese army that Chinese pressure for full recovery of the SMR would intensify. The analysis offered here is substantially different.

7. Various dispatches from the Kwantung Army, Army Ministry, and Foreign Ministry, Aug.–Oct. 1921, in NGB, 1921, 2: 305–13.

8. McCormack, Chang Tso-lin in Northeast China, 62–74; Suzuki Takashi, Nihon teikokushugi to Manshū, 1: 389–98; Ikei, "Dai ichiji Hō-Choku sensō to Nihon." For an overview of warlord politics in the 1920s, see Pye, Warlord Politics, 13–38.

9. McCormack, Chang Tso-lin in Northeast China, 75–110.

10. Bannō, "Japanese Industrialists and Merchants and the Anti-Japanese Boycotts in China," 318–21; idem, Kindai Nihon no gaikō to seiji, 159–61; Suzuki Takashi, Nihon teikokushugi to Manshū, 1: 399–408.

11. On Japanese responses to the immigration law, eventually passed in 1924, see Ariga Tadashi, "Hai-Nichi mondai to Nichi-Bei kankei." For an indication of resurgent interest in settlement, see SMR, Chōsaka, Manmō yori nani o kitai subeki ka. The thrust of this 1924 pamphlet, aimed at a broad public audience, is cautionary and warns against excessive expectations of settlement opportunities in Manchuria.

12. Yoshii's ("Dai ichiji taisen go no 'Manmō' tetsudō mondai") study first drew my attention to the problem of the T'aonan–Tsitsihar and Mukden–Hailung railways, which is central to my larger analysis of Matsuoka's policy. Kaneko ("1920 nendai ni okeru Nihon teikokushugi to 'Manshū,'" pt. 1, 218) touches on this issue in an earlier work.

13. Yoshii, "Dai ichiji taisen go no 'Manmō' tetsudō mondai," 37–38. See also Chi-lin sheng she-hui k'e-hsueh yüan, Man-t'ieh shih tzu-liao pien-chi tsu, Man-t'ieh shih tzu-liao, pt. 2, 3: 728–30. This source is a summary account of negotiations over the T'aonan–Ssup'ingkai railway prepared by Nomura Tadashi, head of the General Affairs Section of the SMR's General Affairs Department some time between 1924 and 1926.

14. Yoshii, "Dai ichiji taisen go no 'Manmō' tetsudō mondai," 37–38.

15. McCormack, Chang Tso-lin in Northeast China, 89–93; Ogata Yōichi, "Tōhoku kōtsū iinkai to iwayuru 'Mantetsu hōi tetsudō mō keikaku,'" 45–46. On railway

construction plans in Inner Mongolia, see Ch'angch'un Consul-General Murakami to Uchida, 12/8/1920, in NGB, 1920, pt. 2, 2: 678–79; and SMR, Chōsaka, *Rinkai tetsudō to shomondai*, 101, 127–29.

16. Huenemann, *The Dragon and the Iron Horse*, 177–86.

17. On the state of the Chang regime's finances, see Nishimura, *Chūgoku kindai tōhoku chiiki shi kenkyū*, 142–57. Nishimura (ibid., 150–51) notes the enormous land-holdings of Chang Tso-lin and other officials of the Three Eastern Provinces.

18. Hirano Kenichirō, "1923 nen no Manshū," 250–52; McCormack, *Chang Tso-lin in Northeast China*, 87–100, 190–91. See also Su, *Man-t'ieh shih*, 401–8.

19. Chang's calculations become clear in subsequent negotiations with Japan; see Chapter 8. Note that the Eastern Conference resolution underscored the importance of railway power in consolidating Chang's rule as a "talking point" in persuading the warlord to cooperate with Japan.

20. DRi, 163–64.

21. Kaneko, *Kindai Nihon ni okeru tai-Manshū tōshi no kenkyū*, 242–50, 402–19. The SMR's Harbin office reported a marked rise in the CER's traffic in 1923 (SMR, Harupin jimusho, Chōsaka, *1923 nendo Tō-Shi tetsudō eigyō seiseki*, 1).

22. See below in this chapter of a discussion of this problem by Matsuoka Yōsuke.

23. Yoshii, "Dai ichiji taisen go no 'Manmō' tetsudō mondai," 38; SMR, Chōsaka, *Rinkai tetsudō to shomondai*, 31–41; SMR, Chōsaka, *Hō-Kai tetsudō to Koryōtō chikkō mondai* (1926), 8–9. See Chapter 8 for further discussion of the problem of business impact.

24. Miwa Kimitada, *Matsuoka Yōsuke*, 36–67; Matsuoka Yōsuke denki kankō kai, *Matsuoka Yōsuke*, 53–142, 144–53; Katō, "Matsuoka Yōsuke to Mantetsu," 66, 83–90.

25. Matsuoka, "Ugoku Manmō," in idem, *Ugoku Manmō*, 29. This article was written in the summer of 1926.

26. Ibid., 27–28.

27. Ibid., 28–29.

28. Matsuoka Yōsuke, "Manmō tetsudō fusetsu sokushin ni tsuite," frame 10. I am grateful to Kaneko Fumio for pointing me toward this source.

29. Matsuoka memorandum to Cabinet Secretary Egi Yoku, General Tanaka Giichi, Kwantung Army Commander Kawada Meiji, and Kwantung Chief Administrator Kodama Hideo, 10/1/24, GSS, 32, 292.

30. "Law and order" in Manchuria would, in fact, become a code phrase for intervention in the language of imperial activism during this era; see the position paper by Hata Eitarō, 3/14/1924, and Hata's notes, 3/5/1924, in NGB 1924, 2: 774 and 783.

31. Matsuoka, "Ugoku Manmō," in idem, *Ugoku Manmō*, 24–29.

32. Matsuoka memorandum, 10/1/24, in GSS, 32, 292.

33. Matsuoka ("Manmō tetsudō fusetsu sokushin ni tsuite," frames 15–16) regarded the need for bribes in negotiations as a function of the "Chinese national

character." He argued strongly for keeping such bribes as small as possible. Matsuoka reveals his frustration and disappointment with Chang in a letter to a colleague in October 1925. In this letter, he also lays out his ideal expectations of an "enlightened" Chinese leader (Matsuoka Yōsuke denki kankō kai, *Matsuoka Yōsuke*, 188–89).

34. Matsuoka, "Manmō tetsudō fusetsu sokushin ni tsuite," frame 12. Matsuoka includes in his proposal a copy of a study prepared by Fujine Jukichi of the SMR's Railway Department, dated Feb. 1923, on the need for reforming railway loan policies (ibid., frames 31–41).

35. Ibid., frame 27.

36. Ibid., frame 37; Matsuoka, "Ugoku Manmō" in idem, *Ugoku Manmō*, 19–20.

37. Matsuoka's essay "Ugoku Manmō" may be regarded as an attempt to present his views to a public audience.

38. Matsuoka, "Manmō tetsudō fusetsu sokushin ni tsuite," frames 25–27.

39. Ibid., frames 14–15, 25–27, 34–41. This interpretation of Matsuoka's arrangement entails some reading between the lines. However, the practice suggested here had precedent. In late 1922, the SMR had footed the bill for the completion of the Ssup'ingkai–T'aonan when loan proceeds to the Chinese side had proved inadequate and the Chinese government refused to borrow additional funds (Yoshii, "Dai ichiji taisen go no 'Manmō' tetsudō mondai," 38–40).

40. Matsuoka, "Manmō tetsudō fusetsu sokushin ni tsuite," frames 27–29.

41. Yoshii Ken'ichi ("Dai ichiji taisen go no 'Manmō tetsudō mondai," 38–40) suggests that endrunning the consortium was a major motivation for this arrangement. Kaneko (*Kindai Nihon ni okeru tai-Manshū tōshi no kenkyū*, 414) agrees and suggests that Matsuoka favored presenting the consortium with a *fait accompli*, reporting the loan after the fact. Concerns about consortium participation played a major role in shaping Japanese policy at this stage. However, by the time the issue emerged with the completion of the T'aonan–Tsitsihar line in 1926 and Chang's decision to opt for a long-term loan, the other powers no longer appeared to be actively interested in participating in Manchurian railway loans, and the problem ceased worrying Japanese policymakers. See also Katō, "Matsuoka Yōsuke to Mantetsu," 69–74.

42. Matsuoka, "Manmō tetsudō fusetsu sokushin ni tsuite," frames 2–3. Matsuoka also added to his proposal an extension to K'ailu of the Chengchiat'un–T'ungliao branch of the Ssup'ingkai–T'aonan line (ibid., frames 20–25).

43. The army's explicit endorsement of Matsuoka's scheme is evident in a note from Military Affairs Bureau Chief Hata Eitarō to Asia Bureau Chief Debuchi, 5/1924, in *NGB*, 1925, pt. 2, 2: 1279 (the note is reproduced in a later memorandum).

44. Mukden Consul-General Funatsu to Foreign Minister Matsui, 5/3/24, in *NGB*, 1925, pt. 2, 2: 1278–79; Yoshii, "Dai ichiji taisen go no 'Manmō' tetsudō mondai," 44–45. The problem of a gap in understanding surfaced in follow-up discus-

sions on the Kirin–Tunhua railway. For Matsuoka's correspondence on this matter in 1925, see Matsuoka Yōsuke denki kankō kai, *Matsuoka Yōsuke*, 181–88.

45. On the political background leading to the formation of the Kiyoura government, see Duus, *Party Rivalry and Political Change in Taishō Japan*, 165–85; on Shōda's role in initiating a review of China policy, see Debuchi Katsuji, "Kiyoura naikaku no tai-Shi seisaku," 6/1924, in *NGB*, 1924, 2: 764. For the proceedings of this conference, see *NGB*, 1924, 2: 766–820.

46. Bannō, *Kindai Nihon no gaikō to seiji*, 155–67.

47. Cabinet resolution, 8/19/24, in *NGB*, 1924, 2: 1280–81.

48. Matsuoka to Katō, 12/11/25, in Matsuoka Yōsuke denki kankō kai, *Matsuoka Yōsuke*, 171.

49. Participants in the 1924 policy conference, including army representatives, reaffirmed this distinction; see Debuchi's draft compromise proposal, 4/2/24, in *NGB*, 1924, 2: 793.

50. Ikei, "Dai niji Hō-Choku sensō to Nihon," 193–216; Suzuki Takashi, *Nihon teikokushugi to Manshū*, 1: 409–18.

51. McCormack, *Chang Tso-lin in Northeast China*, 130–33; Ikei, "Dai niji Hō-Choku sensō to Nihon," 217–24; Suzuki Takashi, *Nihon teikokushugi to Manshū*, 1: 418–20; Bannō, *Kindai Nihon no gaikō to seiji*, 125–32.

52. McCormack, *Chang Tso-lin in Northeast China*, 133–43.

53. SMR, Chōsaka, *Tōnan–Chichiharu tetsudō no kachi*, 6–8, 9–18, 79–80.

54. For Matsuoka's correspondence regarding the Kirin–Tunhua negotiations, see Matsuoka Yōsuke denki kankō kai, *Matsuoka Yōsuke*, 177–211.

55. McCormack, *Chang Tso-lin in Northeast China*, 115–16, 217–18.

56. Kwantung Army Chief of Staff Saitō to Army Vice Minister Tsuno Ichisuke and Tsuno's reply, 5/27/25, in *MDN*, 1925, vol. 6, gaikō 4.

57. Sanbō jichō, "Manmō chihō ni okeru tetsudō seisaku yōkō," 11/1925, in *MDN*, 1925, vol. 6, Library of Congress microfilm, Young classification R103/T619, frames 8672–73.

58. SMR, Chōsaka, Mōko chōsatai, Dai 1 han, *Tōnan–Manshūri kan Mōko chōsa hōkokusho*, vol. 1 (8/1926), 135–39; bessatsu (10/1926), 3–9. The arrest of a mixed team of army and SMR staff engaged in survey work in 1925 in Outer Mongolia created a minor diplomatic row, much to the distress of Debuchi and Shidehara, who were none too pleased with this new excitement about northward expansion (Saitō to Tsuno, 10/12/1925, Debuchi to Tsuno, 11/12/1925, in *MDN*, 1926, vol. 2, sokuryō kansoku 1).

59. Sanbō jichō, "Manmō chihō ni okeru tetsudō seisaku yōkō," frames 8672–73 (see note 57 to this chapter).

60. Ibid., frames 8671–72.

61. Ibid., frames 8672, 73.

62. Three planning documents, dated Feb. 1925 and Sept. 1925, and one undated but probably from 1925, are reproduced in Chi-lin sheng she-hui k'e-hsüeh yüan, Man-t'ieh shih tzu-liao pien-chi tsu, *Man-t'ieh shih tzu-liao*, pt. 2, 3: 847–52.

63. Matsuoka, "Manmō tetsudō fusetsu sokushin ni tsuite," frames 11–12.

64. During discussions between SMR Director Ōkura Kinmochi and Foreign Ministry Asia Bureau Chief Kimura Eiichi in 1926, Ōkura appeared quite defensive about the company's attitude about this line and denied that business interests had anything to do with the SMR's desire to assign the project a low priority (for a summary of the discussions, 7/22/26, see NGB, 1926, pt. 2, 2: 1258).

65. SMR, Chōsaka, *Ten-To keiben tetsudō*, 40–41; idem, *Bujun tan no hanro*, 2. Ironically, two considerations mitigating concern about the threat posed by this line were doubt on the part of company officials that the Kirin–Hoeryong would be completed in the foreseeable future and the fact that it would take years for Chongjin to provide services comparable to Dairen.

66. Discussion recounted in telegram from SMR President Yasuhiro to SMR Tokyo Office, forwarded by Mukden Consul-General Yoshida to Foreign Minister Shidehara, 8/20/26, in NGB, 1926, pt. 2, 2; 1358–59.

67. SMR Tokyo Office to Matsuoka and Matsuoka reply, 4/4/24, in GSS, 32: 422.

68. Correspondence between Matsuoka and President Yasuhiro with regard to the Kirin–Tunhua negotiations, 7/23/25 and 7/24/25, in Matsuoka Yōsuke denki kankō kai, *Matsuoka Yōsuke*, 178–79. See also Katō, "Matsuoka Yōsuke to Mantetsu," 83–93.

69. McCormack, *Chang Tso-lin in Northeast China*, 146–87; Suzuki Takashi, *Nihon teikokushugi to Manshū*, 1: 421–32; Bannō, *Kindai Nihon no gaikō to seiji*, 137–41.

70. Matsuoka Yōsuke denki kankō kai, *Matsuoka Yōsuke*, 188–89.

71. Ugaki, *Ugaki Kazunari nikki*, entry for 12/5/25, 494. For a slightly different translation of this passage, see McCormack, *Chang Tso-lin in Northeast China*, 175.

72. The background for the following discussion draws heavily on Kaneko, *Kindai Nihon ni okeru tai-Manshū tōshi no kenkyū*, 336–70.

73. Nagura, *Nihon tekkōgyō shi no kenkyū*, 271–77.

74. SMR, *Honpō seitekkō saku jūritsu to Minami Manshū* (1924), 5.

75. Yonekura, *The Japanese Iron and Steel Industry*, 117–32. See also Sakurai Tetsu, "Minami Manshū tetsudō no keiei to zaibatsu," 40–46.

76. SMR2, 893–94, 937–38.

77. SMR, *Bujun yūbō ketsugan jigyō rengō kyōgi kaigiroku*, (army view) 40–44, 114–15; (SMR view) 100–103; (navy view) 226–28, 274–76; (army vs. SMR over subsidy) 228–32; (commercial viability as a criterion for war industries) 266–67. This is a transcript of a series of conferences on the shale-oil problem in May 1925. See also SMR, *Nihon no sekiyu mondai to Bujun san yūbō ketsugan no kachi* (1924); SMR2, 798–801. The SMR also continued its work on the distillation of coal in cooperation with

the navy. For a study of Manchuria and navy fuel policy, see Miwa Munehiro, "Kaigun nenryō chō no sekitan ekika no kenkyū."

78. Calculated from SMR, Chōsaka, *Manmō ni okeru Nihon no tōshi jōtai*, 75. For dividend data, see ibid., 118. For an analysis of the larger problem, Kaneko, *Kindai Nihon ni okeru tai-Manshū tōshi no kenkyū*, 358–70.

79. Nishimura, *Chūgoku kindai tōhoku chiiki shi kenkyū*, 175.

80. SMR, Chōsaka, *Waga kuni jinkō mondai to Manmō*, 155–57.

81. Ibid., 149–50.

82. Ibid., 146.

83. Petitions from settler groups are summarized and reported in Mukden Consul-General Funatsu to Foreign Minister Shidehara, 8/22/24, Gaimushō microfilm, S61921, frames 3538–42; Mukden Consul-General Yoshida to Shidehara, 11/7/25, ibid., S61921, frames 3627–29. For a general assessment of the status of the Japanese settler community in 1923, see Hirano Ken'ichirō, "1923 nen no Manshū," 236–43.

84. Shinozaki Yoshirō, *Manshū kin'yū oyobi zaikai no genjō*, 58–72. Shinozaki was an activist in Japanese chambers of commerce in Manchuria.

85. SMR2, 175–78.

86. Matsuoka to Shidehara, 12/5/25, in Matsuoka Yōsuke denki kankō kai, *Matsuoka Yōsuke*, 217.

87. SMR, Chōsaka, *Manmō yori nani o kitai subekika*, 1924 ed., 1.

88. Ibid., 15–17. For admonitions in later editions, see the 1930 ed., 1.

Chapter 8

1. McCormack, *Chang Tso-lin in Northeast China*, 204–17, 222–32; Iriye, *After Imperialism*, 110–15; Usui, *Nitchū gaikō shi*, 12–54. The Japanese government presented an official warning to Chang in the spring of 1926 (Eastern Conference materials, in NGB, Shōwa ki, series 1, pt. 1, 1: 40).

2. On the tariff issue, see Mukden Consul-General Yoshida to Shidehara, 2/24/27, and Shidehara to Yoshida, 2/28/27, in NGB, Shōwa ki, series 1, pt. 1, 1: 128–30.

3. Sakamoto, "Mitsui bussan to 'Manshū'-Chūgoku shijō," 118. See also Kaneko, *Kindai Nihon ni okeru tai-Manshū tōshi no kenkyū*, 473–97.

4. Tsitsihar Consul Shimizu to Shidehara, 12/4/26, in NGB, 1926, pt. 2, 2: 1352–57. The consul's report concerns the SMR's arrangements with the Kuang-hsin kung-ssu, a major official soy merchant in Tsitsihar.

5. Nishimura, *Chūgoku kindai tōhoku chiiki shi kenkyū*, 149–57.

6. Foreign Ministry Asia Bureau report, 7/1926, in NGB, 1926, pt. 2, 2: 1246–47.

7. Yoshii, "'Manmō' tetsudō mondai no tenkai to Tanaka naikaku," 2.

8. Yoshida to Shidehara, 4/23/26, in NGB, 1926, pt. 2, 2: 1395.

9. Transcript sent by Yoshida to Asia Bureau Chief Kimura, 6/1926, of Machino's discussions with Ōkura, 5/25/26, in *NGB*, 1926, pt. 2, 2: 1398; Yoshida to Shidehara, copy of SMR report on conversations with Machino, 7/3/26, in *NGB*, 1926, pt. 2, 2: 1401–2.

10. Army General Staff, "Tai-Ro sakusen no hitsuyōjō Tōnan-Soron tetsudō fusetsu sokushin o yōsu," 7/8/26, in *NGB*, 1926, pt. 2, 2: 1402–3.

11. Yoshida to Shidehara, copy of SMR report on conversations with Machino, 7/3/26, in *NGB*, 1926, pt. 2, 2: 1402.

12. Foreign Ministry, Asia Bureau report, 7/17/26, in *NGB*, 1926, pt. 2, 2: 1250–51. Kimura replaced Debuchi, who had been appointed vice minister for foreign affairs.

13. Foreign Ministry memorandum, "Soron tetsudō ni kansuru ken," 5/5/26, in *NGB*, 1926, pt. 2, 2: 1396–97.

14. For a study of the T'aonan–Solun's projected finances, see SMR, Chōsaka, Mōko chōsatai, dai 1 han, *Tōnan–Manshūri kan Mōko chōsa hōkokusho*, 149–50. This report suggests that the line would more than break even if operated as an extension of the Ssup'ingkai–T'aonan line. Although it was published some months after the Foreign Ministry position paper, the basic information appears to have been available earlier. For data on the T'aoan–Tsitsihar, see SMR, Chōsaka, *Tōnan–Chichiharu tetsudō no kachi*, 8; on the Ch'angch'un–T'aonan, see SMR, Sōmubu, Kōmukyoku, Sekkeika, *Chōshun–Tōnan tetsudō senro tōsa hōkokusho*, 14–16; for the Kirin–Hoeryong, see Chapter 5.

15. Quoted in McCormack, *Chang Tso-lin in Northeast China*, 68.

16. Quoted in Kaneko, *Kindai Nihon ni okeru tai-Manshū tōshi no kenkyū*, 418n.

17. On the policy of withholding permission for the Kirin–Hailung pending agreement on the Ch'angch'un–Talai, see Kimura to Ōkura, 5/11/27, in *NGB*, Shōwa, series 1, pt. 1, 1: 159. Kimura chastised Ōkura for revealing Japan's hand prematurely in the director's discussions with Kirin provincial authorities and in bargaining away the Japanese position too cheaply. Ōkura had apparently indicated a willingness to accept a quid-pro-quo exchange of the Ch'angch'un–Talai for the Kirin–Hailung without including additional demands. Matsuoka's position on railway protests is noted in Minister to Peking Yoshizawa to Foreign Minister Tanaka, 10/6/27, in *NGB*, Shōwa ki, series 1, pt. 1, 1: 278–79. The army raised some mild concerns about protests on the Tahushan–T'ungliao line, which it wanted to see completed (Army Ministry Military Affairs Bureau Chief Abe to Kimura, 7/19/27, in *NGB*, Shōwa ki, series 1, pt. 1, 1: 182). By the time this note was written, the Tanaka cabinet was in office and had concluded its Eastern Conference. Nonetheless, it may be taken as an indication of army attitudes toward the protests. One diplomat, noting the tactical nature of these protests, warned of the danger of "crying wolf" (Mukden Consul-General [acting] Hachiya to Shidehara, 1/8/27, in *NGB*, 1926, pt. 2, 2: 1375–76).

18. For Shidehara's instructions to issue protests, see Shidehara to Yoshida, 8/25/26, *NGB* 1926, part 2, vol. 2, 1359; Shidehara to Yoshida, 11/12/26, *NGB* 1926, part 2, vol. 2, 1382. For cotton trade data, see Remer, *Foreign Investments in China*, 463; for Manchurian trade, see Kaneko, *Kindai Nihon ni okeru tai-Manshū tōshi no kenkyū*, 320. For a somewhat different analysis of Shidehara's policies at this time, see Iriye, *After Imperialism*, 81, 85–86, 110–11.

19. Iriye, *After Imperialism*, 133; Bannō, *Kindai Nihon no gaikō to seiji*, 167–75. Bannō (ibid., 172) notes that the Seiyūkai's campaign against Shidehara's diplomacy began with disputes over the Kuo Sung-ling affair in late 1925.

20. Yoshida to Shidehara, 8/20/26, in *NGB*, 1926, pt. 2, 2: 1357–59.

21. Matsuoka Yōsuke denki kankō kai, *Matsuoka Yōsuke*, 222–24.

22. McCormack, *Chang Tso-lin in Northeast China*, 228. See also Katō, "Matsuoka Yōsuke to Mantetsu," 93–96.

23. SMR, Chōsaka, *Hō–Kai tetsudō to Koryōtō chikkō mondai*, 1–19.

24. Ibid., 15, gives figures for comparative distances between T'ungliao and either Hulutao or Dairen of 268 miles and 492 miles, respectively.

25. Ibid., 8–10.

26. SMR, Chōsaka, *Hō–Kai tetsudō no Mantetsu ni oyobosu eikyō*, 2.

27. SMR, Chōsaka, *Hō–Kai tetsudō to Koryōtō chikkō mondai*, preface, 2.

28. Okura, Matsuoka's successor as the director responsible for external negotiations, cooperated more closely with Kimura; both of them shared a profound skepticism about military railway policy. But there were also limits to that cooperation. Ōkura, for example, supported the Solun project for business reasons, much to Kimura's consternation. The SMR director also sought to delay the construction of the Kirin–Hoeryong line. This impression is drawn from a reading of the transcripts of various conversations between Ōkura and Kimura in July 1926 (Foreign Ministry Asia Bureau study, 7/1926, in *NGB*, 1926, pt. 2, 2: 1246–78).

29. Chang Tso-lin to Yoshida, 10/27/26, in *NGB*, 1926, pt. 2, 2: 1373.

30. Richard Rigby (*The May 30 Movement*, 78) observes that Chang Tso-lin's note of protest over the shootings in Shanghai came as a shock to the British: "It is a credit and a testimony to the strength and universality of the feelings aroused by the Shanghai incident that he [Chang] felt himself obliged to take such a step."

31. See *NGB*, Shōwa ki, series 1, pt. 1, 1: 68–93 for developments through early June 1927; and McCormack, *Chang Tso-lin in Northeast China*, 231–32.

32. Iriye, *After Imperialism*, 143–47; Bannō, *Kindai Nihon no gaikō to seiji*, 162–63.

33. A great deal has been written on the Eastern Conference. For an overview, see Iriye, *After Imperialism*, 162–72; Usui, *Nitchū gaikō shi*, 72–77; and Seki, "Manshū jihen zenshi," 287–91. See also Satō Motoei, "Tanaka naikaku no tai-Chūgoku keizai hattensaku to Mantetsu," 108–22.

34. Saitō Hisashi, "Tai-Man seisaku ni kansuru iken (yōshi)," 6/1/27, in *MDN*, 1927, vol. 4, iken 4.

35. Kimura Eiichi, "Shina jikyoku taisaku ni kansuru ichi kōsatsu," 6/1927, in *NGN*2, 97–101.

36. Yoshida to Shidehara, 3/7/27, and Yoshida to Tanaka, 4/21/27, in *NGB*, Shōwa ki, series 1, pt. 1, 1: 130–31 and 149; Yoshida opinions, Eastern Conference materials, in *NGB*, Shōwa ki, series 1, pt. 1, 1: 28, 59–61. My characterization of Yoshida owes much to Dower, *Empire and Aftermath*.

37. Dower, *Empire and Aftermath*, 63–90, esp. 78–83.

38. Amau opinion, Eastern Conference materials, in *NGB*, Shōwa ki, series 1, pt. 1, 1: 61–64.

39. Iriye, *After Imperialism*, 80–88, 97–122, 161.

40. Eastern Conference materials, in *NGB*, Shōwa ki, series 1, pt. 1, 1: 29.

41. Yoshii, "Manmō tetsudō mondai no tenkai to Tanaka naikaku," 18.

42. It should be noted that, in 1925, at least one prominent Japanese newspaper had described the initial building of the Mukden–Hailung line as a serious threat to the SMR and made no reference to the Sino-Japanese agreement governing this project (*Tōkyō Asahi*, 5/27/25, in Meiji Taishō Shōwa shinbun kenkyūkai, *Shinbun shūsei Taishō hen nenshi*, vol. for 1925, 586–87).

43. Eastern Conference materials, in *NGB*, Shōwa ki, series 1, pt. 1, 1: 56–59.

44. See, e.g., Nish, *Japanese Foreign Policy*, 172–74.

45. Ōe, *Nihon no Sanbō honbu*, 138–50.

46. Yoshida to Tanaka, 4/21/27, and Tanaka to Yoshida, 5/4/27, in *NGB*, Shōwa ki, series 1, pt. 1, 1: 149, 152–53.

47. Tanaka to Yoshizawa, 6/2/27, in *NGB*, Shōwa ki, series 1, pt. 1, 1: 164–65.

48. Ibid., 165.

49. Yoshizawa to Tanaka, 6/10/27, in *NGB*, Shōwa ki, series 1, pt. 1, 1: 168–71.

50. Yoshida to Tanaka, 6/9/27, in *NGB*, Shōwa ki, series 1, pt. 1, 1: 166–168.

51. Eastern Conference materials, in *NGB*, Shōwa ki, series 1, pt. 1, 1: 35. Tanaka's statement is described in these documents as the "foreign minister's instructions" (*kunji*).

52. Ibid., 38.

53. Ibid.

54. Tanaka to Yoshida, 7/20/27, in *NGB*, Shōwa ki, series 1, pt. 1, 1: 183–84.

55. Eastern Conference materials, in *NGB*, Shōwa ki, series 1, pt. 1, 1: 14–15, 29, 44–47, 55–56; Tanaka's instructions on Manchuria, 7/9/27, in *NGB*, Shōwa ki, series 1, pt. 1, 1: 177–79. Tanaka's list also included a 100–mile railway originating from some point on the SMR to the Hsinch'iu coal mine in Jehol (*NGB*, Shōwa ki, series 1, pt. 1, 1: 178–79). This line paralleled the PMR and it is highly unlikely that the Chinese side, even under the best of circumstances, would have agreed to it, par-

ticularly since this very rich mine was located not far from Hsinlit'un on the Ta-hushan–T'ungliao branch of the PMR. This project was first contemplated during World War I when the Japanese acquired access to this coal field in the Twenty-One Demands. It was subsequently set aside as unfeasible. I am not sure what to make of Tanaka's endorsement of this proposal, since it does not appear in any subsequent negotiations. It seems similar to the army's proposal for a Jehol line in 1912. At the same time, its inclusion on the Eastern Conference list might be regarded as a concession to traditionalists complaining about the lack of direct economic benefits from Japanese railway building. On the history of plans for the Hsinch'iu line, see SMR, Chōsaka, *Rinkai tetsudō to shomondai*, 162–63.

56. Tanaka's instructions on Manchuria, 7/1/27, in NGB, Shōwa ki, series 1, pt. 1, 1: 180, 181.

57. Ibid., 179.

58. Tanaka to Yoshida, 7/20/27, in NGB, Shōwa ki, series 1, pt. 1, 1: 183–84. Tanaka noted that Japan should maintain its opposition to a further extension of this line to T'aonan. However, given that such a connection would have formed part of almost any of the possible configurations of a T'aonan–Jehol line, which the Japanese had no diplomatic grounds to protest, it would have been difficult to stand firm on such a policy.

59. See the series of dispatches between Yoshida and Tanaka on this subject, 8/2/27–8/5/27, in NGB, Shōwa ki, series 1, pt. 1, 1: 191–98.

60. McCormack, *Chang Tso-lin in Northeast China*, 238–41; Seki, "Manshū jihen zenshi," 293–94.

61. This appraisal of Tanaka's strategy is based on an interpretation of his exchange of views with Yoshizawa in June 1927 cited in note 47 above. Tanaka clearly saw that a Nationalist victory in North China would force Chang to retreat to Manchuria in order to survive, which would, in turn, give Japan decisive leverage over his future behavior. Yoshizawa fleshed out the possibility of negotiating a bargain with the Nationalists over allowing Chang to maintain an autonomous regime in the territory, provided he made no further attempt to pursue ambitions south of the wall (Yoshizawa to Tanaka, 6/10/27, in NGB, Shōwa ki, series 1, pt. 1, 1: 168–71). In his policy statement following the Eastern Conference, Tanaka hinted at this strategy: "The fact that Chang is facing serious difficulties internally and externally at this time offers a most appropriate opportunity for us to press for the resolution of outstanding issues" (NGB, Shōwa ki, series 1, pt. 1, 1: 176–77).

62. The Yamamoto-Chang talks, along with Yoshizawa's reports, are documented in NGB, Shōwa ki, series 1, pt. 1, 1: 278–333. See also Yamamoto Jōtarō denki hensankai, *Yamamoto Jōtarō denki*, 550–84; McCormack, *Chang Tso-lin in Northeast China*, 241–44; Seki, "Manshū jihen zenshi," 294–96; Iriye, *After Imperialism*, 177–83; Satō Motoei, "Tanaka naikaku no tai-Chūgoku keizai hattensaku to Mantetsu,"

123–39. There is no question that the content of Yamamoto's putative agreements reflected Tanaka's "new imperialist" thinking. The railways that the company president proposed to Chang were essentially the same as those outlined by the Army General Staff in 1925. Ideas contained in the economic and military agreements also closely followed some of the remarks that Tanaka made at the Eastern Conference. *Daikanshō* and bilateral economic cooperation as envisioned by Tanaka, and by Matsuoka himself, were never intended to be translated into formal diplomatic accords unless Japan was fully prepared to establish a protectorate over the territory. Some writers have ascribed a major role to Yamamoto in shaping Tanaka's Manchuria policies and linked him closely to Mori Kaku; see, e.g., Morton, *Tanaka Giichi and China Policy*, 99–101. Yamamoto and Mori shared a long history, dating back to their days as young clerks working for Mitsui Bussan's Shanghai office, where they became acquainted with Matsuoka Yōsuke, acting consul-general in Shanghai. Although dedicated to the cause of empire, Yamamoto does not appear to have shared Mori's military-adventurist bent; he preferred, instead, to emphasize the development of business enterprise in Japan's expansionism. Indeed, although personally loyal to Tanaka and willing to serve what he believed to be his patron's program, Yamamoto's primary interest during his stint as president of the SMR lay in the development of "industrial Manchuria." On Yamamoto's relationship with Mori Kaku, see Togai Yoshio, *Mitsui bussan kaisha no keieshiteki kenkyū*, 260–301. On other aspects of Yamamoto's background and his work at the SMR, see Yamamoto Jōtarō denki hensankai, *Yamamoto Jōtarō denki*, 527–50, 657–91; Egami Teruhiko, *Mantetsu ōkoku*, 99–126; and Kobayashi Hideo, *Mantetsu*, 83–89.

63. McCormack, *Chang Tso-lin in Northeast China*, 244–45; Seki, "Manshū jihen zenshi," 298–99; Yoshizawa to Tanaka, 3/28/28, in NGB, Shōwa ki, series 1, pt. 1, 2: 7–12. In the meantime, the United States became embroiled in a famous controversy over a loan to the SMR; see Iriye, *After Imperialism*, 186–90.

64. Seki, "Manshū jihen zenshi," 297–98; Usui, *Nitchū gaikō shi*, 94; McCormack, *Chang Tso-lin in Northeast China*, 244–45; Iriye, *After Imperialism*, 193–96.

65. Seki, "Manshū jihen zenshi," 299–303; McCormack, *Chang Tso-lin in Northeast China*, 246–48; Iriye, *After Imperialism*, 205–11.

66. Seki, "Manshū jihen zenshi," 303–5; Usui, *Nitchū gaikō shi*, 122–30; Iriye, *After Imperialism*, 211–13.

67. See, e.g, Bamba, *Japanese Diplomacy in a Dilemma*; Iriye, *After Imperialism*. 164, 172, 183–84; and Nish, *Japanese Foreign Policy*, 172–74.

68. Shimada, *Kantōgun*, 56–72; Usui, *Nitchū gaikō shi*, 131–47; Seki, "Manshū jihen zenshi," 305–8.

69. Sagara, *Akai sekiyō no Manshū nogahara ni*, 148–49; for the text of the larger part of this letter, see ibid., 148–50.

70. Shimada, *Kantōgun*, 48. For a biography, see Kimura, *Kōmoto Daisaku*.

71. Sagara, *Akai sekiyō no Manshū nogahara ni*, 148, 150.

72. Seki, "Manshū jihen zenshi," 308–9; Rekishigaku kenkyūkai, *Taiheiyō sensō shi*, 150.

73. Hayashi Kyūjirō, *Manshū jihen to Hōten sōryōji*, 26.

Chapter 9

1. Muraoka to Army Chief of Staff Suzuki, 7/21/28, in NGB, Shōwa ki, series 1, pt. 1, 2: 222.

2. Hayashi's assessment is presented in a series of dispatches to Tanaka in June and July, reproduced in NGB, Shōwa ki, series 1, pt. 1, 2: 18–19, 25, 202, 205, 208, 210, 215–16, 227.

3. Tanaka to Hayashi, "Manmō jikyoku sochi an taikō," 7/18/28, in NGB, Shōwa ki, series 1, pt. 1, 2: 214–15. The new Asia Bureau chief, Arita Hachirō, appears to have endorsed this scheme wholeheartedly as well; see Arita Hachirō, "Tai-Chūgoku ippan oyobi tai-Manmō hōshin ni tsuite," 7/13/28, in NGB, Shōwa ki, series 1, pt. 1, 2: 24–25.

4. Ugaki, *Ugaki Kazunari nikki*, 9/23/29 entry, 692.

5. For an example of Hayashi's rationalization of Chang's delaying tactics, see Hayashi to Tanaka, 1/9/29, in NGB, Shōwa ki, series 1, pt. 1, 3: 2.

6. Nishimura, *Chō Gakurō*, 37–51.

7. Hayashi to Tanaka, 1/22/29 and 1/31/1929, in NGB, Shōwa ki, series 1, pt. 1, 3: 11–12 and 22–24.

8. Tanaka to Debuchi (ambassador to U.S.), copy of instructions to Hayashi, 5/6/29, in NGB, Shōwa ki, series 1, pt. 1, 3: 65–67.

9. Rekishigaku kenkyūkai, *Taiheiyō sensō shi*, 151–53; Shimada, *Kantōgun*, 72–74. Significantly, as early as February, army intelligence reported that Chang was delaying negotiations with Japan and awaiting the downfall of the Tanaka cabinet (Mukden Special Service Unit to Army Vice Minister Minami, 2/24/29, in NGB, Shōwa ki, series 1, pt. 1, 3: 28–29).

10. Nish (*Japanese Foreign Policy*, 165–66, 172–74) offers some insights into the particular nature of Shidehara's second stint as Foreign Minister. For a broader treatment of diplomatic history centered on China during this era, see Iriye, *After Imperialism*, 254–77.

11. DR1, 303–6.

12. See, e.g., Ugaki's (*Ugaki Kazunari nikki*, undated 1919 entry, 204–5) remarks on Chinese nationalism shortly after the emergence of the May Fourth movement.

13. Matsuoka Yōsuke, "Chōkō o sokō shite nanpō Shina kakumei o miru" (5/1927), in idem, *Ugoku Manmō*, 314–15. Matsuoka noted that popular Chinese nationalism was nothing more than simple xenophobia and an attempt to blame foreigners for all the country's problems. Even academics with some sympathy for

China's national aspirations tended to see the anti-Japanese turn of Chinese nationalism as irrational and probably stirred up by outsiders; see Fogel, *Politics and Sinology*, 274–75.

14. Sanbō honbu, *Tai-Shi sakusen wa ikanaru dōki ni te boppatsu suru ya no kenkyū* (1927), in *MDN*, 1927, vol. 6, Shina jōhō 29, leaf 9. This document was forwarded to the Army Ministry by General Honjō Shigeru, military attaché to the Japanese legation in Peking. He notes that the study had been ordered by Major General Araki Sadao in late 1926. The work was largely done by Colonel Doihara Kenji.

15. Minami speech, 8/4/31, in GSS, 7: 150. Iriye (*Japan and China in the Global Setting*, 54) notes that a recognition of the significance of a maturing Chinese nationalism after 1928 persuaded the army to turn toward the use of armed force.

16. Ugaki, *Ugaki Kazunari nikki*, 9/23/28 entry, 690–92. Ugaki outlined three major steps that would need to be accomplished before an active policy, including the possibility of the seizure of Manchuria, could be attempted: the preparation of public opinion, the build-up of Japan's armed forces, and establishment of some understanding with the powers. His views, in this respect, appear similar to Minami's (see below), but his timetable seems to have placed action in a more distant future.

17. Ibid., 9/7/29 entry, 733–34.

18. Ibid., 4/12/29 entry, 719.

19. Kaneko Fumio (*Kindai Nihon ni okeru tai-Manshū tōshi no kenkyū*, 336) considers Mikami's study (SMR, Chōsaka, *Manmō ni okeru Nihon no tōshi jōtai*) one of the most reliable sources on Japanese investment.

20. SMR, Chōsaka, *Manmō ni okeru Nihon no tōshi jōtai*, 277–82.

21. See Chapter 8, note 62, pp. 469–70. For his views on railway policy, see "Mantetsu no gyōseki to sono kokkateki shimei," speech in Dairen, 7/22/29, in Yamamoto Jōtarō denki hensankai, *Yamamoto Jōtarō ronsaku*, 686–87. This speech, made a year after the assassination of Chang Tso-lin, may reflect a later development in his ideas, but it seems consistent with the emphasis of his policies at the SMR from the beginning of his tenure. He clearly favored industrial development in Kwantung and the Zone over new railway building.

22. Yamamoto Jōtarō denki hensankai, *Yamamoto Jōtarō denki*, 657–91. Yamamoto downplayed the importance of Japanese settlement in Manchuria. Manchuria would help to resolve Japan's population problems by providing expanded sources of food, fuel, and raw materials rather than by providing living space (ibid., 654–56).

23. Yamamoto Jōtarō denki hensankai, *Yamamoto Jōtarō denki*, 617.

24. Speech to Osaka keizaikai, 7/31/29, in Yamamoto Jōtarō denki hensankai, *Yamamoto Jōtarō ronsaku*, 706–12.

25. Ugaki, *Ugaki Kazunari nikki*, 1/15/30? entry, 750–51. This entry, sandwiched between two others for 1/14/30 and 1/15/30 and included in the chapter for 1930, is labeled 10/15.

26. SMR, Chōsaka, *Waga kuni jinkō mondai to Manmō*, 207–44.

27. Ibid., 245–46.

28. Petition from the Federation of Residents' Committees of the SMR Zone, 4/10/29, transmitted by Mukden Consul-General Hayashi Kyūjirō to Foreign/Prime Minister Tanaka, 5/28/29, in Gaimushō microfilm, S61921, frames 3991–93.

29. Seki, "Manshū jihen zenshi," 387.

30. S. Ogata, *Defiance in Manchuria*, 37–41; Egler, "Pan-Asianism in Action and Reaction," 229–36. For a more extensive treatment, see Egler, "Japanese Mass Organizations in Manchuria," 78–146. See also Yamaguchi Jūji, *Kieta teikoku Manshū*, 15–20; and Manshū seinen renmei shi kankō iinkai, *Manshū seinen renmei shi*, esp. 48–52 (1929 program) and 402–4 (1931 program).

31. Sata Kōjirō, "Kagakuteki ni Manmō taisaku o miru," 1/24/31, in *GSS*, 7: 134–38.

32. *DR1*, 304–7; Seki, "Manshū jihen zenshi," 405–6.

33. Seki, "Manshū jihen zenshi," 361–70.

34. Ibid., 378–79; *DR1*, 304–06.

35. For an early English-language work on the subject of Sino-Japanese railway competition in Manchuria in 1930–31, see Kingman, *Effects of Chinese Nationalism upon Manchurian Railway Developments*. Background for the following discussion is drawn from Kaneko, *Kindai Nihon ni okeru tai-Manshū tōshi no kenkyū*, 420–8; and Ogata Yōichi, "Tōhoku kōtsū iinkai to iwayuru 'Mantetsu hōi tetsudō mō keikaku.'" See also Satō Motoei, "Dai niji 'Shidehara gaikō' ni okeru Manmō tetsudō mondai kaiketsu kōshō."

36. On Chang's economic development program, see Nishimura, *Chūgoku kindai tōhoku chiiki shi kenkyū*, 205–22; and idem, *Chō Gakurō*, 51–58. On the Northeast Transportation Commission, see Ogata Yōichi, "Tōhoku kōtsū iinkai to iwayuru 'Mantetsu hōi tetsudō mō keikaku,'" 45–48.

37. These developments were reported with some alarm; see, e.g., Ishii Chōtarō, Kirin consul-general, to Shidehara, 6/19/30 and 7/22/30, in *NGB*, Shōwa ki, series 1, pt. 1, vol. 4, 32 and 47–48.

38. The list of the railways in question is compiled from SMR, Tetsudōbu, Ren'unka, *Saikin Tōhoku tetsudō jōsei*, 27–29; Ogata Yōichi, "Tōhoku kōtsū iinkai to iwayuru 'Mantetsu hōi tetsudō mō keikaku,'" 57; idem, "Dai niji 'Shidehara gaikō' to 'Manmō' tetsudō kōshō"; SMR, Chōsaka, *Manmō ni okeru tetsudō no gaiyō*, 78–80; and idem, *Tai-Ha tetsudō chōsa hōkokusho*, 59–60.

39. Kaneko, *Kindai Nihon ni okeru tai-Manshū tōshi no kenkyū*, 425.

40. Shimada, "Tō-Shi tetsudō o meguru Chū-So funsō."

41. Ch'angch'un consul to Shidehara, 7/21/29, in *NGB*, Shōwa ki, series 1, pt. 1, 3: 320.

42. Peattie, *Ishiwara Kanji*, 102–5.

43. Ogata Yōichi, "Dai niji 'Shidehara gaikō' to 'Manmō' tetsudō kōshō," 204.

44. Yoshii, "'Manmō' tetsudō mondai kōshō to 'seron,'" 2–5, 19–28; Tōkyō Asahi, 12/13/30, 12/14/30, 12/21/30. See also Rekishigaku kenkyūkai, Taiheiyō sensō shi, 248–51.

45. Tōkyō Asahi, 12/7/30.

46. Ibid., 12/13/30. According to SMR analysts, "Rumors of German, American, and British investments are nothing more than wild speculation. In reality, nothing of the sort has materialized. That China will suddenly start seeking foreign investment, that each country has secret aims in agreeing to such investment, despite China's confused condition and repeated violation of international good faith, presents no cause for concern" (SMR, Tetsudōbu, Ren'unka, Saikin Tōhoku tetsudō jōsei, 45).

47. Matsuoka, "Manmō mondai to wa nanzo ya?" in idem, Ugoku Manmō, 231.

48. Tōkyō Asahi, 12/20/30.

49. Ugaki, Ugaki Kazunari nikki, 1/18/29 entry, 706.

50. SMR, Tetsudōbu, Ren'unka, Saikin Tōhoku tetsudō jōsei, 34–35.

51. The value of silver Tayang yüan in terms of gold yen fell from near par in 1926 to 0.86 in 1929, to 0.59 in 1930, and to 0.42 in 1931 (SMR, Chōsaka, Manshū Shinagawa tetsudō ensen chihō ni okeru daizu no demawari zōka jijō oyobi sono taiō saku, 40–41). This study was published in Sept. 1931. Another rate comparison study may be found in SMR, Tetsudōbu, Ren'unka, Saikin Tōhoku tetsudō jōsei, 74. It provides rates from Kirin to a southern seaport, citing ¥15.82 per ton by way of the SMR to Dairen as opposed to ¥9.42 by way of the Chinese system to Yingk'ou.

52. SMR3, 2723–24.

53. Newspaper articles stressed the company's dire financial situation and linked it to Chinese railway policy (see, e.g., Tōkyō Asahi, 12/16/30, 12/28/30, 12/31/30).

54. Traffic reaching the PMR's port at Yingk'ou (Hopei—"north of the river") presumably bypassed the SMR altogether and moved entirely along Chinese railway connections. All traffic reaching either Dairen or SMR-Yingk'ou would have to make use of the Japanese trunk line from Mukden south. Significantly, very little traffic from north Manchuria (Tsitsihar-K'eshan) made use of the Chinese Tsitsihar-T'aonan-Chengchiat'un-Tahushan-PMR-Hopei connection.

55. SMR, Chōsaka, Hō-Kai tetsudō no Mantetsu ni oyobosu eikyō, 41–42. This study was prepared in Dec. 1928.

56. SMR, Tetsudōbu, Ren'unka, Saikin Tōhoku tetsudō jōsei, 61–62; SMR, Chōsaka, Manshū Shinagawa tetsudō ensen chihō ni okeru daizu no demawari zōka jijō oyobi sono taiō saku, 66–80.

57. Yamamoto, "Mantetsu no gyōseki to sono kokkateki shimei," speech in Dairen, 7/22/29, in Yamamoto Jōtarō denki hensankai, Yamamoto Jōtarō ronsaku, 686–87.

58. SMR, Tetsudōbu, Ren'unka, Saikin Tōhoku tetsudō jōsei, 61.

59. Tōkyō Asahi, 12/13/30.

60. *Manshū nippō*, 12/4/30, 12/5/30, 12/8/30, 12/12/30.

61. Ogata Yōichi, "Dai niji 'Shidehara gaikō' to 'Manmō' tetsudō kōshō," 182–83. See also Rekishigaku kenkyūkai, *Taiheiyō sensō shi*, 252–53.

62. Ogata Yōichi, "Dai niji 'Shidehara gaikō' to 'Manmō' tetsudō kōshō," 183–85; Shidehara, "Manshū ni okeru tetsudō mondai dakai saku jisshi no kokoroe ni kansuru ken," 12/19/30, in *NGN2*, 169–71.

63. In addition, Shidehara lists a number of other lines, but adds parenthetically "There is a need for the SMR to investigate which of these lines are, indeed, life-threatening." Interestingly, he includes in his tentative list of "life-threatening" lines, a link between T'aonan and T'ungliao. Since this connection represents part of the long-anticipated T'aonan–Jehol line, it is difficult to imagine that he seriously regarded this project as one warranting obstruction. Shidehara also noted that the rumored plans entailed 75 lines totaling 11,280 miles. He believed that many of these were entirely unrealistic, of no value, or prohibitively costly to build. This leaves the impression that he was rather dubious about the seriousness of the overall threat (Ogata Yōichi, "Dai niji 'Shidehara gaikō' to 'Manmō' tetsudō kōshō," 203).

64. Ibid., 185–87, 203.

65. Mukden Consul-General Hayashi asked Shidehara what "all available means" entailed to sound out the foreign minister's resolve (ibid., 187). Shidehara's overall approach would seem to represent Matsuoka's railway policy without the commitment to *daikanshō* and the broader framework of client management.

66. The foreign minister's tough stance was reported in *Tōkyō Asahi*, 12/13/30.

67. Ogata Yōichi, "Dai niji 'Shidehara gaikō' to 'Manmō' tetsudō kōshō," 184. Background materials and "talking points" used by Kimura in these negotiations are reproduced in SMR, Rinji chōsakai, *Iwayuru heikōsen mondai ni tsuite* (8/1931); and idem, *Tetsudō kōshō mondai no kinjō* (9/1931).

68. Ogata Yōichi, "Dai niji 'Shidehara gaikō' to 'Manmō' tetsudō kōshō," 189–98. A faction of the Nationalist coalition, led by Yen Hsi-shan and Feng Yü-hsiang, had broken ranks with Chiang Kai-shek. Chang, who had tried to stay neutral, eventually sided with Chiang and contributed decisively to Nanking's victory, a service for which was rewarded with a broader scope of jurisdiction.

69. Matsuoka, Diet speech, 1/23/31, in idem, *Ugoku Manmō*, 112–13.

70. Seki, "Manshū jihen zenshi," 352–58; Rekishigaku kenkyūkai, *Taiheiyō sensō shi*, 258–64.

71. *Tōkyō Asahi*, 7/7/31.

72. Ibid., 8/18/31.

73. Kobayashi Tatsuo, "Kaigun gunshuku jōyaku," in Inaba et al., *Taiheiyō sensō e no michi*, 1: 100–160; Kunugi Toshihiro, "Gunshuku kara gunkaku e," 103–12. Kunugi suggests that from the perspective of distributing military appropriations, the army hoped that naval arms limitations talks would succeed.

74. Kunugi Toshihiro, "Gunshuku kara gunkaku e," 108–12; Seki, "Manshū jihen zenshi," 374–75, 389–90. See also Kitaoka Shin'ichi, "Rikugun habatsu tairitsu (1931–35) no saikentō," 50–53.

75. S. Ogata, *Defiance in Manchuria*, 20–36; Seki, "Manshū jihen zenshi," 375–77; Rekishigaku kenkyūkai, *Taiheiyō sensō shi*, 244–46; Suzaki Shin'ichi, "Gunbu to fuashizumu undō," 129–31.

76. Iriye, *After Imperialism*, 278–99.

77. Seki, "Manshū jihen zenshi," 387–88.

78. For a discussion of this issue, see Gordon, *Labor and Imperial Democracy in Prewar Japan*, 331–39.

79. "Manshū mondai kaiketsu hōsaku no taikō," in GSS, 7: 164. Dating and authorship based on DR1, 306–7, which paraphrases the document.

80. Peattie, *Ishiwara Kanji*, 49–83, 87–121. See also Seki, "Manshū jihen zenshi," 361–70; Ishiwara Kanji, "Gunjijō yori mitaru Nichi-Bei sensō," 5/20/30, in Tsunoda, *Ishiwara Kanji shiryō—kokubō ronsaku*, 48–49; idem, "Genzai oyobi shōrai ni okeru Nihon no kokubō," 4/1931, in ibid., 58–68; and idem, "Manmō mondai kaiketsu no tame no sensō keikaku taikō," 4/1931, in ibid., 70–73.

81. Shimada, *Kantōgun*, 102–11.

82. S. Ogata, *Defiance in Manchuria*, 53–89; Peattie, *Ishiwara Kanji*, 121–39; Rekishigaku kenkyūkai, *Taiheiyō sensō shi*, 264–85; Coox, *Nomonhan*, 30–43.

83. For a detailed analysis of propaganda and popular responses, see L. Young, *Japan's Total Empire*, 55–114.

84. S. Ogata, *Defiance in Manchuria*, 107–17, 137–75.

85. Ibid., 74–89. See also Furuya, "'Manshūkoku' no sōshutsu."

86. Morishima to Foreign/Prime Minister Inukai Tsuyoshi, 1/12/32, in NGB, Manshū jihen, pt. 2, 1: 344–45.

87. For an account of some of the political developments in the early years of Manchoukuo, see Matsusaka, "Managing Occupied Manchuria, 1931–1934."

88. Iriye, *After Imperialism*, 278–99.

Conclusion

1. For a study of Japanese diplomacy during this period, see Crowley, *Japan's Quest for Autonomy*, 122–86. For domestic political developments linked to the Manchuria Incident, see L. Young, *Japan's Total Empire*, 55–180; S. Ogata, *Defiance in Manchuria*, 137–57; and Berger, *Parties Out of Power*, 80–132.

2. S. Ogata, *Defiance in Manchuria*, 74–89. Also see Furuya, "'Manshūkoku' no sōshutsu," 39–63; Yamamuro, "'Manshūkoku' tōji katei ron," 83–129; Shimizu, "Tai-Man kikō no hensen"; and Yamada, "Manshū tōsei keizai to san i ittai sei no hossoku," 245–95. The choice of P'u-i, the last Ch'ing emperor, as head of state and

subsequently emperor, not only conferred prestige upon the office but also underscored the multi-ethnic character of Manchoukuo. Japanese ideologues condemned Han Chinese nationalism as a form of racial discrimination.

3. Peattie, *Ishiwara Kanji*, 168–81.

4. Journalist John Gunther is quoted as describing Manchoukuo in 1939 as a "proving ground, a testing station for social and economic theory" (Coox, *Nomonhan*, 63). Shiina Etsusaburō ("Nihon sangyō no dai jikkenjo"), a leading figure in the postwar Ministry of International Trade and Industry who served as an economic planner in Manchoukuo, described the territory as the "great proving ground of Japanese industry."

5. Hara Akira, "'Manshū' ni okeru keizai tōsei seisaku no tenkai," 209. Studies of industrialization policy in Manchoukuo in English include Schumpeter and Allen, eds., *The Industrialization of Japan and Manchukuo*; Myers, "Creating a Modern Enclave Economy"; and Nakagane, "Manchoukuo and Economic Development." A pioneering work in Japanese is Kobayashi Hideo, "1930 nendai 'Manshū kōgyōka' seisaku no tenkai katei." The SMR's reorganized research section, the Keizai chōsakai, left a voluminous body of source material.

6. One of the most comprehensive studies of planning in Manchoukuo is Hara Akira, "1930 nendai no Manshū keizai tōsei saku." On the application of Manchurian lessons to planning at home, see Kobayashi Hideo, *Nihon kabushikigaisha o tsukutta otoko*. See also Peattie, *Ishiwara Kanji*, 185–222; and C. Johnson, *MITI and the Japanese Miracle*, 124–32.

7. For a useful summary of Manchurian ideological precepts, see "Proclamation of the Establishment of Manchoukuo," in Tōa keizai chōsakyoku, *Manchoukuo Year Book, 1934*, 58–62. Louise Young (*Japan's Total Empire*, 268–303) discusses radical ideologies in Manchoukuo at length. On Takahashi's idea, see Takahashi Kamekichi, "Manshū kaihatsu no kihonteki shomondai to sono taisaku." For an analysis of Takahashi's Marxism, see Hoston, *Marxism and the Crisis of Development in Prewar Japan*, 76–94. Confucian elements are explicated at length in Jin-ichi Yano, "Wangtao—the Kingly Way," in Tōa keizai chōsakyoku, *Manchoukuo Year Book, 1934*, 100–109.

8. SMR, *Sixth Report on Progress in Manchuria to 1939*, 117. On Japanese settlement policy, see L. Young, *Japan's Total Empire*, 307–98; Okabe Makio, "Manshū nōgyō imin seisaku no tenkai"; Matsumura Takao, "Manshūkoku seiritsu ikō ni okeru imin, rōdō seisaku no keisei to tenkai"; and Wilson, "The 'New Paradise.'" Army planners were cautious from the outset and urged careful selection of immigrants (Kwantung Army, Tōjibu, "Imin hōsaku an," 2/1932, in SMR, Keizai chōsakai, *Manshū nōgyō imin hōsaku*, 3).

9. Although this perspective is most evident in the older historiography, the underlying framework, without explicit reference to "fascism" or "militarism," seems to persist. For a discussion of the idea of Japanese fascism, see Duus and Okimoto,

"Fascism and the History of Prewar Japan." For the classic, Marxist-Leninist theory linking fascism and aggression, see Dimitroff, "Fascism Is War."

10. SMR, Keizai chōsakai, Dai 3 bu, Dai 1 han, *Tetsudō keikaku an*, 1–5.

11. Calculated from Tōa keizai chōsakyoku, *Manchoukuo Year Book, 1934*, 33; Japan-Manchoukuo Year Book 1938, 660–61; Tōa keizai chōsakyoku, *Manchoukuo Year Book 1941*, 116.

12. Suzuki Takashi, *Nihon teikokushugi to Manshū*, 2: 197–200.

13. On developments in Japanese thinking about autarky in the 1930s, see Barnhart, *Japan Prepares for Total War*, 22–33; Bōeichō, Bōeikenshūsho, Senshishitsu, *Rikugun gunju dōin*, 358–412; Nakamura Takafusa, *Nihon no keizai tōsei*, 17–21; and C. Johnson, *MITI and the Japanese Miracle*, 109–11.

14. Koiso set the tone for economic planning in his memorandum "Nichi-Man keizai tōsei jikkōjō no kisō yōken ni kansuru iken," 9/1/32, in SMR, Keizai chōsakai, *Manshū keizai tōsei hōsaku*, 24–26. Radicals strongly opposed his pragmatic approach to planning; see Yamaguchi Jūji, *Kieta teikoku Manshū*, 117.

15. On the SMR's role in the early 1930s, see Hara Akira, "'Manshū' ni okeru keizai tōsei seisaku no tenkai," 209–28; Takahashi Yasutaka, "Minami Manshū tetsudō kabushikigaisha no kaiso keikaku ni tsuite"; Okabe Makio, "Nihon teikokushugi to Mantetsu"; Makita, "1930 nendai ni okeru Mantetsu kaiso mondai"; Hamaguchi, "1930 nendai nakaba no tai-Man seisaku ritsuan ni kansuru ichi kōsatsu"; and Matsusaka, "Managing Occupied Manchuria," 120–27. For contemporary perspectives, see Kojima, "Kensetsuteki tenkan e no daibō"; and idem, *Mantetsu kontsuerun tokuhon*.

16. Chandler, *The Visible Hand*, 1.

17. See, e.g., SMR, Keizai chōsakai, "Manshū keizai tōsei an (kōhen, seisaku hen)," 6/1932, in SMR, Keizai chōsakai, *Manshū keizai tōsei hōsaku*, 63; and Kaji Ryūichi, "Mantetsu kaiso mondai no kentō." Kaji was a member of the SMR research staff.

18. Samuels, *Rich Nation, Strong Army*, 31; Betts, *Uncertain Dimensions*, 80–81. On Gotō's views about the importance of "physical grandeur," see Peattie, "Attitudes Toward Colonialism," 88. For the imaginary traveler's tour of the Zone, see Hoshino, *Economic History of Manchuria*, 122.

19. On Ishibashi Tanzan, see Nolte, *Liberalism in Modern Japan*; on Miyaki Tōten, see Miyazaki, *My Thirty-Three Year's Dream*; on Noro Eitarō, see Hoston, *Marxism and the Crisis of Development in Prewar Japan*, 92–93, 97; and Noro, *Nihon shihonshugi hattatsu shi*, 89–144. On Inukai Tsuyoshi's political career, see Oka, *Five Political Leaders of Modern Japan*, 125–75, esp. 161–75. On the affinities between Hara and the army, see, e.g., J. Young, "The Hara Cabinet and Chang Tso-lin."

20. The argument here is a variant of the "warfare state" hypothesis. For a critical review of the historiography on this subject, see Nelson, "The Warfare State."

21. The classic work in this field is Selznick, *TVA and the Grass Roots.* For more recent examinations, see Scott, *Organizations;* and Galbraith, *How to Control the Military,* 14.

22. Fieldhouse, *Economics and Empire,* 81.

23. Turner, *The Frontier in American History,* 2.

Works Cited

Ajia keizai kenkyūjo, ed. *Kyū shokuminchi kankei kankōbutsu sōgō mokuroku—Minami Manshū tetsudō kabushikigaisha hen.* Tokyo: Ajia keizai kenkyūjo,1979.

Allen, G. C. *A Short Economic History of Modern Japan.* London: Macmillan, 1981.

Amamiya Shōichi. "Shiberiya tettai katei to tōhō kaigi." Special issue: Sekaishi ni okeru chiiki to minshū. *Rekishigaku kenkyū* (Oct. 1979): 21–27.

Anderson, Benedict. *Imagined Communities.* New York: Verso, 1991.

Andō Hikotarō (Waseda study group), ed. *Mantetsu: Nihon teikokushugi to Chūgoku.* Tokyo: Ochanomizu shobō, 1965.

Andō Minoru. "Mantetsu kaisha no sōritsu ni tsuite." 2 pts. *Rekishi hyōron*, no. 117 (May 1960): 13–32; no. 118 (June 1960): 13–36.

Ariga Tadashi. "Hai-Nichi mondai to Nichi-Bei kankei." In *Senkanki no Nihon gaikō*, ed. Iriye Akira and Ariga Tadashi, pp. 65–96. Tokyo: Tōkyō daigaku shuppankai, 1984.

Asada Kyōji. "Nihon shokumin shi kenkyū no genjō to mondai ten." *Rekishi hyōron*, no. 300 (Apr. 1975): 178–98.

———. "Nihon shokumin shi kenkyū no kadai to hōhō." *Rekishi hyōron*, no. 308 (Dec. 1975): 63–86.

———. *Nihon teikokushugi to kyū shokuminchi jinushi sei.* Tokyo: Ochanomizu shobō, 1968.

Asada Kyōji and Kobayashi Hideo, eds. *Nihon teikokushugi no Manshū shihai: jūgonen sensō o chūshin ni.* Tokyo: Jichōsha, 1986.

Asada Sadao. "Washinton kaigi to Nihon no taiō: 'kyū gaikō' to 'shin gaikō' no hazama." In *Senkanki no Nihon gaikō*, ed. Iriye Akira and Ariga Tadashi, pp. 21–63. Tokyo: Tōkyō daigaku shuppankai, 1984.

Baba Akira. "Nichi-Ro sengo ni okeru dai ichiji Saionji naikaku no tai-Man seisaku to Shinkoku." In *Tai-Manmō seisaku shi no ichimen*, ed. Kurihara Ken, pp. 67–73. Tokyo: Hara shobō, 1967.

———. *Nitchū kankei to gaisei kikō no kenkyū.* Tokyo: Hara shobō, 1983.

Bamba, Nobuya. *Japanese Diplomacy in a Dilemma: A New Light on Japan's China Policy, 1924–1929*. Vancouver: University of British Columbia, 1972.

Bannō Junji. "Japanese Industrialists and Merchants and the Anti-Japanese Boycotts in China, 1919–1928." In *The Japanese Informal Empire in China, 1895–1937*, ed. Peter Duus, Ramon H. Myers, and Mark R. Peattie, pp. 314–29. Princeton: Princeton University Press, 1989.

————. *Kindai Nihon no gaikō to seiji*. Tokyo: Kenbun shuppan, 1985.

————. *Taishō seihen*. Tokyo: Minerubua shobō, 1994.

Barnhart, Michael. *Japan Prepares for Total War: The Search for Economic Security, 1919–1941*. Ithaca: Cornell University Press, 1987.

Beasley, William G. *Japanese Imperialism, 1894–1945*. New York: Clarendon, 1987.

Benson, Lee. *Merchants, Farmers and Railroads: Railroad Regulation and New York Politics, 1850–1887*. New York: Russell and Russell, 1969.

Berger, Gordon M. *Parties Out of Power, 1931–1941*. Princeton: Princeton University Press, 1977.

Best, Gary Dean. "Financing a Foreign War: Jacob H. Schiff and Japan, 1904–05." *American Jewish Historical Quarterly* 61, no. 4 (June 1972): 313–24.

Betts, Raymond. *Uncertain Dimensions: Western Overseas Empires in the Twentieth Century*. Minneapolis: University of Minnesota Press, 1985.

Bix, Herbert P. "Japanese Imperialism and Manchuria, 1890–1931." Ph.D. diss., Harvard University, 1972.

————. "Japanese Imperialism and the Manchurian Economy, 1900–1931." *China Quarterly*, no. 51 (July–Sept. 1972): 425–43.

Bōeichō, Bōeikenshūsho, Senshishitsu, ed. *Daihonei kaigunbu: rengō kantai*, vol. 1. Tokyo: Asagumo shinbunsha, 1975.

————. *Daihonei rikugunbu*, vol. 1. Tokyo: Asagumo shinbunsha, 1967.

————. *Rikugun gunju dōin*, vol. 1. Tokyo: Asagumo shinbunsha, 1967.

Brooks, Barbara J. "China Experts in the Gaimushō, 1895–1937." In *The Japanese Informal Empire in China, 1895–1937*, eds. Peter Duus, Ramon H. Myers, and Mark R. Peattie, pp. 369–94. Princeton: Princeton University Press, 1989.

————. "The Japanese Foreign Ministry and China Affairs: Loss of Control, 1895–1938." Ph.D. diss., Princeton University, 1991.

————. "Peopling the Japanese Empire: The Koreans in Manchuria and the Rhetoric of Inclusion." In *Japan's Competing Modernities: Issues in Culture and Democracy, 1900–1930*, ed. Sharon A. Minichiello, pp. 25–44. Honolulu: University of Hawaii Press, 1998.

Chandler, Alfred D., Jr. *The Visible Hand: The Managerial Revolution in American Business*. Cambridge, Mass.: Harvard University Press, Belknap Press, 1977.

Chang Han-yu and Ramon H. Myers. "Japanese Colonial Development Policy in Taiwan, 1895–1906." *Journal of Asian Studies* 22, no. 4 (Aug. 1963): 433–49.

Chang, Richard. "The Failure of the Katsura-Harriman Agreement." *Journal of Asian Studies* 21, no. 1 (Nov. 1961): 65–76.

Chen, Edward. "Japan's Decision to Annex Taiwan." *Journal of Asian Studies* 37, no. 1 (Nov. 1977): 61–72.

Chi, Madeleine. *China Diplomacy, 1914–1918.* Cambridge, Mass.: Harvard University Press, 1970.

Chi-lin sheng she-hui k'e-hsueh yüan, Man-t'ieh shih tzu-liao pien-chi tsu, ed. *Man-t'ieh shih tzu-liao,* part 2, vol. 3. Peking: Chung-hua shu-chü, 1979–87.

Chinese Eastern Railroad, Printing Office. *North Manchuria and the Chinese Eastern Railway.* Harbin, 1924. Reprinted—New York: Garland Publishing, 1982.

Chōsen sōtokufu, Tetsudōkyoku. *Chōsen tetsudō yonjūnen ryakushi.* Seoul: Chōsen sōtokufu, Tetsudōkyoku, 1940.

Chow, Tse-tsung. *The May Fourth Movement.* Cambridge, Mass.: Harvard University Press, 1960.

Clyde, Paul Hibbert. *International Rivalries in Manchuria, 1689–1922.* 2nd ed. New York: Octagon Books, 1966.

Conroy, Hilary. *The Japanese Seizure of Korea: A Study of Realism and Idealism in International Relations.* Philadelphia: University of Pennsylvania, 1960.

———. "Meiji Imperialism: Mostly 'Ad Hoc.'" In *Japan Examined,* ed. Hilary Conroy and Harry Wray, pp. 136–40. Honolulu: University of Hawaii Press, 1983.

Cook, Theodore F. "The Japanese Officer Corps: The Making of a Military Elite, 1872–1943." Ph.D. diss., Princeton University, 1987.

Coox, Alvin. "The Kwantung Army Dimension." In *The Japanese Informal Empire in China, 1895–1937,* ed. Peter Duus, Ramon H. Myers, and Mark R. Peattie, pp. 395–428. Princeton: Princeton University Press, 1989.

———. *Nomonhan: Japan Against Russia, 1939.* 2 vols. Stanford: Stanford University Press, 1985.

Craig, Albert M. "Fukuzawa Yukichi: The Philosophical Foundations of Meiji Nationalism." In *Political Development in Modern Japan,* ed. Robert E. Ward, pp. 99–148. Princeton: Princeton University Press, 1968.

Crowley, James B. *Japan's Quest for Autonomy.* Princeton: Princeton University Press, 1966.

Davis, Clarence B. "Railway Imperialism in China." In *Railway Imperialism,* ed. Clarence B. Davis and Kenneth E. Wilburn, Jr., pp. 155–73. New York: Greenwood Press, 1991.

Davis, Clarence B., and Kenneth E. Wilburn, Jr., eds. *Railway Imperialism.* New York: Greenwood Press, 1991.

Dickinson, Frederick R. *War and National Reinvention: Japan in the Great War, 1914–1919.* Cambridge, Mass.: Harvard University Asia Center, 1999.

Dimitroff, Georgi. "Fascism Is War." In idem, *The United Front*, pp. 262–69. San Francisco: Proletarian Publishers, 1975.

Dingman, Roger. *Power in the Pacific: The Origins of Naval Arms Limitations, 1914–1922*. Chicago: University of Chicago Press, 1976.

DK1, see Bōeichō, Bōeikenshūsho, Senshitsu, *Daihonei kaigunbu*, vol. 1

DR1, see Bōeichō, Bōeikenshūsho, Senshishitsu, *Daihonei rikugunbu*, vol. 1

Dower, John. *Empire and Aftermath: Yoshida Shigeru and the Japanese Experience, 1878–1954*. Cambridge, Mass.: Harvard University Press, 1979.

Duus, Peter. *The Abacus and the Sword: The Japanese Penetration of Korea, 1895–1910*. Berkeley: University of California Press, 1995.

————. "Economic Dimensions." In *The Japanese Colonial Empire, 1895–1945*, ed. Ramon H. Myers and Mark R. Peattie, pp. 128–71. Princeton: Princeton University Press, 1984.

————. "Introduction." In *The Japanese Informal Empire in China, 1895–1937*, ed. Peter Duus, Ramon H. Myers, and Mark R. Peattie, pp. xi–xxix. Princeton: Princeton University Press, 1989.

————. *Party Rivalry and Political Change in Taishō Japan*. Cambridge, Mass.: Harvard University Press, 1968.

————. "The Takeoff Point of Japanese Imperialism." In *Japan Examined: Perspectives on Modern Japanese History*, ed. Hilary Conroy and Harry Wray, pp. 153–57. Honolulu: University of Hawaii Press, 1983.

Duus, Peter, and Daniel Okimoto. "Fascism and the History of Prewar Japan: The Failure of a Concept." *Journal of Asian Studies* 39, no. 1 (Nov. 1979): 65–76.

Eckert, Carter J. *Offspring of Empire: The Koch'ang Kims and the Colonial Origins of Korean Capitalism, 1876–1945*. Seattle: University of Washington Press, 1991.

Eckstein, Alexander; Kang Chao; and John Chang. "The Economic Development of Manchuria: The Rise of a Frontier Economy." *Journal of Economic History* 34 (Mar. 1974): 239–64.

Egami Teruhiko. *Mantetsu ōkoku*. Tokyo: Sankei, 1980.

Egler, David G. "Japanese Mass Organizations in Manchuria, 1928–1945: The Ideology of Racial Harmony." Ph.D. diss., University of Arizona, 1977.

————. "Pan-Asianism in Action and Reaction." In *Japan Examined*, ed. Hilary Conroy and Harry Wray, pp. 229–36. Honolulu: University of Hawaii Press, 1983.

Eguchi Keiichi. "Manshū jihenki kenkyū no saikentō." Special issue: Manshū jihen gojūnen. *Rekishi hyōron*, no. 377 (Sept. 1981): 2–11.

————. *Nihon teikokushugi shiron: Manshū jihen zengo*. Tokyo: Aoki shoten, 1975.

Ericson, Steven J. "The Engine of Change: Railroads and Society in Meiji Japan." *KSU Economic and Business Review*, no. 21 (May 1994): 37–60.

————. "Railroads in Crisis: The Financing and Management of Japanese Railway Companies During the Panic of 1890." In *Managing Industrial Enterprise: Cases from Japan's Prewar Experience*, ed. William Wray, pp. 121–82. Cambridge, Mass.: Harvard University Press, 1989.

————. *The Sound of the Whistle: Railroads and the State in Meiji Japan.* Cambridge, Mass.: Harvard University, Council on East Asian Studies, 1996.

Evans, David C., and Mark R. Peattie. *Kaigun: Strategy, Tactics, and Technology in the Imperial Japanese Navy, 1887–1941.* Annapolis: Naval Institute Press, 1997.

Fieldhouse, Kenneth. *Economics and Empire.* Ithaca: Cornell University Press, 1973.

Fogel, Joshua A. "Integrating into Chinese Society: A Comparison of the Japanese Communities of Shanghai and Harbin." In *Japan's Competing Modernities: Issues in Culture and Democracy, 1900–1930*, ed. Sharon A. Minichiello, pp. 45–69. Honolulu: University of Hawaii Press, 1998.

————. "Introduction: Itō Takeo and the Research Work of the South Manchurian Railway." In Itō Takeo, *Life Along the South Manchurian Railway*, trans. Joshua Fogel. Armonk, N.Y.: M. E. Sharpe, 1988.

————. *Politics and Sinology: The Case of Naitō Kōnan (1866–1934).* Cambridge, Mass.: Harvard University, Council on East Asian Studies, 1984.

Fujimura Michio. "Nisshin sensō." In *Iwanami kōza Nihon rekishi*, vol. 16, pp. 1–46. Tokyo: Iwanami shoten, 1976.

Fujiwara Akira and Imai Seiichi, eds. *Jūgonen sensō shi*, vol. 1, *Manshū jihen.* Tokyo: Aoki shoten, 1988.

Fukuzawa Yukichi. "On De-Asianization." In *Meiji Japan Through Contemporary Sources*, ed. Center for East Asian Cultural Studies, vol. 1, pp. 129–33. Tokyo: The Center for East Asian Cultural Studies, 1969.

Furuya Tetsuo. "'Manshūkoku' no sōshutsu." In *Manshūkoku no kenkyū*, ed. Yamamoto Yūzō, pp. 39–82. Kyoto: Kyoto daigaku jinbun kagaku kenkyūjo, 1993.

Gaimushō. Archives. Microfilm. Washington, D.C.: Library of Congress.

————. *Komura gaikō shi.* Tokyo: Hara shobō, 1966.

————. *Nihon gaikō bunsho*, (multiple volumes). Tokyo: Gaimushō, 1936–1996.

————. *Nihon gaikō nenpyō narabini shuyō bunsho*, 2 vols. Tokyo: Hara shobō, 1965–66.

Galbraith, John Kenneth. *How to Control the Military.* Garden City, N.Y.: Doubleday, 1969.

Gann, Lewis H. "Economic Development in Germany's African Empire, 1884–1914." In *Colonialism in Africa, 1870–1960*, vol. 4, *The Economics of Colonialism*, ed. Peter Duignan and Lewis H. Gann, pp. 213–55. Cambridge, Eng.: Cambridge University Press, 1975.

Gendai shi shiryō, 7, *Manshū jihen.* Ed. Kobayashi Tatsuo and Shimada Toshihiko. Tokyo: Misuzu shobō, 1964.

Gendai shi shiryō, 31–33, *Mantetsu*. Ed. Itō Takeo, Ogiwara Kiwamu, and Fujii Masuo. Tokyo: Misuzu shobō, 1966.

Gooch, G. P., et al., eds. *British Documents on the Origins of the War, 1898–1914*, vol. 4, *The Anglo-Russian Rapprochement, 1903–7*. London: H. M. Stationary Office, 1929.

Gordon, Andrew. *Labor and Imperial Democracy in Japan*. Berkeley: University of California Press, 1991.

Gotō Shinpei. "The Administration of Formosa (Taiwan)." In *Fifty Years of New Japan*, ed. Okuma Shigenobu, pp. 530–33. New York: E.P. Dutton, 1909.

———. *Gotō Shinpei monjo*, Reel 39. Microfilm. Washington, D.C., Library of Congress.

———. *Shokumin seisaku ippan / Nihon bōchō ron*. Ed. Nakamura Tetsu. Tokyo: Nihon hyōronsha, 1944.

Gourvish, T. R. *Railways and the British Economy, 1830–1914*. London: Macmillan, 1980.

Griffiths, Sir Percival. *A License to Trade: The History of English Chartered Companies*. London: E. Benn, 1974.

GSS, see Gendai shi shiryō

Hackett, Roger F. *Yamagata Aritomo in the Rise of Modern Japan, 1838–1922*. Cambridge, Mass.: Harvard University Press, 1971.

Halliday, Jon. *A Political History of Japanese Capitalism*. New York: Pantheon, 1975.

Hamaguchi Hiroko. "1930 nendai nakaba no tai-Man seisaku ritsuan ni kansuru ichi kōsatsu—Manmō kenkyūkai o chūshin ni." In *Kindai Nihon seiji no shosō*, ed. Nakamura Katsunori, pp. 359–84. Tokyo: Keiō tsūshin, 1988.

Hara Akira. "1930 nendai no Manshū keizai tōsei saku." In *Nihon teikokushugika no Manshū*, ed. Manshūshi kenkyūkai, pp. 3–114. Tokyo: Ochanomizu shobō, 1972.

———. "'Manshū' ni okeru keizai tōsei seisaku no tenkai—Mantetsu kaiso to Mangyō setsuritsu o megutte." In *Nihon keizai seisaku shiron*, ed. Andō Yoshio, vol. 2, pp. 209–96. Tokyo: Tōkyō daigaku shuppankai, 1976.

Hara Kakuten. *Mantetsu chōsabu to Ajia*. Tokyo: Sekai shoin, 1986.

Hara Takashi. *Hara Takashi nikki*, vols. 2, 4, 5. Ed. Hara Keiichirō. Tokyo: Kengaisha, 1950–52.

Harada Katsumasa. *Mantetsu*. Tokyo: Iwanami shoten, 1981.

Hashitani Hiroshi. "Chōsen tetsudō no Mantetsu e no itaku keiei o megutte—dai ichiji taisen zengo no Nittei shokuminchi seisaku no ichidanmen." *Chōsen shi kenkyūkai ronbunshū*, no. 19 (Mar. 1982): 151–84.

Hata Ikuhiko. *Senzenki Nihon kanryōsei no seido, soshiki, jinji*. Tokyo: Tōkyō daigaku shuppankai, 1981.

———. *Taiheiyō kokusai kankei shi*. Tokyo: Fukumura shuppan, 1972.

Hayashi Kyūjirō. *Manshū jihen to Hōten sōryōji*. Ed. Baba Akira. Tokyo: Hara shobō, 1978.

Hayashi Masakazu. "Chō Sakurin gunbatsu no keisei katei to Nihon no taiō." *Kokusai seiji*, Apr. 1970, 122–42.

Headrick, Daniel. *The Tools of Empire: Technology and European Imperialism in the Nineteenth Century*. New York: Oxford University Press, 1981.

Hirano Ken'ichirō. "1923 nen no Manshū." In *Kindai Nihon to Ajia—bunka no kōryū to masatsu*, ed. Hirano Ken'ichirō, pp. 235–59. Tokyo: Tōkyō daigaku shuppankai, 1984.

———. "The Japanese in Manchuria, 1906–1931: A Study in the Historical Background of Manchukuo." Ph.D. diss., Harvard University, 1983.

———. "Manshū sangyō chōsa ni tsuite." *Nenpō kindai Nihon kenkyū*, no. 3 (1981): 429–53.

Hirazuka Atsushi. *Itō Hirobumi hiroku*. Tokyo: Shunjūsha, 1929.

Honda Kumatarō. *Tamashii no gaikō*. Tokyo: Chikuma shobō, 1938.

Hoshino Tokuji. *Economic History of Manchuria*. Seoul: Bank of Chōsen, 1920.

Hosie, Alexander. *Manchuria, Its People, Resources and Recent History*. London: Methuen and Co., 1904.

Hoston, Germaine. *Marxism and the Crisis of Development in Prewar Japan*. Princeton: Princeton University Press, 1986.

Huenemann, Ralph W. *The Dragon and the Iron Horse: The Economics of Railroads in China, 1876–1937*. Cambridge, Mass.: Harvard University, Council on East Asian Studies, 1984.

Humphreys, Leonard A. "Crisis and Reaction: The Japanese Army in the 'Liberal' Twenties." *Armed Forces and Society* 5, no. 1 (Fall 1978): 73–92.

———. *The Way of the Heavenly Sword: The Japanese Army in the 1920's*. Stanford: Stanford University Press, 1995.

Hunt, Michael. *Frontier Defense and the Open Door*. New Haven: Yale University Press, 1973.

Hunter, Janet. "Japanese Government Policy, Business Opinion and the Seoul-Pusan Railway, 1894–1906." *Modern Asian Studies* 4, no. 4 (1977): 573–99.

Ikei Masaru. "Dai ichiji Hō-Choku sensō to Nihon." In *Tai-Manmō seisaku shi no ichimen*, ed. Kurihara Ken, pp. 163–91. Tokyo: Hara shobō, 1967.

———. "Dai niji Hō-Choku sensō to Nihon." In *Tai-Manmō seisaku shi no ichimen*, ed. Kurihara Ken, pp. 193–216. Tokyo: Hara shobō, 1967.

———. "Japan's Response to the Chinese Revolution of 1911." *Journal of Asian Studies* 25, no. 2 (Feb. 1966): 213–27.

———. "Ugaki Kazushige's View of China and His China Policy, 1915–1930." Trans. Ronald Toby. In *The Chinese and the Japanese: Essays in Political and Cultural Interactions*, ed. Akira Iriye, pp. 119–219. Princeton: Princeton University Press, 1980.

Imai Seiichi. "Taishō ki ni okeru gunbu no seijiteki chii." *Shisō*, no. 399 (Sept. 1957): 1239–57.

Inaba Masao, Kobayashi Tatsuo, Shimada Toshihiko, and Tsunoda Jun, eds. *Taiheiyō sensō e no michi*, vol. 1. Tokyo: Asahi shinbunsha, 1963.

Inoue Kaoru kō denki hensankai. *Segai Inoue kō den*, vol. 5. Tokyo: Naigai shoseki, 1935.

Inoue Kiyoshi. "Manshū shinryaku." In *Iwanami kōza Nihon rekishi*, vol. 20, pp. 2–42. Tokyo: Iwanami shoten, 1976.

Inoue Manabu. "Nihon teikokushugi to Kantō mondai." *Chōsen shi kenkyūkai ronbunshū*, no. 10 (Mar. 1973): 35–83.

Inoue Yūichi. *Higashi Ajia tetsudō kokusai kankei shi*. Tokyo: Keiō tsūshin, 1991.

———. *Tetsudō ga kaeta gendai shi*. Tokyo: Chūōkōronsha, 1990.

Inukai Tsuyoshi, "Gaikō no konpon o ayamaru gunbi keikaku" (1909). In *Inukai Bokudō shi dai enzetsu shū*, ed. Dai Nihon yūbenkai, pp. 36–45. Tokyo: Dai Nihon yūbenkai, 1927.

———. "Rikugun kakuchō to gunsei kaikaku" (1910). In *Bokudō seiron shū*, ed. Kawasaki Katsu, pp. 218–28. Tokyo: Bunkaidō shoten, 1913.

———. "Taiheiyō mondai no shōrai," (1910). In *Bokudō seiron shū*, ed. Kawasaki Katsu, pp. 237–48. Tokyo: Bunkaidō shoten, 1913.

Iriye, Akira. *After Imperialism: The Search for a New Order in the Far East, 1921–1931*. Cambridge, Mass.: Harvard University Press, 1965.

———. "The Failure of Economic Expansion." In *Japan in Crisis: Essays on Taishō Democracy*, ed. Bernard Silberman, and H. D. Hartoonian, pp. 237–69. Princeton, NJ: Princeton University Press, 1972.

———. *Japan and China in the Global Setting*. Cambridge, Mass.: Harvard University Press, 1992.

———. *Pacific Estrangement: Japanese and American Expansion, 1897–1911*. Cambridge, Mass.: Harvard University Press, 1972.

Ishida Kyōhei. "Shokuminchi kaihatsu shutai to shite no Mantetsu." *Keizai keiei ronsō* 41, no. 1 (June 1979): 2–42.

Ishidō Kiyotomo, Noma Kiyoshi, Nonomura Kazuo, and Kobayashi Shōichi. *Jūgonen sensō to Mantetsu chōsabu*. Tokyo: Hara shobō, 1986.

Ishimoto Kantarō, Aioi Yoshitarō, et al. *Sansen mondai undō keika hōkoku*. Dairen: private publication, 1916. Tōkyō daigaku, Shakai kagaku kenkyūjo, Toshokan.

Itō Takeo. *Life Along the South Manchurian Railway*. Trans. Joshua Fogel. Armonk, N.Y.: M. E. Sharpe, 1988.

Izawa Michio. *Kaitaku tetsudō ron*. Tokyo: Shunjūsha, 1937.

Jansen, Marius B. "Changing Japanese Attitudes Toward Modernization." In *Changing Japanese Attitudes Toward Modernization*, ed. Marius B. Jansen, pp. 43–89. Princeton, NJ: Princeton University Press, 1965.

———. *The Japanese and Sun Yatsen.* Cambridge, Mass.: Harvard University Press, 1954.

———. "Japanese Imperialism: Late Meiji Perspectives." In *The Japanese Colonial Empire, 1895–1945,* ed. Ramon H. Myers and Mark R. Peattie, pp. 61–79. Princeton: Princeton University Press, 1984.

———. "Modernization and Foreign Policy in Meiji Japan." In *Political Development in Modern Japan,* ed. Robert E. Ward. pp. 149–88. Princeton: Princeton University Press, 1968.

Japan-Manchoukuo Year Book, 1938. Tokyo: Japan-Manchoukuo Year Book Co.

Johnson, Arthur, and Barry E. Supple. *Boston Capitalists and Western Railroads.* Cambridge, Mass.: Harvard University Press, 1967.

Johnson, Chalmers. *MITI and the Japanese Miracle.* Stanford: Stanford University Press, 1981.

Jones, F. C. *Manchuria Since 1931.* London: Royal Institute of International Affairs, 1949.

Kagawa Etsuji. *Ōura Kanetake den.* Tokyo, 1921.

Kaji Ryūichi. "Mantetsu kaiso mondai no kentō." *Chūō kōron,* Dec. 1933, 34–39.

Kajima Morinosuke. *Nihon gaikō shi,* vol. 9. Tokyo: Kajima kenkyūjo shuppankai, 1970.

Kamiminochi gunyakusho, ed. *Meiji sanjūshichi-hachinen Kamiminochishi shi.* Nagano, 1906. Tōkyō daigaku, Shakai kagaku kenkyūjo, Toshokan.

Kaneko Fumio. "1920 nendai ni okeru Nihon teikokushugi to 'Manshū.'" 2 pts. *Shakai kagaku kenkyū* 32, no. 4 (Feb. 1981): 149–224; 32, no. 6 (Mar. 1983): 195–286.

———. "1970 nendai ni okeru 'Manshū' kenkyū no genjō." 2 pts. *Ajia keizai* 20, no. 3 (Mar. 1979): 38–43; 20, no. 11 (Nov. 1979): 24–41.

———. *Kindai Nihon ni okeru tai-Manshū tōshi no kenkyū.* Tokyo: Kondō shuppan-sha, 1991.

———. "Sōgyōki no Minami Manshū tetsudō, 1906–1916." *Shakai kagaku kenkyū* 31, no. 4 (Jan. 1980): 171–201.

Kantō totokufu, Minseibu. *Manshū sangyō chōsa shiryō.* 8 unnumbered volumes. Tokyo: Kokkōsha, 1906.

Kantō totokufu, Rikugun, Keiribu. *Manshū ippan shi,* pt. 1, vols. 1, 4. Tokyo, 1911. Kokuritsu kokkai toshokan.

Kantōchō. *Kantōchō shisei nijūnen shi.* Dairen: Manshū nichinichi shinbunsha, 1926.

Kasuga Yukata. "Kan'ei Miike tankō to Mitsui bussan." *Mitsui bunko ronsō,* no. 10 (Nov. 1976): 187–313.

Katō Kiyofumi. "Hara Takashi to Mantetsu: tōsei kakuchō to Manmō seisaku no yūgō." In *Kindai Nihon to Mantetsu,* ed. Kobayashi Hideo, pp. 31–63. Tokyo: Yoshikawa kōbunkan, 2000.

————. "Matsuoka Yōsuke to Mantetsu: Washinton taisei e no tōsen." In *Kindai Nihon to Mantetsu*, ed. Kobayashi Hideo, pp. 64–107. Tokyo: Yoshikawa kōbunkan, 2000.

Kawai Toshizō. "Hariman Mantetsu baishū keikaku zasetsu no kokusaiteki haikei." *Tōyō kenkyū* (Daitō bunka daigaku, Tōyō kenkyūjo), no. 58 (Dec. 1980): 67–79.

Kennan, George. E. H. *Harriman's Far Eastern Plans*. Garden City, N.Y.: Country Life Press, 1917.

Kerr, Austin. *Railroad Politics, 1914–1920: Rates, Wages and Efficiency*. Pittsburgh: University of Pittsburgh Press, 1968.

Kimura Takeo. *Kōmoto Daisaku*. Tokyo: Tsuchiya shoten, 1978.

Kingman, Harry L. *Effects of Chinese Nationalism upon Manchurian Railway Developments, 1925–1931*. Berkeley: University of California Press, 1932.

Kinney, Ann R. *Japanese Investment in Manchurian Manufacturing, Mining, Transportation and Communications, 1931–1945*. New York: Garland Publishing, 1982.

Kitaoka Shin'ichi. "China Experts in the Army." In *The Japanese Informal Empire in China, 1895–1937*, ed. Peter Duus, Ramon H. Myers, and Mark R. Peattie, pp. 530–68. Princeton: Princeton University Press, 1989.

————. *Gotō Shinpei: gaikō to buijiyon*. Tokyo: Chūōkōronsha, 1988.

————. *Nihon rikugun to tairiku seisaku*. Tokyo: Tōkyō daigaku shuppankai, 1978.

————. "Rikugun habatsu tairitsu (1931–35) no saikentō." In *Shōwa ki no gunbu*, ed. Kindai Nihon kenkyūkai, pp. 44–95. Tokyo: Yamakawa shuppansha, 1979.

Kobayashi Hideo. "Gotō Shinpei to Mantetsu chōsabu." In *Kindai Nihon to Mantetsu*, ed. idem, pp. 9–30. Tokyo: Yoshikawa kōbunkan, 2000.

————. *Mantetsu: "chi no shūdan" no tanjō to shi*. Tokyo: Yoshikawa kōbunkan, 1996.

————. *Nihon kabushikigaisha o tsukutta otoko*. Tokyo: Shōgakkan, 1995.

————. "1930 nendai 'Manshū kōgyōka' seisaku no tenkai katei." *Tochi seido shigaku*, no. 44 (July 1969): 19–43.

Kobayashi Hideo, ed. *Kindai Nihon to Mantetsu*. Tokyo: Yoshikawa kōbunkan, 2000.

Kobayashi Michihiko. "Nichi-Ro sengo no Manshū gunji yusō rūto mondai: Ryōjun keiei o chūshin to shite." *Daigaku kenkyū nenpō—bungaku kenkyūka hen* (Chūō daigaku) 4, no. 17 (1987): 81–92.

————. "'Teikoku kokubō hōshin' saikō: Nichi-Ro sengo ni okeru riku-kai gun no kyōchō." *Shigaku zasshi* 98, no. 4 (Apr. 1989): 36–71.

Kobayashi Yukio, "Tai-So seisaku no suii to Manmō mondai (1917–1927)." In *Taiheiyō sensō e no michi*, ed. Kobayashi Tatsuo, Kobayashi Yukio, and Seki Hiroharu, vol. 1, pp. 163–284. Tokyo: Asahi shinbusha, 1963.

Kojima Seiichi. "Kensetsuteki tenkan e no daibō." Special issue: Dai Manshū kaihatsu gō. *Keizai ōrai*, Apr. 1932, pp. 37–44.

————. *Mantetsu kontsuerun tokuhon*. Tokyo: Shunjūsha, 1937.

Koshizawa Akira. *Harupin no toshi keikaku*. Tokyo: Sōwasha, 1989.

————. *Manshūkoku no shuto keikaku.* Tokyo: Nihon keizai hyōronsha, 1988.

————. *Shokuminchi Manshū no toshi keikaku.* Tokyo: Ajia keizai kenkyūjo, 1978.

Kunugi Toshihiro. "Gunshuku kara gunkaku e." In *Jūgonen sensō shi,* vol. 1, *Manshū jihen,* ed. Fujiwara Akira and Imai Seiichi, pp. 83–123. Tokyo: Aoki shoten, 1988.

Kurihara Ken. "Abe Gaimushō, Seimukyokuchō ansatsu jiken to tai-Chūgoku (Manmō) mondai." In *Tai-Manmō seisaku shi no ichimen,* ed. Kurihara Ken, pp. 87–113. Tokyo: Hara shobō, 1967.

————. "Dai ichiji, dai niji Manmō dokuritsu undō to Koike Gaimushō, Seimukyokuchō no ishoku." In *Tai-Manmō seisaku shi no ichimen,* ed. Kurihara Ken, pp. 136–61. Tokyo: Hara shobō, 1967.

————. "Kantō totokufu mondai teiyō." In *Tai-Manmō seisaku shi no ichimen,* ed. Kurihara Ken, pp. 38–47. Tokyo: Hara shobō, 1967.

————. "Nichi-Ro sengo ni okeru Manshū zango sochi mondai to Hagiwara shodai Hōten sōryōji." In *Tai-Manmō seisaku shi no ichimen,* ed. Kurihara Ken, pp. 9–35. Tokyo: Hara shobō, 1967.

Kurihara Ken, ed. *Tai-Manmō seisaku shi no ichimen.* Tokyo: Hara shobō, 1967.

Kurobane Shigeru. "Minami Manshū tetsudō chūritsuka mondai." 2 pts. *Nihon rekishi,* no. 125 (Nov. 1958): 7–12; no. 126 (Dec. 1958): 12–18.

Kuropatkin, Alexei Nikolaevitch. *The Russian Army and the Japanese War.* Trans. A. B. Lindsay. New York: E. P. Dutton, 1909.

Kusayanagi Daizō. *Jitsuroku Mantetsu chōsabu.* 2 vols. Tokyo: Asahi shinbunsha, 1979.

Kuwahara Tetsuya. "Nisshin sensō chokugo no Nihon bōseikigyō no chokusetsu tōshi keikaku: Nakamigawa Hikojirō to Shanhai bōseki kaisha." *Keizai keiei ronsō* 15, no. 1 (June 1980): 112–130.

Landes, David. "Some Thoughts on the Nature of Economic Imperialism." *Journal of Economic History* 21, no. 4 (Dec. 1961): 496–512.

Langer, William. *Diplomacy of Imperialism, 1890–1902,* vol. 2. New York: A. A. Knopf, 1932.

Lattimore, Owen. *Manchuria: Cradle of Conflict.* New York: Macmillan, 1932.

————. *The Mongols of Manchuria.* New York: John Day, 1934.

Lebra, Joyce C. *Okuma Shigenobu: Statesman of Meiji Japan.* Canberra: Australian National University Press, 1973.

Lee, En-han. *China's Quest for Railway Autonomy, 1904–1911.* Singapore: Singapore University Press, 1977.

Lee, Robert H. G. *The Manchurian Frontier in Ch'ing History.* Cambridge, Mass.: Harvard University Press, 1970.

Lensen, George. *The Damned Inheritance: The Soviet Union and the Manchurian Crises, 1924–1935.* Tallahassee: Diplomatic Press, 1974.

Levin, N. Gordon. *Woodrow Wilson and World Politics: America's Response to War and Revolution.* New York: Oxford University Press, 1968.

Lewis, Michael L. *Rioters and Citizens: Mass Protest in Imperial Japan.* Berkeley: University of California Press, 1990.

Lone, Stewart. *Japan's First Modern War: Army and Society in the Conflict with China, 1894–1895.* New York: St. Martin's Press, 1994.

MacMurray, John V. A., comp. *Treaties and Agreements with and Concerning China, 1894–1919.* 2 vols. New York: Oxford University Press, 1921.

Maier, Charles. *Recasting Bourgeois Europe: Stabilization in France, Germany and Italy in the Decade After World War I.* Princeton: Princeton University Press, 1975.

Makita Kensuke. "1930 nendai ni okeru Mantetsu kaiso mondai." *Rekishi hyōron,* no. 289 (May 1974): 36–50.

Mannheim, Karl. *Man and Society in an Age of Reconstruction: Studies in Modern Social Structure.* New York: Harcourt, Brace and World, 1940.

Manshikai, ed. *Manshū kaihatsu yonjūnen shi,* vol. 1. Tokyo: Manshū kaihatsu yonjūnen kankōkai, 1964–65.

Manshū nichi nichi shinbun (Manshū Nippō).

Manshū seinen renmei shi kankō iinkai. *Manshū seinen renmei shi.* Tokyo: Hara shobō, 1968.

Manshūshi kenkyūkai, ed. *Nihon teikokushugika no Manshū,* Tokyo: Ochanomizu shobō, 1972.

Marks, Steven. *The Road to Power: The Trans-Siberian Railroad and the Colonization of Asian Russia, 1850–1917.* Ithaca: Cornell University Press, 1991.

Marwick, Arthur. "Problems and Consequences of Organizing Society for Total War." In *Mobilization for Total War,* ed. N. F. Dreiszinger, pp. 1–21. Waterloo, Ont.: Wilfrid Laurier University Press, 1981.

Matsumoto Toshirō. "Nihon teikokushugi no shigen mondai." In *Taikei Nihon gendai shi,* vol. 4, *Sensō to kokka dokusen shihonshugi,* ed. Nakamura Masanori, pp. 94–114. Tokyo: Nihon hyōronsha, 1979.

———. *Shinryaku to kaihatsu: Nihon shihonshugi to Chūgoku shokuminchika,* Tokyo: Ochanomizu shobō, 1988.

Matsumura Takao. "Manshūkoku seiritsu ikō ni okeru imin, rōdō seisaku no keisei to tenkai." In *Nihon teikokushugika no Manshū,* ed. Manshūshi kenkyūkai, pp. 215–314. Tokyo: Ochanomizu shobō, 1972.

Matsunawa Zensaburō. "Ro-Shi kyōtei ni itaru Tō–Shi tetsudō no riken kaishū to Nihon no taiō." *Gunji shigaku* 13, no. 2 (Sept. 1977): 32–44.

Matsuoka Yōsuke. "Manmō tetsudō fusetsu sokushin ni tsuite" (11/1923). In *Shōwa zaisei shiryō,* comp. Ōkurashō, no. 5, vol. 186. Microfilm, 41 frames.

———. *Ugoku Manmō.* Tokyo: Senshinsha, 1931.

Matsuoka Yōsuke denki kankō kai. *Matsuoka Yōsuke—sono hito to shōgai.* Tokyo: Kōzasha, 1974.

Matsusaka, Y. Tak. "Managing Occupied Manchuria, 1931–1934." In *The Japanese Wartime Empire, 1931–1945*, ed. Peter Duus, Ramon H. Myers, and Mark R. Peattie, pp. 97–135. Princeton: Princeton University Press, 1996.

McCormack, Gavan. *Chang Tso-lin in Northeast China: China, Japan and the Manchurian Idea*. Stanford: Stanford University Press, 1977.

MDN, see Rikugunshō, *Mitsu dai nikki*

Meiji Taishō Shōwa shinbun kenkyūkai, ed. *Shinbun shūsei Taishō hen nenshi*, 1912 and 1925. Tokyo: Meiji Taishō Shōwa shinbun kenkyūkai, 1969–87.

Mercer, Lloyd J. *Railroads and Land Grant Policy: A Study in Government Intervention*. New York: Academic Press, 1982.

MGS, see Rikugunshō, *Manshū gunsei shi*

Mie Rucheng, *Teikokushugi to Chūgoku no tetsudō*. Tokyo: Ryūkei shoseki, 1987.

Minami Manshū tetsudō kabushikigaisha. *Bujun yūbō ketsugan jigyō rengō kyōgi kaigiroku*, N.p., May 1925. Tōkyō daigaku, Shakai kagaku kenkyūjo, Toshokan.

———. *Chū–Tō tetsuro un'yu tōkei*. N.p., n.d. (1930?). Tōkyō daigaku, Shakai kagaku kenkyūjo, Toshokan.

———. *Eigyō hōkokusho*. Dairen: SMR, annual. Reprinted—Tokyo: Ryūkei shoseki, 1977.

——— (Umeno Minoru). *Honpō seitekkō saku jūritsu to Minami Manshū*. SMR: Dairen, 1924.

———. *Mantetsu tōkei nenpō*. Dairen: SMR, 1907–20.

———. *Minami Manshū tetsudō kabushikigaisha dai niji jūnen shi*. Dairen: SMR, 1928.

———. *Minami Manshū tetsudō kabushikigaisha dai sanji jūnen shi*. Dairen: SMR, 1938. Reprinted—Tokyo: Ryūkei shoseki, 1974.

———. *Minami Manshū tetsudō kabushikigaisha jūnen shi*. Dairen: Manshū nichinichi shinbunsha, 1919.

——— (Akabane Katsumi). *Nihon no sekiyū mondai to Bujun san yūbō ketsugan no kachi*. Dairen: SMR, 1924.

———. *Shakakō kōjō gaikyō*. Dairen: SMR, 1924.

———. *Sixth Report on Progress in Manchuria to 1939*. Dairen: SMR, 1940.

Minami Manshū tetsudō kabushikigaisha, Chōsaka. *Bujun tan no hanro*. Dairen: SMR, 1925.

——— (Takeuchi Toraji). *Hō–Kai tetsudō to Koryōtō chikkō mondai*. Dairen: SMR, 1926.

——— (Hirano Hiroshi). *Hō–Kai tetsudō no Mantetsu ni oyobosu eikyō*. Dairen: SMR, 1928.

——— (Miyazaki Masayoshi). *Jikyoku to Tō–Shin tetsudō*. Tokyo: SMR, 1919.

——— (Mikami Yasumi). *Manmō ni okeru Nihon no tōshi jōtai*. Dairen: SMR, 1928.

———. *Manmō ni okeru tetsudō no gaiyō*. Dairen: SMR, 1929.

———. *Manmō tetsudō no shakai oyobi keizai ni oyoboseru eikyō*. Dairen: SMR, 1931.

———— (Nonaka Tokio). *Manmō yori nani o kitai subeki ka.* 3 editions. Dairen: SMR, 1924, 1929, 1930.

———— (Nomura Kiyoshi). "Manshū ni okeru daizu." In SMR, Chōsaka, *Tō-A kankei shiryō ison,* no. 1, pp. 17–34. Dairen: SMR, 1910.

————. *Manshū Shinagawa tetsudō ensen chihō ni okeru daizu no demawari zōka jijō oyobi sono taiō saku.* Dairen: SMR, 1931.

————. *Minami Manshū keizai chōsa shiryō.* 5 vols. Dairen: SMR, 1910.

————. *Rinkai tetsudō to shomondai.* Dairen: SMR, 1924.

———— (Ueda Kenzo). *Ryōga no suiun.* Dairen: SMR, 1911.

————. *Tai–Ha tetsudō chōsa hōkokusho.* Dairen: SMR, 1930.

————. *Ten–To keiben tetsudō.* Dairen: SMR, 1925.

————. *Tōnan–Chichiharu tetsudō no kachi.* Dairen: SMR, 1925.

————. *Tō–Shin tetsudō nanbu sen chihō keizai chōsa shiryō* (1916 study), Dairen: SMR, 1917.

———— (Kudō Takeo). *Waga kuni jinkō mondai to Manmō.* Dairen: SMR, 1928.

Minami Manshū tetsudō kabushikigaisha, Chōsaka, Mōko chōsatai, Dai 1 han. *Tōnan–Manshūri kan Mōko chōsa hōkokusho.* Dairen: SMR, 1926.

Minami Manshū tetsudō kabushikigaisha, Gijutsubu, Senroka. *Tōnan–Chichiharu kan tetsudō yotei senro tōsasho.* Dairen: SMR, 1920.

Minami Manshū tetsudō kabushikigaisha, Harupin jimusho, Chōsaka. *1923 nendo Tō-Shi tetsudō eigyō seiseki.* SMR: Harbin, 1924.

Minami Manshū tetsudō kabushikigaisha, Keizai chōsakai. *Manshū keizai tōsei hōsaku.* Dairen: SMR, 1935.

————. *Manshū nōgyō imin hōsaku.* Dairen: SMR, 1936.

Minami Manshū tetsudō kabushikigaisha, Keizai chōsakai, Dai 3 bu, Dai 1 han. *Tetsudō keikaku an.* Dairen: SMR, 1932.

Minami Manshū tetsudō kabushikigaisha, Rinji chōsakai. *Iwayuru heikōsen mondai ni tsuite.* Rinchō tsuihō 5. Mimeograph. Aug. 1931. Harvard Yenching Library.

————. *Tetsudō kōshō mondai no kinjō.* Rinchō tsuihō 10. Mimeograph. Sept. 1931. Harvard Yenching Library.

Minami Manshū tetsudō kabushikigaisha, Sōmubu, Kōmukyoku, Sekkeika. *Chōshun–Tōnan tetsudō senro tōsa hōkokusho.* Dairen: SMR, 1919.

————. *Kitsurin–Kainei kan kōki tetsudō yotei senro chōsasho.* Dairen: SMR, 1918.

Minami Manshū tetsudō kabushikigaisha, Tetsudōbu, Kōmuka. *Kaigen–Chōyōzan kan yotei tetsudō senro tōsa hōkokusho.* Dairen: SMR, 1919.

Minami Manshū tetsudō kabushikigaisha, Tetsudōbu, Ren'unka. *Saikin Tōhoku tetsudō jōsei.* Mimeograph. 1931. Harvard-Yenching Library.

Minami Manshū tetsudō kabushikigaisha, Tetsudōbu, Un'yuka. *Kamotsu chōsa hōkoku isan—Tetsuryō kamotsu bunkyoku kanku.* Dairen: SMR, 1911.

Minami Manshū tetsudō kabushikigaisha, Un'yubu. *Ekizei ippan: Kitsu–Chō no bu.* Dairen: SMR, 1916.

Minichiello, Sharon A. "Introduction." In *Japan's Competing Modernities: Issues in Culture and Democracy, 1900–1930,* ed. idem, pp. 1–21. Honolulu: University of Hawaii Press, 1998.

Mitani Taichirō. "'Tenkanki' (1918–1921) no gaikō shidō." In *Kindai Nihon no seiji to gaikō,* ed. Shinohara Hajime and Mitani Taichirō, pp. 293–374. Tokyo: Tōkyō daigaku shuppankai, 1965.

Mitsui bunko (Shiryō shōkai). "Mitsui bussan kabushikigaisha torishimariyaku kaigiroku." *Mitsui bunko ronsō,* no. 14, (Nov. 1980): 369–452.

Miura Yasuyuki. *Mantetsu to Higashi Indo kaisha, sono ubugoe: kaigai shinshutsu no keiei paradaimu.* Tokyo: Uejji, 1997.

Miwa Kimitada. *Matsuoka Yōsuke: sono ningen to gaikō.* Tokyo: Chūōkōronsha, 1971.

Miwa Munehiro. "Kaigun nenryō chō no sekitan ekika kenkyū." *Kagakushi kenkyū* 41, no. 4 (Dec. 1987): 164–75.

Miyazaki Tōten. *My Thirty-Three Year's Dream.* Trans. Eto Shinkichi and Marius B. Jansen. Princeton: Princeton University Press, 1982.

Mommsen, Wolfgang J. *Theories of Imperialism.* Trans. P. S. Falla. New York: Random House, 1980.

Morikawa Hidemasa. "Sōgōshōsha no seiritsu to ronri." In *Sōgōshōsha no keieishi,* ed. Miyamoto Mataji, Togai Yoshio, and Mishima Yasuo, pp. 43–78. Tokyo: Tōyō keizai shinpōsha, 1976.

Morley, James William. *The Japanese Thrust into Siberia.* New York: Columbia University Press, 1957.

Morley, James William, ed. *Dilemmas of Growth in Prewar Japan.* Princeton: Princeton University Press, 1971.

———. *Japan Erupts: The London Naval Conference and the Manchurian Incident, 1928–1932.* New York: Columbia University Press, 1984.

Morton, William F. *Tanaka Giichi and Japan's China Policy.* New York: St. Martin's Press, 1980.

Moskowitz, Karl. "The Creation of the Oriental Development Company: Japanese Illusions Meet Korean Reality." *Occasional Papers on Korea,* no. 2 (1974): 73–121.

Motoyama Minoru. "Sansen renraku mondai no rekishiteki kōsatsu." *Keiei keiri kenkyū,* no. 14 (June 1975): 1–19.

MSCS(A), see Kantō totokufu, Minseibu, *Manshū sangyō chōsa shiryō,* nōgyō

MSCS(C), see Kantō totokufu, Minseibu, *Manshū sangyō chōsa shiryō,* shōgyō

MSCS(M), see Kantō totokufu, Minseibu, *Manshū sangyō chōsa shiryō,* kōgyō

Muroyama Yoshimasa. "'Teikoku kokubō hōshin' no seitei." In *Nihon rekishi taikei 4, kindai 1,* ed. Inoue Mitsutada, pp. 1195–216. Tokyo: Yamakawa shuppansha, 1987.

Mutsu Munemitsu. *Kenkenroku: A Diplomatic Record of the Sino-Japanese War, 1894–1895*. Trans. Gordon Berger. Tokyo: University of Tokyo Press, 1982.

Myers, Ramon H. "Creating a Modern Enclave Economy." In *The Japanese Wartime Empire, 1931–1945*, ed. Peter Duus, Ramon H. Myers, and Mark R. Peattie, pp. 136–51. Princeton: Princeton University Press, 1996.

————. *The Japanese Economic Development of Manchuria, 1932–1945*. New York: Garland Publishing, 1982.

————. "Japanese Imperialism in Manchuria: The South Manchuria Railway Company." In *The Japanese Informal Empire in China, 1895–1937*, ed. Peter Duus, Ramon H. Myers, and Mark R. Peattie, pp. 101–32. Princeton: Princeton University Press, 1989.

Myers, Ramon H., and Mark R. Peattie, eds. *The Japanese Colonial Empire, 1895–1945*. Princeton: Princeton University Press, 1984.

Nagao Sakurō. *Shokuminchi tetsudō no sekai keizaiteki oyobi sekai seisakuteki kenkyū*. Tokyo: Nihon hyōronsha, 1930.

Nagura Bunji. *Nihon tekkōgyō shi no kenkyū*. Tokyo: Kondō shuppansha, 1984.

Nahm, Andrew C., ed. *Korea Under Japanese Colonial Rule: Studies of the Policy and Techniques of Japanese Colonialism*. Kalamazoo: Western Michigan University, Institute of International and Area Studies, Center for Korean Studies, 1973.

Najita, Tetsuo. *Hara Kei in the Politics of Compromise*. Cambridge, Mass.: Harvard University Press, 1967.

Nakagane, Katsuji. "Manchukuo and Economic Development." In *The Japanese Informal Empire in China, 1895–1937*, ed. Peter Duus, Ramon H. Myers, and Mark R. Peattie, pp. 133–57. Princeton: Princeton University Press, 1989.

Nakamura Masanori, Emura Eiichi, and Miyachi Masahito. "Nihon teikokushugi to jinmin." *Rekishigaku kenkyū*, no. 327 (Aug. 1967): 1–22.

Nakamura Takafusa. *Nihon no keizai tōsei: senji-sengo no keiken to kyōjun*. Tokyo: Nihon keizai shinbunsha, 1974.

Natsume Sōseki. *Man-Kan tokorodokoro*. 1910. Reprinted in *Meiji hoppō chōsa tanken ki shūsei*, vol. 10, pp. 199–331. Tokyo: Yumani shobō, 1989.

Nelson, Keith L. "The 'Warfare State': History of a Concept." *Pacific Historical Review*, no. 40 (1971): 127–43.

NGB, see Gaimushō, *Nihon gaikō bunsho*

NGN, see Gaimushō, *Nihon gaikō nenpyō narabini shuyō bunsho*

Nihon keiei shi kenkyūjo, ed. *Hanshin denki tetsudō hachijūnen shi*. Osaka: Hanshin denki tetsudō kabushiki kaisha, 1985.

Nihon kindai shiryō kenkyūkai, ed. *Nihon riku kai gun no seido, soshiki, jinji*. Tokyo: Tōkyō daigaku shuppankai, 1981.

Nish, Ian. *Alliance in Decline: A Study in Anglo-Japanese Relations, 1908–1923*. London: Athalone Press, 1972.

————. *The Anglo-Japanese Alliance: The Diplomacy of Two Island Empires, 1894–1907.* London: Athalone Press, 1966.

————. *Japanese Foreign Policy, 1869–1942: Kasumigaseki to Miyakezaka.* Boston: Routledge and Kegan Paul, 1977.

————. *Origins of the Russo-Japanese War.* New York: Longman, 1985.

Nishimura Shigeo. *Chō Gakurō.* Tokyo: Iwanami shoten, 1996.

————. *Chūgoku kindai tōhoku chiiki shi kenkyū.* Tokyo: Hōritsu bunkasha, 1984.

Nochi Kiyoshi and Ōmori Tokuko. "Dai ichiji taisenki no Nihon no tai-Chūgoku shakkan." In *Nihon no shihon yushutsu*, ed. Kokka shihon yushutsu kenkyūkai, pp. 51–87. Tokyo: Taga shuppan, 1986.

Noda Masaho, Harada Katsumasa, and Aoki Eiichi, eds. *Tōkyō-Yokohama dentetsu enkakushi.* Tokyo: Nihon keizai hyōronsha, 1983.

Nolte, Sharon. *Liberalism in Modern Japan: Ishibashi Tanzan and His Teachers, 1905–1960.* Berkeley: University of California Press, 1987.

Nolte, Sharon H., and Sally Ann Hastings. "The Meiji State's Policy Toward Women, 1890–1910." In *Recreating Japanese Women, 1600–1945*, ed. Gail Lee Bernstein, pp. 151–74. Berkeley: University of California Press, 1991.

Nomura Otojirō. "Jēkobu Shifu to Takahashi Korekiyo." *Kokushigaku*, no. 98 (Jan. 1976): 1–24.

Noro Eitarō. *Nihon shihonshugi hattatsu shi.* Tokyo: Iwanami shoten, 1935.

Ōe Shinobu. *Nichi-Ro sensō no gunjishiteki kenkyū.* Tokyo: Iwanami shoten, 1976.

————. *Nihon no Sanbō honbu.* Tokyo: Chūōkōronsha, 1985.

Ogata, Sadako N. *Defiance in Manchuria: The Making of Japanese Foreign Policy, 1931–1932.* Berkeley: University of California Press, 1964.

Ogata Yōichi. "Dai niji 'Shidehara gaikō' to 'Manmō' tetsudō kōshō." *Tōhō gakuhō* 57, no. 3/4 (Mar. 1976): 178–212.

————. "Tōhoku kōtsū iinkai to iwayuru 'Mantetsu hōi tetsudō mō keikaku.'" *Shigaku zasshi* 86, no. 8 (Aug. 1977): 39–72.

Ogoshi Heiriku. *Manshū ryokōki.* 1901. In *Meiji hoppō chōsa tankenki shūsei*, vol. 7, pp. 1–270. Tokyo: Yumani shobō, 1988.

Oh, Bonnie B. "Sino-Japanese Rivalry in Korea, 1876–1885." In *The Chinese and the Japanese: Essays in Political and Cultural Interactions*, ed. Akira Iriye, pp. 35–57. Princeton: Princeton University Press, 1980.

Oka Yoshitake. *Five Political Leaders of Modern Japan: Itō Hirobumi, Okuma Shigenobu, Hara Takashi, Inukai Tsuyoshi, and Saionji Kinmochi.* Trans. Andrew Fraser and Patricia Murray. Tokyo: University of Tokyo Press, 1986.

————. *Konoe Fumimaro: A Political Biography.* Trans. Shumpei Okamoto and Patricia Murray. Tokyo: University of Tokyo Press, 1983.

Okabe Makio. "1920 nendai no Mantetsu to Mantetsu chōsabu." *Rekishi kōron* 5, no. 4 (Apr. 1979): 85–92.

————. "Manshū nōgyō imin seisaku no tenkai—Nagano ken o rei ni shite." In *Nihon fuashizumu to Higashi Ajia*, ed. Fujiwara Akira and Nozawa Minoru, pp. 145–59. Tokyo: Aoki shoten, 1977.

————. "Nihon teikokushugi to Mantetsu—jūgonen sensō ki o chūshin ni." *Nihonshi kenkyū*, no. 195 (Nov. 1978): 66–87.

Okamoto, Shumpei. "Ishibashi Tanzan and the Twenty-One Demands." In *The Chinese and the Japanese: Essays in Political and Cultural Interactions*, ed. Akira Iriye, pp. 184–98. Princeton: Princeton University Press, 1980.

————. *The Japanese Oligarchy and the Russo-Japanese War*. New York: Columbia University Press, 1970.

Ōmori Tokuko. "Nishihara shakkan ni tsuite." *Rekishigaku kenkyū*, no. 419 (Apr. 1975): 36–51.

Osterhammel, Jurgen. "Semi-Colonialism and Informal Empire in Twentieth Century China: Toward a Framework of Analysis." In *Imperialism and After*, ed. Wolfgang J. Mommsen, pp. 290–314. Boston: Allen and Unwin, 1986.

Ōta Ayama. *Fukushima shōgun iseki*. Tokyo: Tōa kyōkai, 1941.

Owen, Roger, and Bob Sutcliffe, eds. *Studies in the Theory of Imperialism*. London: Longman, 1972.

Ōyama Azusa, ed. "Shiryō shōkai: Kantō sōtokufu 'Gunsei jisshi yōryō.'" *Kokusai seiji: Nihon gaikōshi no shomondai II*, no. 2 (1964): 117–27.

————. *Yamagata Aritomo ikensho*. Tokyo: Hara shobō, 1966.

Park, Soon-won. *Colonial Industrialization and Labor in Korea: The Onoda Cement Factory*. Cambridge, Mass.: Harvard University Asia Center, 1999.

Peattie, Mark R. "Attitudes Toward Colonialism." In *The Japanese Colonial Empire, 1895–1945*, ed. Ramon H. Myers and Mark R. Peattie, pp. 80–127. Princeton: Princeton University Press, 1984.

————. "Introduction." In *The Japanese Colonial Empire, 1895–1945*, ed. Ramon H. Myers and Mark R. Peattie, pp. 3–52. Princeton: Princeton University Press, 1984.

————. *Ishiwara Kanji and Japan's Confrontation with the West*. Princeton: Princeton University Press, 1975.

————. "Japanese Treaty Port Settlements in China, 1895–1937." In *The Japanese Informal Empire in China, 1895–1937*, ed. Peter Duus, Ramon H. Myers, and Mark R. Peattie, pp. 166–209. Princeton: Princeton University Press, 1989.

————. *Nan'yo: The Rise and Fall of the Japanese in Micronesia, 1885–1945*. Honolulu: University of Hawaii Press, 1992.

Pratt, Edwin A. *The Rise of Rail-Power in War and Conquest, 1833–1914*. Philadelphia: J. P. Lippincott, 1916.

Presseisen, Ernst L. *Before Aggression: Europeans Prepare the Japanese Army*. Tucson: University of Arizona Press, 1965.

Pye, Lucien W. *Warlord Politics: Conflict and Coalition in the Modernization of Republican China*. New York: Praeger, 1971.

Rekishigaku kenkyūkai, ed. *Taiheiyō sensō shi*, vol. 1, *Manshū jihen*. Tokyo: Aoki shoten, 1971.

Remer, C. F. *Foreign Investments in China*. New York: Macmillan, 1933.

Rigby, Richard W. *The May 30 Movement*. Canberra: Australian National University Press, 1980.

Rikugunshō, comp. *Manshū gunsei shi*, vol. 1. Tokyo: Rikugunshō, 1916.

———. *Meiji gunjishi*, vol. 2. Tokyo: Hara shobō, 1966.

———. *Mitsu dai nikki*. Bōeichō, Bōei kenkyūjo toshokan.

Roman, Donald W. "Railway Imperialism in Canada, 1847–1865." In *Railway Imperialism*, ed. Clarence B. Davis and Kenneth E. Wilburn, Jr., pp. 7–24. New York: Greenwood Press, 1991.

Romanov, B. A. *Russia in Manchuria, 1892–1906*. 1928. Trans. Susan W. Jones. Ann Arbor: American Council of Learned Societies, 1952.

Sagara Shunsuke. *Akai sekiyō no Manshū nogahara ni: kisai Kōmoto Daisaku no shōgai*. Tokyo: Kōjinsha, 1978.

Saitō Seiji. "Kokubō hōshin dai ichiji kaitei no haikei: dai niji Ōkuma naikaku ka ni okeru riku-kai ryō gun kankei." *Shigaku zasshi* 95, no. 6 (June 1986): 1–36.

Sakamoto Masako. "Mitsui bussan to 'Manshū'-Chūgoku shijō." In *Nihon fuashizumu to Higashi Ajia*, ed. Fujiwara Akira and Nozawa Minoru, pp. 106–44. Tokyo: Aoki shoten, 1977.

———. "Sensō to zaibatsu." In *Taikei Nihon gendai shi*, vol. 4, *Sensō to kokka dokusen shihonshugi*, ed. Nakamura Masanori, pp. 48–75. Tokyo: Nihon hyōronsha, 1979.

Sakurai Tetsu. "Minami Manshū tetsudō no keiei to zaibatsu." In *Nihon takokuseki kigyō no shiteki tenkai*, ed. Fujii Mitsuo, Nakase Juichi, Maruyama Shigenari, and Ikeda Masakata, vol. 1, pp. 223–50. Tokyo: Ōtsuki shoten, 1979.

Samuels, Richard J. *"Rich Nation, Strong Army": National Security and the Technological Transformation of Japan*. Ithaca: Cornell University Press, 1994.

Sanbō honbu. *Futatabi waga kuni rikugun sentō nōryoku o zōka sezarubekarazaru yuen o ronji, awasete Chōsen, Manshū ni okeru yusō kikan seibi no hitsuyō ni oyobu*. 1911. Bōeichō, Bōei kenkyūjo toshokan, Miyazaki shiryō, item 48.

———. "Kankoku chūkatsu gun shireikan ni ataru Meiji yonjūninendo sakusen keikaku kunrei." Mimeographed. N.d. (1908?). Bōeichō, Bōei kenkyūjo toshokan.

———. "Kankoku chūkatsu gun shireikan ni ataru Meiji yonjūsannendo sakusen keikaku." Mimeographed. 1909. Bōeichō, Bōei kenkyūjo toshokan.

———. "Kantō totoku ni ataru Meiji yonjūnendo sakusen keikaku kunrei." Mimeographed. 1907. Bōeichō, Bōei kenkyūjo toshokan.

———. "Kantō totoku ni ataru Meiji yonjūninendo sakusen keikaku kunrei." Mimeographed. N.d. (1908?). Bōeichō, Bōei kenkyūjo toshokan.

————. "Kantō totoku ni atauru Meiji yonjūsannendo sakusen keikaku kunrei." Mimeographed. 1909. Bōeichō, Bōei kenkyūjo toshokan.

————. *Man-Kan kōtsū kikan jūbi kansei no kyūmu.* N.d. (1907?). Bōeichō, Bōei kenkyūjo toshokan, Miyazaki shiryō, item 23.

————. *Man-Kan tetsudō keiei ni kansuru ikensho.* 1909. Bōeichō, Bōei kenkyūjo toshokan, Miyazaki shiryō, item 41.

————. "Meiji yonjūnendo Nihon teikoku rikugun sakusen keikaku." Mimeographed. 1907. Bōeichō, Bōei kenkyūjo toshokan.

————. "Meiji yonjūsannendo Nihon teikoku rikugun sakusen keikaku." Mimeographed. 1909. Bōeichō, Bōei kenkyūjo toshokan.

————. *Senji sōheiryoku kettei ni kansuru kaigi gijiroku.* 1920. Bōeichō, Bōei kenkyūjo toshokan, Miyazaki shiryō, item 60.

————. *Tai-Shin sakusen keikaku.* 1911. Bōeichō, Bōei kenkyūjo toshokan, Miyazaki shiryō, item 47.

———— (Koiso Kuniaki). *Teikoku kokubō shigen.* 1917. Bōeichō, Bōei kenkyūjo toshokan.

————. *Tetsudō ron* (1888). In *Sanbō honbu tetsudō ronshū,* ed. Noda Masaho, Harada Katsumasa, Aoki Eiichi, and Oikawa Yoshinobu. Tokyo: Nihon keizai hyōronsha, 1988. (A collection of photo-reproductions of documents; each document is paginated separately.)

———— (Manshūgun sōshirei kan). *Waga rikugun sengo keiei ni kanshi sankō to subeki ippan no yōken.* N.d. (1905?). Bōeichō, Bōei kenkyūjo toshokan, Miyazaki shiryō, item 40.

Sashūkai, ed. *Nomura Ryūtarō den.* Tokyo: Nihon kōtsūkai, 1938.

Satō Motoei. "Dai niji 'Shidehara gaikō' ni okeru Manmō tetsudō mondai kaiketsu kōshō." In *Kindai Nihon to Mantetsu,* ed. Kobayashi Hideo, pp. 151–68. Tokyo: Yoshikawa kobunkan, 2000.

————. "Tanaka naikaku no tai-Chūgoku keizai hattensaku to Mantetsu." In *Kindai Nihon to Mantetsu,* ed. Kobayashi Hideo, pp. 108–50. Tokyo: Yoshikawa kōbunkan, 2000.

Satō Saburō. "Nichi-Ro sensō ni okeru Manshū senryōchi ni taisuru Nihon no gunsei ni tsuite." *Yamagata daigaku kiyō (jinbun kagaku)* 6, no. 2 (Jan. 1967): 21–56.

Satō Tetsutarō. *Teikoku kokubō shiron.* 2 vols. 1908. Reprinted—Tokyo: Hara shobō, 1979.

Schrecker, John E. *Imperialism and Chinese Nationalism: Germany in Shantung.* Cambridge, Mass.: Harvard University Press, 1971.

Schumpeter, Elizabeth Boody, and G. C. Allen, eds. *The Industrialization of Japan and Manchukuo, 1930–1940: Population, Raw Materials and Industry.* New York: Macmillan, 1940.

Scott, Richard W. *Organizations: Rational, Natural and Open Systems.* Englewood Cliffs, N.J.: Prentice Hall, 1981.

Seki Hiroharu. "Manshū jihen zenshi." In *Taiheiyō sensō e no michi,* ed. Kobayashi Tatsuo, Kobayashi Yukio, and Seki Hiroharu, vol. 1, pp. 287–440. Tokyo: Asahi shinbusha, 1963.

Seki Hiroharu and Fujii Shōzō. "Nihon teikokushugi to Higashi Ajia." In *Iwanami kōza sekai rekishi,* vol. 25, pp. 517–61. Tokyo: Iwanami shoten, 1970.

Selznick, Philip. *TVA and the Grass Roots: A Study in the Sociology of Formal Organization.* Berkeley: University of California Press, 1953.

Silberman, Bernard, and H. D. Hartoonian, eds. *Japan in Crisis: Essays on Taishō Democracy.* Princeton: Princeton University Press, 1972.

Shibata Yoshimasa. "Nihon no tai-Manshū tsūka kin'yū seisaku no keisei to sono kinō no jittai." *Shakai keizai shigaku* 43, no. 2 (1977): 37–65.

Shiina Etsusaburō. "Nihon sangyō no dai jikkenjo." *Bungei shunjū* 54, no. 2, (Feb. 1976): 107–14.

Shimada Toshihiko. *Kantōgun.* Tokyo: Chūōkōronsha, 1965.

———. "Tō-Shi tetsudō o meguru Chū-So funsō." *Kokusai kankei,* no. 1 (1970): 25–50.

Shimanuki Takeji. "Dai ichiji taisen igo no kokubō hōshin, shoyō heiryoku, yōhei kōryō." *Gunji shigaku* 9, no. 1 (June 1973): 65–75.

———. "Nichi-Ro sensō igo ni okeru kokubō hōshin, shoyō heiryoku, yōhei kōryō no hensen." *Gunji shigaku* 8, no. 4 (Mar. 1973): 2–16.

Shimizu Hideko. "Tai-Man kikō no hensen." *Kokusai seiji—Nihon gaikō shi no shomondai III,* no. 2 (1967): 136–55.

Shinobu Seizaburō and Nakayama Jiichi. *Nichi-Ro sensō shi no kenkyū.* Tokyo: Kawade shobō shinsha, 1959.

Shinozaki Yoshirō. *Manshū kin'yū oyobi zaikai no genjō,* vol. 2. Dairen: Ōsakayagō shoten, 1928.

———. *Manshū to Aioi Yoshitarō.* Dairen: Fukuchō kōshi gokei kai, 1932.

Shukuri Shigeichi. *Kodama Gentarō.* Tokyo: Taikyōsha, 1938.

Smith, Benjamin E., ed. *The Century Atlas of the World.* New York: Century, 1906.

SMR, see Minami Manshū tetsudō kabushikigaisha

SMR1, see Minami Manshū tetsudō kabushikigaisha, *Minami Manshū tetsudō kabushikigaisha jūnen shi*

SMR2, see Minami Manshū tetsudō kabushikigaisha, *Minami Manshū tetsudō kabushikigaisha dai niji jūnen shi*

SMR3, see Minami Manshū tetsudō kabushikigaisha, *Minami Manshū tetsudō kabushikigaisha dai sanji jūnen shi*

Su Ch'ung-min. *Man-t'ieh shih.* Peking: Chung-hua shu-chü, 1990.

Sun, E-tu Zen. *Chinese Railways and British Interests, 1898–1911.* New York: King's Crown Press, 1954.

Sun, Kungtu C., with Ralph Huenemann. *The Economic Development of Manchuria in the First Half of the Twentieth Century.* Cambridge, Mass.: Harvard University Press, 1969.

Suzaki Shin'ichi. "Gunbu to fuashizumu undō." In *Jūgonen sensō shi*, vol.1, *Manshū jihen*, ed. Fujiwara Akira and Imai Seiichi, pp. 125–69. Tokyo: Aoki shoten, 1988.

Suzuki Kunio. "'Manshūkoku' ni okeru Mitsui zaibatsu: Mitsui bussan no katsudō o chūshin ni." 2 pts. *Denki tsūshin daigaku kiyō* 1, no. 2 (Dec. 1988): 441–53; 2, no. 1 (June 1989): 251–75.

Suzuki Takashi. "'Manshū' kenkyū no genjō to kadai." *Ajia keizai* 12, no. 4 (Apr. 1971): 49–60.

————. "Minami Manshū tetsudō kabushikigaisha (Mantetsu) no sōritsu katei." *Tokushima daigaku kyōikubu kiyō* 4 (1969): 42–62.

————. *Nihon teikokushugi to Manshū.* 2 vols. Tokyo: Hanawa shobō, 1992.

Suzuki Takeo. *Nishihara shakkan shiryō kenkyū.* Tokyo: Tōkyō daigaku shuppankai, 1972.

Takada Sanetarō. "Kokubō hōshin seitei izen no rikugun nendo sakusen keikaku." *Gunjishigaku* 20, no. 1 (June 1984): 16–39.

Takahashi Kamekichi. "Manshū kaihatsu no kihonteki shomondai to sono taisaku." Special issue: Dai Manshū kaihatsu gō. *Keizai ōrai* (Apr. 1932): 13–36.

Takahashi Yasutaka. "Minami Manshū tetsudō kabushikigaisha (Mantetsu) shi kenkyū no genjō to kadai." *Tetsudō shigaku*, no. 2 (Aug. 1985): 55–57.

————. "Minami Manshū tetsudō kabushikigaisha no kaiso keikaku ni tsuite." *Shakai kagaku tōkyū* 27, no. 2 (Apr. 1982): 53–112.

Takayanagi Mitsunaga and Takeuchi Toshizō, eds., *Kadokawa Nihonshi jiten.* Tokyo: Kadokawa jiten, 1981.

Tanaka Giichi denki kankōkai. *Tanaka Giichi denki*, vol. 1. 1958. Reprinted—Tokyo: Hara shobō, 1981.

Tanaka Ryūichi. "Manshūkoku chigai hōken teppai to Mantetsu." In *Kindai Nihon to Mantetsu*, ed. Kobayashi Hideo, pp. 187–218. Tokyo: Yoshikawa kōbunkan, 2000.

Tang, Peter S. H. *Russian and Soviet Policy in Manchuria and Outer Mongolia, 1911–1931.* Durham: Duke University Press, 1959.

Tani Hisao. *Kimitsu Nichi-Ro senshi.* Tokyo: Hara shobō, 1966.

Teikoku gikai shūgiin iinkai giroku, Meiji hen, vols. 33, 55, 62. Tōkyō daigaku shuppankai, 1989.

Teikoku gikai shūgiin iinkai giroku, Taishō hen, vol. 31. Tōkyō daigaku shuppankai, 1989.

Teramoto Yasutoshi. "Manshū kokusai chūritsuka an to Komura gaikō." *Seijikeizaishigaku*, no. 208 (Dec. 1983): 35–44.

—————. "Nichi-Ro sensō go no tai-Man seisaku o meguru Gaimushō to rikugun no tairitsu." *Seijikeizaishigaku*, no. 237 (Jan. 1986): 76–93.

Tetsudōin, Kantokukyoku. *Mantetsu shisatsu hōkokusho.* 1913. N.p., n.d. Tōkyō daigaku, Shakai kagaku kenkyūjo, Toshokan.

Thompson, Virginia, and Richard Adloff. "French Economic Policy in Tropical Africa." In *Colonialism in Africa, 1870–1960,* vol. 4, *The Economics of Colonialism,* ed. Peter Duignan and Lewis H. Gann, pp. 127–64. Cambridge, Eng.: Cambridge University Press, 1975.

Thorne, Christopher. *The Limits of Foreign Policy: The West, the League and the Far Eastern Crisis of 1931–1933.* London: Hamish Hamilton, 1972.

Tiedemann, Arthur. "Japan's Economic Foreign Policies." In *Japan's Foreign Policy: A Research Guide,* ed. James W. Morley, pp. 118–52. New York: Columbia University Press, 1974.

TKN, see Minami Manshū tetsudō kabushikigaisha, *Mantetsu tōkei nenpō*

TKS, see Sanbō honbu, *Teikoku kokubō shigen*

Tōa keizai chōsakyoku. *Manchoukuo Year Book, 1934.* Tokyo: Tōa keizai chōsakyoku, 1934.

—————. *Manchoukuo Year Book, 1941.* Tokyo: Tōa keizai chōsakyoku, 1941.

Togai Yoshio. *Mitsui bussan kaisha no keieishiteki kenkyū.* Tokyo: Tōyō keizai shinpōsha, 1974.

—————. "Saisho ni shutsugen shita sōgoshōsha." In *Sōgoshōsha no keieishi,* ed. Miyamoto Mataji, Togai Yoshio, and Mishima Yasuo, pp. 81–120. Tokyo: Tōyō keizai shinpōsha, 1976.

Tsunoda Jun. *Manshū mondai to kokubō hōshin,* Tokyo: Hara shobō, 1967.

Tsunoda Jun, ed. *Ishiwara Kanji shiryō—kokubō ronsaku.* Tokyo: Hara shobō, 1967.

Tsurumi, E. Patricia. *Japanese Colonial Education in Taiwan, 1895–1945.* Cambridge, Mass.: Harvard University Press, 1977.

Tsurumi Yūsuke *Gotō Shinpei,* vol. 2. 1942. Reprinted—Tokyo: Keisō shobō, 1965.

Turner, Frederick Jackson. *The Frontier in American History.* New York: Henry Holt & Co., 1920.

Uda Tadashi. "Nihon shihonshugi no Manshū keiei." *Shakai keizai shigaku* 39, no. 2 (June 1973): 1–27.

Uehara Yūsaku kankei bunsho kenkyūkai. *Uehara Yūsaku kankei bunsho.* Tokyo: Tōkyō daigaku shuppankai, 1976.

Ugaki Kazunari. *Ugaki Kazunari nikki,* vol. 1. Ed. Tsunoda Jun. Tokyo: Misuzu shobō, 1968.

Usui Katsumi. *Manshū jihen: sensō to gaikō to.* Tokyo: Chūōkōronsha, 1974.

—————. "Nan-Man Tō-Mō jōyaku no seiritsu zengo." In *Tai-Manmō seisaku shi no ichimen,* ed. Kurihara Ken, pp. 126–36. Tokyo: Hara shobō, 1967.

—————. *Nihon to Chūgoku: Taishō jidai.* Tokyo: Hara shobō, 1972.

————. *Nitchū gaikō shi: hokubatsu no jidai.* Tokyo: Hanawa shobō, 1971.

Vevier, Charles. *The United States and China, 1906–1913.* New Brunswick, N.J.: Rutgers University Press, 1955.

von Laue, Theodore H. *Sergei Witte and the Industrialization of Russia.* New York: Columbia University Press, 1963.

Wakuda Yasuo. *Nihon no shitetsu.* Tokyo: Iwanami shoten, 1981.

Weland, James E. "The Japanese Army in Manchuria: Covert Operations and the Roots of Kwantung Army Insubordination." Ph.D. diss., University of Arizona, 1977.

Westney, D. Eleanor. *Imitation and Innovation: The Transfer of Western Organizational Patterns to Meiji Japan.* Cambridge, Mass.: Harvard University Press, 1987.

Willoughby, W. W. *Foreign Rights and Interests in China.* Baltimore: Johns Hopkins Press, 1920.

Wilson, Sandra. "The 'New Paradise': Japanese Emigration to Manchuria in the 1930s and 1940s." *International History Review* 17, no. 2 (May 1995): 249–85.

YAI, see Oyama Azusa, Yamagata Aritomo ikensho

Yamada Gōichi. "Manshū tōsei keizai to san i ittai sei no hossoku." In *Kindai Nihon to Chūgoku,* ed. Ando Hikotarō, pp. 245–95. Tokyo: Kyūko shoin, 1989.

————. *Mantetsu chōsabu: eikō to zasetsu no yonjūnen.* Tokyo: Nihon keizai shinbunsha, 1977.

Yamaguchi Jūji. *Kieta teikoku Manshū.* Tokyo: Asahi shinbunsha, 1967.

Yamaguchi Toshiaki, ed. "Hamaomote Matasuke bunsho." *Nenpō kindai Nihon kenkyū,* no. 1 (1980): 205–70.

Yamamoto Jirō, ed. *Terauchi Masatake kankei monjo.* Kyoto: Kyōto joshi daigaku, 1984.

Yamamoto Jōtarō denki hensankai. *Yamamoto Jōtarō denki.* Tokyo: Yamamoto Jōtarō denki hensankai, 1942.

————. *Yamamoto Jōtarō ronsaku,* vol. 2. Tokyo: Yamamoto Jōtarō denki hensankai, 1939.

Yamamoto Yūzō, ed. *Manshūkoku no kenkyū.* Kyoto: Kyōto daigaku, Jinbun kagaku kenkyūjo, 1993.

Yamamura, Kozo. "General Trading Companies: Their Origins and Growth." In *Japanese Industrialization and Its Social Consequences,* ed. Hugh Patrick, pp. 161–97. Berkeley: University of California Press, 1976.

Yamamura Mutsuo. "Nihon teikokushugi seiritsu katei ni okeru Mitsui bussan no hatten: tai-Chūgoku shinshutsu katei no tokushitsu o chūshin ni." *Tochi seido shigaku,* no. 73 (Apr.–June 1976): 25–46.

Yamamuro Shin'ichi. *Kimera: Manshūkoku no shōzō.* Tokyo: Chūōkōronsha, 1993.

————. "'Manshūkoku' tōji katei ron." In *Manshūkoku no kenkyū,* ed. Yamamoto Yūzō, pp. 83–129. Kyoto: Kyōto daigaku, Jinbun kagaku kenkyūjo, 1993.

Yonekura, Seiichirō. *The Japanese Iron and Steel Industry.* New York: St. Martin's Press, 1994.

Yoshiaki, Takehiko. *Conspiracy at Mukden.* New Haven: Yale University Press, 1963.

Yoshii Ken'ichi. "Dai ichiji taisen go no 'Manmō' tetsudō mondai." *Nihonshi kenkyū,* no. 285 (Apr. 1986): 34–57.

————. "'Manmō' tetsudō mondai kōshō to 'seron.'" *Jinbun kagaku kenkyū* (Niigata daigaku), no. 68 (Dec. 1985): 1–31.

————. "'Manmō' tetsudō mondai no tenkai to Tanaka naikaku." *Jinbun kagaku kenkyū* (Niigata daigaku), no. 69 (July 1986): 1–41.

Young, C. Walter. *The International Relations of Manchuria.* Chicago: University of Chicago Press, 1929.

————. *Japanese Jurisdiction in the South Manchuria Railway Areas.* Baltimore: Johns Hopkins Press, 1931.

Young, Ernest P. *The Presidency of Yüan Shih-k'ai: Liberalism and Dictatorship in Early Republican China.* Ann Arbor: University of Michigan Press, 1977.

Young, John. "The Hara Cabinet and Chang Tso-lin." *Monumenta Nipponica* 27, no. 3 (Summer 1972): 125–41.

————. *The Research Activities of the South Manchuria Railway Company, 1907–1945: A History and Bibliography.* New York: Columbia University Press, 1966.

Young, Louise. *Japan's Total Empire: Manchuria and the Culture of Wartime Imperialism.* Berkeley: University of California Press, 1997.

Glossary of Chinese Place-names

Traditional/Wade-Giles	Pinyin	Characters
Aigun	Aihun	愛琿
Angangki	Ang'angxi	昂昂溪
Anshan	Anshan	安山
Anta	Anda	安達
Changchiak'ou	Zhangjiakou	張家口
Ch'angch'un	Changchun	長春
Ch'angt'u	Changtu	昌圖
Ch'aoyangchen	Chaoyangzhen	朝陽鎮
Chefoo (Chihfu)	Zhifu	芝罘
Chengchiat'un	Zhengjiatun	鄭家屯
Ch'engte	Chengde	承德
Chi'an	Ji'an	輯安
Chientao	Jiandao	間島
Ch'ihfeng	Chifeng	赤峰
Chihli	Zhili	直隸
Chinchow	Jinzhou	錦州
Ch'inhuangtao	Qinhuangdao	秦皇島
Dairen (Talien)	Dalian	大連
Fangcheng	Fangzheng	方正
Fengt'ien	Fengtian	奉天
Fukien	Fujian	福建
Fushun	Fushun	撫順
Fuyu	Fuyu	扶余
Hailar	Hailar	海拉爾
Hailin	Hailin	海林
Hailung	Hailong	海龍
Harbin	Harbin	哈爾濱
Heiho	Heihe	黑河

Traditional/Wade-Giles	*Pinyin*	*Characters*
Heilungkiang	Heilongjiang	黑龍江
Hsinch'iu	Xinqiu	新邱
Hsinlit'un	Xinlitun	新立屯
Hsinmint'un	Xinmintun	新民屯
Hulutao	Huludao	葫蘆島
Hun River	Hunhe	渾河
Imienp'o	Yimianpo	一面坡
Jehol	Rehe	熱河
K'ailu	Kailu	開魯
K'aiyüan	Kaiyuan	開原
K'eshan	Keshan	克山
Kirin	Jilin	吉林
Kungchuling	Gongzhuling	公主嶺
Kwantung	Guandong	關東
Liao River	Liaohe	遼河
Liaotung	Liaodong	遼東
Lienshanwan	Lianshanwan	連山彎
Lungk'ou	Longkou	龍口
Manchouli	Manzhouli	滿洲里
Manchoukuo	Manzhouguo	滿洲國
Maoerhshan	Maoershan	帽兒山
Mergen	Morgen	墨爾根
Mukden	Fengtian	奉天
Nanking	Nanjing	南京
Nonni River	Nenjiang	嫩江
P'aich'üan	Paiquan	排泉
Pataohao	Badaohao	八道濠
Pei'an	Beian	北安
Peking	Beijing	北京
Penhsihu	Benxihu	本溪湖
Petune	Bodune	伯都納
Port Arthur / Lüshun	Lüshun	旅順
Sanhsing (Ilan)	Sanxing (Yilan)	三姓
Shahok'ou	Shahekou	沙河口
Shanhaikuan	Shanhaiguan	山海關
Shantung	Shandong	山東
Solun	Suolun	索倫
Ssup'ingkai	Sipingjie	四平街
Suchiat'un	Sujiatun	蘇家屯

Traditional/Wade-Giles	Pinyin	Characters
Sungari River	Songhuajiang	松花江
Tahushan	Dahushan	打虎山
T'aitzu River	Taizihe	太子河
Talai	Dalai	大賚
T'aoan	Taoan	洮安
T'aolaichao	Taolaizhao	陶賴昭
T'aonan	Taonan	洮南
Tashihch'iao	Dashiqiao	大石橋
Telissu	Delisi	得利寺
T'iehling	Tieling	鐵嶺
T'ientsin	Tianjin	天津
Tsitsihar	Qiqihar	齊齊哈爾
T'umen River	Tumenjiang	圖們江
T'ungkiang	Tongjiang	同江
T'ungkiangk'ou	Tongjiangkou	通江口
T'ungliao	Tongliao	通遼
Tunhua	Dunhua	敦化
Wuchang	Wuchang	五常
Yalu River	Yalujiang	鴨綠江
Yenki	Yanji	延吉
Yingk'ou (Yingkow)	Yingkou	營口